MOSS HART

A Prince of the Theatre

ALSO BY JARED BROWN

The Fabulous Lunts:
A Biography of Alfred Lunt and Lynn Fontanne

Zero Mostel: A Biography

The Theatre in America During the Revolution

Alan J. Pakula: His Films and His Life

MOSS HART

A Prince of the Theatre

A Biography in Three Acts
by

JARED BROWN

BACK STAGE BOOKS
New York

Page 5: Moss Hart in May 1937. Detail of photograph with George S. Kaufman which appears on page 194.

Page 69: Moss Hart in 1948. (Hart Estate)

Page 221: Undated portrait of Moss Hart. Could anyone possibly tell that he concealed a debilitating depression beneath his placid exterior? (Hart Estate)

Quotations from *The Street Where I Live* by Alan Jay Lerner, copyright © 1978 Alan Jay Lerner, used by permission of W. W. Norton & Company, Inc.

Quotations from *Act One* by Moss Hart, copyright © 1959 by Catherine Carlisle Hart & Joseph M. Hyman, trustees, used by permission of Random House, Inc.

Quotations from *You Can't Take It With You*, *Merrily We Roll Along*, *The Man Who Came to Dinner*, *The Fabulous Invalid*, and *The American Way* used by permission of Anne Kaufman Schneider and Kitty Carlisle Hart.

Quotations from *The Beloved Bandit* and *The Great Waltz* used by permission of Cohen & Grossberg, Attorneys at Law (attorneys for the heirs of Moss Hart).

Permission to quote Barnett Hart's lyrics for "The Man Who Came to Dinner" from Bourne Co.

Quotations from *Kitty* by Kitty Carlisle Hart, copyright © 1988, used by permission of Kitty Carlisle Hart.

Acquisitions Editor: Mark Glubke
Cover Design: Mark van Bronkhorst
Interior Design: Jay Anning
Senior Production Manager: Ellen Greene
Text set in Verdigris MVB

Copyright © 2006 Jared Brown

First published in 2006 in the United States
by Back Stage Books, an imprint of
Watson-Guptill Publications,
a division of VNU Business Media, Inc.
770 Broadway, New York, NY 10003
www.wgpub.com

Library of Congress Control Number: 2006922581
ISBN: 0-8230-7890-6

Printed in USA

First printing, 2006

1 2 3 4 5 6 7 8 9 / 14 13 12 11 10 9 8 7 6

For Cynthia Gray

CONTENTS

ACT THREE

Acknowledgments

I appreciate the generous support of Moss Hart's widow, Kitty Carlisle Hart, as well as their children, Christopher Hart and Catherine Hart. All of them were significant sources of information, as were Eddie Albert, Julie Andrews, Jerome Chodorov, Malcolm Goldstein, Robert Goulet, Leonora Hornblow, Anna Crouse Murch, Gregory Peck, Anne Kaufman Schneider, Stone (Bud) Widney, and Dr. Macon Williams. I am especially indebted to Kitty Carlisle Hart for permitting me to see and to quote from Moss Hart's diary, which is available to researchers only with her permission.

Special thanks to Harry Miller, Reference Archivist, and the other members of the staff at the State of Wisconsin Historical Society; and to Susannah Benedetti of the Wisconsin Center for Film and Theater Research. The Billy Rose Theatre Collection at the New York Public Library contained valuable information.

I appreciate the contributions of my editor at Back Stage Books, Mark Glubke, my copyeditor, Cathy Nelson Price, and my agent, Mitchell Waters.

This is the fifth book I have written that my wife, Judy Brown, has read, criticized, reread, and refined. I can only express my gratitude for her contribution and my love.

Alyson Dougherty-Wooldridge, a student at Illinois Wesleyan University, transcribed tapes of interviews, shared her comments about the progress of the manuscript with me, and helped to compile a preliminary index.

This book was written with the help of an Artistic/Scholarly Development Grant from the Faculty Development Committee of Illinois Wesleyan University, and support from the School of Theatre Arts, Illinois Wesleyan University, Nancy B. Loitz, Director.

Moss Hart was a "prince—
not of the blood, but of the theatre."

—Kitty Carlisle Hart, *Kitty*

PREFACE

IN RECENT YEARS, THE BROADWAY THEATRE HAS BECOME PRINCIPALLY A home for revivals and for plays and musicals developed elsewhere: in England and France, in American regional theatres. In the first decade of the twenty-first century, the playwrights who are most highly respected on Broadway for the quality and the frequency of their plays include Martin Mc-Donagh and Brian Friel (Irish) and Tom Stoppard (English, by way of Czechoslovokia). With a few exceptions, such as Paula Vogel, David Mamet, Sam Shepard, and Tony Kushner, American playwrights are barely on Broadway's radar screen.

The career of Neil Simon, who wrote one commercial success after another from the 1950s through the 1980s (and demonstrated in his "Brighton Beach Trilogy" that he was capable of fine, perceptive drama) seems to have faded; his recent plays have not shown commercial appeal and have been anything but adventurous. Stephen Sondheim has been a significant contributor to Broadway theatre for many years, but Sondheim is a composer and lyricist, not a playwright.

By itself, the decline of Broadway as a showcase for American playwrights is not particularly alarming. Regional theatres, off-Broadway, off-off-Broadway, and university theatres in America now offer the opportunities for American playwrights to have their work seen that Broadway once offered. Still, if our culture has been enriched by the addition of such institutions, it has surely been diminished by the decline of Broadway.

In many circles, "Broadway theatre" has become synonymous with conventional, unadventurous plays that are not significantly better than television situation comedies. Audiences see plays that are tailored to the talents of particular performers but have little merit of their own. Broadway has become a tourist attraction, a sort of Disneyland North, no longer a home to challenging, exciting American drama. But that was not the case in the 1920s, '30s, '40s, '50s and '60s. Throughout those decades, the American theatre, a source of vibrant comic invention and affecting, sometimes profound drama, was presented primarily and to best advantage on Broadway.

Now that the American theatre has entered a new millennium, it is appropriate to look back at the most significant playwrights of the twentieth century, those who could be counted upon year after year to produce dramas and comedies that were uniquely American. They once made Broadway the home of many of the world's most exciting plays. Every season from 1920 until about the mid-1960s Broadway audiences could look forward to seeing plays by some of the following dramatists: Eugene O'Neill, Elmer Rice, S. N. Behrman, Robert E. Sherwood, George S. Kaufman, Moss Hart, Lillian Hellman, Thornton Wilder, Marc Connelly, Maxwell Anderson, Arthur Miller, Tennessee Williams; and the list goes on. All but one of these playwrights have been the subject of critical studies or a full-scale biography, detailing the arc of his or her career. The first biography of Moss Hart, who was born in 1904, was not written until 2001: *Dazzler*, by Steven Bach.

Hart's comedies, particularly those written in collaboration with George S. Kaufman, have often been called the finest in American history; the plays he wrote on his own include *Winged Victory*, probably the most significant drama to emerge from World War II; his musical *Lady in the Dark* helped to revolutionize the American musical; his skill as a director helped to shape *My Fair Lady* and *Camelot* and make them milestones of the musical theatre.

If Broadway once stood for a peculiarly American sort of glamour and sophistication, innovation, and excitement, Moss Hart was one of the reasons why. Season after season, for more than three decades, he could be counted upon to write or direct a play or musical that attracted audiences by the thousands from across the United States to Broadway. He was one of several who dominated the Broadway theatre in his time, both by the brilliance of his talent and by the force of his charismatic personality. If few recognize his name any longer, that is a serious loss to American history and culture. This book is intended to help insure that Moss Hart's contributions will once again be seen as precisely what they were and are: milestones of American theatre.

❧

In 1959, at the urging of his wife, Kitty, to whom he often told stories of his boyhood and adolescence, Moss Hart published a memoir entitled *Act One*. The book covers Hart's first twenty-five years, describing his early life in the Bronx and Brooklyn, his relationship with his parents and his younger brother, and the jobs he held when he was a youngster (for the poverty in which his family lived required that he contribute a steady paycheck). Primarily, though, *Act One* tells of a love affair between Moss Hart and the theatre, a love that would eventually be requited when he became one of the foremost playwrights (*The Man Who Came to Dinner*, *Lady in the Dark*, *You Can't Take It With You*) and directors (*My Fair Lady*, *Camelot*) in the United States. In the years covered by his memoir, however, Hart is an outsider attempting to plot the course of a life that will permit him to become active within New York's theatrical community.

Act One ends with the New York production of Hart's first great success, *Once in a Lifetime*. Almost certainly he intended to write at least one more volume of autobiography, but his death in 1961, at the age of fifty-seven, denied the reading public what would likely have been another delightful book. As for *Act One*, although it violated nearly every expectation for theatrical biographies (no gossip, no sex, no portraits, demeaning or idolatrous, of famous performers), it shot almost immediately to the top of *The New York Times* Best Seller list and remained a best-seller for forty-one weeks. It was immediately recognized as a book that transcended other theatrical autobiographies; thoughtful, funny, touching, informative, instructive, and altogether irresistible. Rereading it today only confirms the reaction of the reading public in 1959. Simply put, it is the finest theatrical memoir ever written.

It would be impossible to cover the same ground once again as effectively as Moss Hart covered it in 1959. The present writer can only encourage readers to buy, borrow, or somehow obtain a copy of *Act One*. He can almost assure them that they will be moved (both to laughter and to tears) by Hart's masterfully written tale. Still, for those readers who are unacquainted with *Act One*, the story of his first twenty-five years will be told again in the first two chapters of this book—with additional details based on Hart's correspondence, diaries, scrapbooks, and other items that he chose not to include in his autobiography.

In any case, *Act One* covered only the first twenty-five years of Hart's life. All of his best plays other than *Once in a Lifetime* were written afterward, and he did not begin directing until 1941. Thus: *Moss Hart: A Prince of the Theatre*.

Chapter 1 BEGINNINGS
1904–1930

Moss Hart's maternal grandfather, Barnett Solomon, considered the black sheep in a family of wealthy Jews, married Moss's grandmother against his family's wishes, thereby forfeiting all rights to the family fortune. He and his young wife, Rose, emigrated to America from England where they lived in what Moss called "extremely straitened" circumstances in a cramped apartment in the Bronx. Moss's grandfather worked side by side with Samuel Gompers making cigars, the two of them dreaming of forming an American Federation of Labor.

Moss never knew his grandmother, Rose, but he learned that she was illiterate and loved to have her husband read Dickens aloud to her. When Moss's grandfather, a tyrant within his family, was angry with her, he would punish her by refusing to read, or even to speak, to her. When Rose somehow managed to save enough money to take the family on a trip to England in 1895, her husband "flew into one of his monumental rages," furious that she should have concealed the existence of the money from him when he was down to his last shirt. Still, he deigned to accompany his wife and two daughters to London.

Solomon and Rose's younger daughter, Lillian, met Barnett Hart in London during the trip and fell in love; Barnett emigrated to America a year after the meeting and took up Barnett Solomon's trade. If the younger Barnett, who was born in 1863, and Lily, born in 1870, hoped for an early wedding, they were disappointed. For, if Solomon could not maintain his patriarchal prerogative in any other way, he could at least dominate the family by the force of his personality. He refused to allow Lily and Barnett to marry for six years. When, at last, they were married, they took an apartment together on West 118th Street, but submissively moved back into Solomon's house when he insisted, at the top of his voice, that they do so. He had found living with his daughter Kate impossible, he said, because she was an incompetent, unwilling housekeeper, and he needed Lily to restore order to his life.

Rose had died soon after the family returned to America, but Solomon continued to tyrannize his daughters, Lily and Kate, and tolerated Moss's father with a distinct show of annoyance. Despite the old man's tendency to sulk ("it is the one quirk or quality in people I cannot abide and do not suffer gladly," Moss later wrote), Moss worshipped his grandfather. The old man, in his turn, adored Moss. If Solomon behaved tyrannically, Moss said, he was also "a unique figure of enormous vitality, color and salt."

Aunt Kate "behaved," Moss said, "like a lady of fashion, disdaining work of any sort." From the time she was twenty, she "was supported first by my grandfather and then by my father, whom she detested and who detested her in return," partly because of her superior manner. Also, Aunt Kate believed herself too delicate to help around the house, so that all the housework fell to Moss's mother.

Moss, the first son of Barnett and Lillian, named after Barnett's father, was born into this sullen, destitute family on October 24, 1904. At the time, they lived on East 105th Street in Manhattan. There, Moss was immediately thrust into the turmoil caused by his grandfather's temperament. The old man "generated high drama as his key turned in the door," Moss said, "and I was usually the storm center of both his violence and his tenderness."

The central reality of Moss's early life was poverty. Both his grandfather and his father were thrown out of work by the invention of cigarmaking machines. Barnett Hart, a slight man, was unable to work as a heavy laborer, so the family lived "on the paltry benefits doled out by the Cigarmakers Union" (this according to *Act One*) and the infrequent work he was able to find. When no work was available, Barnett set up a newsstand in the Bronx, but the enterprise was not successful. Unrelieved poverty, Moss said, was "forever in my mouth and the grim smell of actual want always at the end of my nose." The poverty—"a living and evil thing," as Moss later referred to it—was so pervasive that it prevented any possibility of a happy childhood. He wrote movingly of "the overwhelming and suffocating boredom that is the essence of being poor." The successive stream of boarders Lily and Barnett took in to help pay the rent (at 14 East 107th Street, where the family moved soon after Moss was born) added to the emotional burden, for it made the establishment of any closeness within the family impossible.

Barnett Solomon died when Moss was seven, and, although his brother, Bernard, was born that same year, Moss found himself drawn not to his parents or his brother, but to Aunt Kate. For all her eccentricities, Aunt Kate wielded an extraordinary influence over young Moss. It was she, he remembered, who first took him to the theatre. It was she, with her romantic view of life, who showed him that there was more to life than material things and inspired him to escape, if only through the use of his imagination, from the drabness of his existence. She passed on to him her habit of avid reading, often "by candlelight, since there wasn't always a quarter to put in the gas meter." (While other boys were reading *Tom Swift*, Moss, at thirteen, was reading Dreiser's *Sister Carrie*.) Through her courtly demeanor, she showed Moss an alternative to the crudity and brusqueness he was all too often exposed to. She filled him, from an early age, "with a series of bitter resolves to get [himself] out of [poverty]—to escape to a less wretched world."

Aunt Kate received a small monthly stipend from her wealthy relatives in England and used the money exclusively for luxuries. Even when there was no money for gas and precious little for food, Aunt Kate did not permit her allowance to be touched. She used the money to buy books and to visit the theatre every week, after which she then returned home to act out the plays for Moss and his mother, sometimes until two in the morning. When Moss was seven, Aunt Kate invited him to accompany her to see a vaudeville show at the Alhambra Theatre on 126th Street and Seventh Avenue, far uptown in Manhattan. Soon they were seeing productions at a local stock company together, and later, after Moss and his family moved to the Bronx, at the Bronx Opera House at Third Avenue and 149th Street, home to touring companies. Every Thursday and Saturday afternoon the little boy and his eccentric aunt viewed another theatrical performance. Their visits were kept secret, for Moss's parents would surely have disapproved.

The time Moss spent in school was far less rewarding. He attended P.S. 171 in Manhattan from 1910 to 1913, when he and his family lived on East 156th Street; later he transferred to P.S. 10, and, in 1915, to P.S. 51, both in the Bronx.

He was somewhat better than an average student. His report cards for 1910 through 1919 show a preponderance of B's, with a single A and a single C—although his grades for conduct were about evenly divided between A's and B's. He was marked "not proficient" on several occasions, but it's difficult to read his teacher's abbreviations. One seems to be "Ar" (Arithmetic?), another is "Sp" (Spelling? Probably not Speech, for that would more likely have been known as Elocution), another appears to be "Rd" (Reading?). His absences were staggering. In 1911, he was present for fifty-eight days, absent for thirty-two. In 1918, the figures are fifty-five and forty. His attendance was more regular in other years, but never stellar. Many of the absences can be attributed to his brother's many childhood diseases—which meant quarantine for Moss—but surely the Thursday matinees accounted for a few of them.

"About every other month, poor Bernie was laid low with chicken pox, scarletina, croup or measles," Moss recalled years later. He was fortunate never to catch any of Bernie's diseases, and spent his enforced absences from school reading "almost everything in the Bronx branch of the Public Library—good, bad and awful." All in all, Moss thought that he got a far broader and more thorough education from the books he read than from school, which he "cordially detested."

Perhaps Moss's only distinction at P.S. 51 was the occasion on which he won "first honors" in the Junior Four Minute Men Speaking Contest and was selected as Junior Four Minute Speaker. Moss thought enough of his victory to retain the certificate he was awarded and include it in the scrapbook he assembled many years later.

The boys at his school singled him out for teasing, both because his first name was unusual and because of his "manner of speaking," which, he said, included a trace of an English accent, inherited from his parents and grandparents. Also, he "was a trifle too literate, if not downright theatrical—the one a heritage from my family, the other a carry-over from Thursday and Saturday afternoons at the Alhambra Theatre and the Bronx Opera House." Popularity was out of his reach, due in part to his shyness. He was, as he said years later, "an unhappy child."

So the theatre became Moss's refuge, his escape from unpopularity and from poverty, his ticket to romance. The theatre dissipated his unhappiness, for a few hours, anyway. He saw a magical world in which fantasies were played out for a rapt audience so moved that they rewarded the performers with applause. At the Alhambra, the Franklin, and the RKO Royal Theatres he saw "all the great artists of the two-a-day," such as Will Rogers, Nora Bayes, Bert Williams, Sophie Tucker, and Eva Tanguay. Hopelessly stage-struck, he looked forward to a future of uninterrupted theatregoing. But when he was ten, his father and Aunt Kate had a terrible fight, and Barnett ordered his sister-in-law out of the house. She never returned and Moss did not see her again for many years. He was disconsolate, and blamed his father not only for the absence of his Aunt Kate, but for the loss of his precious trips to the theatre. To add to his grievances, he held his father responsible for the family's poverty as well.

Lily was unable to offer comfort to her son. Moss "felt sorrow for her," an emotion that was justified because of the hard life she led, cooking and keeping house not only for her family but for a steady stream of boarders, trying to intervene during the continual battles that raged in the household, first between Aunt Kate and her father and later between Kate and Lily's husband, Barnett. But Moss admitted that although he admired his mother, "I did not like her." For as long as she lived (until 1937) she was rarely more than a peripheral figure in his life.

Moss and his brother, then eleven and five, had their tonsils removed at the same time at a private hospital specializing in tonsilectomies. Moss recalled years later that they "were kept overnight in a ward filled, it now seems to me, with hundreds of screaming children. The place was huge, bare, cold and dark but for a ghostly light through which, at intervals, weird figures in dead white passed to and fro, carrying gleaming instruments of torture."

At twelve Moss took a part-time job at A. L. Levenson's Music Store in the Bronx. There he indulged in dreams of Broadway and the theatre district. "Broadway" represented El Dorado to Moss, a golden land of which he could only dream, for he had never been within several miles of Broadway. One day, however, the store's owner asked him to pick up some music a few blocks from Times Square. As Moss emerged from the subway station, "a swirling mob of happy, laughing people filled the streets, and others hung from the windows of nearly every building. Vendors moved along the crowd selling confetti, noisemakers and paper streamers." Broadway was, it seemed, precisely the glamorous, vivid, exciting place Moss had imagined it to be. But, as he learned, this was a special day: Election Day, 1916, and throngs of people had come to Times Square to await news of Woodrow Wilson's victory over Charles Evans Hughes. Still, his "first look at Broadway was the beginning of a lifelong infection," he said, one that forever remained in his bloodstream.

For most Jewish boys, the months before the thirteenth birthday are filled with Hebrew lessons and religious instruction. The day on which a Jewish boy becomes thirteen is the day of his bar mitzvah, signaling that he has become a man. But Moss Hart never went through that ceremony, and religion was never a meaningful force in his life. (However, it's ironic that many of the jobs—especially the opportunities he received in the theatre early in his career—were provided by Jewish entrepreneurs who might not have given these opportunities to a Gentile.) Later, he strongly identified with the plight of other Jews and felt his Jewishness keenly, but in a cultural rather than a religious sense. For Moss, turning thirteen meant only that he would continue to alternate between school and whatever part-time job he was filling at the moment.

When he was fifteen, Moss was legally eligible to work full-time. His father withdrew him from school so that Moss could contribute to the family's meager finances. Moss's last report card indicates that his father was somehow able to obtain a doctor's certificate of illness, using it to remove Moss from school. But it was economic circumstances, not illness, that prevented Moss from graduating. Although he had hated school, he looked forward to graduation as an important step on his way out of poverty. But the step was never taken; Moss never returned to school.

Ashamed and embittered about his failure to graduate, Moss added this to the list of grievances against his father. Later on, he lied when asked about his schooling. After he became famous he told interviewers that, after his high school graduation, he took courses in creative writing at Columbia University, but this was only his way of dealing with the humiliation he felt. He attributed that sense of shame to his father's actions, and the resentment lingered for many years.

Moss's first full-time job, at a wholesale furriers' near 14th Street in Manhattan, called for him to hang furs inside a foul-smelling storage vault. He remained in that odious job for as long as he could stand the stench that pervaded his clothes as soon as he stepped inside the vault, his dream of somehow finding a place in the theatre keeping him going. "I had no idea how I was to achieve it," he said, "but I knew . . . there was no other world possible for me." Initially he dreamed of being an actor, but any position in the theatre would have suited him.

He was later employed by the National Cloak and Suit Company in the garment district around 23rd Street, the job calling upon him to spy discreetly on the store's customers, seeing to it that no shoplifting occurred. That job offered him one outlet for his theatrical ambitions. On June 26, 1922, he acted in (and evidently wrote) The "National" Revue, an "entertainment" given for the National Cloak and Suit Company. Among the characters in the entertainment were "The Author," "Miss Plot," "Miss Melody," "Miss Jazz," and so on. Moss played "The Author."

Then, suddenly, before he turned eighteen, he stumbled into a theatrical job. He could no longer abide the life he had been living, and one fall day walked resolutely toward Broadway, hoping somehow to find work in the theatre. He went to visit a friend, the only person he knew who was remotely connected to the theatre. The connection was tenuous at best, for Moss's friend worked as an office boy for Augustus Pitou, a booker of small-time acts and plays known as the "King of the One Night Stands."

As it turned out, Moss's friend had quit the job only moments before Moss entered the office. In need of an office boy, Pitou hired the eager Moss—or "Mouse," as he always called him. Seated in the outer office of Pitou's two-room operation in the New Amsterdam building, Moss imposed his gregarious personality on the workplace. Edward Eliscu, a young actor making the rounds of theatrical producers, often stopped at Pitou's office, looking for work. When he stepped off the elevator he often heard laughter coming from behind the office door. The laughter was invariably prompted by Moss, seated in the outer office, Eliscu said. Hart "held court almost daily for a handful of young connoisseurs who gathered to pass judgment on plays, performers, and critics."

Pitou did not present plays on Broadway, but in small towns across America—although occasionally his productions would play briefly in cities such as Chicago or St. Louis or San Francisco. He had a stable of "stars" who were unknown in New York but well established as leading attractions in Port Huron, Michigan, Sheboygan, Wisconsin, and Butte, Montana.

Although Pitou himself seemed to take no real interest in the theatre (other than assuring that his productions managed to get from one city to another in time for the evening's performance), Moss reveled in his new job. He often arrived at the office an hour early, and remained for an hour after everyone left in the afternoon—simply to soak up the theatrical atmosphere. One important benefit of his new job was that, as Pitou's office boy, he was entitled to free tickets from other theatrical offices, and every evening except Saturday (the one night on which free tickets were not available), for as long as he worked for Pitou, he went to see a play.

The early 1920s were a gloriously exciting time for the New York theatre. Eugene O'Neill's early plays were in the process of revolutionizing American drama, substituting maturity in subject and treatment for melodramatic claptrap. Other playwrights, like Elmer Rice, Robert E. Sherwood, and S. N. Behrman would soon follow his example. Musical comedies were juvenile and escapist, but they offered gaiety and vitality. Another form of musical theatre, the revue, most prominently represented by the frequent editions of the *Ziegfeld Follies*, was a sophisticated form of vaudeville, representing glamour and elegance. Moss saw them all: the claptrap as well as the plays that aspired to higher things, the flops (he guessed that "for a space of two years I witnessed more plays that closed in less than a week than any other living mortal, barring the critics who reviewed them") as well as the hits.

Moss's free tickets gave him the means to repay his Aunt Kate for the pleasures she had given him seven years before. He tracked her down, but surreptitiously—not even the mention of her name was permitted in his house—and invited her to accompany him on his nightly visits to the theatre, where they sat in the orchestra rather than the upper balcony. It was to be the last year of Aunt Kate's life, but a year she spent happily beside Moss, having dinner for seventy-five cents every evening at Lorber's restaurant and attending a different play each night.

Anne Nichols, the playwright who supplied Augustus Pitou with all the plays he needed for his various companies each season, struck it rich in 1922 with *Abie's Irish Rose*, a play in which she invested her life savings. (A comedy about a young Jewish man and his Irish sweetheart, and the complications that arise among the couple's parents, the plot served as a template for countless imitators.) It opened on Broadway to execrable reviews but gradually built an audience that became so vast the play broke all records for consecutive performances. As a result, Miss Nichols stopped churning out melodramas and romances for Pitou, who needed to find plays from other sources. Playwrights were found and the plays were produced, but the results were poor. One company in particular, featuring the Irish tenor Joseph Regan, struggled to make enough money in one city to justify taking the production to the next.

In 1923, Pitou turned to his office boy, asking Hart if he would take home a large number of the scripts that had been submitted, hoping that he could find a play to replace the production which was doing so poorly on the road. After reading "batch after batch of manuscripts, one more footling and more foolish than the other," Moss suddenly thought, "Why, I could write a better play than any of these myself." He immediately inserted a sheet of paper into his typewriter and began writing, completing the first act by midnight.

For some reason that Moss himself was at a loss to explain, he did not put his own name on the title page, but used the first names of three acquaintances. The play was initially called

Lad o' Laughter
A Rip-Roaring Comedy
in Three Acts
by Robert Arnold Conrad

but the title was changed when it was discovered that a play called *Lass of Laughter* had been performed only a few years before. The play was then referred to by two titles, *The Hold-Up Man* and *The Beloved Bandit*. (In *Act One*, Hart uses only the title *The Beloved Bandit* when referring to the play.)

Moss showed the first act of his play to Pitou the next morning, recommending it as a play that was "very good," saying that a friend of his had written it. Pitou read it that night, and accosted Moss in the morning. "We found it," the producer said, excitedly. "Don't have to look any further. This is it. If the second and third acts hold up anything like as well, we're home. When can I get the second act?"

"Tomorrow morning," Moss answered, and, that night, stayed awake until five in the morning to write Act Two. Pitou canceled all appointments the next morning as he read "Robert Arnold Conrad's" work, his excitement increasing with each new plot development. "Mouse," he said, "telephone your friend and ask him to see me this afternoon."

Moss exclaimed that Conrad couldn't be reached; he was a lawyer who spent most of his time in court, Moss improvised. Undaunted, Pitou pressed on. "And when do you think he'll have the third act finished?"

"I guess he could have it for you by tomorrow," said the weary Moss. But it took him several days to write Act Three. When he arrived at the office, third act in hand, Pitou was waiting for him. The producer had shown the first two acts to a wealthy friend, Mrs. Henry B. Harris, the night before, he told Moss, and she was as enthusiastic about the play as he was. In fact, she believed the play was good enough for Broadway and was willing to finance the production. "I'm going to bring the company back to New York, rehearse the play here, open in Rochester, play Chicago for four weeks, and then we'll bring it in. It will be my first New York production," Pitou told Moss, adding that he wanted Robert Arnold Conrad to come to his office that afternoon at two o'clock and sign a contract. Moss wanted to confess that he had written the play but found that he was frozen with apprehension. How would Pitou greet the confession? With anger? Resentment? Would Moss be fired from his job?

Pitou read the third act during his lunch, registered his enthusiastic approval, then sat down to wait for the arrival of Robert Arnold Conrad. But when no one appeared at two o'clock—or at three o'clock—or at four o'clock—Moss had to invent a reason. "He must have been held up in court, Mr. Pitou," he said.

"Get your coat, Mouse," Pitou responded. "We'll go down to his office and wait for him, if we have to wait there all day." In the elevator Moss realized that the deception could not continue another minute. Robert Arnold Conrad had no office, of course, so Moss had no recourse but to tell the truth. "Mr. Pitou," he said, bravely, "*I am Robert Arnold Conrad.*"

A long silence ensued as they got off the elevator, walked through the lobby and on to 42nd Street. Then Pitou turned to his office boy. "Mouse," he said, "I don't know whether you know it or not, but when an author writes his first play he doesn't get the regular royalties."

Moss accepted the contract Pitou later presented to him, and, that night, excitedly told his parents about his new status as a professional playwright. But as he remembered it, they greeted the news that their son had written a play and that his work was about to be produced on Broadway "with hardly a lift of an eyebrow." The only thing that seemed to matter to them was that he continue to bring home the fifteen dollars a week he was earning as Pitou's office boy.

Moss had written an old-fashioned, conventional, naïve romantic melodrama. The dialogue, as seen in the following excerpt, was breezy but patently unrecognizable as human speech:

(ROBERT DARE O'DAY STANDS FRAMED IN THE DOORWAY. HE IS TALL, DARK, HANDSOME, WITH A FLASHING, BOYISH SMILE THAT LIGHTS UP HIS COUNTENANCE. . . . HIS SOMBRERO IS PUSHED FAR BACK ON HIS HEAD, HE HOLDS A PISTOL IN EACH HAND, AND A CIGARETTE DANGLES FROM HIS LIPS. HE STANDS FOR A MOMENT GAZING AT [HIS PRISONERS] INTENTLY THROUGH THE CURL OF THE CIGARETTE SMOKE. THEN:)

O'DAY *(with a brilliant smile)*

Gentlemen, and—er—Ladies! You are my prisoners. Sit down. *(They obey. O'Day picks up the paper with the account of the Conway robbery.)* Well, me heartys, I see we've broken into print again. *(He laughs.)*

GRAIL

Ah! So you're the scoundrel.

O'DAY

The very same. *(With a grand gesture)* My card, sir.

GRAIL

(Gingerly taking card and reading) Robert Dare O'Day, D.D. *(Spluttering)* The impertinence of the fellow. D.D.—Doctor of Divinity!—Huh!

O'DAY

A slight error. *Not* Doctor of Divinity!—DAMN DANGEROUS!

HELEN

(in an ecstasy of bliss) Oh, I think he's *wonderful*!

A director, Priestly Morrison, was hired, and the company, including its star, Joseph Regan, assembled for rehearsals. Moss was allowed to attend rehearsals after four o'clock, but before that time he was required to function as the office boy, "closing the windows, emptying the wastebaskets, stamping the mail and then taking it to the post office on my way to the subway." When the company left New York City for Rochester, the event marked several milestones in Moss's life. He had "never ridden in a Pullman train or eaten in a dining car, and I had never stayed overnight in a hotel." He enjoyed privacy, for the first time in his life, in his hotel room. "I did not know until that moment how starved I had been for privacy, what a precious refreshment to the spirit it is," he wrote in *Act One*. "There is no such indulgence in the realms of poverty, and only those who have lived without it can know what a prime luxury privacy is."

Moss remembered the opening performance in 1923 at the Lyceum Theatre in Rochester, New York, as an unrelieved disaster, and he was grateful that Robert Arnold Conrad was still billed as the play's author. In *Act One* he described in considerable detail the misery and humiliation he experienced at the play's failure. The audience "knew what was wrong with [the play] before the first act was half over. It was a fake. It was a composite of all the plays Anne Nichols had written . . . and while I doubt that any of those efforts would have won an accolade from a student of play-writing, they were at least true to their genre. Of their kind, they at least had the virtue of honesty—and *The Beloved Bandit* was a dishonest facsimile."

But newspaper accounts of the opening night don't seem to be describing the same event. The press and the audience—the house was sold out—evidently enjoyed the play and production. One critic said, "From all indications, this combination play with music, is going to be thoroughly well-liked in Rochester. All the elements that make for success as an entertainment are comprised in this production."

Another critic agreed: "To build a play which will prove adequate to the needs of a singing actor has always proven a difficult task for the dramatist . . . These requirements have been met in an admirable manner by Robert Conrad." The critic offered a synopsis of the play:

> Mr. Regan assumes the role of an operatic singer who masquerades as a bandit. It so happens that his first victims prove to be an elderly man and his two daughters and he does not find sufficient excitement or satisfaction in simply holding them up while he relieves them of any valuables they may have, but he proceeds to detain them in a California mountain shack where he forces the father to scrub the floor and imposes other household duties upon the two daughters and the parent's secretary. Then he proceeds to "exercise" his voice with the result that the prisoners immediately become thrilled and one of the young women forthwith proceeds to fall in love with the supposed bandit. In a most pleasing manner and captivating tone Mr. Regan sang "The Bandit's Song," "Love Will Lead the Way" [and other songs, written by an unidentified composer and lyricist] to the complete satisfaction of last night's audience.

The synopsis and the dialogue quoted earlier reveal that Moss's description of his work as "a dishonest facsimile" of the romantic melodrama was an honest judgment. On the other hand, the playwright was nineteen years old and a novice, the play had been written in less than a week, and American drama—except for Eugene O'Neill's plays, the sophisticated comedies of George S. Kaufman and Marc Connelly, and those of a very few others—was only beginning to emerge from its infantile stage. Would anyone expect anything more than a rather slapdash, imitative piece under those conditions? All in all, Moss Hart's first effort may have been no better than other plays of its kind (that is, a play written as a vehicle for the star, in this case Joseph Regan, and one that aspires to do nothing more than amuse an undemanding audience), but—despite some ludicrous· dialogue and events—it is not a great deal worse, as readers of early twentieth-century American drama can attest.

Still, Moss recalled the week in Rochester as "perhaps the most dismal week I have ever spent with a play." He remembered no performance attended by more than thirty people, invariably sitting "in silence throughout the performance, and as the final curtain fell, they clumped silently up the aisle and left the theatre in the same glum fashion they had entered it." Moss dutifully watched every performance in order to make suggestions for improvements to the actors and the director, but the experience was so excruciating that it created in him a lifelong aversion to seeing his own plays.

From Rochester the company moved on to Chicago, where the play met with the disastrous reception Moss mistakenly attributed to the audiences in Rochester. The Chicago audience laughed derisively at the play's revolting green set, its acting and its dialogue, and it wasn't long after the opening curtain that people began rising from their seats and leaving the theatre. Later, in Pitou's hotel room, Pitou and Mrs. Harris agreed to close the production the following night, foregoing the planned Broadway production and absorbing a loss of forty-five thousand dollars.

Two days later, when Pitou and Moss returned to New York, Pitou said that, having lost money on *The Beloved Bandit*, he would have to economize by eliminating Moss's job. His secretary and the elevator operator could handle what had been the office boy's duties. Moss disconsolately took the subway home to the Bronx.

Or so he remembered the sequence of events. In fact, Pitou was able to recoup some of Mrs. Harris's investment with subsequent performances of *The Hold-up Man*, or *The Beloved Bandit* in Youngstown, Ohio, Dubuque, Iowa, Fort Wayne, Indiana, and elsewhere. Pitou signed Gerald Griffin, "the singing comedian," to appear in the play. The "cyclonic comedy of youth, music, laughter and song," as it was advertised, played at the Park Theatre in Youngstown in September 1925, with the author's name given as Moss Hart, not Robert Arnold Conrad. Sheet music for at least one of the songs from the production was issued and sold. Griffin, the singer, gave Hart an auto-graphed copy of the song "Sunset Hour" in October.

For the programs distributed during these performances, Moss wrote a brief introduction: "I think you will like THE BELOVED BANDIT. It has been written to entertain and amuse, and, we hope, send you home laughing and happy. If it accomplishes this last, it has served its purpose."[1]

The posters for the play included a different sort of note: "NOT A PICTURE. It's an Augustus Pitou Attraction." This may seem to have been an innocu-ous and unremarkable notice, but, in fact, the message it conveyed was omi-nous for the theatre outside New York. Moviegoing was becoming such a habit throughout America that the stage was struggling to retain its audi-ence. Movies were cheaper to attend, their production values were generally higher than any road production could achieve—and this was still in the silent era. Two years later, in 1927, the first talking picture, *The Jazz Singer* with Al Jolson (which was really a silent film with musical numbers), was re-leased. And after the movies began to talk, the theatre's hold on its audiences became even more tenuous. Augustus Pitou had good reason to be con-cerned for the future of his enterprises, and one can understand his need to

---

1 According to Edward Eliscu, he collaborated with Hart on *The Beloved Bandit*, and both agreed that they would be credited as co-authors—although, in the event that Eliscu would direct the production, his name would not be listed as playwright. Pitou was never told that Eliscu had co-written the play. Later, when the production was in preparation, Hart told Eliscu not to attend rehearsals because "it would be too confusing for Priestly Morrison . . . to communicate with two authors." Thus, Eliscu says, he had nothing to do with the production and Pitou never knew that he had a hand in writing the play. Whatever Eliscu's feelings may have been, he never tried to take the credit that was (in his account, at any rate) properly due him.

Many years afterward, Hart sent Eliscu "a fondly inscribed copy" of *Act One*. In his autobiography, Eliscu says, "I anticipated reading a mellow, funny account of our joint venture. But in the book's otherwise well remembered, warmly told story, I found no mention of my co-authorship of the play. I wrote Moss, praising *Act One*, gently pointing out a few inaccuracies. I referred to our . . . collaboration by thanking him for his gallantry in assuming sole responsibility for [*The Beloved Bandit*]." Why Hart would have denied Eliscu credit—both at the time *The Beloved Bandit* was written and when he told of the events in *Act One*—is utterly baffling. A playwright who achieved most of his success working with collaborators surely would not have felt diminished by confessing that his first play had been written with another playwright. Perhaps he felt that Eliscu's contribution was insignificant, unworthy of credit. In any case—presuming that Elis-cu's account is accurate—Hart's behavior was odd, to say the least. But it is only one of many instances when the incidents described in *Act One* prove, upon close inspection, to have been so thoroughly embroi-dered that they offer only a distorted (or, at best, a partial) view of reality.

economize when he let Moss go. However, the loss of his job was a terrible blow for Moss, both because it severed his connection with the theatre and because he desperately needed an income, for his parents' economic situation was at its bleakest.

Fortunately, Edward Chodorov, a young friend of Moss's, had been offered the job of directing plays for William J. Perlman, owner of a little-theatre group at the Labor Temple on 14th Street in New York. Perlman, who also owned a summer camp—Camp Utopia in Lackawaxen, Pennsylvania—suggested that the well-read, articulate, flamboyant Chodorov might also be appointed social director of the camp if he proved capable of handling the Labor Temple job. Chodorov, in turn, approached Moss about being his partner in the little-theatre venture (each would direct three one-act plays) and his assistant at the summer camp. Moss was initially skeptical as he had no experience in either position, but as few other prospects were in view, he accepted Chodorov's proposal.

Only two nights later Moss met with the casts of the three one-act plays that comprised the first production he was to direct for the Labor Temple. Rehearsals were held three nights a week (until the final week or so, when four or five evenings would be devoted to rehearsals), during which Moss gradually gained confidence in his ability to direct his cast of amateur performers. The director of a play must, of course, know and understand every aspect of the play being worked upon, and Moss said that directing made him "aware almost for the first time of the inner structure of a play." He focused upon what the author hoped to achieve in his work and the means by which he intended to achieve it. "The mechanism and construction of a play began to hold far more interest for me than the actual staging of it," he wrote, leading him to become a voracious reader of plays.

On January 28 and 29, 1926, Moss directed the Labor Temple Players in *The Flattering Word* by George Kelly (the author of successful comedies and dramas on Broadway and the uncle of actress Grace Kelly), a double bill with O'Neill's *The Dreamy Kid*, directed by Chodorov. In a subsequent production of Ibsen's *Ghosts*—one of the most complex and challenging plays ever written, and a play that a second-time director probably should not have chosen to produce with amateur actors—Moss not only directed but played the role of Oswald when the actor assigned the role quit the production only a week before the performance was scheduled. Moss felt the production was ghastly and that his own performance was no better, but, he said, the audience was polite if not enthusiastic. And despite the play's failure, William J. Perlman, who saw the performance, offered Chodorov and Hart the positions of Social Director and Assistant Social Director at Camp Utopia.

Chodorov told Moss that they would need a supply of sketches and songs, "especially the newest stuff from the musical comedies" when they reached Camp Utopia. But how to get this material? Chodorov said, mysteriously, "There are ways." Hart described them in *Act One*:

> There were indeed ways, as I was to learn in the following weeks, or at least Eddie's ways, of collecting the necessary material for a social director's portfolio. One of them was for us to arrive on the sidewalk in front of the theatre of a reigning musical comedy hit just before intermission time. We then mingled with the audience as they emerged into the lobby at the end of the first act, picked up a program that someone inevitably dropped and left on the lobby floor, and brandishing the program conspicuously in front of us, walked back into the theatre with the audience to see the second act.
>
> Though this system restricted the amount of material we could steal, the authors of musical comedies and revues invariably save some of their heavy ammunition for the second act, and there were always reprises of songs from the first act. There were a few theatres, of course, that issued intermission checks to the audience to stop just such banditry, but there were not many of these. . . . The *Follies* was very necessary for us to see, for it contained not only a large amount of special material in skits, but Fanny Brice as well, of whom I was to do an impersonation for several summers thereafter.
>
> After each show, it was our practice to go straight to Eddie's house and between us piece together all the material we had stolen from the show with the help of a pocket flashlight and notes scribbled on the program. . . . We were very often able to piece together whole sketches word for word, and what we couldn't remember we wrote ourselves.

Perhaps the best aspect of going to summer camp, from Hart's point of view, was escaping the crowded apartment in which his family and their boarders lived in the Bronx. At last he would be able to break out of "the dark brown sameness" he had experienced all his life. "The thought of escaping from another city summer, with its front stoops and fire escapes filled with tired, sweating adults and squalling children, into a world of green lawns and shady trees" made him giddy with anticipation.

Hart's stint as assistant social director at Camp Utopia included the writing (with Chodorov) of *The Utopian Follies*, a revue in eighteen scenes, in 1926. Moss appeared in eleven of the eighteen. In subsequent summers, Hart was hired as social director by several other summer camps, all of which served the same purposes but differed in their degree of affluence. The guests, the great majority of them Jewish and most of them young adults, came to the country to get away from city life for a few days or weeks. At any given time there might be as few as two hundred or as many as fifteen hundred guests in attendance, all expecting to be entertained throughout the day, whether in the social hall, on the tennis courts, or in the swimming pool. Some of the young women hoped to meet future husbands, and nearly everyone of both sexes anticipated a summer romance.

The burden of providing the entertainment—of all sorts, at any time, for the guests—fell entirely on the shoulders of the social director and his staff. Entertainments might consist of songs and sketches, comic monologues, impressions of celebrated performers, or complete plays. Once a week "an original musical comedy," written as well as performed by the social staff, was presented. Being a social director (or his assistant) meant serving as Master of Ceremonies for any occasion that might arise and leading the guests in song during campfire nights. It meant socializing with the guests at mealtimes. It meant offering to dance with any girl who might not have been asked by a male guest (and, since women always outnumbered the men at the camps, the male members of the social staff were always kept busy, attempting to insure that no female guest could ever say she had a disappointing time), or serving as a tennis partner for a guest who was looking for an opponent. It meant decorating the social hall for Costume Night and cleaning up after the evening was over. It meant maintaining a perpetual smile and always being ready with a funny remark offstage as well as on. It meant giving lessons in palm reading and tap dancing. It also meant many hours of labor and precious little time for strolling among the "green lawns and shady trees" he had looked forward to. Still, Hart was successful in his job, Edward Chodorov remembered, because he was popular and romantic looking, and a skilled guitar player and singer.

Those who became social directors—among those who subsequently filled the job were Danny Kaye (prominently featured in Hart's 1940 production *Lady in the Dark*) and Phil Silvers—often went on to bigger and better things, but the work was hard, the hours were long, the guests demanding, the compensation skimpy. For Hart, social directing was only an odious chore. Moreover, it "provided me with a lifelong disdain for the incredible contortions of the human spirit at play, and a lasting horror of people in the mass seeking pleasure and release in packaged doses."

In spite of all his frenzied summer activities at Camp Utopia, Hart had time to formulate a plan for his future. He knew beyond doubt that he wanted to make his living in the theatre. He considered stage management, but stage managers' jobs were among the most difficult to come by. He still harbored an ambition to be an actor, but his performance in *Ghosts* had been discouraging. By process of elimination, he realized that his best chance for success was as a playwright. His one experience as a dramatist—*The Beloved Bandit*—had turned out disastrously, but that play had been written in haste by an immature young man who knew next to nothing about playwriting. Now, older by a year and well-read in modern drama, he felt himself qualified to write for the theatre.

Certainly his background qualified him as an astute observer of the theatrical scene. He objected strongly to a negative review J. Brooks Atkinson (who later dropped the "J") wrote in *The New York Times* of a now-forgotten play called *My Country* by William J. Perlman, the owner of Camp Utopia and the director of the Labor Temple. Whether his letter was written purely out of conviction or whether loyalty to his employer was also involved is a matter of conjecture, but Hart composed and mailed a long, detailed, well-reasoned rebuttal to the dramatic editor of the *Times*, calling Atkinson's review "unreasonable and unfair." Regardless of the validity of Hart's opinions, his letter illustrates his passion about theatrical matters.

The letter also indicates that Hart's taste, even at the age of twenty-two, inclined toward satirical comedy. Perlman's play, which satirized various ethnic groups, "is undoubtedly a problem play," Hart wrote. "In fact, it might have been turned into a tragedy; but what's the use? Life is sufficiently serious without stressing its tragic side. If we can laugh good-naturedly at one another's eccentricities—and that is what we laugh at in *My Country*—it is a healthy sign for the coming of a more tolerant age."

Hart's decision to become a playwright was bolstered by the many plays he had seen in New York while in the employ of Augustus Pitou. His frequent theatregoing served as a sort of playwriting apprenticeship. Viewing the best plays set a good example of what he, as a playwright, should aspire to, but seeing the bad ones also had value, for their pattern of inept dialogue, weak characterizations, and inadequate plots all showed him what to avoid.

If he were to become a playwright, he realized, he would need time—time to consider the ideas he wished to explore, time to select those characters and incidents which would best convey the ideas, time to refine the dialogue and mold all of the other elements a good play requires. Full-time jobs would deprive him of the time he needed, but he could carve out the time, he reasoned, if his daytime hours were free. Perhaps he could earn enough money to help support his family by directing amateur productions at night—not only at the Labor Temple but in other venues—and by serving as a social director in the summertime. If so, he could spend all his other waking hours writing the play or plays that would finally bring him recognition in the theatre.

When Camp Utopia closed in September, Hart spoke to William J. Perlman, requesting that he be put in charge of the little-theatre group at the Labor Temple (Edward Chodorov had gone off to South Africa as a member of a theatrical touring company). Perlman agreed, and also expressed a willingness to recommend him for another directing position in the Bronx.

Hart's directorial duties wouldn't begin for a few months, and, unwilling to return to a non-theatrical job unless absolutely forced to do so, he decided that this was a good time to try his luck as an actor. Hart was friendly with the office boy of George Tyler, a successful producer. Believing that his friend might give him some valuable information about casting, Hart visited Tyler's office. There was nothing at the moment, he was told, but his friend could get him in to see Mr. Tyler if he would wait patiently. Hart sat in the waiting room with other hopeful actors until one of them mentioned that a revival of Eugene O'Neill's *The Emperor Jones* was scheduled for the Mayfair Theatre and that the producers were looking for an actor to play Smithers. The aspirants in the waiting room scoffed at the opportunity, for the pay was only twenty-five dollars a week. But for Hart, twenty-five dollars was ten dollars more than he had been earning with Pitou. He waved goodbye to his friend, slipped out of the waiting room, and walked to the Mayfair, a small theatre on 44th Street, east of Broadway.

In the theatre's office Hart announced his interest in the role of Smithers. A man seated behind a desk handed him a script of the play and told him to read it aloud. Fortunately, Hart had already read the play (it had been produced five years before at the Provincetown Playhouse) and, even more fortunately, he had no difficulty in adopting the Cockney accent the role called for, for his father spoke with a distinct Cockney accent. Hart's reading must have been good—or perhaps the management was desperate—for the man behind the desk offered him the role. He told Moss to go immediately to the stage to begin rehearsals with the company.

Charles Gilpin, a brilliant black actor, was directing as well as playing the leading role—a role he had already played more than a thousand times, including the original production of O'Neill's play. He was so impressive in the role that O'Neill later said, "As I look back on all my work, I can honestly say there was only one actor who carried out every notion of a character I had in mind. That actor was Charles Gilpin . . . in *The Emperor Jones*." Had Gilpin been white he would have been recognized as one of America's greatest actors, but racial prejudice limited him to playing only black characters, of which there were few in American drama. *The Emperor Jones* offered him an opportunity to use all of his remarkable talents. But that was, in essence, the only role available to him. And the fact that, between theatrical engagements he was forced to take jobs as an elevator operator, a barbershop attendant, and a Pullman car porter left him embittered. Now, at the age of forty-eight, he was thoroughly dependent on alcohol.

Gilpin ran through the first scene, in which only Jones and Smithers appear, with Hart. "Stolidly and wearily," Gilpin gave Hart his blocking, then asked, "Did they tell you when we open?" Hart hadn't the faintest idea. "Day after tomorrow," said Gilpin. "You better learn the words fast."

That night, after telling his parents that he was about to become an actor—and once again finding his news received with a distressing lack of enthusiasm, except concerning the additional ten dollars he would be making—Hart went to his bedroom to learn his lines.

The production opened as part of a double bill (the other play was *In 1999* by William de Mille, the brother of Cecil B. de Mille and father of choreographer Agnes DeMille) on November 10, 1926. For some unknown reason, Hart moved this date forward by four years in *Act One*, one of several peculiar inconsistencies in that book. One cannot excuse these inconsistencies by maintaining that Hart's memory was simply playing tricks on him, for he quotes verbatim from the reviews he received in *The Emperor Jones*, reviews clearly dated 1926 rather than 1922. Perhaps he felt that the story would somehow seem more intriguing or romantic if he had been eighteen rather than twenty-two at the time of the production.

Apparently, Hart manipulated the truth with some regularity when he wrote *Act One*. George S. Kaufman evidently believed that to be so, for he told Howard Teichmann soon after Hart's autobiography had been published, "I'm very pleased for Moss that *Act One* is on the best seller list. I simply feel that it should be under fiction instead of non-fiction."

In any case, Hart, less than a month after having observed his twenty-second birthday, was playing a dissolute sixty-year-old man—with only two days of rehearsals. Gilpin gave a brilliant performance (although, dulled by alcohol, his subsequent performances were barely adequate, and in some he was able to do little more than recite his lines while reeling about the stage) and the newspaper critics said so the next day. As one would expect, the notices all concentrated upon the play and Gilpin's performance, but Hart was not neglected. One critic said "Moss Hart as Smithers, the Cockney, is a delight both to the eye and ear." Another said "Moss Hart . . . does the cheap Cockney trader to perfection." A third managed to contain his enthusiasm: "Moss Hart adequately portrayed a Cockney trader" was all he had to say. *The Emperor Jones* was a success, running for fifteen weeks at the Mayfair.

Although Hart's name was listed correctly in the program, a number of publicity blurbs sent out by the producers listed "Marcy Hart" as a member of the cast. Since Moss's nickname was "Mossie," one wonders if the person in charge of publicity overheard the name and mistook it for Marcy.

But that was only a small irritation, for Hart's career as an actor had been launched, his debut had been successful—and it had all happened so easily! Surely he would progress from here to greater things. As it happened, though, Smithers was the first and, with one minor exception, the last role he acted professionally in New York.

The failure to be cast in another play soon led Hart to a conclusion he could not escape: "in spite of a lucky beginning, in spite of passion and dedication, I would never be more than a passable actor and at best an adequate one—and there is no more damning word to apply to acting than 'adequate.'"

At home, the struggle for economic survival was as great as ever. One subtle shift in the family's dynamic occurred without Hart's having noticed it: as the primary money-earner, he found that he had gradually assumed the role of head of the household. "My mother turned to me and not to my father, even in the smallest crises of daily living," Hart said, "and . . . I realized that in these last few years my father had receded more and more into the dim background and I had replaced him." Perhaps it was this subtle displacement that was responsible, but Hart's brother, Bernie, was always sullen in Moss's presence. Although Bernie and Moss slept in the same bed, they almost never communicated, had no affection for one another, were virtual strangers. Moss made attempts to bridge the gap, and, when they didn't work, tried to understand why his brother resented him so, but without success.

Hart resumed his occupation as a director of amateur productions in early 1927. Eventually he held a remarkable number of such positions. For the Park Players of the Young Folks League of Congregation Shaari Zedek, he directed four one-act plays on May 21, 1927, performing a leading role in one of them. Then, in November of that year, he became Dramatic Director for clubhouses of the Young Men's Hebrew Association in the Bronx, Brooklyn, and Newark. For the Brooklyn Jewish Center, which listed Hart as "Director,

Social Activities" in January 1928, he wrote and performed as well as directed. One of the plays he presented was George Kelly's *The Show-Off*, which he also directed that year for "The Y Players."

Hart preferred directing modern plays such as *The Show-Off*, but they were still under copyright and would have cost money for royalties, money that the YMHAs did not possess. So, every once in a while, he directed a contemporary play under a title he had invented. *The Trial of Mary Dugan* became *What Price Justice?* and *Beggar on Horseback* became *Dreams for Sale*, the authorship attributed to such fictitious writers as James L. Baker and Michael Crane.[2] Other plays were presented under their own titles. Hart directed an ambitious season for the "Y" Players in 1928–29, consisting of recent American successes such as *The Royal Family*, *Broadway*, *They Knew What They Wanted*, and *Anna Christie*.

According to Dore Schary (who acted in several of the productions Moss directed, and who later rose to prominence as the head of MGM studios), the ambitious plays Hart chose—far more challenging than the conventional fare offered in community theatres—were selected "not for the benefit of the players, but, as he confided to me, for this own tempering, schooling, and benefit."

Schary described his first meeting with Hart, who wore "a green velour hat, a wide black tie and long pointed Barrymore-style shirt collar. Twenty-three years old, he was earning a precarious living as an itinerant director of little theatre groups. But you would never have guessed it. He behaved as if he were a highly successful Broadway director who was gracing us with his time and talent, provided we proved to him that we were worthy of those gifts. It was that resolute air of independence and authority that Moss wore during all his life that was so impressive to me."

In April 1929, the New Jersey Federation of the YMHA and YWHA offered a bill of four one-acts at the Jewish Community Center in Jersey City. One of them, *The Valiant*, was directed by Hart. That must have been an especially busy month, for *The Center Follies*, "An Intimate Musical Revue in Sixteen Scenes"—with Hart appearing in one of them—was "Conceived and Staged by Moss Hart" on April 6, 1929. Also in 1929, Hart was director of an organization called "The Stagers" at the YMHA.

He directed three one-acts and wrote one of them, *Anything Might Happen* (a variation of *The Beloved Bandit*) for "The Masquers" of the YMHA and supervised "a *Y Follies*, written by the members of the Dramatic Society." A

---

2 Or so Hart said to interviewers and repeated in *Act One*. Programs of the time show that *The Trial of Mary Dugan* and *Beggar on Horseback* were presented under their own names, however.

group called the American Co-Optimists enlisted Hart's services for their productions of three one-act plays at the Mayfair Theatre (where Hart had played Smithers in *The Emperor Jones* a few years earlier).

Hart was obviously fascinated with *The Emperor Jones*, for he directed it once again for the Center Players, this time reprising his role of Smithers. He tackled a number of other plays more than once; among them were *The Show-Off* and *Ghosts*. He played Oswald in *Ghosts* both for the "Y" Players in Newark in early 1930 and for the Labor Temple Players, although, on the latter occasion, he did not serve as director.

Shortly after he wrote his first great success in the Broadway theatre, Hart felt sufficiently knowledgeable about the amateur theatre movement in America that he consented to write an article in a New York newspaper about it. He made the point that "amateurs have a higher mission [than providing easily digested entertainment], which the Jewish groups seem quick and eager to recognize—and that is to study, select and present the very finest dramaturgy, even if only to a small neighborhood following. Amateurs alone can afford to be so discerning, for they are not oppressed and swayed by box office exigencies and need heed only the dictates of their own taste." Hart hoped particularly for Jewish plays. "We need someone to do for the Jewish soul what Eugene O'Neill has done for the American. . . . I sometimes hope that some day I may have something to contribute. It is a dream worth keeping alive—to create the Jewish prize play, to be the Meistersinger who will stir our people with a glorious epic . . ." Hart never wrote such a play, but evidently he made the attempt, for *The New York Times* in 1930 said that the early (unpublished and unproduced) plays Hart wrote "dealt with distinctively Jewish subjects."

Directing plays with amateur groups between November and May paid just enough to enable his family to live, and the summer season began immediately afterward, bringing with it Hart's salary as social director. But September and October posed a problem, and Hart filled in with various nontheatrical jobs. For a week he was a floorwalker at Macy's, for several more weeks he worked on the night shift at *The New York Times* doing clerical work—and managed every week to bring home a paycheck.

After his first summer job at Camp Utopia as Eddie Chodorov's assistant, Hart was promoted to the position of social director at the Half Moon Country Club in Vermont, where he was also able to acquire menial jobs for his father and his brother, jobs that paid no salary but offered board and lodging—and, if they were lucky, tips from the departing guests. Meanwhile, his mother moved to a furnished room for the summer, where Hart sent her ten dollars from his salary each week to pay for her room and board.

One of the crises Hart had to face before summer camp began was finding the money to provide a suitable wardrobe, for every social director was expected to be outfitted in a sport coat and white flannel trousers at the very least. At Camp Utopia, as assistant social director, he could get away with his own meager wardrobe, but that would not do for his new position at the Half Moon Country Club. Hart asked the club's owner, "Mr. Axeler" (as Moss called him in *Act One*), for an advance on his salary so that he could buy suitable clothes. Mr. Axeler said he could not provide an advance but suggested that Hart go to Geller's clothing store on Eighth Avenue in Manhattan, pick out whatever he wanted, and charge it to Axeler, who would send the clothing to the Half Moon Country Club where it would be waiting when Hart arrived. This resulted in the first in a lifelong series of buying frenzies, undoubtedly with the hope that wearing expensive clothing would enable him to blot out his memories of poverty. As he said,

> Though I had never had the wherewithal with which to indulge myself, I was at that time and for a long time afterward absolutely clothes crazy. It amounted to a hunger for clothes I could never seem to satisfy. I professed to scorn the high-style outfits most male guests paraded around camp in, but secretly I envied them. I craved and coveted the sky-blue turtleneck sweaters and the striped jackets with brass buttons, with a multicolored handkerchief peeking discreetly out of the breast pocket, and a tie that matched, and white suede shoes with patent leather tops. I craved those absurd getups with a real passion.

He bought clothes passionately, indiscriminately, going "a little berserk." After selecting a jacket and slacks, he ordered sweaters, shirts, socks, ties, sandals, a smoking jacket, cravats. "By the time I finished, I had bought in all about $135 worth of clothes—an amount of money that in those days would have outfitted at least three people for two summers. . . . I staggered out of the store as a drunk might stagger into the dawn from an all-night bar, wonderfully warm inside and satisfied to the core, my thirst quenched at last."[3]

Unfortunately for Hart, he never saw the clothes again. The owner of the clothing store, knowing the treacherous Mr. Axeler all too well, refused to send the clothing until he received payment—and Mr. Axeler had no intention of paying a cent. Hart had to make to do with clothing taken from the stock of costumes every camp had on hand for party nights—a routine he found pro-

---

3 Hart implies in *Act One* that he had never had access to new, fashionable clothing before. However, Dore Schary's description of Hart's appearance in 1927 paints a very different picture.

foundly humiliating—until the end of June, when Mr. Axeler finally gave him twenty-five dollars, enough to buy a sports jacket and slacks.

Wherever he served as social director, Hart invariably tried to present plays that were several cuts above the level of the usual entertainment provided at summer camps. At the Half Moon Country Club, for example, he staged *The Emperor Jones*, this time playing the leading role of Brutus Jones. And often these courageous choices proved to be embarrassing mistakes, for the guests had no interest in serious drama and were apt to walk out angrily in the middle of the performances or laugh loudly and inappropriately at scenes and dialogue that were intended to be tragic.

One of the guests who saw the performance of *The Emperor Jones* at the Half Moon Country Club was Joseph Hyman, a businessman in his middle to late twenties, who would have a significant influence on Moss Hart's life. Despite the derisive laughter that greeted the production, Hyman was impressed with Hart's work. As the two talked afterward, Hart spoke of his ambition to be a playwright and Hyman said that, for his part, he hoped to leave his family's business and become a theatrical producer someday.

The summer at the Half Moon Country Club was a nightmare for Hart and for his brother, Bernie, but Moss's father enjoyed himself so thoroughly that he underwent a thorough change of personality: "he became a loquacious, merry and delightful human being [who] quickly established himself as a camp favorite," Moss said. He came alive, blossoming "in a hundred different enjoyable ways. . . . as his loneliness was replaced by the newly discovered pleasure of being accepted for the sunny creature he really was." In his later years, too, Barnett Hart (who was generally known as "The Commodore," for reasons no one can remember) was a jaunty soul.

If the hard work at the Half Moon Country Club was draining, at least Moss would pick up a hefty paycheck at the end of the summer. Or so he thought. But Mr. Axeler left the camp before paying any of the staff, leaving his partners to cope with the disgruntled entertainers, waiters, dishwashers, and cooks. Like Moss, most of them had let their salary accumulate over the summer, expecting to receive it in a lump sum. Although Axeler's partners—evidently as sadly deceived by Axeler's treachery as everyone else—provided money for Barnett to take the train back to New York, they could only afford to give Moss and Bernie train tickets as far as Albany, after which they were forced to hitchhike.

When they arrived in the Bronx, they needed to come to a decision immediately about where the family was to live, for Lily was still renting a furnished room. And a new apartment would cost money—$200, Hart estimated—

money for rent, money for a deposit, money to move their furniture. In this moment of their greatest desperation, Hart turned to Joe Hyman, who had professed an interest in Hart's future. Hyman immediately handed two hundred dollars in cash to Hart, a gesture for which he never ceased to be grateful. Hyman also gave jobs to Barnett and to Bernie.

With Hyman's gift, the family took a new apartment in Sea Gate, a community on the edge of Brooklyn, an apartment that none of them had ever seen but that relatives in Brooklyn had told them about. Hart was determined to escape from the Bronx, a place he associated only with tawdriness and want. The new apartment, consisting of three small rooms, was barely large enough to contain the family's furniture, but that mattered less than the escape from the Bronx.

True to the vow he took in 1926, Hart spent his mornings and afternoons writing plays. The first attempts were primitive and unsatisfactory, but with each new play Hart came a step closer to finding his own voice and style. Still, his progress was agonizingly slow and frustrating. At times he felt he was making no progress at all.

Summers continued to be spent at summer camps. The Crescent Country Club, for which Hart directed plays during the winter, offered "A Summer School of the Theatre on the shores of Lake Champlain" in upstate New York, in which courses in History of the Drama, Playwriting, Stage Direction, Acting, Voice Control, Stage Lighting, Makeup, Dramatic Criticism, and assorted other subjects were taught. The country club's brochure identified "the heads of the faculty" as Philip Gross and Moss Hart.

In time, Hart's status as social director changed markedly for the better. By 1929 he was, as he said, "the most highly paid [$200 per week], the most sought-after social director of the Borscht Circuit," as the string of hotels catering primarily to Jewish customers in the Catskills was known. At the Flagler Hotel he had a personal staff of twenty-six people, a substantial budget to work with, and he was able to provide much more polished entertainments than he had presented in earlier years. So impressive was Hart's reputation that guests of nearby hotels attempted to see the productions he mounted—but on Saturday nights the shows were always sold out, and several hundred people had to return in disappointment to their hotels. At the Flagler, Hart's presentations of recent Broadway successes were taken seriously by the audiences, which rarely failed to fill the fifteen-hundred-seat theatre.

His work at the Flagler gave Hart a self-confidence he had never before possessed. The salary also allowed him to dress in the manner he thought befitting a young director. While at the Flagler, Hart appeared in and directed Assistant Social Director Dore Schary in a production of *The Valiant*. Hart also wrote "An Intimate Musical Revue in Fifteen Scenes" called *The Flagler Scandals of 1929* and appeared in some of the sketches. He performed his by-now-famous (in summer camp circles) impression of Fanny Brice in one of them. He directed *Homeward Bound*, "A Nautical Musical Comedy in Two Acts," and appeared in it along with Schary. Also at the Flagler Hart presented his own play, *Anything Might Happen*, for the second time. (Still another performance of that play—the script of which is now lost—was given in 1929 for The Y Players.)

Years later, at Moss Hart's eulogy, Dore Schary recalled how impressive Hart's work was to his colleagues: "Those who worked with him in community centers and in the beleaguered bastions of the Borscht Circuit watched that development and were convinced that Moss would make his way with firm and long strides. He directed us on-stage through plays of Ibsen, O'Neill and Shaw with the same authority he brought to staging [old vaudeville and burlesque] sketches like Floogle Street or Belt in the Back."

By September 1929, Hart had been directing amateur groups and serving as social director for various camps for several years. He had used all but the summer months to write plays, all of them heavily dramatic, and "each successive play had been better than the one before," Hart said, "of this I was convinced." Although Richard J. Madden of The Richard J. Madden Play Company turned down a play called *Panic* that Lester Sweyd[4] submitted to him on Hart's behalf, his letter of rejection contained some encouraging words: "If Mr. Hart has anything else I would certainly like to read it," Madden said, and he mentioned Moss's "splendid talents."

Undaunted by Madden's rejection, Hart retitled the play *No Retreat* and submitted it to the Hampton Players of Long Island, who accepted the play for production in the summer of 1930. *No Retreat* premiered on July 16 of that year, with Albert Van Dekker (who later dropped the "Van") and Henry Howard, experienced actors with Broadway credits, included in the cast. A newspaper critic said that "the three acts were replete with exciting complica-

---

4 Sweyd was a friend of Hart's who had no theatrical ambition for himself but was a fervent "believer" in talent. In Hart's words, Sweyd "was forever accosting play readers, secretaries, casting directors, and even office boys, or whomever else he could waylay in the streets and alleys around Times Square, and saying . . . 'Keep your eye on a writer called Moss Hart—he's a comer'. . ." Sweyd remained a strong supporter of Hart's for many years, eventually presenting him with an enormous scrapbook containing clippings of his interviews and reviews of Hart's plays.

tions." The play concerned a rivalry between father and son, both actors, who were rehearsing a play in which both would appear, each trying to outshine the other. *No Retreat* was successful enough that a magazine article devoted to the summer theatre scene said that "it is rumored [that the play] will receive [a] Broadway production." The renowned producer Jed Harris purchased an option on *No Retreat* for a production on Broadway, according to a newspaper report in January 1930. (Harris told Lester Sweyd that *No Retreat* "was the best back-stage play he had read.") No such production came about, but one presumes that Hart was pleased with the success of his play. However—and curiously—he has nothing whatever to say about *No Retreat* in *Act One*.

Nor does he say a word about a musical called *Jonica*. Frieda Fischbein, acting as Hart's agent, got Moss an assignment to write the book (that is, all but the music and the lyrics) for the musical in collaboration with Dorothy Heyward, who wrote the short story "Have a Good Time, Jonica," on which *Jonica* was based. The musical, with lyrics by William Moll and music by Joseph Meyer, opened initially at the National Theatre in Washington, D.C., on March 23, 1930, under William B. Friedlander's direction. In the play, Jonica, an innocent miss from Buffalo who has just left a convent, travels to New York to be a bridesmaid at the wedding of an old family friend; the musical chronicles Jonica's various encounters along the way. As one newspaper story described those encounters, "On the Pullman train she loses a precious strand of pearls, there is a pistol shot and excitement, and some unexpected happenings that operate to delay the wedding. It was all ironed out somehow so that orange blossoms and wedding bells arrive at the end of Act Two." That may sound like a slim reed on which to hang a musical, but it was not untypical of musical comedy plots of the day, which existed only to provide excuses for songs and dances. Heyward and Hart evidently did a competent job, for John J. Daly, writing in *The Washington Post* on March 26, said that while "what had taken place on the boards of the National [was] by no means in ship shape . . . *Jonica* has certain indefinable traits of worthiness." About the book, he said: "While the story becomes a bit cluttered on the way to its finale, it can be detected all the way; which is something that can not be said of the average musical comedy plot."

From Washington, *Jonica* moved on to Atlantic City, where it began a week's run at Nixon's Apollo Theatre on March 31. There it received less qualified praise from the critics. "A lively and merry musical comedy," said J. J. Farrell, "abounding in smart-cracks and agile dancing, with colorful backgrounds and some satisfactory tunes." E. F. Smith, in the *Atlantic City*

Press, wrote, "*Jonica* can be recommended as a tonic that requires no thinking, just looking, listening and chuckling."

Jonica then opened on Broadway, where it ran at the Craig Theatre for five weeks, beginning on April 7. It received what could be described as mixed reviews, many of which were pasted (as clippings, often without the names of the critics or the newspapers they wrote for) into Hart's scrapbook. One critic, although he said the musical "had all the essentials for hit entertainment," added that when it "attempted to tell a hodge podge story, it was bogged with a playwright's perplexities." But Lee Somers said, "Don't pass it up. It is the peppiest, most youthful and most enjoyable offering of its kind all season." He did qualify his praise somewhat when he noted, "When we staggered forth into the open at 11:40, after three hours and 10 minutes of it, we had precious little idea what it was about, but we were all acutely conscious of having enjoyed almost every moment of it." Walter Winchell enjoyed none of it, however. He called it "tedious . . . conventional and sometimes banal." Finally, another critic said, "*Jonica* proved to be a fairly lively show compounded, in equal parts, of musical comedy clichés and banalities and of a knowing, slightly insane humor that sprang out in unexpected places and made some of the soggier portions endurable."

In any case, although *Jonica* was something less than an overwhelming success, Hart ignored its existence entirely when he wrote *Act One*. Nor did he refer to it after he had become successful when he gave newspaper and magazine interviews—although he willingly told anyone who would listen about *The Beloved Bandit*. All of Hart's plays that reached Broadway were bound and kept in his personal library—except for *Jonica*. One can only conclude that he felt *Jonica* to be insignificant and hoped that it would be forgotten; perhaps he was even ashamed of it. It was, however, his first play to reach Broadway, and, as such, represented what would seem to have been a milestone.[5]

More important, perhaps, was Hart's use of "a knowing, slightly insane humor" (in the words of the critic quoted above) in *Jonica*, for it was just that quality that served him so well later in the 1930–31 season, when his new play, an unequivocal hit, announced to the world that a promising new American playwright had arrived on the scene.

---

5 Moreover, the play caught the attention of Billy Rose, the famous producer, who was putting together a revue in which his wife, Fanny Brice, would star. Rose informed several newspapers that Hart would write some of the sketches. Although the sketches were not written—or possibly written but not performed—the mere fact that Billy Rose acknowledged Hart's talent in this way was surely significant.

Chapter 2 ONCE IN A LIFETIME
1930–1931

DESPITE THE PRODUCTIONS GIVEN *No Retreat* AND *Jonica*, HART must have felt that his playwriting career was not proceeding as successfully as he would have liked, or so one would assume by his omission of those plays from his account of his early career in *Act One*. When he attempted to analyze what was wrong with his work, however, he was unable to identify the problem. But a letter rejecting one of his plays from Richard J. Madden offered a possible answer. "Since by far the best part of the plays you have sent us have been the comedic moments, why not try writing a comedy?" Madden asked, adding, "I am inclined to believe very strongly that you could turn out a good one." Hart was puzzled, since, in his own mind, the plays he had submitted contained virtually no comic material at all (presumably, *Jonica* had not been submitted to Madden). Nor was he particularly interested in writing comedy, seeing himself as a spiritual brother of Eugene O'Neill, whose plays were saturated with a bleak outlook on life. The comic playwright whose work appealed most to Hart was George Bernard Shaw, but Shaw's plays were comedies only on the surface; his use of humor was clearly intended as a tool to most effectively express his social convictions. And, Hart felt, the plays he had been writing were clearly inspired by those of Shaw and O'Neill. His impulse was to write another such play—but to do so meant risking another failure.

Taking stock of his situation, Hart guessed that he had, at best, only three more years during which he would be in demand as a social director, because, the cyclical nature of the business being what it was, others were bound to take his place. Time was running out if his strategy to become a successful playwright was going to work. He reasoned that since Richard J. Madden was a professional, it would perhaps be wise to take his suggestion rather than risk another letter of rejection, so he decided to try his hand at a comedy.

But what sort of comedy? The only American comic playwrights Hart admired were George S. Kaufman and Marc Connelly, who wrote in a satirical vein. *Merton of the Movies*, *To the Ladies*, *Dulcy*, and *Beggar on Horseback*, all co-written by Kaufman and Connelly, were works he respected. They would serve as good models, he thought. So, sitting on a beach near his apartment in Brooklyn in September 1929, Hart put pencil to yellow pad and jotted down a title: *Once in a Lifetime*. The title was generic enough to be used for almost any play he wrote; moreover, it reflected his mood, for he was certain that this play would be his one and only comedy.

Although Hart had spent his entire life on the East Coast, he was an avid reader of *Variety*, the weekly newspaper published in Los Angeles that chronicled show business, with an emphasis on the movies. From *Variety*, Hart felt that "the wonderful absurdity of the Hollywood scene" could serve as the basis for a comic play.

Talking movies were still a novelty in 1929, but it was clear to Hollywood that the days of the silent film were over. The transition to talkies offered monumental problems, though. Sound equipment needed to be developed and employed in the production of movies. Theatres all over the country needed to be refitted in order to play the talkies. And where would the actors for these new pictures come from? Many of the performers in silents had been trained in pantomime and gesture, but few had stage experience or expressive voices. Some spoke with incomprehensible foreign accents; some male stars had voices that were considered unacceptably high pitched; some women spoke with gratingly harsh voices. Here was a subject ripe for satirical treatment.

Another inspiration for Hart's play was the original Broadway production of *June Moon* that he watched from the upper balcony of the Broadhurst Theatre. Taken by George S. Kaufman and Ring Lardner's clever dialogue, he was all the more determined to write a comedy in such a style.

Once in a Lifetime focuses primarily on three characters, May, Jerry, and George, members of a second-rate vaudeville team. After seeing *The Jazz Singer*, Jerry sells the act to finance a move to Hollywood where he and his partners intend to open a school of elocution—about which they know exactly nothing. Still, through a combination of ingenuity and dumb luck, George, who may be generously described as a dim bulb, rises to the top of the movie business, partly by dumbly repeating slogans he reads in *Variety*. His every imbecility is mistaken for genius, such as when he forgets to turn on the lights for an entire scene, which the critics interpret as deliberate—and brilliant—experimentation. In an "industry" populated by idiots, the play suggests, the biggest idiot of all will naturally rise to the top.

Wisecracking May and the go-getter Jerry provide a romantic interest. The subsidiary roles provide a kaleidoscope of lunatic characters: the Hollywood gossip columnist, based on Louella Parsons; the young aspiring actress without a hint of talent, whose only audition piece consists of Kipling's "Boots," recited with metronomic regularity; the megalomaniacal studio head and his cringing subordinates; a gifted playwright imported at great cost from New York and given nothing at all to do; and a vast array of minor roles.

The play was written in less than three weeks, an achievement that did not entirely please its author. All of his previous plays (with the exception of *The Beloved Bandit*) had emerged from a slow, laborious process, generally taking four to six months. He was concerned that the ease with which *Once in a Lifetime* was written was a sign that he had composed another superficial play. On the other hand, he had never found writing a play so enjoyable, which seemed a good sign. But was it funny? He had no idea. It had, he felt, "a fresh and impertinent quality," but that alone wouldn't necessarily make audiences laugh. The way to find out if he had been successful, he decided, was to read his play to the actors in the amateur groups with which he was associated in Brooklyn and Newark. These were amateurs of a high order, many with aspirations to become theatre professionals. They were familiar with the plays on Broadway and would, Hart thought, be able to give him a sound judgment about his play.

Nervous at first, Hart began gaining confidence as his listeners laughed at his dialogue, the laughs increasing throughout the first act. But the response to the rest of the play was less gratifying. "I had written a very funny first act, a somewhat unfulfilled and commonplace second act and a quite flat third act," he later said. Still, despite its flaws it was clear that the play "had a wonderful surging vitality," a quality that, if it could be sustained throughout, might bring the second and third acts up to the level of the first.

Dore Schary, then active with the Newark group, persuaded Hart to send his play immediately to Jed Harris, a universally disliked man noted for his sadistic behavior, but the most successful producer on Broadway. Harris responded by telegram, summoning Hart to meet him in his suite of rooms at the Madison Hotel. Filled with excitement, Hart took the subway from his Brooklyn home to the Madison, only to be told, after sitting in the lobby for three hours, that Mr. Harris would not see him until the next day. But the next day the experience was the same: Hart waited in the lobby until late afternoon, when he was informed that Mr. Harris would be unable to see him until the following morning. At ten o'clock on the third day, Hart arrived at the hotel, prepared for more long hours of frustration, but, to his surprise, was told to go right up to Mr. Harris's suite. Harris called out from his bathroom to Hart, "Come in, come in." To Hart's astonishment, Jed Harris's face was covered with shaving cream, but he was otherwise stark naked. Nervous and embarrassed, Hart heard Harris say, "I read your play last night, and I liked a great deal of it." As he dressed, Harris offered a lengthy, pungent critique of *Once in a Lifetime*—but without giving a hint that he might be willing to produce it. As he picked up his coat, he asked Hart, "Are you going downtown? Good, you can drop me."

In the taxi, Harris continued his wide-ranging discussion, covering not only Hart's play but all aspects of the current theatrical scene. The brilliance of Harris's monologue was such that, not until Harris had left the cab to enter the Morosco Theatre did Hart realize that he had been stuck for the taxi fare. He grudgingly paid the driver, then took the subway back to Brooklyn.

He had no idea what to do next. Harris had not committed to a second meeting, much less the promise of a production. Hart shared his frustrations with a group of young men he met with frequently for coffee at Rudley's restaurant (or at the Automat, Childs, the Tavern, or the Cadillac Cafeteria, depending on the source of the information). One of them was Lester Sweyd, who, unknown to Hart, sent the producer Sam H. Harris (no relation to Jed) his copy of *Once in a Lifetime*. After hearing from the producer's office, Sweyd conveyed the news to Hart that he was to meet with Sam Harris's general manager, Max Siegel, at the Music Box Theatre that afternoon. At the meeting, Siegel showed Hart a telegram from Sam Harris, who was visiting Irving Berlin at Berlin's home in Palm Beach, California. "LIKE PLAY ," it said. "ASK THE YOUNG AUTHOR IF HE WOULD BE WILLING TO MAKE A MUSICAL OF IT WITH IRVING BERLIN ."

Hart thought the proposal preposterous. For some reason that Hart himself could not understand when he looked back upon it afterward, he stood up, said, "I do not write musical comedies, Mr. Siegel. I'm a playwright. I write plays—*only* plays," and headed for the door. (Hart said in 1959, "I blush a little still . . . when I think of the conceit, the self-importance and the pomposity of the words I used . . ." It also seems odd that he so forcefully expressed the notion that he did not write musical comedies when he must, at this time, have been working on *Jonica*. On the other hand, perhaps it was his dissatisfaction with *Jonica* that prompted him to insist he would not tamper with the script of *Once in a Lifetime*.)

Siegel was not offended. He told Hart with a smile that he would wire Sam Harris to say that Hart was not interested in a musical version of the play and ask if Harris would be interested in producing *Once in a Lifetime* without music. Still in his pompous mood, Hart answered that "another producer [Jed Harris] is interested in the play much as it is without songs and dances, so he [Sam Harris] had better make up his mind." Of course, Jed Harris had expressed no such interest (although Hart still fervently hoped for a Jed Harris production), but Hart was undeterred. "Mr. Harris is a quick decider," Siegel said. "You may have an answer tomorrow morning."

Sure enough, the following morning Max Siegel received a telegram from Sam Harris—who believed, on the basis of *Once in a Lifetime*'s knowing satire that Hart was a Hollywood insider—saying, "TELL YOUNG AUTHOR I WILL PRODUCE HIS PLAY IF GEORGE KAUFMAN LIKES IT AND AGREES TO COLLABORATE." When Siegel read the telegram to Hart, the young author was stunned. Kaufman! George S. Kaufman! The great man of the theatre himself! Co-author of the only American comedies Hart favored, the director of many successful productions, a renowned wit who was a regular member of the Algonquin Round Table group, Kaufman had already assumed the status of an idol in Hart's mind. The prospect of working with his hero outweighed the chance of Jed Harris's producing his play. "Tell him yes," Hart said to Siegel.

Lester Sweyd and Hart's other friends who met regularly over coffee (the group included aspiring playwright Eddie Chodorov, Sam Levene, later regarded as one of the theatre's finest character actors, Oscar Serlin, who later became a producer, Preston Sturges, who went on to success in films as a writer-director of brilliant satires, and Archie Leach, a young actor from England—all of whom were later to make their mark on American comedy) were outraged when they heard Hart's news. "You're just handing your play over to Kaufman," one of them said. Another shouted, "He'll get *all* the credit! They won't even know you had anything to do with it!" From still another: "You might just as well say 'By George S. Kaufman' and leave it at that!" Yes, Hart tried to explain, he was aware that he might be overshadowed by Kaufman, but this was his opportunity to work with and be instructed by a man he admired more than any other.

Hart telephoned Jed Harris to say he was withdrawing his play, explaining that he had an opportunity to collaborate with George S. Kaufman. Hart expected a torrent of abuse, but Harris accepted the news pleasantly, asked if Kaufman had already read the play, and, when Hart said that he was uncertain, Harris gave Hart Kaufman's home telephone number. "You call him right away and tell him that Jed Harris says that this is just the play he ought to do."

Everything seemed to be conspiring in Moss's favor, he thought. But what he could not know was that Jed Harris and George S. Kaufman were not on speaking terms; they were, in fact, in the midst of a monumental feud, and the surest way to sabotage a possible collaboration with Kaufman was for the malevolent Jed Harris to suggest it.

Hart called Kaufman and passed on Jed Harris's message, with the result Harris must have intended. "Even as I spoke the words I was dimly conscious of their peculiar ring," Hart later said. Kaufman replied, after a long silence, "I would not be interested in anything that Jed Harris was interested in," and hung up.

The disconsolate Hart was amazed, when, the next morning, Max Siegel called to say that Kaufman had read Moss's play, had liked it, and wanted to meet with the young author that afternoon. Hart, elated, threw his arms around his mother and shouted, "We're going to be rich." When she gave him her usual condescending smile, Hart said, "I'm going to work with George S. Kaufman!" But the name meant nothing to Lily, who could only respond, "That's very nice. If you're going to bring him home to work with you, I hope you won't do it until after next week. We're having the painters next week."

Later that afternoon Hart saw George S. Kaufman for the first time. "That first glimpse of George Kaufman," wrote Hart,

> made all the caricatures I had seen of him in the Sunday drama sections through the years come instantly alive. The bushy hair brushed straight up from the forehead into an orderly but somehow unruly pompadour, the tortoiseshell glasses placed low on the bridge of the rather large nose, the quick, darting eyes searching incisively over the rims, the full sensuous mouth set at a humorously twisted tilt in the descending angularity of the long face—each single feature was a caricaturist's delight. . . .
>
> Though it was a rather mild October day, he sat in the chair in his overcoat, and around his neck was wrapped a long blue woolen scarf that hung outside the coat and came almost to his knees. His legs were twisted or, rather, entwined one under the other in the most intricate fashion, so that one wondered how he would ever get out of the chair if he had to do so quickly, and one arm was stretched clear around the back of his neck to the opposite side of his head where it was busily engaged in the business of scratching the back of his ear.

When Siegel introduced them, Kaufman only lifted one finger of his hand and wearily said, "Hi." "Even the one finger was lifted slowly and with infinite lassitude," Hart said. Kaufman seemed too exhausted to speak, so Siegel took over, telling Hart that Kaufman was willing to collaborate on the play. Hart turned to Kaufman for some sign of enthusiasm, but there was only "another long silence, and a long drawn-out and mournful sigh." Still, Kaufman finally roused himself enough to ask when he and Hart could have their first working session. Hart was ready to begin immediately, but Kaufman, amused at Hart's naïve enthusiasm, suggested they begin the following morning at his house on East 63rd Street.

Hart began to express his gratitude to Kaufman and to let him know how much he admired him, but Kaufman immediately leapt out of the chair and bolted from the room. It was Hart's first exposure to Kaufman's total aversion to sentimentality of any kind.

Siegel handed Hart an advance royalty check for five hundred dollars—more money than Hart had ever possessed. Exultant, Moss returned to Brooklyn and placed the check on the dining room table for his parents to see. Surely this time they could not fail to be impressed. But Lily said, skeptically, "I suppose you know what you're doing, taking all that money, but I wouldn't touch it until after you've worked with this Mr. Kaufman for a while—in case he asks you to give it back." Even his mother's cool reception of the news caused only momentary irritation, however, for Hart was too thrilled at the prospect of working with Kaufman to be deflated. He spent a sleepless night in anticipation of their first working session.

On the top floor of his house, Kaufman greeted his new partner with the lifting of one finger and a weary "Hi," followed by a long sigh. Turning to Hart, he said, "Er"—a form of address that never varied during the collaboration on *Once in a Lifetime*. Perhaps Kaufman could never recall Moss's name, or perhaps, as Hart conjectured, he was too shy to use "Moss," and Kaufman, at forty-one, felt that addressing Moss, who was twenty-five, as "Mr. Hart," would be absurdly formal. In any case, the only thing he called his colleague throughout the entire process of their collaboration on *Once in a Lifetime* was "Er." (On the other hand, a sign of Hart's reverence for his new partner can be seen in *Act One*, written nearly thirty years after *Once in a Lifetime*, in which Hart always describes his collaborator as "Mr. Kaufman.")

"The trouble begins in the third scene of the first act," Kaufman said. "It's messy and unclear and goes off in the wrong direction. Suppose we start with that." They went to work on it as soon as Kaufman washed his hands, an invariable prelude to writing. Kaufman made massive cuts with a pencil, then handed the script to Hart, who discovered that the structure of his scene remained intact, "but its point was unmuddied by repetition, and the economy and clarity with which everything necessary was now said gave the scene a new urgency." This was Kaufman's unvarying technique: to cut to the bone, tossing out everything that did not further the action or embellish the portrayal of the characters. For Hart, whose talent was, in his own words, "raw and undisciplined," Kaufman provided precisely the corrective he needed.

Despite Hart's occasionally gauche behavior (he constantly smoked cigars, which Kaufman detested; he insisted on telling Kaufman how grateful he was to him, which Kaufman couldn't abide; he grew increasingly hungry each day, his stomach growling, wolfing down the cookies and cake brought by the maid at four o'clock, or surreptitiously munching on candy bars, whereas Kaufman seemed oblivious to the necessity of food) and Kaufman's eccentricities (he often lay flat on his back when they discussed a scene, he ran swiftly to the bathroom to wash his hands at the conclusion of each session, thereby avoiding Hart's inevitable speech of gratitude), the two made slow but steady progress in rewriting *Once in a Lifetime*. Although Hart remained idolatrous of Kaufman, he had no problem disagreeing whenever he felt a new line failed to serve its purpose or a scene was being reshaped incorrectly.

Kaufman was never cantankerous or abrupt with Hart, only formidably industrious, often working until Hart, who was still directing amateur productions in the evening (some of them the plays of Kaufman and Connelly) would nearly collapse from exhaustion.[1]

One morning when Hart reported for work at East 63rd Street, he saw Kaufman "in conversation with a handsome woman whose luxuriant hair, brushed straight back from her forehead in a high pompadour, was tinged a bluish-gray." Hart couldn't imagine who this could be, but "Mr. Kaufman lifted the usual one finger in greeting, and then seeming to summon up all the social grace he possessed for the effort, he said, 'Moss Hart—Beatrice Kaufman.'" Since Kaufman did not introduce her as his wife, Hart assumed that Beatrice must be his sister. Also, he knew that Kaufman had his own bedroom and could not envision a married couple with separate rooms.

When she left, Kaufman announced that "Beatrice is having people for tea" that afternoon and made it clear that the two of them were expected to attend. The "tea" turned out to be a party to which some of the most renowned artists and publishers in New York had been invited. Hart mingled wide-eyed with Harpo Marx, Ethel Barrymore, Herbert Bayard Swope, Robert Benchley, Alexander Woollcott, Neysa McMein, Alfred Lunt and Lynn Fontanne, Robert E. Sherwood, Helen Hayes, George Gershwin, Leslie Howard, Heywood Broun, Dorothy Parker, and Franklin P. Adams, among others. The conversations he overheard stimulated him beyond measure; they also revealed to him that George and Beatrice Kaufman were man and wife.

Hart had only been invited to the party because he happened to be working upstairs with Kaufman, but the episode presented a world so attractive to him

---

1 Hart didn't dare give up his little-theatre directing, for, if *Once in a Lifetime* were not successful, he would have no income at all.

that he was determined to become a member of it one day. Moreover, he was overcome with admiration for Beatrice Kaufman. "She had the gift of imbuing even the smallest of daily undertakings with an enkindling gaiety and an intoxicating flavor," he said. "It was a gift which was peculiarly hers and hers alone."

But Hart rarely saw Beatrice when he rang the bell each morning at Kaufman's house. The maid showed him to the workroom upstairs, and there he and Kaufman stayed until it was time for Hart to depart.

Work on *Once in a Lifetime* went slowly, primarily because of Kaufman's perfectionism. He thought nothing of spending two hours on a single line of dialogue, or an entire day discussing an exit or entrance. Rewriting, Hart discovered—at least, rewriting as practiced by George S. Kaufman—resembled "a combination of the Spanish Inquisition and the bloodiest portions of the First World War."

By March 1930, Kaufman and Hart had rewritten the second act and had completed an outline of the third, at which point Hart had his first meeting with his producer, Sam H. Harris, whom Hart found "an irresistible human being." Although not the least bit physically prepossessing, Harris's kindliness, amiability, and incisive intelligence won Hart over immediately. "Everyone in the theatre adored him," Hart said. Fortunately, Harris took to Hart as quickly as the younger man had taken to him, and the two got along famously.

Two events gave Hart the courage to inform the owners of the Catskills' Flagler Hotel that he would not be returning as social director that summer. One was the out-of-town opening of *Jonica* in March 1930; the second was the encouraging meeting with Sam Harris. Now committed entirely to working throughout the summer rewriting *Once in a Lifetime*, Hart returned to work with Kaufman.

Once in a Lifetime was scheduled for a spring tryout in the last two weeks of May 1930. It was the custom at the time for Broadway-bound plays to give out-of-town performances in the spring, close for the summer while the author or authors revised the play, then play at another out-of-town venue in the fall before opening on Broadway. (Within ten years, the spring tryout system would be abandoned, for the cost of such a system was high.) So the play would have to be ready very soon in order for it to be cast and rehearsed in time for the performances scheduled for Atlantic City.

One of the central characters in *Once in a Lifetime* is Lawrence Vail, a frustrated playwright from New York who is brought to Hollywood at great expense only to languish in an office, unable to learn what movie it is he's supposed to be working on. Vail's predicament was based on reality. Since Holly-wood was embarking on the production of talking pictures, it needed writers to produce literate dialogue. A fair number of New York-trained playwrights were imported by Hollywood at the beginning of the talkie era, and some, like Vail, were given lamentably little to do. Kaufman asked Hart what he would think of Kaufman's playing the role of Vail. Hart agreed enthusiasti-cally to Kaufman's suggestion.

The following week the third act was completed, and the next day the au-thors met with Sam Harris to discuss casting the remaining roles. Kaufman and Harris chose the actors, always consulting Hart before proceeding. For Hart, the excitement of the casting and the rehearsals that followed were even greater than the thrill of writing the play.

Kaufman directed *Once in a Lifetime*, as he normally directed all the plays on which he collaborated. At the first rehearsal, with the massive cast gathered to read the script aloud, Kaufman began simply by saying "Act One—Scene One," and the actors began reading. For Hart the experience was excruciating, for the lines he had labored over so carefully sounded flat and lifeless. But Kaufman and Harris were undisturbed, knowing that the first table reading of any play is always disappointing. The actors, nervous about being called upon to read for the first time and wanting to ease rather than plunge into their roles, often speak in a monotone.

But as the actors began to become more comfortable, the read-through improved. The second act was given a more lively reading than the first, the third a more spirited reading than the second. At the next rehearsal, Kauf-man blocked the play—that is, arranged the actors' traffic patterns—and, gradually, Hart could see the production taking shape. Meanwhile, designers were at work on the sets and costumes, which were, in both cases, mammoth enterprises. The play called for six sets—several of them extremely elabo-rate—and costumes for sixty-eight actors. Hundreds of props were needed, among which were six live pigeons and two Russian wolfhounds.

By the eighth day of rehearsal, the actors were ready to give their first run-through. Hart was as disappointed by the run-through as he had been by the read-through. And, as rehearsals progressed, he became concerned that the details of the production would never be in place by the time the play was scheduled to open. He became progressively more anxious as the date of the first performance loomed nearer, finally suffering a full-fledged anxiety at-tack when the company went to Atlantic City for the dress rehearsals and a week of performances. For an hour before the first dress rehearsal Hart lay on his hotel room bed staring at the ceiling, in a "frozen panic." The panic subsided and he went to the theatre, only to have it recur as soon as he entered. Every light cue, every change of scenery or costume, seemed to take an eternity. Kaufman did not appear to be flustered, but Hart was desperate with worry, and remained in anguish throughout the dress rehearsals.

Hart's suffering became even more acute on the opening night—May 26, 1930, some seven weeks after *Jonica* had opened in New York. Accompanied by his friend and benefactor Joe Hyman, who was visiting from New York, Hart made his reluctant way to the Apollo Theatre.

During the week's run in Atlantic City (and again the following week in Brighton Beach) George S. Kaufman played not under his own name but as "Calvin Brown." Since he did not appear as Lawrence Vail until the second act, Kaufman watched the first act from the house, pacing furiously back and forth behind the last row of the orchestra, as was his custom during performances. Hart was uncertain whether he, as co-author, should pace at Kaufman's side, but decided instead to begin from the opposite end, crossing and re-crossing Kaufman as they met in the center.

Listening to the audience react to his play for the first time was almost unbearably stressful. But the first act was greeted with continual laughter and tumultuous applause. Joe Hyman told Hart that the play—if the rest of it remained on this level—was a certain hit. Kaufman's scene at the opening of Act Two was met with the biggest laughs of the evening. But suddenly, as if a faucet had been turned off, the laughter stopped. For the rest of the second act and throughout the third, the audience's response to the play became progressively less enthusiastic. In the final scene (the one that Kaufman and Hart thought was the funniest in the play) there was no laughter at all, the silence punctuated only by coughing. (As Hart's future collaborator Alan Jay Lerner observed, when members of an audience cough during a performance it is not an ailment, it is a criticism.) The third act ended with only perfunctory applause.

Joe Hyman's only word to Hart was, "You got an act and a half of a hit. What you need pretty badly is the other half." Hart returned to the hotel and Kaufman's room, where Kaufman was already at work, revising the play. "We'll be working all night," he informed Hart. Again, as he had the first time they met, Kaufman cut the script "to the bone," demonstrating that much of the dialogue was repetitive and unnecessary. At 7:30 A.M. the work session concluded—only because Kaufman needed a brief nap before meeting the cast for a rehearsal scheduled for eleven o'clock.

Reviews in the Atlantic City newspapers were better than might have been expected. One critic wrote that Kaufman and Hart "have concocted a hard-hitting, wisecracking indictment of Hollywood . . . with most of the sock absorbed by a coating of rich and hilarious comedy." Another said the play "is filled with brilliant and amusing lines from beginning to end . . . [It] is not to be missed."

But audience reaction told a different story, and Kaufman knew that only major surgery could save the play. He and Hart wrote feverishly throughout the week, inserting new material at each performance and excising great quantities of the old. In Hart's view, the "savage and ruthless cutting job accomplished exactly what [Kaufman] had meant it to do: it revealed . . . *Once in a Lifetime* . . . as a play of sound satiric viewpoint but very little substance." Despite all of the unexpected plot twists, the clever wisecracks, the deft characterizations, something was obviously missing. And finding the solution was no easy matter.

Hart admired Kaufman's incredible stamina, but wondered why any sane playwright would want to direct his own piece, for it meant watching the play at night, rewriting furiously until dawn, rehearsing the new material from 11:00 A.M. until breaking for dinner, then beginning the process all over again.

The production then played Brighton Beach, Brooklyn, for a week, in the New Brighton Theatre, not far from where Hart and his family lived. It marked the first time that a legitimate play was performed at the New Brighton, hitherto used as a vaudeville house. Finally, seeing their son's name on posters advertising *Once in a Lifetime*, Lily and Barnett had become convinced that Hart was not quite as hopeless as they had supposed. When he returned from Atlantic City, they could not restrain their exuberance. Nor could the Harts' neighbors, who told Moss again and again that they couldn't wait to see his play. Everyone had heard about the good Atlantic City reviews and Hart's parents had read an enthusiastic notice in *Variety*. But Hart was filled with trepidation.

The Brighton Beach engagement began on June 2. The lobby of the theatre on the opening night was filled with Broadway regulars, Hart saw, for the trip from Manhattan to Brighton Beach was an easy one. Most of them, he felt, hoped the production would fail, and his heart sank.

But the audience responded warmly to the first act, as they had in Atlantic City. Again, however, the laughs began to dissipate in Act Two, then stopped almost completely in Act Three. Although the authors were presenting a thoroughly revised play, the audience reaction had hardly changed. Joe Hyman caused Hart to erupt with fury when he said, "What happened to all that work you were supposed to be doing? This is the same play I saw in Atlantic City." The play had, in fact, undergone massive changes, but the new material was no more successful in maintaining the audience's initial enthusiasm than the original material had been.

Again, however, nearly all of the Brooklyn critical notices were favorable, although most reviewers stipulated that work needed to be done on the play before it opened on Broadway. The *Standard Union*, for example, called *Once in a Lifetime* a "hard-boiled, wise and witty play, but one which in its present state unfortunately reaches the end of its tether before the second act is played out." Robert Garland, the critic for the *New York Telegram*, made the trip to Brighton Beach and reported, "Even in its pre-Broadway showings, *Once in a Lifetime* is a swell show. There's dialogue such as Mr. Kaufman alone can write, and, although the bigger and brighter Kaufman pace is not maintained unflaggingly until the end, there's every reason to suppose that no little stepping-up and pulling together will be done before Broadway sees the comedy in September or October."

Garland's attribution of all of the funny lines to Kaufman was a typical response, but he, and all those who expressed the same opinion, were wrong. One of the Brooklyn reviewers had gone so far as to say, "judging by the records of both names [i.e., the authors] listed on the program last night, the first act and a half of *Once in a Lifetime*, which is very good indeed, was written by George S. Kaufman and the rest by Moss Hart." However, the original script of *Once in a Lifetime*—that is, the script as Hart wrote it, before Kaufman began working on it—is still in existence, and a reading of it demonstrates conclusively that many of the characterizations, situations, and funniest lines were written by Hart. Indeed, the line that invariably got the biggest laugh and that everyone quoted as a typical Kaufman wisecrack (when Lawrence Vail, the frustrated playwright, is told by a page for the umpteenth time that Mr. Glogauer, the head of the studio, is on number six [i.e., set number six] or number four or number eight, Vail replies, "Listen son. I'm going to the men's room. If Mr. Glogauer wants me, I'm in number three") appears in Hart's original script.

Which is not to suggest that Kaufman's contribution was not essential to the play's success. The last two acts of Hart's original play did, as his little-theatre friends told him long before Kaufman became involved, become tedious, and the play could not have succeeded without substantial rewriting.

Years later, in 1953, Hart came across his original manuscript of *Once in a Lifetime* and noted in his diary, "I began to turn the pages idly, afraid in a sense to read it, and I must admit I was struck by the talent it showed. It was quite well constructed, the lines extremely funny, and I think perhaps if a manuscript like this were submitted to me today I would have to admit that the author had real talent for the theatre."

But in 1930, Hart was filled with despair. When he went backstage after the Brighton Beach opening, Kaufman was already gone, having driven back to Manhattan with Sam Harris. The next morning Hart called Kaufman to find out when he should arrive for the day's rewriting session. Kaufman said, "I think we both need a respite for a couple of days before we tackle it again."

Later in the week, after Kaufman made his final exit (his character appeared only in the second act), he said to Hart, "Come back to my dressing room at the end of the show so that we can talk for a few minutes, will you?" Hart believed that Kaufman was ready to begin the nightly rewriting sessions again. But Kaufman's comment was totally unexpected. "I'm certain now that I haven't anything more to offer to this play," he said. "Someone else, or maybe you alone, would be better than I would be from here on. I've gone dry on it or maybe I've lost my taste for it." After a long, agonizing silence from Hart, Kaufman continued, "I'm sure you'll get it done again. There's a lot of good stuff there and you may suddenly get an idea that will crack the second and third acts."

Hart asked Kaufman, with faint hope, if his decision was final. When Kaufman assured him that it was, Hart turned toward the door. Kaufman raised one finger as a farewell gesture. Hart managed to say, "Goodbye," and left Kaufman's dressing room.

Hart tried to console himself. Although no other management would be interested in producing a play that even George S. Kaufman had been unable to fix, he would begin on another play, and whatever he chose to work on would be better for the instruction he had received from Kaufman. He would need to return to his jobs at summer camps, but he could survive that, too.

The rationalizations numbed his pain for a few moments, but then reality intruded. He would be devastated if *Once in a Lifetime* were not completed. He realized that it was imperative for him to somehow persuade Kaufman to return to the play. But what tactic could he use? He dared not appeal to sentiment, for Kaufman was unsentimentality personified. Rather, Hart would have to approach Kaufman with a new idea that would stimulate him to return to work.

The next morning Hart returned to the beach where he had written the original draft of *Once in a Lifetime*, again equipped with pencils and a yellow pad. Knowing that he would need to formulate his idea quickly or Kaufman might turn his mind to other projects, he spent the day devising notions for new second and third acts. He memorized the new scenario he had created, repeating it to himself so that he could describe it to Kaufman without resorting to notes. Then, the next morning, to Kaufman's surprise, he showed up at 158 East 63rd Street. Kaufman agreed to listen to Hart's ideas while he, Kaufman, ate breakfast.

An hour passed before Hart finished his careful recitation, by which time Kaufman was lying face up on the floor. He arose and said to Hart, "How soon could you move in here?" Hart tried to conceal his astonishment and delight as Kaufman continued, "That's a full summer's work you've laid out, you know, with evenings included. We could get into rehearsal by August, I think, if you moved in here and we worked straight through." Hart returned to Brooklyn, packed a suitcase, and, for the second time that day, boarded the subway for Manhattan.

Virtually every day and night of that hot, humid New York summer was consumed with hard work, as the collaborators created dialogue for Hart's new scenes, found that the scenes would not work as they hoped, then began again. They did take a break on one particularly uncomfortable weekend, Kaufman going to Long Island to play in a croquet tournament, Hart going to the Flagler Hotel, where he "was welcomed back like a reigning opera star" and spent the weekend entertaining the guests. But the experience convinced him that he could never return to social directing. Even more than before, he was dedicated to reshaping and refining *Once in a Lifetime*.

Kaufman returned refreshed, and the collaborators were able to complete the second act within a week. Now, though, the scheduled rehearsals in mid-August were looming, and, not only did the third act have to be completed, but the authors were occupied with recasting the play and meeting with the designers, for two elaborate new scenes had been added. Still, four days before the first scheduled rehearsal, they completed the rewrite with a new, bigger, even more spectacular and even wackier third act set in a nightclub. Beatrice Kaufman was asked her opinion about the new third act. She made clear that she did not like it at all, an ominous sign as far as Hart was concerned, for he had developed a healthy respect for her opinion.

With some of the leading roles recast, rehearsals began at the Music Box Theatre. Kaufman and Hart had, from the beginning, wanted Jean Dixon, who had played a wisecracking woman with great success in *June Moon*, to play May. Dixon, concerned that playing a similar role might be a bad career move, had turned it down. Now, though, having seen a dress rehearsal of the Atlantic City version of *Once in a Lifetime*, and having enjoyed it, she accepted the role.

Again the actors mumbled their way through the first reading, but Hart, no longer a neophyte at listening to initial read-throughs, thought he could detect a spark from the new actors that had been missing before.

Still, he called the next three weeks "perhaps the worst . . . I have ever spent in rehearsal in the theatre." Uncertain that his labors with Kaufman had improved the second and third acts, he waited with trepidation for the opening in Philadelphia. He had particular cause for concern, for his income stream had dried up. When *Once In a Lifetime* was running in Atlantic City and Brighton Beach, Hart had had to give up his little-theatre work. Only the fact that his brother Bernie was working for the first time insured the family a steady income.

The three weeks' run at Philadelphia's Lyric Theatre began on September 1, 1930. As always, the first act played to nearly continual laughter. Kaufman's scene in the second act (he was now acting under his own name) played as well as ever. Then the new material was introduced—and the remainder of the second act continued to elicit laughs in a way it never had before. Hart, Sam Harris, and Max Siegel grinned at one another, satisfied that the problems that had seemed so intractable had finally been solved. Hart eavesdropped among the audience in the lobby during the intermission. Although intermission talk is often about other matters, this time the audience was talking about the play, and in the most enthusiastic terms.

The third act began with a gratifying response—laughter *and* prolonged applause—to the outrageous nightclub set. But then the laughs began to diminish. Finally, in the middle of the act they stopped altogether. The great third act difficulty that had plagued *Once in Lifetime* from the beginning had not been conquered. Kaufman whispered to Hart as the act was nearing its end, "We're too close to a hit now not to get this right. Meet me in the room in half an hour."

Hart and Kaufman worked through the night, pausing only to read the newspaper reviews. One critic, who called Kaufman "the play's chief author," said, "the mark is seldom missed, so continually is Mr. Kaufman's clever touch in evidence." But it was the "seldom" that stood out, for that clearly referred to the intractable third act. Another reviewer was more explicit: the play "contains enough 'gags' to keep a studio gag-man busy for a year," it said. "Where it loses force is in the matter of tying these gags into smooth running form. . . . The last act alone has enough comedy material for an average play, containing the best burlesque of the evening, but by the time one gets to it, there is just a little tired feeling." And H. T. Craven called the play "too diffuse and too long."

A rewritten third act was introduced on the second night of the run, and, although an improvement, failed to sustain the excellence of the first two acts. Again, and for many nights thereafter, Kaufman and Hart worked overnight, creating new scenes—but, each night, audience response to the last act was disappointing, and the new scenes were discarded. All the frenzied rewriting seemed to bring the playwrights no closer to success.

A heat wave was partially responsible (theatres were not air-conditioned in 1930), but poor word of mouth also took its toll and the size of the audiences fell off drastically in the second week. The audiences lessened to such a degree that the hundred or so people sitting in the cavernous theatre could not give Kaufman and Hart a good indication of whether the new material they were continually inserting was working or not. The morale of the actors and authors progressively declined.

A few days before the Philadelphia performances ended, Kaufman took a train to New York to meet his wife, who was returning from Europe. Before he left he said to Hart, "I think we ought to face the fact that we may have to settle for what we've got. We must give the company a chance to play the same show four nights in a row before we open in New York."

"What do you think our chances are in New York with this last act?" Hart asked.

"Not wonderful, if you want my honest opinion," Kaufman said. "Well, no one can say we didn't try. We're freezing the show Thursday night."

Sam Harris took Hart out for a beer after Kaufman left. They remained in the speakeasy until it closed, with Harris giving Hart his opinion of *Once in a Lifetime*. Hart found Harris's analysis difficult to grasp at first, for his conversation was "enigmatic and circuitous," but, as the two were about to leave, Harris made a particularly perceptive comment. "I wish, kid, that this weren't such a noisy play."

"Noisy, Mr. Harris?" said Hart. "What do you mean by a noisy play?"

"It's a noisy play, kid. Just think about it. Except for those two minutes at the beginning of the first act, there isn't another spot in this whole play where two people sit down and talk quietly to each other. Maybe *noisy* is the wrong word, but I've watched this play through maybe a hundred times, and I think one of the main things wrong with it is that it tires an audience out. I can almost feel them beginning to get tired all around me. That stage is so damn full of actors and scenery and costumes and props all the time they never get a chance to catch their breath and listen to the play."

Harris's criticism was on target. From Hart's initial draft of the play until that moment, the third act had been spectacular, even overwhelming, and the continual rewrites made it ever more so. But Harris's comment finally allowed Hart to see that the very quality for which the playwrights had striven was actually sabotaging the play.

After dropping Harris off at the hotel, Hart walked around the streets and parks of Philadelphia all night. Seated in a child's swing at four o'clock in the morning, swinging as high as he could go, "in a sudden flash of improvisation" he realized how to solve the problem Harris had pinpointed. The nightclub scene should be discarded entirely and the character of Lawrence Vail, who had only one scene in Act Two, should be brought back onstage in Act Three for a quiet scene with May on the train from Hollywood to New York. That would provide a less frenzied episode before the big finale in Hollywood. "Everything clicked into place with an almost mathematical accuracy," Hart said. "New lines began tumbling into my mind faster than I could remember them."

When Kaufman returned in time for the next day's matinée, Hart could not restrain himself, pouring out his idea as Kaufman was putting on his makeup. "I see what you mean," Kaufman said, "but it's too risky. It's too big a change to make with only three days left."

Afterward, at the hotel, Hart repeated his new idea, but in greater detail. He pleaded with Kaufman to take a chance. Slowly, Kaufman looked up at him. "You have as much right to say yes to anything about this play as I have to say no," he said. "If you feel this strongly, why don't you skip the show tonight and stay here and make a rough draft that we can work on when I get back." Then he wearily made his way back to the theatre for the evening's performance.

Writing an entirely new scene in a few hours was not possible, but Hart had a rough draft ready for Kaufman when he returned from the theatre. Kaufman read the draft, then, thinking of the nightclub scenery that would be thrown away, he strode to the typewriter. "Well, here goes twenty thousand dollars' worth of scenery," he said, and they went to work.

The actors, bone-weary and insecure, took the news that a substantial portion of the third act had to be memorized and rehearsed with glum resignation.

Worse, the new scene had to be played that very night, for it was Friday and the Philadelphia production was closing the following night. The new material could not be judged unless played before an audience, and there were precious few audiences remaining.

Hart watched the new scene from the last row of the balcony. May, played by Jean Dixon, "was seated alone in the Pullman car," Hart wrote, "but her aloneness in a train that was obviously headed back to New York told [the audience] all they needed to know without a line's being spoken. They made the leap for us themselves without a word of exposition, and the stage, quiet and silent for once, seemed to create by its wordlessness the exact sense of drama and climax that we had previously tried so hard to achieve, without success." Then Kaufman entered as Lawrence Vail, and the audience laughed with the knowledge that Vail, too—who, the scene made clear, had just been released from a Flagstaff, Arizona, sanitarium that catered to writers recovering from nervous breakdowns—had given up on Hollywood. "I knew," Hart said, "that our search for the right last act had ended." And the quiet scene on the train provided just the right setup for the explosive finish. For the first time, *Once in a Lifetime* was successful from the first curtain to the last.

The company returned to New York and the Music Box Theatre for two final rehearsals before the opening. Hart, back in Brooklyn, made an important discovery. His brother Bernie, who had always seemed distant and behaved sullenly, seemed like a different person, "witty, beguiling [and] sweet-natured." Moss had barely seen his brother for a year, and Bernie had changed in many ways, the physical being the least of them. "His diffidence had vanished," Hart said, "and with it the withdrawal from me and his silence." Bernie gave Moss a scrapbook, filled with clippings from every newspaper that had printed an article about *Once in a Lifetime*, and Moss was deeply touched.

Hart's relationship with his parents also seemed to have improved. He felt, perhaps for the first time, that they understood and accepted him—and he, in turn, felt closer to them than before.

In Manhattan, final rehearsals were underway. In the hallowed tradition of the theatre, the afternoon of the final dress rehearsal was a nightmare of missed entrances, doors that refused to open, costumes that—although they had fit the actors perfectly in Philadelphia—now had the actors complaining that they were too small and too tight. Fortunately, however, the evening rehearsal went smoothly, although the actors, playing without benefit of an audience, seemed to Hart to be "completely hollow."

Sam Harris, seeing Hart's distress, invited the author to his office in the theatre for a drink. For the next five hours, Hart listened in silence as Harris, pouring himself one drink after another, reminisced about his past experiences in the theatre—and then proceeded to describe the plot of *Once in a Lifetime*, scene by scene, down to the smallest detail. Hart, desperately wishing that Harris would finish so that he could catch the last subway for Brooklyn, but too polite to interrupt, fought a losing battle against weariness. But Harris continued, imitating the actors' voices, speaking each line of the play, describing the scenery and the lighting. At last, Harris stopped speaking and Hart opened his eyes. Harris was standing in front of him, saying, "Go on home and get a good night's sleep, kid."

When they got outside, they saw that dawn had broken. Harris realized there was no point in Hart's going home to Brooklyn, since Kaufman had called a rehearsal for 11:00 A.M. Knowing that Hart would not be able to pay for a hotel, Harris slipped a one hundred dollar bill into Hart's hand, then stepped into a taxi. Hart, feeling that this was no time to be frugal, strode to the Astor Hotel, asked for a suite, arranged to have a masseur come to his room at nine in the morning, a barber and manicurist at nine forty-five, and a large breakfast sent in at ten thirty. He overtipped the bellboy and, after opening the window to look for a moment at his name on the marquee of the Music Box Theatre, fell into a deep and satisfying sleep, savoring a luxury he had never experienced before. The bill, when everything was totaled, came to eighty-five dollars, including tips for everyone. Hart hurried down the street to the Music Box.

After the morning's rehearsal, Hart spent the afternoon riding in a hansom cab around Central Park—four times—with his friend Joe Hyman. He felt temporarily worry-free, although the opening performance was only hours away. Surely that evening, September 24, 1930, would prove to be one of the most momentous occasions in his life.

At the theatre, the actors were all beset with opening-night nerves, and Hart, plagued by the fear that attacks most playwrights on a first night, was not in a condition to calm anyone down. He rushed to the rear of the orchestra seats for the first-act curtain, almost bumping into Kaufman, who had already begun pacing back and forth.

Broadway opening nights always attracted a celebrity-studded crowd. On this occasion, Al Jolson and his wife Ruby Keeler, Paul Muni, the four Marx Brothers, Fredric March, Jesse Lasky, and Adolph Zukor were among those in the audience. The house was full, all the critics in their places. Hart's family was there, as were his friends from the group that used to meet regularly for coffee.

The curtain rose, but there was still one more crisis to be dealt with. The electrician had forgotten to turn off the giant fans that were used to cool the theatre, and not a word could be heard from the stage until he switched them off a minute or two after the performance began. The actors, realizing that important exposition would be missed if they did not start the scene from the beginning, simply repeated the dialogue that had not been audible, and, from that moment on, *Once in a Lifetime* was "played and received," said Hart, "like a playwright's dream of a perfect opening night." Each act played better than the one before. The final curtain was greeted with tumultuous applause, the actors taking curtain call after curtain call. Then George S. Kaufman, dressed as Lawrence Vail, stepped forward and raised his hand, cutting the applause short. What he had to say took only a moment. "I would like this audience to know," he said, "that eighty percent of this play is Moss Hart."

Hart made his way backstage, his eyes moist, but most of the audience seemed to have preceded him. "A solid mass of humanity crushed one against the other into every available inch of space," he said, audience members congratulating the actors and talking excitedly to one another. Hart couldn't make his way into any of the dressing rooms, including Kaufman's, but managed to wave to as many of the performers as he could. He walked up to the stage where his family and friends were waiting for him. Joe Hyman took everyone to a restaurant, where they waited for the morning newspapers with the critics' reviews.

The critics were rhapsodic. In 1930, New York City supported many newspapers, and with more than twenty reviews one might expect one or two of the critics to withhold praise or at least to express an occasional reservation. But the verdict was unanimous: the play was an unalloyed success. Brooks Atkinson of the *Times* described it as "a hard, swift satire—fantastic and deadly, and full of highly charged comedy lines." Gilbert W. Gabriel of the *American* called it "an often fiendishly funny presentation." Percy Hammond thought it a "hilarious travesty." Walter Winchell in the *Mirror* said it was "the funniest comedy" of the season, and Whitney Bolton said *Once in a Lifetime* was "at once the funniest and most satisfying play in New York, a robust and outrageously comic evening." A survey of the twelve most influential critics in New York revealed that all twelve had raved about the play. Magazines such as *The New Yorker*, *Time*, *The Nation*, and *Commonweal* all later printed equally enthusiastic notices. A number of the critics, however, ignored Kaufman's curtain speech and gave the lion's share of the credit to the older playwright while all but dismissing Hart's contribution.

After the first notices came out on opening night, Hart's family returned to Brooklyn, but Moss, delirious with happiness, remained in the restaurant with Joe Hyman until four-thirty in the morning. Afterward, standing on the sidewalk, Hart realized that he was ravenously hungry, so he and Hyman went to another restaurant where his friend treated Hart to a celebratory breakfast. Throbbing with the thrill of success, Hart felt "taller, more alive, handsomer, uncommonly gifted and indomitably secure with the certainty that this is the way life will always be," he said.

With fifteen dollars still in his pocket (left over from the hundred dollars Sam Harris had given him) and applause still ringing in his ears, Hart decided that he would never again ride in the subway, which had become for him a symbol of the poverty he so detested. He took a taxi home to Brooklyn, dreaming—literally, for he fell asleep during the ride—of the ways he would spend the money that would soon be coming his way. And the money would amount to a great deal, for Kaufman had insisted that Hart receive sixty percent of the box office income.

When he arrived at home his parents and brother were asleep. Hart stood in the kitchen waiting for water to boil for coffee, and looked at the shabby apartment with its frayed carpet and worn furniture. Suddenly a thought occurred: "to walk out of [the squalid apartment] forever—not piecemeal, but completely—would give meaning to the wonder of what had happened to me, make success tangible, decisive."

He woke his family and announced that they were all moving to Manhattan that very day. "And we're not taking anything with us," he said, "not even a toothbrush, a bathrobe, pajamas or nightgown. We're walking out of here and starting fresh." His mother, stunned, asked where they were going. "To a hotel," Hart said, "until we find an apartment and furnish it."

Lily insisted on taking her pictures and other souvenirs, and Hart relented to the extent that he allowed her to pack one suitcase. She burst into laughter and began to pack. In less than an hour, they were in a taxi, riding across the Brooklyn Bridge, headed for the Edison Hotel on 47th Street, near the Music Box Theatre. Hart told the driver to stop for a moment at the playhouse. Hundreds of people stood in line, hoping to buy tickets, the line snaking out of the lobby and down the block. Entering the box office, Hart asked for and received an advance payment of five hundred dollars. "Come around any time," the box office manager said. "We'll be here for a long, long time."

Hart, embarked on a career that would yield many successes—though none quite so unexpected and glorious as *Once in a Lifetime*, perhaps—returned to the taxi and rode, with his family, to their temporary home in the Edison Hotel.

ભૂ

Once in a Lifetime ran for 305 performances on Broadway, a run of significant proportions in 1930. It won the Roi Cooper Megrue Award for Hart and Kaufman (Hart's name was first in the play's billing), "given to a member [of the Dramatists Guild] whose play, produced in New York, makes an audience a little brighter and a little more cheered up when it leaves the theater than when it came in." Critic and anthologist Burns Mantle included *Once in a Lifetime* in his collection of best plays of the year.

Soon after the Broadway opening, casting was held for a Los Angeles production, with Hart serving as director. He left for Hollywood in December 1930, accompanied by some actors from New York. The plan called for most of the actors to come from Hollywood. Ironically, the plan failed because of the precise problem *Once in a Lifetime* satirized: the actors in the film community had insufficiently trained voices. So most of those who performed in the Los Angeles production were Broadway actors. Aline MacMahon, who had played May during the spring tryout in Atlantic City and Brighton Beach and had been replaced by Jean Dixon, was cast as May in Los Angeles.

If Hart suspected that he would be looked upon with suspicion by the Hollywood community, he was wrong. *Theatre News* reported that he "is being wined, dined and feted in Hollywood by the very people he is supposed to have belittled and shown up in an unfavorable light." According to an article from a Los Angeles newspaper, Hart was "lionized in a big way on the West coast." The story noted that he "was immediately overwhelmed with invitations, finally having an expensive imported car"—reported in another article to be a Rolls Royce—"placed at his disposal by Sid Grauman, the big Hollywood showman." Hart's income from *Once in a Lifetime* allowed him to indulge in extravagances of all sorts. One that he particularly savored was to hire a valet.

But Hart spoke in disparaging terms about life in Los Angeles. "The celebrated Hollywood parties are excessively dull," he told a newspaper reporter. "The main impression you get out of Hollywood is a sense of instability. Everyone is working from option to option. Nobody comes out with a frank opinion for fear it will be carried to the ears of an overlord. Everything is politics."

The Los Angeles production of *Once in a Lifetime* opened on February 26, 1931, at the Mayan Theatre. Hart was scheduled to play Lawrence Vail, but he fell ill and was replaced by the assistant director, Robert Sinclair (who had been an assistant stage manager when the play opened in New York). Sid Grauman, the owner of the Mayan Theatre, arranged for a publicity stunt to increase the play's notoriety, conspiring to have two women loudly claim that Grauman had slandered Hollywood by producing *Once in a Lifetime* and hit him with their purses as he made his way into the theatre.

Ever since it had been announced that the play was coming to Los Angeles, a good deal of speculation had circulated. How would Hollywood react to being ridiculed? Would audiences jeer at the play? Would they walk out in significant numbers?

As it turned out, the audience, which included nearly every major film studio executive—more than had ever been gathered together under one roof, according to one account—seemed to enjoy the production thoroughly (although Louella Parsons, an object of ridicule in the play, expressed her disdain on many occasions in her column), and the critics, with one exception—*The Los Angeles Evening Express*—gave it high praise.

Hart made a quick recovery from his illness and joined the cast several nights after the opening. Since the critics had already attended the production, Hart's appearance was not considered newsworthy and no reviews of his performance exist. One newspaper did mention several weeks later, however, that Hart "is justly being praised for his portrayal . . . Hart's diction is especially good—which some other actors might observe with profit." On the other hand, some of Hart's friends said just the reverse, maintaining that he mumbled his lines to the point of incomprehensibility. In the end, Hart withdrew from the cast, once again the victim of illness, this time a case of influenza.

Sergei Eisenstein, the legendary Russian film director, was then in Hollywood, under contract to Paramount. After seeing the play, Eisenstein said, "Believe me, *Once in a Lifetime* is under-written. I have been here six months on a very big salary and I have, like the author in the play, done nothing."

While in Hollywood, a number of film studios inquired about Hart's availability for writing screenplays. He turned down the offers at first, saying "I would rather attempt a new play every season and sell the rights to the movies," but he eventually decided to accept. However, he insisted, he would do all the writing in New York and would be exempt from having to attend studio conferences or become enmeshed in studio politics. "I won't have to appear in Hollywood at all," he said, "except for a possible two or three weeks during the actual filming." However, despite the imbecilities of the Hollywood community he satirized so bitingly in *Once in a Lifetime*, he said that he intended "to take picture writing seriously. As a matter of fact I intend to go at it in dead earnest."

Early in April 1931, the *Once in a Lifetime* company moved to San Francisco, Hart resuming the role of Lawrence Vail. Then he left the company—which continued playing on the road until November—to return to New York. Kaufman had announced his intention to leave the New York cast on April 30, 1931, and Hart took over the role on the next day. Again, there are no critical notices of Hart's performance to report, but it may be noted that Jean Dixon told Malcolm Goldstein[2] that she was not impressed with Hart's performance. In any case, he did not play the role for long. A newspaper reported, "Mr. Hart has given up acting to complete his new drama, *Twentieth Century*."

Another source gave the title as *Twentieth Century Limited* and noted that it was to be a non-comic play. Whatever the correct title, the project was not completed.[3]

A subsequent, successful production of *Once in a Lifetime* was given in London in February 1932, under the management of Charles B. Cochran. Jean Dixon, Hugh O'Connell, and Grant Mills all repeated their New York roles.

The final chapter in the saga of *Once in a Lifetime* was written when Carl Laemmle Jr. of Universal Pictures purchased the rights to the play in order to make a film version—to the dismay of some other studio owners. Rumors circulated that Laemmle would emasculate the play, removing its deepest satiric thrusts. Other rumors implied that the locale would be shifted to New York, with Broadway producers becoming the butt of the humor. But Laemmle explained to *The New York Times* that he had no such plans. "I intend to make the screen version almost exactly like the play," he said. "My aim is not to convert satire into slapstick comedy, but to produce the play on the screen as faithfully as common decency will permit."

Kaufman and Hart had nothing to do with the screenplay, which was directed by Russel Mack. *The New York Times* reviewed the film on October 29,

---

2   when he interviewed her for his book *George S. Kaufman: His Life, His Theater*, 1979.

3   In 1932, Ben Hecht and Charles MacArthur's play, *Twentieth Century*, was produced. But their zany farce was not at all the sort of play Hart was working on.

1932, saying, "much of the caustic humor of the stage work has been retained, but here and there some of the sting in the original has been taken out." Perhaps the sting that was excised might have offended the "common decency" Laemmle mentioned. The film was, however, "far better . . . than it was thought would be turned out," the critic Mordaunt Hall concluded.

Aline MacMahon, the original May who repeated her role in the road company, played it again in the film. Other actors included Jack Oakie and Gregory Ratoff. All the performances were enthusiastically reviewed.

Whether or not the film preserved the brilliance of the play would have been relatively unimportant to Moss Hart. Many of his plays were filmed, but in only one case did he take a hand in the process. "If you sell something to the movies," he often said, "take the money and run."

The income from the various productions of the play and the movie of *Once in a Lifetime* made a fortune for both Kaufman and Hart. For Moss, it gave him not only the respect accorded a bright young playwright, but freedom from the poverty that had always gripped him and his family in the past. True to his vow, he never rode the subway again; he never denied himself material pleasure; he spent freely, joyously, enjoying every moment of his hardwon success. But his pleasure in material gains did not interfere with his progress as a playwright, for he was to turn out one hit play after another, both with Kaufman, with other collaborators, and finally on his own.

INTERMISSION

Moss Hart's memoir, *Act One*, concluded with the opening night performance of *Once in Lifetime* in New York in 1930. That Hart was utterly besotted with theatrical matters can be seen in what *Act One* never mentions. No event that does not touch directly upon Hart's ambition or upon the theatre is referred to in the memoir, although America and the world were going through cataclysmic changes during Hart's young manhood. When Hart was nineteen, the twenty-ninth president of the United States, Warren G. Harding, died, his memory disgraced by the Teapot Dome and related scandals that lasted until 1927; when he was twenty-one, the Scopes "Monkey Trial" was held in Tennessee, pitting the forces of science against those of fundamentalist religion; in sports, Babe Ruth's powerful swing—his sixty home runs in 1927 considered a mark so astounding that it would last forever—was winning greater popularity for baseball than ever before, in spite of the nearly mortal blow the sport suffered when eight members of the Chicago "Black Sox" threw the World Series of 1919. That Hart did not even take note of the stock market crash of October 1929 that gave rise to the Great Depression is remarkable. One could argue that Hart and his family were so poor to begin with that the Depression had little effect on them personally, but it would have been impossible not to have observed the effect on American society.

That Moss Hart recorded none of these events in *Act One* is neither surprising nor lamentable, for his memoir was intended not as a historical study of his times but as a deeply personal, highly focused view of the author's determination to win a foothold in the theatre, and in that aim it succeeds brilliantly. Nevertheless, the environment in which Hart rose to maturity is conspicuously absent.

That environment is important to note in these pages, for, although the momentous events experienced by the nation did not affect Hart directly, they did help to form the cultural and political fabric that formed his audience's life experiences.

Nor did Hart investigate the cultural milieu in *Act One*. Music and literature are ignored entirely. Even significant events in the theatre are bypassed without mention, except insofar as they directly affected Hart. For example, he notes the prominence of the *Ziegfeld Follies* because he was able to borrow material from it for his stints as a social director at various summer camps, but ignores it as a symbol of the glamour and gaiety of the 1920s, a plaything of the rich. Other theatrical phenomena of the 1920s are overlooked altogether. The Theatre Guild—so instrumental in reshaping American attitudes toward drama, provoking interest in previously unknown European plays, and stimulating the careers of such young, experimental American playwrights as Eugene O'Neill, S. N. Behrman, Elmer Rice, Sidney Howard, and John Howard Lawson—is ignored. So is Eva Le Gallienne's Civic Repertory Theatre, which presented a repertory of plays from Europe's past and present in generally outstanding productions. No mention is made of *Show Boat* (1927), the first American play to employ a significant societal theme (miscegenation), combine it with popular music, and win a large audience. Even the little-theatre movement in which he took part is explored only in the most personal terms, although it was helping to redefine American perspectives toward the theatre by offering plays of greater substance than most Americans throughout the country had seen in the past.

Beyond question, Hart was aware of these events but chose to omit them from his autobiography because they would wrench the book out of focus. And the excellence of his memoir demonstrates that his decision to concentrate on his own experience was correct. Still, it is worth noting that Moss Hart's struggles and achievements were not fought out and won in a social, cultural, or theatrical vacuum.

American-written plays seen on Broadway prior to 1920 were, almost without exception, formularized, immature, and trivial. Most writers of talent and the ambition to innovate concentrated on fiction and poetry, for the theatre was not a hospitable medium.

But the milieu was thoroughly altered in the '20s. Despite the existence of "the road" (everything outside New York City) and the little-theatre companies that dotted America, Broadway was, without question, the theatrical mecca of the era. Any American who aspired to a playwriting career wished his or her plays to be produced on Broadway. Broadway success generally led to success on the road and to subsequent little-theatre productions. It often resulted in sales to the movies, further popularizing the plays from which the films were derived. In an inversion of the prevailing situation before 1920, when significant artists avoided the professional theatre in New York, accomplished artists of all kinds—poets, composers, novelists, painters, architects—were in the years after 1920 all drawn to Broadway.

Eugene O'Neill's *Beyond the Horizon*, which won the Pulitzer Prize for Drama in 1920 after its Broadway run, signaled a new, more mature approach to dramatic literature. Before the decade was over he would also write *Anna Christie*, *The Hairy Ape*, *All God's Chillun Got Wings*, *Desire Under the Elms*, and *Strange Interlude*, all concerned with eternal human problems, all written in the highly varied forms O'Neill believed appropriate to their content, and all still considered milestones of American drama. His plays are flawed, sometimes by the inability to master a dramatic form he had not yet explored, sometimes by excessive length, but the flaws are those of too much ambition, not too little.

The difference between the superficial entertainments produced on Broadway before 1920 and that decade's attempts to come to grips with the most profound issues confronting humanity can be seen in O'Neill's credo:

> The playwright of today must dig at the roots of the sickness of today as he feels it—the death of the old god and the failure of science and materialism to give any satisfactory new one for the surviving primitive religious instinct to find a meaning for life in, and to comfort its fears of death with. It seems to me that anyone trying to do big work nowadays must have this big subject behind all the little subjects of his plays or novels, or he is scribbling around the surface of things.

Although O'Neill's view of life was particularly bleak, the acceptance of his unconventional views and experimental forms by Broadway audiences and critics paved the way for others to express their deeply held beliefs, often in forms that had never before been seen on Broadway. Elmer Rice's *The Adding Machine* in 1923 presented the dehumanization of mankind in the face of advancing technology in expressionistic form; his *Street Scene* in 1929 showed the brutality of New York tenement life in a harshly realistic light. Marc Connelly, working with George S. Kaufman, employed expressionism in their 1924 satire, *Beggar on Horseback*. Maxwell Anderson and Laurence Stallings collaborated on a searing anti-war play, *What Price Glory?* in 1924; Anderson and Harold Hickerson indicted American justice and argued on behalf of anarchism in *Gods of the Lightning* in 1928. Paul Green's *In Abraham's Bosom* (1926) displayed the ugliness of racism, as did O'Neill's *All God's Chillun Got Wings*. Sidney Howard's *They Knew What They Wanted*, a comedy-drama of 1925, explored the experience of the recent immigrant to America. Robert E. Sherwood created a comedy in the manner of Bernard Shaw in 1927's *The Road to Rome*. Philip Barry wrote wittily of the follies of the upper classes in *Holiday* (1928). All of those plays, and many others like them, presented ambitious, compassionate, experimental dramas and comedies, reflecting a view of the American experience that, for the most part, Broadway had hitherto ignored. Thus, a veritable explosion of daring, sophisticated, and innovative drama was produced regularly on Broadway in the '20s, the plays existing side by side with the old, comparatively shallow entertainments, offering theatregoers a choice between maturity and superficiality.

In the 1920s, visits to New York from foreign theatres (among them the Moscow Art Theatre, the Irish National Theatre, and the Habima Players, presenting Jewish drama in productions by Jewish artists) further enriched the lives of thousands of theatregoers. And the productions they presented did not supplant new American drama; rather, they stimulated the careers of American playwrights whose best works could be favorably compared to plays written anywhere in the world.

Broadway in the '20s was vital, electric, often thrilling. Outstanding Broadway successes were the talk of New York, then the talk of the country and the world. Broadway was, at least for a time, the focal point of the American artistic spirit. As such, it assumed an importance unknown before. Along with importance came glamour, romance, excitement, sophistication. The Broadway theatre was indeed worthy of the passion Moss Hart felt in making every effort to become a part of its magical aura.

જી

American playwrights of the 1920s who favored experimentation over convention and wished to express their most fundamental beliefs, liberated by the success of Eugene O'Neill's dramatic work, turned in large measure to intensely dramatic fare. But the work of Philip Barry, S. N. Behrman, George S. Kaufman, and Marc Connelly served as reminders that, throughout history, comedy has commented upon philosophical issues and social inequities as effectively as tragedy. In ancient Greece, Aristophanes was as influential as Euripides; Shakespeare's *Twelfth Night* and *Much Ado About Nothing* are as incisive and as memorable as *Othello* and *Macbeth*; the sting of Molière's comedies and farces was sufficiently sharp to keep the targets of his satire (hypocritical clergymen and empty-headed aristocrats, for example) in a perpetual state of outrage; Oscar Wilde brilliantly skewered the well-made play in *The Importance of Being Earnest*; George Bernard Shaw's comedies effectively displayed the follies of nineteenth- and twentieth-century British society. In short, many of the finest dramas have been cast in comic form.

As all accomplished comic artists have known, comedy can do far more than entertain. It can act as a corrective to inappropriate behavior and intolerant attitudes; it can puncture pomposity and bigotry; it can expose the follies of humanity. Humor can express what might otherwise be unpalatable, cast a fresh light on issues of substance, unmask charlatans. In short, an outstanding comedy is no less consequential than the most finely wrought tragedy.

Some of the most memorable comics (performers as well as writers) have possessed temperaments that would seem to preclude the creation of comedy.

Molière, known in his day as a magnificent comic actor as well as playwright, was a melancholic, not given to offstage humor. Mark Twain's cynicism is well known. Woody Allen has never concealed his obsession with death and suffering. That some writers have chosen to explore comic terrain in order to blot out their own psychic pain is a commonplace. Most humorists, to be sure, have had sunnier dispositions, but, clearly, great comedy can emerge from apparently unlikely sources.

Just as Moss Hart coolly assessed his strengths and weaknesses as a dramatist in the late 1920s, eventually deciding that satirical comedy was his métier, other writers have reached the same conclusion. Like Hart, they discovered that, although they might have been temperamentally drawn to a stark drama, undiluted by humor, their theatrical and literary gifts were better suited to the comic approach. They possessed precisely those qualities needed for the creation of well-crafted, incisive comedy: wit, an understanding of paradox, a sense of timing, the recognition that comedy is often based upon the collapse of expectation, the ability to create characters who are at once individuals and prototypes, the aptitude for inventing a structure in which one comic incident follows another, each funnier than the one that preceded it.

Moss Hart's critically acclaimed and most popular plays sprang from the comic impulse. He was one of twentieth-century America's finest comic craftsmen. But, like Molière, who yearned but failed to be recognized as a non-comic playwright, Hart was not content only to exploit his comic gifts. Throughout his career, he wrote plays that he hoped would be accepted as dramatic, rather than comic, pieces. And, like Molière, like Woody Allen, he was significantly less successful on those occasions. Some of his non-comic plays are worthy of re-evaluation, for they were underrated at the time they were written. Nevertheless, it is clear that Hart's legacy is his contribution to comedy in America.

In a letter he wrote to Brooks Atkinson in the late 1940s, Hart stated the philosophy that served him so well throughout most of his career. While working on a new comedy, Hart bemoaned the current state of the theatre, in which—after victory over Hitler and Mussolini, after the dropping of the atomic bomb on Hiroshima and Nagasaki, in the midst of the struggle against Stalin—the comic view seemed to have been misplaced. "It just damned well seems to me," he said,

> that there must be a way of making some comment on our troublous times in
> terms of humor and a little gaiety. Are we never to laugh again? Must every-

thing be [a somber drama such as Lillian Hellman's] *Another Part of the Forest* or even [Arthur Miller's] *All My Sons?* Every writer, I'm sure, myself included, wants to be part of this strange and tortured era and have his say, but isn't anyone ever going to say it with the saving grace of a little levity? . . . to join in the battle in terms of laughter instead of lecture, gaiety instead of gloom? At any rate, that's what I'm trying to do—make my particular comment but say my say lightly and with fun.

Comedy, Hart argued, can speak as eloquently as the most searing drama. His most widely admired plays are the proof.

69

Chapter 3 OTHER PROJECTS, OTHER COLLABORATORS
1932–1934

IT HAS BEEN SAID THAT CARY GRANT "INVENTED HIMSELF." THAT IS, THE man who began life in poverty in England as Archibald Leach envisioned the kind of person he would like to become: debonair, attractive, poised, mysterious—and he so thoroughly mastered that persona that he used it in virtually every screen performance he ever gave. Nearly all the public assumed that the Cary Grant they saw on the screen—who, no matter what the particular requirements of his character, was almost always debonair, attractive, poised, and mysterious—was identical to Cary Grant himself, which could not have been further from the truth. For Cary Grant was bedeviled by self-doubt and insecurity, and was reputed to be sexually ambivalent. So successfully did Archie Leach create "Cary Grant," however, that he seemed to the public to be untouched by the problems with which everyone else is beset.

Moss Hart can be likened to Cary Grant in many respects. He, too, was born into and grew up in poverty. He, too, dreamed of another life, a life in which he would become a wealthy, witty, dapper, self-assured man, a respected playwright and director. He hoped to become a man whose opinions on many subjects would be sought, for his knowledge and erudition (especially where the theatre was concerned) would be highly valued. And, like Grant, rumors of his bisexuality were widespread. But Hart, like Grant, became what he envisioned. He earned the respect of everyone in the theatrical community through the excellence of his plays and the virtuosity of his directing; and those skills brought him a great deal of money and worldwide fame. But many aspects of his personality (self-confidence, a relaxed manner, a jaunty air) were the calculated creation of the insecure boy from the Bronx.

It is a fascinating coincidence—or was it more than coincidental?—that Moss Hart and Archie Leach knew one another in New York when they were in their early twenties, meeting regularly with their friends for coffee at Rudley's. The group often discussed their plans for the future. One wonders if Hart and Leach also discussed the ways in which they hoped to reshape their personas and whether Hart's plan to assume a personality that he could maintain in his work and in his social interactions affected Archie Leach, or vice-versa.

∾

George S. Kaufman, Hart's professional idol, offered the prototype of what Moss would like to become. And the areas in which he excelled were precisely those Hart strove to emulate. Kaufman was the American theatre's great craftsman, succeeding at whatever task he took on. He rarely broke new ground; rather than a pioneer, he took the plays he worked on to higher levels of achievement. Hart's goal seems to have been the same.

In other ways, too, Hart's career seems to have developed logically from Kaufman's example. Kaufman worked almost exclusively in collaboration. Hart became his most famous partner, but Kaufman also wrote plays with Marc Connelly, Edna Ferber, John P. Marquand, Ring Lardner, Nunnally Johnson, Leueen McGrath, Howard Teichmann, and others. Either Kaufman persuaded Hart that collaboration was an ideal method for the creation of theatrical pieces or Hart came to that conclusion on his own, but the first fifteen of Hart's plays to reach Broadway were all written in collaboration.

Kaufman was also one of the most prominent directors in the theatre, particularly in comedy. It is fair to say that, for more than twenty years, every comic playwright's dream was to have his or her play directed by George S. Kaufman. With *Of Mice and Men* in 1937 he demonstrated his expertise as a director of non-comic plays, as well. Whenever Kaufman directed a play or musical on which Hart collaborated, Hart was a constant presence at rehearsals, often making suggestions. It was only a matter of time before Hart, like Kaufman, began directing plays on Broadway, first a play written by other playwrights, then works of his own.

Even when Kaufman received no credit, he often acted as a "play doctor," giving advice about other playwrights' works either when the plays were in written form or in rehearsal. Hart soon became known as a man to whom others could turn when a show was in trouble as well.

Certainly Hart did not set out to mimic George S. Kaufman's career—but no one could have provided a finer model. Hart's ambition, to succeed on Broadway as a versatile man of the theatre, had been realized by Kaufman. Kaufman was a wealthy man who, though not ostentatious, could afford to go wherever he chose whenever he chose. Hart, a product of the slums, was determined to make enough money so that he, too, could travel when he wished, give dinner parties for his friends and those with whom he hoped to become friendly, attend the theatre as often as he liked, and purchase anything that struck his fancy. If Kaufman's methods would offer him such rewards, it is understandable that Hart would have wished to follow his example.

Many of Kaufman's attainments had been made possible by his gift for writing satirical comedy. Now that Hart had demonstrated that he, too, was a skilled satirist, it was only natural that he should have tapped into this vein again and again, as he did, especially during the first decade of his Broadway career.

All of these considerations must have been on Hart's mind as he contemplated his next theatrical ventures, but first he was obligated to fulfill the screenwriting commitments he had agreed to during the Los Angeles production of *Once in a Lifetime*.

In the 1930s, Hart regarded his screenwriting as no more than a job. Movies were useful in that the income they produced allowed him to maintain what was rapidly becoming an opulent lifestyle and allowed him to work on whatever theatrical projects he liked. But movies gave him no satisfaction whatever, and he was indifferent to film as an art form. It is revealing that in his voluminous scrapbook, in which every detail of his theatrical career was elaborately chronicled, Hart did not keep a single clipping about the films he worked on in the 1930s. Instead, he suffered through screenwriting as if he were being held in artistic bondage, and whenever he spent time in Hollywood he couldn't wait to complete his contract and return to New York.

Though it might seem difficult to feel sorry for a man who was exploiting the film studios for financial gain, it should be noted that the agonies he felt while writing for the screen were real. Movies served primarily, almost exclusively, as a bank from which he drew enormous sums of money. Contrasting the boredom he felt in Hollywood with the excitement of working in the theatre, he said, "You were safe [in Hollywood]. You were miserable, but you were safe. You sat at your typewriter and hated yourself, but in the evening you could leave and forget it until the next morning. You didn't eat it and sleep it and drink it the way you did in the theatre."

Hart wasted no time showing his contempt for Hollywood. Asked to say a few words on the radio at the first film premiere he attended, he commented, "Well, here I am out here, and if this is God's country He can have it."

Hart's quip seems a bit arrogant, but he appears to have arrived at his negative opinion for good reason. When he arrived in Hollywood to write for MGM, Irving Thalberg, the head of the studio, instructed two of his employees to meet Hart at the train station and rush him to his office. When they arrived, Hart was handed the treatment of a story for which he was to write the dialogue. After three weeks he had completed the assignment, only to be told that he had been given the wrong synopsis. The studio, he was informed, had decided a year before to discard the treatment.

Later, at a story conference, Hart jestingly suggested to a producer that he write a screenplay about an elderly Jew who enters into an agreement to lend money to a Venetian merchant. In return, the Jew demands a pound of flesh if the merchant is unable to repay the money on the agreed-upon date. He proceeded to outline the entire story of *The Merchant of Venice*. The producer listened attentively, then shook his head. "I'm afraid it will never go," the producer said.[1]

If nothing else, Hart's employment in Hollywood brought with it a luxury for his family as well as himself. He rented a mansion above the Sunset Strip in 1932, followed by a home in Beverly Hills the next year, in both of which he lived with his brother and parents.

Assessing Hart's precise contributions to the films he worked on is nearly impossible, for several reasons. Some of the work he did was uncredited (perhaps because he preferred not to have his name associated with the resultant films); some of it was radically altered by the producer or director; all of it was co-written with various screenwriters of varying abilities; and some of the films themselves no longer exist.

He co-wrote *Flesh* (evidently he was responsible for "dialogue only"), an MGM film directed by John Ford and released in 1932. Wallace Beery played Polikai, a German wrestler who falls in love with Nora (Karen Morley), an American dancer who marries Polikai, then leaves him. Subsequently, Polikai kills Grant (Ricardo Cortez), the father of Nora's child. *Variety*'s verdict was that the film was "not bad, could have been better." Indeed, it would seem that *Flesh* was neither more nor less significant than any of a hundred other movies of the time.

He may have contributed to *Make Me a Star*, a film adaptation of the Kaufman and Connelly success, *Merton of the Movies*, but credit was given to Sam Mintz, Walter DeLeon, and Arthur Kober. Either Hart did not wish to have his name included or his contribution was not significant enough to justify it.

Hart wrote *The Masquerader* with Howard Estabrook for Samuel Goldwyn in 1933, an adaptation from a play by John Hunter Booth. In the film, Ronald Colman plays the dual role of Sir John, a dope-addicted member of

---

1 History repeated itself in 1939, when Hart was asked by another Hollywood producer what he was working on. "A new movie scenario," Hart replied, "all about a young prince of a mythical kingdom who is informed by his father's ghost that his death is to be avenged upon an unscrupulous uncle who usurps the throne. So this young prince stages a play to watch the face of his uncle as the crime is re-enacted. There's some love interest, too. But the girl goes mad because the prince broods too damn much. Like the idea?"

The producer thought a moment, then shook his head. "I don't know," he said. "A mythical kingdom story would be a tough proposition after Selznick's *Prisoner of Zenda*."

Parliament and his cousin, who is persuaded to step in and give a speech for the drugged politician. He does so, with great success, and, when Sir John dies, takes his place forever, fooling even Sir John's wife. *Variety* praised *The Masquerader* as "a fine production," but said it was burdened "with too much story handicap." *Newsweek* called it "The first amusing and believable tale of English politics and society . . . made of all places in Hollywood." Hart also worked on an original screenplay, *The March of Time*, for MGM. The film was to chronicle the legitimate theatre from the 1880s until 1933. Although *The March of Time* was never filmed, Hart filed away the idea and used it as the basis for a play he would write five years later.

Hart arranged with MGM to postpone the remainder of his contract for a year. In April 1933, he returned to New York, eager to begin a project for the theatre. George S. Kaufman made clear that he was eager to work with Hart again, but Kaufman had already committed to other projects and needed to see them through before he could renew his partnership with Hart. That was one reason they did not immediately begin working on another play together. Another was Hart's friends' advice that he needed to establish his own reputation unless he wished to be known forever as Kaufman's junior partner.

If Hart did not immediately resume his collaboration with Kaufman, he was certainly influenced by Kaufman's example. Although Kaufman was perhaps best known as the author of plays, he also co-wrote a number of successful musical comedies. He excelled at directing musicals as well, despite the fact that he confessed to having no love for music. Hart was not a musician, but he, too, was certainly capable of writing for the musical theatre. In 1932, he reconsidered the assertion he had made to Max Siegel in 1929 ("I'm a playwright. I write plays—*only* plays").

At the time Hart made that rather self-important proclamation, he might have believed that Sam Harris, whose suggestion it was to turn *Once in a Lifetime* into a musical, was a philistine. But Hart had grown to know and respect Harris, and no doubt he wondered whether Harris's suggestion might have merit after all. Harris's instinct that Hart's play might have served as the basis of an excellent musical was not nearly as bizarre as Hart first thought. In many ways, in fact, *Once in a Lifetime* was a musical comedy without the music. The broadness of the characterizations, the structure of the piece, its very nature seemed to call out for songs and dances. Hart resisted the idea of writing a musical in 1929, but, after *Once in a Lifetime* proved successful, his attitude changed. The fact that the Pulitzer Prize in 1931 went to a musical,

Of Thee I Sing (with book by George S. Kaufman and Morrie Ryskind, music and lyrics by George and Ira Gershwin), may have supplied the final impetus for Hart to try his hand at the form, as well. Even the Pulitzer judges had proclaimed that musical comedy was not necessarily an inferior form. Musicals did not have to be as vapid as *Jonica*. If written with distinction, a satirical musical could be just as pointed as a satirical play.

For many reasons, then, none of Hart's next three projects in the theatre were written with George S. Kaufman, and all of them involved music. Sam Harris had signed Hart to a five-year contract giving Harris the right to produce anything Hart wrote for the stage during that period. In 1931, Hart plunged into the first of several collaborative projects, *Face the Music*, a "musical comedy revue" with music by Irving Berlin, which Harris produced in 1932. Kaufman co-directed the musical with Hassard Short, a renowned British choreographer-director of the period. Short staged the musical numbers while Kaufman was responsible for all of the other scenes.

Hart had met Berlin after returning to New York from the California tour of *Once in a Lifetime*. While dining with Sam Harris, Hart mentioned that he had spent much of the transcontinental train ride thinking of sketch possibilities for a *Music Box Revue*, which, if it came to pass, would be one of a successful series of revues that had been presented under that name. Harris became excited by Hart's ideas and shouted for a telephone to be brought to the table. He called Irving Berlin (who was co-owner, with Harris, of the Music Box Theatre), saying, "Come right down here, Irving. Moss Hart has an idea for a new *Music Box Revue* and I like it."

Berlin was tied up and unable to join them that night but did arrange to lunch with them at Sardi's the following day. For Hart, although he had opted not to work with Berlin on *Once in a Lifetime*, the opportunity to meet the composer was another dream come true, offering the possibility of working with one of his idols. As a boy working in Mr. Levenson's music store, he had first learned to appreciate Berlin's songs. And, on the occasion of the first *Music Box Revue*, to which Berlin contributed, Hart had waited at the stage door, watching the famous songwriter enter the theatre.

At lunch, one of Hart's sketch ideas intrigued Berlin, but the composer announced that he was not interested in working on another revue. He was, however, eager to collaborate on a musical comedy, and suggested that Hart's sketch idea might serve as the basis for a book musical. When Hart's film commitments were completed, Berlin invited him to move into his house on Long Island for two weeks so that they could discuss the idea in a leisurely fashion.

Two weeks turned into four months, during which time the prospective musical was the exclusive subject of conversation. "Writing a show with Irving Berlin is tantamount to entering a monastery," Hart said. "Family, friends, personal life, all of them disappear into the dim distance, to be remembered at odd moments when you were not writing a musical comedy. For you not only write a show with Irving Berlin, you live it, breathe it, eat it, and were it not for the fact that he allows you to sleep not at all, I should also say sleep it." Berlin worked best late at night, beginning at midnight, and Hart agreed to work on Berlin's schedule. However, he found it almost impossible to sleep during the day, as Berlin did, and attributed the insomnia that plagued him for the rest of his life to the period of his collaboration with Irving Berlin.

After the prolonged stay at Berlin's Long Island home, Hart and the composer worked for eight more months in New York City. With Berlin, Hart experienced at least as much turmoil as he felt in his collaboration with Kaufman: "high elation one moment and profound despair the next; great delight in each other's work . . . in the morning [when their work day was ending] and a complete reversal" at night. Hart, who described himself as a "nervous type," found an intensity in Berlin that he had not encountered before. "Compared to Irving Berlin," he said, "I am Buddha incarnate." Hart was so exhausted by insomnia and nerves that, he said, "I found myself walking about in a world resembling nothing so much as the settings of the motion picture *The Cabinet of Dr. Caligari.*"

Face the Music, the musical that resulted from their collaboration, was produced in the midst of the Depression. It tapped into the vein of political satire Kaufman and Ryskind explored in *Of Thee I Sing*, but in a much more genial way than *Of Thee I Sing*'s savage mockery. *Face the Music* was unlike many of the plays and films of its period in that, rather than ignoring the economic crisis that gripped the country, it was set in a Depression milieu and managed to find humor in it. The play dealt with the hearings then being held by Judge Samuel Seabury into police and political corruption in New York. Testifying before the Seabury Commission, policemen and political officials claimed that the money missing from the city's treasury had not been stolen; rather, they had prudently stored away the funds in "little tin boxes." A scandal of such proportions arose that, eventually, the Seabury Commission hearings resulted in the resignation of Mayor Jimmy Walker.[2]

---

2 Another musical in which the little tin boxes played a prominent role is *Fiorello*, with music by Jerry Bock, lyrics by Sheldon Harnick, and book by Jerome Weidman and George Abbott. *Fiorello* opened on Broadway in November 1959.

The New York portrayed in *Face the Music* is but a shadow of its former self. Tiffany's, Cartier's, and Elizabeth Arden's once-vaunted dignity is a thing of the past, as hawkers outside their shops peddle their wares for a pittance ("Two for the price of one!" "Some real bargains today, folks. How about a diamond for your sweetheart!")—to no effect, for all the best people are shopping at Woolworth's. A character named Kit Baker, a former musical comedy star, announces that she can "be had for just coffee and cakes, or coffee and rolls, or, in a pinch, just plain coffee." In contrast, a Mrs. Martin Van Buren Meshbesher, whose policeman husband has collected enough little tin boxes to afford himself and his wife a luxurious existence (Mrs. Meshbesher is bedecked with diamonds, emeralds, and four wristwatches), declares, "My husband's business has just blossomed the last year. My God, how the money rolls in." Thus the basis of the musical is established: the contrast between the grotesquely rich and the very poor.

Face the Music also aimed satirical thrusts at the then-current state of show business. The Depression had forced economies everywhere, but the economies portrayed in the musical were particularly loony: the Palace Theatre offering a vaudeville featuring Ethel Barrymore, Eddie Cantor, Aimee Semple McPherson, Albert Einstein, and Al Jolson, for example—along with a free lunch. At the Roxy Theatre one could see four films and get a room and bath for a dime.

In the musical lampoon Hart and Berlin fashioned, Mrs. Meshbesher and her husband agree to back a production called *The Rhinestone Girl* by Hal Reisman, a down-on-his-luck Broadway producer. Only the police, it's suggested, could possibly afford to put up the backing for a musical, for they have corralled all the money in the city. What Reisman doesn't know is that the Meshbeshers, along with the other backers, all of whom have dipped into public funds, are subsidizing his production only to get rid of some of the money they've stolen before it can be discovered by the investigators. Reisman, a producer with a notorious reputation for incompetence, seems an excellent bet to lose every cent; indeed, *The Rhinestone Girl* appears to be headed for spectacular failure.[3]

Eventually, however, the Meshbeshers and their policemen allies who backed the production are brought to trial. Judge Seabury orders the offenders to ten years in jail, but, in the tradition of musical comedy, all ends happily and spectacularly: Reisman infuses his show with sex, becomes successful, and makes a fortune for all those who were down on their luck. In the final

---

3 Mel Brooks's film and subsequent stage musical, *The Producers*, are based on a variation of this idea.

scene, Reisman, who has for some obscure reason been posing as a waiter in a little country town, decides to return to New York and present a show entitled *Investigations of 1932, Glorifying the American Policeman*.

Finding an appropriate title for a play is often a difficult proposition, but *Face the Music* proved to be especially challenging. Among the titles considered, then discarded, were *Nickels and Dimes, This Town of Ours, Curtain Going Up, Footlights, Let's Do a Show, Off the Beat, Standing Room Only, Brass Buttons, Round the Corner, Stand Up and Cheer, Wings Over Broadway, Grand Slam, Manhattan Madness,Gotham Gleanings, The Big Town, Crying Out Loud* and *Louder and Funnier*, among many other possibilities. It was Irving Berlin who finally hit upon *Face the Music*.

Hugh O'Connell, who had played George so successfully in *Once in a Lifetime*, was cast as the wealthy chief of police, Mr. Meshbesher, and the popular Mary Boland played the malapropian Mrs. Meshbesher.

Face the Music tried out at the Shubert Theatre in Philadelphia on February 3, 1932. A critic for the *Philadelphia Inquirer* was enthusiastic. "The audience, which filled every seat in the house and overflowed into the standees in the rear, laughed until it was tired," he said. "It chuckled appreciatively at the whimsy of the songs . . . which are . . . set to tuneful, catchy music." He added that Mary Boland "proved a riot throughout." A later report, on February 8, described all the Philadelphia reviews as having been "raves," and said, "Since its opening it has builded [*sic*] into smash proportions."

After that successful tryout, *Face the Music* opened at the New Amsterdam Theatre in New York on February 17, with Jimmy Walker and Governor Al Smith in attendance. (One wonders how Walker reacted to the musical, in which his administration was accused of permitting if not fostering corruption, but his response is not on record.) Brooks Atkinson appreciated the show's "impudent sense of humor" and reserved special praise for Mary Boland, who was particularly adored by the opening night audience. Another critic called *Face the Music* "a good show, a hilarious show, a tuneful one, and one that is constantly entertaining. The customers loved it." Richard Lockridge wrote in the *New York Sun*, "It will go, and should go, at once among the things which no one will want to miss." And Robert Garland, in the *World-Telegram*, said, "even if Mr. Hart's libretto weakens infrequently, even if his wisecracks are once in a great while neither as wise nor as witty as might be expected, Mr. Irving Berlin's words and music are as Berlinian as any he has written."

The success of the production—it ran for a respectable 165 performances (and would probably have played longer but for the withdrawal of Mary

Boland, who had to go to Hollywood to fulfill a film obligation)—was due at least as much to Irving Berlin's tuneful songs as it was to Hart's book. "Let's Have Another Cup o' Coffee," sung by two young unemployed performers who are eating five-cent dinners at the Automat at Broadway and 47th Street, told of the prosperity that seemed right around the corner, and was the show's biggest hit—and, in its tongue-in-cheek optimism, became a sort of anthem for the Depression.

Mary Boland, her movie completed, began a tour of *Face the Music* in Boston on November 22, 1932. New York's theatregoers obviously wanted more of *Face the Music*, too, for the show reopened on January 31, 1933, at the 44th Street Theatre, and gave an additional thirty-two performances.

One could not make a case for *Face the Music* as a ground-breaking musical. Although it dealt with topical material in a satirical way, its structure was conventional, its ending predictably silly, in the fashion of musicals of the time. Hart must have been pleased, though, at Atkinson's recognition of him as someone who "can look after himself as a wit. There is an undercurrent of genuine humor in his most poisonous barrages," Atkinson said, "which are sharp and deadly." In a later article, however, Atkinson lamented the "sometimes barren" humor and said the musical was "not an unalloyed delight."

Indeed, the book, which was largely nonsensical, existing primarily to accommodate some good jokes and tuneful songs, was more sophisticated but no more innovative than the book for *Jonica* had been. The satirical thrust of the musical, however, along with the use of topical elements, gave *Face the Music* a greater distinction than the typical musical comedy of the kind could claim. *Face the Music* had the temerity not only to deal with an inflammatory subject, but to name the names of those Hart thought were particularly corrupt. One of the original New York reviews summed up *Face the Music*'s pluses and minuses quite well: "It's a worthy successor to *Of Thee I Sing*, [but] it doesn't entirely measure up to it. It resorts to slapstick instead of satire. It becomes merely burlesque. All of which doesn't mean that *Face the Music* isn't a howl. It most emphatically is."

The modern American musical, in which musical numbers do not stop the progression of the plot but are smoothly integrated into the dialogue and propel the story forward, and in which the songs reveal elements of character more subtly and profoundly than dialogue could do, had only recently been invented. (*Show Boat* in 1927 had contained some of these elements.) Hart would eventually be regarded as an architect of the modern American musical, but in 1932 he expressed no such ambition. Perhaps he was thinking about it, though, for he said, "I happen to think that a musical comedy or a revue can, in its own special way, be important."

With some conspicuous exceptions (such as *Show Boat* and *Porgy and Bess*), American musicals of the 1920s and '30s deserved the adjective "frivolous." Why, then, did Hart think that musical comedy can be "important?" Perhaps for the same reason that the nineteenth-century German composer Richard Wagner wrote music-dramas (the term he preferred to "operas"): if the greatest dramatic art could be seamlessly blended with the greatest musical art (drama should be "dipped in the magic fountain of music," Wagner wrote) the resultant form should be more emotionally satisfying and more powerful than either drama or music alone. Wagner suggested a fusion of Shakespeare and Beethoven to illustrate how magnificent the finest music-dramas could be. It is doubtful that Moss Hart had Shakespeare or Beethoven in mind, but his aspirations for the musical may have exceeded anything that had been produced in the early 1930s. No one could claim that *Face the Music* had advanced the form of the American musical, but it was only the first link in a chain Moss Hart forged. Eventually a musical he wrote (*Lady in the Dark*) and another he directed (*My Fair Lady*) could accurately be described as having broken new ground.

If nothing else, *Face the Music* furthered Hart's reputation as the boy wonder of Broadway. Still only twenty-eight, Hart had firmly established his theatrical reputation and was in demand as a screenwriter. And not only had his dream of success come true, he was now invited to the same sorts of parties he had once been so awed by at the Kaufmans' house. He gave many parties of his own, having moved into a townhouse on East 57th Street and having spared no expense in decorating it. Most of the guests represented the theatrical elite of New York. His income permitted him to travel, and he spent several months trekking across France, Germany, Switzerland, Austria, Italy, and Yugoslavia in the summer of 1932. And, on top of all his achievements and good fortune, he was immensely likable and attractive, both to women (some of whom hoped to snare this very eligible bachelor) and to men (who found him a good, congenial friend and, perhaps, an object of romantic interest). Although he was known for his wit, he never used it in a venomous way. As George Cukor, who came to know him well, said, "He was very funny, but never unkind."

One of the famous people he came to know in the early 1930s was Edna Ferber, the prominent novelist and playwright, who had herself collaborated on several occasions with George S. Kaufman. Ferber took Hart under her wing soon after the success of *Once in a Lifetime*. Although she was nearly twenty years older than Hart, she was deeply attached to him for many years, often dining with him. He turned to her for advice, frequently calling or writing her whenever he was out of New York. In the words of Ferber's biographer Julie Goldsmith Gilbert, Hart "provided her with the only maternal instincts she ever had." Certainly the relationship was not sexual—in later years Hart wondered aloud if Ferber was celibate—but their emotional bond was strong.

Asked to describe her impression of Hart, Ferber used the following five adjectives: "gentle, kind, witty, generous, companionable." Although Hart and Ferber later had a prolonged feud, they were ultimately reconciled. It may have been simply impossible for anyone to stay angry with Moss Hart for long.

One can hardly exaggerate the level of urbanity, charm (Garson Kanin called Hart "the most charming man that ever was") and self-possession Hart projected to the world. Everyone who knew Hart found him an ideal companion, a man of great warmth, a friend who could be relied upon to provide help when needed, a witty—but not malicious or cynical—commentator on current events and all things theatrical. To know him was to envy his equanimity, his cultivation, and his elegance. His turns of phrase were widely quoted and anecdotes about his activities were in constant circulation. He was gentle and considerate; he was a good listener who would never fail to draw out and encourage his conversational partner.

In Hart, urbanity combined with boyish exuberance. Indeed, Rosamond Gilder, who wrote an article about him in the 1940s, said that he "seems to be perpetually at the centre of an electric storm. His personality vibrates with intensity, with ideas, emotions . . . He is dynamic . . . a man with a great zest for the complexities of living . . . One of the most glitteringly successful playwrights of the day, he has not yet learned to be blasé—about an opening night, about the money that has rolled into (and out of) his pockets, about his work, his friends, his possessions, or about the theatre."

In appearance, Hart was tall—over six feet—slender (the huge appetite he possessed as a youth, when he gobbled down whatever food he could find at George S. Kaufman's house, tapered off as he grew older), and possessed of wavy dark hair, which he began to lose while in his 20s. Blessed with attractive features, he "looked like a matinee idol," said fellow playwright S. N. Behrman. Because of his hairline, which came to a peak in the middle of his forehead, then receded to his temples, his bold nose and his severely arched eyebrows, he was often described as "Mephisophelean" or "Satanic." But the devilish look contrasted with his behavior, which "was that of an amiable boy," Brooks Atkinson said, "with enthusiastic gestures and eager, curious eyes."

Dore Schary said, "His head was always held high as if he were about to issue a command or answer a question or search out a truth. His eyebrows were always arched, sometimes as if in disbelief, at any sign of ineptitude or fraud or discourtesy. Other times, they gave him a look of amused interest. Sometimes, of imperial disdain."

Judging by early photographs of him, when he was in his twenties he looked considerably older than he was. As he aged, his appearance changed very little, except for the slowly receding hairline.

He spoke with a resonant baritone voice, his speech precise and cultivated. In conversation, he shifted easily from one topic to another. "His nimble, challenging mind leaps about so in talk," wrote an interviewer, "that a chat with Hart sometimes leaves one with the slightly unsettled feeling of having been tossed in a blanket."

Everything about Hart—his appearance, his voice, his manner of dress— was theatrical. He might have stepped directly out of a play about the humorous activities of the upper class, a play by Philip Barry or Noël Coward, perhaps. If Hart had been a song, he would have been written by Cole Porter. Walter Kerr later said of him, "His style was something a curtain could always have gone up on." His style can be seen in this description by Kitty Carlisle—his future wife—of his entering a restaurant: "He didn't just walk in: he made an entrance, his overcoat on his shoulders like a cloak; he looked like a great actor, and every head turned." His enthusiasm for life, his spontaneity, his *joie de vivre* may have seemed to those who first met him as if they might be a pose, but they soon discovered that these qualities were unfeigned (if slightly theatricalized). "When he entered a room the lights came on," Edna Ferber said. "There was nothing exhibitionistic about this. He just carried with him a built-in incandescence."

Romantic attachments to women were a late development in Hart's life, but a new world of relationships with the opposite sex opened to him after *Once in a Lifetime* succeeded in New York. Initially, he used his new affluence to thank a woman to whom he owed a debt of gratitude. He bought a set of tailored dinner clothes and, the first time he wore them, invited Beatrice Kaufman to accompany him to dinner and the theatre.

Soon after, he began to date women closer to his own age. For various reasons—his character, his dynamism, his success, his sizable income—he was attractive to many women, a number of whom accompanied him to dinner, to parties and to the theatre. So many women's names were linked to Hart's, in fact, that his friends despaired of his becoming truly serious about any one of them. One evening, when he escorted the actress Edith Atwater to a restaurant, Oscar Levant, seated at another table, said, "Here comes Moss Hart with the future Miss Atwater."

Greta Garbo was among the many women who flirted openly with Hart, her manner suggesting that she had more than a flirtation in mind. He chose not to pursue the relationship. Hart and Kaufman were both attracted to still another actress, who made it clear that she preferred Hart.

But he showed no inclination to marry, despite the urging of some of his friends. Cole Porter and Monty Woolley were convinced that Hart was a repressed homosexual, suggesting to him, "You haven't been laid until you've been laid by a man who knows the ropes," according to Porter's biographer, Charles Schwarz. However, Porter and Woolley were unsuccessful in bringing Hart "out of the closet," if, indeed, he was concealing his sexuality. At least one man claimed to have had an affair with Hart in 1939.

Whenever his friends' matchmaking urges became too insistent to suit him, he stated that his heart still belonged to a schoolteacher who had died, making any thoughts of marriage impossible for him. Not wanting to cause him emotional distress, his friends dropped the subject. On one occasion, however, during a private conversation, Beatrice Kaufman sympathetically mentioned the schoolteacher. Hart looked at her, astonished. "My God," he said, "You didn't *believe* that, did you?"

Perhaps Hart's relationship with Beatrice Kaufman made it difficult for him to consider other women he knew as possible marriage partners. He looked upon Beatrice with a mixture of filial feeling—she was considerably older than he was—and romantic attachment. In his romantic feelings, he was not alone. Her charm and wit caused many men to fall in love with her, among them Oscar Levant and Alexander Woollcott. It would be inaccurate to term Hart's friendship with Beatrice a love affair, but there is no question that Hart admired her deeply and preferred her company to that of any other woman.

She was "not in the conventional sense a beautiful woman," Hart said of her, "but she had uncommon distinction, an individual style, and a unique and singular quality of her own that lent to everything she said and did a special radiance."

Beatrice became his confidant, the person he could share his concerns with, ask for advice, and know that he would always receive a sympathetic, heartfelt response. He looked to her for understanding and was never disappointed. If George S. Kaufman was Hart's mentor in his working life, Beatrice Kaufman filled the same function in his emotional and social life. In turn, Beatrice came to feel great affection for the young man whom she had seen evolve from a wide-eyed naïf into a man of the world, sensing, correctly, that they had much in common.

ↄ৹

In July 1932, Hart returned to Hollywood to fulfill his contract with MGM. He rented a large home in the Hollywood hills, above Sunset Boulevard, where he lived with his mother, father, and brother Bernie. One of the projects on which he worked was a projected film musical, *I Married an Angel*, with lyrics by Lorenz Hart (no relation to Moss) and music by Richard Rodgers, who found Moss "an intense . . . fellow, fairly bursting with ideas." *I Married an Angel* was intended for Jeanette MacDonald, who had just been signed to an MGM contract. Hart adapted a Hungarian play about a banker who does indeed marry an angel, thus fulfilling his greatest wish. Within a month the screenplay and score were completed, but Louis B. Mayer decreed that fantasies were no longer commercial and the production did not go forward.[4]

Soon afterward, Hart received word from Irving Berlin that the composer wished to discuss the possibility of their working together again, and, given Hart's eagerness to work in the theatre rather than in Hollywood, he readily agreed—especially when Berlin sweetened his offer. He gave Hart a loan of $5,000—not an inconsiderable sum during the Depression—and proposed to finance a trip to Bermuda, where they would work on the new project. MGM gave Hart a leave of absence, with the understanding that he would resume his contractual obligations at a later date. As the discussions with Berlin progressed during a stay in Bermuda, an idea emerged: this time they would dispense with plot altogether and write a musical revue. But this revue would be different from others. They agreed that most of the revues they had seen had been unsatisfactory, because, in their opinions, no meaningful thread linked the songs and sketches together. But they hit upon the idea of using headlines from the daily newspapers as the connecting material. Every song and sketch would be introduced by a headline invented for the occasion

---

4 In 1938, Rodgers and Hart converted *I Married an Angel* into a Broadway production, but they used a translation from the Hungarian rather than Moss's adaptation. He received no credit whatever for his oblique contribution to the production. The 1942 MGM musical of the same name, though starring Jeannette MacDonald and Nelson Eddy and carrying through some plot elements, bore little overall resemblance to any of its previous incarnations.

and projected on the front curtain.

The virtue of their notion was that the newspaper format would hold the material together in a way that was rarely seen in revues (an article in *Stage* magazine conceded that other shows had offered "topical skits," but "never before an entire evening planned, written, and acted as a burlesque parade of the planet's momentary preoccupations"). It also offered sufficient latitude so that *any* idea, so long as it was topical, could be dramatized or turned into a song.

Watching *As Thousands Cheer* would replicate the reading of a newspaper. Individual scenes thus dealt with news events, the society page, the comics, advice to the lovelorn, and other newspaper features. Excited by the ideas he and Berlin had conceived, Hart and the composer wrote the first act in Bermuda in March and April 1933. Hart wrote the sketches for Act Two in Skowhegan, Maine, at the home of Jean Dixon, his leading lady in *Once in a Lifetime*. Unlike the continual outbreak of nerves produced by *Face the Music*, Hart and Berlin had a very different experience. "Either we had grown less nervous and more used to each other," said Hart, "or we had learned a bitter lesson; I do not know. But the work moved smoothly and without strain."

Although each song and each sketch in *As Thousands Cheer* differed from every other, the material was held together by its topical nature. Some of the headlines projected before the scenes included "World's Wealthiest Man Celebrates 94th Birthday" (John D. Rockefeller Jr. attempts to give Radio City to his father as a birthday gift. When the old man turns on John Junior with a knife, the younger Rockefeller runs for his life); "Josephine Baker Still the Rage of Paris," "The Funnies," "Lonely Hearts Column," "Prince of Wales Rumored Engaged" (the King and Queen of England lecture the Prince of Wales about his love life), and "Franklin D. Roosevelt Inaugurated Tomorrow" (Herbert Hoover is seen with his wife in the process of vacating the White House prior to the Roosevelt inauguration, acidulously commenting upon their successors while Mrs. Hoover insists on taking a set of silver spoons with her). The latter was considered particularly shocking, for political satire in the Broadway theatre had in the past always been generalized; here, for the first time in an American musical, the actual personages were portrayed and burlesqued. Joan Crawford, Barbara Hutton, Aimee Semple McPherson, Josephine Baker, Will Hays, Lynn Fontanne, and Douglas Fairbanks Jr. also figured as characters in the sketches, identified by name, the scenes often showing them in a wickedly unflattering light.

One of the sketches satirizes the ever-brilliant but sometimes-bizarre young playwright-actor-songwriter Noël Coward, driving the staff of a hotel mad with his quickly alternating moods and impossible demands. In another, "Joan Crawford to Divorce Douglas Fairbanks, Jr.," Will Hays, then the watchdog of morality for motion pictures, tries to put the best possible spin on the impending divorce. Hays says proudly, "I want to say . . . that this is a divorce the industry can be proud of! It's clear—no sex in it! It's a divorce any Woman's Club in the country can point to with pride. . . . If there was an Academy Award for the best divorce of the year, I'd give it to this one!" But the amiability shown by Crawford and Fairbanks breaks down when they envision the newspaper headlines. He wants first billing, but she insists that her name should come first. Then they bicker about who should be given credit for the idea of divorcing. Joan says, "If my name doesn't come first then I just won't *get* the divorce, that's all. Does Constance Bennett's name come second when *she* has her divorces? I should say not!" Hays attempts to salvage the situation, but the vanity of the two stars continues to wreak havoc as the sketch comes to an end.

Author and composer believed firmly in the production concept. When skeptics watched rehearsals and insisted that the public would not sit still for a revue without a tap dancer or a group of pretty chorus girls, Hart and Berlin resisted all attempts to include time-honored musical conventions. They sought a revue containing more adult, more satirical, bolder material than revues had included in the past. "I had not come out of Hollywood for just a pleasant success," Hart said. "If the show fulfilled my hopes for it, then I wanted a *hell* of a success."

Success was threatened for a time because of the need to replace several of the songs not long before the New York opening. In a revue without connecting tissue no song was more appropriate than another, but in *As Thousands Cheer*, each song had to have topical significance. Hart said, "If a musical show is in trouble, it is indeed in trouble. You can't blandly and bodily remove musical numbers without finding that your pace, variety, and even actual viewpoint of the show are turned around, to say nothing of the fact that chorus boys and girls, fast as they are, can't make a costume change in less than two minutes."

In four days, working virtually without sleep, Berlin wrote four songs, a new opening, and a new finale. Composing music was no problem for him ("music streams from him as from a faucet," Hart said) but lyrics were another matter. He agonized over every word, every rhyme, every metaphor.

Hassard Short directed the musical numbers and lit the production. Although Hart received no credit, he directed the sketches. Sam H. Harris was the producer once again, and *As Thousands Cheer* was presented in Harris and Berlin's Music Box Theatre, which, because of its intimacy, was the ideal home for the revue.

Casting posed many problems. Beatrice Lillie, Edna Mae Oliver, Cicely Courtenidge, and others were approached, but declined. According to Hart, the responses ranged from "My name must go first!" to "How many songs do I have?" to "I wouldn't *think* of sharing billing!" to "I've never had anything but Dressing Room Number One in my life!"

Hart's greatest hope was that Marilyn Miller, the acclaimed singer and dancer and the highest paid female musical comedy star of her time, would appear in the production. Miller, who had won fame in the *Ziegfeld Follies*, had also starred in *Sally* on Broadway in the early 1920s, when Hart was a teenager. He was enchanted by her, seeing her in *Sally* no less than thirty-seven times. She became for him "an unattainable ideal, a sort of 'vision,'" he said. In May or June 1933, Hart was invited to a dinner party at which Miller would be one of the guests. He arranged to be seated next to her and, during the course of dinner conversation, they became friendly. It then struck him that she would be an ideal star for *As Thousands Cheer*. She was immediately interested. "Pictures bore me," she said. "I want to get back on the stage again and get the feel of an audience. Let me see what you've written when it's finished." Later, impressed by the sketches and the score, Miller signed a contract.

Ultimately, Clifton Webb, Helen Broderick, and Ethel Waters joined Miller as featured performers. All of them were talented and popular, but some proved difficult to work with. As rehearsals proceeded throughout July and August 1933, the performers' temperaments caused continual trouble. One crisis followed another, as Hart recounted: "The crisis of who followed what sketch. The crisis of who had the spot next to the finale. The crisis of who opened the show. The crisis of who closed the show." Hart found himself spending most of the rehearsal time soothing the performers, "pouring flattery into the not unwilling ears of Marilyn Miller [and driving] Helen Broderick to tears by my own nervous impatience and frayed nerves." Despite all his attempts to flatter Marilyn Miller, she remained quarrelsome throughout rehearsals. She called Hart at three in the morning during the Philadelphia tryout, screaming to him so irritatingly about how little she was appreciated in spite of all her hard work that Hart hung up on her. Later, contrite, he called her room and attempted to apologize, but she shouted, "How dare you speak to me like that! I'm not a chorus girl! How dare you!" She invoked the spirit of the man who used to present her in the *Follies*, Florenz Ziegfeld, comparing Hart unfavorably to the legendary showman. Hart, unable to control his temper, shouted, "Mr. Ziegfeld is dead, my dear, and the sooner you get that into your head the better," and hung up the phone again. Their volatile relationship continued until one night, when, after a performance, Hart went to Miller's dressing room and, without a word, patched up their differences. "Without sending in my name," he said, he "knocked briefly and went in. We dutifully fell into each other's arms."

Clifton Webb, who later became known to film audiences as a straight comic actor but was in fact a skillful singer and dancer, also had the opportunity in *As Thousands Cheer* to create devastating impressions of Mahatma Gandhi, Noël Coward, and John D. Rockefeller Sr. Ethel Waters was brilliant in singing "Heat Wave" (in "Heat Wave Strikes New York") and "Supper Time," an almost unbearably moving song about a widow trying to decide how to tell her children that their father would never be returning home. The scene, headlined, "Unknown Negro Lynched by Frenzied Mob," was surely one of the most original and daring ever included in a musical. Many of those connected with the production tried to persuade Hart and Irving Berlin to eliminate the scene, but they—and Sam Harris—insisted that it remain in the production. It did, and its poignancy gave the revue a more profound dimension than it would otherwise have possessed. It demonstrated as decisively as had ever been previously demonstrated that musicals could deal effectively with serious, even painful, subjects.

"Supper Time," "How's Chances," "Harlem on My Mind," and "Heat Wave" have become classics of American popular song, but perhaps the most famous of Berlin's songs in *As Thousands Cheer* was "Easter Parade," in a scene from the rotogravure section of the "newspaper." Burns Mantle described it as "the grandest finale any revue ever had."[5]

The first tryout performance of *As Thousands Cheer* was at the Forrest Theatre in Philadelphia on September 9, 1933. Trouble was brewing, as Hart discovered when he arrived in Philadelphia after having settled his parents, who were visiting from California, in a New York hotel. He arrived in Philadelphia tired and irritable, but his spirits lifted when he watched the finale,

---

5 Few songs have had as extensive a history as "Easter Parade." The music was originally composed in 1917 for a song called "Smile and Show Your Dimple." Under its new title, it was featured in the 1942 Bing Crosby–Fred Astaire film *Holiday Inn*, and later served as the title song for the 1948 MGM film featuring Judy Garland and Fred Astaire. By then the song had become a great national hit and the inevitable accompaniment to the Easter holiday.

which played extremely well, and he repaired to Sam Harris's room at the hotel expecting to find Berlin and Harris in high spirits.

Instead, both looked tired to the point of exhaustion. They explained that a problem so monumental had arisen that they were at a loss how to deal with it. A new song for Ethel Waters had been inserted during the matinee that afternoon, and she had stopped the show with it. Not everyone was pleased with Waters' success, however, and Harris and Berlin feared that the issue was about to erupt in ways that could threaten the show's potential success.

Only moments later, Clifton Webb sent a message through his agent, Louis Shurr, to Harris's room. "Mr. Harris," Shurr said, "I want you to know I did everything I could to prevent this. I told Webb he was crazy. I told him he had no right to do it." Harris read the letter with apparent calm, but his stomach was churning. Webb insisted that Waters' song be cut or moved to another spot, because his song, which followed it, was suffering. If Harris wouldn't move her song, Webb insisted on a better number for himself. Moreover, if his demands weren't met, he, Webb, threatened to quit the show before the scheduled opening in New York.

Harris turned to Shurr and said, "Louis, you go back and tell Webb to go ahead and walk out. That number for Ethel Waters stays where it is. I'm not going to kid you. We can't replace Webb in this show. It means the show closes as of tonight. That's too bad for these boys here and for all the other people, and for me, too, but I can't help that. You go back and tell him that he not only doesn't have to open in New York on Saturday, he doesn't even have to play the show here tomorrow night. The show is closed."

Shurr, taken aback, said he would repeat Harris's sentiments to his client. After waiting an hour with no word from Webb or Shurr, Hart, convinced that the show was closed, walked gloomily down the hall to his room. "I began to think, a trifle longingly, I confess," he said later, "about Hollywood."

The next morning, Hart awoke and called Irving Berlin. "Any news?" he asked. No, Berlin responded, but told Hart he needed to be in the lobby in fifteen minutes, for a meeting with the cast had been called for ten o'clock. Hart hurried out of bed, dressed, met Berlin and Harris, and the three of them walked to the theatre to deliver the news to the company that the show was canceled. When they entered the stage door, they saw, to their surprise, Clifton Webb draped elegantly and calmly against the proscenium arch. They realized that Webb's presence represented an unspoken signal that he was conceding the battle. The show would go on.

As the rehearsal progressed, Hart "was only conscious of a great personal excitement," he said. "I had a show again! To the devil with the critics, and to hell with Hollywood! I had a show again."

Afterward, Hart listened attentively to all of Webb's complaints, and, he says, "agreed with everything. Moreover, I lied whitely and told him that Berlin had promised to write a new number for him after we opened. I don't think he believed me any more than I believed him when he said that he loved the idea of Ethel Waters stopping the show." But that particular crisis was over.

Perhaps racism rather than jealousy accounted for Webb's position. Marilyn Miller, Helen Broderick, and Webb all spoke to Irving Berlin, expressing their distaste about sharing a curtain call with Ethel Waters, who was black. Berlin dealt with the situation calmly and decisively. If his stars objected to an interracial bow, he said, he would be glad to eliminate *all* curtain calls. None of the performers was willing to go without applause, so they agreed to accept Waters' presence in the curtain call reserved for the show's stars.

As Thousands Cheer opened on September 30, 1933, at the Music Box. Hart suffered through the first night, spending most of the evening retching in the men's room. He had had the same reaction during previous opening nights.

Hart explained in *Act One* why he always felt so queasy whenever one of his plays was presented to an audience for the first time:

> No one really knows anything much about a play until it meets its first audience; not its directors, its actors, its producers, and least of all its author. The scenes he has counted on most strongly, his favorite bits of fine writing—the delicately balanced emotional or comedic thrusts, the witty, ironic summing up, the wry third-act curtain with its caustic stinging last line that adroitly illuminates the theme—these are the things that are most likely to go down the drain first, sometimes with an audible thud. . . . the acid test of a play is usually its very first [performance]. It is that first audience that I most fear, for regardless of what miracles of rewriting may be undertaken and even brilliantly carried out, the actual fate of a play is almost always sealed by its first audience.

Elsewhere, he wrote, "I have tried telling myself that in China they will still go on planting rice regardless of what happens to the show; that in Germany they will go on re-arming and preparing for the next war no matter what Brooks Atkinson says tomorrow morning; I have tried getting drunk; I have tried staying cold sober. None of it does any good. I am filled with a numb, unspeakable terror, and though I am aware that it is all pretty adolescent and silly, all this carrying on, the misery is none the less real for all that."

Fortunately, the production of *As Thousands Cheer* went smoothly, "each of the sketches [unfolding] like a delicious treat," in the words of Berlin's biographer, Laurence Bergreen. In the *Times*, Atkinson gave his "approval to every item on the program," calling the show "enormously exhilarating" and "a superb panorama of entertainment. . . . It is all crisply written, adroitly presented and wittily acted." Burns Mantle called the revue "an ultra smart musical entertainment, a spoofer's delight, a satirist's holiday." John Anderson said, "To say that it lives up to its promise is to express mildly the raptures it caused . . . by its smart and unfaltering humor, its swiftness, its beauty, and its boldness." Heywood Broun said it was "the best revue I've ever seen."

Other critics agreed, and the public purchased enough tickets to guarantee a successful run. Some Republicans walked out when they saw the portrayal of Mr. and Mrs. Herbert Hoover; some were offended at the parody of the British royal family in "Prince of Wales Rumored Engaged"—one English newspaperman filed a story headed "Gross Insult to the Crown"—and "Unknown Negro Lynched by Frenzied Mob" engendered a good deal of controversy. But the various controversies failed to hurt business in any measurable way, for the revue gave 400 performances in New York, a run of considerable length. When, in the middle of the run, Sam Harris announced that *As Thousands Cheer* would have to close because Clifton Webb—whose performance was thought to be essential to the show's success—needed a vacation, articles in the New York press appeared, pleading with Harris to keep it running. "It has become a civic institution," said one.

The success of *As Thousands Cheer* in New York prompted Harris to send out a road company, which extended the popularity of the show to several other American cities. The response on the road was generally favorable, although some cities questioned the revue's "spiciness." Also, the very topicality that made *As Thousands Cheer* so successful in New York created something of a problem on the road, since, by the time the road company reached St. Louis or Chicago, the events referred to in the show no longer reflected the headlines of the day. However, Hart periodically worked on new sketches to take the place of the pieces that had lost their topicality. Inserted first in the New York production, they would then be incorporated into the production on the road. Many observers of the musical theatre believe that *As Thousands Cheer* was the finest musical revue ever produced. Critic Cecil Smith, looking back at the genre in *Musical Comedy in America*, said that it "has never been surpassed in hilarity, vitality, or the encompassing talent of all those involved."

The money Hart made from *As Thousands Cheer* permitted him to indulge more freely in the periodic spending sprees for which he was becoming notorious. During his lifetime, Hart made an enormous amount of money—and spent nearly all of it. By 1959, he had made more than five million dollars. "I have none of the money left," he said, "and I have no regrets." His drab boyhood, when his family was too poor to buy Christmas presents for one another, led to a frenzy for spending money, often on the most unlikely objects. (In a rare moment of seriousness about the subject, Hart himself called his extravagance "senseless," but his friends were more tolerant, understanding that his free-spending manner allowed him to exorcise his poverty-ridden upbringing.) Charles, the valet he hired in California, remained in his employ until Charles died. Hart spent a fortune on clothing, including the most expensive silk underwear and an inordinate number of elegant neckties. He acquired a prodigious number of objects made of gold: cufflinks, belt buckles, garters, pens and pencils, cigarette cases, and even a gold tobacco pouch. "He didn't buy things by ones," said Bennett Cerf, "he bought things by sixes, whether they were dressing gowns, porch swings, desk sets, household pets, or houses to put them in." But Hart's fame and fortune, and the conspicuous consumption that followed, couldn't be resented, for he remained so delighted with each acquisition, so unspoiled, so generous to his friends and family (indeed, he lavished such expensive gifts on them that they wondered how even a successful playwright and screenwriter could possibly afford it) that everyone found his extravagance endearing.

Whenever he was in a store, he said, "I feel as if every bit of merchandise on every shelf is trembling with desire to belong to me." Whatever happened to please him at the moment was the item he had to purchase. "No false economy" was his motto.

The urge to spend and to elevate his standard of living occurred the moment he began to make enough money to permit a change in his circumstances. Soon after moving himself and his family to the Edison Hotel after the opening performance of *Once in a Lifetime*, he moved yet again, settling the family in a suite of rooms at the Ansonia Hotel. There, he hired a decorator to transform the apartment into something resembling an extravagant theatrical set. Each window in Hart's room was covered by four sets of curtains, one of net, one of chiffon, another of satin, with brocaded velvet covering them all. "I never had any curtains when I was poor, so I thought I'd like to have plenty," he explained.

Having decided that once he had sufficient means he would never ride in the subway again, he took taxis everywhere, even if his destination were only a block or two away. He rebelled against the necessity of awaking early as he had to do before he became an established playwright by determining never to rise until the late morning, preferably not until noon. And, except in the most unusual circumstances, he maintained that luxurious schedule.

To say that Hart took immense pride in his success would be putting it mildly. One would have a difficult time identifying anyone else who took such an ingenuous delight in his achievements. One writer compared his enjoyment of success to "a volcanic eruption." Edna Ferber said, "I have never known anyone who so savored every luscious morsel of his own victory over hardship."

Shortly after the opening of *As Thousands Cheer*, Hart, holding no grudges, went to Boston, where the road company was playing, to speak to Webb, Broderick, and Waters about appearing in a sequel, to be entitled *More Cheers*, which Hart and Berlin hoped to produce in late 1934. The playwright and composer took an ocean liner to Italy in July—with Berlin's upright piano, equipped with a shifting keyboard that allowed him to play in any key, placed in his suite. Except for an eleven-hour stop in Naples, they devoted the trip to discussions about the songs and sketches for *More Cheers*.

When they returned to the United States, Sam Harris announced that the new revue would begin rehearsals on Thanksgiving day and open late in December. However, *More Cheers* was never produced. The wisdom of presenting a sequel seemed questionable in light of the emphatic failure of *Let 'Em Eat Cake* by the Gershwins, George S. Kaufman, and Morrie Ryskind, the sequel to *Of Thee I Sing*. Then, too, Marilyn Miller, Berlin and Hart's choice to star in *More Cheers*, had died at the age of thirty-eight of a sinus infection that inflamed her brain (or, as gossip had it, of syphilis, the disease to which her husband had succumbed).

In spite of the demise of *More Cheers*, the pace of Hart's professional life was not slowed, as he immediately threw himself into a project suggested to him by Hassard Short. Short persuaded him to see *Waltzes from Vienna*—an operetta he had staged in London—during Hart's 1932 European vacation. The production was successful, but Short believed that a new book was needed in order for the operetta to be successful in the United States. The book was the only element that would require changes, for the music (by Johann Strauss Sr. and Johann Strauss Jr.) and the lyrics (by Desmond Carter) would again be used. Indeed, the main attraction of the production would be the familiar music of the Strausses.

Hart insisted that he "could not abide" operettas, but, to his surprise, he "was more or less delighted with the whole affair." When Short told Hart that the American producer Max Gordon wanted him to adapt the book, Moss agreed.

Hart's commitment to *The Great Waltz* (as the American production was retitled) was less consuming than most of the productions he wrote or directed. The assignment was a commission rather than a project he had helped to conceive. The plot of the operetta had already been determined, the music and lyrics were written, and his job was limited to supplying the dialogue between songs. Proceeding swiftly, he wrote the book during a working holiday in Charleston, South Carolina.

The story was that of Johann Strauss Jr.'s attempts to make his career independent of his famous father—and Johann Strauss Sr.'s jealousy of his son's success. A rivalry between father and son had been at the core of *No Retreat*, Hart's play presented by the Hampton Players in 1930, so he was no stranger to the conflict explored by the operetta.[6]

In *The Great Waltz*, as in reality, Johann Jr.'s success surpasses that of his father. The final curtain descends as the younger Strauss conducts "The Blue Danube" while all Vienna celebrates his accomplishment.

Hart said that what he tried to do in the book "is to divorce operetta from all the made-to-order folderol that usually stands for a plot. I have tried to write a play that stands on its own, aside from the songs and dances that will accompany it . . . a story of real people who might conceivably have dwelt in nineteenth-century Vienna, and not the stock characters that usually haunt the larger musical attractions."

Any honest assessment would have to conclude that he was only partially successful. In his workmanlike book, subtlety was sacrificed for clarity. In a conventional musical, the dialogue scenes must be attenuated in order to accommodate the musical numbers, but in an operetta featuring Strauss waltz after Strauss waltz, every sentence was made to do the work of ten. An example:

YOUNG STRAUSS

God knows I've every faith in your good judgment, Father, but I've got faith in myself, too. Isn't that a necessary part of my equipment?

OLD STRAUSS

Faith, son, and a youthful, optimistic view of one's own ability, are two very different things.

YOUNG STRAUSS

I've passed that stage. I've had all that knocked out of me. Do you think anyone can fight for existence as a musician for five years and not get a true idea of his actual ability?

---

6 MGM's 1938 film does away with the father-son conflict entirely.

OLD STRAUSS

My dear boy, are you telling me about musicians? Do you think I don't know?

YOUNG STRAUSS

What about all those lean months between—before I could bring myself to ask you [for help]. You know nothing of them, and you actually know nothing of what a fight it really is.

OLD STRAUSS

O, don't I!

YOUNG STRAUSS

How can you? You haven't had to fight. Almost from the very first you've been successful—and for years you've been "The Waltz King."

The dialogue reveals the difficulty of having to pack a great deal of exposition into every line while attempting simultaneously to delineate the characters and forward the action.

Hart was more successful in creating the character of Ebeseder, a shop owner, through whom he was able to inject some of his characteristic humor, undercutting the notion of "Viennese charm." In an early scene Ebeseder is greeted by a maiden, who says,

"Well, Mr. Ebeseder! A typical Vienna morning, isn't it!" He replies: "It certainly is. A typical Vienna morning! Sunlight of burnished gold—the streets a very dream of fair women—a musical enchantment in the air—and over everything a subtle, pervading charm!" Then, after a momentary pause, he continues, "I *hate* it! I'm so damn full of Viennese charm it's turning my stomach. . . . [M]y God, I've had forty-five years of Viennese charm! Day in, day out—charm—always charm! The women are charming, the men are gallant. The city itself drips charm from every street corner. It *does* something to a man. . . . I'm breaking up under all this charm. I'd give anything for a nice, ungracious, bad-tempered human being."

The production was scheduled to be given in the Center Theatre in Rockefeller Center. The theatre had been built as a movie house but suffered because of the proximity to Radio City Music Hall only a block away. Thus, two years after it opened, it was turned into a legitimate theatre. But its proportions were far too large for conventional theatrical production. The space was beautifully appointed but enormous, the auditorium holding 3,822 spectators. Anything but a gigantic musical production would have been dwarfed by the vast stage, so hundreds of performers and musicians were engaged for the enterprise. But, as the gargantuan theatre made inevitable, the production elements overwhelmed the play and perhaps the music as well. The spectacle—for "spectacle" is a more apt description than "play"—included "an imposing display of fireworks" as well as a movable orchestra that began at pit level, was elevated to the level of the stage, glided across the stage, then divided into a staircase, all the while producing lush Strauss melodies.

For the production, Hassard Short served not only as director and lighting designer but as creator of "mechanical effects." Without doubt, he was the prime mover in the proceedings, for it was the spectacular production rather than the play that received the most notice.

The Great Waltz opened on September 22, 1934. Some of the performers had appeared in *Waltzes from Vienna* in England; others were Americans cast specifically for *The Great Waltz*. But both the play and the actors' contributions were barely noted. For perfectly understandable reasons, the critics tended to review the theatre and the spectacular production rather than the operetta. Burns Mantle in the *Daily News* saluted "the turntables that whirl the scenery about before your eyes and then lift it up and push it back on a series of elevators that work with startling smoothness and effect." Bernard Sobel in the *Mirror* called it "the most beautiful musical spectacle I have ever seen." Another critic said that the hope of Max Gordon and his associates was to "surpass in grandeur and grace all previous musical plays." And, the critic added, "the expenditure obtained the desired results. . . . Some of the unfolding of the plot is a bit dull and slow moving, but you do not mind, for the surrounding production is so vivid and breath-taking in its splendor."

Brooks Atkinson felt that *The Great Waltz* was "a stupendous show," but one in which "a great orgy of brilliant costumes, whirling scenery and mechanical effects drugs the imagination more than it nourishes." Still, "it is impossible not to admire the resourcefulness, the courage and the artistry that have gone into this enterprise." Atkinson was certainly of two minds about the production, however, for elsewhere he called it "dull and weighty." Ultimately, he blamed the vastness of the Center Theatre for the blandness of the presentation, saying that the theatre was "too large for spirited entertainment."

By all accounts, *The Great Waltz* was a show to admire but not one to love. The task of filling the Center Theatre with a production grandiose enough to attract the public and maintain their interest was an achievement not to be derided, but, if the theatre is, at its best, about the subtle interchange of emotion between actors and spectator, *The Great Waltz* was unable even to hint at that quality. The audience marveled at the production, but failed to become involved in its human dimension.

Still, the immense spectacle attracted spectators to each performance by the thousands. *The Great Waltz* ran for 298 performances, then, after a hiatus, returned for 49 more, reopening at the Center Theatre on August 5, 1935. And Hart, after having endured the stresses of working with the demanding George S. Kaufman and the manic Irving Berlin, joked that the Strausses—both long dead—were his favorite collaborators.

Bernard Hart worked on one of his brother's productions for the first time, serving as an assistant stage manager for *The Great Waltz*. Ironically, while working on a play in which Johann Strauss Jr. was often mistaken for his father (and resented the compliments he received for music he had not written), Bernie was often mistaken for Moss. Backstage visitors, hearing the name Hart, congratulated Bernie on his adaptation of the book. Bernie said that he received two offers from Hollywood studio heads who confused him with his brother.

Throughout *The Great Waltz*, Moss Hart's attention was divided between that project and another that, one suspects, was much closer to his heart. Long before the operetta opened, he developed an idea for a play he wished to share with George S. Kaufman, and traveled to London to tell him about it. Only a week after the premiere of *The Great Waltz* at the Center Theatre, a renewal of his collaboration with George S. Kaufman opened in New York.

Chapter 4 KAUFMAN AND HART, TOGETHER AGAIN 1934–1936

EVER SINCE *ONCE IN A LIFETIME* HAD PLAYED IN CALIFORNIA, HART had been developing the idea for a play about the history of an American family from 1899 to 1929, using the major events of the period as backdrop.

"HAVE STARTED FIRST ACT OF NEW PLAY ," he wired to Sam Harris from California. "COMPLETELY FULL OF IT. WON'T TELL YOU A WORD ABOUT IT UNTIL IT IS FINISHED, BUT THINK IT'S A WHALE OF AN IDEA. DON'T DARE TO TALK ABOUT IT."

In a subsequent telegram to Harris, he offered a few more details: "TENTATIVE TITLE FOR NEW PLAY IS 'WIND UP AN ERA.' HOPE YOU LIKE IT. MAY HAVE TWO ACTS FINISHED WHEN I REACH NEW YORK ."

When he arrived in New York, the first act and half of the second were complete. "I've never been so enthusiastic about anything before in my life," he told Harris.

Then, however, Noël Coward's *Cavalcade*—which turned out to employ the same concept, although the family in his play was British—opened in London in 1931. Even in its details, the two plays were remarkably similar. *Wind Up an Era* began with the sinking of the *Lusitania*, for example, and *Cavalcade* incorporated the sinking of the *Titanic* into its plot. Hart, reading about Coward's play, decided that his idea needed to be recast in a different format. At first he thought to dramatize the history of the Rockefeller family, but eventually discarded that idea as well. At last he settled on the notion of an episodic play about the career of an individual playwright (spanning eighteen years rather than thirty) that would deal with failed hopes and expectations.

Trying to wrestle the material into theatrical form, Hart took a freighter to the West Indies, disembarking at Jamaica. But progress on the play was stalled until he hit on the notion of beginning the play in the present day (1934), then moving backward scene by scene.

Uncertain of the worth of his idea, Hart felt the need for a collaborator. He had feared, after *Once in a Lifetime*, that a partnership with Kaufman would likely result in the older man becoming the dominant force, to the detriment of Hart's own development and self-confidence. Now, however, as the successful writer of several musicals, Hart was more secure. No longer frightened by (although perhaps still in awe of) Kaufman, he broached the notion of their collaborating together on a new play.

In turn, Kaufman had hoped to renew his working relationship with Hart and was eagerly waiting for the younger playwright to call upon him. "I very quickly knew when I met Moss on which side my bread was buttered," he said later. So when Hart presented his idea, Kaufman immediately expressed his willingness to collaborate on the project. The two of them spent several weeks exchanging ideas, discussing the particulars of individual scenes and writing some preliminary dialogue.

The project represented a significant departure for both writers. The play would not take advantage of the gifts they had developed so skillfully, for it would eschew comedy altogether. Indeed, the play would come as close to a modern tragedy as Kaufman and Hart ever wrote. And they would continue to write serious drama together with nearly as much frequency as comedy.

Their play revolves around the playwright Richard Niles and his two closest friends. Niles, when we first see him, is forty, at the peak of his success but jaded and unfulfilled. His friends once held the highest hopes for Niles's aspirations to become a meaningful artist—he had once shown great promise—but his success has been achieved by writing superficial comedies. As a result, he has lost his integrity and become unprincipled. As the play progresses, we see him and his friends go backward in time, from middle age to youth, from cynicism to idealism. During the course of the play Niles abandons the wife who loyally supported him before he achieved success; he rejects the producer who had produced his first play; and he disappoints the friends with whom he went to college and who had such high hopes for him, leaving them disillusioned and embittered. Jonathan Crale, Niles's former classmate, accuses him of writing "a whole mess of nice polite *nothing*" and having no claim to be regarded as an artist. Julia Glenn, a writer who was once in love with Niles, becomes a sloppy and abusive alcoholic, because, it would seem, of her disillusionment.

In order to lend verisimilitude to the scenes set in the past (episodes occur in 1934, 1927, 1926, 1925, 1924, 1923, 1922, 1918, and 1916), Kaufman and Hart spent many hours in the library poring over advertisements, want ads, and columns from old newspapers and magazines. They read books of reminiscences, all with the aim of discovering details that would lend each scene in the play a vividness it would otherwise lack. How did Americans feel about Woodrow Wilson's trip to Paris? Had cellophane come into use in 1922?

Hart, obligated to return to California, asked Kaufman to join him there for further work sessions. Kaufman did so, and, in Palm Springs in March 1934, they completed the remaining dialogue in five weeks. They wrote the play first in chronological order, then reversed it, adding whatever material was necessary for the reverse time scheme to make sense. Later, in New York, they completed a revision, and met with Sam Harris to discuss a production in the fall.

Their original title, *All Our Yesterdays*, was changed to *Career* and then to *Merrily We Roll Along*. Given the serious tone of the play, the title was meant ironically, but it might have been the worst possible choice, for it conveyed a sense of brightness and fun—especially considering that it came from the authors of *Once in a Lifetime*—and set up an anticipation in its audiences that the play could not (and did not wish to) fulfill.

The use of a reverse chronological order in *Merrily We Roll Along* was employed perhaps for the first time in the theatre.[1]

Some characters in the play seemed to bear more than a passing resemblance to real people. Julia Glenn, the witty but neurotic and promiscuous writer who once loved Niles, seemed to be very Dorothy Parker-like, and a skillful pianist was thought to be George Gershwin. A columnist asked Kaufman if Gershwin was indeed the model for Sam Frankel. Kaufman only smiled noncommittally.

About the model for Julia Glenn, Kaufman admitted that "there are certain Parkeresque traces [but] we deny categorically, specifically, and in minute detail, that we ever intended Julia Glenn to be Mrs. Parker." He made the perfectly reasonable point that every character in every work of fiction is based on the author's observation of life; thus the character is likely to contain some elements of reality mixed with elements from the author's imagination. For his part, Hart added, "There are other women who drink and write short stories, too." Dorothy Parker ignored the controversy, choosing not to see the play. "I've been too fucking busy and vice versa," she said.

Rehearsals began on September 3, 1934, under Kaufman's direction, while Hart was working on *The Great Waltz*, which opened only nineteen days later. With two plays in rehearsal concurrently, Hart spent his afternoons at rehearsals of *Merrily We Roll Along* and his evenings watching rehearsals of *The Great Waltz*.

---

1 Ludwig Tieck's nineteenth-century play, *The Land of Upside Down*, begins with the Epilogue and ends with the Prologue, but is otherwise structured chronologically. J. B. Priestly used a reverse chronology in *Time and the Conways*, but that play was written in 1936, two years after *Merrily We Roll Along*. Contemporary theatregoers are more familiar with the device, for, in recent years, such plays as *Betrayal* by Harold Pinter and *Sight Unseen* by Donald Margulies have employed irregular time schemes.

The cast of *Merrily We Roll Along*, like that of *Once in a Lifetime*, is extraordinarily large, calling for ninety-one actors and extras. No "stars" were used in the production, although many of the actors were respected and experienced performers. Nine different sets and two hundred fifty costumes were required. Because the production was so complex and so expensive, Sam Harris decided to forego the usual out-of-town tour, substituting five New York previews instead, all given for invited audiences only. That meant that the play was rehearsed for a bit less than three weeks, a startlingly brief rehearsal period. Why Kaufman agreed to this schedule is hard to comprehend, given the many difficulties inherent in the production.[2]

Perhaps the brevity of the rehearsal process forced the creators to use their time more efficiently. After each rehearsal, Kaufman, Hart, and Sam Harris discussed the progress of the production in a drugstore near the theatre, over coffee and cake.

Hart's favorite theatre, the Music Box, was selected as the venue for *Merrily We Roll Along*, which opened on Saturday, September 29, 1934, only a week after the premiere of *The Great Waltz*. The reviews for the play were respectful, some of them even reverential. The critics attributed a profundity to the play that it did not possess. Typical of the responses was John Anderson's: he called the play "steadily engrossing, courageous, and you'll pardon the expression, provocative," although he also noted that "beyond a certain point it loses the edge and meaning of its momentum." Brooks Atkinson's assessment was almost wholly positive: "[T]he theatre has acquired stature again with the production of *Merrily We Roll Along*, which . . . is [a] resolute, mature-minded drama." The play is "likely to move you deeply," he added. John Mason Brown called it "superlatively good theatre . . . No modern playwrights that I know of have drawn so merciless a picture of the ruthlessness, the vulgarity, and the cruel forgetfulness of contemporary backstage life as Mr. Kaufman and Mr. Hart have drawn in *Merrily We Roll Along*." Gilbert W. Gabriel described it as "a play of unusually interesting intent, extraordinarily vivid effect." Rowland Field said that it was "a drama of the first importance."

Some of the critics wished the play had been structured more conventionally. Percy Hammond wanted the authors to "let *Merrily We Roll Along* stand

---

2 Peculiarly, the actors were not paid for these preview performances, although the stagehands were. Actors' Equity had become the accepted union for actors in 1919, but the practice of not paying the actors their performance salaries for previews indicates that actors' rights were not yet fully protected in 1934.

on its feet instead of its head," and Burns Mantle said he was "bewildered" by the time scheme.

Hart told a newspaper reporter, George Ross:

> We find ourselves mildly surprised . . . by discussions as to whether *Merrily We Roll Along* has a valid reason for being played backwards—is it just a stunt perpetrated for the sake of novelty—would it not be a better play if the order of the scenes were reversed? We also find ourselves, not angry, but terribly hurt.
>
> The accusation that [the chronology] is merely a stunt implies that it is an arbitrary mechanism having no relation to the inherent scheme of things as revealed in the play.
>
> This we emphatically deny. It could be told in no other way. Played forward, or in the conventional manner, the play would have no point. Played backward, the audience is allowed to see each character create his individual and inevitable tragedy.
>
> The thing that attracted us to the idea from the very beginning was the notion that each member of the audience became an ally of the authors.
>
> An audience watching *Merrily We Roll Along* unfold in retrogressive fashion experiences, as we experienced, the unique sensation of being in the position of some high God for whom time does not exist and destiny holds no secrets.

Some works of art age gracefully and others, for various reasons, do not. Although the play contended for the Pulitzer Prize (losing to *The Old Maid* by Zoë Akins), *Merrily We Roll Along* seems now to be an amazingly inert, clumsy, didactic, and banal play. It is difficult to understand why Kaufman and Hart spent so much time and effort on *Merrily We Roll Along*. Aside from the reverse time scheme there is little to recommend it. The characters are crudely developed, often seeming more like caricatures, the plot all too obvious. When Niles, at the end of the play, delivers the valedictory address at his college, speaking Polonius' lines, "To thine own self be true / And it must follow, as the night the day, / Thou canst not then be false to any man," one feels that the authors' point is being driven home with a sledgehammer.[3]

Since each episode preceded in dramatic time the scene that followed it in literal time, the authors had to include substantial amounts of exposition in each scene. The play is so clumsy in this respect that it nearly obliterates the impact of the reverse time scheme. And the dialogue, coming from two playwrights whose skill at writing dialogue was even then highly regarded and soon became

---

3 In an early draft, the play ends just *before* the graduation ceremony. Richard, it is clear, is about to give the valedictory speech, but the audience is left in the dark about its content. The ending of this draft is more subtle than the ending that Kaufman and Hart elected to use; perhaps they felt that a subtle ending wouldn't be sufficiently clear or sufficiently powerful.

legendary, is often almost embarrassingly awkward and unbelievable. The following passage, involving Althea, Niles's second wife, and Ivy, an actress Althea believes is sleeping with her husband, is taken from the first scene:

ALTHEA

(taking a moment to survey [Ivy])
I have just discovered, Miss Carroll, why you were so right for the part.

ALTHEA

"Most beautiful of our younger actresses." "Starry eyed and translucent." Well, perhaps you won't be so starry-eyed now! *(With a quick movement she picks up the bottle of iodine, which DAVID had set down. In a flash she uncorks it and hurls the contents into IVY's face. The dark stain splotches over her white evening gown. IVY screams.)*

RICHARD

Christ!

ALTHEA

(hysterically laughing and crying) There goes your hit, Richard! Didn't think I'd do that, did you? I'll do it all the time! To your hits and your women!

The overwrought nature of the scene, not far removed from nineteenth-century melodrama, is not its only defect. In addition, the climactic moment of the play thus occurs in the first scene (a logical development in a play that moves backward in time), so that every other scene is anti-climactic. The play therefore becomes progressively less interesting as it "rolls along."

Although it includes such highly dramatic events as a suicide, many sexual affairs, physical violence, and so on, the play has no real life. Furthermore, it lacks any significant idea beyond the obvious: that artists should not sell out, for such behavior will lead only to recriminations and bitterness. There is no profundity, only facile stagecraft.

Just as the clown always wishes to play Hamlet, the writer of farces and comedies yearns occasionally to express his most fundamental beliefs without the use of humor. This is certainly his privilege, and, in fact, Hart eventually demonstrated that he was not out of his depth with non-comic material, going on to write several "serious" plays that were intriguing in their ideas and in their expression. In his collaborations with Kaufman, however, the comic plays tended to succeed, the "serious" plays to fail, both as works of art and as commercial properties.

An example of the failure of *Merrily We Roll Along* to age gracefully can be found in Brooks Atkinson's history, *Broadway*, written in 1970. The critic, who had expressed such admiration for *Merrily We Roll Along* in 1934, revised his opinion completely thirty-six years later, saying, the play "was not a contribution to thought or literature, and it came with ill grace from two of Broadway's most successful playwrights."

In 1934, in spite of critical approbation, the play failed to catch on with the public, running for 155 performances, only about half the run of *Once in a Lifetime*. Some members of the audience, at least, were resentful that the play they were seeing was not the sort of satirical comedy they had hoped for from Kaufman and Hart. Because of the great expense required to mount such a large production, the play lost money. One might assume that such an outcome would not have bothered the authors, whose point in writing the play was to extol the virtue of artistic integrity over the mere making of money. But, of course, they hoped for a longer run and commercial success for *Merrily We Roll Along*.

Despite the failure in New York, Sam Harris sent out a road company, but it performed for only two weeks to smallish audiences in Philadelphia, after which the tour was brought to a premature end. Hart's disappointment in the play's failure—his first—was bitter. *Merrily We Roll Along* was a soundly written drama, he maintained, and deserved a better reception.

Writer Herman Mankiewicz's description of *Merrily We Roll Along* succinctly summed up the difficulty of taking the play seriously: "It's about this playwright who writes a play and it's a big success, and then he writes another play and *that's* a big success, all his plays are big successes, and all the actresses in them are in love with him, and he has a yacht and a beautiful home in the country and a beautiful wife and two beautiful children, and he makes a million dollars. Now the problem the play propounds is this: how did the poor son of a bitch ever get in this jam?"

In spite of such sardonic comments, the play fired the imagination of other creative artists nearly fifty years later. In 1981, at the suggestion of producer-director Hal Prince, Stephen Sondheim and George Furth adapted the Kaufman and Hart work as a musical. Although the characters were altered (the playwright in the original play becomes a composer who gives up music to produce films in Hollywood, for example, and the events of the play are shifted to a later era), the structure is the same, as is the title. Ironically, given the play's theme, Hal Prince's motivation was to produce a moneymaking musical. However, the Broadway production of the musical folded quickly, despite some fine work by Sondheim. The casting of the musical did not help, in the opinion of many who saw it, for the performers were simply too young and inexperienced to play the characters in the early scenes. Jonathan Tunick, the musical's orchestrator, observed in words reminiscent of Mankiewicz's jibe years before: "As for the plot, in which our hero writes a couple of musicals and then becomes a movie producer, I don't think the average playgoer understands that the highest aspiration of mankind is to write Broadway musicals, and anyone who doesn't is contemptible."

Since its original production on Broadway, the musical version of *Merrily We Roll Along* has been revised several times and produced in Washington, D.C., Seattle, and San Diego with more seasoned performers, resulting in somewhat greater critical success. It was performed most recently in 2002, at the Kennedy Center in Washington, D.C.

❧

It is notable that many of Moss Hart's plays were about the theatre, and understandably so, for he was a man of the theatre. The theatre was the milieu in which he was most comfortable; success in the theatre was what he most craved. *Once in a Lifetime* focused on three vaudevillians and their takeover of Hollywood; Hal Reisman in *Face the Music* is a producer, Kit Baker a musical comedy singer; theatrical personages (Noël Coward, Joan Crawford, Douglas Fairbanks Jr., et al) are portrayed to humorous effect in *As Thousands Cheer*; and Richard Niles in *Merrily We Roll Along* is a playwright. Nor would these be the last instances of Hart's use of theatrical personalities and theatrical situations in his plays. The tendency to concentrate so heavily on what he knew best is at once a secret of Hart's success and, on the other hand, a limiting factor. Perhaps this repeated focus on the same topic is why his career has rarely been treated by critics as that of a major American playwright, despite the financial and critical successes of many of his individual plays.

In 1935, Hart returned to Hollywood to fulfill the screenwriting obligations he had been permitted to postpone in order to write *As Thousands Cheer*. He wrote a treatment for *Broadway Melody of 1936* (again using the theatre as the background of the action), for which he was nominated for an Academy Award. (The nomination was for the "story." The screenplay was written by Jack McGowan, Sid Silvers, and Harry Cohn.) The year 1935 must have been a lean one for film stories, for the plot of *Broadway Melody* is so inane that it nearly defies description. Jack Benny plays a gossip columnist who continually enrages Robert Taylor, playing a Broadway producer, by hinting in print that Taylor's relationship with the wealthy society woman who is backing his show is less than platonic. Taylor vents his anger by punching Benny after each incident. Enter Eleanor Powell, only five years earlier Taylor's high school sweetheart, now an aspiring actress hoping to be cast in Taylor's new show. Somehow, though, Taylor has completely forgotten her. But she and Benny cook up a scheme to pass her off as a famous Parisian star, leading to the conventional happy, if improbable, ending.

It seems likely that the story for *Broadway Melody of 1936* was drawn from a screenplay Hart had written for MGM in 1934, *Miss Pamelo Thorndyke*. That unproduced screenplay dealt with three Broadway gossip columnists. Never a man to waste an idea, Hart condensed the three columnists into one, changed the particulars of the story, and turned *Miss Pamelo Thorndyke* into *Broadway Melody of 1936*.

The film was one of four *Broadway Melodies*, and is regarded as one of the best. If so, it owes its success more to Eleanor Powell and Jack Benny than to the story or screenplay.

Hart left Hollywood with his usual sigh of relief. He then spent an eventful year collaborating with Cole Porter on a musical satire of royalty entitled *Jubilee*. Hart had first met Porter in Paris on his 1932 trip abroad after the success of *Face the Music*, carrying a letter of introduction from Irving Berlin. After reading Berlin's letter, Porter invited Hart to meet him the next afternoon at the Ritz Bar. At the meeting, Hart passed on to Porter a package he had been asked to give to the composer by a mutual friend. Hart described his reaction as Porter opened the package.

> It was a box that bore the Cartier label, and in it reposed a pair of gold garters with his initials in diamonds. My provincial eyes bulged, but they almost popped out of my head as I saw the perfectly composed Mr. Porter calmly lift his trouser leg, revealing another pair of gold garters, remove them, put the new garters on, nonchalantly call out, "Here, Jim!" to the barman, and toss him the old, gold garters.

"People don't *do* such things," thought Hart, echoing a line from *Hedda Gabler*.

In 1933, he had visited Porter and his wife, Linda, at their home in Paris. Porter, "more than anyone else I know," Hart said, "has somehow captured the secret of living successfully—of having 'fun' in the true sense of the word."

Cole and Linda Porter embodied many of the qualities Hart admired: they were rich, smart, gifted, equally at ease in the world of the theatre and in the world "of fashion and glitter," as he described it. Altogether, "a wonderful pair," he wrote.

> Their house in Paris was exquisite, one of the most beautiful houses I have ever seen, and Linda Porter, a legendary beauty herself, lent something of her own

radiance and splendor to their life together so that everything and everyone in their house seemed to shine and sparkle with a little of her own special grace. . . . Together, the Porters bloomed in a scintillating world that seemed uncommonly festive . . .

Hart failed to mention that the Porters' lives together were complicated by Porter's homosexuality. Nor did he refer to the fact that Porter invented many episodes that supposedly had taken place in the past. If Hart was at all disturbed by Porter's tendency to rearrange his life and legend to suit himself, he never said so. Indeed, he seems to have admired the songwriter unreservedly.

On the last night of his visit with the Porters, Porter casually mentioned, "Let's do a show together, eh?" Two years later, in 1935, when Porter and Hart were lunching at Jack and Charlie's in New York, Porter raised the subject again. After having dealt with weighty dramatic issues in *Merrily We Roll Along*, Hart was ready for something in a much lighter vein. But, after briefly describing an idea for a musical he had conceived, Hart

> brushed it aside with something else that was very much on my mind that day. "I think I came to a decision this morning," I said. "I'm going to drop work completely for a while. There are always ideas—plays to be written—but always at the expense of something else. I don't want to settle for that quick trip to Europe wedged in between work and rehearsals. I'm going to take a year off. . . . I'd like some sun."

Porter thought about Hart's remarks for a moment, then said, "Why not do both? I like that idea of yours for a musical. And if it's sun you want, what about the South Seas? What about Bali? What about Africa? What about"—he paused to let the effect sink in—"what about the world? Why don't we [write the musical] and go around the world at the same time? I could leave next week." They left the restaurant, stopped at Cook's Travel Agency to leaf through travel folders, then booked passage on the *Franconia*, which was scheduled to begin sailing on a 144-day, round-the-world trip only six days later.

At some point, Porter specified that Max Gordon would have to be the producer. "That won't be possible," Hart replied, "I'm under contract to Sam Harris. He let me do *The Great Waltz* as a favor to Gordon, but I wouldn't dare ask him to let another piece go."

"Maybe they'd like to do it together," Porter suggested. As a result, Gordon and Harris co-produced *Jubilee*, based on the concept Hart outlined to Porter over lunch at Jack and Charlie's. The producers committed to the production although, at that point, it was only an idea with no book, music, or lyrics. Still, they agreed to engage a theatre in Boston for the out-of-town try-out in September 1935, another in New York in October, and to hire Hassard Short to direct the musical numbers.

The ever-convivial Porter brought with him enough companions to insure a continual party on the *Franconia*. Among them were Linda Porter, her maid, and three of the Porters' friends, including Monty Woolley, whom Porter was considering as the director of the work he and Hart would write. Hart was concerned that Porter would be too distracted to work, but Porter was more disciplined than Hart had expected. For one thing, he brought his piano on board, a sure sign that he intended to work whenever a lapse in the partying and sightseeing allowed. For another, as Hart discovered, Porter was a perfectionist who, when at work, would not stop until he was satisfied that he had produced the most finely crafted song of which he was capable. Although Porter was an eager sightseer, refusing to pass up any opportunity to explore places he had not before visited, "flying over Africa, climbing through ruined temples in India," watching native dancing in Bali, he would then disappear for days at a time and emerge with complete and polished songs. Hart learned "that the jaunty and debonair world of Cole Porter disappeared completely when he was at work. . . . The secret of those gay and seemingly effortless songs was a prodigious and unending industry. He worked around the clock." Hart described Porter as "the most self-indulgent and the most pleasure-loving of any man I have ever known," but "indulgence and pleasure both stopped dead the moment song-writing began."

"The first ten days of the trip were given over to a detailed discussion of the general architecture of the show," Hart said, although that did not preclude spending many relaxing hours on deck. Within two weeks, the outline of the musical was complete enough for Porter to begin working on the score. Porter was interested, Hart discovered, not only in writing songs that might become successful on the radio or on recordings; "he was scrupulous about what each particular song was to say in relationship to the score as a whole, and he polished and worried over so simple a song as 'Why Shouldn't I' until it gleamed like the perfect little song it is."

The other passengers learned that Porter and Hart were writing a musical together and did not hesitate to offer suggestions. When anything unusual happened on the ship, someone would ask the authors if the incident would turn up in their musical. Hart tried to work on deck, but found that the constant questions and comments of the passengers made it impossible. His favorite question came from an elderly woman, who asked him one day, "Mr.

Hart, do you get your ideas first and then write, or do you write first and then get the ideas?" After that he worked in his cabin.

When he was not writing the book for *Jubilee*, Hart wrote a forty-four-page account of the trip. He detailed his responses to such places as Kingston, Jamaica, Panama City and the Panama Canal ("My mind always reels in the face of these stupendous feats of engineering but my heart fails to beat any faster and, while I admit I am stunned by the magnitude of the Canal, I am also forced to admit that I am more impressed by a particularly tricky turn of phrase in one of Mr. Somerset Maugham's short stories"), Hilo and Honolulu, Pago-Pago, Samoa and the Fiji Islands ("whatever has been written of the beauties of these magic islands is true"), the interior of New Zealand (which Hart found stifling, except for the Glow Worm Caves at Waitons, "a series of huge cavities in the earth, ceiling and walls of which are covered with millions of glowworms, every single one of them glowing with an unearthly brilliance," which "are worth going to the other end of the world to see"), India, Australia, Bali ("a traveler's paradise" with "the handsomest people in the world"), Port Moresby, Kalibahi, Semarang, and a ten-day airplane flight over Africa, with stops in Mombasa, Zanzibar, and Madagascar. Hart's diary was never published, which is a shame, for it is a delightful and perceptive travel book.

Despite working on *Jubilee* and on his diary, Hart had plenty of time to socialize in and around the ship's pool or nap in a deck chair. He caught up on his reading, and whenever the ship docked he indulged his passion for shopping. The diary includes this passage:

> I now confess, unashamed, that I am an incurable shopper. I buy everything. Silly, useless, senseless, wonderful things. Across my forehead, branded, as it were, in Neon lights, the word "Sucker" is largely written, so that I imagine in the far bazaars and compounds of the places we are yet to go the glad cry has already risen that Hart is on the way. Down from the topmost shelf will come the faded native baskets, the war drums, the dusty glass beads, the native headdress, and I will buy them all. They will clutter up my cabin, they will give me a devil of a time with the customs men, they will finally gather dust in my apartment and ultimately the janitor will fall heir to most of them. But I will have had my fun. . . . I will have bought something I liked when I saw it, instead of waiting until we got to where it was cheapest. I will have wasted a startling amount of time, energy and money. But I will have had my fun. And I am convinced, by this time, that it is the suckers of the world who have all the fun.

Curiously, one of the stops on the *Franconia*'s itinerary was Hollywood. Hart was glad to visit with old friends such as Aline MacMahon and Irving Berlin, but he couldn't wait to resume the trip. "I had no desire to see [Hollywood] again," he confided in his diary. "I know it well [and] I dislike it intensely. . . . There is the same sickening toadying to the ones in power at the moment, the same rigid caste system to the social goings-on, the same dismal talk of who previewed what picture last night, and the same senseless spending of money."

Hart was himself a prodigious spender, of course, but the money he spent was his own, whereas his reference to the "senseless spending of money" in Hollywood applied to the lavish, often unnecessary expenditures of backers' investments connected with filmmaking.

The first act of *Jubilee* was finished in New Guinea, the second act begun on the day the ship landed in Kalabahi. When the *Franconia* reached Cape Town, most of the book had been written—a week ahead of the schedule Hart had set for himself. At Rio de Janeiro, Porter completed the score. "THE TITLE IS JUBILEE," they wired Sam Harris in the middle of the South Atlantic. "WE'LL TELL YOU ALL ABOUT IT WHEN WE GET HOME." By the time they reached New York, they had covered thirty-four thousand miles. At the dock, the mothers of both Porter and Hart welcomed them home. When Lily and Moss were alone in the taxi taking them to their apartment, Lily told her son, "You know—that Mrs. Porter—she's very nice, very nice for a country woman."

Hart and Porter, both of whom claimed to be suffering from attacks of stage fright, read the script and sang the songs to Harris and Gordon on June 5, 1935. Despite the nervousness of the author and composer, the producers gave their enthusiastic approval to the material. The show's perfectionist creators continued to discuss improvements, however. The weekend before rehearsals were to begin, Hart and Porter were visiting at a friend's farm in Ohio. Hart tentatively expressed his belief that the second act needed a more exciting song. Porter, he said,

> was surprised, but quickly agreed with me. Thereafter silence fell, and shortly after that the usual withdrawal began. I might just as well have been strolling through the woods by myself. Early on, I might have mistaken this for annoyance, but I knew by now that he was already at work, and mentally made a note that with luck, we might have the song for the third week of rehearsals. . . . The next morning he called me into the living room and closed the doors. He placed a scribbled sheet of notepaper on the music-rack of the piano and then played and sang the verse of "Just One of Those Things." No word of either verse or chorus was ever altered.

The musical's plot chronicles the adventures of a bored royal family, about to celebrate their jubilee celebration in a mythical kingdom. They take advantage of a threat of revolution to run away to the city where they conceal their identities and gleefully, uninhibitedly, disguise themselves as ordinary citizens. Queen Katherine's greatest desire is to meet Charles Rausmiller, the swimming champion now famous for playing Mowgli, the ape man, in the movies. They meet, and he gives her swimming lessons. King Henry's ambition extends no further than to learn a rope trick. The Princess Royal falls in love with a playwright and the Crown Prince with a nightclub dancer. Eventually, however, the identity of the royal family is revealed, and they grudgingly return to the dreary duties of monarchy. The contrast between the family's tightly controlled life in their kingdom and their enjoyment in behaving more spontaneously in the city is the musical's mainspring and the source of much of its humor.

Porter's music was strongly influenced by the trip around the world. From Samoa he borrowed rhythms from a native dance that led him to compose "Begin the Beguine;" in Jamaica a trip through a botanical garden inspired a song called "The Kling-Kling Bird on the Divi-Divi Tree;" a ballet entitled "Judgment of Paris" emerged from musical themes heard on Bali.

As in *As Thousands Cheer*, Hart used living people as characters in *Jubilee*, but, in this case, they were not portrayed under their own names. Johnny Weismuller became Charles Rausmiller ("Mowgli"), Elsa Maxwell became Eva Standing, and Noël Coward became Eric Dare (whose last name is an antonym for "coward"), the playwright with whom the princess falls in love. They were treated not as objects of satire but with good-natured humor.

Hart's comic technique was so polished by this time that his original, handwritten script was not terribly different from the final version. That technique employed the creation of personages whose chief characteristics were drawn in a few broad strokes, but stopped short of caricature; the use of incongruous juxtapositions; dialogue that carefully built to a laugh line, often a wisecrack; the ability to delay, by the use of carefully constructed dialogue and visual images, the audience's wish to laugh until the precise moment when the suppressed laughter could no longer be controlled, resulting in an explosion of mirth; the creation of situations full of comic potential that were fully exploited; and a sense of economy, so that no scene was overextended, no line a word longer than necessary.

The book of *Jubilee* might have had more substance, but there can be no question of the author's remarkable comic facility.

The casting of the leading roles took place in Hollywood; primarily, it seems, because Hart and Porter were determined to have Mary Boland, whose performance in *Face the Music* had been so highly praised, play the queen. Their tactic was successful, as MGM agreed to lend Boland to the producers for six months in exchange for a share of the profits in *Jubilee*. Boland's name was displayed over the title, a sign of the high regard in which she was held by Broadway audiences.

One of the actresses considered to play the princess was Kitty Carlisle, an actress-singer in her mid-twenties then playing opposite the Marx Brothers in the film *A Night at the Opera*. She was invited to Hart and Porter's suite in the Beverly Wilshire Hotel, where Hart read a portion of the script and Porter sang some of the songs for her. Carlisle was, by her own admission, "dying to get to know Moss Hart." She had heard a good deal about him and her expectations were great. She was not disappointed. "I thought he was the best-looking, most arresting man I'd ever seen," she said.

She sang one of the songs for the authors, but was not cast as the princess. Still, a contact had been made that had much more than professional connotations, for in 1946, Kitty Carlisle became Mrs. Moss Hart. Her regret about not being cast in *Jubilee* was more personal than professional. "If they had engaged me," she said, "I might have had ten more years with Moss."

Other actors who were cast in Hollywood included Melville Cooper as the meek king and fifteen-year-old Montgomery Clift as the prince. Meanwhile, Hassard Short, who was responsible for the musical scenes, auditioned performers in New York.

Monty Woolley, the former head of Yale's drama department, was hired to stage the dialogue scenes; Short lit Jo Mielziner's sets.[4] The producers wound up spending $155,000 on the production, considered to be a lavish outlay of money in 1935.

Hart found this rehearsal process a rather bewildering experience. Never having worked with Cole Porter before, he had no way of anticipating the composer's peculiarities or his seeming indifference to the tensions of rehearsals. During runthroughs of the production, Porter would sit in the front row with a group of friends, loudly discussing their plans for lunch, while his valet mixed martinis in a large cocktail shaker. The cast was understandably upset by the distraction, but Porter was, after all, the composer, and could not have been evicted from the theatre, even if Hart had had the courage to ask him to leave.

Hart, always anxious during the rehearsal process, said that Porter's treatment of rehearsals as "a glorious party . . . just so much more fun," increased

---

4 Mielziner, who also designed *Merrily We Roll Along*, was on his way to becoming the dominant set designer during Broadway's golden age, creating the sets for virtually every major show of the '30s, '40s, and '50s.

his anxiety. But Porter remained serene regardless of the crises that may have been occurring on stage. Hart observed that Porter

> refused to worry; he refused to fret; he refused completely to let a disastrous dress rehearsal spoil his plans for a midnight supper party that night. In short, after the hair-trigger Mr. Kaufman and the nervous Mr. Berlin, Mr. Porter was a collaborator I knew not how to cope with. I do not mean to suggest that he was unfeeling; he was not; but the mere fact that he was able actually to sit in a seat through an entire opening night, that he was even able to sleep blissfully and peacefully the night before the opening, was enough to drive me frantic.

Even when Monty Woolley and Hassard Short came into such conflict that Woolley had to be fired, Porter—despite his friendship with Woolley—remained extraordinarily placid.

Jubilee was first seen in Boston for a two-week run on September 22, 1935. Rumors had circulated that the British royal family might be ridiculed in the production, but the fears of the British Foreign Office that the musical might be offensive were dispelled when the characters were shown to be inhabitants of a kingdom that was clearly mythical. According to a report in *The New York Times*, Boston's first nighters found the show "big, beautiful, amusing, spectacular and for the most part in admirable taste. . . . a musical show that is regarded as setting new standards." A subsequent report said, "There is about [*Jubilee*] an air of well-bred opulence, a mingling of smartness and substance"—an observation that might have been made of any number of Cole Porter shows. Hundreds of people had to be turned away, as every seat was filled for every performance.

Still, cuts and emendations were made in Boston in an effort to tighten the show another notch. Although the audiences and critics in Boston thought the production ideal as it was, Hart, Porter, and the producers realized that there was still work to be done. The work was made more stressful when, the day before the company's arrival in Boston, Hart, Porter, the two producers, and Mary Boland received letters stating that, if they left Manhattan, they were putting their lives at risk. (Later, on opening night in New York, still more threatening letters were received. Then, in mid-November, three backstage fires were set, causing the cancellation of a performance. From then on, private detectives patrolled the backstage area. George Eells, Cole Porter's biographer, hints that the culprit was "a disgruntled stage mother." Steven Bach states unequivocally in *Dazzler* that Hart's Aunt Kate set the fires—although, according to Moss's account in *Act One*, Kate had died about a decade earlier. Bach, attempting to justify his claim, made every effort to track down

Kate's death certificate, wishing to show that she was still alive in 1935. However, he says, "No search could locate definitively Aunt Kate's death records in New York.")

Sam Harris and Max Gordon jointly presented *Jubilee* in New York at the Imperial Theatre on October 12, 1935, nine days short of Hart's thirty-first birthday. Percy Hammond said, "*Jubilee* is the most satisfactory fete of its kind that this pleasure-seeker has seen in what might be called ever so long." Burns Mantle called it "the smartest musical comedy, and the most satisfying, that has been produced in an American theatre within the length of trustworthy memories." Robert Garland was far less enthusiastic, however. Although he conceded that "there was fun; there was satire; there was beauty a-plenty," he added, "*Jubilee* didn't quite come off with the éclat that had been predicted" by those who had seen it in Boston. There was not enough fun, satire, or beauty "to eke out an evening."

The overwhelmingly positive response to *Jubilee* in Boston and the excited word that filtered back to New York raised expectations to a level that—at least for some—the show could not quite meet. John Mason Brown in the *Post* said,

> So much has been heard in advance about *Jubilee* and so much has come to be expected that the production was forced to fight an unfair battle with its reputation. To say that it did not emerge from this battle as a victor on all counts is not to suggest that *Jubilee* fails to stand head and shoulders above most musical comedies . . . It is merely to state that it is not the inspired sort of lunacy which Mr. Porter himself has taught an admiring world to identify as 'the top' [in *Anything Goes*, presented in 1934]. Chiefly for this reason it is disappointing.

Neither "Begin the Beguine" nor "Just One of Those Things," both eventually regarded as classics, had a significant impact in 1935. The song that received the most notice was "Me and Marie," long since forgotten.

The public's response to *Jubilee* was less than ecstatic. It played for 169 performances on Broadway, a respectable, but, considering the expenditure, rather disappointing run.

Just as the run of *Face the Music* had to be curtailed after Mary Boland left the cast, so it was in *Jubilee*. She left in order to fulfill her film contract and no satisfactory replacement could be found. Hart, too, returned to Los Angeles in December 1935, where he rented the rather spectacular home of Frances Marion, a noted screenwriter, while she was in Europe. Hart planned not to write a film but to relax and learn to play tennis.

Shortly afterward, Republic Studios released *Frankie and Johnnie*, a film

Hart had co-written in 1933, featuring Helen Morgan and Chester Morris, and filmed at the Biograph Studios in New York in early 1934. The screenplay was based on Jack Kirkland's stage adaptation of the popular ballad, which had played in New York several seasons earlier. Whatever the merits of the screenplay might have been, the final product was described by *Variety* as "unusually slovenly entertainment." Censorship undoubtedly had something to do with the defects of the movie, which was shelved for two years while the studio recut it. *The New York Times* mentioned some clumsy "scissoring" in their brief 1936 review. Whoever was at fault, the *Times* concluded, "It does us [the audience] wrong."

In any case, Hart's passion was not for Hollywood but for New York. He reveled in being called "Broadway's current wonder boy" in an article in the 1930s. And the appellation was not inappropriate, for he had written seven plays for Broadway in five years, most of them critically and financially successful. Another article from the *Newark News* claimed that Hart was "making more money per week than has ever been earned by any living dramatist." Although Hart declined to specify his exact income (from both the theatre and films), the interviewer asked if he was making more or less than $3,000 per week. "More," Hart replied. $3,000 per week in 1934 is roughly equivalent to an annual salary of $2,500,000 in the year 2005.

The driving force behind Hart's frenetic activity was not so much the income he generated—although it was certainly a factor—but the desire to get the most out of his abilities. As long as he remained creative, the ideas virtually tumbling out, each one rapidly succeeding the one before, the expression of those ideas fresh and appealing to audiences, he intended to continue his hectic pace. It seems in retrospect that Hart feared that his talent might dry up one day, and that he was determined to make full use of that gift until it deserted him.

Hart had considered dramatizing Jacob Wasserman's novel, *The Maurizius Case*. A sorrowful story about a judge who, many years after sentencing a prisoner, comes to learn that his verdict was unjust and loses his sanity as a result, the novel seemed to have considerable dramatic possibilities. In September 1935, Hart began a series of telephone calls to Wasserman's family in Zurich, inquiring about dramatic rights. Hart optioned the novel, but lost enthusiasm as six months passed in negotiations. "It finally turned out to be too much trouble—too many Wasserman heirs, contracts lost in the mail, etc.," *The New York Times* reported. At last Hart notified the Wasserman estate that he was no longer interested, and the estate returned some of the option money.

Having collaborated with Cole Porter, Irving Berlin, Richard Rodgers and Lorenz Hart, Moss was ready to return once again to the partner he admired most, George S. Kaufman, and this time the relationship continued for several years. Except for contributing some sketches to two musical revues, Hart's next six plays were all collaborations with Kaufman.

The agent for writer Dalton Trumbo sent the galleys of Trumbo's as-yet-unpublished comic novel *Washington Jitters* to Hart, and Hart believed that it offered a good vehicle for adaptation by himself and Kaufman. He said jocularly that he was "toying with an idea that will change the American political scene unless Mr. Roosevelt gets wind of it." In January 1936, Trumbo's agent led the writer to believe that Hart had already agreed to adapt the novel, but, in fact, *Washington Jitters* was only one of several possibilities Hart was considering.

Kaufman joined Hart in Los Angeles in the spring of 1936 to discuss adapting Trumbo's novel, but after two days they decided against it, perhaps because the plot of *Washington Jitters*—in which a bumbling sign painter becomes, through a series of comic incidents, president of the United States—is somewhat reminiscent of the plot of *Once in a Lifetime*. Kaufman then asked, "What about your other idea?" referring to a notion Hart had mentioned several months earlier about a family living happily together, barely aware of the outside world, determinedly pursuing their own happiness in ways that would have seemed utterly mad to an outsider. What, Kaufman asked, if each member of the household was trying to achieve a different goal, oblivious to the goals of the others? The suggestion sparked Hart's imagination, and he began offering ideas of his own. The more they exchanged possibilities for the play, the more intrigued they became.

In just three days, they created detailed portraits of all of the characters who would appear in the play, for they intended to focus more upon character than upon plot. The character outline served as the framework for what would become the best-known and best-loved play of the Kaufman and Hart partnership, *You Can't Take It With You*, written and produced in 1936. The comedy is, as W. David Sievers described it in *Freud on Broadway*, Kaufman and Hart's "great essay on integrity and fulfillment."

The play includes zany characters who, despite their outrageous behavior, are curiously endearing; a satire of conventional behavior; and a critique of the American business ethic. The thin plot line the authors developed is not a detriment but an asset to the play, for it permits the audience to focus attention all the more on the gentle lunacy of the characters.

Insofar as the play has a theme, it is a simple one. Kaufman expressed it in a letter to his wife, Beatrice: "the way to live and be happy is just to go ahead and live, and not pay attention to the world." In many respects, this was the same theme expressed with a heavy-handedness uncharacteristic of Kaufman and Hart in *Merrily We Roll Along*. In *You Can't Take It With You*, however, the authors found just the right tone to express their point of view. Their characters *embody* the notion that the pursuit of money is no substitute for joy and fulfillment. Ethan Mordden wrote in *The American Theatre*, "Many of the plays [of the 1930s] dealt with disoriented characters—alienated either by epic environmental pressures they don't understand or because they understand and dislike their environment. In *You Can't Take It With You* the screwballs have their world in order; it's everybody else who's disoriented."

After creating the outline but before beginning to write the dialogue, the authors wired Sam Harris:

DEAR SAM, WE START WORK ON NEW PLAY TOMORROW MORNING. CAN YOU TIE UP AT ONCE JOSEPHINE HULL, GEORGE TOBIAS, FRANK CONLAN, OSCAR POLK? WE ARE ENGAGING HENRY TRAVERS HERE. MOSS AND GEORGE.

Using the detailed character outline they had devised enabled the authors to work with remarkable swiftness, especially considering Kaufman's usual laborious working method. Whereas the rewrite alone of *Once in a Lifetime* took six months, *You Can't Take It With You* was written in five weeks.

The play, set in Grandpa Vanderhof's living room, is home to the Sycamore family. Grandpa, seventy-five, spends as much time as he can watching graduation ceremonies at nearby Columbia University, amused by the solemnity of the occasion and the pomposity of the speakers. Penny Sycamore, his fiftyish daughter, decided years before to become a writer because a typewriter was delivered to the house by mistake. She has been working for eight years, but, as she points out, the first two years don't count because she was learning how to type. Paul, her husband, makes fireworks in the basement with Mr. De Pinna, who delivered ice to Grandpa's house six years ago and decided to stay. Essie, Penny and Paul's daughter, dances about the house in ballet slippers whenever the mood strikes her, and it strikes her frequently. When she isn't dancing, she is in the kitchen making candy, which she packages and sells. Ed, Essie's husband, plays the xylophone and creates whatever strikes his fancy on an old printing press—menus for dinner, posters, leaflets. He idly, randomly includes some of the leaflets in Essie's candy boxes. Rheba, the maid, and her boyfriend Donald take care of the cooking and feed the snakes, which writhe in an aquarium. Donald is on welfare, and likes it that way—except for the necessity of standing in line every Wednesday for half an hour to pick up his welfare check because "it breaks up my week." Grandpa's house is, as the opening stage direction says, "a house where you do as you like, and no questions asked." Although the Depression may be in full swing outside the house, it never interferes with the innocent fun the characters experience in Grandpa's living room.

Because Grandpa, who is a bit of a philosopher, sees no sense in paying income tax, he has never filed a return. An auditor for Internal Revenue shows up one day, insisting that Grandpa pay taxes from 1914, the year income tax was begun in the U. S., through 1936. Grandpa, who quit work many years ago but collects about four thousand dollars a year from a rental property, wants to know why he should pay; what's the government planning to do with his money? The auditor enumerates some of the uses to which income taxes are put: battleships, for instance. Grandpa answers that he doesn't want any battleships. Losing patience, the auditor shouts that he won't argue; Grandpa owes back taxes and that's that. "Well," says Grandpa, "I might pay about seventy-five dollars, but that's all it's worth."

Only Alice, Essie's sister, is remotely normal. For one thing, she actually works for a living. She is in love with Tony Kirby, her boss's son, and accepts his proposal of marriage, but is afraid that Mr. and Mrs. Kirby will never get along with the Sycamores. Tony brings his haughty parents to Grandpa's house for dinner, but, because he wants them to see Alice's family as they really are, purposely arrives the evening before the agreed-upon date. The Kirbys enter in full evening dress just as Penny, in a smock, is painting Mr. De Pinna, skimpily costumed as a discus thrower, while Ed plays the xylophone for Essie, who is dancing like a dervish for Kolenhkov, the Russian dancing teacher. Simultaneously, Grandpa tosses darts at a dartboard, and Gay Wellington, the actress whom Penny met on a bus and invited to be in the play she's currently writing, lies in a drunken stupor on the sofa.

Tony's parents, as stuffy as two human beings could possibly be, put up with the Sycamores for a few awkward moments, but their tolerance is exhausted by one act of eccentricity after another. At last, before Donald and Rheba have a chance to serve dinner, the Kirbys announce that they cannot stay any longer. Just as they head for the door, however, three FBI agents enter. They have discovered the quotation from Trotsky ("God Is the State; the State Is God") and the other slogans ("Dynamite the Capitol! "Dynamite the Supreme Court!") that Ed has innocently printed and included in Essie's boxes of candy, and accuse the hapless young man of fomenting violence. A coincidental explosion of "a whole year's supply" of fireworks from the basement scatters the G-Men and ends the second act.

After spending the night in jail, even the Kirbys are reconciled to the Sycamores. Grandpa persuades Mr. Kirby that happiness is not dependent upon the accumulation of money—a belief that audiences everywhere and at all times (but especially during the Depression) would like to share, even if the hard reality is that a reasonable amount of money is necessary for happiness to exist. The play ends with Grandpa saying grace as everyone, including Mr. Kirby, sits down for dinner:

> Well, Sir, here we are again. We want to say thanks once more for everything You've done for us. Things seem to be going along fine. Alice is going to marry Tony, and it looks as if they're going to be very happy. Of course, the fireworks blew up, but that was Mr. De Pinna's fault, not Yours. We've all got our health and as far as anything else is concerned, we'll leave it up to You.

Other characters, such as Kolenkhov's friend, Olga, the penniless Russian Grand Duchess (no longer recognized as such in Russia, thanks to the Bolshevik revolution) who makes delicious blintzes, add to the play's riotous good humor.

The carefully constructed plot never threatens the comedy's focus on the charm of the characters. In its careful balance of character, plot, and dialogue, *You Can't Take It With You* is perhaps the most accomplished of the Kaufman–Hart plays and one of the best-achieved American comedies. S. N. Behrman, an outstanding playwright in his own right, went further still. He said that he always thought Oscar Wilde's *The Importance of Being Earnest* the funniest play ever written, but changed his mind after reading and seeing *You Can't Take It With You*, which, he maintained, should take its place alongside *Earnest*. The Kaufman and Hart play is, he observed, "a classic farce, dateless as Wilde's play is."

You Can't Take It With You gives the impression of chaos and anarchy, but it is highly organized chaos, tightly controlled anarchy. Another significant accomplishment in the play is the authors' treatment of the characters. Despite assembling perhaps the greatest collection of good-natured lunatics ever put on a stage, the authors do not condescend to their characters. Quite the opposite, in fact. They obviously regard them with affection.

The overall effect of the play is touching and sweet. All of the characters in the Vanderhof household may be naïve dreamers, but the audience accepts their dreams and wishes them success. Hundreds of plays, movies, and television shows have attempted to mine the humor of a loving, eccentric family, but none has come within miles of succeeding as well as *You Can't Take It With You.*

Unlike all of their other comedies, Kaufman and Hart chose not to employ the wisecrack as the principal form of humor in *You Can't Take It With You.* Funny lines exist by the bushelful, but they emerge from character and situation. For example, during the strained conversation between the Sycamores and the Kirbys on the night of the Kirbys' visit, the following dialogue occurs:

MRS. KIRBY

I think it's necessary for everyone to have a hobby. Of course it's more to me than a hobby, but my great solace is—spiritualism.

PENNY

Now, Mrs. Kirby, don't tell me you fell for that. Why, everybody knows it's a fake.

MRS. KIRBY

(freezing) To me, Mrs. Sycamore, spiritualism is—I would rather not discuss it, Mrs. Sycamore.

PAUL

Remember, Penny, you've got one or two hobbies of your own.

PENNY

Yes, but not silly ones.

Penny's line is guaranteed to bring down the house. There is nothing inherently funny about the line itself, but the audience's knowledge of Penny's peculiar hobbies makes her comment irresistibly comic.

Later in the same scene, Penny, hoping to put the Kirbys at their ease, suggests that everyone play a word-association game. The Kirbys join in reluctantly, writing down the first thing that comes to their minds as Penny reads off a list of words ("potatoes," "bathroom," "lust" and "sex"; "Everybody got 'sex'?" she inquires). Mr. Kirby's answers are entirely predictable. He associates "potatoes" with "steak," "bathroom" with "toothpaste," "lust" with "human," and "sex" with "male." Mrs. Kirby, on the other hand, offers some surprises. Perhaps the funniest scene in *You Can't Take It With You* occurs when Penny reads Mrs. Kirby's responses.

PENNY

Now we'll see how Mrs. Kirby's mind works. Ready? This is Mrs. Kirby . . . "Bathroom—Mr. Kirby." . . .

KIRBY

(turning to his wife) I don't quite follow that, my dear.

MRS. KIRBY

I don't know—I just thought of you in connection with it. After all, you are in there a good deal, Anthony. Bathing, and shaving—well, you do take a long time.

KIRBY

. . . What was the next word?

PENNY

(reluctantly) Honeymoon.

KIRBY

Oh, yes. And what was Mrs. Kirby's answer?

PENNY

Ah—"Honeymoon—dull."

KIRBY

(murderously calm) Did you say—dull?

MRS. KIRBY

What I meant, Anthony, was that Hot Springs was not very gay that season. All those old people sitting on the porch all afternoon, and—nothing to do at night.

KIRBY

That was not your reaction at the time, as I recall it.

PENNY

(brightly, having taken a look ahead) This one's all right, Mr. Kirby. "Sex—Wall Street."

KIRBY

Wall Street? What do you mean by that, Miriam?

MRS. KIRBY

(nervously) I don't know what I meant, Anthony. . . . It's just that you're always talking about Wall Street, even when— *(she catches herself)* I don't know what I meant.

The way in which Kaufman and Hart's dialogue elicits one laugh after another, building the tension, leading to the final revelation which brings the greatest laugh of all, represents comic technique carried to perfection. The word-association scene is one of the most brilliantly accomplished in modern comedy.

Kaufman and Hart's original title, *Foxy Grandpa*, wasn't quite what the authors were looking for. During the next several months, *Money in the Bank*, *They Loved Each Other*, and *The King Is Naked* were considered, but none seemed quite right. *Grandpa's Other Snake* was vetoed by Beatrice Kaufman. At last, *You Can't Take It With You* (one of Grandpa's lines) was chosen, but with some reluctance. Sam Harris liked it, though, and persuaded the authors to keep it. Eventually they agreed with him that it was an ideal title for the play.

That summer, Hart became involved in one of the many instances of George S. Kaufman's infidelity to his wife. Although Kaufman and Beatrice were devoted to each another, neither expected fidelity. Thus, Kaufman conducted a series of love affairs, one of which was with Mary Astor, the film actress, who kept a detailed and rather lurid diary of her relations with Kaufman. In July 1936, a Los Angeles newspaperwoman discovered the diary and published excerpts from it in the *Herald-Express*. (The New York *Daily News* headlined its version of the story, "Diary of Astor Love Bares Kaufman Tryst—'Ecstacy.'")

Kaufman, in the forlorn hope that the diary was a fake, asked Hart to examine Astor's journal, especially such apparently racy sections as "He fits me perfectly . . . many exquisite moments . . . twenty—count them, diary, twenty. . . . I don't see how he does it . . . he is perfect." Hart told Kaufman he believed that the diary was authentic. Astor had indeed written the words, but Hart suggested that they referred to the number of Kaufman's successful plays, not to whatever exquisite moments he may have provided between the sheets.

Astor feared, correctly, that her former husband, Dr. Franklyn Thorpe, would attempt to use the incidents chronicled in the diary to retain custody of their daughter.[5] Thorpe advised his lawyer to subpoena Kaufman as a witness in the trial.

Kaufman, trying to avoid the process servers, went to Hart's Hollywood home, closely followed by newspaper reporters. In an incident that takes on the coloration of a Kaufman–Hart farce, Kaufman tried to hide himself behind the drapes in Hart's living room while Hart dealt with the press, denying that Kaufman was in the house. This left Hart open to the charge of interfering with a legal officer in the course of his duties. Still, he remained loyal to his friend and mentor, hiding him in a laundry basket, covering it with dirty

---

5 In 1935, when Astor and Thorpe had divorced, Thorpe was awarded custody of the daughter. The following year, Astor contested the ruling, hoping that it would be overturned. In response, Thorpe sued Astor and entered her diary as evidence of her lack of moral fitness.

clothing, and having the basket, the clothing and Kaufman hauled into a laundry truck. The truck drove Kaufman to the railroad station, whereupon a train took him to New York. The judge in the case sent a deputy sheriff to look for Kaufman in Hart's house, but, of course, did not find Kaufman.

The incident ended when the California judge, realizing that Kaufman was out of his jurisdiction, impounded the diary and settled the case between Astor and her husband on August 13, 1936, awarding her custody of her daughter for nine months each year.

Meanwhile, Sam Harris booked theatres for the out-of-town tryouts and Broadway run of *You Can't Take It With You*, signed the actors Kaufman and Hart had requested, and arranged to hold auditions for the other roles. An accomplished xylophone player was needed to play Ed, and Harris found one in George Heller.

After casting was completed, Kaufman directed, as he always did, although Hart was a constant presence at rehearsals and felt no compunctions about making suggestions. As with other Kaufman productions, only two and a half weeks were allocated for rehearsals prior to the out-of-town performances.

More than seven hundred props were needed for the production, requiring the attention of three property men. Although the play called for only a single set, nearly every inch of space was utilized for props. Mechanical snakes, a ship's model hanging from the ceiling, a skull from which Penny idly takes pieces of candy while writing her plays, a tusk of ivory, a hand-carved African war shield, a key to the city of Buffalo, a Piranesi print, and a string of wampum were all strategically placed around the set.

Kaufman and Hart were confident of the play's virtues and believed that critics would ratify their opinion, but were apprehensive how well their fantastic, almost plotless play would be received by audiences that had consistently demonstrated they preferred realism to fantasy.

Beginning on November 26, 1936, the first out-of-town performances were given in Princeton, New Jersey (where it became apparent that one of the actresses was unsatisfactory and was replaced). A two-week run in Philadelphia at the Chestnut Street Opera House began on November 30. The normal crisis atmosphere of pre-Broadway performances was avoided, as only minor rewriting was necessary.

As with *Jubilee*, rapturous out-of-town notices preceded *You Can't Take It With You*'s arrival in New York. A report from Philadelphia in *The New York Times* said, "the whole question with the audience is whether back muscles, strained by paroxysms of laughter, and chest muscles, sore with the effort of restraining guffaws, will be equal much longer to keeping their owners upright in their seats." In this case, however, when *You Can't Take It With You* opened at the Booth Theatre in New York on December 14, expectations were met and perhaps exceeded. Critics and audiences alike were charmed by the play, which Atkinson found the authors' "most thoroughly ingratiating comedy." The *Journal's* John Anderson added that by the end of the evening the audience was "still laughing at the delirious doings." Robert Coleman in *The Daily Mirror* called *You Can't Take It With You* "a glorious and riotous evening's fun." *Time* noted that "the playwrights have conjured a species of dramatis personae which transcends plot, bursts the bonds of the established theatre and mounts into the stratosphere of great literary lunacy."

One potential complication was avoided when Kaufman saw to it that the final scene of *You Can't Take It With You* would end while the play running next door at the Shubert, *Idiot's Delight*, was still in progress. The final scene in *Idiot's Delight*, featuring loud bursts of cannon fire and air-raid sirens, would be clearly heard in the Booth, and Kaufman's timing was intended to avert that possibility. One night, however, *You Can't Take It With You* ran longer than usual. The explosions from the Shubert occurred at the quietest moment in the Kaufman–Hart play, just as Grandpa was offering his invocation as the family sat down to dinner, leaving the bewildered audience to wonder why God was so thunderously rejecting Grandpa's prayer.

Eight months after the opening, Brooks Atkinson revisited the performance. "Some of the original actors have let down and are playing only for the mechanical laughs in the script," he said, but he exempted Josephine Hull as Penny, Frank Conlan as Mr. De Pinna, and George Tobias as Kolenkhov from this criticism. His greatest praise, however, was reserved for Henry Travers, "still a dry and droll delight as Grandpa, filling the whole play with the sardonic benevolence of his acting." Film buffs familiar with Henry Travers's performance as James Stewart's angel in *It's a Wonderful Life* can imagine how delightful Travers's performance was in *You Can't Take It With You.*

The play ran for 837 performances in New York, the longest run of any Kaufman–Hart production, earning everyone connected with it a fortune.

Theatregoers across America wanted to see *You Can't Take It With You*, and Sam Harris spared no effort promoting the four companies he sent on the road. He collected the New York critics' reviews into a brochure and sent it to all mayors, theatre managers, secretaries of chambers of commerce, and newspapers of towns with a population of ten thousand or more around the country, suggesting that, if a road company would not be playing near their city, they should consider busing a group to New York. In some cities, that was unnecessary. In Chicago, for example, *You Can't Take It With You* played for so many weeks that historians scurried to discover whether or not it was the longest-running play the city had ever seen.

A controversy of major proportions erupted when, in May 1937, *You Can't Take It With You* was awarded the Pulitzer Prize as the outstanding American play of 1936. Two months earlier, The New York Drama Critics' Circle had given their prize for the year's best play to Maxwell Anderson's *High Tor*, with *You Can't Take It With You* failing to receive a single vote. Some observers were aghast at the Pulitzer decision. It was one thing to delight an audience with comic inventiveness, they said, but a play of such little depth should not be awarded a Pulitzer Prize. *You Can't Take It With You*, John Mason Brown said in the *Post*, was "unusually entertaining and immensely lovable" but "a box-office play, pure and simple minded." Even Hart's great friend Edna Ferber disapproved of the Pulitzer decision, although she probably never mentioned it. In her diary, however, she wrote, "George and Moss awarded the Pulitzer for *You Can't Take It With You*. No play of this year deserved it. Certainly not that one." On the other hand, the New York *News* and the *Times* ran editorials about the selection, both endorsing the Pulitzer judges' decision.

Kaufman took the news about winning the Pulitzer in stride. His victory a few years earlier for *Of Thee I Sing* may have made the honor seem routine. But Hart was thrilled. To win such an award at the age of thirty-two was immensely gratifying. He pasted the telegram he received announcing that *You Can't Take It With You* would receive the Pulitzer and the subsequent letter confirming the prize into his scrapbook.

Some observers remain decidedly unconvinced that *You Can't Take It With You* is a play worthy of any award. Joseph Wood Krutch, writing in 1957, conceded that the play "had a considerable claim to" the Pulitzer Prize, but lamented the authors' willingness "to descend to the lowest level of banality when the occasion seems to invite it." A more recent (1983) criticism by John Simon began, "It is a sorry theater in which *You Can't Take It With You* becomes a classic." He called the play's humor "consistently primitive." Somewhere in the land, then, there are those who take little or no enjoyment from *You Can't Take It With You*. For most, however, it is impossible to watch a production or read the play without smiling throughout, and full-fledged laughter is difficult to subdue. As Robert Benchley put it in *The New Yorker*, "it is so funny that even when you are not laughing, you get a glow, for it is not only funny but nice."

A London production opened late in 1937 but bewildered the British critics and public. Lionel Hale in *The News Chronicle* had some complimentary things to say, but called the play a "rebottling of old wine." The *Times* of London was much harsher, saying, "George S. Kaufman and Moss Hart have converted the stage into a madhouse of irrelevant bad manners unseasoned by wit. With the best will in the world one can find little to commend the play except its brevity." The run, too, was brief: it closed in a week. In 1983, however, the managers of the Royal National Theatre recognized the mistake the British critics and public had made forty-six years before, and staged *You Can't Take It With You* to considerable acclaim. Irving Wardle, reviewing the play for the *Times* of London on August 5, called it "one of the comic experiences of a lifetime . . . [The] superbly plotted comedy . . . seems simply to be bouncing along from one disconnected episode to the next."

In November 1937, a woman named Virginia Gordon accused Kaufman and Hart of stealing her unproduced 1934 comedy, *Rash Moments*, which she had sent to the playwrights, and using it as the basis for *You Can't Take It With You*. The judge found her case to be entirely without merit, assessed her for court costs, and instructed her to pay her lawyer's $500 fee.

In Hollywood, *You Can't Take It With You* was purchased by Columbia Studios for a then-record price of $200,000. When the film version opened on September 6, 1938, the play was still running in New York. Normally, the box-office receipts for a play would fall precipitously if the filmed adaptation was playing only blocks away. In this case, though, the play, now moved to the Imperial Theatre, continued to play before sold-out houses for eleven more weeks. It marked the first time in Broadway history that a play and a film based on the play ran simultaneously.

The picture, with outstanding direction by Frank Capra and screenplay by Robert Riskin, richly deserved the Academy Award it won as Best Picture of 1938.[6] But it is much closer in tone and style to Capra's *Meet John Doe* and *Mr. Smith Goes to Washington* than it is to Kaufman and Hart's *You Can't Take It With You*.

In the film, James Stewart and Jean Arthur play Tony and Alice, in roles that have been vastly expanded from those in the play. Spring Byington as Penny is excellent and Lionel Barrymore as Grandpa is effective (if a trifle heavy-handed) as well. But the film is really about Mr. Kirby, played superbly by Edward Arnold, and his conversion from hardhearted banker to humani-

---

6 Capra also won as Best Director. Kaufman and Hart did not contribute to the screenplay.

tarian. Not only is Kirby's philosophy—that the purpose of life is to accumulate as much money as possible without regard to human consequences—pitted against Grandpa's (who, in the film, becomes an active proselytizer for his beliefs, rather than, as in the play, an amused observer), but the two characters become bitter antagonists. An entirely new premise is invented for the movie: Kirby connives to buy Grandpa's house in order to turn the entire block on which Grandpa lives into a munitions factory. He succeeds, but, when Tony tells his father that he is quitting the business and leaving his family, Kirby finally sees the error of his ways and is converted to Grandpa's way of thinking. The story of a madcap family becomes, in the film, only the backdrop for Kirby's change of heart.

Other less substantial changes included Donald Meek playing the role of Mr. Poppins, a character invented for the film version. Gay Wellington and the Grand Duchess are dropped altogether (since their presence in the play is hardly integral to its central idea, these characters were the logical choices to eliminate). And as in most adaptations of play to film, additional locations are included.

Thus, the picture is light-years from the comedy written by Kaufman and Hart. It presents an alternate version of the situation, and does so with great skill. Frank S. Nugent, the film critic for *The New York Times*, found the film less funny than the play—which is surely true, since the film makes few attempts at arousing laughter—but the characters "far more likable, far more human." Perhaps, however, it is more just to say that the play and the film, both excellent, see the issues raised by the material very differently; one is intended to be (and succeeds as) a gentle but hilarious comedy, the other is intended to be (and succeeds as) the agonizing emotional journey of a ruthless businessman.

Despite the unquestioned achievement of the film, the play is in no way diminished. *You Can't Take It With You* has been revived again and again in New York and in theatres across the country. (A revival of the play on Broadway in 1966 directed by Ellis Rabb was an immense hit. Anne Kaufman Schneider—George S. Kaufman's daughter—credits it with having begun the steady stream of revivals of the Kaufman–Hart plays on Broadway.) It has become a staple of the non-professional theatre as well. Different productions of the play were televised in 1945, 1950, 1979, 1984, and 1987. Each revival seems to demonstrate that the characters have become no less lovable over the course of time, the play no less charming.

Now at the peak of his career, Hart took his accomplishments and good fortune without permitting them to inflate his ego. He could look upon his success with a sense of irony and turn it into an anecdote, poking gentle fun at himself. Soon after the success of *You Can't Take It With You*, for example, he decided, on a whim, to visit the school in the Bronx he had attended more than twenty years earlier. He remembered that the principal had been named Mr. Cartwright, and Hart sought him out, not knowing whether or not the principal was still in charge or even alive. When he knocked on the door of the principal's office, however, Mr. Cartwright looked up from his desk, peered without recognition at Hart, and said, "What do you want?"

"My name is—Moss Hart," said Hart, hoping for a light bulb to go off somewhere. But Mr. Cartwright's expression did not change. "I—uh—I used to go to school here when I was a boy. My name is—Moss Hart."

"Well, what do you want?" asked the stern principal.

"Why—nothing. I just thought I'd—my name is Moss Hart. I just happened to be near by, and thought I'd—uh—you know."

After an awkward, silent moment, Mr. Cartwright continued, "Is that all?"

"Well," said Hart, "is it all right if I just go through the school—look around?"

The principal gave Hart a pass, and Hart wandered the halls of the school until he found the classroom in which he had spent so much time as a ten-year-old. When a teacher opened the door, she looked at Hart with a puzzled expression.

"My name is—Moss Hart," he offered, still hoping that someone—*anyone*—from his old school would recognize him and make a fuss over him.

"Oh, yes," said the teacher. "You're the father of one of the boys, aren't you?"

"No, no. I write—plays. Plays. I used to go to this school, so—"

"Oh, come right in," the teacher said, and turned to the class. "Boys, this is—what is the name?"

"Moss Hart."

"Yes. He used to go to school here. Sit right down, Mr. Hart."

Squeezed into a small chair, Hart suffered through the next two hours, then returned to Mr. Cartwright's office to thank him for the pass, hoping that the principal would by now have realized that his visitor was *the* famous Moss Hart. Mr. Cartwright, still seated at his desk, looked up and asked: "What do you want?"[7]

---

7 Several versions of this story exist. The version quoted here—and the dialogue—is taken from George S. Kaufman's account.

Another story that Hart liked to tell about himself concerned the occasion when, one day in the mid-1930s, he ran into an old acquaintance from the grammar school he had attended in the Bronx. Hart was strolling along the Lower East Side, dressed in his usual perfectly tailored suit, looking for antiques, when a pushcart peddler put his arm around him. "Moss Hart, you old so-and-so, you look like you robbed a bank," the peddler said. "What are you doing to make all that dough?"

"I am a playwright," Hart answered. "Five of my plays have had long runs on Broadway."

"Dope that I am," said the peddler, hitting his forehead with his hand. "Why didn't *I* think of that?"

As the owner of a beautifully decorated New York townhouse, the possessor of every item he could desire, the highly respected author of one Broadway success after another, and a man of considerable polish and charm, one might be tempted to see Moss Hart's life as one unmixed blessing after another.

However, a dark cloud hovered over him for the rest of his life, for a profound depression overwhelmed Hart when he was thirty. Perhaps, as some of his friends thought, the depression stemmed from anxiety over Hart's relationship with Kaufman, upon whom he felt himself utterly dependent, relying on him for advice and seeing him as a father figure. Hart believed, so the thinking goes, that his talent was minuscule compared to that of his partner, and that he would be unable to succeed on his own. Marc Connelly observed, "Moss is in such a state of genuflection toward George all the time that I don't know how they ever get a play written. Moss really wants to be George's son."[8]

---

8 Connelly's scathing remark might be at least partly explained by the fact that he preceded Hart as a collaborator with Kaufman.

Chapter 5 DRIVEN
1936–1939

THE PACE OF HART'S PLAYWRITING CAREER WAS BREATHTAKING IN THE late 1930s. From 1936 until 1943, Hart wrote five plays with Kaufman, contributed to two revues, conceived, wrote the book for and directed a groundbreaking musical, and, for the first time working without collaborators, wrote one of the most significant American plays to emerge from World War II.

The source of Hart's frenzied theatrical activity was his view of the theatre as a fascinating adventure and his determination to remain at the top of his profession, even at the expense of developing other aspects of his life. Perhaps he felt that devoting time to any other activity would dull his ability as a playwright; perhaps he was concerned that he would no longer have the energy to create at the same pace when he reached his forties. At any rate, he subordinated every other activity to work during the late 1930s. Or, looked at from another point of view, he may have thrown himself passionately into his work in order to avoid examining aspects of his life he chose not to deal with. To take only one example, he seems not even to have considered marrying and having children until after 1945.

His world, at least until 1938–39, was circumscribed by the theatre. "Moss never saw himself as anything else but a playwright," Dore Schary said. "He had a single-mindedness . . . Moss's interest in community affairs was limited to the community of the theater." Mussolini may have come to power in Italy; the struggle for control of China was in full swing; the Depression was raging throughout the world; Hitler was preparing to invade Czechoslovakia; Franklin D. Roosevelt was reshaping the American political landscape— but few of these events occupied Moss Hart's thoughts in the 1930s unless they could be turned into dramatic material. An avid reader, both of newspapers and of literature, he was by no means unaware of the turmoil raging in the world, but politics, the threat of war, and the economic plight of the nation could be dealt with by others. In 1936 Moss Hart's purpose in life was to create entertainments that would allow people to forget, at least momentarily, the forces beyond their control. And, of course, he was also motivated by the desire to create the most comfortable life possible for himself—an ambition that could only be satisfied by perpetual success in the theatre.

His drive required that he no sooner complete one project than he begin another. And one project at a time was often not enough to satisfy his need for perpetual involvement in the theatre. Often he juggled two or three different activities, with the result that, on at least one occasion, he was represented on Broadway by as many as three plays or musicals simultaneously. Indeed, the projects on which he worked between 1936 and 1939 were so numerous—and many of them overlapped to such an extent—that it is virtually impossible to describe his work on one production without discussing one or two others simultaneously.

Even while he was writing *You Can't Take It With You*, Hart (working on his own) contributed a sketch to *The Show Is On*, a revue with music and lyrics by various artists (including Dietz and Schwartz, Hoagy Carmichael, Rodgers and Hart, the Gershwins, and Vernon Duke). His sketch, "Mr. Gielgud Passes By," written for Reginald Gardiner (who was featured in the production with Beatrice Lillie and Bert Lahr), was a lampoon on John Gielgud playing Hamlet. Fifteen years later, NBC asked Hart to revise it for a television appearance by Rex Harrison.

A review from Boston on November 8, 1936, indicated that *The Show Is On* "will need some polishing" before going to Broadway. It received much more than "polishing;" five musical numbers were added by the time the production arrived in New York on Christmas night, just eleven days after the premiere of *You Can't Take It With You*. The new songs seem to have made the difference, for Brooks Atkinson said the revue "skims gayly through an evening of radiant high-jinks." The production ran for 237 performances at the Winter Garden Theatre.

An article in the New York *World-Telegram*, written on December 22, 1936, noted that, although Hart had written only one sketch for *The Show Is On*, the management obviously wanted to capitalize on his prominence. "The houseboard in front of the Winter Garden credits [Hart with] most of the dialogue," the article's author stated.

Late in 1936, Hart also was involved in Clare Boothe's play *The Women*. He and Kaufman invested in and doctored Boothe's comedy, although the dialogue of the play evidently remained hers alone.[1] In any case, *You Can't Take It With You*, *The Show is On* and *The Women* all ran simultaneously on Broadway in 1936–37, and all of them were either co-written by or influenced by Moss Hart.

---

1 Hart also invested in *Stage Door*, written by Kaufman and Edna Ferber for the 1936–37 Broadway season.

Hart's second ambition—to live as luxuriously as he could—was made possible by his many theatrical successes. And, as George S. Kaufman's partner and close friend, he wished to emulate his mentor's lifestyle as closely as possible. Consequently, in 1937, with the enormous profits from *You Can't Take It With You* supplementing the income from his other stage and film work, Hart bought a seventy-nine-acre plot of land with an old farmhouse in New Hope, Bucks County, Pennsylvania, only a few miles from Kaufman's country home.

Of all the houses Hart owned (and his passion for spending caused him to buy several; at one time he owned three homes simultaneously), this one—Fairview Farm—was his favorite. Hart bought the house and grounds after having seen them only once, and from a moving car, at that. Only after the purchase was made did he discover how dilapidated the property was and how much effort would be necessary to turn it into the country retreat he wanted.

Hart contracted to have a well drilled. Several months and seventeen wells later, the drillers finally found water. As the house had no bathrooms, Hart installed them everywhere. Other additions included a modern kitchen, a swimming pool, a tennis court, and a houseful of antique furniture. Later he added a separate wing, which included his office, an enormous playroom, and four guest rooms. A pair of sheepdogs came later; within three years they were the parents of thirteen more.

Hart wanted a shaded yard, so he ordered the planting of more than 3,600 fully-grown trees—3,500 pine trees, as well as an assortment of 139 elm, maple, and other shade trees, some as much as fifty feet tall. Trees were designed to do a specific job, Hart felt, and he became impatient if they didn't begin performing immediately. "When Moss plants a tree, he sits down under it and waits five minutes for it to give shade," his brother Bernie observed.

Hart grew vegetables at Fairview Farm, but the cost of producing them was excessive, to say the least. He joked that each radish grown at the farm cost him $115. He furnished the rooms with television sets, although barely anything was being televised in the late 1930s and early 1940s, when he bought them. He installed a sound system through which the same music could be played in every room, on the tennis court, and by the swimming pool, and added many other expensive items to enhance life in the country. Hart asked George S. Kaufman how he liked the renovations Hart had introduced. "Well, Moss," Kaufman said, "it just goes to show what God would have done if He'd had the money."[2]

---

2 Kitty Carlisle recalled this wisecrack having been made by Kaufman, but Hart attributed it to Alexander Woollcott.

Altogether, there were seven full-time employees at the farm, one of whom was Hart's valet, Charles, who also served as the butler. Charles and Raymond, the caretaker, were frequent participants in the games of croquet and backgammon that were constantly in progress during parties. Once, during a bridge game at the farm, a woman wondered why her partner seemed so familiar. After a moment she realized that he was the man who had served the dinner an hour before.

When Raymond considered taking another, more challenging, job, Hart took decisive action and bought a hundred pigs so that Raymond would have something to keep him busy. Hart knew that it was well worth a few thousand dollars to keep everything running smoothly at Fairview Farm, the place where he could be most relaxed and which served as his anchor for nearly twenty years.

In time, many of Hart's friends also bought homes in Bucks County. In addition to Kaufman and Hart, Ruth and Augustus Goetz, Oscar Hammerstein II, and S. J. Perelman all had retreats within a few miles of Fairview Farm.

Hart was trapped (although it was a trap of his own devising) in a pattern he could not escape. In order to meet the extraordinary expenses of Fairview Farm, he needed to work furiously. Only the frantic pace of his professional life would permit him to live in such ostentatious luxury. But his work required that he spend most of his time in New York and Hollywood, not in Bucks County. And Fairview Farm was hardly his only home. He leased a four-story apartment at 461 East 57th Street, near Sutton Place, in May 1939. Hart spent money extravagantly throughout his life, with most of the money going into his homes. "Buying houses all over the place" was his most enjoyable activity, he once said. "There is no greater fun for me than buying a new house and doing it over, stem to stern." Among the properties he owned at different times were an apartment on Park Avenue, another on East 57th Street, another on 73rd Street, a house in Beach Haven, New Jersey, and another in Palm Springs. He did show extreme restraint in resisting his impulse to buy a cottage in Jamaica and a flat in London.

He also continued to add to his collection of expensive clothes and objects, buying a cowboy suit for $1,000—at a time when $1,000 could buy a lot of cowboy suits. He bought a pair of elephant tusks, a prodigious number of monogrammed items of clothing, including dressing gowns, underwear, shirts, and ties. After buying a dog, he enjoyed the animal so much he bought seven more. As his friend Leonora Hornblow said of him, "He was determined to have a good time, to have fun, in spite of the Depression, in spite of troubles in the theatre or troubles with films."

Although Hart's investments and lavish lifestyle required that he continue to write as much as possible in order to keep the income stream flowing, he reduced his commitment to Hollywood in the late 1930s, for the work had become too depressing for him to contemplate. A decade later, when he became enthusiastic about a particular film, he would return to Hollywood, but he no longer wrote screenplays on a regular basis simply to increase his income.[3]

The Show Is On and *The Women* may have required only a minor expenditure of time and effort on Hart's part, but the same could certainly not be said about the next Kaufman–Hart collaboration. They discussed several possibilities, among them a revue intended for the Marx Brothers, tentatively titled *Curtain Going Up*, for which Irving Berlin would write the score. Groucho declined, however, reasoning that he had spent many years in the past doing revuelike material in vaudeville, and had no wish to return "precisely where I was fifteen years ago."

In January 1937, Hart journeyed to Hollywood at MGM's behest. His task was to write a musical for Greta Garbo and other studio luminaries. The mind reels at the thought of Garbo in a musical—and perhaps Hart's mind reeled as well, for he was unable to complete a screenplay. Within a month, he returned the advance payment of ten thousand dollars to the studio. The reason, he said, was that he wished to write a play instead. MGM offered to pay him twice the salary originally agreed upon, but Hart was not attempting to negotiate a higher wage. Suffering another bout of depression, he appealed directly to Louis B. Mayer, the head of the studio, to release him from his contract. Mayer was the soul of affability until he realized that Hart was serious. Infuriated by the notion that a mere writer would dare to walk out on his studio, Mayer flew into a rage, screaming and pounding the table. Hart later told his friend Jerome Chodorov about the experience, and Chodorov recalls the incident clearly. Mayer "turned into an ogre, a monster," he said, "as he denounced Moss and denounced all New York writers. This guy, this punk from New York telling him he wanted to get out was an insult, a terrible insult to the industry and to him. Moss said it was frightening the way he transformed himself from a sweet old uncle to a terrible bastard." Hart was firm, however; he never wrote a musical for Garbo.

---

3 Hart's attitude toward the movies is clearly demonstrated in a stage direction in *The Fabulous Invalid*. After the theatre has been converted to a movie house, Kaufman and Hart describe the stage picture: "Gone are the dignified houseboards and everything that John Carleton [the fictional theatre owner in the play] stood for. The whole effect is loud, garish, movie."

Kaufman ventured west to visit Hart, hoping they might conceive the idea for another jointly written production. They considered but decided against a number of possibilities for the stage, one of which was a revue about the writing of a revue, with music by George Gershwin and lyrics by his brother Ira. In the original conception, Kaufman and Hart, playing themselves, would appear on stage with the revue's two stars, Ina Claire and Clifton Webb, also portraying themselves. Sam Harris, they hoped, would appear as well. Eventually, however, Kaufman and Hart decided not to pursue the idea. Perhaps the notions that looked so fresh on Tuesday evening appeared stale on Thursday morning; or perhaps it became apparent that the schedules of Kaufman, Hart, Harris, Claire, and Webb would not coincide.

Kaufman and Hart considered other projects but they failed to come to fruition. Norma Shearer asked them to write a screenplay for her in 1937, but they declined. They discussed—but did not pursue—writing a musical about the material Hart would later cover in *Act One*: his early years in the Bronx and Brooklyn, followed by the production of *Once in a Lifetime* and Hart's consequent move with his family to a hotel in Manhattan. They considered writing a musical for Marlene Dietrich. Hart suggested a musical dealing with his current (and lifelong) preoccupation, psychoanalysis. But Kaufman, a skeptic on the subject, was only moderately enthusiastic. They worked together on an outline and completed a first act, which they showed to Dietrich, but Kaufman's less-than-eager attitude ultimately prompted them to abandon the idea and look for another.

At last they hit upon the notion of a full-length musical gently satirizing the then-current administration in Washington. Franklin D. Roosevelt was, in 1937, beginning his second term inauspiciously. His anger at the Supreme Court, which was dismantling some of his New Deal programs, had led him to propose appointing additional justices as a way of protecting those programs—"packing" the court, in the words of his critics. The result was a serious dip in the president's popularity. Still, Kaufman and Hart thought that a friendly spoof of the Roosevelt administration might serve as the basis for an appealing musical. The unique element was that FDR would be the leading character and portrayed under his own name—a concept then regarded as bold and daring. Although both Calvin Coolidge and Herbert Hoover had been depicted in revues, this would be the first occasion in which a sitting president would be portrayed as the leading character in a book musical.

Kaufman and Hart, concerned that the notion of portraying President Roosevelt in a play would be highly controversial, revealed their idea to Sam

Harris, but asked him not to share it with anyone. They believed the key to audience acceptance would be a charismatic portrayal of FDR by a highly respected actor. In their letter to Harris they asked if he could find them an actor who could convincingly portray the president with "dignity and distinction, but . . . also be able to play certain scenes with a broad sense of humor."

Harris recommended Charles Winninger, but Winninger, once a Broadway performer, was by 1937 a busy character actor so involved in films such as *Show Boat* and *Nothing Sacred*—and so comfortable living in California—that he had no wish to return to the New York stage.

Kaufman then suggested that George M. Cohan, the legendary actor-producer-playwright-songwriter, would be ideal. Not only was Cohan held in extremely high regard by the theatregoing public, he was also regarded as the very essence of patriotism. He claimed to have been born on July 4th (although he had actually been born on the 3rd), and his song hits included such patriotic standards as "Yankee Doodle Dandy" and "You're a Grand Old Flag." Surely no one could take offense, Kaufman reasoned, if Cohan—almost as great a national institution as the president himself—were to play Roosevelt.

Kaufman's idea struck Hart and Harris as an ideal solution. However, all three feared that Cohan would reject the suggestion, for many reasons. He was living in comfortable retirement and had given no indication he wanted to return to the theatre, he had never before performed on stage in a musical he hadn't written and composed, and he was a conservative Republican, firmly opposed to Roosevelt's policies. He might feel that an appearance as Roosevelt would lead observers to believe that he had abandoned his conservative principles.

Kaufman and Hart knew that Sam Harris had a special relationship with Cohan, however, for Harris and Cohan had once been partners and friends. Harris cabled Cohan, who was vacationing in Europe, and offered him the lead in a musical with a book by Kaufman and Hart. Without seeing the script, Cohan accepted, attesting to the respect in which Kaufman and Hart were held.

After Cohan's acceptance, Richard Rodgers and Lorenz Hart were asked to write a musical score. Persuading them to join the venture was difficult, for Kaufman said openly to Rodgers that the songs would be much less important than the book to the show's success. He also insisted that he and Moss receive a larger share of the profits than the songwriters. Finally, Rodgers and Hart, who had worked once with George M. Cohan on a film, detested the actor for his arrogance and egotism and had vowed never to work with him again. Cohan, for his part, was outwardly contemptuous of Rodgers and Hart.

Moss assured Rodgers that the experience he and Lorenz Hart had had with Cohan would not be repeated. For one thing, he said, Cohan had behaved disagreeably in the film only because he felt that he was being mistreated by the studio. For another, Moss insisted—falsely—that Cohan had great respect for Rodgers and Hart. Finally, Moss reminded Rodgers that Sam Harris would be around to intervene if Cohan were to behave temperamentally.

Moss's arguments were persuasive. The songwriters "were aware that we couldn't get just anybody for the part," Rodgers said. Furthermore, "It needed an outstanding star, and whatever we might feel about him personally, Cohan was exactly that, possibly the only one in the musical theatre who could play Roosevelt." After some agonizing, Rodgers and Hart accepted the assignment.

Rodgers articulated why he thought *I'd Rather Be Right* (then titled *Hold On to Your Hat, Boys*) could be not only an amusing musical but an important statement:

> . . . creating such a musical comedy at this time was in itself an affirmation of the freedom we [Americans] had always enjoyed and had long taken for granted. Hitler, who had come to power in Germany the same year Roosevelt first took office, had already instituted repressive measures against non-Aryans and "enemies of the state." Abolition of all forms of dissent was also a part of Mussolini's Fascist regime in Italy and of the aggressive military leaders in Japan. Spain was in the midst of a civil war led by Franco, with the blessing and backing of Hitler and Mussolini. . . . [But the United States] was one of the few nations on earth where people weren't afraid of their leaders. We could talk against them, we could vote them out of office—and we could even put them up on a Broadway stage as the butt of ridicule in a song-and-dance show.

Rodgers and Hart worked quickly to compose the score, then collaborated with Kaufman and Hart as they integrated the score and the book. The writing of the show was completed in June 1937.

Moss returned to New York in July to discuss casting with Sam Harris. According to a newspaper account, he also visited his parents for a few days at the Berkeley-Carteret Hotel in Asbury Park, New Jersey, where they were spending the summer. Steven Bach claims, however, that Lily "and Barnett—and her sons—had drifted so far apart that she was vacationing alone when she suffered a coronary thrombosis" that resulted in her death on September 6, 1937. She was sixty-seven years old. Hart returned from Bucks County, Pennsylvania, where he and Kaufman had been working on *I'd Rather Be Right* at Barley Sheaf Farm, Kaufman's estate, and arranged for a funeral service to be held at the Riverside Memorial Chapel in New York City on September 8. Lily was buried in Mt. Neboh Cemetery in Brooklyn. Bach implies that Hart did not attend the funeral. Based upon Hart's actions—or inaction—he seems to have considered Lily's death little more than an irritating interruption in his theatrical career.

Hart seldom spoke about his mother, for whom he felt little affection. He did place a telephone call to Edna Ferber, however, during which he spoke to her emotionally and at length about his mother's death. Otherwise, however, he seemed to treat her death with indifference. Perhaps he believed Lily to be unbalanced, and therefore a threat to his success. In later years, Hart told of peculiar occurrences in which his mother may have played a part. Most bizarre was the appearance of crossbones carved into Hart's apartment door and at the foot of his bed, accompanied by the warning, "Beware!" According to Hart, the crosses first appeared when he was a child of six. Then, wherever his family moved—Brooklyn, Manhattan, Hollywood—the crosses and their warnings reappeared. Hart's father reported the incidents to the police, who assigned an officer to guard the Harts' domiciles, but without result. Hart hired private detectives, who sat in the dark waiting for an intruder or intruders, but none appeared. One evening, his parents were waiting for him at his home when he returned to find the symbols carved on his bedstead.

After much discussion, Lily, Barnett, Moss, and Bernie, unable to identify any acquaintance who might be responsible for following them around the country in order to persecute them, began to suspect one another. Then, after Lily died, the carving of the crosses ceased. Hart never said publicly that she was responsible for the incidents, but his story implied that he had his suspicions. The intriguing mystery, obviously rich in implications, was never solved.

Although Hart never said so, it is possible that he also suspected his mother of sending threatening letters and setting backstage fires during the run of *Jubilee* in 1935.

⌘

Work on *I'd Rather Be Right* resumed when George M. Cohan returned to the United States and heard the score for the first time. Cohan sat comfortably in the living room of an elegant East Side apartment, the home of one of Rodgers's friends. Moss sang the songs with Rodgers and another pianist accompanying him. Moss "didn't have a trained voice," Rodgers said, "but he had excellent enunciation and an oddly charming way of putting over a song." Cohan, his arms folded, his expression dour, listened to each song without the slightest reaction. After the presentation, he finally arose, took a few steps to Rodgers, said, "Don't take any wooden nickels," and walked out, leaving everyone in a state of near-shock.

Fearing correctly that Cohan was about to withdraw from the show, Moss and Kaufman now turned their attention to flattering and soothing Cohan. Insofar as he remained in the production, they succeeded, but Cohan's participation led to frequent trouble. For one thing, he never failed to take the opportunity to express his disdain for Rodgers and Hart, with whom he battled frequently during rehearsals. He referred to them only as "Gilbert and Sullivan," which he evidently regarded as devastating sarcasm.

One expression of Cohan's disdain occurred during the first out-of-town performance at the Colonial Theatre in Boston on October 11, 1937, when Cohan without warning substituted some of his own lyrics for those written by Lorenz Hart, followed by a comment addressed directly to the audience. Not only was this professionally unethical, but Cohan's lyrics belittled Roosevelt, reversing the musical's emphasis. When the lyricist, justifiably furious, complained to Sam Harris (as producer) and to Kaufman (as director) about Cohan's behavior, they promised that the episode would not recur. Indeed, they somehow managed to persuade the irritable and patronizing Cohan to curb his ad-libbing.

However, the next morning an account of the incident and its resolution appeared in the New York *Herald-Tribune*. Cohan was furious. Convinced that Rodgers was behind the article, Cohan seemed once again on the verge of pulling out of the production. But Moss, Kaufman, and Harris, trying to mollify both the actor and the songwriting team, persuaded Cohan that Rodgers had had nothing to do with the article's appearance. Once again, the crisis abated.

From Boston, *I'd Rather Be Right* moved to Baltimore, where many government officials saw the production. When those officials refused to say publicly what they thought of the musical, it added to the already-growing belief in New York that *I'd Rather Be Right* must be a brazen, controversial, irreverent production, thus whetting the appetite of subsequent audiences.

Broadway theatregoers, excited by the out-of-town reports, were enthusiastic about seeing a musical that would brashly satirize American politics. The prospect of seeing the president impudently caricatured seemed irresistible. "*I'd Rather Be Right* may well have been the most eagerly awaited musical of all times," Rodgers said. "Gags from the show were repeated all over town even before the official New York premiere."

The creators themselves were persuaded that their work was bold and unconventional. "All four of the authors were jesting all Summer and through rehearsals," *The New York Times* reported, "about the prospect of spending a long Winter in jail because of the provocative content of the show and its audacious razzing of persons in high places."

Pre-opening ticket sales were also boosted because of the audiences' enthusiasm for a collaboration between Kaufman and Hart, Rodgers and Hart, and the revered old showman, George M. Cohan, making his first musical appearance in ten years.

The Boston production caused *The New York Times* to editorialize that the mere existence of *I'd Rather Be Right* was a tribute to democracy and to Americans, who "love to laugh at plays satirizing or burlesquing their public men, . . . elections, platforms and promises." The anticipation on the part of theatregoers led to an extremely strong advance sale (somewhere between $250,000 and $300,000, whereas the cost of production was $150,000).

As with several of Moss Hart's previous works, the anticipation could not possibly live up to the reality of the actual production. And *I'd Rather Be Right* was particularly vulnerable, for it simply was not a distinguished work. The book was far below the usual Kaufman and Hart standards, and the songs were much less distinguished than Rodgers and Hart's customary output.

As a result of the creators' cold-eyed appraisal of the Baltimore production, they knew that their show was in trouble. Kaufman and Hart asked Noël Coward to help them on some rewrites and invited Coward to restage some scenes. Rodgers later admitted that the score "may not have been one for the ages." Only "Have You Met Miss Jones" is remembered as one of Rodgers and Hart's better songs.

I'd Rather Be Right turned out to be a pallid, unadventurous spoof, especially when compared to *Of Thee I Sing*, the genuinely audacious political satire Kaufman had helped to create earlier in the '30s. And if *I'd Rather Be Right* seemed a bit flat in 1937, it now seems even more so. Like *Merrily We Roll Along*, it has not aged at all well. Somehow Boston and Baltimore accepted the show as bold political satire (quite an astonishing response to a musical that is neither bold nor satirical and only marginally political), but its inadequacy could not be concealed from New York audiences. Its jokes, aimed at easy targets, are, at best, slightly amusing. The plot, intended as inspired comic foolery, consists instead of a soggy collection of predictable episodes.

I'd Rather Be Right focuses on two ordinary young Americans, Peggy and Phil, who just happen to meet Franklin D. Roosevelt strolling through Central Park. They are unable to get married because of the Depression, they tell him, and ask him to help them out. He can do so only by balancing the federal budget, which would encourage Phil's boss to give him a raise. "Kids," he says, "I'll tell you what [I'll] do. I'll *try*. I'll try real hard and see if I can . . . because I want to see you two married, if it's the last thing I do as President."

Roosevelt conceives of several hare-brained schemes, including imposing a tax on post offices and calling on American women to give up cosmetics and donate the savings to the federal treasury. But the president, who is portrayed throughout as an amiable bumbler, is unable to bring the budget into balance. However, he leaves Peggy and Phil with a fervent speech favoring democracy and individual initiative, thus convincing them that a wedding will somehow solve all their problems. Moreover, he promises to run for a third term, specifically for their benefit. At the end of the musical, the audience learns that the entire plot has been only a dream!—a shopworn device that at least has the merit of explaining why the characters have behaved in such ridiculous fashion. Phil proposes, Peggy accepts, and the curtain descends.

Songs and dances in *I'd Rather Be Right* feature members of the Supreme Court jumping out from behind rocks and bushes—they declare everything unconstitutional, including the Constitution itself—and Cabinet members and chorus girls entering from nowhere to perform songs and dances. President Roosevelt periodically breaks into a tap dance. At one point, the president drives the Chief Justice of the Supreme Court offstage with a "beanshooter." Roosevelt's mother, Republican presidential nominee Alf Landon, political adviser Jim Farley, and Secretary of Labor Frances Perkins are portrayed among a gallery of recognizable figures. The Federal Theatre Project is mocked on several occasions—in part, perhaps, because that taxpayer-subsidized program was in direct competition with such commercial enterprises as *I'd Rather Be Right*. A group of Federal Theatre performers bursts into song, because, as they say, whenever they encounter three people gathered together, they are supposed to give a show. Another gag occurs when Roosevelt asks his secretary to bring him the Wagner Act, and two acrobats named Wagner are brought onstage to perform.[4]

Such a description may give the impression that the script and score approached inspired lunacy, but *I'd Rather Be Right* is merely silly. It settles for

---

4 The Wagner Labor Relations Act established the National Labor Relations Board.

easy laughs, never even attempting to deal with the most significant political issues of the day, such as Roosevelt's efforts to pack the Supreme Court. In the printed version of the script, *I'd Rather Be Right* is billed as "a Musical Revue," which was meant perhaps as an acknowledgment that the not-very-funny gags, irrelevant songs, and easy caricatures did not add up to a comprehensible book musical. It is surprising that Moss Hart, who resisted the temptation to turn *As Thousands Cheer* into a conventional revue, had no such compunctions when it came to *I'd Rather Be Right*.

I'd Rather Be Right opened in New York at the Alvin Theatre on November 2, 1937. Cohan, who had to perform in an ankle brace on opening night, the result of an accident suffered a few nights earlier, exerted his usual hold over the theatregoing public and the critics, although the show itself did not meet with approval.

John Mason Brown expressed the belief that the audience cheered only because of Cohan's performance, and he was probably correct. Richard Lockridge, writing in the New York *Sun*, questioned why out-of-town audiences seemed to have found the tired satire so brilliant. Others noted that the musical was undistinguished either by its book or its score. Its only claim to notoriety, they suggested, was the appearance onstage of an actor representing the president—but George Jean Nathan, writing in *Newsweek*, said, "Why the idea of calling George M. Cohan Franklin D. Roosevelt should have engendered so intense an interest I cannot figure out." Brooks Atkinson gave the musical credit for being "playful," but said, "that is hardly enough for a first-rate musical show. . . . *I'd Rather Be Right* [is] a clever and generally likeable musical comedy, but it is not the keen and brilliant political satire that most of us have been fondly expecting."

Still, *I'd Rather Be Right* ran for 290 performances in New York—presumably on the basis of its large pre-sale—then went on tour. Commercially, the production was a success. But a financially successful show is not the same as a well-achieved theatrical work. One cannot imagine *I'd Rather Be Right* succeeding today, not only because the current attitude toward politicians is so much less respectful than it was in 1937, but because the comedy of the play is so bland.

Cohan's disdain for the songs of *I'd Rather Be Right* remained evident throughout the run. However, to his credit, he never again attempted to alter Lorenz Hart's lyrics nor to alter the characterization of FDR that Kaufman and Hart had created. Except for one final appearance (in *The Return of the Vagabond* in 1940), *I'd Rather Be Right* was Cohan's final production on Broadway, where he had experienced enormous success since his debut in 1904.

Kaufman must have felt that the failure of *I'd Rather Be Right* was an aberration, for he told a newspaper interviewer that although he had worked successfully with many other playwrights, Moss Hart was his favorite collaborator. Kaufman's declaration left no doubt that his partnership with Hart would continue.

After a brief holiday on the West Coast in January 1938, Hart and Kaufman discussed and began to write a comedy centering around a family. They worked on the play during a boat trip from California to New York. By the time they reached the Panama Canal, however, they were no longer so enthusiastic. They decided the play bore too close a resemblance to *You Can't Take It With You* and abandoned it.

In March, the partners began two more projects for the stage which were to open on Broadway within two weeks of each other, and on which they worked concurrently. One was a revue, *Sing Out the News*, to which Hart and Kaufman contributed two sketches and considerable revision of others. Moreover, Hart invested $25,000 in the production, matching Kaufman's investment. (The show was budgeted at $100,000.) *Sing Out the News* was also the first occasion on which Hart was billed as the producer, sharing billing with Kaufman and Max Gordon.

Nominally, the author of the sketches was Charles Friedman, but Harold Rome, the composer of the revue, said that Kaufman and Hart contributed significant amounts of material. The revue was intended as a Broadway sequel to Rome's hugely successful *Pins and Needles*, a satirical musical revue produced in 1937 by the International Ladies' Garment Workers Union, which offered a distinctly left-wing commentary on the issues of the day.

Harold Rome hoped that the new revue would make few concessions to standard musical and comic entertainment, favoring an even more hard-hitting, uncompromising approach than *Pins and Needles*. He was distressed to find that Kaufman and Hart's plan was to combine social commentary with satirical humor, some of which would be aimed at left-wing targets. Rome particularly resented Kaufman, who, he felt, paid no heed to his objections.

Throughout the summer of 1938, Rome, Friedman, and Max Gordon paid periodic visits to the farms of Kaufman and Hart in Pennsylvania to work on the revue. In the process, a good many of Friedman's original sketches were rewritten by Kaufman and Hart (although they neither sought nor received program credit), who later continued their revisions during rehearsals. The more highly polished sketches remained socially oriented, but less pointed. Although neither Hart nor Kaufman directed *Sing Out the News*,

both were often present at rehearsals, as would be expected of the co-producers. Their interest in the production reflects Hart's growing awareness of
world events and his understanding that he could not remain oblivious to
them. Further, it was perhaps his first realization that his skill as a writer
might be put to social use. Still, the writers saw themselves primarily as paro-
dists. Thus, although both by now were committed Democrats, they saw
nothing wrong with poking fun at Roosevelt and the Democratic Party.

Sing Out the News began rehearsing in July for a tryout run in Philadelphia
beginning on August 29. The Philadelphia reviews indicated that the production was in need of considerable revision, and it was rumored that Kaufman would replace Friedman as director. However, the new play that Kaufman and Hart were writing was also scheduled for a Broadway production in
September, and Kaufman, already set as director, chose to spend his time on
his own play. Still, when *Sing Out the News* opened, the credits read: "Directed
by Charles Friedman, with a bow to George S. Kaufman."

The run of *Sing Out the News* at the Music Box Theatre began on September 24, 1938. Reviews praised the production, but, falling considerably short
of raves, they failed to ignite public interest. The general view was that, despite its virtues, *Sing Out the News* was less incisive than *Pins and Needles*.
Atkinson's review was typical: "It is a neatly written and attractively produced
satirical revue about current persons—brisk in pace and New Deal in philosophy. . . . Some of it may be a little pale and wan . . . but most of it is crisply
amusing." Some of the paleness of *Sing Out the News* was undoubtedly due to
the failure of the creators to share a common point of view. Rome and Friedman were motivated at least as much by social conviction as by the desire to
produce entertaining material, while the primary goal of Kaufman and Hart
was to write the funniest comic sketches of which they were capable. In the
process, the revue's theme often became muddied, the social focus obscured.

Sing Out the News closed after 105 performances. Despite its moderate
production cost, the backers lost their entire investment. Poorer by $25,000,
Hart could not afford to slow the pace of his work even if he had wished to.

The other Kaufman–Hart project of 1938 was intended to reflect directly
Hart's lifelong love affair with the theatre. The year before, he proposed to
Kaufman that they write a play chronicling the great moments of Broadway
history, thus reminding audiences of the importance of the theatre to the
American experience.

The event that specifically triggered Hart's imagination occurred during
the out-of-town performances of *I'd Rather Be Right*, when, unable to sleep, he

began looking through his collection of old *Theatre* magazines. The first issues he looked at were from the early 1900s, and included fine illustrations of Broadway productions of the period. Enchanted by the illustrations and the articles, Hart mentioned his enthusiasm to Kaufman the following day.

Months later, the playwrights began work on a play about a fictional playhouse, the Alexandria, that had once been the most beautiful and admired theatre on Broadway. Scenes would be shown from a representative sample of American plays, from the beginnings of the American theatre until the present day (1938). In the course of the play, the Alexandria would fall into disrepair and be rescued by a group of young actors. Thus the Alexandria was a metaphor for the state of the legitimate theatre, which always seems to be on its last legs but always manages to recover. The authors titled their play *The Fabulous Invalid.*[5]

As the partners so often did, they discussed the actors who might be cast in the play before completing the writing. In this case, they hoped that Alfred Lunt and Lynn Fontanne would wish to participate, employing their versatility to play many roles. The Lunts were intrigued by the concept, but eventually decided to pursue other projects.

By that time, Kaufman and Hart had discovered that many of the plays from which they had intended to extrapolate scenes, beginning with the comedies and dramas of the colonial era, continuing through the nineteenth century and into the twentieth, were unworthy of revival. Except for a handful of plays, American drama written before 1900 was hardly distinguished. Even though such great European playwrights as Bernard Shaw, Anton Chekhov, August Strindberg, and Henrik Ibsen were thriving in the 1870s, '80s, and '90s, most American theatres opted instead to present trivial farces and melodramas. Discouraged, Kaufman and Hart decided to drop the idea of a theatrical cavalcade and work on another play instead.

They began discussing new possibilities while traveling by boat from California to New York by way of the Panama Canal. But they kept returning to their idea of a play about the American theatre, and by the time they reached the Caribbean they had once again focused their attention on *The Fabulous Invalid*. Now, however, it would exist in somewhat different form; only plays from the twentieth century would be included.

By the time their journey was over, the play was finished. The authors were pleased with the quality of their work, and were confirmed in their opinion

---

5 The phrase "the fabulous invalid" has been used ever since to characterize the theatre. Hart claimed that he and Kaufman were the first to use it.

when Kaufman, with Hart in attendance, read *The Fabulous Invalid* to Sam Harris, who expressed interest in producing it.[6]

Shortly before *The Fabulous Invalid* opened in New York, however, Hart was approached by Alexander Woollcott to write a play with a leading role for him to play. Woollcott, egg-shaped and owl-faced, was one of the most famous men in the United States, a critic of such influence that a word from him could make or break a play or novel, a raconteur whose witticisms and invective were constantly quoted, a frequent visitor to the White House and the homes of the world's most famous artists and statesmen. His fame was based partly on his remarkably long list of accomplishments: critic, radio personality, lecturer, spokesman for various worthy causes, and devotee of real-life murder mysteries.

Woollcott had a charming and generous side, but also could be notoriously rude. Hart found that out in 1929, at the first party he attended at Beatrice Kaufman's house, with the premiere of *Once in a Lifetime* still months away. The aspiring twenty-five-year-old playwright attempted to speak to Woollcott. Seeing that Woollcott was leafing through a mystery novel that Hart had recently finished, he said, "You'll like that book very much, Mr. Woollcott."

Woollcott looked slowly up at the young man and asked malevolently, "How would *you* know?" A moment later, Hart, flushed with embarrassment, edged his way to the door and ran downstairs to the safety of the street.

Years later, after Hart had established himself as a major American playwright, he and Woollcott became friendly. Still, one had to be wary of Woollcott's penchant for venomous remarks, even those that were meant to be taken humorously. So, when Woollcott suggested that Hart write a play in which he could play the central role, Hart didn't know whether or not to take him seriously.

The idea was not entirely outrageous, for Woollcott had some acting experience. In 1931, he had appeared in a play written by S. N. Behrman, *Brief Moment*, playing a character not unlike himself. Throughout the play he lay on a sofa, "occasionally exploding into typical Woollcottian invective," in the words of Beatrice Kaufman and Joseph Kennedy, who edited Woollcott's letters. Woollcott wrote most of his own dialogue, he claimed, "because

---

6 To illustrate how *The Fabulous Invalid* and *Sing Out the News* overlapped, it was on May 25, 1938, that Kaufman read *The Fabulous Invalid* to Sam Harris and his staff for the first time. The very next day, Charles Friedman and Harold Rome presented their revue material for Kaufman, Hart, and Max Gordon.

[Behrman's] dialogue simply cannot be spoken." Seven years later, when Woollcott was lecturing at the University of Chicago, Behrman enticed him into appearing in a similar role in his *Wine of Choice*, which played in Philadelphia on a tryout tour. Again, according to Woollcott, he completely rewrote his own part.

On a Sunday afternoon in 1938, when no performance of *Wine of Choice* was scheduled, Woollcott drove to Fairview Farm for an overnight stay. Woollcott's visit turned out to be an upsetting one for everyone. He made one irritating demand after another, insisting, for example, that he would not go to bed unless a milkshake and chocolate cookies were prepared for him, demanding that all the heat in the house be turned off, and refusing to sleep in any room other than Hart's bedroom. He also accused Hart's servants of dishonesty. When Hart looked at his guest book after the weekend was over, he found that Woollcott had written, "I wish to say that on my first visit to Moss Hart's house I had one of the most unpleasant evenings I can ever recall having spent."

Evidently Woollcott meant the inscription as a joke, for he insisted that Hart accompany him to Philadelphia to see *Wine of Choice* the next night. Hart did so, and, somewhat to his surprise, enjoyed Woollcott's performance.

Afterward, in Woollcott's hotel, while sipping brandies, Hart suggested that he and Kaufman might just write the play Woollcott had proposed. "By 4 o'clock in the morning we were both enchanted with the idea," Hart said: "Mr. Woollcott, because he was no doubt already envisioning a great Bernhardt tour—the horses unhitched from his carriage and the bewitched Midwest townspeople strewing roses in his path."

When Hart awoke the next day, the idea no longer seemed quite so promising, but he had said that he would mention it to Kaufman, "and having been the recipient of some Woollcottian rages before this, I decided I must at least carry out my part of the drunken romanticism of the night before." He drove to the Kaufman farm and discovered that Kaufman liked the idea. Although no one would describe Woollcott as a brilliant actor, a play tailored especially for him, one which could capitalize both on his abilities and his reputation, would, the writers thought, be an intriguing challenge. Kaufman then added, sardonically, "All we have to have now are three funny acts."

Hart then mentioned that Woollcott had been a recent houseguest of his and described the critic's outrageous behavior, concluding with, "Wouldn't it have been awful if he had broken a leg and been on my hands for the rest of the summer?"

Kaufman and Hart looked at one another and both began to smile. Hart had just suggested a workable premise for the Woollcott play.

After telling Woollcott of their decision to proceed with a play in which he would play a major role, the critic urged them to begin immediately. Indeed, he would soon be needing another play, for, after three months on the road, *Wine of Choice* ran only briefly in New York. However, Kaufman and Hart could not immediately turn their attention to the Woollcott play, since *The Fabulous Invalid* had not yet been produced. They did assure him, however, that it would be ready for the 1939–40 Broadway season.

Kaufman and Hart then returned to *The Fabulous Invalid*. The play, already in rehearsal, needed a great deal of rewriting, but the authors, distracted by the Woollcott episode, either failed to recognize the need or simply ran out of time.

In the first act of *The Fabulous Invalid*, the Alexandria Theatre, at its height of popularity and influence, is presenting a play featuring a married couple, Paula and Laurence. At the end of the "performance," the actors are shown in their dressing room, preparing to attend a champagne supper. Suddenly, Paula collapses and dies. Laurence, traumatized, fatally shoots himself. Although their bodies are borne away on stretchers, their ghosts arise, to join other phantoms, most importantly the ghost of Jim, the genial doorman. Jim tells Paula and Laurence that they can go to heaven if they wish, but warns them that they will find no theatre there. Since the world of the theatre *is* heaven for Paula and Laurence, they choose to remain in the Alexandria as long as the building continues to stand.

The ghosts watch appreciatively as fifty-two scenes and musical numbers from twenty-six American plays and musicals, ranging from 1900 to the late 1920s, are shown. Some of the scenes consist of only a few lines and most are less than thirty seconds long. Each of the scenes presented in the play is reproduced—through scene and costume design, as well as acting style—faithfully in the manner of the period.

Suddenly, a crash of discord from the orchestra introduces an ominous note: theatres are going dark all over New York and companies are closing on the road. The ghosts of Paula and Laurence fear that their beloved theatre is dying. Another discordant crash introduces more bad news: the ten percent tax on all plays introduced during the World War is endangering the theatre's survival; the strike of Actors' Equity in 1919 arouses great hostility among theatrical producers; the Depression and the advent of talking films all threaten the continued existence of the theatre. Ultimately, the Alexandria is to be converted to a movie palace. Despite an appearance by the ghost of Shakespeare, who reassures Paula and Laurence that the institution of the theatre is indestructible, they remain concerned that the theatre will not survive.

In the second act, the Alexandria is seen once again, but garishly repainted. Now converted to a movie house, the theatre is to be auctioned off, to become either a garage or a bus terminal. The ghosts of Paula and Laurence appear, lending John W. Carleton, the Alexandria's former owner, moral support in his bid to save the theatre. But he is outbid, and the Alexandria becomes a tawdry burlesque house with equally shabby entertainment. The police raid the theatre and arrest the performers. As they're led away, the ghosts of Paula and Laurence are told by an emissary from heaven that, unless the theatre is saved they will have no choice but to go to heaven.

Later, after the Alexandria has been boarded up and abandoned, Paula and Laurence prepare to leave, lamenting the conversion of 42nd Street from its former elegance to an area populated by an Army and Navy store, a flea circus, and a Chock Full O' Nuts coffee shop. At the last moment, however, a group of twelve or fifteen young men and women enter, look the theatre over, and discuss their plans to renovate it and produce plays there. Their leader, patterned on Orson Welles, begins a rehearsal of the group (patterned on Welles's Mercury Theatre company). The Alexandria, it seems, will return once again to its former nobility. The ghosts, now joyful, embrace as the curtain falls.

Of all the Kaufman–Hart collaborations, *The Fabulous Invalid*, although highly ambitious, is the least well-achieved. It is understandable that these two stage-struck writers would wish to communicate their enthusiasm for the theatre to the public. Moreover, it is admirable that they attempted to break out of the realistic form that had brought them so much success in the past. But the deficiencies of the play far outweigh its virtues. It is almost embarrassingly maudlin; its conventions (such as the theatre ghosts) are such clichés that they are almost laughable.[7]

The characterizations are so sketchy that no character rises above the level of the banal. Shakespeare's appearance is gratuitous, at best. The dialogue is unbelievable and transparent. Most objectionable, though, is the preposterous exaggeration of the legitimate theatre's dignity and the reduction of every

---

7 At the end of the play, with the Alexandria again peopled by actors, the ghost of Jim the doorman "smiles at Paula and Larry," in the words of the stage directions. He "draws his pipe from his pocket, and tilts a chair against the wall. Comfortably settled, he lights his pipe, looks up toward the heaven that now seems far away." Such sentimental business would be more appropriate in a parody.

other form of entertainment to tawdriness. An unpleasant attitude of snobbery lies at the core of the play.

Moreover, the scenes and musical numbers from the twenty-six selected American plays were bound to fail. Performers from 1938 (none of them "stars," many of them relatively obscure) were forced to compete with the audience's memories (or the imagined performances) of such legendary performers as the Barrymores, Mrs. Fiske, Elsie Janis, and others—an impossible task which inevitably led to disappointment.

The Fabulous Invalid can today be viewed only as spectacle—and the projection of greatly enlarged old theatrical posters on a screen as well as the many sets and costumes made it spectacular, indeed—but almost completely inadequate as drama.

For the same reason that *Merrily We Roll Along* did not have an "out-of-town" tryout—the immense size of the production—*The Fabulous Invalid* also offered New York previews rather than a preliminary road tour. Not only did the cast require seventy-three actors, but the massive set, which reproduced both the interior and the exterior of the Alexandria Theatre, made touring impossible.

Neither the critics nor the public found much merit in *The Fabulous Invalid*, which opened at the Broadhurst Theatre on October 8, 1938. Atkinson called it "an enormous theatre parade . . . and [an] often remarkably pungent illustrated lecture on the theme that the theatre never dies. . . . There is a great story in this succession [but] it needs to be written. It needs an exultant literary style; it needs coherence, pith and insight into its theme." The style of the play, Atkinson said, "is so alien to Mr. Hart's and Mr. Kaufman's familiar abilities that the writing . . . is either threadbare or on the verge of being maudlin." In a subsequent article, Atkinson compared *The Fabulous Invalid* unfavorably to Kaufman and Hart's earlier works. The play closed after a mere sixty-five performances.

Some observers questioned the inclusion of scenes from so many deservedly forgotten melodramas. As the writer of a letter to *The New York Times* noted, "It is unfortunate that the choice has been made of plays that were box office successes rather than those that were important." Kaufman and Hart had read 165 plays in order to find scenes to include in *The Fabulous Invalid*. But in the paring-down process, many of the most significant American plays (such as *Continental Divide* and *The Faith Healer*, William Vaughn Moody's forward-looking dramas of 1906 and 1909) were omitted and too many of the inconsequential melodramas and farces (such as the long-forgotten *The*

Music Master, Within the Law, and *The Lion and the Mouse*) remained, emphasizing those plays that had been commercially successful rather than those that, by their quality, changed the course of American drama.

Most evaluations of the works of Kaufman and Hart rank *The Fabulous Invalid* as the least successful of their collaborations. Rosamond Gilder in 1944 called it a "weighty affair." Hart himself later referred to it as "unmourned and over-sentimental." Indeed, among the many oddities concerning *The Fabulous Invalid* is that it is such a mawkish play. Given Kaufman's aversion to sentimentality, it's astonishing that he co-wrote the piece.

Looking back on the remarkable amount of activity for which Kaufman and Hart were responsible in the fall of 1938, it seems miraculous that *The Fabulous Invalid* was able to get into production at all. *Sing Out the News,* co-produced by and unofficially co-authored by Kaufman and Hart, opened on September 24, 1938, and *The Fabulous Invalid* premiered on October 8 under Kaufman's direction. It seems impossible that one production or the other would not have suffered. Given their reception, it seems clear that both *Sing Out the News* and *The Fabulous Invalid* required more attention than they received. The authors' focus was only split further by their plans to write a play for Alexander Woollcott.

Hart had a well-deserved reputation as a versatile and busy man of the theatre, who, even while writing one play, could dash off a screenplay here, several revue sketches there, all the while helping out friends with their productions on the side. But too much activity can lead to shoddy results. Hart seems to have come to this realization soon after *The Fabulous Invalid,* for his furious pace slackened before long. He wrote only one play in 1940, another in 1941 (although he did begin directing on Broadway in that year), and none at all in 1942, while preparing for a single play in 1943. By his standards, his pace in the 1940s and '50s would seem downright glacial.

A bizarre outgrowth of *The Fabulous Invalid* was a lawsuit for $24,500 brought by the Federal Nut Company against Kaufman and Hart. Offended by the line in the play grouping their subsidiary, Chock Full O' Nuts, together with a flea circus on 42nd Street, Federal Nut alleged that the reference was intended to harm their coffee business. In court, the judge asked Kaufman and Hart whether they had ever held anyone or any institution up to ridicule in their previous plays. Kaufman, explaining that his plays were intended as satires, replied that he had lampooned the president of the United States on several occasions. *I'd Rather Be Right* was one, but Kaufman, working independently of Hart, had also mocked the office of the presidency in two other musicals. The judge then turned to Hart. "Have you ever held anyone up to ridicule?" he asked. Hart could have chosen any of a number of people from *As Thousands Cheer*, but he mentioned only the king and queen of England, thinking either of that revue or of *Jubilee*. The judge asked if Kaufman and Hart had been sued by any of the people they had satirized. Kaufman answered, "No, only Chock Full O' Nuts." The judge ruled in favor of the playwrights, sending the message that satire was still permissible in New York.

The next logical move was for Kaufman and Hart to return to the play they had promised Woollcott. But Beatrice Kaufman urged her husband and Hart to write a play that would speak out much more firmly against the fascist threat of Hitler and Mussolini than *Sing Out the News* had done, eschewing humor to make a passionate declaration of their faith in freedom and democracy. The playwrights were skeptical at first, uncertain of their ability to write such a drama, but Beatrice's advocacy awakened Hart's social consciousness, and Hart eventually succeeded in persuading Kaufman.

Ultimately, Kaufman came to realize that a play of the sort Beatrice suggested had to be written. He and Hart, both Jews, generously supported Jewish organizations. Given the Nazi threat to Jewish identity in Europe, both wished to state their convictions in unmistakable terms. They began preparations for their new enterprise even while *The Fabulous Invalid* was still in performance. Neither the authors nor the producers (Sam Harris and Max Gordon) intended to make much money if the play succeeded financially, for all agreed to donate part of the profits to political charities.

Before they could begin, Alexander Woollcott asked what had happened to the play Kaufman and Hart had promised him. The playwrights, perhaps feeling somewhat ashamed of their cavalier treatment of Woollcott, journeyed to Woollcott's summer home in Bomoseen, Vermont, to tell him that the play for him would have to be delayed yet again. "Mr. Woollcott received this news in the manner of the Dowager Empress of China," Hart said, "receiving the humble petition of a couple of coolies, and relented to the extent of saying he would change his plans once more, but that was all."

In October 1938, the co-authors returned to the play Beatrice Kaufman had urged them to write: *The American Way*, an indictment of fascism and a celebration of democracy. It would use three stages, the action moving cinematically from one to the other as one scene "dissolved" into the next. The action would cover more than forty years. The cast would call for approximately two hundred fifty actors (many of them extras, paid at $15—later raised to $18—a week) and a large orchestra, part of which would appear on stage as "The Community Novelty Band." The authors were determined to create the effect of a vast historical pageant.

The central character of *The American Way* is Martin Gunther (played by Fredric March), a German immigrant who arrives in the United States shortly before 1896, and is joined in that year by his wife, Irma (played by March's real-life wife, actress Florence Eldridge), and their two children. They settle in Mapleton, Ohio, where Martin, a cabinetmaker, is saving money to buy his own shop and studies to become an American citizen. In time he achieves his ambitions, and his shop is eventually transformed into a factory. Later another is built, attesting to Martin's growing success. Martin becomes a fervent American patriot and a pillar of his community. His standing is jeopardized, however, when Irma refuses to allow their son Karl to join the army during the World War. Irma's family still resides in Germany and she can't bear the thought of Karl fighting against—and possibly killing or being killed by—her own brothers. Townspeople accuse the Gunthers of being slackers. Martin argues that it is Karl's duty to fight for his adopted country, and his argument prevails. Karl goes overseas, but, when the doughboys return, Karl is not among them; he has died on the battlefield.

Mapleton goes through the Depression, and many of its citizens become embittered. Martin loses his money, but his faith in America is not shaken. (And the loss of his fortune does not seem to adversely affect his lifestyle—which may reflect the inability of Kaufman and Hart to comprehend the desperation of those who had no foothold on the economic ladder.) Still, a sizable percentage of Mapleton's population, associating the Depression with a failure of participatory democracy, becomes attracted to totalitarianism. The Gunthers' grandson, also named Karl, is enamored of a fascist group that promises easy solutions to America's economic and political problems. On the night of Martin and Irma's fiftieth anniversary celebration, young Karl, after arguing the meaning of "America" and "freedom" with his grandfather, runs off to meet with the fascists in a picnic grove. As Karl is being initiated into their group, Martin tries to break up the meeting. The fascists grab and beat him, leading to his death. Young Karl tries to intervene but is restrained. When the fascists leave, young Karl, remorseful, takes his grandfather in his arms and carries him back to Mapleton. In the town square, citizens mourn Martin's death, solemnly singing "The Star Spangled Banner" as the curtain falls.

Martin is portrayed as an ideal American citizen: thoughtful, articulate, hardworking, ambitious.[8] In contrast, his grandson, Karl, is a dangerously confused young man, caught up in turbulent social currents he can barely comprehend. His despair is exemplified when he shouts at Martin just before going off to join the fascists, "Go ahead—wave the flag. Let the bands play. But if you stop listening to 'The Star-Spangled Banner' for a minute, you can hear this whole rotten system crashing around your ears."

Although the America portrayed in the play is idealized, the warts have not been entirely removed. In some respects, *The American Way* succeeds in its aim, effectively contrasting the American way of life with the growing fascist menace. And, for an America in turmoil in 1939—isolationists were in the ascendant, contending that faraway events in Europe were none of America's business and that foreign dictators were no threat to the United States—the ending would have been either a stirring rallying cry to come to the aid of nations threatened by fascism or an affirmation of isolationist principles.

The play, a truly vast panorama of American life, was conceived as a remarkable visual spectacle, employing the arrival of a ship and a reconstruction of the immigration hall at Ellis Island, as well as many other complete sets. For most of its length it is a pageant rather than a play, for the plot includes little conflict until the final scene of the first act. Rather, episodes from various historical periods are shown against the background of such events as the McKinley–Bryan presidential campaign of 1896, Lindbergh's flight to Paris in 1927, and the inauguration of Franklin D. Roosevelt as president in 1933.

Such historical pageants with many scenes create inevitable problems, many of which the authors were unable to solve. For example, the audience continually needs to be informed when the scene they're watching is taking place and what has happened to the characters since the last time they were seen, or, if this is the character's first appearance, identifying him or her. Thus, one character is made to say, "Well, you can't say I haven't kept up with the times. Yes, sir, I opened up the first beauty shop in Mapleton." Another says, "Here I am—twenty-one years old. I've never had a job in my life . . . I've been trying for three years and I can't get one." Verisimilitude is continually sacrificed for clarity in the dialogue.

The scenes fly by with such haste (albeit skillfully, for the use of three stages made it possible for one scene to "fade" into another without a moment's pause), packing so much information into each episode, that few

---

8 But not Jewish. The writers were at pains to give their play a universal significance that, they feared, might have been compromised if their main character was Jewish.

scenes are given time to develop their potential. With hundreds of characters, only a handful are individualized, and even those in rudimentary fashion. The spectator yearns throughout much of the play for the action to stop so that the audience can focus on the leading characters. When, at last, the conflict between Martin and young Karl is allowed to be played out, the play is at its most compelling.

The mammoth Center Theatre, with its nearly 4,000 seats, housed *The American Way*. The orchestra pit was covered over, permitting the actors to play scenes as close to the audience as possible. An orchestra conducted by Oscar Levant was stationed six floors above the auditorium, its music (composed by Levant) played through speakers. Two directors—Kaufman and Hassard Short (who was billed as "Technical Director")—were employed to coordinate the massive production. The stage manager required six assistants to run each performance. Thirty tons of scenery were hung from steel cables above the stage. Each of the sets, some of them motorized, was coordinated to descend and ascend noiselessly. Hundreds of lighting instruments were added to those already hanging in the Center Theatre, and the lighting board was supplemented with two auxiliary boards. Thirty-eight child actors were quartered in dressing rooms, chaperoned by their mothers, when not onstage.

Several previews preceded the official opening, on January 21, 1939.[9] The date marked the first time the Center Theatre had ever been used for a nonmusical production. The producers hoped to attract visitors to the World's Fair, which would open in New York in April.

Some of the notices were overwhelmingly favorable. For example, John Anderson in the *Journal American* wrote of an extraordinary theatrical phenomenon:

> No audience that I can remember in my time on the aisle has been so shaken with emotion as we all were at the Center Theatre on Saturday when in the last few moments of *The American Way* a vast rising rumble began at the back of the enormous theatre and swept forward until nearly 4,000 playgoers were on their feet while the on-stage singers finished "The Star Spangled Banner" and brought the curtain down before people too choked to move. Then followed an uproar that marked this as not a play nor a spectacle so much as a dedication. . . . [This was] no time to sit in judgment, but to stand at attention.
>
> Few there, I suppose, could have failed to see in that frankly tear-stained moment that the audience had become a part of the play, and the play a part of us.

---

9 The authors had hoped to open the show on Christmas Day, 1938, but were unable to complete preparations on time.

Sidney Whipple of the *World Telegram* said, "Vivid life and glowing inspiration, superb propaganda and unashamed sentimentality, comfortable humor and heart-wrenching drama have been combined in a spectacular pageant . . ."

But Richard Watts in *The New York Herald-Tribune* was more reserved. The play "is more expert in its spectacular effects than in its more personal drama," he said. "To appreciate *The American Way*, you must look at it as what it is, a colorful spectacle, rather than a play." Brooks Atkinson, although he praised the first act as "a profoundly moving evocation of gay and rueful memories, recapturing some of the precious lost innocence of our lives" and also expressed admiration for "the authors and actors [who] endow *The American Way* with patriotic authority that is both solemn and stirring," had reservations about the "leaden moments, particularly in the second act."

All of the critics praised the leading actors, particularly Fredric March, whose role called not only for him to age forty-three years in the course of the evening, but to hold the play together with the strength of his performance.

The critics, seated in the orchestra, got a very different impression than did audiences in the balconies. One newspaper complained that the "more intimate scenes were almost completely lost in the great reaches of the playhouse."

Kaufman and Hart returned to the production after the opening, revising some of the dialogue and staging. Because Atkinson complained in his review that Martin's murder was "no more savage in the staging than a college cane rush," the writers modified the scene and, in his staging, Kaufman made the attack more savage and realistic.

The cost of *The American Way* was so great ($225,000) that only unequivocally enthusiastic reviews could have made it financially successful. A large pre-sale insured its early success. The box-office gross for one week exceeded $41,000, a record for the next ten years. Ultimately, however, even though it ran for 244 performances, the production lost sixty thousand dollars. The hope that visitors to the World's Fair would buy tickets in great numbers proved to be false. Though the prices were lowered in August (from a top of $3.30 to $2.20, with some of the orchestra seats available at $1.65), it did little to stimulate business.

The American Way won a number of awards for its authors and its leading actors. Patriotic service crosses were given to Kaufman and Hart by the United States Flag Association for their service in arousing "the patriotism of every American who sees this stimulating play." Awards were given to March and Eldridge by various organizations, including the National Conference of

Christians and Jews, which awarded them badges of tolerance, symbols of their support for democracy, freedom and brotherhood; and the Drama Study Club's plaque for "the foremost achievement in the American theatre for the season." Hart attended the luncheon when the plaque was presented in April.

Just as a lawsuit had been brought against Kaufman and Hart for allegedly having stolen a play they retitled *You Can't Take It With You* in 1936, so they were accused of stealing an idea that became *The American Way*. Again, however, the suit was dismissed.

Edward Mann, one of the extras in *The American Way*, asked Kaufman and Hart if they would consider inviting agents, managers, and talent scouts to a special invitation-only performance, during which some of the extras could perform scenes. Kaufman and Hart sat on an audition board along with March and Eldridge. Together, they selected fifty of the extras to give a performance in September 1939. Hart's generosity in agreeing to give of his time represented another step in his becoming a more compassionate individual, willing to sacrifice some of the hours he would otherwise spend in generating new plays so that he could help those less successful than himself.

RKO Pictures bought the rights to *The American Way*, allowing most backers to recover their investments, but the film was never made. When *Abe Lincoln in Illinois* was released in 1940 to generally favorable reviews but did not return a profit, RKO decided with typical movie studio foresight that the American public did not want patriotic movies. (Following that line of thought, if *The Wizard of Oz* had not been successful, MGM might have stopped making musicals!)

As late as February 1942, reports indicated that the film of *The American Way* might be made after all. Columbia Pictures bought the rights from RKO; again, however, the plans came to nothing.

The earnestness of *The American Way*, along with its occasional effectiveness, deserves praise. Indeed, Kaufman and Hart were more successful with *The American Way* than they had been with other episodic productions that emphasized drama over comedy, such as *Merrily We Roll Along* and *The Fabulous Invalid*. Still, the play clearly confirms the belief that the writers' mutual talents were far better suited to satirical comedy than to any other form.

Alexander Woollcott was on a lecture tour in California when *The American Way* opened. Without his repeated reminders that Kaufman and Hart had promised to begin work on a play for him, the authors promptly turned their attention to a new project, this time a musical comedy written with Cole

Porter to feature W. C. Fields. However, Woollcott unexpectedly returned to New York (canceling three scheduled lectures), and, in Hart's words: "I received the royal command to come to dinner that night. . . . We had barely sat down when Mr. Woollcott wanted to know when he could hear the first act of his play. I blurted out the truth. Not only had we not written a line of it, but we had almost completed the first act [of the musical with Cole Porter]."

Woollcott exploded in anger. On the basis of Kaufman and Hart's promise, he said, he had turned down requests to appear on the radio and had refused lecture tours. If the play were not ready to be performed at the time the writers had specified, Woollcott stood to lose a great deal of money. Hart could only apologize sheepishly, vowing to get to work with Kaufman right away.

But that was not enough for Woollcott, who then suggested to Kaufman that the two of them—Woollcott and Kaufman—write the play together. Kaufman replied that he would not dream of dissolving his partnership with Hart, but he assured the critic that the play would eventually be ready as promised.

Indeed, Kaufman and Hart began outlining the plot the very next day, after informing Cole Porter that they would be unable to proceed with the planned musical until they completed Woollcott's play. As it turned out, none of the writers ever returned to the musical and W. C. Fields continued to perform in the movies.

Still, Hart's need for continual activity prompted him to become involved in one more project before the play for Alexander Woollcott went into rehearsals. Along with many other writers, composers, and actors, Hart invested money in a musical revue (established as a non-profit enterprise) called *From Vienna*, in which Beatrice Kaufman presented a group of Viennese refugees. He served as an unofficial adviser to the production, watching rehearsals and offering comments to Charles Friedman and Hassard Short, the directors. The revue, opening on June 20, 1939, ran for seventy-nine performances.

After that brief diversion, Hart returned to the Woollcott play. When playwrights write vehicles for specific actors, undistinguished drama often results. In the case of the play for Alexander Woollcott, however, the opposite occurred. The Woollcott play became one of Kaufman and Hart's greatest triumphs, cementing their reputations as the finest American comic writers of the twentieth century.

Chapter 6 KAUFMAN AND HART: THE FINAL PLAYS
1939–1942

ALTHOUGH MOSS HART WAS ONLY THIRTY-FIVE YEARS OLD IN 1939, his playwriting career was in need of rejuvenation. His past several productions had all been moderate successes at best. Collaborating with Kaufman was no longer encouraging either man to produce his best work. Hart's friends' prediction of years before, that he would always be subservient to Kaufman as long as they worked together, had not proven true, but it was undeniable that the relationship which had produced *Once in a Lifetime* and *You Can't Take It With You* was no longer as fruitful as it had once been.

The partnership, though still highly regarded in the Broadway theatre in 1939, had been dealt a blow by the tepid responses to *The Fabulous Invalid* and *The American Way*. If Kaufman and Hart insisted on pursuing drama instead of comedy, some observers said, they were likely to be relegated to the ranks of second-rate playwrights.

Hart's own reservations about the collaboration were more and more on his mind. His wish to write a play about psychoanalysis had been stymied by Kaufman's indifference; perhaps a break was necessary to allow him to write on subjects about which his partner had no interest. Hart hoped, too, that breaking with Kaufman—traumatic though it might be for both of them—would relieve his depressive states.

If Hart was contemplating the breakup of the partnership in the late 1930s, he did not share his thoughts with anyone else. Indeed, he and Kaufman finally set to work in 1939 on the play they had promised Alexander Woollcott, completing it the following year.

"We decided to use only public aspects of [Woollcott's] character," Hart said, about the approach to the play, tentatively titled *Prince Charming*. "That is, to be guided in the plot by his lecture tours, his broadcasts, his charm, his acidulousness, his interest in murders, and all of this had to be worked into the plot of the play. Those things were the core of the play, and the plot was something that had to be worked around them."

Although Sheridan Whiteside, the Woollcottian character they invented, was invested with many of Woollcott's most odious characteristics, he was also conceived as a character of venomous but irresistible humor, which, the playwrights believed, would surely appeal to Woollcott. In addition, Whiteside would be confined to a wheelchair throughout the play, and Woollcott, whose extreme corpulence limited his mobility, would surely welcome the opportunity to play a leading role without many physical demands. Whiteside was, in Hart's words, a "tremendously caustic but basically sentimental fellow with a heart underneath of tempered steel, with perhaps a bit of acid."

Since their play's leading character was to be a thinly disguised portrait of Woollcott, Kaufman and Hart felt strongly that they should not proceed further without his consent. When the moment came for the authors to present the first act of their script to Woollcott (which they did by reading it aloud to him), they assumed that he would be delighted, but his response was far less gratifying. In the play, the portrayal of Sheridan Whiteside was, to put it mildly, less than flattering. Besides, Woollcott claimed in a letter to Lady Sybil Colefax, "It had been my parting instruction [to Kaufman and Hart] that my role should be as different from me as possible. I was considerably taken aback to find that they had done a cartoon of me." The critic told the authors he would need a week to think over whether or not he would consent to their use of his persona as a character in their play.

Woollcott also pondered whether he would accept the role, should the play go forward. In the ensuing week, while Kaufman and Hart worked on the second act, Woollcott cogitated. On the one side was his intuitive negative feeling: "It struck me that it would be alienating and even offensive for me to come forward and say in effect, 'See how rude and eccentric I can afford to be. Dear, dear, how amusing I am, to be sure.'" On the other side was his perception that the play was very funny and his hunch that it would be successful.

Finally, he decided that he could not possibly play the role, although he did not insist that Kaufman and Hart put aside their work on the play. Woollcott suggested Robert Morley, the fine English comic actor, as a possible Whiteside.

After completing the first draft of the play, the authors contacted Morley, but his schedule was already full and, unenthusiastic about Kaufman and Hart's third act, he did not wish to rearrange his other commitments. The authors were forced to look elsewhere.[1]

Adolphe Menjou also turned down the role. At last they settled on a relative unknown, Monty Woolley, who was then playing small roles in films and on Broadway. He had performed as the ballet impresario in *On Your Toes* in

---

1 Morley later played Whiteside in London.

New York in 1937 and King Edward VII in *Knights of Song* in 1938. Additionally, Hart knew Woolley from their association on *Jubilee* and believed that he could do justice to the role. He was right; the role gave Woolley the opportunity to become a leading player, both on the stage and in films, for the first time.

In what they now called *The Man Who Came to Dinner*, the Woollcottian Sheridan Whiteside, a famous celebrity, is touring the Midwest. Whiteside is described as a "critic, lecturer, wit, radio orator, intimate friend of the great and near-great, . . . the idol of the air waves." He also richly deserves to be called an egomaniac, for never has there been a more self-centered character. Shortly before he is scheduled to give a speech in Mesalia, Ohio, Whiteside falls and fractures his hip. Forced to convalesce in the home of Mr. and Mrs. Ernest Stanley, Whiteside threatens to sue them for $150,000. He insists upon exclusive use of the library and the living room, adding that the family is to leave the telephone untouched so that Whiteside's calls will not be blocked. Moreover, they are forbidden to use the front door; instead, they are to confine themselves to the service entrance. Whiteside proceeds to turn the stodgy family upside down with his outrageous demands and the bizarre behavior of his theatrical friends, who visit him throughout the play. Harpo Marx served as the model for Banjo, the manic, fun-loving, woman-purusing brother of Wacko and Sloppo, and Noël Coward's persona served as the basis for Beverly Carlton.[2]

Lorraine Sheldon, an actress of dubious distinction who has slept her way to the top, is a composite of all the Hollywood stars of limited talent Kaufman and Hart had known or imagined. Some of Lorraine's characteristics, though—her flightiness, love of gossip, and her tendency to behave with the grandest theatricality offstage as well as on—were derived from Gertrude Lawrence.

During the play, Whiteside outrages the Stanleys by encouraging their son Richard to leave home to become an itinerant photographer; he also advocates the marriage of their daughter to a labor organizer at Mr. Stanley's factory. Primarily, though, his objective is to hold on to the indispensable services of his secretary, Maggie Cutler, by disrupting the growing relationship between Maggie and Bert Jefferson, the young newspaperman (and aspiring playwright) with whom she falls in love. Later, however, after conspiring to give Bert's play as a starring vehicle to Lorraine, thereby succeeding in his wish to

---

2 This marked the third time Hart used Coward's personality in a play, once under his own name, twice in thinly-veiled disguises.

come between Maggie and Bert, Whiteside repents. With the help of Banjo, Lorraine is trapped inside a mummy case and the coast is clear for Maggie and Bert.

Before Whiteside can carry out all his plans, the local doctor informs him that he is perfectly all right—the doctor has been reading the wrong person's X-rays—but Whiteside, allowing the doctor to believe that his mammoth tome, *Forty Years an Ohio Doctor; The Story of a Humble Practitioner*, is a brilliant work that Whiteside wants to help rewrite, swears the doctor to secrecy so that he can remain in the household until all of his schemes come to fruition.

Mr. Stanley, driven nearly mad by Whiteside's behavior, his enormous phone bills, his guests (including an ax murderer), the gifts he receives (among which are four penguins that can only eat whale blubber, eels, and cracked lobster), tries to evict his famous guest. He nearly succeeds, until Whiteside, an avid reader of murder mysteries, recognizes Mrs. Stanley's sister Harriet as the notorious Harriet Sedley, who gave her mother forty whacks with an ax, then gave her father forty-one. Whiteside threatens to announce his discovery over the radio unless Mr. Stanley relents concerning Whiteside's eviction, his daughter's marriage, and his son's freedom to begin a career as a photographer. Whiteside is victorious on all counts, but when he triumphantly walks out of the house, he slips on a piece of ice and is carried back inside, shouting that he will increase the size of his lawsuit against the Stanleys to $350,000. Mrs. Stanley faints as the final curtain descends.

Cole Porter, who had traveled around the world with Hart and Woolley four years earlier, composed an original song for the play, an ingenious parody of Noël Coward's characteristic style. The lyrics were sometimes attributed to Porter, sometimes to Kaufman and Hart. Since no official credit was given, either possibility exists.

The characters in the play fall into three groups. Whiteside, Lorraine, Banjo, and Beverly Carlton, all of whom are involved in the theatre or the movies, are highly exaggerated caricatures whose levels of energy are prodigious. Contrasting with them are characters such as Maggie and Bert, as well as the Stanleys' children, who represent normality. Most of the others—the gawky Miss Preen, the ever-frustrated Mr. Stanley, his silly and star-struck wife, and the wraithlike Harriet—fall somewhere in between.

You Can't Take It With You was set during the Depression and the incidents in the play were conditioned by the characters' responses to that momentous event, but one would never know from the text of *The Man Who Came To Dinner* that the play took place in an environment of economic deprivation. The

Stanleys and their friends are all wealthy, as are the show-business types, who fly or sail here and there with no thought of the expense involved.

Despite the ingenious plot and the delightful supporting characters, the mainspring of the humor can be found in Whiteside's inspired insults. The first line of the play, heard from offstage, occurs when a nurse, Miss Preen, enters the living room from the library in full uniform, Whiteside shouting, "Great dribbling cow!" Later, when Miss Preen attempts to comfort him, he sneers, "You have the touch of a sex-starved cobra!" When Whiteside, seated in a wheelchair, first sees the Stanley family, their servants, and friends, all of whom are waiting for the great man to utter deathless prose, he turns to Maggie, saying icily, "I may vomit." Then he turns his baleful stare at two of Mrs. Stanley's friends. "Who are these two harpies standing there like the kiss of death?" he asks. When a matron drops the calf's foot jelly she brought for him, he says, "Made from your own foot, I have no doubt." And, a few moments later: "And now will you leave quietly, or must I ask Miss Cutler to pass among you with a baseball bat?" He refers to Miss Preen as "Miss Bed Pan;" he greets Banjo by asking, "How are you, you fawn's behind?"

Whiteside's dialogue is amusing even when he is not spouting invective. For example, when Whiteside, the epitome of outrageous behavior, is asked a perfectly reasonable question, he moans, "Is there a man in the world who suffers as I do from the gross inadequacies of the human race?" When he gets down to work, he dictates a telegram to Maggie: "Send a cable to Mahatma Gandhi, Bombay India: 'Dear Boo-Boo: Schedule changed. Can you meet me Calcutta July twelfth? Dinner eight-thirty. Whiteside.'" Gandhi is only one of the world's most influential people with whom Whiteside is involved. During the course of the play he receives telegrams or phone calls of condolence from H. G. Wells, Walt Disney, Lucius Beebe, and many others.

Miraculously, the pace of the play never slackens from beginning to end. The danger of such a scheme is precisely the hazard *Once in a Lifetime* suffered from until shortly before its opening night on Broadway—that a breakneck pace can exhaust an audience. In *The Man Who Came to Dinner*, however, the play, a miracle of construction, is always exhilarating, never fatiguing.

In rehearsals, Monty Woolley made no attempt to imitate Alexander Woollcott's manner in his portrayal of Whiteside, developing instead a character of his own. John Hoysradt, a student at Yale in 1926 when Woolley headed the drama school, was cast as Beverly Carlton. Carol Goodner, an American actress who had gone to England in 1924 and remained to become a leading performer, returned to the United States to play Lorraine. Other featured actors included Mary Wickes as Miss Preen, David Burns as Banjo, and Ruth Vivian as Harriet. All proved to be excellent, as did Edith Atwater as Whiteside's secretary. Hart and Atwater, frequently in each other's company after rehearsals and performances, appeared to those who knew them to be becoming romantically involved.

Altogether, the cast of *The Man Who Came to Dinner* includes thirty-six characters. The large number of characters was typical of a Kaufman and Hart play. In a concession to increasing production costs, however, the play called for only one set, the Stanleys' living room, whereas all of the previous collaborations, except *You Can't Take It With You*, required many locations.

Rehearsals were held in the Music Box Theatre, with Donald Oenslager's set in place and completely furnished—an unusual luxury. But Kaufman, the director, wanted the actors to become comfortable with their stage environment from the first rehearsal, and in this case the single set made such an arrangement possible. Furthermore, since Sam Harris, the co-owner of the Music Box, was producing the play, there was no need to use a rehearsal hall.

The Man Who Came to Dinner had only nineteen days of rehearsals before giving its first performance before an audience. Actors' Equity permitted a four-week rehearsal period, but Kaufman, who had allocated only nineteen rehearsals to *Merrily We Roll Along* as well, obviously preferred a short, intense rehearsal period.

Kaufman devoted the first four days of rehearsals to read-throughs. After three days spent blocking the production, the first run-through was held with only Monty Woolley—whose role was far longer than anyone else's—carrying his script; all others' lines were committed to memory.

Often, Kaufman rehearsed the third act first, then the second, and finally the first, perhaps because he wanted to be sure that each act was as strong as another. Eventually, of course, as the out-of-town opening approached, he ran the play in its proper order.

Hart was present at all rehearsals, often conferring with Kaufman. Their conversations might last only a few seconds or might extend for ten or fifteen minutes. At one point, early in the process, Kaufman held a whispered conversation with Hart before a scene was about to begin. He was then heard to say, "You may be right, but let's run it through this way and see how it plays."

When a scene was played, Kaufman and Hart would normally sit side by side, often exchanging whispered comments.

Although Kaufman was always the one who addressed the actors, Hart clearly served as an unofficial co-director. At one point, for example, after watching the scene in which Whiteside comes to the silent realization that Harriet Stanley is actually the notorious Harriet Sedley, Hart stood up and verbalized his opinion for all to hear. "I think we've got to build this, George," he said. "I'd like to have him snap his fingers as he looks at the picture—and I'd even go so far as to have him say, 'I knew I'd seen that face before.' You've got to let the audience realize the significance of what he's discovered and I don't think the facial expression is enough."

Initially skeptical, Kaufman gave Hart's suggestion a try and discovered that it improved the scene considerably, eliminating any possible confusion the audience might experience.

On another occasion, Kaufman asked Hart, "Don't you think it would be better to insert 'Quiet, please' instead of 's-s-s-sh' there? It flows better." Hart pondered for a moment, then agreed to the change with a nod.

"I think, too," Kaufman said, "that we'll need a new exit line for John Hoysradt [as Beverly Carlton]. Something with a little more bite."

Hart retreated to the back of the theatre, pacing back and forth, conceiving a new exit line while Kaufman continued to watch the actors from his seat in the front row.

Kaufman and Hart regarded the script they had written only as the clay from which the performance would emerge. Many lines were changed during rehearsals as the authors heard their words spoken. Neither collaborator hesitated a moment to change the wording of a line—or to add new lines—if the alteration would improve the production.

Periodically, the authors would turn the rehearsal over to Hart's brother Bernie, who served as stage manager, while they repaired to Sam Harris's office for a rewriting session. They would emerge with freshly typed pages that would then be distributed to the actors. Sometimes the rewrites took the form of cutting extraneous material; sometimes they shifted the focus of a scene from one character to another; sometimes they expanded on points that needed elaboration. According to Morton Eustis, who observed the rehearsals, the rewrites invariably improved the play, making it clearer, funnier, sharper.

Whenever a visitor sat in on a rehearsal, Kaufman and Hart were concerned to find exactly where a laugh occurred on a given line. Then the playing of the moment would be constructed to lead to the laugh. This might involve telling an actor to emphasize a certain word or to take a breath at a specific moment.

"So it goes," said Morton Eustis, "day in, day out, for three weeks: heightening here, keying it down here, building it up, tearing it down, and cutting, cutting, cutting."

Pre-Broadway performances began in Hartford, Connecticut, in September 1939, followed by a two-week run in Boston, opening on September 25. Few changes were needed, although performing before a live audience necessitated inevitable modifications. At times, despite the elaborate preparation, a laugh did not occur where Kaufman thought it would, or the audience responded more enthusiastically to a moment than had been anticipated. The unexpected reactions prompted alterations in the rehearsals that continued to be conducted before the show arrived in New York.

One significant change in Hartford involved the introduction of the mummy case in which Lorraine is carried out of the Stanleys' house. The original scheme—Banjo's wrapping Lorraine in a blanket with the help of a bizarre surrealist painter named Miguel Santos (a parody of Salvador Dalí)—proved to be insufficiently funny, resulting in Santos's character being written out of the play. Introducing a new scene required time, and Sam Harris postponed the New York opening from October 10 to October 16.

Another improvement had nothing to do with rewriting. In Boston, Kaufman and Hart were puzzled by the variation in Monty Woolley's performances; one night his timing was perfect, the next night it would be a trifle off. At last they realized that the variation could be traced to whether or not he had had a cocktail before dinner. Neither Kaufman nor Hart was brave enough to confront Woolley directly, but asked Edith Atwater to be their emissary. She complied, and there was no more drinking before performances.

When the play opened at the Music Box on October 16, 1939, the production, though a good deal sharper for its out-of-town run, was substantially the same as the play that had been rehearsed in New York.

Richard Watts in *The New York Herald-Tribune* called *The Man Who Came to Dinner* "genuinely hilarious . . . good, smart, brittle fun." He found the play "decidedly funnier, if far less likable than *You Can't Take It With You.*" Richard Lockridge, critic for the *New York Sun* described the play as "joltingly funny . . . great fun." John Mason Brown's review in the *Post* said *The Man Who Came to Dinner* was "as gay, giddy, and delectable a comedy as our stage has seen in years." Brooks Atkinson described the piece as "the funniest play of this season . . . a fantastic piece of nonsense, with enough plot to serve and a succession of witty rejoinders to keep it hilarious." All the critics praised the actors, particularly Monty Woolley, and Kaufman's first-rate direction.

One evening early in the run Noël Coward sat next to Hart, who was a bit apprehensive about Coward's reaction to Cole Porter's parody of his songwriting style. "I got it immediately," Coward said, "and I pinched Moss Hart. It was devastatingly right."

So successful was *The Man Who Came to Dinner* that the audience did not mind when one performance was delayed until nine o'clock so that Monty Woolley could appear on the radio program *Information Please*. Although the curtain time had been advertised in advance, speakers were set up onstage to broadcast the radio program for the benefit of viewers who had missed the announcement and arrived at eight o'clock.

After the failures of *The Fabulous Invalid* and *The American Way*, the success of *The Man Who Came to Dinner* was particularly gratifying to its authors. Kaufman said that he preferred *The Man Who Came to Dinner* to *You Can't Take It With You*. Hart said that *The Man Who Came to Dinner* represented the partnership's best work. The run of the play on Broadway exceeded that of any Kaufman–Hart collaboration except *You Can't Take It With You*, playing for 739 performances, an exceptionally long run in 1939–40.[3]

Like *You Can't Take It With You*, *The Man Who Came to Dinner* has been performed at various educational and regional theatres throughout the United States for many years. And, unlike the earlier play, *The Man Who Came to Dinner* was as successful in England in its first production there as it was in the United States.

When plans were being made for American road companies, Alexander Woollcott decided that he was now ready to play Sheridan Whiteside. His first choice was to play the role in Chicago, but Clifton Webb had already been cast in that production (which ultimately toured to Pittsburgh, Toronto, Detroit, and Rochester, among other places). Thus Woollcott played Whiteside in the West Coast tour, with the understanding that he would repeat the role on the East Coast afterward. Kaufman and Hart both traveled to Los Angeles to supervise rehearsals.

Woollcott wrote to Beatrice Kaufman on January 28 that he was "wrestling silently with an attack of asthma," but that, otherwise, things were going well. "We seem to rehearse quite a lot," he said, adding that he hoped Beatrice would not see the play until San Francisco, by which time Woollcott was confident that his portrayal would be polished. The first West Coast performance was given in Santa Barbara on February 9, 1940, with Kaufman, Hart, and Sam Harris among those in attendance.

---

3 When the play gave its seven-hundredth performance on June 11, 1941, it became the eleventh longest-running play in Broadway history to that time.

The production arrived in Los Angeles on February 12. Woollcott fought through a case of laryngitis to give what a reviewer termed "a vastly entertaining performance, though a few captious folk who had seen the New York production were heard to say that he seemed less like Alexander Woollcott, somehow, than Monty Woolley does." Cheered by the audience during the curtain calls, Woollcott stepped forward to announce that he planned to sue the authors for $150,000 (echoing his line in the play). Among the laughter was heard one loud boo, which, witnesses said, came from the general direction of Harpo Marx.

Woollcott's voice failed him entirely on February 15, whereupon Kaufman stepped in to play Whiteside for a single performance. Perhaps Woollcott's illness should have made him realize that he needed to conserve his energy. Even an actor in good physical shape must be careful not to exhaust himself too greatly, and Woollcott, vastly overweight and underexercised, was in dreadful shape. Moreover, he refused to cut back on his other activities, so that he was busy from early morning until after each evening's performance. On February 19 he wrote to his friend, the actress Cornelia Otis Skinner, "The playing time in the theatre uses up so few hours out of a man's day that I have more time for writing than I have things to say, and as much opportunity for broadcasting as I want."

Still, Woollcott delighted in playing the role, even if he realized his own limitations as an actor. In a letter to Beatrice Kaufman from San Francisco on April 1, he confessed, "You may take it from me that I was pretty lousy" in the early performances. He believed that he improved, however: "It was at Fresno that I began to be comparatively good, and by this time I am giving a performance I wouldn't mind your seeing."

Hart did not see Woollcott at his self-professed best. He and Kaufman both returned to New York on February 19 while the production was still in Los Angeles. Eventually, Woollcott achieved a level of excellence that might have surprised even the authors. Reviewing his performance in April, Cecil Smith, writing in the *Chicago Tribune*, acknowledged that Woollcott was "only partly an actor" but "somehow," he said, "his Sheridan Whiteside emerges a fully delineated and greatly lovable figure, testy and childish, enamored of his own verbal gifts of vindictive metaphor and vivid pictorial imagery, yet withal completely human and quite worth all the fuss that is made about him." Although Smith felt that Woollcott's portrayal lacked "acerbity and callous cynicism," he preferred Woollcott's performance to that of Monty Woolley.

Woollcott was struck down by a heart attack on April 23. Sam Harris, Kaufman, and Hart realized that Woollcott's presence had by that time become a prime source of audience interest and that closing the play for a time would be wiser than substituting another actor. The road production closed and Woollcott, after several weeks in the hospital, returned to Bomoseen, his summer home in Vermont, for a lengthy recuperation. By September he had shed more than thirty pounds and had begun to feel substantially better.

Sam Harris insisted that the actors receive only one-eighth of their salaries during Woollcott's hospital stay. Actors' Equity objected and Harris was required to fully compensate the performers.

By the end of 1940, Woollcott announced that he was ready to resume playing Sheridan Whiteside. *The Man Who Came to Dinner*, with Woollcott in the leading role, began its East Coast tour in Philadelphia in January, 1941.

The following month, the company was playing in Washington, D.C. Woollcott wrote to Lynn Fontanne on February 21 that the week before, Hart, "thinking to surprise everybody," flew in for the first performance, "greedily intent on responding to the first cry of 'Author! Author!' which might be raised on the opening night. Unfortunately he got the wrong week and swept up to the National Theatre only to find it occupied by *Tobacco Road*."

Woollcott received a favorable notice from the critic for *The Washington Post*. Although there were times "when Mr. Woollcott may be deemed a bit on the elocutionary side, there are a great many more times when he seems to be exclusively and explosively himself. . . . Mr. Woollcott is a tremendously acceptable Mr. Woollcott."

Franklin D. Roosevelt attended a public performance of *The Man Who Came to Dinner* on February 25, marking only the third time Roosevelt had gone to the theatre as president. One hopes that he liked what he saw or conversation would have been strained afterward, for Woollcott stayed at the White House during the run of the play in Washington.

In Baltimore on February 9, 1941, Woollcott gave a curtain speech after the performance: "Due to the magnificent reception given us by this audience," he said, "I feel called upon to deny a nasty rumor which has been circulated about this character. Sheridan Whiteside is actually a composite of the two authors, and he combines, although you may find it hard to believe, the best features of each."

Another stop on the tour was Montreal. As Woollcott told the writer Alan Campbell (Dorothy Parker's husband) in a letter, "As Canada was then at war and we were not, I naturally felt uncomfortable at the prospect of our raiding Canada and carrying off some of their money." Hart, Kaufman, and Harris all felt the same, and all donated their salaries and their percentages to British War Relief. The Queen's Canadian Fund received a total of $7,500.

Woollcott was again hospitalized in April, 1942. As he wrote to his friend, Lady Sybil Colefax, "The hospital was in Syracuse, N.Y., where I had played *The Man Who Came to Dinner* myself. More recently, the enormously successful movie of it has made it familiar to everybody. In consequence, each of the three nurses summoned to the job when I arrived went on duty most apprehensively, probably each with a dirk [dagger] concealed in her stocking."

Among the many subsequent performances of *The Man Who Came to Dinner* was a production in late July 1941, at the Bucks County Playhouse, in which Kaufman played Whiteside, Hart played Beverly Carlton, Edith Atwater reprised her role of Maggie Cutler, and Harpo Marx himself played Banjo. A large contingent of Broadway theatregoers traveled to Bucks County on opening night. Among those who attended were Oscar Levant, Max Gordon, Brian Aherne, Kurt Weill, Michael Todd, and Hassard Short.

Harpo was, of course, famous for not issuing a word in his performances, so, for many who saw the performance, they heard his voice for the first time. Memorization was not easy for him, but he learned his lines perfectly, threw in a good deal of comic business not in the original script, and did a thoroughly creditable job. Most viewers felt that his performance was the clear highlight of the production.

Requests for tickets by Kaufman and Hart's Pennsylvania friends and neighbors was intense. Several matinees were added to satisfy the demand, but many customers had to be turned away.

On July 14, 1941, Hart played Whiteside for a week at the Cape Playhouse in Dennis, Massachusetts. Edith Atwater, who was seldom out of Hart's view in the late 1930s and early 1940s, played Maggie. On the opening night, Hart's false beard began slipping during the first act and he played the remainder of the act with his chin in his hand. Despite that handicap, he seems to have given a strong performance, if the critic of the *Cape Cod Standard-Times* can be believed. Hart's Whiteside, said the critic, "was not the portly, explosive gentleman of culture of Monty Woolley on the New York stage, but it was a genuine portrait of the talented old scoundrel, suave, mellow-voiced, incisive and cynical." The notice was not entirely favorable, however. "What the characterization needs is more force on occasion, more of the explosive quality that Woolley had," the critic noted. "However," he said, "some may prefer

[Hart's interpretation] to Woolley's. For an actor's first night," he concluded, "it was a remarkable performance."

Still again, a writer attempted to bring suit against Kaufman and Hart for stealing his idea. Vincent McConnor and two others had written a play entitled *Sticks and Stones* and sent it to Kaufman in 1936, attempting to generate his interest in collaborating with them. McConnor's partners refused to join in the suit, but McConnor charged that their play's main character, like *The Man Who Came to Dinner*, was based upon Alexander Woollcott. Kaufman testified that he had turned McConnor's script, unread, over to his secretary, who wrote "a polite note" to McConnor. The secretary corroborated Kaufman's testimony. Accepting Kaufman's word, the judge dismissed the case.

Although Kaufman and Hart had often shown their disdain for movies in the past, they announced in March 1940, that they planned to be intimately involved with the film version of *The Man Who Came to Dinner*. They would write it, they said, direct it, and, with Sam Harris, produce it. The filming was planned for the summer of 1941.

Warner Bros. purchased the film rights to the play for $275,000—then a record amount—but the project was jeopardized when Woollcott, asked to give his permission for a film to be made based on himself, refused to do so. He was afraid, he said, that the character in the movie might be changed in such a way as to subject him to ridicule. Perhaps, however, his greater wish was to force Kaufman and Hart to express their gratitude to him for allowing the play to go forward in the first place. "I thought and still think of [the $12,375 Warners offered him] as a token payment acknowledging the considerable indebtedness to me in the matter of the whole venture, which neither you nor Hart had ever recognized or at least admitted," Woollcott told Kaufman.

At last, however, Woollcott agreed to give his permission. But he took a bit of revenge when he invited Hart to sit on the platform during one of Woollcott's lectures, at the end of which Hart was to offer a few remarks. During the lecture, Woollcott began without introducing Hart, seated beside him, but Moss was not perturbed, knowing that he would be introduced when Woollcott's lecture concluded. However, Woollcott ended by saying to the audience, "I'm sure you're wondering who this young man is who has been sitting here all evening. Well, so am I." And with that he waddled off the platform, leaving Hart red-faced in his chair.

Casting an actor to play Whiteside in the film proved difficult, for, as *The New York Times* reported in May 1940, "The press representatives of many of the screen's major actors have hinted darkly that Warners were pleading with their clients to accept the role"—which, decoded, meant that their clients were vying for the part. Among them were John Barrymore, Orson Welles, Charles Laughton, and Robert Benchley. The one actor who openly declared his interest was Hart's old friend from New York, Cary Grant.

In March 1941, the studio announced that Grant would play the role, necessitating a considerable revision in the scenario. Kaufman and Hart saw the play slipping away from them, and their desire to make the film diminished. They withdrew in December 1940. The responsibility for writing the screenplay was assigned to Julius G. and Philip J. Epstein. In their version, Whiteside and Maggie Cutler (who, sources indicated, would probably be performed by Rosalind Russell, although some rumors suggested that Olivia De Havilland would play the role) would be romantically involved. The Epsteins explained that the film would be much like *His Girl Friday*, in which the leading man prevents the leading lady from marrying a rival in order to win her himself.

Howard Hawks had agreed to direct the film if Cary Grant could be persuaded to play Whiteside. Undoubtedly, a film along the lines of *His Girl Friday*, which had been directed by Hawks, with Grant and Russell in the leading roles, would have been enormously entertaining. But it would not have retained the comic flavor of the Kaufman and Hart play.

A conflict about the casting broke out at Warner Bros. One faction favored Grant, while the other hoped that Whiteside would be played by—or at least in the manner of—Monty Woolley.

As a result of the controversy, Cary Grant withdrew on April 8, 1941, reopening the possibility that the film would be a reflection rather than a distortion of the play. Eventually, Warners decided to reproduce the play as faithfully as possible in the movie. William Keighley was assigned to direct. Monty Woolley replaced Cary Grant as Whiteside. Bette Davis was cast as Maggie Cutler, Reginald Gardner as Beverly Carlton, Ann Sheridan as Lorraine Sheldon, and Jimmy Durante—whose character seemed to be much more like Jimmy Durante than Harpo Marx—played Banjo. The movie successfully reproduced the madcap atmosphere of the play, with few changes to the original Kaufman and Hart script.

Bosley Crowther of *The New York Times* called the movie "the niftiest comedy of 1942 . . . here, in the space of something like an hour and fifty-two minutes, is compacted what is unquestionably the most vicious but hilarious cat-clawing exhibition ever put on the screen, a deliciously wicked character portrait and a helter-skelter satire, withal."

Unlike most films, *The Man Who Came to Dinner* is largely confined to a single room, but the limitation doesn't harm the movie at all. The tempo of the film is breakneck, as was the rhythm of the Broadway production. Although the picture does not precisely duplicate the stage production, cutting some lines thought to be too racy for the movie audience here, adding a bit of business there, it does not stray far. Bosley Crowther was especially taken by Monty Woolley's performance: "His zest for rascality is delightful, he spouts alliterations as though he were spitting out orange seeds . . ." In all, Crowther said, the film, like the play, is very much like a "river of incidents and wisecracks plunging over a precipice."

The most notable performance in the film, other than Woolley's, was not delivered by any of the newcomers but by Ruth Vivian, who repeated her Broadway role as Harriet. Her ethereal portrayal, with just a hint of madness, is perfection.

The play also marked a turning point for Hart, although the result was not immediately apparent. He found that the ambition that had sustained him for so long seemed to have lost its luster. He was no longer stage-struck. The excitement of writing one play or musical after another, being hailed as a theatrical prodigy, maintaining the life of a celebrity and a wit, suddenly all seemed a bit hollow. He saw before him the prospect of churning out one comedy after another and found it bleak. What had once been thrilling would, he feared, become routine. Perhaps his collaboration with Kaufman, successful although it frequently was, had led him to this point. He saw the need to break free, to move in a new and different direction.

But breaking up, as they say, is hard to do. Hart was not quite ready to sever his partnership with Kaufman, but the inevitability of the break was clear. *The Man Who Came to Dinner*, in which all their comic gifts were utilized to the fullest, was the final great achievement of the partnership, for, although they did write one more comedy, it was a pale imitation of their earlier works and a clear signal to Hart that he needed creative stimulation that Kaufman could no longer provide.

The Kaufman–Hart partnership continued, if briefly, but the same cannot be said of Hart's relationship with Edith Atwater. The beautiful, dark-haired thirty-year-old actress married the actor Hugh Marlowe in November 1941, an event that took Hart by surprise. Jerome Chodorov, Hart's friend, recalled in 1999 that Hart was shocked and upset when he heard the news. Indeed, when Hart saw Marlowe (who was no longer married to Atwater) at a cocktail party in January 1954, Hart confided to his diary that he vividly remembered his "feelings of deep hostility toward [Marlowe] when he was married to Edith Atwater."[4]

∾

The United States did not become a participant in the war until the attack on Pearl Harbor in December 1941, of course, but the fighting in Europe was a great concern to Hart, as it was to millions of other Americans. Early in 1941 he volunteered to serve on a committee of the American Theatre Wing, attempting to raise funds for British War Relief. In March of that year, he and Kaufman took part in a benefit performance.

They were also looking for an idea for a new play. Their reputations secure as the masters of madcap comedy, the partners felt impelled to write another one—precisely the sort of trap Hart feared falling into. The expectation of the public was that their collaboration would continue indefinitely, turning out one comic masterpiece after another.

After working for a time on an outline about the comic adventures of customers in a barbershop, they rejected it as unsatisfactory, turning instead to a plot that drew inspiration from their own adventures as scions of country estates.

The idea that led to *George Washington Slept Here* seemed promising. Hart's experience as the purchaser of an old house on a farm in the country had cost him not only a fortune to refurbish but a great deal of time. Kaufman, too, had been through much the same process, although, unlike Hart, he left the details of the renovation to his wife. Their combined misadventures held the potential for a rollicking comedy. The notion of a city-dweller who attempts to combine the pleasures of rural living with the comfort of the city in an old, ramshackle house in which George Washington supposedly once slept, was, they felt, a promising idea. Furthermore, the set would be designed to resemble Hart's country house, even to the stone fireplace and the Dutch door to the living room. One can imagine the authors' and designer's enjoyment over the inside joke that would be gotten only by those few who had visited Fairview Farm.

But both playwrights must have felt that something was intrinsically wrong with the play. Even during the writing of *George Washington Slept Here*, Hart was thinking as much about his next enterprise—one that would, once and for all, establish his individuality as a playwright—as he was about the collaboration with Kaufman. For several reasons, Hart realized that he could

---

4 After divorcing Marlowe, Edith Atwater remarried twice. She died of cancer in Los Angeles in 1986, at the age of seventy-four.

no longer postpone severing his professional relationship with Kaufman. For one, the collaboration was no longer yielding fresh material. Second, he had long been advised by friends and by professional counselors that he should establish his own identity as a playwright. Perhaps most important, he wished to explore ideas that Kaufman did not care to investigate. Foremost among them was Hart's interest in psychoanalysis. He and Kaufman had made an attempt to use psychoanalysis as the basis of a musical, but Kaufman's lack of interest in the subject prevented its achievement. Working on his own, however, Hart could explore the territory that the partnership had made impossible.

This must have been the subject of many of Hart's sessions with Dr. Lawrence Kubie, for in 1941, the psychoanalyst advised Hart that his psychological well-being depended on his breaking with Kaufman.[5]

Thus, Hart told Kaufman that he was formulating ideas about the book of a musical he intended to write without Kaufman's help. Kaufman may have realized that their collaboration was soon to be at an end, but, although he offered no resistance when Hart said that he would be embarking on projects independently, he clearly wished otherwise. Losing his longtime partner, the collaborator with whom he felt most comfortable, was a blow, according to his daughter, Anne Kaufman Schneider.

Joseph Fields and Jerome Chodorov asked Hart to direct their new play, *My Sister Eileen*—but even Hart realized that that would be one project too many. Instead, he passed the play on to Max Gordon with the suggestion that Kaufman direct it, perhaps in an attempt to divert Kaufman's attention from the impending breakup of the Kaufman–Hart partnership. Kaufman agreed to direct the Fields and Chodorov comedy, and spent considerable time working with the authors on the script. No doubt *George Washington Slept Here* suffered because of both its authors' simultaneous involvement with other projects.

In the Kaufman–Hart play, Newton Fuller, a New York businessman of modest means, purchases an abandoned farmhouse in Bucks County, for he has become captivated by the sales angle that the real-estate agent successfully promoted: George Washington once slept there. Newton envisions the magnificent shape the house will take when restored, whereas Annabelle, his cynical wife, is able only to see the house's present state of dishevelment. Furthermore, she hates both the house and the idea of living in the country.

---

5 According to Scott Meredith in *George S. Kaufman and His Friends*, p. 556. Meredith contends that Dr. Gregory Zilboorg was the analyst in question, but Hart was definitely consulting Dr. Kubie in 1941.

Mr. Kimber, the property's laconic caretaker, informs Newton that there is no running water, no cesspool, no bathrooms, and no closets. And, as Newton discovers when he attempts to sit in a rocking chair, the furniture is falling apart. Still, his enthusiasm is undimmed, although it is tested when, a month later, Mr. Kimber announces that the cost of the renovation will be far higher than originally anticipated, the well diggers have not yet located water, the trees Newton has planted are in danger of being blighted, and the seventeen-year locusts have arrived. And the worst blow of all occurs when Newton is told by a neighbor that George Washington never slept in the house; Benedict Arnold did.

After two months, the house has been made attractive and livable but is still without water. Newton's bank account is exhausted, a payment of five thousand dollars to the bank is due, and his only hope is to persuade his wealthy uncle Stanley, from whom he expects a generous inheritance, to give Newton a sizable advance payment. But Uncle Stanley informs the astounded Newton and Annabelle that he went broke in 1929 and hasn't got "a God-damned cent."

The Newtons' daughter Madge, her boyfriend, Steve, and a group of their friends figure in the plot, but their presence has little to do with the play's central premise. Their existence adds nothing to the play and is often simply distracting. The same can be said of many of the other subsidiary characters. Katie, the cook; Raymond, Annabelle's obnoxious fifteen-year-old nephew; Rena, an actress with the local summer stock company; her vain husband, Clayton, and others, all seem to have wandered in from a different play—*You Can't Take It With You* or *The Man Who Came to Dinner*, perhaps.

The playwrights employ theatrical effects in an attempt to animate the comedy. Act One ends with a bolt of lightning; later, Newton chases a man who's running off with his daughter with a rifle he grabs from the mantelpiece; and the play concludes with the characters drunkenly destroying the house, even to the point of chopping holes in the roof and the walls with an axe, allowing rain from a hurricane to flood the premises. But all of these devices add up to very little. George S. Kaufman's daughter, Anne, who has seen many productions of *George Washington Slept Here*, says that audiences invariably respond negatively to the ending. "It's not funny," she says, "and people don't like it."

A few moderately funny scenes enliven the proceedings, but, all in all, it is an uninspired piece of work. Many of the scenes have no organic relationship to the dramatic action, and thus serve only as fillers. The flaws in the comedy would almost certainly have been capable of repair by a fully committed Kaufman and Hart, as they had demonstrated so often in the past. But with both the partners distracted, the flaws simply overwhelmed the play.

Nor was the rehearsal process satisfying. Jean Dixon, as Annabelle, playing a role similar to the one she had played a decade earlier in *Once in a Lifetime*, was wary about repeating herself. Moreover, she did not get along with Ernest Truex, who played Newton; and Truex was resentful that Dixon had been given the funniest lines and attempted, through the use of extraneous business, to draw attention to himself. Dixon argued so vehemently with Kaufman that some of her dialogue was tasteless that she walked out of rehearsal, announcing that she was withdrawing from the play. The argument was patched up and she returned, but an atmosphere of tension never abated throughout rehearsals. When the play ran in New Haven during its out-of-town tryout, she again requested that Kaufman and Hart let her go. She and Truex were still battling and she could foresee no resolution. However, Kaufman insisted that she honor her contract.

The play opened in Hartford on September 21, 1940, where, despite a favorable response from audiences, its weaknesses became apparent to the authors. However, the modifications made in Hartford, New Haven, and Boston were not enough to rescue a show that was as ramshackle as the building Newton and Anabelle Fuller were attempting to renovate.

Truex severely sprained his ankle in Boston, forcing a cancellation of a performance. He was indulging in some blocking of his own invention, trying to get a laugh by stepping from a table onto a wheelbarrow—a bit of business that Kaufman had tried to cut, fearing that it could result in just the sort of accident that occurred. Although an understudy traveled with the company, he could not take Truex's place because Kaufman and Hart had revised the play so frequently that the understudy had not had time to learn the lines. The play, scheduled to open on Broadway on October 7, was postponed for a week.

A second postponement was forced when Berton Churchill, playing Uncle Stanley, died on October 10. Churchill, sixty-four years old, was found unconscious in his room at the Hotel Lincoln. He was taken to the hospital, but died of uremic poisoning. Dudley Digges, the actor cast in Churchill's place, was given a week to rehearse the role.

Once again, Sam Harris displayed an ungenerous spirit after Digges's week of rehearsal. He claimed that the cast was not entitled to be paid for the week, since Churchill's death was "an act of God." Again, Actors' Equity filed a formal objection, causing Harris's decision to be overturned.

At the premiere of *George Washington Slept Here* on October 18, the play was coolly received by most critics. While Sidney Whipple of the *World-Telegram* appreciated it ("a thoroughly enjoyable play and one full of laughter") and Richard Watts Jr. of the *Herald-Tribune* found it "vastly amusing" if "pretty mechanical," Burns Mantle's review in the *Daily News* called the play "Class B Kaufman-Hart," Richard Lockridge said in the *Sun* that the authors' previous successes had caused him to hope for more than "a moderately amusing little play" and John Mason Brown of the *Post* found that it could "not hold a candle to *The Man Who Came to Dinner*, [nor is it] to be mentioned in the same breath with *You Can't Take It With You*."

But it was left to Brooks Atkinson to offer the most thoroughly negative opinion. Atkinson called *George Washington Slept Here* "a labored and empty enterprise [which] reaches to the bottom of the barrel . . . Mr. Kaufman and Mr. Hart have gone through the motions of playwriting without taking much fresh enjoyment in what they are doing."

Truex's attempts to win laughs for himself at the expense of the other performers were successful at least as far as Atkinson was concerned, for the critic lauded Truex's performance as the best the actor had ever given. Still, the performer most often singled out for praise by the critics was Percy Kilbride—not yet famous as a result of the "Ma and Pa Kettle" movies—as the doleful Mr. Kimber.

Generally, Kaufman and Hart's plays went on extensive tours after their Broadway productions. *George Washington Slept Here* was an exception, for the peculiar reason that this one-set comedy—normally the dream of a producer who wishes to send a play on tour—was simply too expensive to operate profitably. Turning the chaos in the farmhouse of Act One to the tidy, well-decorated look of Act Two during a brief intermission required twenty-three stagehands (as compared to nineteen actors).

For unfathomable reasons, *George Washington Slept Here* proved to be a bonanza in summer stock and in community theatres. More productions of *George Washington Slept Here* were performed in stock in 1941 than any other play. Again in 1942, the play proved wildly successful in stock.

Warner Bros., having made an enormous profit from the film of *The Man Who Came to Dinner*, bought the rights to *George Washington Slept Here* for $250,000 and made a rather pallid film comedy featuring Jack Benny and Ann Sheridan—reversing the situation so that the wife wanted the house and the husband was the skeptic. Percy Kilbride again played Mr. Kimber. In general, critics thought no more of the movie than they had of the play, although in at least three respects, the film improved on the stage comedy. The extraneous characters are either minimized, or—in the case of Madge's friends—eliminated altogether; and when Newton (renamed Bill in the film) pursues Madge's suitor with a rifle, the business culminates in a reasonably clever joke, whereas the action in the play led nowhere. Best of all, the characters do not demolish the house at the end of the film.

The wellsprings of creativity had obviously run dry with *George Washington Slept Here*. Every other play written by Kaufman and Hart had been adventurous, an attempt to explore new territory. Several of the plays—*Merrily We Roll Along*, *I'd Rather Be Right*, *The Fabulous Invalid*, and *The American Way*—had not been successful, but each represented an attempt to say something the partners felt needed saying, in a new and different way. *George Washington Slept Here*, on the other hand, was little more than formulaic, warmed-over material, the characters far less well-developed than those in *Once in a Lifetime*, *You Can't Take It With You*, and *The Man Who Came to Dinner*, the situation formulated no more skillfully than had been done by a hundred writers of comedy before.

Kaufman's unhappiness at the end of his professional relationship with Hart was, at least in part, based on his genuine affection for Moss. Various aspects of Hart's personality and activities amused Kaufman. "Nothing happens to Moss in the simple and ordinary terms in which it happens to the average person," he said. "The most normal of human experiences is crowded with drama where Moss is concerned."

For example, Kaufman enjoyed telling about Hart's marathon visits to his dentists. One visit lasted from eleven o'clock in the morning until nine o'clock at night—and Hart, certain that Kaufman would not believe him, had his dentists (for there were several of them, working on him in relays) sign an affadavit certifying that Hart had actually been in the dentist's chair for ten hours. And that visit paled in comparison to a later one, when the appointment began at 10 A.M. and lasted until two o'clock in the morning.

In March 1942, Hart underwent more marathon sessions with his dentist. So debilitating were they that he was unable to think about writing a play. "But if I were," he told a friend, "I have the title. It's *The Yanks Are Coming*."

George S. Kaufman continued to write plays with other collaborators, but his remaining plays reveal all too clearly how much he missed Moss Hart. Still, Kaufman and Hart remained close friends, visiting each other's houses several times a week, holding daily telephone conversations, and, whenever one of them was traveling, exchanging letters.

However, Hart, who needed Kaufman's approval as a father-figure and an icon as well as his friend and partner, wished that Kaufman would at least occasionally show some sign of warmth. Although Kaufman felt closer to Hart than to any other man, their relationship did not include genuine intimacy, for Kaufman simply would not permit it.

Soon after the fiasco of *The Fabulous Invalid*, Hart dined with Kaufman before leaving New York on what Hart described as "a long journey—a difficult journey—for me. George knew the import of that journey. I did not spend that last evening in New York with my family," he said. "I spent it with George, for George in many ways was more father to me than my own father." Hart hoped for some advice or, at the least, for some word from Kaufman that he would be missed, but Kaufman said nothing. "Not once," said Hart, "did he mention my leave-taking or the reason for my going. When it came time to go, he saw me to the door, and lifted that inevitable finger of his in his gesture of goodbye. That was all." Hart left feeling dejected, even bitter. But, when he arrived home, "there on my desk was a three-page, single-spaced typewritten letter, hand-delivered while he had sat opposite me saying nothing of what he felt— the letter saying what he found himself incapable of saying to me face-to-face. How sad that he should have known that he could not say the words to me himself, but how marvelous that he should have written the letter beforehand." Kaufman's daughter, Anne, says that the story gibes with her recollection of Hart's relationship with her father. Kaufman "really loved Moss," she said. But if Hart had any problems, Kaufman "wouldn't have wanted to hear about it. He didn't like getting involved. He was very austere, my father. I adored my father," she added, "but warm he wasn't."

However, the public image of Kaufman and Hart in the early 1940s was that of intimate friends, noted wits, and men about town. Their lives were well-chronicled, their ideas accorded considerable attention, their witticisms regularly recorded.

Although they were to write no more plays together, no announcement to that effect was ever made, and the public still thought of them as a team. Their working relationship fascinated readers and theatregoers. People wanted to know what Hart brought to the collaboration and which contributions were Kaufman's. One writer conjectured that "Mr. Kaufman supplies the discipline and Mr. Hart the spirit." Or, as others maintained, Hart supplied the ideas and Kaufman wrote all the funny lines. Was Kaufman alone responsible for the rewriting or did Hart do his part as well, others wondered. In fact, the partnership of Kaufman and Hart was a true collaboration, an intermingling of concept and language, each man contributing significantly. As Hart said (and Kaufman agreed):

> . . . every line and idea, including the idea of the play itself, was so tightly woven into the mosaic of collaboration that it would be impossible to tell who suggested which or what, or how one line sprang full-blown from another. When the basic idea of a play was a good one, our collaboration worked well, and when it was not, it did not work at all. The mechanics of collaboration in the plays we did together remained as simple as putting a fresh sheet of paper into the typewriter and laboriously plugging away until that page satisfied both of us.

Different plays required different methods, but Brooks Atkinson's description of their working relationship offers several useful generalizations:

> They first discuss various ideas casually, sometimes letting an idea develop at random for several months before they take it seriously. When they feel that an idea has become sufficiently tangible, they go to work on a daily schedule in some place where they can be free from interruption. . . . At first they continue talking for two or three weeks, hoping to enlarge and clarify the idea and to run up stray notions into fantastification. The whole thing begins to change proportion and direction once they get both heads working at it systematically. When the details of character and narrative have begun to take shape, Mr. Kaufman and Mr. Hart start putting them on paper, Mr. Kaufman usually sitting at the typewriter, Mr. Hart roaming the house and hoping for interruptions. An orderly person who likes to attack everything on plan, Mr. Kaufman feels happy if they produce four pages a day. They are likely to overwrite the first draft, confident that it is easier to improve a play by cutting than by expanding.

The authors always had elements of production in mind when they were writing a play. Early in the process, sometimes even before they began composing dialogue, they would consider the actors they wished to cast. They also envisioned a specific space for the play they were creating, writing with the Music Box Theatre in mind or the Alvin or the Winter Garden. In many cases the playhouse itself would help determine the shape the play would take. An intimate theatre like the Music Box demanded an intimate play (although "intimate" for Moss Hart was always a relative term, for his smallest plays required significant numbers of actors); a vast space such as the Winter Garden required a more spectacular production. The scale of Hart's plays—those he wrote with George S. Kaufman as well as the others—tended to be immense: large casts calling for great numbers of costumes, and numerous, often highly elaborate sets. But Hart was not deterred by size and complexity. If anything, they seem to have fired his imagination. He loved to tax the theatre's resources to their fullest extent.

☙

The Kaufman–Hart partnership produced some plays that could reasonably be called comic masterpieces (*Once in a Lifetime, You Can't Take It With You, The Man Who Came to Dinner*), and it is for those plays the team will be remembered and admired. It is astonishing, however, how extraordinarily threadbare some of their collaborations (*Merrily We Roll Along, The Fabulous Invalid, The American Way, George Washington Slept Here*) were. It is difficult to think of another writer or writing team, from any era, writing in any genre, whose work was so remarkably uneven. Still, the partners will forever be remembered for their successes.

Kaufman's impact on Hart's life and career was great. He served as a mentor on several levels: as a playwright, as a director, and as a father figure. Without Kaufman, Hart would probably never have achieved a breakthrough with *Once in a Lifetime*, the success that made all his future successes possible. Although Hart was now determined to strike out on his own, his debt to Kaufman was—as he realized—incalculable.

INTERMISSION

Moss Hart was a social creature, and, when he himself was not giving a party, he rarely turned down an invitation. In fact, he spent so much time giving and attending parties that one sometimes wonders how he found time to work at all. But his socializing must have nourished his creativity in some way, for the amount of work he produced indicates how often he was able to channel his energy and intensity into his writing.

However, the drive to work continually took a steadily mounting toll. Although to the outside world Hart was everything he wished to be—witty, charming, dashing, theatrical, sophisticated—he paid for his suave exterior with inner turmoil. The depression that made it difficult to get through so much as a day without a visit to his psychoanalyst was only the most visible manifestation of his need for perpetual activity and continued success. He was compulsively neat and suffered when anyone else failed to meet his standards of orderliness. He was unable to break his habit of smoking—cigars, especially when he was young, cigarettes, and a pipe (or, rather, pipes, for he owned more than a hundred of them). Smoking contributed, to a degree, to the sophisticated image he wished to create, but it contributed also to a history of illness, as did his propensity for eating the richest foods.

Hart's chronic insomnia must also have made it difficult to focus on his work. The nights he spent with one or two hours of sleep—or with no sleep at all—are beyond counting. Fortunately, his enormous energy allowed him to work in spite of the weariness he often felt after a sleepless night.

Though Hart's insomnia was troubling, it also provided him with some choice anecdotes. One of his favorites concerned a Tuesday night in the 1930s in London. Exhausted by travel, social events, and professional projects, he decided that he would have to leave in the midst of a party at the Savoy Grill, return to his hotel room and get a good night's sleep—twelve hours' worth, if possible. As soon as he climbed into bed, he fell asleep, noticing, just before nodding off, that the clock on his bedstand said nine o'clock. When he awoke the next morning at nine-thirty, he was entirely refreshed. He rang Room Service, ordered a hearty breakfast and, while waiting for his breakfast to arrive, showered and shaved, whistling all the while.

When Room Service brought Hart's breakfast they also brought a newspaper. Looking at the date, he was somewhat annoyed. "You've brought me yesterday's newspaper," he said. "No, sir," came the reply, "that is this morning's newspaper." Beginning to suspect the truth, Hart asked, "What time is it?" He was told that it was ten o'clock. "What day is it?" "Tuesday, sir," came the reply. He had been asleep for exactly half an hour. After thinking over the alternatives for a moment, Hart donned his formal dress once again and re-joined the party at the Savoy Grill.

It would be wrong to conclude from this anecdote that Hart's insomnia was not a great burden to him. But because Hart spoke without hesitation about these matters—spoke wittily, charmingly about them, often turning them into delightful stories—one might be tempted to believe that his diffi-culties were not nearly as acute as they were in actuality and that his depen-dence upon psychoanalysis was merely faddish. But sleep disorders led to many nights of torment, as a perusal of the diary he kept for one year in the 1950s indicates. "Again no sleep," he wrote on February 9, 1954; "woke up depressed . . . I have been dreaming nightmarish dreams constantly for the past week," he noted in May; "up all night and finally at about 6:30 gave up trying to sleep at all. . . . I was ill all day and unable to work" he lamented on June 16. His lack of sleep increased his need for professional psychiatric help. For Hart, psychoanalysis wasn't a matter of fashion. He could not function without it.

Perhaps the rapidity of Hart's rise contributed to his feelings of inade-quacy. One day in 1930 he had been a poor boy from the Bronx; the next he was the toast of Broadway. Indeed, these may have played some role in his ill-ness, but long afterward—when he was a successful playwright and director on his own, no longer working in collaboration with Kaufman—the need for analysis did not subside.

Hart told Beatrice Kaufman about his depressed state, and she, a psycho-analytic patient and an advocate of psychoanalysis, recommended that he consult Dr. Gregory Zilboorg. When Hart worked on the West Coast writing films, the analytical sessions continued, this time with Dr. Ernest Simmel. Later Hart became acquainted with Dr. Lawrence S. Kubie, who, he felt, had particular insight and understanding into his condition, and Hart became a regular—often daily—patient for years to come. On numerous occasions Hart began his day with a visit to Dr. Kubie and consulted him again in the late afternoon. The two of them maintained a doctor-patient relationship for years, and, for Hart, it was—other than his wife and children—the most im-portant relationship in his life. He subordinated everything else to it, includ-ing work, permitting nothing to interfere with his psychoanalytic sessions.

But Hart continued to have episodes of depression throughout the years he consulted analysts. Perhaps the problem can be attributed primarily to the analysts themselves, for two of them can be said to have had either seri-ous character flaws or to have engaged in unorthodox, possibly destructive methods—or both. Zilboorg, for example, who, in the words of Stephen Farber and Marc Green, the authors of *Hollywood on the Couch*, "was a flamboyant showman who wore a black cape and sported an enormous handlebar mustache," was accused of ethical misconduct before the New York Psychoanalytic Association. A panel of twelve psychoanalysts voted in favor of censure, but Zilboorg's threat of a lawsuit caused the full membership to drop all charges.

Kubie, described by Farber and Green as "a prickly personality [who] found himself in conflict with . . . most of his American colleagues," welcomed celebrity clients, as did Zilboorg. Both men seemed to crave the publicity and prestige that such a clientele guaranteed. Among Kubie's patients were the pianist Vladimir Horowitz and—in later years—Tennesee Williams. Both Horowitz and Williams were homosexuals, and Kubie considered homosexuality an illness to be cured. In his book, *Neurotic Distortions of the Creative Process*, he referred to "the culturally noxious assumption, devoid as far as I can see of the least fragment of truth, that one must be sick to be creative." Consequently, he encouraged Horowitz and Williams to break off their homosexual liaisons and form relationships with women. Erika Freeman, a New York analyst, maintained that Kubie advised Horowitz "to lock himself in a room whenever he felt homosexual urges coming on." In Williams's case, Kubie persuaded the playwright to break with his male lover; Williams did so, but his homosexual orientation did not change.

Celeste Holm, who knew Hart in the 1940s, believed Hart to be homosexual, but claimed that "he didn't want to be." Although she detested Kubie, she maintained that Kubie's treatments permitted Hart eventually to engage in romantic relationships with women.

One cannot know precisely what condition led Hart to seek psychoanalysis, although his anxiety that he would never be able to work creatively without collaborators seems to have played a part, as did the fear that his creative powers would one day desert him. Perhaps, too, he revealed to his analysts that he was attracted to men, but that is no more than speculation.

Hart's episodes of depression were so severe that, at one point, he even contemplated suicide. In December 1937, he wrote to his friend Dore Schary, "The going is still tough—but I can report that I'm still fighting. Last week I came very close to what is called putting an end to it all—but I threw the stuff away, and I don't think I'll ever come that close again." The following year, he told Schary, ". . . I'm making progress with the Doctor—painful and oh so slow, but I'm much better than I've been in months. At least that awful mania to destroy myself doesn't sweep over me every other night."

Although Hart often believed that he had conquered his depression and that he would one day be able to function without psychoanalysis, he was never able to enjoy life for a sustained period without falling again into despair. His illness often made it difficult for him to write. Later, in the 1940s, he underwent a long, terrible bout of writer's block. Somehow, this highly skilled playwright, with a substantial record of well-deserved success, found it nearly impossible to marshal his resources and complete a play. The result was torment.

His depression affected him in other ways as well. There were times when he thought he would be unable to function at all, so bleak was his outlook. The fact that he did function, even on his worst days, and that most people were unable to discern his distress, is a remarkable achievement in itself.

Hart never concealed the fact that he consulted Dr. Kubie on a regular basis. He freely told friends, acquaintances, and newspaper interviewers that he was undergoing, and was fascinated by, psychoanalysis. One reporter noted in 1937 that Hart was "given to talking about it on the slightest provocation or on no provocation at all." But only those closest to him were aware of the depths of the despair that would plague him when he was overcome by depression. To those who knew him at a remove he seemed perpetually genial, pleased with his lot in life, comfortable with himself and with others.

As a reporter for *The New York Times* noted when interviewing Hart for a story in 1943, "To the casual eye there is no vestige of whatever took him to a psychoanalyst in the first place. Moss Hart is an attractive-looking man in a nice Satanic way and he has an easy friendly personality with quotable witticisms popping out every three minutes." Even such an acute observer as his long-time friend and partner George S. Kaufman failed to comprehend the depths of his melancholia. Kaufman was not a believer in psychoanalysis and actively tried to dissuade Hart from participating. In a letter Kaufman wrote to his wife, Beatrice, in the late 1930s, he confessed his puzzlement about Hart's reliance on his physician. He said that he and "others who have been around him say they never see any signs of unhappiness. He looks marvelous, and to me that's that."

Success, far from being a panacea, was another source of stress for Hart. "The great mystery of unhappiness is not the story of a failure," he said. "A man who is a failure complains about fate, about bad breaks, and you can understand it. But when you're completely successful and you're unhappy, it becomes a mystery. Most of the successful people I know are unhappy." The most prized sign of Hart's success—his winning of the Pulitzer Prize for *You Can't Take It With You*—precipitated one of his worst bouts of depression. "I practically had to be carried feet first to my analyst's couch," he said.

Many years later, Hart may have discovered the dread that caused his periods of depression. He told *Esquire* magazine that his greatest anxiety was "the fear that every writer lives with. That time will pass him by, and he will, as Ben Hecht has said, 'rot upon the vine in full public view.'"

Had effective medications for anxiety and depression been available in the 1930s and '40s, Hart might not have had to rely so completely upon psychoanalysis. But such medications did not exist until a decade later. Thus, the analysts who recommended that Hart see them as frequently as every day were simply attempting to provide him with the best treatment available.[1]

On the other hand, the twice-daily regimen Dr. Kubie sometimes employed was definitely irregular. (Kurt Weill told his wife, Lotte Lenya, in 1942 that Hart spent an hour each morning and two and-a-half hours each afternoon with Kubie.) The connection between patient and physician became—or, at least, was in danger of becoming—a dependent, rather than therapeutic, relationship.

It is striking that so many of Hart's friends felt that only they knew of his depressive states. His outward geniality and easy manner convinced them that others could not possibly discern his suffering. One of them, for example, said, "I doubt if anyone . . . was aware of it." Perhaps only the most perceptive of his friends did recognize his inner torment—but Hart had a number of perceptive friends. Beatrice Kaufman was one, of course. Another, Bennett Cerf, said: "All of his life, Moss Hart suffered periodic attacks of almost unbearable depression. Analysis provided only a partial cure. Never once, however, did I know him to let his own troubles keep him from throwing himself completely into performing a task he had undertaken, or heeding a call for help from one of his innumerable friends." Dore Schary recognized "the inner struggles which [Hart] conquered by raw moral and physical courage." Brooks Atkinson also commented on Hart's "genuine and possibly dangerous" melancholia; Edna Ferber said that she was "aware of his periods of deep and terrible depression."

If Hart never hid his reliance on psychoanalysis, it is nevertheless likely that a casual acquaintance would have been unaware of his anguish, for, as

---

1 For a patient to see his or her analyst three times a week was not regarded as excessive during the 1930s and '40s, although daily visits were unusual. Less wealthy patients could not have afforded daily treatment, of course, but money was no object in Hart's case.

Alan Jay Lerner said of him, "Moss was always able to listen, sympathize, empathize and comment with perception and wit" when any of his friends was in trouble, although "When one is plagued by [the] kind of emotional anguish [Hart suffered from] there is nothing more difficult than the simple act of listening when others speak. . . . He never inflicted his suffering on others. He was the most gallant man I ever knew."

Leonora Hornblow, who first met Hart in 1938 and, with her husband Arthur, was among the Harts' closest friends, shared Lerner's view of Hart's character. "Moss had wonderful manners," she said. "He never, ever burdened you with his troubles, whether a show was going well, whether he'd had a fight with someone. He made light of it." But she was most struck by Hart's ability to listen sympathetically. "Unlike many good conversationalists," she said, "he was an attentive listener." George S. Kaufman's daughter Anne commented similarly: "He was a wonderful listener to people who had problems."

Occasionally, despite his best efforts, Hart's mask of relaxed geniality would slip. Jerome Chodorov, the brother of Eddie Chodorov and a friend of Hart's from the days they grew up in the Bronx, described a particularly revealing incident in which Hart, though in the midst of depression, made a heroic effort to conceal it:

> He tried to cover it up, but he didn't always succeed. I have a snapshot on my wall of my wife, myself and Moss at Malibu. I noticed as we sat down to have the picture taken that he was very depressed. But he forced a grin, a terrible grimace. He didn't want to be seen at any time in a state of desperation. He didn't want to look depressed, he wanted to be thought of as a happy, successful guy with no problems.

Chodorov, who himself underwent psychoanalysis for depression, spoke on occasion to Hart about their mutual difficulty. "Sometimes Moss would let down a veil," he said; "he would admit the seriousness of it." At one point Hart said to him, "I just can't seem to get over these depressions."

*Moss Hart's father, Barnett, who,
later in life, called himself "the
Commodore." Kitty Carlisle Hart said
that no one could remember why.
(Courtesy of the Moss Hart Estate)*

*Moss Hart's mother, Lily, in the 1920s.
Moss "felt sorrow for her" difficult life,
he said, "but I did not like her."
(New York Public Library)*

*Moss Hart at about age fifteen, when his
father withdrew him from school and he
began to work full-time. (Hart Estate)*

Moss Hart, far right, working at a summer camp in the 1920s. In time,
he became the most prominent social director in the Catskill resorts.
(Hart Estate)

George S. Kaufman and Moss Hart, the toast of
Broadway throughout the 1930s. (NYPL)

May 1937: Perhaps the most famous photo ever taken of George S. Kaufman and Moss Hart, Broadway's leading comedy playwrights from 1930 until they dissolved their partnership ten years later. (NYPL)

Jean Dixon (left) and Spring Byington in the original 1930 *Broadway production of Kaufman and Hart's* Once in a Lifetime, *Moss's first great success. (NYPL)*

Left to right: Sally Phipps, Charles Halton, Hugh O'Connell, and Walter Dreher in the original 1930 Broadway production of Once in a Lifetime. (NYPL)

▼ Left to right: Marilyn Miller, Clifton Webb, and Helen Broderick in the original 1933 Broadway production of Moss Hart and Irving Berlin's As Thousands Cheer. Not pictured is the fourth star of the production, Ethel Waters. (NYPL)

Walter Abel (left) and Kenneth McKenna in the original 1934 Broadway production of Kaufman and Hart's Merrily We Roll Along. *(NYPL)*

Jessie Royce Landis as Althea Royce, second from left, and other cast members in the original Broadway production of Merrily We Roll Along. *(NYPL)*

◀ *Left to right: Mitzi Hajos, George Heller, Paula Trueman, Oscar Polk, Frank Wilcox, Henry Travers (seated), and Josephine Hull in the original 1936 Broadway production of Kaufman and Hart's* You Can't Take It With You. *(NYPL)*

▼ *Kaufman and Hart (standing, center) with the entire cast of the Broadway production of* You Can't Take It With You. *Producer Sam H. Harris is center, seated at the table. (NYPL)*

▶ *Acrobats Jack Reynolds and Sol Black with George M. Cohan as Franklin Delano Roosevelt, along with Evelyn Mills (Sistie) and Warren Mills (Buzzie) in the original 1937 Broadway production of* I'd Rather Be Right. *(NYPL)*

▼ *Showstopper George M. Cohan in his masterful portrayal of FDR in the 1937 production of Kaufman and Hart's* I'd Rather Be Right, *with songs by Richard Rodgers and Lorenz Hart. (NYPL)*

◄ *Fredric March and Florence Eldridge as settled grandparents in the original 1939 Broadway production of Kaufman and Hart's* The American Way. *(NYPL)*

▼ *An example of the lavish sets featured in the original 1938 Broadway production of Kaufman and Hart's* The Fabulous Invalid. *(NYPL)*

*Mary Wickes as Miss Preen and
Monty Woolley as Sheridan Whiteside
in the original 1939 Broadway
production of Kaufman and Hart's*
The Man Who Came to Dinner.
(NYPL)

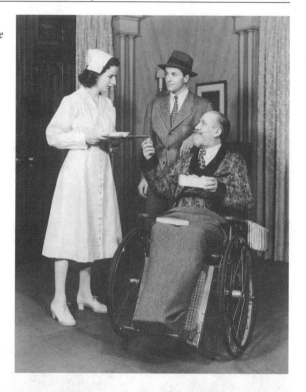

*Alexander Woollcott as Sheridan
Whiteside in Kaufman and Hart's*
The Man Who Came to Dinner.
*Woollcott played the role on tour after
Monty Woolley originated it on
Broadway. Also pictured is Claudia
Morgan as Maggie Cutler. (NYPL)*

Moss Hart (left) as Sheridan Whiteside on tour with The Man Who Came to Dinner, *June 1945. The production toured U. S. military bases in the South Pacific (the "foxhole circuit") for almost three months. (NYPL)*

Moss Hart (wearing a beard for his performance as Sheridan Whiteside) with Major Maurice Evans, discussing the itinerary for the South Pacific tour of The Man Who Came to Dinner. *(NYPL)*

March 1938: Kitty Carlisle in an MGM publicity photo as she would have appeared not long after she first met Moss Hart. (NYPL)

August 11, 1946: Moss Hart and Kitty Carlisle exchanging marriage vows before Justice of the Peace John Simon in New Hope, Pennsylvania. Kitty said she was nervous and a reporter described Hart as "jittery." Moss was forty-one, Kitty thirty-four. (Photo: Corbis)

*Gertrude Lawrence in the original 1941
Broadway production of Moss Hart, Kurt Weill,
and Ira Gershwin's groundbreaking play with
music (as Hart always called it),* Lady in the
Dark. *Hart said he "adored" Lawrence but told
Julie Andrews that he often found her
"maddening." (NYPL)*

Moss Hart rehearsing the cast of Winged Victory *in 1943. Hart contributed all of his income from the production to the Army Emergency Relief fund. (Hart Estate)*

A table-reading of Winged Victory, 1943. *Most of the women who played roles in the production were wives of the Air Force men. (NYPL)*

Winged Victory. *All of the actors were members of the Air Forces, but some had professional theatrical experience before the war. (Hart Estate)*

*Newlyweds Moss and Kitty Carlisle Hart in the late 1940s. Moss chose all
of Kitty's clothes, helping to insure that both were models of elegance. Kitty
said, "I felt I was in a continuous drawing-room comedy." (Hart Estate)*

Moss and Kitty Carlisle Hart on vacation early in their marriage.
Kitty said she found Moss "endlessly interesting and diverting and
stimulating." On their fifth anniversary, Moss told her, "You have
given me the purest happiness I have ever known." (Hart Estate)

Left to right: Leonora Hornblow, writer Arthur Hornblow,
publisher and television personality Bennett Cerf, Phyllis Cerf, Kitty
Carlisle, and Moss Hart camping it up in the 1950s during a
tropical vacation. (Hart Estate)

Kitty Carlisle as Alice Waters in Moss Hart's original 1954 Broadway production of Anniversary Waltz. *Hart wrote in his diary that Kitty was "extremely deft, with a sure comedic sense, and surprised everyone, including me." (NYPL)*

Macdonald Carey (left), rehearsing a scene with Moss and Kitty Carlisle Hart for the original 1954 Broadway production of Anniversary Waltz. *This marked the only time that Kitty and her husband worked together on Broadway. (NYPL)*

Domestic bliss: Moss and Kitty Carlisle Hart photographed at home with their children, Chris and Cathy, in the mid-1950s. (Hart Estate)

Legendary photographer Richard Avedon took this portrait of Chris and Cathy Hart in the late 1950s. (Courtesy of Richard Avedon Estate)

▲ *Julie Andrews as Eliza Doolittle in the original* 1956 *Broadway production of* My Fair Lady, *directed by Moss Hart. Hart spent a grueling weekend coaching her in every aspect of the role. Andrews later called him "my Svengali." (NYPL)*

◄ *Left to right: Robert Coote, Rex Harrison, Stanley Holloway, and Julie Andrews in the original production of* My Fair Lady, *which some have described as the greatest musical of all time. (NYPL)*

"*I Could Have Danced All Night*": *Julie Andrews (now converted from a Cockney flower girl into a reasonable facsimile of "a lady") and Rex Harrison in the original 1956 production of* My Fair Lady. *(NYPL)*

▲ *Robert Coote as Colonel Pickering, with Julie Andrews and Rex Harrison in the original 1956 production of* My Fair Lady. *They are performing "The Rain in Spain," which never failed to bring down the house. (NYPL)*

◄ *February 1958: Julie Andrews, Frederick Loewe, Moss Hart, and Kitty Carlisle Hart preparing to travel overseas for the London opening of* My Fair Lady. *(NYPL)*

▶ *July 22, 1960: Moss Hart (left), Alan Jay Lerner (center), and Frederick Loewe at Lerner's summer home in Sands Point, Long Island, during a break from their work on the creation of* Camelot. *(Hart Estate)*

▼ *Robert Goulet (right), well-known for his clowning during rehearsals of* Camelot, *is pictured here with Julie Andrews and other members of the original 1960 Broadway cast. The production was directed by Moss Hart. (NYPL)*

Moss Hart, barely recognizable after suffering his second heart attack, and Kitty Carlisle Hart take in some New York theatre in October 1961, just two months before Hart's death. (NYPL)

Kitty Carlisle Hart, still ravishing in her 80s. She was, at this time, chairman of the New York State Council on the Arts. Beverly Sills called her "a living landmark." (Hart Estate)

Kitty Carlisle Hart with her two children, Christopher and Catherine, in a recent photograph. (Hart Estate)

Kitty Carlisle Hart, at age 94, receiving an emotional standing ovation when appearing at a Lincoln Center tribute to herself and to Moss Hart in October 2004. To her immediate right are Robert Goulet and Michael Feinstein. (Hart Estate)

ACT THREE

Chapter 7 NEW DIRECTIONS
1940–1944

H ART BELIEVED THAT A "PLAYWRIGHT MUST HAVE THE COURAGE TO make mistakes" and he put that to the test in 1940, immediately after his break with George S. Kaufman.[1]

Three years earlier, he had proposed that he and Kaufman write "a show based upon free association." When Kaufman gave him a quizzical look, Hart added, "It's the psychoanalytical technique. You lie down on a sofa and let your mind drift and you come through with everything that flashes across your consciousness." The idea, intended as a musical for Marlene Dietrich, came to nothing, but Hart remained fascinated by the notion, and continued to develop it.

In 1939, he conceived of the play as almost entirely dramatic, containing only a single song for the leading actress and incidental music. But in the fall of that year, at the Hapsburg Restaurant in New York, Hart met with Kurt Weill, the exiled German composer who had already written widely admired music for *The Threepenny Opera*, *The Eternal Road*, and *Knickerbocker Holiday*, among other productions. Each admired the other's work and each expressed interest in working together, although both insisted they had no interest in a conventional musical. "We were both completely disinterested in doing a show for the sake of doing a show, in Broadway parlance," Hart said, "and the tight little formula of the musical comedy stage held no interest for either of us."

At their next meeting, Hart explained his wish to present a play with incidental music focusing upon psychoanalysis. Weill was interested, but believed the idea could best be achieved with a full score. Eventually, Hart agreed that musical segments throughout the play could be used to represent the dreams of the principal character and revised his approach. Music, he saw, could be as integral to the play he envisioned as dialogue. But, since the music was to be almost completely limited to the main character's dreams, a scenario needed to be written before Weill could begin composing.

---

1 The break wasn't total. Hart enlarged his presence on Broadway when, in May 1940, he joined Kaufman, Max Gordon, Joe Hyman, and Marcus Heiman in purchasing the Lyceum Theatre. The partners owned unequal shares; Hart's amounted to 12½%. The venture was successful, earning a significant profit before the group sold the theatre in 1945.

Early in 1940, Hart telephoned Ira Gershwin in Los Angeles, inviting him to write the lyrics. Gershwin, who would be collaborating on a full score with a composer other than his late brother George for the first time, agreed. All were determined not to allow the play to become a conventional musical, Hart always referring to it as a "play with music," never as a musical. Hart began writing the dialogue on March 1, then collaborated with Weill on outlining the dream scenarios—which Weill eventually referred to as "three one-act operas of about 20 minutes length each"—and Gershwin joined his partners in New York in early May.

Gershwin recalled one session at Fairview Farm, when the three collaborators "discussed for many hours the format of the Second and Third Dreams. . . . After all three of us had suggested various notions, Moss left us for an hour or so and returned from his library with . . . two pages he had just typed for me."

Work proceeded at a furious pace. According to Gershwin, the collaborators worked for twelve to sixteen hours a day for sixteen weeks during "one of the hottest summers New York had ever known."

The play on which Hart and his partners were working was to be the first American play, musical or non-musical, to explore the process of psychoanalysis, and the musical sequences would, he hoped, enrich the play rather than dominate it. Although the psychoanalytic process would inevitably have to be simplified in the play, Hart's aim was to demonstrate as honestly as possible the way in which a particular patient's dreams reveal the subconscious fears that lead her into depression and shape her destiny. Originally, he titled the work *I Am Listening*; eventually it was changed to *Lady in the Dark*.

Hart knew only too well how intractable a problem depression could be. He had been wrestling with it for a decade, often taking successful steps toward recovery, then relapsing. The time compression of a play, however, dictated that the patient's progress be more or less regular, leading ultimately to a breakthrough, that, it is suggested, will be lifelong.

Because the central character, Liza, is involved in a love affair and winds up with another man, the possibility existed that the play would become a conventional romantic comedy, but Hart never wavered in his determination not to allow that to happen. He regarded *Lady in the Dark* as a serious drama, and, although he included comic episodes, they did not overwhelm the serious intent.

The play stemmed primarily from Hart's own experience, but he freely fictionalized the dilemmas of Liza Elliot, the "Lady" of the title. Liza, the successsful editor of a women's fashion magazine, is living with a married man who is unable to secure a divorce from his wife. Although Liza believes herself to be perfectly content with that arrangement, she finds herself unable to make decisions and suffers bouts of depression, leading her to consult a psychoanalyst, Dr. Brooks. In the course of the play, Liza reveals her dreams and nightmares to him. The dreams take the form of musical interludes, one showing Liza as a child, another as an adolescent, and another in the various stages of adulthood. Although Liza is impatient with the amount of time required by the analysis and rejects the analyst's conclusions on several occasions, her symptoms do not abate and she keeps returning to him, trying to sort out her feelings for three men in her life: Kendall Nesbitt, her lover; Randy Curtis, a film star who is posing for a photographic spread in Liza's magazine; and Charley Johnson, the magazine's advertising manager, whose independence and cynicism arouse Liza's resentment. Fantasies about the men are interspersed with Liza's frequently painful dreams.

Utimately, Dr. Brooks's interpretation of Liza's dreams result in a diagnosis: her depression, he says, stems from her parents' treatment of her when she was a child (one of her most vivid dreams shows Liza, as a child, wearing her mother's cape soon after her mother dies; her father angrily takes the cape from her, seemingly rejecting his daughter). Moreover, Dr. Brooks suggests that her satisfaction in running the magazine is in reality a substitute for her desire to be loved; her attempts to conceal her femininity in order to be a more effective businesswoman are repressing her true character; and her advertising manager, Charley Johnson, a man she thought she despised, is the man she truly loves. Armed with the analyst's diagnosis, Liza emerges from her depression, breaks off the affair with Kendall Nesbitt, and begins a relationship with Charley Johnson.

Lady in the Dark cannot be listed among the great American musicals (it is generally categorized as a musical, despite Hart's preference for "a play with music"), for it is flawed in many respects. Liza's emergence from depression, as portrayed, is psychologically facile, taking place with lightning speed. The play's central notion, that a woman who earns her living in a world generally controlled by men is emotionally distraught because she is forced to conceal her femininity, seems rather primitive in light of our current understanding of psychology. The male characters in the play are all too obviously portrayed as contrasting types for Liza to choose among.

Despite its faults, however, *Lady in the Dark* can certainly be described as adventurous, even groundbreaking. The combination of a subject as profound and mysterious as the workings of the subconscious mind and incidents suitable for a musical comedy represented an important step on the road to maturity for the American musical theatre. Liza is a multi-dimensional character, and the play, beyond being cleverly constructed, is ultimately moving.

Fully aware of the possibility that *Lady in the Dark* might be non-commercial, Hart wrote to Dore Schary in the fall of 1940, "It's completely experimental . . . and I may go right on my ass. But it's a very adventureous [*sic*] thing to have done, and I don't care if it's an absolute failure."

Hart's respect for George S. Kaufman's knowledge had not diminished since his decision to write independently. He showed the script of *Lady in the Dark* to Kaufman, eager to see if his former partner found it theatrically effective; he also showed it to Beatrice Kaufman, wishing primarily to see if she believed that it accurately reflected the psychoanalytic experience. Both praised it highly.

Perhaps because Hart so frequently referred to *Lady in the Dark* as "a play with music," the Broadway rumor mill asserted that Kurt Weill's contribution had been limited to writing incidental music. Hart explained to newspaper reporters that Broadway gossip was incorrect. Weill's score, he said, would be as important to the play as Hart's book.

Hart said that *Lady in the Dark*, as conceived by himself and Weill, was "a show in which the music carried forward the essential story and was not imposed on the architecture of the play as rather melodious but useless addenda." He was proud that the score was "part and parcel of the basic structure of the play. One cannot separate the play from the music, and vice versa," he said. "More than that, the music and lyrics carry the story forward dramatically and psychologically."

Sam Harris served once again as Hart's producer. Harris persuaded Paramount Pictures to invest $35,000, but much more money would be required. As the plans for staging the musical sequences became more elaborate, requiring several revolving stages and costumes numbering in the hundreds for a cast of sixty-one, the cost of production rose to a then-unprecedented $137,000. Hart said to Weill, "You see, we had a nice little lunch at the Hapsburg last fall—and here is the result."

Harris showed the script to Marshall Field, the wealthy Chicago department store owner, who tentatively agreed to fund a major portion of the production. A complication ensued, however, when Field specified that his investment would depend upon the favorable opinion of his psychiatrist, to whom he sent the script. Field's analyst found fault with some of the details, causing Dr. Kubie, Hart's consultant, to fly to Chicago for a conference. Only after they came to an agreement did Field notify Harris that his funding could be counted upon.

Hassard Short choreographed *Lady in the Dark*'s musical sequences, but Hart was responsible for the overall direction, a position for which he was well qualified.

Hart's first choice to play Liza Elliot in *Lady in the Dark*—when the play was still primarily dramatic rather than musical—was Katharine Cornell, whom he had seen years before in Bernard Shaw's *Candida*. Hart, a stagestruck teenager at the time, had pawned his overcoat in order to be able to see the performance. After the final curtain, he waited outside the stage door, shivering in the cold, for Cornell to emerge. When she did, Hart, one of a large group of fans, believed that she smiled directly at him. On the subway ride to Brooklyn that night, he vowed that one day he would write a play for her.

Years later, after Hart had achieved success, he and Cornell were on a first-name basis. "Kit," he told her in 1939, "I'm going to write a play for you right away." He promised to read the first act to her as soon as it was completed.

In March 1940, Hart visited Cornell and described the play as it was then evolving. By that time, however, he suspected that, with the growing musical demands of the production, Cornell would not be suitable for Liza.

Edith Atwater, not yet married to Hugh Marlowe, asked Hart early in the summer of 1940 if he would consider her for the role of Liza. As infatuated as Hart may have been with Atwater, he was not about to give her a role for which she was unqualified. "This requires someone who can sing," he told her, and, as he pointed out, she had never sung on a Broadway stage. She promptly began an intensive series of vocal lessons, which lasted throughout the summer. In September, she tried out on the stage of the Music Box Theatre—enabling her to say that she had, after all, sung on a Broadway stage. However, Hart believed that her musical abilities were too limited.

On a Sunday night in May, Hart was scheduled to rehearse a sketch with Kaufman that they would perform at a British War Relief benefit. Another of the participants was Gertrude Lawrence, one of the world's most renowned actresses, a performer as accomplished in song and dance as in straight dramatic roles. By 1940, Lawrence thought her days as a musical performer were over, but for the Relief benefit she sang a romantic song. "As I watched her sing and dance," Hart said, "I knew that here, irrevocably, was the Lady of *Lady in the Dark*."

He did not mention his certainty when he read the script of his play to Sam Harris and his staff. After the reading, the staff began to discuss casting. About

Liza there was virtually no discussion. Almost in chorus everyone in the room shouted "Gertrude Lawrence!" When they contemplated what they would do in case Lawrence would not be available, they could think of no alternative. Like Hart, they believed that Gertrude Lawrence was the only choice.

In March, Hart asked Lawrence to join him for a drink at the Plaza, where he asked if she would be interested in hearing his play. She was extremely interested, she said, and invited Hart to her apartment the next day. After Hart's reading of the first act, Lawrence's fervor was difficult to contain. "It was more than exciting, she kept repeating," said Hart. "It was an adventure in the theatre and something she had always hoped for as an actress." Just at the point when Hart thought she was about to commit herself to the production, however, she told him that her astrologer had warned her to do nothing until April 7. And, since April 7 was still two weeks away, she couldn't possibly make a decision until then.

Hart spent the next two weeks at Fairview Farm in Bucks County, completing the play on April 6. Gertrude Lawrence called that morning to ask if the play was finished and to say that Noël Coward was arriving from England the next day. "I never do anything without Noël's advice," she said. "You must read the play to Noël and if he says 'yes' I'll do it."

Knowing that Coward, who was on a war mission for Britain, would have other things to do than to listen to a new play, Hart faced their meeting with trepidation. Still, he called Coward on the morning of the seventh and explained his situation. Coward agreed to visit Hart for lunch and hear the play the next afternoon.

"The book seemed to have the authentic ring of success," Coward wrote in his autobiography, *Future Indefinite*. He sat expressionless through the reading, but commented as Hart came to an end, "Gertie ought to pay you to play it." However, as Coward soon discovered, "Gertie, as usual, was undecided, she wouldn't say 'Yes,' she wouldn't say 'No'; Moss, treading for the first time this well-worn path of anxiety and frustration, implored me, almost tearfully, to reason with her. He seemed so agitated, so obviously headed for a nervous breakdown, that I agreed to coax her, or, failing this, bash her into definite acceptance."

Hart and Coward walked together to the theatre where Lawrence's current play, Samson Raphaelson's *Skylark*, was running. After the final curtain, the three of them discussed Coward's enthusiastic reaction to the play in Lawrence's dressing room. Lawrence agreed to play Liza and Hart thought that his difficulties were over. But Coward said to him after Lawrence was out of earshot, "Now your troubles are really beginning."

Surprised, Hart asked, "But Gertie said 'yes,' didn't she?"

"That's just the point, my boy," Coward answered. "Gertie said 'yes.'" Over the course of the next four months, Hart would come to understand Coward's meaning.

Two days later Lawrence read the entire manuscript, said she loved it, and added, "Now we must read it to Fanny Holtzman," her lawyer and business manager, without whom, she said, she could not think of signing a contract.

Hart described Fanny Holtzman as "a small, delicate, mouselike creature given to wearing floppy hats in the Spring and creating a first impression of wistful helpfulness." In fact, as he came to learn, she was "about as helpless as the Bethlehem Steel Company and as delicate as Jack the Ripper." Hart read his play to Holtzman, with Weill and Gershwin playing and singing the score. Holtzman, impressed, said, "We'll have it all settled by the end of the week." Again, Hart thought that Gertrude Lawrence's participation in *Lady in the Dark* was certain.

Before the end of the week, however, Holtzman had exhausted Hart with demands on behalf of her client. "I would leave [Holtzman's office] after a two-hour session, limp and bedraggled," said Hart, "only to be called to the telephone fifteen minutes later, no matter where I was, for at least a forty-five minute conversation." At last, however, when Holtzman had arranged the most lavish possible terms for Lawrence, including a weekly salary of $3,500, a percentage of the gross receipts, a summer holiday of three months, and, as Hart joked, "my farm, the Music Box Theatre, Sam Harris's house in Palm Beach, half of Metro-Goldwyn-Mayer, [and] a couple of race horses," the contract was finally drawn up and Hart looked forward to the next morning, when all the principals would assemble for the signing.

However, Holtzman informed Hart that Lawrence had left for Massachusetts for a week and the signing would have to be delayed. At that point, the playwright expressed anger and impatience. He "insisted somewhat rudely," Hart said, "that I had had enough of Fanny and Gertie and that unless Fanny went up there and brought back a signed contract the following Monday the whole thing was off."

During the wait, Hart contacted Irene Dunne's agent to see if Dunne would be available to play Liza if Lawrence decided against playing the role. Before the agent could check with his client and get back to Hart, Moss received a telegram from Lawrence to say that she had been married the night before, and, as Hart said, "I suppose it was utterly beyond her to sign two contracts at once."

Irene Dunne's agent telephoned to say that his client was definitely interested in playing Liza. Armed with that information, Hart called Lawrence, told her about Irene Dunne, and asked her to make up her mind there and then, "or this was the end of it."

Lawrence, with an air of total surprise, cooed, "But darling, I said 'yes' months ago, didn't I? Whatever are you troubling your little head about? I am coming into town on Monday—let's have lunch at Voisson's and I will bring the contract with me all beautifully signed." Hart wired Hollywood to cancel all negotiations with Irene Dunne, and met Lawrence at Voisson's on the appointed day.

"Darling, the most awful thing has happened," she told him. "I left [the contract] in Cape Cod and Fanny is drawing another one this very minute. We will have it for you the day after tomorrow." Two days later, Holtzman brought the signed contract to Hart at Sam Harris's office—but, Hart noted with desperation, Lawrence "had not initialed any of the additional clauses, so that the contract was completely useless." In just an hour, Lawrence would be leaving for Los Angeles to begin touring in *Skylark*, an engagement that would consume five months.

Holtzman rushed to the theatre where the final rehearsal of *Skylark* was taking place. Meanwhile, Hart, Weill, and Gershwin met for what had originally been intended as a work session; none of them could concentrate, however, as they waited for the phone to ring. When it did, Holtzman made one final demand: the play must open at the Music Box or the whole thing was off. "Fine," Hart shouted, "the whole thing is off. I will be here for fifteen minutes longer, and if that contract is not here by then just tear it up." Evidently his show of temper was precisely what was needed, for the signed and initialed contract arrived within the next fifteen minutes.

Hart, who had never told Katharine Cornell about his pursuit of Gertrude Lawrence, hastily sent her a letter "to explain my silence and the reason why." He stated that he felt "pretty badly" and was suffering from "a heavy sense of guilt at not having let you know what was going on," but that "the play fairly reeks of music now [and] there was some doubt in . . . our minds you know, about there being too much music for you, and as Weill and Gershwin went on with their part of it, it became more and more apparent that we ought to have someone almost musical comedy to handle it."

Another casting complication occurred on November 13 when the Group Theatre announced that Victor Mature would play the leading role in Irwin Shaw's *Retreat to Pleasure*. Unknown to the Group, however, Mature had signed a contract the day before to appear in *Lady in the Dark*. Hart, alarmed by the Group's announcement, sought assurances both from Mature and from his agent, Louis Shurr, that the actor had not agreed to perform in the Group's play. Two days later the Group bowed out, saying that Mature had led them to believe he wished to act in *Retreat to Pleasure* but had not informed them he had already committed himself to *Lady in the Dark*. The Group took special care to point out that "Mr. Hart was an innocent party in the mix-up."

Later, Mature claimed surprise when he discovered that he was expected to sing in the production, although it seems astonishing that he would have signed a contract without that knowledge. In any case, he possessed good vocal equipment and enrolled in a course of singing lessons to increase his facility.

Another actor who tried out for *Lady in the Dark* was Gregory Peck, not yet a film star. "I went to [Hart's] office upstairs at the Plymouth Theatre," Peck recalled early in the year 2000.

> I saw him alone, and I was very, very impressed, both by his accomplishments in the theatre and by him. As I remember, he was elegantly tailored, he seemed to be in a cloud of cologne, and was very sophisticated. He walked up and down while he told me about the play and the part of [Charley Johnson]. He apparently sized me up while he was talking, because he ultimately decided not to audition me, saying I was too young. I think Moss telling me that I was too young was his gracious way of telling me that he didn't see me in the role; he was letting me down easy. But I was invigorated and elevated by the experience. He treated me like I was a legitimate member of the profession. I rushed out of there and immediately went to tell all my friends about the interview. He gave me encouragement and hope.

One role had already been cast. Danny Kaye would play Russell, an effeminate photographer. Hart saw Kaye for the first time at La Martinique early in 1940, at the suggestion of Ben Bernie. "I hate night clubs," Hart said, but Bernie "kept at me, saying 'you must see a new young fellow.' I shirked it a great deal, but finally one night I did go to see it and I was very taken by this young man, and he came to the table afterwards, and I said to him, 'I'm writing a show now for next fall and I'm going to write a part in it for you.'"

Afterward, Hart wondered how he could keep his promise, for, he said, "I had no thought of writing a part [of the sort Danny Kaye could play] originally but," bowled over by the talent and versatility of the comedian, "I broke the first act open which I'd partly completed and put the part in, wrote it for him, and engaged him." The decision proved to be both wise and dangerous. Wise, because Kaye immediately demonstrated that he was a brilliantly talented performer; dangerous, because the character Hart wrote for him is far too broadly and comically drawn to mesh smoothly with the tone of *Lady in the Dark* and has little relation to the play's theme. His comic scenes threaten to turn *Lady in the Dark* into the conventional comedy Hart wished to avoid.

Nonetheless, the decision to cast Danny Kaye proved to be a key to the popularity of the production, for Kaye was brilliant, especially in the musical number included especially for him. On the other hand, the most substantial criticism to be leveled at *Lady in the Dark* is that the character created for Kaye has no meaningful relation to Liza's concerns.

In November 1940, Gertrude Lawrence's tour of *Skylark* came to an end. She immediately traveled to Fairview Farm for two weeks of discussions and rehearsals with Hart. The two weeks were essential, for, despite the size and complexity of *Lady in the Dark*, Hart and Hassard Short, the choreographer, had given themselves only three weeks to rehearse the production before its out-of-town opening.[2]

Hart felt confident that he could mount the production in the time allotted, but was concerned about Lawrence's possible behavior in rehearsals:

> If Gertie conducted her professional life in the same haphazard and scatter-brained way in which she conducted her business life there would be real trouble ahead. I privately decided that the first time Gertie came late to rehearsals and the first time I noticed any dawdling and shilly-shallying I would go right to the mat with her and fight it out, for, when rehearsals begin, the actress is trapped quite as much as the producer and author, and at least you fight on equal terms.
>
> My fears were groundless. From the first moment of rehearsal Gertie was the very antithesis of her contract-signing self. A brilliant and intelligent actress I knew her to be, but what I did not know was that she was a perfect angel once past a stage door. Sensitive and kind and completely conscientious, I would have to drive her out of the theatre at night, and there was one element of a working relationship with Gertie that I have never experienced in working with any other actress. That element was fun—rehearsals were unalloyed fun.

Only one obstacle caused tension in rehearsals. Danny Kaye was, in Hart's words, "a very bad rehearser, he's no good at all without an audience." Neither Sam Harris nor Gertrude Lawrence had ever seen Kaye perform, and they grew increasingly nervous that he would not be capable of playing his role with flair. Hart continued, "About the second week of rehearsal Miss Lawrence and

---

2 However, while Hart rehearsed the actors in one studio, Gertrude Lawrence said, "the chorus was busy in another, and the dancers in another. Little by little we began to fit the separate pieces together, and it was amazing to see how they dovetailed."

Mr. Harris came to me and asked me to let [Kaye] go, [because] he just wasn't going to make it. I said I was sure he was, and they were just as certain that he wasn't and they said, quite rightly, that sometimes night club comedians disappear when the footlights light up."

Hart had seen the electric effect Kaye had had upon the audience at La Martinique and insisted on retaining him in the play. He knew that "Tschaikowsky," a number that called for Kaye to rattle off the names of fifty Russian composers in fifty seconds and was especially suited to Kaye's comic style—which Kaye would sing while Lawrence was onstage, seated on a swing, watching—was likely to be a sensation in performance.[3]

That, too, created a problem, however. If "Tschaikowsky" (which Ira Gershwin had written sixteen years earlier, but had never before appeared in a musical) stopped the show, as Hart firmly believed it would, it might overshadow Gertrude Lawrence, thus throwing the production out of kilter and irritating the leading lady.

For days, Hart spoke to Gershwin and Weill, saying, "Please, for goodness' sake, get a song for Gertrude Lawrence," one that she could perform immediately after "Tschaikowsky." At one all-night session at the Essex House in Boston, Hart offered encouragement and criticism while Weill and Gershwin wrote "The Saga of Jenny," a character who, like Liza, couldn't make up her mind—just as Gertrude Lawrence had been unable to decide whether or not to appear in *Lady in the Dark.*

The next day Hart took the song to rehearsal and sang it to Lawrence, who responded, "This is not a song for me, this is for Ethel Merman, and it's not very funny anyway." Hart assured her he agreed on both counts (although he actually felt otherwise), but added, "You must do it, we have a right to hear it, we're out of town and if it's no good it'll be cut, but you have to sing it." He added that a new song would be written for the New York production if "The Saga of Jenny" was unsuccessful in Boston. Lawrence finally acquiesced, saying, as she often did in rehearsals, "You're the boss, Moss."

Disliking the song, Lawrence did everything she could during the next rehearsal to sabotage "The Saga of Jenny." "In rehearsal, when a star doesn't like the number she's been given," Hart said, "the way she does it is [just to mumble the lyrics; she] not only walks through it but tries to kill it, show her dislike, and this is the way she rehearsed it."

---

3 Kaye gradually increased the speed of the song. By April 1941, he was down to thirty-nine seconds. Later he shaved another second off the running time. In June of that year, Ripley's "Believe It or Not" claimed that Kaye sang "Tschaikowsky" in thirty seconds.

Meanwhile, Kaye was becoming concerned that, as Hart said, "if his song went over and her song did not, his song would be cut." And Kaye had come to like "Tschaikowsky" enormously.

Hart described the audience's reaction to Kaye's song: "On the opening night, [the response to] Danny was thunderous. Remember, this is the first theatre audience that had ever seen him in a major part. And the effect was electric, and they kept applauding and applauding and at the back of the theatre I was saying 'Ssh,' to try to quiet them, knowing that the more they applauded the more likely the song was to be cut. Danny kept bowing to Gertie as if to indicate that she would sing next, and, of course, the more he bowed, generously, the more they applauded."

Maurice Abravanel, conducting the pit orchestra, sensed that "The Saga of Jenny" would have to follow "Tschaikowsky" immediately in order to have maximum impact. Although some dialogue and recitative were supposed to bridge the two songs, Abravanel did not wait for the applause for "Tschaikowsky" to end; instead, he cued the trumpets to begin the fanfare introducing "The Saga of Jenny." The trumpets stopped the applause for Danny Kaye, Lawrence jumped from the swing to the stage floor, and went immediately into her song. As Hart recalled, she "then sang 'Jenny' as she had never rehearsed it. She did it with bumps, grinds, a strip tease, and completely topped him. And no one was more pleased to see her do this than Danny Kaye and myself."

Both songs remained in the production and, as performed by Kaye and Lawrence, both were brilliantly successful every night, never failing to win ovations. That changed, however, when Danny Kaye left the production. No other performer has been able to make "Tschaikowsky" appear to be anything other than what it is: a musical number inserted in the middle of the production that has no meaning except to display Danny Kaye's remarkable tongue-twisting ability.

Other than the spat over "The Saga of Jenny," Lawrence made the rehearsals into a pleasant and rewarding experience, Hart said, thanks to her "shining good nature and her own special magic."

If rehearsals went smoothly for Hart and the actors, the same could not be said for the scenic designer, Harry Horner. The play called for scenes to alternate between the doctor's office, Liza's office, and her fantasies. Stage directions in the script included such instructions as "Doctor's office fades into Park Avenue apartment house" and "Night club unfolds as a rose." Horner, determined not to use the conventional method of shifting scenery with curtains opening before and closing after each scene (because, he said, "a careful reading of the script convinced me that a curtain between each scene would slow or completely dam the flow of the story"), instead chose to use a pair of turntables. He soon realized, however, that so much scenery was called for that two turntables would be insufficient, and hit upon the scheme, then radically new, of using four turntables, to be turned mechanically by a system of gears.

Horner explained his plan to Hart, Short, and Harris, evoking a surprised comment from Hart. "Did I write something that complicated?" he asked. Horner assured him he had. Harris commented that he intended to tour *Lady in the Dark*, a plan that would eliminate the possibility of using the gear system, for the scheme would require far too much time to set up and take down in each theatre on the tour. Horner settled for turntables that would be manually operated.

Even with Horner's modifications, the scenic and costume requirements for *Lady in the Dark* were so extravagant that Harris considered an extensive tryout tour too formidable. Instead, the production played in only one city, Boston, for three weeks before its New York engagement.

Hart suffered a case of pleurisy in Boston, and, at a post-show party in his room at the Ritz-Carlton Hotel on January 3, his temperature rose to 102. As the partygoers realized how ill he was and began to leave, Hart, whose love for social interaction knew no bounds, cried out, "I'm sick! You can't leave me all alone!" The next day he recovered sufficiently to attend the rehearsal at the Colonial Theatre.

The Boston tryout, beginning on December 20, was played before enthusiastic critics and packed houses. One Boston notice, written for *The New York Times*, called it "a big show and an entertaining one that runs all the way in mood from psychiatric problems through excursions into fantasy, sentiment and varied humors, to the bright cheerfulness of a circus interlude." The critic, noting that "Sam H. Harris seems to have spared no expense in the production," described the "revolving stages to transform one scene into another, somewhat [resembling] the movie flash-back and fade-in, imaginatively devised and skillfully managed." He noted, however, that the production was too long, running well past 11:30 on the opening night. Elinor Hughes, in the *Boston Herald*, called *Lady in the Dark* "the handsomest, most novel and generally entertaining show in a long time;" Elliot Norton's review in the *Boston Post* was equally enthusiastic: "it is unique and, not to play with the phrase, it is also extraordinary; handsome, ingenious, in some ways inspired."

While in Boston, Hart asked George S. Kaufman to watch a rehearsal, hoping that his friend could suggest ways to eliminate some material without cutting into the play's core. Many musicals have suffered from the problem of excessive length, but cutting is not an easy process, for every element in a play or musical exists for a reason, and to cut one element will necessarily affect another. Still, Kaufman and Hart, working together, were able to pare *Lady in the Dark* to a reasonable length without harming its overall structure.

The production was scheduled to open in New York on January 16, 1941, but Gertrude Lawrence came down with a serious case of influenza, a disease which was then rampant on Broadway. Gene Kelly and Vivienne Segal, starring in *Pal Joey*, were unable to appear that night and Al Jolson had to cancel a performance of *Hold On To Your Hats*. Lawrence's illness caused Sam Harris to postpone the opening of *Lady in the Dark* for a week.

Rehearsals continued, however. Lawrence was too ill to appear in the dress rehearsal of January 15, and, since her understudy was also suffering from the flu, Hart volunteered to walk through the role, carrying the script. Knowing every moment of the play intimately, he had no difficulty—until the lights dimmed and the revolving stages began to turn. Aware of apparent chaos all around him, Hart had no idea where he should go in order to avoid the moving scenery and the actors, some scurrying on to the stage, others rushing into the wings. An assistant stage manager, who had been given the responsibility of guiding Gertrude Lawrence safely to her dressing room during the scene changes, ran onstage, took Hart by the hand, and led him out of danger. "God!" shouted Hart, "Who'd be crazy enough to write something like this?"

Lawrence emerged from the hospital to which she had been confined to give two previews, followed by the opening performance at the Alvin Theatre on January 23, returning to the hospital on each occasion (although she did attend an opening-night party at the Waldorf-Astoria).[4]

Hart sent her a letter, thanking her for her work in the production, adding, "For the first time in a good many years, you've helped me to recapture that sense of wonder and excitement I came into the theatre with. I've come to each rehearsal [with] that old sense of adventure, and through all our little agonies I've been sustained by your shining good nature and essential kindness."

---

4 As late as February 9, Lawrence continued to commute from the hospital to the theatre. "The nurses and doctors are trying to build me up so that my system will refuel itself," she said. "But every matinee day I lose a pound and a half, and then they have to go to work and help me get it back." The doctors only permitted her to perform, she said, "if I would stay here all the time I'm not at the theatre."

All of the reviews were positive, but many contained qualifications. Two who were wholly enthusiastic were Brooks Atkinson and John Mason Brown. *Lady in the Dark* "uses the resources of the theatre magnificently and tells a compassionate story triumphantly," wrote Atkinson in the *Times*. "Mr. Hart has written a dramatic story about the anguish of a human being. Kurt Weill has matched it with the finest score written for the theatre in years. Ira Gershwin's lyrics are brilliant. Harry Horner's whirling scenery gives the narrative a transcendent loveliness." The cast, Atkinson said, "is excellent throughout." He had special praise for Gertrude Lawrence, Danny Kaye, and Macdonald Carey, who played Charley Johnson, the advertising manager with whom Liza falls in love. "No one but Miss Lawrence could play a virtuoso part of such length and variety," he said. Finally, Hart's direction was commended as "excellent throughout."

Brown called *Lady in the Dark* "little short of miraculous, [boasting] virtues as a production which are as difficult to overestimate as it is hard to underestimate the seriousness with which it deserves to be taken as a literary drama." He added that "Gertrude Lawrence has never given a more fascinating, disciplined, or compelling performance."

Other critics expressed reservations. The general critical consensus was that the acting and production elements were thrilling, but that *Lady in the Dark* was overlong, that its portrait of psychoanalysis was oversimplified, and its conclusion too obvious. Richard Lockridge said, "Fantasy, reality and the song and dance were copiously mixed, sometimes behaving like oil and water." He opined that the subject of mental disturbance had not been well served by the musical format. Burns Mantle called *Lady in the Dark* a spectacle, "for there is more show than substance in it," although he approved of the "fine individual scenes, with Miss Lawrence always at the peak of her talents." He also noted the "marvelous stage effects, most skillfully maneuvered," and felt that "Mr. Hart's use of a psychoanalyst's consulting room as the basis of a dream play must be counted an inspiration." Richard Watts in the *Herald-Tribune* agreed with Mantle's assessment "that *Lady in the Dark* is a show, rather than a play." He called the "propaganda for the soul-curing virtues of psycho-analysis . . . rather on the primitive side" but "as a feat of showmanship . . . it is unquestionably brilliant. . . . [The production] is sure to be [a] vast success." Indeed, the critics agreed that the production's virtues overwhelmed whatever objections might exist to the play itself.

Noël Coward, when he saw *Lady in the Dark*, "watched, spell-bound, the brilliant assurance with which [Gertrude Lawrence] wove her way through the intricacies of that varied and difficult part. . . . [H]er performance was magnificent, no one else could have done it."

Cecil Smith, in his book *Musical Comedy in America*, summed up the achievements of Hart, Weill, and Gershwin:

> The contrast of the tailored modernity of the office and the clipped dialogue that took place within it with the riotous decorations and unpredictable free associations of the dream scenes made these musical episodes doubly effective. Like the pieces of a jigsaw puzzle, the dream passages fitted into the surrounding narrative with constantly increasing intelligibility; at the end, but only then, it was possible to see the dexterity with which the action, spectacle, lines, lyrics, and music had been put together with uncommon lucidity and purpose.

Smith added his voice to that of Gertrude Lawrence's many admirers, lauding her "many-sided performance, in which each new facet was as arresting as the last."

Weill's music, all the critics agreed, was the finest he had written in America. Despite the effectiveness of the production numbers in the dream sequences, Weill's most haunting song was "My Ship," a melody that Liza dimly remembers throughout the play, then, as she reaches an understanding of her true nature, sings quietly, helping her and her analyst achieve a psychological breakthrough.

Many of the critics may have expressed reservations, but the public accepted the play wholeheartedly. *Lady in the Dark* ran for 467 performances on Broadway, most of them before standing-room-only crowds. The play owed its origin to Hart's fascination with the psychoanalytic process, of course, but the production's popularity with audiences owed at least as much to its opulent production numbers and its spectacular scenery and costumes.

Danny Kaye's small role in *Lady in the Dark* propelled him to stardom. Kaye, who began, as Hart did, as a social director for a summer camp in the Catskills, continued to give two shows a night at La Martinique while playing in *Lady in the Dark*. Soon afterward, he was whisked off to Hollywood where he gave a string of brilliant comic performances in various films.

As outstanding as Gertrude Lawrence was in *Lady in the Dark*, she occasionally drove Hart to distraction. One night when he stopped in to watch a performance, he saw to his dismay that the audience paid no attention to Victor Mature's dialogue during a scene in which Lawrence continually adjusted his collar and fussed over him, causing the audience to focus upon her rather than him. "For God's sake, Gertie," Hart said to her afterward, "leave him alone." Lawrence complied, but in her own way. At the next performance

Hart saw, he was aghast when Lawrence sat on a sofa, lit her cigarette as Mature began speaking and kept the match lit until he finished. The effect on the audience was hypnotic. Every eye in the house remained on Gertrude Lawrence and, although Mature's speech was perfectly audible, no one listened to a word. Years later, Hart told Julie Andrews that although he "adored" Gertrude Lawrence, he often found her "maddening."

As Lawrence's contract stipulated, she took an eleven-week vacation from June 15 to September 2, 1941. Her performance was so integral to the success of *Lady in the Dark* that Sam Harris closed the play until she could return. In previous years, shows that were not particularly successful would often break for the summer in the un-air-conditioned New York theatres, then reopen in the fall. To break the momentum of a successful production was unprecedented, however; never before in Broadway history had a production as triumphant as *Lady in the Dark* taken such a long break. At the last performance before Lawrence's vacation, Hart sent a wreath of flowers to her with the inscription, "Rest in peace." The need to close the show, re-rehearse it and go through another opening added $23,000 to its cost.

Nearly all of the New York theatre critics revisited *Lady in the Dark* when it reopened on September 3. Gertrude Lawrence was still magnificent, they agreed, but the replacements for Danny Kaye, Victor Mature, and Macdonald Carey were somewhat less successful than their predecessors had been.

The show's schedule continued to change, depending on Lawrence's wishes. It closed on December 22 for a brief holiday recess until Christmas night. Whenever Lawrence was ill—as she was on October 17, 1942—performances were canceled rather than having the understudy go on, for theatregoers would almost certainly have insisted upon seeing the actress who had become synonymous with Liza Elliot. Kurt Weill wrote to Ira Gershwin that he feared Lawrence, whom he characterized as "moody and temperamental," might not "go through with the show the whole season. From the way she is acting now, anything might happen." As it turned out, however, his fears were groundless.

Cities across the country clamored to see the production. Sam Harris sent out a national tour with Gertrude Lawrence in the fall of 1942 and throughout the following theatrical season, including a return to Broadway on February 27, 1943, for an additional eighty-three performances. All in all, *Lady in the Dark* gave 777 performances in twelve American cities. The play helped to explain and popularize psychoanalysis to theatergoers—and later to moviegoers. It was one of Hart's most profitable ventures, earning him nearly

$300,000 in royalties. With the immense profits from *Lady in the Dark*, Hart built an addition to his house at Fairview Farm in April 1941, calling it "the Gertrude Lawrence Memorial Wing."

During the early performances of *Lady in the Dark*, *The Man Who Came to Dinner* and *George Washington Slept Here* were also playing on Broadway. It was not the first time that a single playwright had been represented by three plays running simultaneously, but the feat was sufficiently unusual that a number of newspapers commented upon it and congratulated Hart on his achievement.

When the published version of *Lady in the Dark* was issued, the preface was written by "Dr. Brooks." The actual author, though, was Dr. Kubie, upon whom Hart relied for analytical help for many years and to whom he dedicated the play. Kubie wrote that "for the first time on any stage, the struggle of a vigorous and gifted human spirit to overcome deep-seated, unconscious, self-destructive forces is portrayed accurately. . . . From the technical psychiatric point of view the portrayal, both of [Liza's] illness itself and of its evolution out of her normal life, is accurate in the subtlest details. . . . As a case history this is wholly accurate; and at the same time it could be the document of almost any human life." Kubie admitted that "as a portrayal of psychoanalysis itself there are a number of technical flaws to which the analyst might object," including the asking of too many direct questions ("the procedure as it is portrayed is more active, more directly challenging, more provocative, than would be characteristic of the ordinary analytical situation"), the nature of the dream scenes (which, Kubie said, "are not dreams at all, but rather a series of rococo fantasies built around a core of valid dream ideas"), and the brevity with which Dr. Brooks arrived at the core of Liza's problems. Still, "the essential spirit" of psychoanalysis had been preserved, "the ordinary playgoer leaves the theater under a spell" and "goes back to see the play repeatedly, with a deepening pleasure and understanding . . . because he has been awakened to a realization that subtle and powerful psychological forces play beneath the surface of his own life and of the lives of those around him."

Lady in the Dark was bought by Paramount Pictures for $283,000, representing the largest amount spent to acquire film rights either to a play or novel to that time (*The Man Who Came to Dinner* had been the previous record holder). Mitchell Liesen, the director, doubted that the film would be a commercial success. Most audience members would reject the notion of psychoanalysis, he feared. As a result of Liesen's expressed concerns, Paramount did not permit any reference to psychiatry in its advertising. In addition, they added a scene at the beginning of the movie, in which a general medical practitioner advised Liza to seek psychoanalysis, patiently explaining to her (and to the audience) that analysis should be considered as acceptable treatment rather than quackery.

The picture took twenty-two weeks to shoot, far longer than originally planned. Newly created dream sequences, filmed in color to contrast with the black-and-white of the realistic scenes, were added, making the film an hour longer than the play. A patronizing view of movie audiences dictated the length: Liesen and Paramount executives believed that the film not only had to portray Liza Elliot's story but to offer a crash course in psychoanalysis for the unitiated. Additional songs (by Johnny Burke and James Van Heusen) were written and a number of Weill and Gershwin's songs were either abridged or eliminated.

Paramount hoped that Gertrude Lawrence would repeat her stage triumph, but Lawrence refused to take a screen test at the urging of her lawyer, Fanny Holtzman, who argued that Lawrence, the "first lady of the Drama—a Goddess," should not be subjected to the indignity of a test. Irene Dunne let it be known that she had not lost her interest in playing Liza. Greta Garbo told Hart that she wished to be considered. Ultimately, however, the role was given to Ginger Rogers.

Edward Chodorov, Hart's friend from Camp Utopia in the late 1920s, was announced as the probable screenwriter, but, in the end, Frances Goodrich and Albert Hackett were responsible for the screenplay.

The film, released in 1944, pleased the critics. Jesse Zunser in *Cue* magazine called it "a dandy show—done with brilliance, imagination, good taste and a fine humor." He added, however, that "Ginger Rogers in the title role is no Gertrude Lawrence, and the subtleties of Miss Lawrence's wonderful characterization are lost somewhat in the more forthright handling of the part by Miss Rogers." Archer Winsten called the movie "a delight" in his review in the New York *Post*. Bosley Crowther in the *Times* said, "never, in this writer's memory, has the screen mounted such a display of overpowering splash and glitter . . . Imagine the gaudiest creations of all the fancy dressmakers in the trade; imagine the most resplendent spectacles of the Music Hall rolled into one . . . [T]he studio . . . has completely shot the works and turned out a Technicolored march-past [*sic*] that puts such previous screen parades to shame." However, the spectacle overwhelmed Liza's story, Crowther felt. "Most of the wistfulness and pathos of the original Moss Hart play has been left out."

Peculiarly, although Liza hummed snatches of "My Ship" throughout the film, as she had in the play, the entire song was never performed, leaving the audience confused about its significance. Ginger Rogers told Ira Gershwin that she "had made a charming rendition and had no idea why it had been cut."

Rogers wrote in her autobiography that "*Lady in the Dark* was not one of my happiest assignments. . . . Mitch [Liesen]'s interest was in the window draperies and the sets, not in the people and their emotions. As far as I'm concerned, he made hash out of Moss Hart's very original, very meaty story."

Gertrude Lawrence had been so successful as Liza Elliot onstage that her admirers in England hoped to see her play the role. As late as 1948 she attempted, with Hart's help, to mount a London production, but it never came about. Lawrence died on September 7, 1952, at the age of fifty-four.

Hart's achievement in taking the lead as author of *Lady in the Dark* was immensely gratifying to him. For years theatrical observers had hinted that Hart without Kaufman would be incapable of creating a major work. At last, however, he had proven them wrong. More important, perhaps, he had demonstrated to himself that he was capable of seeing a project through from start to finish. In the past, as Jerome Chodorov said in 1999, whenever Hart wrote a play "he wondered if it was Kaufman or somebody else who really did the work. You see what a neurosis can do."

Of course, *Lady in the Dark* was greatly enhanced by Kurt Weill's music, Ira Gershwin's lyrics, and Hassard Short's musical staging. But there was no question that the driving force from beginning to end had been Moss Hart. His success gave him the courage to tell Kaufman that he planned to write independently from then on, although he did not rule out the possibility of resuming their collaboration if a project arose that would be mutually appealing.

Hart told a columnist, Robert Rice, that he was no longer drawn to the sort of play he and Kaufman had written. "One reason for writing *Lady in the Dark* was my increasing disinterest for plays with plots; for what is known as 'the well-made play,'" he said. "I've become much more interested in characters than in stories." He further explained that his own psychoanalytic experiences were a determining factor in breaking with Kaufman. ". . . [O]ver the last few years I've literally sabotaged every serious idea I've had for a play. . . . [M]y psychoanalyst made me resolve that the next idea I had, whether it was good or lousy, I'd carry through. . . . And now, as the result of *Lady*'s success, and my own trend along a path of playwriting that isn't George Kaufman's *métier*, I can afford not to feel obligated to write a play every year, or to continue to work with George just for the sake of collaborating with him."

Lady in the Dark was not only a break with Kaufman as a collaborator, but a break from the kinds of plays with which Kaufman and Hart had attained so much success. For Hart, it marked a turning point in his career, for he devoted the remainder of his life to writing plays and screenplays that (with the single exception of *Light Up the Sky* in 1948) did not rely on satirical humor, witticisms, and wisecracks. Hart's decision to write in a wholly different style was a genuine act of courage, for he had attained great renown for his brilliance as a comic playwright, a renown that he willingly forsook in order to explore very different territory. However, his decision to change course was never entirely accepted by the public or the critics, some of whom continued to expect a comic romp whenever a play by Moss Hart was produced.

His new stature as a librettist drew the interest of other theatre professionals. Richard Rodgers and Oscar Hammerstein II, recognizing Hart's skillful and innovative use of the musical form, asked him to write the book for *Oklahoma!* in 1942 and *Carousel* the following year, according to Jerome Chodorov. Hart turned them down, however, realizing that his view of the world would clash drastically with Oscar Hammerstein's wide-eyed, naïve—but brilliantly accomplished—lyrics.

Hart was as pleased by the praise for his direction of *Lady in the Dark* as he was by the enthusiasm for the play itself. Years before, he had directed one amateur and summer camp production after another, and the experiences proved themselves to be a good apprenticeship for directing in the professional theatre. However, he wished in the future only to direct plays he had written, he said.

Thus, it was something of a surprise when he consented to direct *Junior Miss*, a play by Joseph Fields and Hart's old friend Jerome Chodorov. The authors asked him to direct their comedy and Hart said, "It's much too good in my opinion, to pass up. I love the play and know I'm going to have an exciting time doing it."

Junior Miss, about the comical problems of two adolescent girls, was derived from a series of short stories by Sally Benson. (Another series of Benson stories, written for *The New Yorker*, became the basis of the film *Meet Me in St. Louis*.) Hart invested in the production (as did Max Gordon, the producer, George S. Kaufman, Joseph Hyman, and the authors), which paid a handsome profit. Hart did not receive a salary for directing *Junior Miss*, opting, at Kaufman's suggestion, to receive a share of the weekly box-office receipts. This had been always been Kaufman's practice, and Hart now adopted the same procedure. If the plays he directed did not achieve success, his compensation would be low, perhaps nonexistent. On the other hand, extremely successful productions yielded him enormous profits.

Junior Miss began rehearsals in mid-October 1941, played for two weeks in Boston, and opened at the Lyceum Theatre in New York on November 18, 1941, to general acclaim[5]. Brooks Atkinson said, "it ought to make everyone very happy, indeed. For somehow it manages to capture the problem of living in the same house with two adolescent girls in just the proper mood of wonder and alarm." As to the direction, Atkinson said Hart staged the play "resourcefully and in high good humor."

John Anderson agreed that Hart "directed it expertly," but Wilella Waldorf, writing in the *Post*, dissented. She found *Junior Miss* "a surprisingly poor piece of playwriting, decidedly below par as Broadway standards go," and said that Hart, as director, "has sometimes rendered this distressing fact more obvious by his frantic attempts to cover it up." None of the actors, she said, "had much help from either playwrights or director."

Still, Waldorf was distinctly in the minority regarding Hart's direction. *Junior Miss*, the first play Hart directed on Broadway that he did not write, not only continued a professional directorial career that began with his direction of the West Coast company of *Once in a Lifetime*, but became, over time, his primary occupation. After *Lady in the Dark*, he would write only five more plays (in addition to contributing to some revues), but he would direct eleven plays and musicals.

For many years Hart had observed George S. Kaufman's directorial style, so it is not surprising that he adopted many of Kaufman's techniques. For instance, Kaufman was notorious for his attention to detail. To take one example, the timing of an offstage door slam in *The Man Who Came to Dinner* was worked and reworked for a full ten minutes. Hart, too, gained the reputation of a director for whom no detail was too small to overlook.

Kaufman was more concerned with timing than with any other aspect of the productions he directed. If he determined that a speech would be most effective if it was delivered in twenty-seven seconds, he would not settle for twenty-six or twenty-eight. Aspects of characterization were sometimes sacrificed on the altar of precise timing. Hart, too, focused upon timing, but, unlike his mentor, he was equally concerned with character development.

---

5 One specific result of the *Junior Miss* production was a romance Hart began with Paula Laurence, a member of the cast. According to Laurence's goddaughter, Stephanie Zimbalist, who made her revelation to Campbell Robertson of *The New York Times* many years after the fact (at a memorial dinner for Laurence in 2006, several months after Laurence's death), Laurence "was engaged to Moss Hart." The reporter then asked for Kitty Carlisle's reaction. Carlisle, who married Hart five years later, doubted that Hart's relationship with Laurence had progressed so far. "I don't think so," she said. "He took her out, but I don't think he ever asked her to marry him."

greatest contrast between Kaufman's directorial style and Hart's was in their approach to actors. Kaufman took great pains to establish an intimacy with each actor. When he offered direction, he spoke so quietly to the actor that no one else could hear. Hart's preference was to speak in a conversational tone with each actor, perhaps in the hope that other actors would intuit his approach to the direction of the play by listening to what he had to say. "Moss wasn't a whisperer," said Jerome Chodorov; "he talked up."

Like Kaufman, Hart was the antithesis of the loud, dictatorial, sadistic director that has become established in the public's mind. If the public's expectation of a director was someone who races about, nerves jangling, shouting at actors and technicians, periodically giving way to fits of temperament, Hart would have disappointed. He was quiet, methodical, reasonable, thorough, infinitely patient, never undercutting an actor's self-confidence, never fighting to establish his supremacy over other members of the production team. "The actors loved him," Chodorov said, "and rightfully."

Eddie Albert, who appeared in *Miss Liberty* under Hart's direction in 1948, echoed Chodorov's sentiment. He said of his experience, "it was nothing but a joy, and we had a wonderful time. There were no problems. It was heaven. Moss Hart was a man of real class."

Hart's versatility as a director stimulated the demand for his services. Because he had written successfully for comedies and dramas, musicals and revues, he had an understanding of all theatrical forms. Furthermore, his experiences as playwright and producer served him well in his directorial function, for he was able to see all sides of the theatrical equation. As Alan Jay Lerner said of him: "He was a superb constructionist and could put his finger on the most subtle dramatic weakness. He appreciated the actor's craft and always sought the best. He understood the producer's problems and the economic limitation, and was as practical as he was creative." Years later, Hart directed *My Fair Lady* and *Camelot*, both of which were the creation of Lerner and Frederick Loewe. Lerner said of the experience of working with Hart:

> To work with a director who is an outstanding creator in his own right has its allures, but can also be a terrifying experience. Only those writers who have been directed by Moss Hart can fully appreciate the tact, delicacy and sensitive understanding with which he went about his job. Never once did he try to superimpose his ideas on you. He saw the play through your eyes, and if he felt that in places you were becoming myopic or astigmatic he became your glasses to enable you to see your own work clearer. Were there ever a disagreement, you won. If you were proven right, he was the first to admit it. If you were

proven wrong, he was the easiest person to be wrong with. For in either case, it was always accomplished with warmth and humor.

Hart did not boast of his directorial ability to others, but took quiet pride in it. In his diary he recorded the following in 1954: "In some ways I think I am a very good director indeed—perhaps one of the best."

That year a young playwright watched Hart rehearse for a week with the cast of *Anniversary Waltz*. Throughout the week the playwright spoke not a word, leading Hart to believe that he was unimpressed. At the end of the week, however, the playwright sent Hart a letter, saying, "I watched you and I saw the dignity with which you treat people. This is a rare quality and you use it as if you genuinely understood the importance of the individual."

One of the director's fundamental responsibilities is to put the actor at his ease so that he may give the best performance of which he is capable. That responsibility must not interfere with the need for the director to establish control over his production, however. When Hart directed, that never occurred. As Bennett Cerf said, "Once rehearsals of a new play start, a new and very formidable Moss Hart emerges from the wings. Gone are the charm, the semi-serious self-deprecation. In their place is a stern, demanding general, in absolute control of his troops. . . . Why do they bow so meekly before him? Because they know from the moment the cast assembles on the very first day that a master is in control."

ↄ

If Moss Hart's focus had been primarily on his work from the time he was a teenager, that outlook changed during the Second World War. Even before the Japanese attack on Pearl Harbor, Hart's attention had turned from his own concerns to larger issues. *You Can't Take It With You* was, in a sense, Kaufman and Hart's response to the economic system that had produced the Depression; Hart had incorporated significant social themes into *The American Way*; his involvement with *From Vienna* had been prompted by his social conscience; and even his contribution to *Sing Out the News* demonstrated his interest in using his comic gifts to promote social betterment.

But it was the war that caused him to change drastically and permanently, from a man nearly obsessed by his career to one who gave generously—both in terms of his money and his time—to worthy causes. He became much more aware of aspects of life, such as politics, he had earlier chosen to ignore. As a result, the frenetic pace he had long maintained as a playwright slowed significantly, but he compensated by making many contributions to his profession, his country, the state of Israel, and to Jews around the world.

In January 1940, a committee was established by the American Theatre Wing to raise funds for British War Relief. Hart served with Kaufman and others as a member. He both wrote material for, and performed in, sketches at fundraising benefits. In April 1941, he wrote a portion of a radio program raising funds for British War Relief.

After America's entry into the war, Hart made every attempt to become directly involved. On January 10, 1942, after having been rejected by the army because of his age (nearly thirty-eight), he applied for a commission to the Navy, which turned him down because of "insufficient education." Nothing could be done about his age ("I guess I'm just too old for this war," he said), but he was consoled about his lack of formal education by the fact that he gave a lecture at Columbia University later that same day.[6]

In 1942, Hart, once again working with Kaufman, wrote several sketches for "The Lunchtime Follies," noontime entertainments designed to raise the spirits of factory workers engaged in the war effort. The first production, *Fun to Be Free*, was given by volunteer performers at the Todd Shipyards in Brooklyn on June 22 after a "tryout performance" on Long Island the week before. Some five thousand helmeted workers, carrying sandwiches and desserts, crowded around a makeshift stage, watching two Kaufman–Hart sketches; "Washington, D.C." and "The Man Who Went to Moscow" (with David Burns, the Banjo of *The Man Who Came to Dinner*, playing Hitler) and listening to vocalist Anne Francine sing a song by Harold Rome, who accompanied her on the piano. The entertainment, which also included dance numbers, lasted for forty-five minutes.

Hart served as master of ceremonies, explaining why the Theatre Wing was sponsoring the "Lunchtime Follies." At the end of the presentation, a navy lieutenant spoke to the laborers about the significance of the work in which they were engaged.

Hart's co-chairman of "The Lunchtime Follies" was George Heller, who years before had performed in *You Can't Take It With You*. The enterprise continued for three years, during which Kaufman and Hart contributed several additional sketches, including "The Paperhanger" and "Dream On, Soldier." These sketches, while minor contributions to the Kaufman–Hart canon, served their purpose admirably.

---

6 This was Hart's version of the events. But Steven Bach has evidence that Hart took steps to ensure that he would not be drafted. "According to Department of the Army records," Bach notes, Hart "requested and was granted a deferment because of a dependent father and his claim that he had a breakdown and had been under psychiatric treatment for six years."

On April 5, 1943, Kaufman and Hart acted in a sketch they co-wrote at Madison Square Garden, in a show given for the benefit of the Red Cross. Others who appeared in the presentation included Ethel Merman, Helen Hayes, Paul Muni, Gypsy Rose Lee, Alfred Lunt, Ray Bolger, Tallulah Bankhead, and Fredric March, all volunteering their services.

The *National Jewish Monthly* saluted Hart for his "selfless interest in the plight of your fellow Jews and your great services to the cause of the refugees [from Nazi Germany and occupied countries]. You're one swell guy," it concluded.

But Hart's greatest contribution to the war effort was a play he wrote entirely on his own, the first such effort of his professional career. The project began when Lieutenant Colonel Dudley S. Dean, executive manager of the Air Forces Branch of Army Emergency Relief, conceived the notion of a presentation to explain to the general public the inner workings of the Air Force. He explained his idea to Lieutenant Irving Lazar, whose experience as an agent at the William Morris Agency qualified him as a theatrical expert.

Or, in the version Lazar told in his autobiography, *Swifty*, it was Lazar who set the wheels in motion. Lazar said that a captain showed him a directive from General Henry H. ("Hap") Arnold, the commander of the Army Air Force, suggesting a benefit production for AAF Emergency Relief that would be similar to Irving Berlin's musical revue, *This Is the Army*, which had raised a good deal of money for the army. Lazar said that he "told the captain I could give him a show that would make Berlin's production look tame," and, on the basis of very little more than his bravado, was introduced to General Arnold, who told Lazar to begin assembling the talent necessary for a benefit production.

In any case, Lazar subsequently encountered Hart sipping a cocktail in the Oak Room of the Plaza Hotel. Lazar approached Hart, said, "You don't know me," but explained that General Arnold had assigned him to put a benefit production together, and posed a question: "Would you like to do a show for the Air Force?" Hart, a bit surprised by the directness of Lazar's approach, but concerned that he was still not contributing sufficiently to the war effort, neither declined nor accepted. Instead, he answered, "Call me tomorrow."

The following day Lazar called Hart, saying, "It's all set." When Hart said that he would need to hear from someone higher in the chain of command, Lazar assured him that he would soon be contacted by General Arnold. Then, depending upon whose account one believes, Lazar sent Hart a telegram, signing General Arnold's name to it (Lazar's version), or, as a result of Lazar's urging, General Arnold sent the telegram asking Hart to meet with the general at the Pentagon on Wednesday afternoon (Hart's version). In any case, Lazar was able to arrange a meeting between the general and the playwright.

The meeting began awkwardly. After Lazar introduced Hart to Arnold, it took Moss only two minutes to realize that the general had no idea who he was. Hart, embarrassed, tried to exit gracefully, but Lazar jumped in, praising Hart's theatrical expertise and producing a scrapbook with reviews of Hart's plays. Now understanding the reason for the meeting, Arnold asked, according to Lazar, "Do you think you can do this show for the Army Air Force in the dignified way it should be done?" and Hart responded, "General, if you want me, I'll do it."

Hart wrote a lengthy newspaper article describing the remainder of the encounter:

> General Arnold managed to convey so quickly his excitement, his zeal, his passion and his sense of wonder at what is called the Army Air Forces that I managed to forget the four stars on his shoulder and was soon swept up in what I might roughly term his own sense of theatre. . . . Our first talk ended with General Arnold asking how I intended to go about writing . . . I replied that since I knew nothing about the Air Force whatever I thought it would be sensible for me to take a trip to an airfield and see what went on. He smiled at this and suggested instead a tour of the various air bases throughout the country, ending up with, "When can you be ready to leave, Mr. Hart?" "Oh, in about three days," I replied blithely, shook hands, and three days later I was strapped into an Army bomber and on my way to Fort Worth, Texas.

Before departing, Hart spent an evening with Beatrice Kaufman, whose relationship with Hart had deepened to such an extent that she despaired at the idea of not seeing him for the duration of his absence. For years she and Hart had conversed nearly every day; now she was forced to endure an enforced absence that she knew would be painful. They spent the evening before he left New York in each other's company, attempting to soothe the pain of their imminent separation.

In May 1943, he began a two-month tour of Army camps and airfields. Despite his own congenital airsickness and nervous stomach, he traveled in the bomber provided for him, seeking material for his play. During those eight weeks, Hart, who had spent his adult life in the company of theatre folk, said, "I learned more about my country in terms of people than I had ever learned before."

As he took off in a plane for the first time, "The first thing they did," Hart explained, "was to set up a table, typewriter, and chair in the bomb-bay, strap a parachute on me, zoom a couple of thousand miles straight up in the air, and say to me, 'So, go ahead, write the play.'" But Hart did not begin writing until the two-month observation tour ended.

In Fort Worth, he was informed of training methods in the chart and statistical room of the air base by General Yount, the head of the Flying Training Command. He was then flown to Keesler Field in Mississippi. Hart traveled twenty-eight thousand miles in all, during which he observed the life of the Air Cadet at every stage: from induction to graduation. He was attempting to "cover in eight weeks the entire training program of fifteen months and to follow, step by step, each phase of a pilot, bombardier or navigator's training from the time he entered the Air Forces in civilian clothes until the day he embarked in his own ship with his own crew for combat duty."

During Hart's two-month tour he lost fifteen pounds. On one occasion in Kansas, the plane on which he was flying ran into a tornado. The flight crew seemed to deal calmly with the crisis, but Hart was frightened "nearly to death." Only when they were safely on the ground did the pilot admit that he, too, had been terrified.

Hart, famous for sleeping until noon, changed his habits entirely during the tour, becoming completely immersed in Army life. He arose every morning at 4:30 A.M., ate with the men, and performed every task the men performed.

When the men slept—lights were out at nine o' clock—Hart organized his notes, rarely falling asleep until midnight. As he said, "it added up to quite a day."

At each stop Hart dressed in a private's uniform and attempted to blend in with the soldiers. No one except the commanding officers at each field knew that he was a playwright gathering material, rather than a recruit. In case some suspected that Hart, as much as twenty years older than many of the men ("I must have seemed the oldest-looking cadet" in the Air Force," he said), was not what he claimed to be, he carried false papers. He slept with the men in the barracks and ate in the cafeteria. His disguise allowed him not only to observe the men but participate in activities with them, gathering the material that would eventually be used to make up a play—material that would not simply be a factual account of Air Force training procedures, however, but a detailing of the emotions felt by each cadet as he went through every step in the process.

Hart not only observed but experienced "the highlights of each phase [of training] and each transition . . . for each phase an aircrew man passes through is a special dramatic and emotional experience."

At Columbia, Missouri, Hart took part in and observed the college training program. "I arrived at the college at dawn," he said, "to find that a group
was going up for the first ride in what is correctly termed a Puddle-Jumper, or
what the boys themselves call a Maytag Messershmitt. This, their first ride in
a plane after four months of cleaning latrines is quite an event and I wanted
to be part of it, so I promptly became part of the group and went up too."

The next stop was Santa Ana, where Hart and the cadets went through
"three days of exhaustion and terror" in preparation for the classification
tests. "I went through the same tests they did, and a curious thing happened,"
he said. "By 11 o'clock the morning of the first day of the tests I completely
forgot that I was only a middle-aged playwright in search of material for a
play. I wanted to pass those tests more than anything else in the world." He
never found the nerve to ask whether or not he was successful.

On the day of classification, the cadets were informed whether, on the
basis of their test scores, they were to become pilots, bombardiers, or navigators. It was, Hart said, "one of the most exciting and dramatic moments I
have ever been present at, and I found myself pulling quite as hard as any one
of them to see that they got the classification their hearts were set on."

From Santa Ana, Hart was flown to a flight training school. "I spent my
first day with a group who were getting their clothing issue and the excitement at receiving their first flying jackets and flying suits, their parachutes,
their helmets and their goggles was something to behold."

Basic and advanced flying training came next, with Hart "rather breath-
lessly [keeping] to my program of taking each successive step with them and
doing everything they did." Finally, in July, Hart observed graduation ceremonies at a base in the desert, finding the enthusiasm of the cadets—now
officers—touching. As he discovered, "graduation is not the end, but the beginning. These young officers, fresh out of their first day in the sacred
precincts of the Officers' Club ship right to operational training units where
they meet the crews they are to fly with and the ships they are to fly."

Hart accompanied one crew to the embarkation field "and stayed with
them down on the flying line till that last moment when they took off . . . for
combat. No play and no playwright can ever quite do justice to the poignancy
of that particular moment."

The sophisticated man of the theatre was moved by the gallantry of the young
men whose training he chronicled. Hart wrote of the impressions he formed:

A strange and wonderful kind of camaraderie develops among the boys in the
Air Force. I was at one field the week a class was to graduate, and I got to know

some of the boys. They were all quite excited because their mothers and girls were coming for the ceremony—the mothers to pin the wings on, and the girls the bars. . . .

These American kids are a whole new breed. They work incredibly hard for what is really the privilege of dying. I've seen so many acts of individual heroism outside of combat.

All in all, the seven months Hart spent touring the airfields, writing, and directing the play were "the roughest and toughest seven months in my life," he said, "and there were several times I wished I were dead."

After months of collecting information, Hart returned to New York with "a suitcase full of notes." Irving Lazar's notion had been that Hart would write a revue, using the talents of famous Hollywood performers in the Air Force such as Clark Gable, James Stewart, and Henry Fonda, but Hart was determined to write a play that would detail the progress of an Air Force cadet and would feature, not well-known actors, but, in Lazar's words, "good working talents who were young enough to be in active military service."

Hart spent the next two days deep in thought, trying to conceive an appropriate structure for the as-yet untitled play. His reverie was interrupted by a call from Washington, however, informing him that he must decide on an opening date immediately, for Hart's plan was to cast the male roles in the play entirely with soldiers, and the Air Force needed considerable lead time in order to arrange auditions, and, for those who were cast, to arrange release time from their units. He chose November 2, 1943, as the date for the pre-Broadway opening and set to work. It was, he said, the most difficult task he had ever faced, as he hoped to write something "very simple, very un-Broadway." In order to do so, "I had to find a whole new way of writing—like learning to walk all over again." His goal was to "put down the thing that is the Army Air Force in terms of the men rather than the planes." Daunting as his task was, everything came together quickly, and the play was completed in a few weeks.

As Hart was adding the finishing touches, Irving Lazar and Lieutenant Ben Landis traveled to 125 air bases, interviewing soldiers who had potential as actors, musicians, singers, and technicians. In all, some seven thousand applicants were considered; three thousand of them applied to work on the play.

Hart's drama focuses on three young men from a small town in Ohio,[7] pairs them with three other aspiring pilots—one from an Oregon farm, another from

---

[7] Ohio seems to have represented all of America outside New York to Hart, who set *The American Way* and *The Man Who Came to Dinner*, as well as the opening scenes of his new play there. Moreover, Liza, in *Lady in the Dark*, came to New York from Ohio.

a wealthy family in Texas, and another from Brooklyn—and follows them for a year throughout every stage of training, then into combat in the South Pacific. At the end one of the six has been killed in action, another has been wounded, and the others return to the plane they have decided to call "Winged Victory."

Nineteen scenes in all show the men's arrival at cadet barracks, their attendance at military lectures, their examinations before classification boards, and other slices of military life. Many of the scenes provide the audience with factual information about the nature of air force training, but the emphasis is always on the emotions of those whose lives are being affected. The tone of the scenes varies from tragic to humorous, although the wisecracking humor associated with Hart's earlier work is limited to the dialogue of the cadet from Brooklyn. The one constant in the play, however, is a mute tension that permeates every scene: whether the men will receive the assignments they desire, whether they will succeed in their training, whether they will survive in combat. The men's wives, mothers, and girlfriends are also portrayed, in scenes dealing with their fears, frustrations, and hopes. One of the most poignant sequences shows three of the wives following their husbands from one camp to another, living in cheap hotel rooms. (Thirty-nine civilian actresses, many of them wives of soldiers, portrayed the women.) All the scenes, taken together, make up a cross-section of wartime America.

Hart was under some mild pressure from the military. Major General Barney M. Giles asked him to tone down a scene in which, as a result of the classification board's meeting, some cadets, to their intense disappointment, are assigned to become navigators and bombardiers rather than pilots. The general wrote that the disappointment was "overemphasized. . . . I should hate to have [the play] in any way contribute to a feeling . . . that any important distinction in value or recognition exists . . . in the various positions in our aircrews. I wonder if you would give this a little thought and see if the possibility of any such impression can be eliminated." Hart decided to leave the scene as he had written it, thus showing as realistic a portrait as possible of the men's reaction to their training.

Though the play is not free of clichés—patriotic, idealistic speeches, the blustering cadet from Texas, the cynical but plucky kid from Brooklyn—one cannot but admire Hart's skill, not only at chronicling the progress of the cadets, but at the infusion of sincere, affecting emotion. To be sure, the propagandistic nature of the play (above all, Hart was intent on paying tribute to the gallantry of the young men in the Air Forces) and its occasional sentimentality may now, more than sixty years later, be looked upon as weaknesses, but as a wartime enterprise, designed to raise money for Army Emergency Relief, the piece is a superb effort. The play, although intended to inform, is not overly didactic. One can understand why critics described it as "moving, inspiring and stimulating" (as critic Lewis Nichols did). The work is excellently crafted; it has energy and honesty; it skillfully shows the life of the men in the Air Force, tracing their development from raw recruits to fighting men. The characters, and the audience, feel the excitement—and often the pain—of going through each phase.

On September 15, more than five hundred soldiers from air camps and bases arrived in New York to participate in final auditions for Hart's still untitled play. Time was getting short, for Hart wished to begin rehearsals in October and to open the play in Boston, play there for two weeks, perform for a week in Washington, D.C., then open on Broadway around Thanksgiving.

Hart's task was to select three hundred men for the cast of the play he announced would be known as *Winged Victory*. He was free to choose soldiers of all ranks, but neither pilots nor cadets could be considered, for their priority was combat.

He then organized and directed the play's production, a mammoth enterprise. All the male members of the cast were enrolled in the Air Forces. A few—such as Lieutenant Tim Holt, Sergeant Peter Lind Hayes, Privates Freddie Bartholomew, Karl Malden, Don Taylor, Barry Nelson, Red Buttons, Edmond O'Brien, Lee J. Cobb, and Paul Stewart—had had professional acting experience, but, for most, this marked the soldiers' first time on a stage.

Sergeant David Rose, an accomplished musician, was recruited by Lazar to write incidental music for the play based on Army songs and to conduct the orchestra of forty-five Army musicians. A chorus of fifty soldiers sang Army songs. Corporal Harry Horner, who had utilized revolving stages when, as a civilian, he designed *Lady in the Dark*, used the same scheme again as the designer of *Winged Victory*.

Hart's legendary generosity, formerly lavished on his family and friends, now extended to the enormous cast. He regularly picked up the meal checks for the air cadets during rehearsals. He endeared himself to the company by learning the names of all three hundred members of the cast within a week and calling each actor by his first name. Moreover, when the soldier-actors informed him that they were not receiving enough money to live with some degree of comfort in New York, Hart flew to Washington. After a meeting at the Pentagon, he returned to announce that everyone's per diem had been raised by two dollars (to be taken from box office receipts).

The production cost of $100,000 was raised by a civilian committee headed by Broadway producer Gilbert Miller. Miller and nineteen others each contributed $5,000, with the understanding that they would recover their investment if the play were successful, but that all profits would go to Army Emergency Relief.

The official producer of the play was the United States Army Air Forces of Army Emergency Relief. Joseph Hyman served as civilian liaison, planning all the details of the production.

The play was priced to be affordable to nearly everyone. Balcony seats were sold for $1.65 (except for Saturday night, when the price jumped to $2.20). Tickets for $1.10 were available during weekday matinees.

Hart refused any pay for the work he did on *Winged Victory*, donating whatever he might have earned to the Army Emergency Relief fund. Later, when he wrote and supervised the film based on the play, he donated his salary to the Air Force Benevolent Society. In all, *Winged Victory* took two years of Moss Hart's life, during which he took no compensation whatsoever. His commitment cost him a great deal economically, but enriched him in many profound ways. He subsequently referred to the experience as the most rewarding of his life.

Employing George S. Kaufman's method, Hart opted for a brief, intense rehearsal period, despite the complexity of the production. *Winged Victory* rehearsed for only two and a half weeks. The logistics of the production were difficult—even finding sufficient backstage space for three hundred performers was a challenge—but military discipline prevailed throughout the rehearsal process, imposing order on what otherwise might have been chaos. Officers were placed in charge of transportation, supply and materials, and medical care.

Even the enormous number of cast members and the brevity of the rehearsal period did not change Hart's calm, placid demeanor. "It was astounding to watch Moss as a director," Lazar observed. "He never yelled. If something bothered him, he would always go up to the stage, pull the actor aside, and speak to him privately and gently . . ."

The male members of the company were housed three to a room at the Narragansett Hotel. Military drills were held in the morning; special courses on playwriting and theatre techniques were arranged for those men who were not actively engaged in rehearsing on any given day.

Prior to the New York opening, a special exhibition of scene designs, color sketches, and Hart's original script was displayed at the Museum of the City of New York, beginning on October 25. The exhibit also featured photographs of Hart's tour of army camps and bases.

Early in the rehearsal process, the company gave a reading of the play for military officers, flown to New York for the occasion. Everyone was apprehensive about the brass's response, but Hart defused the tension by addressing the officers before the reading. "I am reminded," he said,

> of the story of the acrobat who performed the death-defying feat of sliding on one foot from a wire stretched across the third balcony to center stage. After a heroic introduction followed by a tumultuous fanfare, a little old man steps from the wings, his tights hanging loosely about his legs. He eyes the wire, then scans the audience. Again his eyes travel up the length of the wire, and then with a sigh, turns again to the audience: "If you want to see an old Jew get killed, I'll do it."

Everyone shared in the laughter and the reading proceeded to the satisfaction of the military observers.

The play opened at the Shubert Theatre in Boston on November 2, 1943, before a full house that included many Army officers. Not even the length of the play—three and a half hours—marred a "tumultuous reception," as *The New York Times* characterized it. Elinor Hughes, the Boston critic, summarized her response by calling *Winged Victory* "an enormously impressive spectacle which also manages to be an honest and stirring play." During the twelve-day Boston run, receipts totaled $53,000.

The first New York performance was given on November 20, 1943, at the Forty-fourth Street Theatre, with members of the Army, Navy, and Air Force, the governor of Connecticut, and members of Congress mingling with the usual opening night throng.

Traditionally, first-night audiences on Broadway rush for the exits as quickly as possible after the final curtain. In this case, however, an ovation continued for eighteen curtain calls and did not subside until Hart was persuaded to make a curtain speech. He spoke briefly. "I have just heard on the radio that we have just bombed Berlin again," he said. "That's what this play is about."

Lewis Nichols in the *Times* called *Winged Victory* "stirring, moving and, what is more important, a most human play" acted with "understanding, dignity, humor and warmth." Hart's writing was praised as "moving," his direction described as "masterful. . . . Mr. Hart has taken all the strands of what could have been sprawling confusion and has bound them into a fine, rapidly moving show."

The notices were nearly unanimous in praise of the play, the acting and directing, the settings, and the musical direction. Ward Morehouse said in the *Sun* that "The American theater rose to magnificence" with *Winged Victory*. "Here is a thrilling show, a combination of play and spectacle that dwarfs all else of the current season and beside which the majority of productions of the present decade and century shrink to mediocrity." Howard Barnes in the *Herald-Tribune* called it "a brilliant play on any terms as well as the greatest of all war shows." John Chapman joined the enthusiastic chorus in the *Daily News*: "It is big, but simple. It is thrilling, yet tender. It is funny and it will make you weep." And Burton Rascoe in the *World-Telegram* called it "a thrilling spectacle, full of emotional drive. It is spine-tingling and it wrenches your heart. It is earthy and glamorous, ribald and romantic, tragic and glorious, and it is instructive."

Rosamond Gilder wrote in *Theatre Arts* that Hart has "served the theatre by proving beyond argument that a play can be serious, even didactic, and at the same time superb entertainment; he has served himself by adding yet another cubit to his stature as a playwright."

George Jean Nathan rejected the play's artistry, however, writing, "I assume that this newspaper pays me not to be a patriot but to be a theatre critic." In his review, Nathan quoted some lines, purportedly from the play, to illustrate his contention that the play failed aesthetically. Hart wrote an angry rebuttal, accusing Nathan of being "repertorially inaccurate and intellectually dishonest." According to Hart, "Most of the lines you quoted from the play were never spoken on the stage of the 44th Street Theatre opening night. As a matter of fact, they were out during rehearsals and were never even spoken in Boston. You have been guilty of critical malpractices before and it is high time that someone called you to account for this, because your review was inaccurate, dishonest and snide."

But Nathan's review was clearly a minority report. More representative of the response to the play was the Donaldson Award for Outstanding Achievement in the Theatre Hart received as "Best Director of the 1943–44 season" for *Winged Victory*.

President and Mrs. Roosevelt expressed interest in having *Winged Victory* performed at the White House (without scenery) early in December. Eventually a performance was arranged for January 24, 1944, but the enormous cast size made the idea of a White House production too unwieldy and it had to be canceled.

General Arnold, busy with military duties, was unable to see the play until early in 1944. After watching a performance, he notified Hart by telegram of his approval. For Hart, Arnold's praise was the most important recognition he received. Despite the general admiration for the play, he said, "I kept waiting until you had seen it—and now that you have and that you have liked it, means more to me than I can tell you. . . . If there is such a thing as inspiration, it seems to me that it came in my first talk with you; and if I have been able to capture that indefinable something called the 'spirit' of the Air Forces, it had its beginning as I listened to you tell, at that first meeting, of the magic and the wonder and the miracle that is the AAF."

General George C. Marshall, Chief of Staff of the War Department, attended the performance with General Arnold. He wrote to Hart, saying, "It was an outstanding show and one which I thoroughly enjoyed from beginning to end."

General Arnold inscribed the published version of Hart's copy of *Winged Victory*: "With full appreciation of your highly successful efforts in starting from scratch and completing this play which so effectively portrayed the aims—ideals—and workings of the Air Forces." For his part, Hart dedicated the book to General Arnold.

An advance sale of $168,000 for the theatrical production insured the return of the backers' investments. Although the weekly operating cost of the play was $50,000, checks totaling $100,000 were mailed to the investors on January 10, 1944. Every week thereafter *Winged Victory* turned over approximately $25,000 to the Army Emergency Relief fund.

A one-hour version of *Winged Victory* with the original cast was broadcast on the "Radio Hall of Fame" in December 1943. Bob Hope and Jimmy Durante, among others, made special appearances. Hart received a citation "for his distinguished contribution to the literature of World War II."

Winged Victory closed on Broadway after 212 performances, but only so that it could be made into a film. Twentieth Century-Fox obtained the rights to the play by donating a million dollars to Army Emergency Relief. Hart went to Hollywood in mid-December 1943 to write the screenplay and supervise the filming with the director. It was the only time in Hart's career that he wrote the screenplay for a film made from one of his plays.

The screenplay, which varied little from the play, was completed on February 29, 1944. Since the play was cinematic in its structure there was little difficulty in adapting it to the screen. It is perhaps true, as Bosley Crowther said in his review of the picture in *The New York Times*, that film "was the medium which was most appropriate to it all the time."

Hart recognized that he would be likely to have less control over the picture than he had over the play. However, bearing in mind General Arnold's lament about "what usually happened when Hollywood made a picture about the Air Force," he was determined to maintain the play's integrity. Consequently, Hart wrote Arnold that he would remain in Hollywood until the picture was completed. "My feeling," he said, "is that the only way I can be sure that the whole fabric and texture of the play is captured completely by the screen is to stay right here, and in addition to writing the play for the screen, see to it very thoroughly that it is presented in as simple and as honest a way as the play is." He committed himself to a full year in Hollywood, a commitment he would normally have avoided at all costs.

The film was originally scheduled to be directed by William Wyler, but was eventually turned over to George Cukor. The servicemen who made up the Broadway cast, chorus, and orchestra repeated their roles in the film, traveling by troop train from New York to California along with the technicians, who were also Air Force men. They were housed in a GI encampment near the ocean in Santa Monica, about seven miles from the film studio. On May 31, only a few days after they arrived, every member of the cast was given a screen test. Filming took place from June 15 until September 25, with scenes filmed at more than twenty military camps in California. The battle scenes, set in New Guinea, were filmed at a Marine Corps base, where a jungle of "coconut palm trees" (actually eucalyptus trees whose trunks were covered with painted paper towels) were purchased for $50 each and replanted.[8] Some street scenes were filmed in San Francisco, where the scenes of embarkation took place.

Darryl Zanuck, the film's producer, gave ten-week contracts to the wives of the soldiers, some of whom played small roles, while others were used as extras. The larger female roles were played by Twentieth Century-Fox contract performers such as Jeanne Crain and Judy Holliday.

Although the filming went smoothly, the long stay in Hollywood took its toll on Hart. Joe Hyman, in July 1944, reported in a letter to a mutual friend that Hart was "sick as a dog as usual."

The movie was favorably reviewed. Bosley Crowther called *Winged Victory* "one of the most successful films about this war. . . . a stunning production." He noted that "all the poignancy and zeal" of the play were preserved in the picture. And although Crowther regretted the sentimentality of some of the scenes, he said "there is no question that Mr. Hart captured much of the gallantry and pathos of youth rushing toward dangerous adventures with surface enthusiasm and inner dread."

---

8 After the filming, the Marine Corps used the site as a jungle training course for men heading for combat.

Variety said that *Winged Victory* "was a memorable evening in the theatre—and the picture is no less worthy. . . . Its appeal has the punch of an Army backfield." The critic noted the many "poignant scenes" and praised Cukor's direction as well as Hart's screenplay.

Immediately after shooting was completed for the film, the company began rehearsals on September 28 for a twenty-eight-week road tour of the play, beginning with a performance in Los Angeles on October 9, then playing in San Francisco, St. Louis, Philadelphia, Washington, D.C., Pittsburgh, Chicago, and many other venues, ending its run in Richmond, Virginia, on April 21, 1945. As on Broadway, most of the women in the play were acted by the soldiers' wives, thereby saving money on the salaries that would have been necessary for professional actresses.[9]

The road tour alone played before 837,000 persons and took in $1,124,656.62. In Chicago, *Winged Victory* broke *Lady in the Dark*'s record for the highest-grossing production ever given in that city.

In February 1946, after the war's conclusion, Joseph Hyman turned over an additional check to the Army Air Forces Aid Society of $1,414,620. General Arnold wrote Hart a letter expressing his appreciation:

Dear Moss:

Not quite three years ago I can remember when *Winged Victory* was just an idea without even a name. Through your special talent this idea grew into a stage play and motion picture which proved a forceful factor in the great struggle in which we were engaged. . . . I am sure that it must give you a warm feeling as it does me, to realize that these funds will be used to repair the ravages and suffering caused by war among personnel and their families whose efforts and sacrifices saw us through to victory.

Two years later, a reunion of three hundred members of the *Winged Victory* company was held in New York. Peter Lind Hayes, Ray Middleton, Edmond O'Brien, Red Buttons, and David Rose, among others who had contributed so successfully to the 1943 production and 1944 film, assembled at the Savoy Plaza to pay tribute to Moss Hart, a man who wrote and directed an outstanding play, and contributed to morale that helped, at least to some degree, to win the war.

☙

For Hart, the change in his character brought about by events leading up to and during World War II was permanent. For the rest of his life he sought to

---

9 The professional actresses' salaries ranged from $46 per week to $165. The starlets in the movie were replaced by stage actresses.

use his talents for worthwhile social endeavors. He publicly supported Franklin Roosevelt in his bid for a third presidential term in 1940, and, in return, the Roosevelts welcomed him as a visitor to the White House. In 1944, he contributed to a newspaper article (along with Fredric March, Lillian Hellman, and others) entitled "Why I Will Vote For Franklin D. Roosevelt."

In 1947, Hart was one of several speakers on a radio program, "Hollywood Fights Back," that announced its opposition to the House Committee on Un-American Activities, which was conducting hearings into alleged Communist infiltration of the movies. Opposition to the hearings was led by the Committee for the First Amendment, of which Hart was a member, along with Humphrey Bogart, Lauren Bacall, Leonard Bernstein, George S. Kaufman, and others.

Two months later, Hart joined with other playwrights and screenwriters in filing an anti-trust suit against the Motion Picture Association of America, its president, Eric Johnston, individual movie studios, and the Association of Motion Picture Producers in an attempt to end the studios' and the associations' ban on writers with alleged Communist leanings.[10]

In March 1948, Hart spoke on behalf of the Stop Censorship Movement, a group formed "to combat the rising menace of censorship threatening to engulf and stifle freedom of expression in every field of the creative arts in America."

Hart was encouraged by developments in the Middle East. He wrote to Brooks Atkinson in 1948, "Like yourself, I feel that the State of Israel is here to stay, and for the first time in many months I feel the winds of the world blowing fresher. . . . And I don't mean just Israel—I mean the world and men generally. We're beginning to learn a little, aren't we? Slowly and painfully, to be sure, but we're beginning."

In the 1940s, Hart successfully ran for office (as president of the Dramatists Guild, then the Authors League). He became co-chairman (with George S. Kaufman) of the legitimate theatre committee of the United Jewish Appeal, raising hundreds of thousands of dollars. He raised money for Holocaust survivors. He became a trustee of the Dramatic Workshop. He served as a member of a committee to select young American actors for a scholarship to study at the Old Vic in London. He spoke at commencement exercises. He spoke out publicly on issues confronting artists, particularly writers. He gave lectures on playwriting for the benefit of the American Theatre Wing.

---

10 The suit was dismissed on technical grounds later in 1948.

The global awareness that Hart evidenced in the 1940s continued in the 1950s. Furthermore, his position as head of the Dramatists Guild and his expanding commitment to non-theatrical matters led him to take overt political stands.

In 1952, he spoke out strongly and courageously against the political witch hunts conducted by Senator Joseph McCarthy and others. He announced his support of Adlai Stevenson in his presidential campaign of 1952.

In May 1954, Hart acted as Master of Ceremonies at a meeting of Americans for Democratic Action, introducing Eleanor Roosevelt and Supreme Court Justice William O. Douglas. The entertainment lasted until half past two in the morning, but Hart, generally apprehensive about such matters, "was quite unnervous and rather enjoyed doing it," he said. "Kitty [Carlisle, to whom by then he was married] told me I was very good and did an excellent job, and . . . I rather think that I did all right."

Again in 1956, Hart worked to elect Adlai Stevenson president. In October, Hart combined with Oscar Hammerstein II, Alan Jay Lerner, and author Herman Wouk to produce a closed-circuit telecast to raise money for the Stevenson campaign, which was, for the second consecutive time, limping to an unsuccessful close.

Stevenson expressed his gratitude in a letter, saying, "Your support and encouragement mean a great deal to me and I want you to know how very grateful I am."

The man who had been consumed by his career, turning out one play after another with astounding speed, giving little thought to the welfare of others, became the antithesis of his former self. As the pace of his playwriting slowed, he discovered and employed aspects of his humanity that had long lain dormant.

Chapter 8 MARRIAGE AND CHILDREN
1945–1950

W HEN *WINGED VICTORY* CLOSED IN 1945, HART WAS ONLY FORTY
years old and seemingly in the prime of his playwriting career. He
had no reason to suspect that his fertile imagination would fail him. Although he would live for seventeen more years, however, he would write only
three more plays produced on Broadway. Despite the writing of three screenplays, sketches for two revues, and an autobiographical memoir, Hart felt his
ability to write plays—the one thing that mattered more to him than anything
else in the world—slipping away. He suffered a massive case of writer's block
that lasted until the end of his life.

The time between composing plays was used to continue his directing career and to begin work on a memoir of his early life, a project that would take
him more than fifteen years to complete.

Having earned no money on *Winged Victory*, Hart had to return to work as
quickly as possible, so he turned out three sketches for Beatrice Lillie for a musical revue, *Seven Lively Arts*, which opened on December 7, 1944, with Hart's
sketches—and Lillie's performance—gaining the best reviews. *Seven Lively
Arts* was a modest success (Howard Barnes in the New York *Herald-Tribune*
called it "both inspired and ordinary"), running for 183 performances.

Hart simultaneously worked on another project, directing Norman Krasna's
Dear Ruth for his brother, Bernie, who was making his debut as a producer,
sharing the title with Joe Hyman. The play, like *Junior Miss*, was a comedy
about adolescent girls. In this case, they become entangled in the romantic
story of a lieutenant, a veteran of twenty-five combat missions, who comes
home to claim the girl he's never met but whose photographs have been sent
to him. *Dear Ruth* opened on December 13 at Henry Miller's Theatre, less
than a week after the opening of *Seven Lively Arts*. "Moss Hart has directed it
to perfection," Lewis Nichols enthused in the *Times*, and Howard Barker in
the *Herald-Tribune* was equally enthusiastic, citing "Moss Hart's superb direction." On the other hand, Burton Rascoe's notice in the *World-Telegram*
was scornful. "Badly directed," he said. "The play wavers back and forth between a standard soap opera romance and third-rate farce; it is timed too fast
for one and too slow for the other."

Reviews for the play ranged from Ward Morehouse's favorable verdict ("a genial and warming comedy") to Rascoe's disdainful judgment ("lifeless, machine made"). Nichols liked the play ("it has a bubbling humor and a speed all its own"), although he acknowledged that "there is nothing whatever new in it."

Audiences cast their votes by eagerly purchasing tickets. *Dear Ruth* ran until July 1946, for a total of 680 performances.

Two performances were notable. On April 8, 1945, *Dear Ruth* was given a special Sunday evening performance for the officers and enlisted personnel of the United States Naval Training Station at Norfolk, Virginia. And on October 24, Hart, who was always concerned about the need to introduce playgoers to Broadway at an early age, agreed with Hyman and Bernie Hart to offer a ten-cent matinee for 945 high school students from thirty high schools, plus a number of children with physical disabilities who were homebound. The theatrical unions cooperated to allow the low-priced performance.

Not content with having spent two years of his life working on *Winged Victory*, Hart offered his services as director and lead actor in a production of *The Man Who Came to Dinner* to be given at military bases in the South Pacific—known as the "foxhole circuit." He said, "Don't ask me why, but I couldn't sit out the war at the Stork Club. . . . I felt I wasn't doing enough for the war effort." As a result, USO-Camp Show Overseas Unit 453 was formed. General H. H. Arnold wrote to Hart on January 7, 1945, "Delighted to hear that you're taking *The Man Who Came to Dinner* overseas."

Just before Hart's departure for the South Pacific, the Kaufmans gave him a farewell party. George Kaufman wrote a sketch called "Moss Hart at the Analyst's" and played Hart in the sketch, while Martin Gabel played Dr. Kubie. A sample of the dialogue:

KUBIE

Tell me, Moss—have you forgotten that this is an anniversary?

MOSS

Anniversary?

KUBIE

You're beginning your twenty-fifth year of analysis today.

MOSS

You don't mean it? Twenty-five years! (*He sits up.*) Well, well! (*He shakes hands with the Doctor.*) Say, you're pretty good-looking—I never saw your face before.

KUBIE

I like yours too. I've always seen it upside down.

MOSS

Well, back to work. (*Lies down again.*) What year is this?

KUBIE

This is 1945.

MOSS

1945, huh? I haven't slept since 1941.

KUBIE

On my records it mentions a nap you had in 1943.

MOSS

It does?

Kaufman worked Hart's relationship with Joe Hyman into the sketch. Moss's deeply-felt gratitude for the two-hundred-dollar loan Hyman had made to him years before, a loan that permitted Moss to write *Once in a Lifetime* without having to worry about taking a job—and Moss's continual references to Hyman's kindness—was satirized:

KUBIE

Joe Hyman . . . who is that again?

MOSS

Oh, Joe Hyman is a wonderful man, wonderful! He did a great thing for me once, and I'd do anything in the world for him. I [directed] *Dear Ruth* for Joe Hyman—I wrote *Lady in the Dark* for Joe Hyman—I write everything for Joe Hyman. He gets half of everything I make.

KUBIE

He must be a very great friend.

MOSS

He is. He did something for me when I was much younger, and I'll never forget it. I was broke, and I'd written a letter to a friend of mine, and I wanted to mail it, and I had no stamp. And Joe Hyman came along and *gave* me a stamp, just like that.

KUBIE

That was three cents.

MOSS

No, three-cent postage hadn't come in yet—it was two cents. But it wasn't the money—It was what he said when he gave it to me. Naturally, being his stamp I thought he'd want to stick it on the letter, but that wasn't the way Joe did things. He just gave me the stamp—I'll never forget the expression on his face—and he said, "Here, Moss. Take this stamp and stick it."

Among the actors in *The Man Who Came to Dinner* was Dora Sayers, who, like Edith Atwater, her predecessor in the role of Maggie Cutler, was an actress with whom Hart had a romantic relationship.

Another actor in the company was making his debut. When Charles Matthies, Hart's valet, said that he had always hoped to perform onstage one day, Hart arranged for him to play the butler, John.

Hart reduced the cast size from thirty-six to fourteen for the tour. Although none of the performers had appeared with the production on Broadway, it was billed throughout the tour as "the New York cast." Featured were Haila Stoddard, Janet Fox, Dina Merrill, and Robert Downing, who not only played the doctor but served as the company manager and the stage manager.

Although Hart had performed Sheridan Whiteside once before, he found it difficult to commit all the lines to memory. "Never would have made the role so long if I'd known I'd have to handle it myself," he said.

Rehearsals began on February 1, 1945. The production was given first at Camp Kilmer in Seattle on February 16, before the company headed overseas on February 27. It played Oahu's Army and Navy bases for three weeks, then toured bases in the central and southwest Pacific for two months in the spring of 1945. One review of Hart's performance in an Army newspaper was moderately enthusiastic, calling his performance "pretty good in the part that he helped create."

On the basis of a letter to Hart from Colonel L. G. De Haven on April 21, 1945, it seems likely that the production was a good one and achieved the desired result of pleasing the servicemen who constituted the audience. "*The Man Who Came to Dinner* is ideally suited for men overseas and I'm sure it has and will receive the same highly enthusiastic reception from other units as it did from us," Colonel De Haven wrote. "It goes without saying that you and the other members of the talented cast did more than justice to the ever witty dialogue of your famous play."

The tour was interrupted briefly when Hart was confined to a naval hospital for treatment of a fungal disease and a painful earache. After completing the performances, the troupe returned to the States on June 12.

In 1937, George S. Kaufman, Hart's model as a director, had scored one of his greatest successes with the production of John Steinbeck's *Of Mice and Men*. Kaufman, whose strength until that time was perceived to lie only with comedy, directed Steinbeck's moving drama with a sure and subtle touch. One of the most poignant moments occurred after Lennie, the gentle, mentally impaired giant, accidentally kills Curly's wife. Lennie confesses to George, his friend and protector, "I done a bad thing, George," after which George, choking with emotion, realizes that he must kill Lennie before his friend can be caught by his pursuers.

In 1945, Hart also broke new ground when he turned his directorial hand to an intensely serious drama, Robert Turney's *The Secret Room*. One can only assume that Hart agreed to the assignment as a favor to Bernie Hart and Joe Hyman, the producers, for he was highly skeptical about the quality of the play, which Lewis Nichols described as "a most improbable melodrama . . . about a psychopathic lady with a love of children and a lust for killing [which] doesn't make too much sense . . . [and spells] complete defeat for the evening." Hart, who had long counseled his friends never to say *Yes* when their instinct was to say *No*, failed to follow his own advice in the case of *The Secret Room*.

He was at a loss in attempting to direct the play, ultimately allowing his actors to be as melodramatic as the play itself. Audiences in Boston were unable to suppress giggles at those moments that were intended to elicit pity and terror.

In an agony of indecision about how to salvage the production, Hart called Kaufman, asking his mentor to come to Boston to offer any suggestions that might be useful. Kaufman headed straight for Hart's room at Boston's Ritz-Carlton hotel, knocked at the door, and heard a pitiful whimper: "Come in." Hart was seated on a bed, looking forlornly out the window at the Boston Commons. Slowly, he turned to look at Kaufman, revealing bags under his eyes, and moaned, "I done a bad thing, George."

The Secret Room was by every measure the greatest fiasco with which Moss Hart was ever associated. It opened in New York on November 7, 1945, to unanimous scorn (Louis Kronenberger was "bored stiff;" Robert Garland found the play "tortuous, contrived;" Ward Morehouse called it "preposterous," and wondered why Hart had chosen to direct it; "He must have seen things in the script that were by no means visible to me"). Of course, Hart had accepted the assignment only out of loyalty to his brother and his old friend. *The Secret Room* closed, mercifully, after a mere twenty-one performances.

During Hart's tour in *The Man Who Came to Dinner*, he had frequently written to Beatrice Kaufman, perhaps his closest friend. Her feeling of loss was intense, and Moss felt the separation just as keenly. He wrote to her first from Seattle, the embarkation point for his trip, then from the South Pacific, detailing his periodic depressions, the inconveniences he encountered on the tour, and his attitude toward his fellow actors.

When he returned from the South Pacific, he found Beatrice in deteriorating health, although neither knew how close she was to death, which occurred as the result of a cerebral hemorrhage on October 6. She was only fifty-one. Since George S. Kaufman was so deeply in grief, the task of informing Beatrice's adult daughter, Anne, of her mother's death, fell to Moss. He could not bear telling Anne that Beatrice was dead, however, and said only that her mother was extremely ill and that Anne should return home from Boston.

Moss tearfully eulogized Beatrice at her funeral. Another speaker, Bennett Cerf, said of her, "She was the core and the connecting link of scores of people in every walk of life who owe some of their success today to her ever-ready counsel and sympathy . . ." The service was attended not only by her friends in the arts, but by prominent political figures as well.

Her death was a dreadful blow to her husband, who had relied for many years on her judgment, and felt for her a strong, enduring friendship. Although they were not compatible sexually, they were bound by deep ties of affection.

And, of course, her loss was devastating for Moss. Many people wondered why Moss Hart remained a bachelor until he was forty-one, since many women liked and admired him and he took a good number of them out to dinner, to parties, and to the theatre. Perhaps his tie to Beatrice was so profound that he could find no one to compare with her. Almost surely, his relationship with Beatrice was not sexual, but they were the deepest spiritual companions. Or, as Anne Kaufman Schneider, Beatrice's daughter, conjectured, perhaps she derided the young women to whom Hart was attracted. Anne Schneider also suspects that the fact that he did not marry until after Beatrice's death—and quite soon after, at that—would seem to be more than coincidence.

The chain of events that led to Hart's marriage began with an invitation he extended to playwright Norman Krasna before the opening of *Dear Ruth* to spend a weekend at Fairview Farm. Krasna asked if he could bring a female friend with him, the singer and actress Kitty Carlisle. "If I can get her away from her mother," Krasna told Hart, "I think I can get her to marry me." Hart seemed less than impressed by Krasna's date, treating her rather coldly. After the weekend, he told Krasna that Kitty Carlisle would be a bad match for him. Marriage, Hart said, would be a serious mistake.

Kitty Carlisle had appeared on Broadway in *Champagne Sec*, *Walk With Music*, and *White Horse Inn*. Her films included *Love in Bloom* and *A Night at the Opera*. Distinguished men, such as Sinclair Lewis and George Gershwin, had fallen in love with her, but she remained unmarried until 1946.

Although Hart and Carlisle had first met in 1935 and again when she visited Fairview Farm as Norman Krasna's date, it wasn't until both attended a party at Lillian Hellman's apartment in the summer of 1945 that Hart felt attracted to her. He called her the next morning, inviting her to "21" for lunch. She was nervous, concerned that she might say something gauche to a man of whom she was in awe, thinking of him as "a wit and part of the smart-talking successful theatre group." But he disarmed her immediately. Rather than dominating the conversation with stories about his successes, he asked her about herself. "He was quite different from what I expected," Kitty said, "not brittle, and although the wit was there it was gentle and we laughed a lot. He was a wonderful listener." After a long lunch, he invited her to spend a weekend at Fairview Farm.

Hart must have confided in a number of his guests that Kitty held a special appeal for him, for, Carlisle said, "one by one Moss's friends drew me aside and said, 'Be patient; you will be so good for each other.'"

They spent a great deal of time together in the following months, engaging in long, private conversations. He told her about his depressions with unprecedented candor. "I found I wanted to make up for all his unhappiness," Carlisle said. "There was something so dear, so childlike, so appealing about him; he touched my heart." She asked him about his sessions with Dr. Kubie. What did they speak about and what did Kubie have to say? Hart "told me that one of the first rules of analysis was that the patient was not allowed to discuss anything he told his analyst," she said. And Hart remained true to his avowal. Never, in their fifteen years together, did he discuss his analytical sessions.

She did ask him at one point, however, "Are you homosexual?" According to Carlisle, Hart replied, "Absolutely not," then told her (in Carlisle's words) that "there had been a couple of [men] who made passes at him. And that was it."

They traveled together to Chicago, where Carlisle was performing at the Blackstone Hotel. Later, in New York, at a party at the Plaza Hotel, a group of Hart's closest friends—George S. Kaufman, Jerome and Rhea Chodorov, Garson Kanin and Ruth Gordon, Mr. and Mrs. Harold Rome, and Max Gordon—made Kitty uncomfortable, for she felt they were sizing her up as a possible wife for Hart. The tension diminished, however, as she felt she "was being regarded more and more benignly."

Looking at photographs of Edith Atwater, Dora Sayers, and Kitty Carlisle, one is struck by the similarities in their appearance. Perhaps Hart imagined an ideal of femininity that he never ceased to pursue, and found its perfect embodiment in Kitty Carlisle.

Kaufman had little difficulty discerning Hart's attitude toward Kitty Carlisle in comparison to his attitude to the other women with whom he had been involved. "This afternoon I am having . . . drinks with Mossie," he wrote to his daughter, Anne, "and it seems that romance is really in the air between him and Kitty. A week from Monday he goes to Miami to spend some time with her, and it would not surprise me if it were marriage this time."

When Hart was in California casting his new play, *Christopher Blake*, he called Carlisle in New York and spoke obliquely about marriage—too obliquely for Carlisle's taste. She wanted an unequivocal proposal and received one during an evening they spent together at Fairview Farm. She accepted at once.

Weeks before the marriage date a small crisis was averted when Hart took Kitty's side against George S. Kaufman. At Fairview Farm, in the midst of a large party, Carlisle and Kaufman were playing a game of gin rummy. Carlisle, always nervous around Kaufman, studied her hand and, in what she described as "a terrible baby-talk voice," made what she immediately realized was an inane comment. Kaufman looked at her imperiously, then said, in a sharp tone, "We don't talk baby talk around here." Carlisle said,

> There was a sudden hush in the room. Tears sprang to my eyes. To have George S. Kaufman reprimand me in front of all those people! I held my breath: what would Moss do? I knew what George meant to him—part mentor, part father, and most respected friend.
>
> After what seemed to me an eon, Moss spoke up: "Around here, and in this house, she can say anything she wants."

Hart's comment made clear that he was thoroughly, unalterably committed to Kitty Carlisle, even at the risk of offending his former partner.

On August 11, Moss Hart and Kitty Carlisle were married in a small civil ceremony in New Hope, near Fairview Farm. He was forty-one, she thirty-four.

Kitty found out about Hart's financial extravagance almost immediately. The day after their marriage, she was startled to look out her window and see trucks moving many of the trees across the lawn. "I didn't like the placement of those trees," Hart told her, "so I'm moving these over there and those over here."

Norman Krasna, when he had courted Carlisle, had worried about winning over her mother. Hart had no difficulty. He charmed her by calling her not by her name, Hortense, which she detested, but by its French translation, Hydrangea, and by engaging her in repartee. He "brought out the best in Mother," Carlisle said.

Shortly after the wedding, the couple appeared together in *The Man Who Came to Dinner* at the Bucks County Playhouse, with Hart as Whiteside and Carlisle as Maggie Cutler. (Only a few weeks before the wedding, she had appeared there in *Tonight or Never*.) In a subsequent production she played the actress, Lorraine Sheldon. Hart and Carlisle appeared together on several occasions at the Playhouse, never failing to draw large crowds.

Kitty Carlisle Hart was deeply devoted to her husband, and remains devoted to his memory as this book is being written. Her love for him was and is total, unqualified, as was his for her. Alan Jay Lerner said, "they were not only an ideal couple, they were *the* ideal couple."

"I was once asked on a TV interview what I liked most about Moss," Carlisle said. "I said everything, and that was the truth. I was so proud that he chose me. . . . I found him endlessly interesting and diverting and stimulating." When asked if she didn't find it suffocating to have her husband around the house every day (since he wrote at home), she replied, "I adored it. I resented every moment that he wasn't with me."

And he was as smitten as she. "From the day he met Kitty he never looked at anybody again," Anne Kaufman Schneider told me. "Moss and Kitty were a perfect marriage. Perfect."

If Hart had engaged in sexual activities with men prior to his marriage to Kitty Carlisle, it seems virtually certain that he no longer did so afterward. Kitty seemed to fill all of his needs: psychological, emotional, and sexual. He rearranged his working schedule, writing at home, so that he could be with her as often as possible. He insisted that they lunch together daily. "We lived in each other's pockets," she said. "Moss hated to let me out of his sight. We slept in a double bed, and he wouldn't even let me leave the bed to go in to the children when they were sick."

On the date of their fifth anniversary, Hart wrote to his wife,

> Is there a way of saying 'Thank you' for the greatest gift one human being can give to another? In these five years you have given me the purest happiness I have ever known—and my love for you has grown and deepened with each year. How can I find words to thank you or even tell you how much you mean to me? . . . Perhaps I can only go on loving you more—though that does not seem possible.

Bennett Cerf said that one of the reasons for the marriage's success was that Kitty "gave [Moss] just the right amount of opposition to his most outrageous extravagances before admitting graciously, 'You were absolutely right, Mossie. The room wouldn't look the same without that $600 flower pot in the corner.' That always made Moss's joy in his newest possession complete."

Hart's enthusiasm for selecting clothes now extended to Kitty. He chose her outfits ("I never bought a dress he didn't pass on" during their marriage, she said), her jewelry, and her perfume.

Even in a perfect marriage, some unhappy events occur. On Christmas day 1946, the Harts' apartment at 4 East 65th Street was broken into. The Harts were in New Hope, but Moss's valet, Charles, had brought expensive wedding gifts to the apartment only a few days earlier.

Twenty-five thousand dollars of jewelry, clothing, and gifts were stolen, according to Hart's account. The police version set the loss at fifteen thousand. The burglars got into the building by ringing the bell of another apartment, going upstairs in the service elevator, and entering the Harts' apartment with a passkey or a celluloid impression. They removed closet-door hinges on the second and third floors, leaving wood shavings in the bedrooms, the living room, and the drawing room.

When Hart discovered the theft, he was indignant that the thieves had passed up his neckties. "I rather resent that," he said. But the burglars left little else, for fourteen of Hart's suits and six overcoats were stolen. Only a frayed sports jacket remained. The thieves also left several valuable paintings on the walls.

Fortunately, Kitty's clothes were insured, but Hart's were not. Needing something to wear, Hart called Danny Kaye, who, being precisely the same size, provided a suit and an overcoat.

Although the thieves were never discovered, the man to whom the stolen property was given was arrested and booked on January 20, 1947.

It was not Hart's first experience with burglary. His apartment had been ransacked in December 1943, with thieves stealing items worth six thousand dollars. And in November 1946, burglars attempted to force the front door to the 65th Street apartment, but were unsuccessful.

Hart's approach to his work changed radically after his marriage, perhaps because he had never before known anyone he wanted to be with as completely as he wished to be with Kitty Carlisle. At one time the most industrious of writers, he now sought every opportunity to avoid writing. "When Moss was writing at the farm," Carlisle said, "he worked in full view on the lawn, not with his back to the house, so anyone who went by could be hailed: 'Any messages? Anyone phone? Could I have a glass of water?' Company was what he wanted, not solitude. . . . I discovered that I had married the most gregarious of men, one whose entire life was dedicated to the avoidance of the quill and the typewriter."

When Hart and Carlisle, early in their married life, traveled from New York to California on the *Superchief*, Kitty "quickly realized that 'order,' Moss's watchword, also applied to trains. Five minutes after we boarded, our compartment was a home away from home, the cushions arranged just so on the seats, books on the table, and Moss's pipes lined up in perfect symmetry on the windowsill."

During their marriage, Kitty observed, "I felt I was in a continuous drawing-room comedy. Conversation was an art, and people sharpened their epigrams ahead of time. Once in a while I would hear Moss muttering to himself while he was shaving. I'm convinced he was orchestrating the conversations for our dinner party that evening." The dinner parties, sometimes at the Harts', sometimes at the Kaufmans', sometimes elsewhere, were an almost nightly event.

They attempted to have a child soon after they were married, but Kitty suffered a miscarriage. The next attempt was more successful. Christopher Hart was born on January 14, 1948. Another child, Catherine, followed on June 17, 1950.

When Christopher Hart was in his first year, Moss wrote to Brooks Atkinson that his son was

> cute as a button, but he doesn't *do* anything yet. For a man who plants trees in the morning and expects them to give shade by the afternoon, this is maddeningly slow. I don't expect miracles, but I'd like him to *do* just a little more than smile and eat. He might as well learn as early as he can that his father is not the most patient of men. By the way, he did have his first lesson as to what life is really like a couple of days ago. He was to receive his first injection for whooping cough, and we put him outside in his carriage while we waited for the Doctor to arrive. Very shortly thereafter, a bird shit in his face, and very shortly after that, the Doctor arrived and jabbed him in the arm with a needle and he yelled bloody murder. I carefully explained to him that life was rather like that, and he was a fortunate little boy to be finding it out so early. He was not amused.

As the years went by, Hart, the product of poverty and an unhappy childhood, was determined to bring up his own children in happier circumstances. He and his wife, he said, "try to be aware of what's going on between the children and ourselves, below the surface as well as on the top." The children, expected to work hard at school, were allowed to watch television only rarely. But their summers, most of them spent in Beach Haven, were entirely free.

As a boy, Chris Hart was sometimes embarrassed by his parents' prominence. He recalled one Sunday when they went to see the Disney movie *Old Yeller*. "We were standing in line for the movie and it started to rain," he remembered.

> And I don't know quite how it happened but an usher or the manager, somebody, recognized them and said, 'Do come in.' It meant walking in front of all those people and I said, 'No, no, don't do that, come stand in the rain with me.' They said, 'No, you're welcome to stand in the rain, darling, but we're going inside.' I tried to stand in the rain for as long as I could, but then, of course, I scurried inside as well. They felt, and rightly so, that they earned their celebrity status and that one of the perks was occasionally not having to stand in the rain with everyone else.

Catherine Hart's most powerful memory of her father is "making him laugh" when she was a child, "and realizing the power of that, and how good that made me feel. I remember how responsive he was and how receptive, and it was wonderful."

Just as Hart had overseen the decoration of his various apartments when he was single, he continued to do so as a married man. Over the course of his lifetime, he made several interior decorators wealthy, and eventually became a skilled decorator himself. He decorated the apartments in New York he and his family occupied and took great pride in his work.

Kitty Carlisle described the pinnacle of Moss's career as a decorator:

> Moss's predilection for decorating hit a new high . . . when he went to London for rehearsals of *My Fair Lady* [in the late 1950s]. He arrived at the Savoy Hotel early in the morning. Herman Levin, the show's producer, had reserved a suite for him. Moss had not stayed there before, and he was expecting something very elegant and grand. He took one look around, turned to the morning-coated assistant manager and said, "It won't do. Get your decorators and your painters." The manager protested: "Mr. Hart, it's terribly early." "The earlier the better," Moss said. The hastily summoned decorator realized that she and Moss were kindred spirits. She took him right down to the storeroom to pick out the furniture. . . . The entire suite was refurnished and repainted within twenty-four hours, and was long known as the Moss Hart Suite.

Although marriage to Kitty Carlisle was everything Hart hoped it would be, his depressions still occurred regularly. Carlisle described his tactics for dealing with his melancholia:

> Moss handled his depressions extremely well and tried valiantly not to take them out on his family and friends. He believed that if you're at a party, you have an obligation not to impose your misery on the company. I tried to help him find his way out from what he called the black umbrella of despair. I would suggest we not go out, so that he wouldn't have to make a continuing effort to spark the party. But he would answer, "You don't escape *from* life, you escape *into* it." So off we'd go to one of the never-ending . . . parties. He did it so well that no one except me ever knew the effort it cost him.

If anyone could offer an antidote for depression, it was Kitty. Her attitude toward life was wholly positive, as the following anecdote from her friend, Anne Kaufman Schneider, illustrates: "She told me one time that she had gone to a party and done something she was unhappy about, drank three glasses of wine or something. Whatever she did, when she woke up the next morning she thought, 'Oh dear, I shouldn't have done that.' She got up and went into the bathroom, looked at herself in the mirror and said, 'Kitty, I forgive you.' And that was that. She was finished with it. It was gone, which is healthy beyond words. I don't think Moss had that."

When Hart's personal life seems to have been at its happiest he wrote his most unsettling play. Bernie Hart and Joseph Hyman, now Hart's regular producers, presented *Christopher Blake* at the Music Box Theatre on November 30, 1946, with the playwright also serving as director.[1]

Eschewing comedy altogether, Hart wrote a play about a twelve-year-old boy whose parents are divorcing and the subsequent agonies he suffers. As in *Lady in the Dark*, his protagonist's subconscious is probed. In this case, it is his fantasies rather than his dreams that are played out.

In the first scene, Christopher is being awarded a medal by President Truman for having achieved world peace. The president asks Christopher's parents to join him during the ceremony. But when they reveal they have just obtained a divorce, Christopher shoots himself. His parents reunite tearfully and an honor guard gives Christopher a twenty-one-gun salute. Thus, Christopher fantasizes, as so many children do, how badly his parents will miss him after he is gone.

Similar fantastic episodes are interspersed with realistic scenes of Christopher in the judge's chambers and in the courtroom, where he is asked to select the parent with whom he wishes to live. Bewildered and unhappy, Christopher cannot choose.

---

1 Sam Harris, Hart's producer since 1930, had died in 1941.

Other fantasy scenes—each requiring a new set and many characters—include Christopher as the great playwright J. Roger Bascom, whose new play about a divorced couple is so movingly written that Mr. and Mrs. Blake reunite; a poorhouse run by a cruel superintendent in which Christopher's parents are institutionalized and from which Christopher—the richest man in South America—can free them, but refuses because they deserted him when he most needed their help; and an imaginary courtroom run by a sadistic judge.

The divorce, we learn during the realistic scenes, was precipitated by an affair Mr. Blake had but deeply regrets. He pleads with Mrs. Blake to forgive him. The judge encourages the Blakes to reconcile, but she is unwilling to forgive his affair. In a long, convoluted final scene, Mr. and Mrs. Blake argue the issue, with Christopher present but silent. Mrs. Blake is shown to be a hard, unforgiving woman who married her husband only because she sought security. Mr. Blake is revealed as rather weak, unable to function without a loving partner. At last, Christopher is forced to choose whether to live with one parent or another. He sobs that he wants both, but ultimately chooses his father, not because he is the stronger of the two, but because he needs Christopher more. Christopher's decision seems unbelievably wise and mature for a twelve-year-old. It also seems to be an altogether too-convenient way of resolving the play.

The play's realistic scenes clash jarringly with the fantasies. In hindsight, it seems apparent that Hart would have profited had he decided either to write a wholly realistic or a wholly expressionistic play.

Perhaps, in fact, he wrestled with that question. Evidently he gave some thought to a more thoroughly expressionistic play than the one that was eventually produced. He wrote an alternate ending to the play that never got beyond the handwritten stage. In the alternate version, Mr. and Mrs. Blake turn their backs on Christopher during the final scene (as Christopher tries to decide between them) and move off into the darkness. Chris's final speech and the subsequent stage directions indicate just how radically different an ending Hart was considering.

CHRIS

Mom! Dad! (He turns frantically to the Judge) Help me! Help me! What'll I do? You're a judge—why don't you help me? I thought you were going to tell me what to do! Why don't you tell me what to do? Why don't you help me? (As the Judge has started to speak all the big doors have opened, and out of them, to take their places [as] in a ball game, pour the creation of Christopher's fantasies. President Truman, the General, the Newsreel Photographer, the Headmaster, Miss

Holly, the People of the Poorhouse, the Bailiffs, the Spectators in the Courtroom and the Judge [several illegible words]. Silently, they all take their places in
the ghostly game as the Judge continues to speak.) (Pushed aside by the players,
Christopher shrinks helpless against the big center door, as the lights dim.)

Had Hart used this frightening final image, the play would have been more
poignant, ambiguous, and adventurous. Undoubtedly, commercial pressures militated against such an approach, for audiences are thought to like
tidy endings. But it is unfortunate that Hart did not follow his instinct, for the
pat, unbelievable resolution of the play as produced is largely responsible for
Christopher Blake's failure as a work of dramatic art.

The play has many virtues. It is compassionate, sincere, imaginative, bold,
and highly theatrical. All of the ingredients of a moving, insightful drama are
present. However, some of the scenes, particularly the scene between Mr.
and Mrs. Blake, are overlong, overwrought, and entirely too loquacious,
leading to the contrived and unbelievable ending.

Equally problematical is the sheer size of the play. Another director
might have encouraged Hart to scale *Christopher Blake* to a smaller dimension, for the drama focuses tightly on the boy, his parents, and the judge
who will decide Christopher's fate. But Hart the playwright was wedded to
the notion of a large cast (more than forty actors, not including extras) and
numerous sets (designed, once again, by Harry Horner, whose expertise
with turntables—five of them, in this case—was again employed) and Hart
the director was unable to see the flaw in that scheme. Other producers
than Hart's brother and his friend Joe Hyman might have persuaded him to
reduce the size of the play. But if either attempted to guide Hart in another
direction, he failed. The result was a cumbersome, massive production that
almost completely overwhelmed the intimate story of Christopher Blake.
The production cost of $180,000 was one of the highest for a non-musical
production to that time.[2]

An invited audience watched a run-through of *Christopher Blake* without
sets and costumes before the production gave its first performance. The
story, unencumbered by massive sets, communicated itself movingly and effectively to the audience, convincing Hart that his play was bound for success.

But the pre-Broadway tryout was disastrous. Because the scenery was so
cumbersome, the New Haven opening was canceled altogether. Then, in
Boston, nearly everything went wrong. The turntables failed to revolve dur-

---

2 Rising production costs in the theatre eventually convinced Hart that government subsidy was the
only appropriate remedy. He said so in an article he wrote for the *Harvard Crimson* in 1960.

ing the dress rehearsal, instead gouging the stage floor and destroying the set. Hart, as theatrical as ever, "ran up the center aisle," in Kitty Carlisle's words, "and in despair threw himself face down on the carpet, beating the floor with his fists." The accident caused a week's postponement in the Boston opening.

The play was not enthusiastically greeted in Boston, although Elinor Hughes, writing in the *Boston Herald*, offered a spirited defense, calling *Christopher Blake* "both entertaining and serious, spectacular and moving, a labor of love and something quite away from the previous pattern established by other Hart plays." Although it has provoked disagreement . . . I can and will say that it deserves success and has been well worth the doing."

Hughes also offered a general appreciation of Hart's work ethic:

His name is practically synonymous with popularity, but I know of no one in the theatre who works harder or takes less for granted. His self-deprecation is as genuine as his ability to perform prodigies of work is unquestioned, which helps to explain in part, at least, why he has no enemies and can count his friends by the hundreds.

Does he worry, nearly knock himself out and spend sleepless nights before an opening? Unquestionably. But it is not from lack of organization, planning and knowledge of technique; rather, he is a perfectionist and nothing ever turns out quite as well as he had planned and hoped.

The reviews of the New York opening were respectful but generally unfavorable. Robert Garland called the play "a sort of Broadway grab-bag overfilled with ideas and inventions." Many of the ideas are "significant," he conceded, and "many of the inventions are fresh, most of them . . . striking," but the realistic scenes are no more than "a three-dimensional soap opera." Louis Kronenberger professed "great respect for what Moss Hart wanted to do in *Christopher Blake*," but lamented that the play "is not a success." Richard Watts called the drama "a curiously unsatisfying combination of fantasy and realism that was gravely handicapped by its elaborately cumbersome presentation." Brooks Atkinson, in what was otherwise a favorable review, noted that "although half the play exists in the sphere of imagination, [Hart] is unwilling to leave much of it to the imagination of the audience." *Time* complained that the "general effect [was] top-heavy."

Hart, deeply disappointed by the critics' notices, sent an angry letter to John Chapman (who titled his review "*Christopher Blake* Suffers From the Curse of an Aching Hart") about Chapman's "frivolous" and "vulgar" review of the play.

Joe Hyman suggested revisions in January 1947. He oversaw some changes in the production while Hart was on the West Coast, eliminating some scenes and rearranging the order of others, but nothing helped. In fact, the changes only angered some theatregoers. One of them wrote to Hyman, saying that he had seen the play primarily because he had read about the scene at the White House, which was omitted from the performance he saw. Later, he heard that the White House scene had been restored. He asked for and received free tickets to see the play again.

Christopher Blake closed after 114 performances, too few to return the backers' investments. Hart was profoundly distressed by the failure of a play that he characterized as "a serious and honest effort" in which he had, for the first time in his career, maintained a non-comic tone throughout. However, he himself eventually conceded that *Christopher Blake* was "smothered in production."

The observations of W. David Sievers, in *Freud on Broadway*, a study of psychoanalysis and American drama, are cogent. The author notes that "The poignant and deeply troubled inner world of this child of divorce is somehow not entirely captured nor his relationship to his parents fully explored. . . . The parents fail to arouse empathy. . . . [Christopher's] choice to remain with his father is made without agony . . . His fantasies are, in fact, unrelated to this choice and provide little insight into it."

From the outset, Hart, believing that his play would be successful, and hoping for a large sale to the movies, set the asking price at $500,000, the highest ever for a non-musical production. As the play proceeded through its disappointing pre-Broadway performances, the asking price declined. The lukewarm New York reviews certainly did not encourage offers in the $500,000 range. According to various reports in the newspapers, Universal Studios bid $275,000 and Warner Bros. $305,000. In December 1946, the Warner Bros. offer was accepted.[3]

The film, *The Decision of Christopher Blake*, was beset with problems from the beginning. The director disagreed so strongly with the studio's decision to cast Alexis Smith as the mother that he walked off the picture. Instead,

---

3 According to Irving Lazar, the actual price was $150,000. Lazar claimed that Jack Warner had seen a preview of *Christopher Blake*, had been moved deeply, and had said to Lazar, "I want this play." A rule of the Dramatists Guild prohibited selling the motion picture rights until a play had run for three weeks, but, Lazar said, he told Warner at the intermission, "Jack, don't tell anybody. Let's just make a pact [for $150,000] . . . He agreed and we shook hands." After the lukewarm reviews, Lazar "called Jack to remind him of our agreement. . . . He knew the play was a flop, but he lived up to his commitment and paid in full."

Peter Godfrey directed Ranald McDougall's adaptation. The film emphasized the play's weaknesses and neglected its strengths. The courtroom fantasy, perhaps the play's strongest scene, is omitted; the parents' bitter conflict is easily resolved into an artificially happy ending; and the performances are stilted and unconvincing. *Variety*'s critic had faint praise, calling the film "passably interesting," but Bosley Crowther described the movie as "a hollow affair." He lamented the severe alterations in the screenplay, calling them "most injudicious."

In all, *Christopher Blake* was one of Hart's least satisfactory professional experiences. Feeling that he had been punished by critics who refused to accept anything other than comedy from him, he took a vacation from the theatre lasting more than a year. Still, although he wrote no plays during that time, he was elected president of the Dramatists Guild in November 1947, replacing George S. Kaufman. He was subsequently elected to three more two-year terms. During his tenure, the Dramatists Guild wrestled with several thorny problems, among them the ban against blacks in theatres in Washington, D.C. The Guild allied itself with Actors' Equity in opposing the ban. It also took the position that black actors should not be limited to playing roles written for black characters. "When Negro citizens are presented exclusively [as servants] an imbalance results, and their integration in American life is improperly set before the world," a Guild statement said. "We must correct this situation, not by eliminating the Negro artist, but by enlarging his scope and participation in all types of roles and in all forms of American entertainment." Kitty Carlisle said that Hart ran the Dramatists Guild (and the Authors League, for which he served as president from 1955 to 1961) with an iron hand. When an issue had been decided to his satisfaction, rather than call for a vote, he would simply say, "That's it!"

On February 3, 1947, Darryl Zanuck announced that Hart had been contracted to write the screen adaptation of Laura Z. Hobson's novel *Gentleman's Agreement*, for Twentieth Century-Fox. It was to be one of Hollywood's first films about anti-Semitism, and the mere announcement that the film would be made stirred protests, both from anti-Semites and from some Jews who feared that the picture might increase intolerance.

Some of Hollywood's élite shared that concern. Although most of the film world's studio heads and creative talent were Jewish, the public was largely unaware of their ethnicity—and the studio heads, in particular, took pains to conceal their Jewishness from the public. Their hope was that moviegoers would think of Hollywood pictures only as representative of "American" values.

Hart, who was not religious but proud of his cultural heritage, was eager to work on *Gentleman's Agreement*. Aside from *Winged Victory*, it was perhaps the only film he worked on with complete enthusiasm, as it dealt with a subject on which he wished to take a stand. When he told Kitty that he regarded writing the film as "a labor of love," she said he should write the screenplay for nothing. Unwilling to go quite that far, he told Irving Lazar, who was by then his agent, that he would be willing to write *Gentleman's Agreement* for the minimum salary permitted by the Screen Writers Guild—which was precisely what he received.

In Hart's screenplay, as in Hobson's novel, the protagonist, Phil Green, a Christian journalist, is asked by John Minify, the editor of *Smith's Weekly*, to write an article on anti-Semitism. Not wishing merely to recite a statistical litany of the effects of anti-Semitism on millions of Jews, Green (played by Gregory Peck) decides on a novel angle for his story: he will masquerade as a Jew in order to feel directly the pain of being attacked or rejected on the basis of his (presumed) religion.[4]

When Hart said publicly that his screenplay would pull no punches, at least one studio head, Louis B. Mayer, called Zanuck, urging him to tread carefully. According to Gregory Peck, Mayer said, "Why stir up a lot of controversy? Eighty million people a week are going to the movies in America. Why muddy the waters and stir up a controversy?" Zanuck told Peck that he responded, "Look, I bought a best-selling book. It's created a national sensation and I'm going to make a movie out of it that will create another national sensation. We've got a great story to tell. I've got Moss Hart, Elia Kazan [to direct], Gregory Peck, Dorothy McGuire, and John Garfield, we're all gung-ho and we're going to make this movie."

After Zanuck told Hart about Mayer's telephone call, Hart incorporated a scene in the screenplay that introduced a Jewish character named Irving Weissman, the magazine's principal investor. In the scene, at a meeting attended by Weissman and the magazine's staff, editor John Minify announces his plan to have Green write an article on anti-Semitism. Wiessman urges Minify not to proceed. "Do you mind my saying as an old friend that I think it a very bad idea, John," he says, "the worst, most harmful thing you could possibly do now." When asked why, Weissman continues, "Because it'll only

---

4 Although it is no more than coincidental, it is nonetheless interesting to note that Hart masqueraded as an Air Force cadet while gathering material for *Winged Victory*, and the protagonist of *Gentleman's Agreement* takes on the identity of a Jew in order to acquire knowledge for his magazine article on anti-Semitism.

stir it up more, that's why. Let it alone. We'll handle it in our own way. . . . We've been fighting it for years and know from experience the less talk there is about it the better." Minify brushes Weissman's protests aside and encourages Phil Green to go forward with his article.

As a "Jew," Green suffers both direct and implied insults, one after another. He comes to realize, as he never had before, the viciousness of anti-Semitism. Perhaps the most poignant moment in the film occurs when Green, attempting to check into the "Flume Inn," demands to know whether or not the hotel is restricted to Christians. The manager evades a direct response, but makes it clear that Jews are unwelcome. Peck's reaction combines outrage, uncertainty about how to respond appropriately, and the awareness that if he protests he will be labeled a "typical Jew"—all with virtually no dialogue, a striking example of the actor's film technique.

As with most screenplays, Hart's version underwent several revisions, some by Darryl Zanuck, some by the director, Elia Kazan. The final shooting script was influenced by all three, but Hart's voice was clearly dominant.

Hart, who only a few years earlier had turned down Gregory Peck when the actor auditioned for *Lady in the Dark*, was "instrumental in getting me" the role in *Gentleman's Agreement*, Peck said. He called the making of the picture "an exciting venture. . . . we all thought we were quite courageous in breaking new ground by making the very first film [actually, the second; *Crossfire*, released earlier in 1947, was the first] on the subject of anti-Semitism."

One of the best performances in the film is given by Celeste Holm as a fashion editor who attempts unsuccessfully to conceal her love for Phil Green. Holm asked Hart to recommend her to Zanuck. Like Hart, she said she was unconcerned about billing or the amount of her salary; she wanted only to be a part of a film that she recognized would be important. At the time, Holm was known primarily as a singer, having performed on Broadway in *Oklahoma*, *Three Little Girls in Blue*, and *Carnival in Costa Rica*, but *Gentleman's Agreement* changed the arc of her career and won her the Academy Award for Best Supporting Actress.

Although virtually every moment of the film is charged with tension, leaving virtually no room for comedy, Hart managed to include the question he was asked by a passenger on the *Franconia* in 1935. A woman at a party asks Gregory Peck, "Mr. Green, do you get your ideas first and then write, or do you write first and then get your ideas?"

A rumor has persisted ever since 1947 that Hollywood's studio heads met with Darryl Zanuck after *Gentleman's Agreement* was edited and offered to buy the negative and all copies of the film in order to keep it from being released. Gregory Peck, who had never heard the rumor, told me in 1999 that he doubted its authenticity. He could not imagine that some of the studio bosses would have had anything to do with such a scheme, citing Jack Warner of Warner Bros. and Harry Cohn, head of Columbia Studios, who were making "some films which were critical of the society and the culture—daring producers for their time. I don't believe that story," Peck said; "I think it's baseless."

Late in June 1947, Hart completed the screenplay for *Gentleman's Agreement* and announced that he intended to take an extended vacation. He and Kitty enjoyed a long belated honeymoon before he began working on a new play.

Gentleman's Agreement opened in New York in November. Bosley Crowther, reviewing the film for *The New York Times*, expressed his belief that the film was not only powerful, but a considerable improvement on the novel. "The shabby cruelties of anti-Semitism . . . have now been exposed with . . . even greater forcefulness in the motion-picture version of the novel . . . every point about prejudice which Miss Hobson had to make in her book has been made with superior illustration and more graphic demonstration in the film." For Hart, Crowther had only praise: "Shaped by Moss Hart into a . . . taut and literate . . . screen play of notable nimbleness and drive, the bewilderments of Miss Hobson's hero become absorbing and vital issues on the screen and the eventual outcome of his romance [with the character played by Dorothy McGuire, who tries to persuade Peck not to continue his noble charade] becomes a matter of serious concern."

Cecelia Ager, writing in *PM*, said

> *Gentleman's Agreement* is a great movie. But [it] is still more; it soars beyond. It is the first movie to show that ideas can be as exciting as emotions. . . . *Gentleman's Agreement* marks a shining milestone in the development of the movies; it covers the movie industry with glory; it sets up an illustrious new standard; it will attract a vast new group whose attention and respect the movies have rarely compelled before.
>
> Moss Hart, who wrote the screenplay, has given [the film] a dramatist's sense of mounting climax; has transmuted the book's anemic, cerebral romance into the fully-realized passionate love story of a mature man . . . and woman; has developed the book's one-dimensional illustrations of a point, into people; has made their revelations and conflicts the natural, inevitable, dramatic revelations of whole, rich, human personalities.

Some observers suggested that Gregory Peck's character was incredibly naïve in discovering the extent of anti-Semitism in American society. Others objected that the film's message was blunted by having a Christian pose as a Jew; they argued that a Jew should have been the primary character. But John Garfield, playing a Jewish friend of Peck's, is seen to be victimized by discrimination, somewhat mitigating the criticism.[5]

Perhaps, in fact, a film whose central character was Jewish could not have been made in 1947. In any case, as Crowther noted, the film "should be profoundly effective in awakening millions to unsuspected cruelties.[6]

Gentleman's Agreement won the New York Film Critics' award and, in addition to Celeste Holm's Oscar, the Academy Award as best film of 1947. The National Board of Film Critics voted their agreement. Twentieth Century-Fox, which was the beneficiary of the awards and the good publicity, showed their gratitude to Hart, whom they had grossly underpaid, by giving him an enormous Chrysler station wagon.

In the theatre during 1948, Hart was represented by a single sketch for a revue, *Inside U.S.A.*, but the sketch was an old one Hart had written for Beatrice Lillie that had been dropped from *Seven Lively Arts* (but which Lillie had performed in England). First seen in Philadelphia, *Inside U.S.A.* moved to Broadway, where it opened at the Century Theatre on April 30. In Hart's contrivance, Beatrice Lillie played an irritatingly superstitious maid whose eccentricities drive a Broadway actress, nervous about her opening night, nearly to distraction. The sketch was singled out by most of the critics as a highlight (many of them called it *the* highlight) of the revue. The show was successful, running for 337 performances, more than fifty of them taken over by theatre parties, at which the entire house was bought out by a single group, who would then sell the tickets at inflated prices in order to raise money for one organization or another.

---

5 An irony is that Phil Green's secretary in the film (played by June Havoc) reveals that she is a Jew who changed her last name from Walovsky to Wales in order to get a job with the magazine for which Green is writing his exposé. But one of the movie's leading players also felt the need to change his name: Julius Garfinkle became John Garfield in order to find work in the theatre and films, a common practice among Jewish-born performers who later became icons of WASP audiences, including Kirk Douglas and Lauren Bacall.

6 Years later, the director, Kazan, concluded that *Gentleman's Agreement* was "too damn polite. The film is too nice. It doesn't get inside the parts of anti-Semitism that persist and hurt. . . . Zanuck had the theory, which I didn't agree with, that every social problem and every human problem can be solved through the mechanics of a love story." Dorothy McGuire, as Phil Green's fiancée, is portrayed as an essentially decent woman whose unconscious anti-Semitism is gradually revealed to her. Ultimately, her generosity to Dave Goldman (Garfield's character) in lending him the home she has built in Darien, Connecticut, so that he can move his family to the East Coast and take a job in New York, leads to a reconciliation with Phil Green, and ends the film.

When Hart began work on another play in the spring of 1948, he grudgingly set out to accommodate the critics' expectations that he would write comic material. If they wanted a broad comedy in the Kaufman–Hart style, he would provide it. However, he would not entirely forswear the serious, thoughtful note that had characterized his work since *Lady in the Dark*. The result was an ambitious play, *Light Up the Sky*, that switches from broad satirical comedy to serious drama without fully succeeding at either. Perhaps as a result of his efforts to unify the diverse elements, Hart said he found *Light Up the Sky* "a more difficult task than any of my efforts . . . since *Once in a Lifetime*."

Hart began writing the play while in California, then completed it at Fairview Farm, where there were fewer distractions. Uncharacteristically, his play required a relatively small cast (thirteen characters) and a single set.

Hart described his play as "a simple story about show people who love each other, get into trouble, detest each other and then find out that they need each other. In my own simple way," he said, "I was only trying to do what every other writer is attempting today—make a significant comment on the behavior of people [but] in terms of gaiety and laughs instead of sober preachment."

Light Up the Sky is nearly plotless. During the first act, various theatre people are shown in Irene Livingston's suite of rooms at Boston's Ritz-Carlton Hotel hours before the first performance of a play by a young, idealistic playwright, Peter Sloan. The flamboyant director, the crass, wealthy producer, interested only in the play's money-making potential, his vulgar wife, the temperamental star (Irene), and her poison-tongued mother all gather to toast what most of them are certain will be a triumphant opening night. The broadly drawn characters are clearly intended to arouse the audience's scorn as well as laughter.

Contrasted to all of the stereotypical characters is Owen, a realistically portrayed, middle-aged, sensible, ironic, knowledgeable, urbane playwright who wrote two of Irene's earlier successes but has nothing to do with Peter Sloan's play. He is present only as an observer whose interest is in persuading the others to aspire to artistic integrity. Owen, clearly intended as a self-portrait of Moss Hart (Owen has been writing professionally for eighteen years, as had Hart in 1948; Owen is president of the "union" as Hart was president of the Dramatists Guild), seems somewhat out of place in *Light Up the Sky*. His laconic, philosophical comments about the clash of art and commerce evidently carry the play's meaning, but the flamboyance of the other characters makes it nearly certain that they will be the focus of the audience's attention. Hart confirmed that Owen was his alter ego when, in a rehearsal,

Sam Levene, playing the producer, asked if Owen "was meant to represent somebody established like George Kaufman or William Saroyan." Hart responded, "The hell he is. He's me."

The second act shows the characters' reaction to the unexpected failure of Peter Sloan's play. Sloan wishes to revise and strengthen his work; the producer wants to add jokes and dancing girls. The act consists mostly of bickering among most of the characters, with Owen's sensible remarks, serving as a counterpoint, gradually altering the tone of *Light Up the Sky*. In the third act, the reviews of Sloan's play come in: to everyone's surprise, the critics have dubbed the play a work of brilliance, needing only some minor polishing. The characters patch up their differences and come together in order to improve the play.

Some of the scenes and characters in the final version of *Light Up the Sky* are not fully integrated into the play. One character, Irene's husband, makes an occasional appearance, but has no real function. Another, Miss Lowell, a young woman writing Irene's memoirs, is present only to provide exposition. A scene in the second act features a group of Shriners noisily and drunkenly celebrating in the halls of the Ritz-Carlton. Their scene may be amusing but has little relation to the rest of the play. All of these characters receive only the sketchiest of characterizations.

Many of the other characters were rather clearly based on real-life models. The producer and his wife, for example, were thinly disguised versions of Billy Rose and his then-wife, swimming star Eleanor Holm; the leading actress was obviously modeled on Gertrude Lawrence.

Billy Rose threatened to bring a lawsuit against Hart. Although he admitted privately that he had no chance of winning, Rose hoped to prevent a movie sale, knowing that film studios were reluctant to become involved with any properties that were in litigation. Rose succeeded in his intention, for no film of *Light Up the Sky* was ever made—one of the few such instances in Hart's career.

An enterprising newspaper invited Rose to review the play. In the notice, Rose said, "It's my belief that Moss is an essential component of some of these [characters]. For instance, Sidney Black, the theatrical producer . . . is partly me to be sure, but I submit that he's partly Moss Hart—the part of Moss Hart that he would like to pin on somebody else. Psychoanalysts call it 'projection,' but, as I see it, it's the old trick of saving face by pretending the face doesn't belong to you." And, Rose said, the idealistic young playwright in *Light Up the Sky*, whom many took to be Moss Hart at the beginning of his career, is what "Moss wishes he had been—a serious, talented, straight-forward sort of guy who had something to say, and wasn't going to trade his right to say it." In implying that Hart had allowed commercial pressures to dictate the course of his career, no doubt Rose felt that he gained some measure of revenge for Hart's acid-tipped portrait of Sidney Black.

Hart claimed to be astounded that anyone would see real people as the models for his characters, and offered the standard disclaimer that the characters "are all bits and pieces of the thousands of people I have encountered in my theatrical experiences," but the parallels are so strong that it is difficult to take his disavowal seriously.

Hart hoped that Gertrude Lawrence would play the role based on her personality; failing that, he wished that Greer Garson would play the role. He wanted Mary Boland to play the actress's mother. Ultimately, Virginia Field played the actress and Phyllis Povah the mother. He wrote the role of Carleton Fitzgerald, the volatile director, specifically for Glenn Anders, who played it on Broadway.

When *Light Up the Sky* was announced for Broadway production, the producers, Bernard Hart and Joseph Hyman,[7] announced that they would not accept theatre parties, in which all the seats were purchased by a single source, which then sold the tickets at extremely high prices, generally to raise money for an organization.

Moss had come to believe that theatre parties were causing significant problems. Those who had bought tickets came to the theatre in a grumpy mood, he said, certain that they would not get their money's worth, and determined to show their disdain. The actors were upset because members of the audience were inattentive and refused to laugh at appropriate times or to applaud enthusiastically. And members of the public were irritated because tickets were unavailable when the houses were purchased by theatre parties.

The anti-theatre-party stand caused an uproar among ticket agents, for several other productions adopted the same policy as *Light Up the Sky*. Perhaps as a sop to the agents, a theatre party was allowed to buy out the house for a preview of *Light Up the Sky*. Joe Hyman insisted that this did not violate the policy, for he considered the preview more a rehearsal than a performance.

The action of *Light Up the Sky*, showing the difficulties of mixing the ingredients of a new play to proper effect, was reproduced in the play's production, for the first performance of *Light Up the Sky* in New Haven revealed significant weaknesses, causing endless post-mortems. Kitty Carlisle said, "Conferences took place in clumps of two or three all over our hotel suite and in the halls, or with everybody all at once in the living room. The suite was filled with well-

---

7 Hart, his brother Bernie, and co-producer Joe Hyman all put up a significant percentage of the production costs. George S. Kaufman and Irving Lazar invested lesser amounts.

wishers and not so well-wishers. Moss was not only the author, he was also the director; and when changes were made, he had to write them, give them to the cast next day, and redirect the scenes that were altered. People came and went, worn out and bleary-eyed, but Moss plowed on and rewrote and redirected an act and a half within ten days. It was an experience that made him swear he'd never again be both writer and director of the same play."

Early in 1948, Alan Jay Lerner and Kurt Weill had written a musical entitled *Love Life*. Hart, asked his opinion after the pre-Broadway opening in New Haven, told them that they had essentially written two musicals: a satirical first act and a realistic second act. Now, Lerner and Weill saw the New Haven opening of *Light Up the Sky*. Afterward, in Hart's hotel room, Weill remarked without irony that the problem with Hart's play was that the first half was a comedy and the second half a drama. Hart had been correct in his criticism of *Love Life*; Weill was no less correct in his judgment about *Light Up the Sky*.

The play, much revised, then moved to Philadelphia (with its running time reduced by thirty-three minutes), then to Boston (where a new second act was inserted). Eventually, the original third act was scrapped and a new one substituted. All in all, eleven characters were either dropped from or added to the original script. Perhaps the continual and extreme changes contributed to the difficulties Hart had in unifying the proceedings.

Light Up the Sky opened at the Royale Theatre on Broadway on November 18, 1948. In the program and in the published version of the play, a quotation appears from "The Idle Jeste," attributed to Old Skroob: "Mad, sire? Ah, yes—mad indeed, but observe how they do light up the sky." Brooks Atkinson puzzled over the quotation, both in his review and in his Sunday piece; he had attempted to locate the reference, he said, and failed. Little wonder, for "The Idle Jeste" was a figment of Hart's imagination and Skroob was an anagram for Brooks Atkinson himself, created by Hart, his wife, and Jerome Chodorov one afternoon at Schrafft's.

Atkinson's review described *Light Up the Sky* as "a loud, broad, tempestuous comedy that is acted at top speed." He also noted, however, that (as Hart had earlier confided to him) the play was originally "intended as a Shavian comedy with serious overtones about the human frailties of human beings." Atkinson does not belabor the point (his review is quite favorable), but Hart's intention, as he described it, could clearly not be discerned in the play's final form.

As to Hart's direction, Atkinson said "the performance races around the stage like a volcanic circus, everybody shouting, everybody making exits and entrances and slamming doors."

Joseph Wood Krutch, writing in *The Nation*, found the play "a great deal more entertaining than I . . . expected it to be." Krutch believed the play's abrupt turn from highly exaggerated comedy to serious drama was a virtue. George Jean Nathan, beginning his review by noting that he was familiar with Hart's "ire, which has erupted with gusto on the one or two occasions when I have timidly ventured to reflect on the magnitude of his genius," confessed that *Light Up the Sky* "has some very funny stuff in it" but is also "forced and spurious."

Most of the critics thought the play an enjoyable if minor contribution to Moss Hart's output. John Chapman called it "a noisy and rollicking comedy . . . good dirty fun." William Hawkins said that Hart "turned up with an extremely funny, high riding comedy that is pitiless in its comment on the theatre while brazenly in love with it."

Only a few weeks after the play closed in New York, a condensed version was telecast on CBS in June 1949. *Variety* called it "one of the top TV treats of the season [containing] a spark seldom found in the comedy department of video dramatics."

Still, *Light Up the Sky* is far from Hart's best work. In its acerbic portrait of actors, producers, and directors, it is similar to but less effective than *Once in a Lifetime*. It is also somewhat reminiscent of the satire on show business by Hart's friends George S. Kaufman and Edna Ferber, *The Royal Family*. Again, however, *Light Up the Sky* suffers by comparison. The play also includes several scenes and characters that are not fully integrated into the action—a sure sign of hasty rewriting. On the other hand, one cannot overlook the play's commercial success. Not only did it prove popular on Broadway, it has been successfully revived in recent years in Chicago, Los Angeles, and elsewhere. Regional and academic theatres are currently producing the play nearly as often as the longtime staples *You Can't Take It With You* and *The Man Who Came to Dinner*.

Hart himself, in discussing the play four years after the New York premiére, said that he "had hoped, in *Light Up the Sky* . . . to say a number of things I wanted to say under the masquerade of hard-hitting comedy," but, despite its popular success, the play "was a disappointment to me personally, for I did not succeed at all in my own terms."

Some playwrights claim to be indifferent to critical opinion about their work, though that was not true of Moss Hart, for whom the critics' views were of great importance. When he objected to a critic's response to one of his plays, he did not suffer in silence. More than once he fired off a letter, accusing the critic of insensitivity or incompetence.

Hart's relationship with Brooks Atkinson, whose critical acumen he admired, went beyond the usually rather remote association of playwright and critic. For understandable and valid reasons, most theatrical artists prefer not to become close to those whose profession it is to judge their work. To establish a friendship might seem to be asking for friendly critical treatment, a favor that the critic could not possibly bestow while maintaining his independence. Furthermore, since the theatrical artist risks a negative critical response every time he or she is involved with a production, establishing a friendship with a critic and hoping that it will endure risks personal as well as professional rejection on a regular basis.

But around 1936, Hart asked Atkinson to meet him regularly for lunch or dinner so that they could discuss their perspectives on the theatre. One might attribute Hart's suggestion to naïveté or to calculation, but the latter does not seem to have been a significant factor. The playwright, respecting the critic, sincerely wanted to exchange ideas about the state of the theatre. Atkinson was at first suspicious of Hart's motives, but, after their first dinner at the Hunting Room of the Astor Hotel, he relaxed, secure in the knowledge that the playwright was not trying to use friendship to influence the critic's reviews. Their meetings, during which Hart's plays were seldom discussed, were invariably pleasant, despite occasional disagreements about the merits of specific plays.

It was understood that their friendship would not prevent Atkinson from writing a negative review of a play of Hart's when he felt that a negative review was merited. And, to be sure, the critic did not hesitate to offer an unfavorable review on occasion. "But," Atkinson said, Hart "never grumbled or complained . . . at least to me."

In general, Hart's opinion of critics was not high. "Their idea of what constitutes a good performance is remarkably fluid," he said, "and their standards change alarmingly from season to season." He was particularly upset by what he saw as a failure on the part of most critics to evaluate acting intelligently. "They are notoriously unable to divorce the actor from the part he is playing. Acute and artful as they are in judging the merits of a play, their skill seems to leave them entirely when it comes to evaluating a performance. You will find them saying, 'Miss So-and-So was colorless and uncertain in the first act but marvelously effective in the last act' when it should have been obvious that Miss So-and-So's part was no good at all in the first act but excellent in the third." And most critics, he maintained, knew "almost nothing about directing."

Hart felt that all critics had prejudices, although some of them, he conceded, might have been subconscious. One critic, he felt, "is a sucker for what he likes to imagine is the unorthodox actor." Another would automatically give a good notice to any actor who played a scene with a child or a dog. Most of all, he wished critics would conquer their tendencies to find each play either brilliant or entirely unworthy. There were such things, he thought, as "interesting mistakes"—plays that were less than fully satisfactory, but demonstrated enough skill or sufficient aspiration that the playwrights should be praised for their efforts.

⁊

Even the finest theatrical craftsmen, those who have achieved consistent success in the theatre over a long period of time, are subject to lengthy periods of frustration. The example of Oscar Hammerstein II is often cited. After writing the lyrics for *Show Boat* in 1927 and winning justified acclaim, Hammerstein suffered through twelve consecutive failures until he began his partnership with Richard Rodgers in 1943, re-establishing his credentials as one of the finest librettists in the theatre. Moss Hart's string of theatrical frustrations, which began with *The Secret Room* in 1945 and continued through *Light Up the Sky* (a commercial success but, in Hart's own view, an artistic failure) in 1948, did not end with *Miss Liberty*, a musical he directed in 1949.

Few musicals have been as eagerly anticipated as *Miss Liberty*. Irving Berlin, the by-then legendary composer of so many Broadway hits, fresh from *Annie Get Your Gun*, wrote the music and lyrics. Robert E. Sherwood, one of America's leading playwrights ever since the 1920s (and a four-time winner of the Pulitzer Prize) wrote a musical book for the first time.[8] Joining them were Moss Hart as director and Jerome Robbins, already established as a leading light in the world of ballet, as choreographer. Eddie Albert, an appealing comedian, was featured with the accomplished young dancer Allyn Ann McLerie. And the subject, a newspaper photographer's search for the girl who posed for the Statue of Liberty in 1885, set against the background of the circulation war between two New York newspapers, the *Herald* and the *World*, seemed an ideal plot line for a musical. New York audiences fairly trembled with anticipation, buying enough tickets to fill the house for months long before *Miss Liberty* opened. The production chalked up a sizable advance sale of $430,000.

Berlin told observers that *Miss Liberty* had no pretensions to unconventionality. He would be satisfied, he said, if the musical was simply "a good old-fashioned commercial smash hit."

Eddie Albert recalled the excitement of the first rehearsal on May 13, 1949, when the actors, scripts laid out in front of them, were addressed by Moss Hart, who, after greeting them and saying what a marvelous musical Sher-

---

8 Hart and Sherwood had, years before, discussed the notion of co-writing a musical for the Marx Brothers. Beyond his contributions to the theatre, Sherwood had earned distinction as a speechwriter for Franklin D. Roosevelt and as the author of *Roosevelt and Hopkins*. He was also a fan of Irving Berlin's songs, proof of which was his ability to sing not only the first verse of each song but the second.

wood and Berlin had written, began the read-through by saying simply, "And now, the most beautiful words in the English language: Act One, Scene One."

But nearly everything that could go awry went awry—with a vengeance. Three songs were scrapped after the first run-through, and most of those that remained were well below Berlin's usual standards. Much of Sherwood's book was found to be unfunny and talky, and, despite Hart's pleas, Sherwood's approach to the necessary revisions was slow, both because he was suffering from trigeminal neuralgia and because he was drinking prodigious amounts of alcohol in an attempt to relieve the pain. During rehearsals, Hart would occasionally try to cut a line here or there, but, as Eddie Albert recalled, Sherwood would then come to life, saying, "Uh, I beg your pardon."

Some changes were obviously needed, however, and Hart made as many as he could without alienating Sherwood. In addition to cutting, Hart added some comic lines, for he felt that *Miss Liberty* was far less funny than a musical comedy ought to be.

The rehearsals began to go more smoothly, Albert remembered, due largely to Hart's influence. "He was very intelligent and very courageous," Albert said, "although he had to be very political, too. Each one of them [Sherwood, Berlin, and Hart] assumed that he was nothing but gold and diamonds—and they were, actually." Allyn Ann McLerie's recollections of the rehearsals were the polar opposite of Albert's. As a relative beginner in her first major role, she hoped to receive considerable help from Hart, but felt let down by his cavalier attitude. "Everything," she said, referring to the early rehearsals, "was sad. Everything was bad."

Rehearsals were held in New York at three different venues (the Music Box Theatre, the New Amsterdam Roof, and a rented studio), then *Miss Liberty* began a road tour in Philadelphia on June 13. Curiosity about the first performance was so great that an unusually large contingent of visitors from Broadway and elsewhere trooped to Philadelphia. Although two of the three Philadelphia newspapers praised the production, the opening night alarmed the show's creators, for the final curtain did not descend until 11:40, the second act was in clear need of extensive revision, and the problems were sufficiently severe that a postponement of the New York premiere, originally planned for July 4 (obviously an ideal date on which to open a play called *Miss Liberty*), was discussed. An additional week was added to the Philadelphia engagement, turning a three-week run into a four-week run,9 and the Broadway

---

9 The producers announced that the Philadelphia run of *Miss Liberty* was being extended due to popular demand, but the need to improve the production before its Broadway opening was the real reason.

opening was delayed by a bit more than a week. The New York premiére occurred at the Imperial Theatre on July 15, 1949.

Hart, Berlin, and Sherwood co-produced the musical, and all invested heavily in the production. At first, each intended to hold a one-third interest. Eventually, others were permitted to put up part of the $200,000 production cost, Hart's share being reduced to twenty-two percent. As was his custom, Hart did not accept a fee for directing, instead receiving three percent of the gross receipts.

The first words of Brooks Atkinson's review told the critical tale: "To come right out and say so in public, *Miss Liberty* is a disappointing musical comedy," he said. "It is built on an old-fashioned model and it is put together without sparkle or originality." Words such as *competent, routine, pedestrian,* and *pallid*—certain to scuttle any show, much less one as eagerly awaited as *Miss Liberty*—jump off the page.

Atkinson further damned the production in his Sunday piece. "*Miss Liberty* can hardly be distinguished from any other mediocre song-and-dance show," he said, "for it is done to a worn formula without imagination or originality." About Sherwood's book, he commented: "Almost any competent hack might have done as well by the story and might have written some brighter lines."

The critics, as a group, gave *Miss Liberty* a lukewarm reception. Three of them wrote favorable notices, three were distinctly unfavorable, and the rest were in between. "Only pretty fair," summarized Richard Watts Jr., while Ward Morehouse called the show "gravely disappointing."

Hart's direction received praise, even from those who were unenthusiastic about the show as a whole. Morehouse noted that "Moss Hart has applied some directorial magic in pulling everything together" and Robert Garland said "Under Moss Hart's affectionate direction, *Miss Liberty* moves its plot and people from one typically Irving Berlin hit to another." ("Let's Take an Old-Fashioned Walk" is probably the best-known song from the musical. Although the score is a pleasant one, it hardly qualifies as a collection of hit songs, despite Garland's description.)

Miss Liberty limped along for 308 performances, a passable run for most productions, but a distinct disappointment for a musical that had been so eagerly anticipated—and for a show that had cost so much to produce. Furthermore, the number of empty seats increased dramatically in the latter half of the run. Hart's royalties as director were offset by the loss he took as an investor, for production costs on Broadway were increasing alarmingly after the war.

At least the production brought Hart and Berlin closer together, as the composer told Kitty Carlisle. "Regardless of the outcome," he said, the closer relationship "is worth a lot to me."

Chapter 9 AN UNDERAPPRECIATED PLAY; A BRILLIANT SCREENPLAY
1950–1954

THE HARTS' FINANCIAL SITUATION WAS BECOMING PRECARIOUS. Neither *Christopher Blake* nor *Miss Liberty* had been successful, *Gentleman's Agreement* had been written for minimum salary, and *Light Up The Sky* had produced only a moderate return. Hart had accepted no remuneration either for *Winged Victory* or for the South Pacific tour of *The Man Who Came to Dinner*. Over the course of his career he had made a fortune, but the money had been spent freely, and seven years of minimal income had further drained his account.

Some money came in as a result of periodic radio and television appearances, but he was generally a guest, receiving the minimum salary. For a brief time in 1950 he was the master of ceremonies on a quiz show called *Answer—Yes or No* for NBC, bringing all his wit and urbanity to bear. Jack Gould, writing in *The New York Times*, predicted that *Answer—Yes or No* would become "one of the better TV quiz games." He had particular praise for Hart: "To a much greater degree than most other quiz shows, Mr. Hart's contribution has managed to capture some of that adult charm which once made 'Information Please' the darling of the airwaves. . . . Mr. Hart is doing a most competent job, keeping the proceedings moving along without sacrificing the engaging informality that gives the show its flavor." But the show did not catch on despite critical approval, running only from April 30 until July 23.

So, for the first time in many years, it was necessary for him to go to Hollywood to write a screenplay that would earn him enough money to subsidize his theatrical career in New York. He went to work for Samuel Goldwyn, who had long sought to bring a story based on the tales of Hans Christian Andersen to the screen. According to one version, Goldwyn had already read and rejected twenty different screenplays for the movie before he hired Hart.

Goldwyn's notion was to ignore biography altogether. *Hans Christian Andersen* would be a fairy tale, much like those told by the great tale-spinner himself. Only Andersen's name, the film's period (the 1830s), and the titles of some of his stories were based on reality.

Frank Loesser, the composer and lyricist of *Guys and Dolls*, had already been hired to write the songs for *Hans Christian Andersen*. Unlike the conventional Hollywood procedure, in which, as Goldwyn said, "the producer of a musical would say [to the composer after the screenplay had been completed], 'Let's have a song here, here and there,'" Loesser and Hart worked together from the outset. "We'd bat the ideas back and forth," Loesser said. "For instance, the story outline Moss did had Hans going from the island of Odense, where he started out as a cobbler, to Copenhagen. We tried to figure out how important that trip was to the general development of the character and the forward movement of the story. Should Hans 'sing' his way to Copenhagen or should he just show up there?" Loesser and Hart worked together for eight months, taking great pleasure in their collaboration, before giving the completed screenplay to Goldwyn.

Hart's script was often charming, always workmanlike. However, because the dramatic content of the film is lighter than air, charm was made to work overtime. Hans (Danny Kaye), a small-town cobbler whose passion is telling stories to children, is expelled from the small village of Odense because he disrupts the schoolmaster's lessons. Accompanied by his apprentice, Peter, Hans travels to Copenhagen where he falls in love with and writes a ballet for a beautiful ballerina (Renée Jeanmaire) who is married to the ballet master (Farley Granger), a young man of mercurial temper. In his remarkably naïve way, Hans hopes to win the ballerina's love by writing stories for her that can be used as the basis for ballets. Finally, after the ballerina assures him that she loves her husband, Hans, now a celebrity, returns to Odense.

Hart's screenplay is so uncharacteristically muted that one presumes he was prevented from increasing the dramatic content by the producer's insistence. Whoever is responsible, however, the script could certainly have used a bit less *Gemütlichkeit*, a less simple-minded hero, and greater conflict. Hart explained that he was only able to go so far. "The spirit of the film set the pattern for the writing," he said.

Danny Kaye was reunited with Hart for the first time in ten years. His gentle performance contrasted greatly with his flamboyant characterization in *Lady in the Dark* and in so many films. But Kaye played Hans with just the right level of delicacy and tenderness the film demanded. Kaye brings a luminous charm to the screen, especially in his scenes with children.

Goldwyn hoped that the film would become a classic for children. No one was prepared for the storm of controversy that erupted when the Danish government expressed outrage over the movie. On March 15, 1952, while the film was still in production, the Danish Foreign Office considered registering a formal protest, claiming that Goldwyn's version of Hans Christian Andersen "would insult the memory of the beloved fairy tale writer." A spokesman for Goldwyn countered that the producer "never intended to make a literal story of Andersen's life. The studio has used the best talent available to make a beautiful production based on certain portions of Andersen's fairy tales."

In April, the Danish Foreign Office offered to produce its own version of Andersen's life, one that would conform with historical truth. They asked that Goldwyn show their film concurrently with his. Goldwyn rejected the request.

In July, Danny Kaye journeyed to Copenhagen, hoping to mend fences. At a heavily attended press conference, he explained that "for years and years this has been Goldwyn's secret and sincerest wish—not a biography, just another fairy tale, an entertaining film built on an incident which might have taken place in Hans Christian Andersen's life." Kaye presented the script of the film to the Danish Prime Minister, Erik Eriksen. He was greeted tumultuously by Danes, who made clear that, if they had any argument, it was with Samuel Goldwyn, not with the film's charismatic star.

Kaye proceeded from Copenhagen to Odense, Hans Christian Andersen's birthplace, where he tried out Andersen's traveling boots, lay on his bed, and sat at his desk. These actions, which aroused widespread criticism, nearly neutralized the positive impression Kaye had made in Copenhagen.

The following day, Kaye, attempting to repair the damage, appeared on Danish radio, giving a one-hour program for charity. Again, the public seemed satisfied, forgiving him his behavior in Odense.

Meanwhile, in California, the film was previewed for a generally enthusiastic audience. Nevertheless, Goldwyn insisted on some rewriting and reshooting. Hart agreed, for his response to the preview was "how terrible" it was. The added material helped, and, despite Hart's reservations, everyone else connected with the film believed it would be a great success.

Just before the opening of the film, however, the Danish-American controversy began anew. Arne Soerensen, a Danish film critic, saw the picture in November at a special benefit performance and wrote in his newspaper, *Information*, "It will cost America's reputation [in Denmark] so much that it will take the United States Information Service in Denmark fifty years to make up for the loss."

Soerensen claimed that the film created a German, rather than a Danish, atmosphere. The words *Hans* and *Copenhagen* received German pronunciations and the actors were dressed in Bavarian clothing. And, of course, the character in the film bore no relation whatever to the historical Hans Christian Andersen.

American critics were unconcerned about the controversy in Denmark. Bosley Crowther, reviewing the film for *The New York Times* on November 26, 1952, called it "as pretty and graceful a picture as has come down the rocky pike this year," and praised Loesser's songs, although he disliked the "syrupy script of Moss Hart. . . . Mr. Hart has not created a character for Mr. Kaye to play, let alone a credible reflection of the famous Danish teller of tales. His Hans Christian Andersen is lumpish, humorless and wan." Crowther said that Kaye, restricted by the script, appears to be "a sort of amiable village dunce."

Variety was less critical. Its reviewer called *Hans Christian Andersen* "a charming fairy tale . . . done with the taste expected of a Samuel Goldwyn production. . . . the Moss Hart screenplay . . . follows a simple line in keeping with the plot simplicity and stress on sympathetic charm."

But the Danish government was still upset. In December, the Foreign Office issued a pamphlet called "The Real Andersen," which they hoped would be circulated to movie audiences at showings of *Hans Christian Andersen*. Again, Goldwyn refused to comply, although he did include a sentence that appeared just after the film's credits and before the story begins: "This is not a story of [Andersen's] life, but a fairy tale about this great spinner of fairy tales."

Despite Hart's own reservations about the film, he was nominated by the Screen Writers Guild as "author of the best American [film] musical" for *Hans Christian Andersen*.

One suitably impressed young viewer was Christopher Hart, four years old when the movie was released. "My favorite thing on my birthday for the next two or three years was to have eight or nine screaming classmates come to our house to watch the picture," he said. It's certain that, despite the limitations of the film that are apparent to adults, children by the millions were enthralled.

Although writing a film offered no particular difficulty for Hart, playwriting was becoming a more and more formidable enterprise. Hart found himself unable to conceive any material he considered worthy of dramatization. In a pattern that repeated itself several times during this period, he would begin a project, realize its inadequacy, and drop it. He yearned to write another play, one that would bring him a satisfaction he had not felt since *Winged Victory* in 1943. For several years he found "nothing that excited or pleased me," as he put it, "and I was determined not to put that blank piece of paper in the typewriter until I did."

Irving Lazar, Hart's agent, was puzzled by his client's seeming inability to begin a new play. "It took me years," Lazar wrote in 1995, "to understand that under [Hart's] surface confidence and charm was a man so profoundly insecure and anxious that he [was] convinced he would never write anything decent again."

In 1951, however, Hart read and was profoundly moved by a novel of Edgar Mittelhölzer's entitled *Shadows Move Among Them*. He wrote to Mittelhölzer in England, seeking and receiving permission to adapt the novel for the stage. In a letter written in December 1951, Mittelhölzer cautioned Hart "not to be afraid of disappointing me, for I know what difficulties must face you in trying to convert the book into a play, and I am prepared to witness great changes." He said that he was "thrilled to see what new form you will give the work" and had complete "confidence in your ability to do justice to *Shadows*."

Hart had never before adapted material written for another medium to the stage, and he was apprehensive about making the attempt, but working on the adaptation stirred his creative juices as they had not been stirred for years. In an article written shortly before the play opened, he wrote, "The very difficulties of Mr. Mittelhölzer's novel attracted me and I was drawn back again and again by the prospect of departing almost completely from the style and content of all my other work."

Still, the process of adaptation proved difficult. "Far from being a help, as it would seem, [adapting] an existing book is a hindrance," said Hart. "The printed page has a legality, an authority, and it's very hard to get away from it."

The novel, a complex philosophical and psychological story about the contrast between an apparent paradise in the jungle of British Guyana and the pressures of life in "civilization"—as well as a young man's guilt over the death of his wife—may have seemed unlikely material for Moss Hart, the renowned writer of satirical comedy, but he threw himself into the project with intense enthusiasm. He wrote it, he maintained, "because it represented a challenge to me as a writer; a departure from anything I had ever done before: in style, in content, in my whole creative personality."

Any adaptation of a novel must sacrifice some elements, and a theme in *Shadows Move Among Them*, the ominous nature of the "shadows" of the past (the myths and conventions that govern peoples' behavior), was eliminated in Hart's play. Undoubtedly for that reason Hart was unable to accommodate Mittelhölzer's request that the title of the novel be preserved in the play.

The title he eventually chose (the first several drafts are called, simply, "An Untitled Play"), *The Climate of Eden*, is intriguing because it is as ambiguous as every other element in the drama. Does the title suggest that the world of the play is an unspoiled paradise, an Eden? Or is the title meant ironically?

However, the play preserves (and sometimes elaborates on) the complex nature of the characters. Most of the plot remains intact. The play is mysterious, ambiguous, wistful, mystical, elusive—qualities which some of the critics believed to be assets, others weaknesses. The tone is often foreboding.

The play focuses on Gregory Hawke, a thirty-one-year-old Englishman on the verge of a nervous breakdown. It is unclear whether or not the death of Gregory's former wife, Brenda, was an accident, a suicide, or a murder. In any case, Gregory holds himself responsible and is tormented by the thought that Brenda's spirit is trying to destroy him. Unable to cope with life in England, he asks his uncle in British Guyana, the Reverend Gerald Harmston, if he can live with Harmston and his family until he can conquer his alcoholism and his melancholia. Harmston is a most unusual clergyman, neither the stuffy preacher so often portrayed in some plays and films nor the kindly, genial caricature of others. Instead, he is a visionary, who, in the words of C. W. E. Bigsby, "hopes to create a utopia intended to serve as a bright contrast to all the ills of Western civilization." Harmston subscribes to no particular doctrine other than goodness: his sermons promote freedom and he devotes himself to disseminating culture (through books and phonograph records, for example) to the Guyanese people. God, if He exists at all for Harmston, is a loving, benevolent figure. Harmston, impatient with Gregory's neuroses, tells the young man that they are of two different worlds: Gregory is looking for conclusions, but those who live in the jungle prefer mystery.

The Harmston family is portrayed as eccentric but admirable. Harmston's elder daughter, Mabel, falls in love with Gregory and, indulging in the freedom her father espouses, sleeps with him. Harmston and his wife inform Gregory that they have no wish to dictate Mabel's behavior; if Mabel and Gregory wish to sleep together, her parents have no objection. Mabel has already had an affair, sanctioned by her parents, with a native Guyanese man. (One of the tenets of Harmston's teaching is the encouragement of premarital sex. The arrival of a supply of contraceptives occasions an announcement from the pulpit.) However, although Harmston is perfectly prepared for Gregory and Mabel to live together, he does not approve of their getting married.

Olivia, Mabel's twelve-year-old sister, is a thoroughly developed character, showing all the characteristics of a precocious adolescent. She has a fierce crush on Gregory and feels deeply ambivalent about Mabel. Olivia asks Gregory directly if he murdered his wife, but Gregory evades the question, leaving it shrouded in mystery—as are so many elements of *The Climate of Eden*. At one point, Olivia tells Gregory that Mabel was bitten by a snake and killed. The audience, like Gregory, is convinced that Mabel is dead, but, it turns out, Olivia has been lying.

All of these characters, as well as the others who inhabit the play, are developed intriguingly. Harmston is portrayed as an admirable, intelligent man, but something of a dictator, both within his family and in his relationship with the natives. He has a tendency toward violence (he beats his servant and slaps his children when he feels they need to be disciplined), but he is at the same time a loving, tender father and a beloved minister. The contradictions in his personality are not resolved in the play; they simply exist side by side, as contradictions exist within many human beings. Harmston's tendency to violence is more thoroughly explored in *Shadows Move Among Them*, in which he upsets his wife and children, although they accept Harmston's authority unquestioningly. In the novel, Gregory goes so far as to call Harmston "fascistic." The novel is as much about the pathology of the Harmstons as it is about Gregory's neuorsis. Indeed, Gregory seems a good deal less neurotic in the novel than in the play. By the end of *Shadows Move Among Them*, it is clear that Harmston's philosophy is no more than a very fancy justification for dictatorship. A valid criticism of the play is that Hart chose not to dramatize this material, instead portraying Harmston as a benign, though flawed, figure.

Eventually, Gregory's hallucinations, suicidal longings, and dependence on alcohol subside, thanks to Harmston's counsel, although the play by no means offers a conventional happy ending.

Frederick Fox provided an ingenious two-level set which accommodated scenes set in the Reverend Harmston's house, in the church, on the front porch, and in the jungle. The set permitted the play to move in cinematic fashion from one location to another.

Shortly before the play's scheduled opening in late 1952, Hart wrote, "I think *The Climate of Eden* is by far the most interesting piece of work I have ever done for the theatre." However, he was fearful that the play would not be received well. "It's not always a good thing—when you shift [style and tone] suddenly, as I have, it leaves [critics and audiences] unsettled." However, Hart said "that a writer has a certain number of good years—so many books or plays—and during those years he has to gamble."

In nearly every respect, *The Climate of Eden* inhabits a different world than that represented in all of Moss Hart's other plays. He preserves the elliptical quality of Mittelhölzer's novel, and often increases it. The tone of the play is leavened by humor, but it is a gentle humor, unprecedented in Hart's earlier work.

He also directed *The Climate of Eden*, and went to England on the *Queen Elizabeth* in 1952 to cast many of the performers. His most fortuitous discovery was Rosemary Harris, who played Mabel, then went on to a long career in England and in the United States. Brooks Atkinson described her performance in *The Climate of Eden* as "radiant . . . all grace and loveliness."

Penelope Munday, a fourteen-year-old British actress cast as Olivia, caught the precociousness of her character "brilliantly," Atkinson said; she "is almost like pure spirit in the quicksilver quality of her acting." Munday was selected by Daniel Blum, the editor of *Theatre World*, for an award for her performance.

In the pivotal role of Gregory, Hart made a somewhat less successful selection. Judging by some of the reviews, Lee Montague was unable to convey Gregory's attractive side, concentrating perhaps too strongly on Gregory's neuroses. Hart eventually came to believe that he had cast the role incorrectly, but, by the time he had reached that conclusion, it was too late to make any changes.

The pre-Broadway tryout of *The Climate of Eden* took place in Washington, D.C., in August. As Kitty Carlisle said, "Almost no one in Washington wanted to see *The Climate of Eden*—there were fifty people in the theatre [one] afternoon, and we were worried about paying the actors. After the matinee, Moss and Bernie and I sat in a sad, dusty little park opposite the theatre, terribly dispirited, staring at the ground." Bernie Hart looked at his disconsolate brother and said, "Never mind, Moss. We got out of Egypt, we'll get out of Washington."

The out-of-town tryouts failed to attract an audience, but the author and producers (Bernard Hart and Joseph Hyman) hoped that New Yorkers would respond more positively to the play's ambiguities. Despite the excellence of much of the writing in the play, however, it failed to win public support. Some meritorious works of art simply do not interest the public, and such was the case with *The Climate of Eden*.

The play opened to mixed reviews at the Martin Beck Theatre on November 6, 1952. Brooks Atkinson commented, "in the final analysis it must no doubt be said that Mr. Hart has not succeeded," although he conceded that there were "a number of tender and touching scenes." In spite of his reservations about the play, Atkinson called Hart's production "entrancing," but the overall tone of the review was less than enthusiastic. The prestige of *The New York Times* was so great that a mixed notice from its critic had the potential to keep the public away. Recognizing that fact, Atkinson sent a note to Hart, saying, "There is so much that is good in your play that I hate to see it go down so fast. That is one of the many cruelties of show business." And, indeed, Atkinson's review ended any chance *The Climate of Eden* might have had for a successful run in New York.

Other critics agreed with Atkinson. Walter Kerr, although he called the play "earnestly written and brilliantly mounted," was unmoved, and Robert Coleman dismissed it as "more irritating than fascinating." John McClain in the *Journal American* saluted the play's "taste and intelligence . . . moments of high humor and pathos . . . pervaded with gentle philosophy," but "thought the story hopelessly cluttered."

However, a number of the reviewers were deeply moved by the play. One of them, Ward Morehouse, told Hart in a letter, "There's a great deal of beauty in the play, wonderful scenes and some of your best writing. I shall be seeing it again and again. My congratulations on a fine job."

Richard Watts Jr. wrote in his review that *The Climate of Eden* was "a striking, original and absorbing play, staged and acted with force and distinction." Louis Kronenberger included *The Climate of Eden* in his *Best Plays of 1952–53* and John Chapman selected it as one of the "Golden Dozen" in *Theatre '53*. The play received one vote as the New York Drama Critics Circle's "best new American play." (The winner was William Inge's *Picnic*.)

Some of the critics wrote follow-up articles, attempting to encourage the public to purchase tickets to *The Climate of Eden*. John Chapman was one. His original review called *The Climate of Eden* "an eerie, fascinating, lovely play . . . given a glowing performance." In a subsequent meditation on the play, Chapman said, "No playwright has worked harder in and for the theatre [than Moss Hart], or more successfully, and few have been as venturesome. Hart's newest piece, *The Climate of Eden* . . . is an adventure for him and for the playgoer, too . . . [I]t is the most original drama so far this season, and in writing, staging and acting the most distinguished. Yet . . . *The Climate of Eden* has started off at the box office less boisterously [than other productions]. Now it is up to the audiences to make the piece a success." Chapman conceded that the play "does have a loose end or two, but these technical defects are negligible. [The play has] great warmth, deep affection in it as it tells the stories of many people in a strange mission." But the public refused to budge. The play closed after only twenty performances.

Hart wrote to his friend Atkinson after the opening, but before the closing notice had been posted:

Well, I made a valiant try. Like Mr. [Adlai] Stevenson [who had just lost the 1952 presidential election to Dwight D. Eisenhower], I'm too old to cry and it hurts too much to laugh . . . but I have no regrets. This was the way I wanted to walk, and if my steps faltered, the road ahead is the direction I want to go. . . . I have taken more from this failure than from many a success.

I agree with you about [*The Climate of Eden's*] imperfections as a play; its unfulfilled quality . . . No one was more aware of its lacks than myself, though I had hoped that its very imperfections rose above the drab stuff we have been getting, and that a reach of this sort was what the theatre needed. I am proud of some of the writing in it—a good deal more proud than if I had written a tight, facile little play [although] we haven't a chance of running beyond this week or next.

I find myself in a state of utter exhaustion, but . . . I'll [soon] pick up the outside world again—and can we have one of our lunches?

Attempts were made by those who were moved by the play to bring *The Climate of Eden* to a wider audience than the few who had seen it in New York and in its pre-Broadway performances. A condensed version was performed on WNTA-TV in New York in 1952 and again in 1960.

On October 6, 1953, the play was revived off-Broadway at Current Stages, opening on October 6, and running for 138 performances. Atkinson found the production "uncommonly good . . . a sensitive and often touching performance." Although Atkinson repeated some of his earlier criticisms of the play, he now found much more to praise: "Mr. Hart's sketch of the hospitable, unspoiled missionary family living under the tyranny of a benevolent prophet with a vision of joy and purity is a beautiful piece of work—work of art, in fact. . . . Some of the philosophical comments in *The Climate of Eden* are extraordinarily aware; and some of the writing is as delicate as a lyric poem."

Theatre Arts magazine, which published a commercially successful play each month, adjusted its policy in order to include *The Climate of Eden* in its May 1954, issue. The editors "feel strongly that it is a worthwhile play, one worthy of presentation in text form; the editors also feel that its publication here may serve as a stimulus to production by theatrical groups throughout the country."

In 1955, the play was produced at Hunter College, in New York City. A priest objected vigorously, calling the play "disgustingly repelling . . . there is a gentle deriding of religion and of morals . . . If the play is put on at Hunter as it was written by Moss Hart, there will be many a blush, many an embarrassed person." Charles Elsom, the director of the Theatre Workshop at Hunter, assured Hart "that we are sitting as tight as we can, though the pressure . . . is somewhat uncomfortable." Hunter presented *The Climate of Eden* late in March 1955, with a minimum of cuts. However, despite the best efforts of some believers in the play, the brief Broadway run doomed it to obscurity; it has rarely been produced since 1955.

Hart made every effort to interest a British producer-director to present *The Climate of Eden* in London. His friend Garson Kanin took the script to Laurence Olivier, recommending that Olivier might wish to direct the play. Olivier wrote to Hart in February 1954:

> My dear Moss,
>
> I have just finished this afternoon reading *The Climate of Eden* . . . I am terribly impressed and moved by it . . . Of course it is quite an undertaking, and my interest is not much good unless I get others interested in it . . . May I have your permission to try and work something out? I can think of no people better than Ralph Richardson [as Harmston] and Denholm Elliott [as Gregory Hawke] for the two leading men—can you? As time goes on and I become more familiar with it, it might be I would feel bold enough to ask you to consider one or two changes, but I don't know this because right now I am a bit bowled over by it.

Hart was "very pleased indeed at [Olivier's] interest and the possibility of his doing it," he noted in his diary. "It might be a minor triumph of sorts to have him do it in London and to have it a success."

Until 1968, all plays presented for public performance in England were subject to the approval of the Lord Chamberlain, who had total authority to alter or forbid the performance of any play. Olivier submitted *The Climate of Eden* to the Lord Chamberlain's office and received a letter from the assistant comptroller, N. Gwatkin, granting permission to produce the play only if certain changes were made. These included "elimination of the mention of contraceptives, no reference to Jesus Christ, no suggestion of pre-marriage living together," and the omission of various lines such as "before I pee on your new trousers," "Well, for one thing it has an indecent sound," "Oh, stop pretending you're so modest and say it," "the feel of his chest pressing down on your two breasts," and "kiss my bottom." These demands, which seem utterly preposterous, at least left the door open for public production of the play. (Tennessee Williams's great drama *A Streetcar Named Desire* had been refused permission altogether only a few years before.)

Olivier wrote to Hart, "There is a certain amount of reasoning that can be done with the Censor, but only a certain amount, you understand." Olivier asked if Hart would be willing to do some "re-writing [of] the second act and *generally* unsensationalise the goings-on a bit, which I believe, if you could see your way to doing, might be to the play's advantage. . . . The tough one is, of course, the advice on living together before marriage. As to contraceptives etc., I could probably go in to bat with the Lord Chamberlain's Office and get away with 'special medical supplies' or some such phrase."

Olivier's greatest fear, however, was that Richardson would not be interested in the role of Harmston and he could think of no one else who could play it satisfactorily.

"Denholm Elliott loves the play and would love to do it," he wrote to Hart. "I haven't got an answer from [Dorothy] Tutin yet, but I've got a feeling that she might not want to play a [twelve]-year old . . . Richardson is going to be very difficult to get."

Garson Kanin followed up with a letter to Hart late in February. "Ralph Richardson, Larry reports, is a little worried that the other parts will overshadow him," Kanin said, "and is also worried that the censor here might remove some of his most colorful material."

In June, Olivier regretfully pulled out because of his total involvement with the film of *Richard III*, which he not only produced and directed, but in which he played the leading role.

"Not being able to undertake the direction of the play myself, which was my first great wish, I have since tried, and vainly I am afraid, to find a producer to whom I would care to entrust the piece," Olivier said. In any case, Olivier could see no solution to the casting problems: "The only person who was willing and able and enthusiastic was Denholm Elliott. Dorothy Tutin was too involved, and apart from Richardson I couldn't think of anybody else with sufficient magnetism or an unadulterated enough personality to take the leading role."

Three years later, Hart discussed a production with the prominent English actor and director Anthony Quayle. Although Quayle said that he found the play "a really fascinating piece of work," he also "found something subtly unsatisfactory about it—though I must confess I find it the very devil to try and analyse what I mean." Quayle thought the ambiguity that lies at the core of the play a weakness. "I really couldn't quite make out if the Harmston family and their way of life, was meant to be a truly innocent state," he said in letter of January 1957, "a real 'garden of Eden,' while Gregory was a man basically sickened by civilisation, who couldn't breathe their 'climate'—or whether the Harmstons had got something more than a little wrong with them, themselves. . . . [T]hat is all very well in a book . . . but in the theatre, it seems to me that the author must be more explicit."

Unwilling to alter the very element that gave *The Climate of Eden* its haunting quality, Hart decided to look elsewhere. He submitted the play to Tony Richardson, Associate Artistic Director of the English Stage Company, in 1958. Richardson, like Olivier, was impressed. "I find [the play] very fascinating, and am showing it to other members of the Artistic Committee at the moment," Richardson reported in a letter of May 12, 1958. But the other members of the committee must have been less fascinated, for the English Stage Company also decided against mounting a production.

Hart was devastated by the failure of *The Climate of Eden* on Broadway and the lack of a British production (it was "a failure that hurt," he said). He was particularly bitter about the "tantalizing and frustrating" nature of the failure, he said; "frustrating because the audiences who saw the play in its brief run were enthusiastic and deeply moved; tantalizing because half the critics found the play good and even those critics who did not like it were unusually reluctant and gentle in their disapproval."

Despite his relative youth (he was forty-eight when *The Climate of Eden* opened), Moss Hart never completed another play.

ϛ

Barnett Hart, Moss's father, seemed to blossom in the years following his wife's death. He became a jaunty, lovable eccentric, known to one and all as the Commodore because of the yachting cap and white suits he habitually wore. He wrote dreadful songs in honor of each of Moss's plays (called, for example, "You Can't Take It With You," "George Washington Slept Here," and "Lady in the Dark") that he would sing at the drop of a hat. As a surprise for his father's birthday one year, Moss arranged for Irving Berlin to publish a song by the Commodore. Berlin graciously agreed and even took time to discuss the musical arrangement with Barnett Hart, suggesting that he change two notes in the final verse. But the Commodore needed no help, he assured Berlin, patting him on the shoulder and saying, "Now listen, boy, you tend to your song writing and I'll tend to mine."

The lyrics of "The Man Who Came to Dinner," the song published by Irving Berlin, Inc., are representative of the Commodore's songwriting efforts:

Be very careful, when you're inviting a friend,
You never know when he's going to go.
Anything can happen for your hospitality.
May it never happen to you. Just what happened to me.
The Man Who Came to Dinner, what a man, what a man!

Somehow he fell, now he isn't well,
All he needs is rest.
A patient now, he's a wow! wow! wow!
Thank God he's leaving on the six o'clock train.
Think of it when he was gone, he fell again upon the lawn,
They picked him up and brought him back again,
Yes they picked him up and brought him in,
He looked around and said with a grin,
"The Man, the Man, The Man Who Came to Dinner's here again."

Although the Commodore endeared himself to virtually everyone (Kitty Carlisle loved him dearly), the relationship between Moss and Barnett remained strained, as both found it difficult to bridge the gap that had grown so wide during Moss's childhood. However, late in 1953, the Harts visited Florida and Moss experienced "a touching moment," as he wrote in his diary. During "one of the evenings we spent with Pop . . . he suddenly reached out and held my hand. I let him hold it and continued to hold his. It was one of the few moments of physical contact we have ever had between us and I was neither uncomfortable nor awkward about it." It was the beginning, he hoped, after some thirty-five years of bitterness, of reconciliation.

Still, in June of the following year Hart noted that despite his pleasure that the Commodore "looks very hale and hearty and is absolutely amazing for his age [ninety-one], I am making a very great effort to have some kind of relationship with my father. But I am afraid it is not going very well. I am sad about this but I am afraid there are too many loveless and strange years in between for us to try to make anything of this now. . . . Kitty reports that when I am there he is quite a different person. I apparently make him very uncomfortable."

The Commodore lived until 1960, dying in Florida at ninety-seven.

∾

On November 18, 1952, shortly after *The Climate of Eden* opened on Broadway, Hart traveled to Boston at the behest of the producers of the revue *Two's Company*, featuring Bette Davis.

The show was in trouble, and the producers sought Hart's opinions. They were so impressed by his evaluation that they asked him to take over the revue's direction, but Hart, already contracted to Warner Bros. to write a screenplay for a new version of *A Star Is Born* and intending to travel to California in less than two months, turned down the offer.

He did, however, consent to begin a project with his longtime friend and mother-surrogate, Edna Ferber. Ferber, older than Moss by nineteen years, had a well-deserved reputation for imperious behavior. For example, she was deeply upset that she was not the first to be informed when Kitty was pregnant with Cathy. She wrote the Harts an indignant letter, saying "I'm the girl who is The Last To Know. Just why you didn't want to tell me when I was [visiting] at New Hope is one of the things I'll never understand."

Despite Ferber's prickly personality, Hart agreed to work with her when she proposed that they collaborate on adapting her novel *Saratoga Trunk* into a musical. She envisioned a score by Rodgers and Hammerstein, although Hart, knowing that they were already working on another project, suggested Harold Arlen instead. Ferber, pretending, one imagines, never to have heard of Harold Arlen ("Who is this Arlen fellow? What's he done? What are his credits?") scoffed at the idea. Hart, who had not been enthusiastic about *Saratoga Trunk* in the first place, was irritated by Ferber's reaction. Nevertheless, he and Ferber began work on the musical, drawing up an outline and sending it to Rodgers and Hammerstein. The songwriters offered suggestions for improvement in the *Saratoga Trunk* proposal, offering a detailed analysis of the material Ferber and Hart had submitted, but made clear that they would be unable to work on it. They were certain *Saratoga Trunk* "can be a big hit and a beautiful show," Rodgers and Hammerstein said. "For several reasons, however, the other story we are considering [*Pipe Dream*] is more interesting to us." Ferber refused to accept their rejection as final, telling Hart that she was certain Rodgers and Hammerstein would change their minds.

But every day Hart was more convinced that the material was simply not good enough to be revived and musicalized. In private he referred to Ferber's novel as "Saratoga Junk," and word may have gotten back to her; if it did, she surely would have been furious. In any case, the working sessions on *Saratoga Trunk* became more and more difficult, eventually turning into acrimony. Hart soon decided he did not wish to continue; "I simply cannot work with her," he told his wife.

Kitty warned him that Ferber would undoubtedly be upset by his decision and he must take care to be tactful when informing her. But the meeting went badly. That *Saratoga Trunk* was dropped, to Ferber's intense annoyance, is almost incidental to the hostility that resulted. Later that same day, Ferber called Kitty to complain that Hart had called her "old granite face," and that she would never forgive him his remark. Although Hart insisted that he really said simply that Ferber was "as stubborn as a piece of granite," the two writers were soon enmeshed in a monumental feud. Hart insisted he could not work with Ferber;

she maintained that he had treated her viciously and inexcusably. Ferber wrote an anguished letter to Kitty Carlisle, claiming that for twenty-five years she had given Hart nothing but "friendship, understanding, appreciation and respect," and he had repaid her with "a barrage of the most savage and uncalled-for abuse, . . . such undeserved vindictiveness, such venom, as . . . I have ever heard directed at me (or at anyone)." She claimed not to have resented his decision to abandon *Saratoga Trunk*, but could not resist adding, "I was, and am, ashamed for this man who was, I had thought, a friend."

Hart was as outraged at Ferber as she was at him. Running into her accidentally in 1954, he attempted to be cordial, saying, "Hello, Edna," and taking her hand. "She dropped it as though my hand were radio-active and cut me dead," he confided to his diary. "This ends my friendship with Ferber. I have behaved in the most scrupulous fashion and I intend to make no further efforts. I am convinced as I have been for a long time, that Edna is actually a mean spirited and petty human being."

For years afterward, Hart did his best to avoid Ferber. However, when Cathy Hart was five, her father took her and Chris to see *Peter Pan*, then one of Broadway's most successful musicals. After the production, he escorted them backstage to meet Mary Martin, who played Peter. While they were in Martin's dressing room, Edna Ferber came in, wishing to introduce her great-niece to Martin. Hart said that he and Ferber "looked right through each other and never spoke a word." As he and the children left the room and began walking down the corridor, Cathy, feeling the tension between her father and the woman they had encountered, asked whom he had just ignored so elaborately. "That, my child, was Captain Hook," Hart replied.

Later, when Ferber was contacted by the producer Robert Fryer about *Saratoga Trunk*, she wrote a formal letter to Hart, believing (or pretending to believe) that he might sue her, since they had worked together briefly on an outline. She maintained that "anything you would want considered would, of course, be necessarily cleared if there's a play in the future." Hart assured her that "There is nothing to 'clear.' Whatever the outline contained stemmed directly from the book—my contribution was purely a technical one—and if it is at all helpful, so much the better. Moss." Under Robert Fryer's auspices, Morton Da Costa wrote a book for *Saratoga Trunk*. As it turned out, Ferber's association with Da Costa also ended in unpleasantness and recriminations, although the eventual musical made of *Saratoga Trunk*—renamed *Saratoga*—did have a brief Broadway run.

The feud between Hart and Ferber continued for four years, but was forgotten when they ran into each other in London. Neither said a word about their long period of estrangement, Kitty Carlisle said, but both obviously felt that the tension between them had existed long enough. Afterward, they remained friendly until Hart's death, when Ferber was chosen as one of several friends to deliver the eulogy.

ↄ

In January 1953, Hart and his family moved to Palm Springs, where he began writing a screenplay for the musical adaptation of *A Star Is Born*. He believed the script could be completed in several months, but work continued into the spring, whereupon the Harts vacated the house they were renting and moved to Santa Monica.

An earlier version of *A Star Is Born*, released in 1937, was written by Dorothy Parker, her husband Alan Campbell, and Robert Carson. Featuring Janet Gaynor, Fredric March, Lionel Stander, and Adolphe Menjou, the film was much admired by critics and moviegoers. The version Hart wrote for Judy Garland (making her film comeback after a four-year absence), James Mason, Jack Carson, and Charles Bickford was a triumph, surpassing the original in nearly every respect. Skeptics had wondered how it would be possible to turn the film into a musical without destroying it, but Hart, Harold Arlen (who wrote the music), and Ira Gershwin (lyrics) solved the problem. Many songs were written for Garland, but all of them stemmed from her occupation in the film (as a singer-actress), thus maintaining a realism unusual in musicals.

The history of *A Star Is Born* began in 1932, with a film entitled *What Price Hollywood?* that employed the story later used in *A Star Is Born*. *What Price Hollywood?* was directed by George Cukor, who would direct the Judy Garland version twenty-two years later.

Both the 1937 and 1954 versions of *A Star Is Born*[1] tell the story of Esther Blodgett, an aspiring performer who arrives in Hollywood, is taken under the wing of the alcoholic film star Norman Maine, and sees her career rise spectacularly under his tutelage. They fall in love, and Esther (renamed Vicki Lester) marries Maine, whose career is declining as rapidly as that of Esther/Vicki is rising. Maine learns how to deal with his alcoholism at a clinic, but after his rehabilitation, while attending the races, he is snubbed by those who once deferred to him. His degradation is complete when Matt Libby, the studio's publicity director who has long detested Maine, punches him savagely, leading onlookers to conclude that "Norman Maine is drunk again." Eventually, after Vicki has become the leading actress in Hollywood and Nor-

---

1 Still another version, directed by Frank Pierson and featuring Barbra Streisand and Kris Kristofferson, was released in 1976.

man, unable to find work as an actor, has sunk to the level of vagrancy, he walks into the ocean, committing suicide.

Both films are effective, well-written pieces; Hart uses a good deal of the 1937 screenplay, some of it almost verbatim; but when he does make a change it nearly always represents an improvement, converting scenes of treacly sentiment into believable episodes in which the characters are developed with psychological complexity. *A Star Is Born* is Moss Hart's best work for films, a work that can rank alongside *You Can't Take It With You*, *Once in a Lifetime*, and *The Man Who Came to Dinner* as Hart's most accomplished contributions to the theatrical arts. For his part, Hart was more enthusiastic about *A Star Is Born* than any other film he ever worked on.[2]

Judy Garland impressed Hart not only with her talent but with her character. Although he recognized her neuroses and occasionally drew back from them, he found her "completely enchanting . . . one of the wittiest and most intelligent creatures I have ever known and certainly one of the few actresses who is a person in her own right apart from her talent."

Kitty Carlisle said that Hart was not only fond of Garland, but "sorry for her," because of her many emotional problems. "There was something very appealing about her—very appealing, very sweet. One wanted to protect her, take her in your arms and make sure that no harm befell her."

On an evening in California before *A Star Is Born* was released, the Harts attended a party at Irving Lazar's house with Garland, her husband Sid Luft, and many others. Garland, woefully insecure to begin with, was deeply offended when one of the guests cruelly asked her, "Why did you let your mother die in a parking lot?" In tears, she ran to the bathroom. Not until some time had passed did Sid Luft become alarmed and begin to look for his wife. He opened the bathroom door to find Garland weeping, according to Kitty Carlisle. (Irving Lazar maintained that Garland had attempted to commit suicide.)

Hart spoke to Garland at length the next day, then wrote her a sympathetic letter, to which she responded:

> How can I possibly tell you how much that note means to me. I can only tell you that I read it every day . . . and shall continue to read it every day and also every time I get low—or scared from the painful lack of confidence I've lived

---

2 It is the only bound film script he wrote that he kept in his library. Two inscriptions face the title page. The first, from producer Sid Luft, says: "Dear Moss—Where would we be? What would we have done? I owe so much." The second, from Judy Garland, says: "If I can only say it—the way you've written it— *I'll be home!* God bless you."

with for so many years. That I should feel this is, I know, illogical, senseless, foolish. But it's there and it's very real to me.

That's why your letter is so important. It made me realize that you know me very well—more than I ever dreamed. And oh what a comfort it is to know that I have a true friend in you. Such a wise and knowing friend, Moss dear . . .

Again I say bless you for my treasured letter. I'm so proud to have you for my friend.

Hart returned to New York after completing the screenplay. Afterward, he kept in close touch with Cukor, the director, to see how the filming, which began in October 1953, was progressing. Cukor wrote a series of long, detailed letters apprising Hart of the way he intended to shoot each scene and what color process he had chosen to use; he asked if Hart would approve of minor changes in the dialogue; he asked Hart's opinion of his ideas for various bits of business.

So detailed and so frequent were Cukor's letters that he said in one of them, "I trust that you're not sore at me for this continued harassing."

On the contrary, Hart maintained his interest in the film throughout the process. In October, replying to a letter from Cukor, he suggested ways in which a scene could be rewritten to greater effect. In other letters and telegrams he proposed changes of various kinds in his screenplay. One spoke of "minor tatting and hemstitching to be done" to the script. Unlike the general procedure in moviemaking, when the writer's screenplay is often freely rewritten by the producer, director, and studio head, Hart's script seems to have been adhered to scrupulously. When Cukor requested modifications, Hart generally agreed; but there were occasions when he stated his preference for the scene as he had written it, and the final version of the film demonstrates that Hart's wishes were observed.

Hart returned to California in mid-January 1954, to see a rough cut of *A Star Is Born*. He was appalled. "It may be that I had heard too much about how very good it was or that I am always filled with anxiety in looking at something of mine for the first time; . . . but certainly I was shaken by what I saw," he confided to his journal. "The only saving grace, it seemed to me, was that Judy was spectacular. She is an extraordinary actress of depth and emotion and very rarely goes over the edge into sentimentality." Hart was less enthusiastic about James Mason and about George Cukor's direction, which he found uneven. "I squirmed through three hours of it, . . . then at five in the morning I had quite a skirmish with Judy, who wanted me to re-write a love scene. She can be quite difficult . . . However, I can forgive her anything."

Hart, again in New York, received a letter from Cukor on February 10, telling him that the director and Warner Bros. had cut a scene from the film without Hart's permission, which "infuriated" the playwright. He "sent them a scorching wire."

February 16 brought "a number of letters and telegrams from Hollywood in answer to my angry one. I've apparently stirred up quite a hornet's nest out there and I am rather pleased that I have."

At the end of March 1954, Cukor complained to Hart that the studio had attempted to eliminate a good many important elements from the film, but said that he was restoring them. He was, he said, "paying strict attention to your [Hart's] cutting notes." And, indeed, both Hart and Cukor felt that the rough cut was much too long.

The director dined with Hart and Carlisle at Sardi's on May 6. Cukor told of various battles he had had with Jack Warner and others about the film; each story was constructed so that Cukor emerged as a hero fighting off the suggestions of Philistines. Although Hart was "very fond" of Cukor, finding him "an extremely nice and dear person," he doubted Cukor's version of events.

Eventually, Jack Warner replaced Cukor in the editing room because he had become so enamored of the footage that he refused to permit any substantial cuts. Friends and colleagues even persuaded him to restore footage that had previously been discarded, with the result that the film grew continually longer. In May, after hearing reports from people who saw a second rough cut of the movie, Hart became concerned that the film would be weakened by excessive length. He wrote to Warner expressing his point of view. He was "apprehensive," he said, "that what appears to be a fine picture might be jeopardized by a too-loving eye or an unwillingness to relinquish some parts for the good of the whole." He expressed his willingness to suggest places where cuts could be made and asked Warner to send him a copy of the rough cut.

But Warner responded that, after seeing the film, "I personally cut out about 1,500 feet. . . . Between you and me, Moss, there will be very little to cut in this picture . . . The writing, direction and performances of the people themselves are so good that there is nothing that really can be cut." He also indicated that he did not wish to send the film to Hart because it was not yet completely scored. "However," he said, "once we get the picture finished and previewed and find anything wrong on which I think you can be helpful, I will telephone you."

Warner added, "I am taking the responsibility for editing this picture." Consequently, George Cukor did not see the edited version until a preview on August 4. Despite Warner's enthusiasm ("DEAR MOSS . . . JUST IMPOSSIBLE TO FIND WORDS TELL YOU HOW PICTURE WENT OVER IN BOTH PREVIEWS. A STAR WAS REALLY BORN AGAIN. WITH DEEP APPRECIATION FOR THE WONDERFUL THINGS YOU DID BEYOND THE LINE OF DUTY"), Cukor was deeply upset. He wrote to Hart:

> How right I was to kick up that fuss when I heard that [Warner] had been "at" the picture. I won't go into detail about how heavy a hand he used in his depredations—how inept and insensitive—because you might rupture [a] disc. He snipped here and there, seemingly without reason. He succeeded in muddying things up, making scenes pointless and incomprehensible—all this without losing any footage to speak of. . . . I pointed out to him that I knew *this* material better than he did and that it was unfair to the picture not to take advantage of my experience, knowledge, etc. After a lot of wrangling I won my point. I don't think I convinced him, but the picture is being cut the way I think it should be.

Still, despite what he considered to be Warner's inept editing and the excessive length, he reported that the previews were "extraordinary occasions. Judy generates a kind of hysteria from an audience. This was especially noticeable at the first preview in Huntington Park. They yipped and screamed and carried on about the musical numbers; . . . I was worried that this response was excessive. However, the next night the picture had the same impact on the audience, without the racket."

Cukor, again supervising the editing, added that he intended not only to recut the picture but to eliminate some material, amounting to about twelve minutes.

In Warner's letter to Hart of May 28, the studio head had told Hart that the film would run approximately three hours and fifteen minutes. When the final version was released Cukor had cut it to about twenty minutes shorter than Warner's estimate.

A Star Is Born, as edited by George Cukor, is one of the great American motion pictures. All of the elements from script to acting are brilliantly achieved. The audiences that saw the movie early in its run agreed. A telegram from Jack Warner to Hart conveyed the reaction of the audience at the premiere in Los Angeles on September 30: "OPENING LAST NIGHT WAS FANTASTIC ACCLAIM FOR JUDY EVERYONE BEYOND ANYTHING EVER WITNESSED IN A THEATRE."

Hart attended the premiere in New York on October 11. Police lines held back fans who were trying to get autographs from the celebrities who arrived regularly in limousines. The experience of seeing the film was exciting and satisfying. Hart said,

The picture itself, while infinitely too long, I consider an absolute triumph . . . The real triumph, however, belongs to Judy. Though I did a first-rate crafts-man-like job, Judy Garland has without doubt a tinge of authentic genius. She plays one scene toward the end of the picture [the scene in which she pleads with Charles Bickford, as the studio head, to give her husband a job] as well as I have ever seen anything played in my life on either stage or screen. The pic-ture would have benefited enormously by being 30 minutes shorter, but I am making no complaints. On the whole, it is an excellent job, both on my part and on George Cukor's part, too; and of course Judy is a phenomenon.

The notices for *A Star Is Born* were rapturous. Bosley Crowther began his review in *The New York Times*, "Those who have blissful recollections of David O. Selznick's [1937 version of] *A Star Is Born* as probably the most affecting movie ever made about Hollywood may get themselves set for a new experi-ence that should put the former one in the shade."

The review in *The Hollywood Reporter* enthused: "the entire film is done with such taste that not a single element of it seems overdone or unnecessary. The superb screenplay by Moss Hart keeps a personal story at all times dom-inating the magnitude of the production. George Cukor's direction, briskly paced, combines heartbreaking tragedy, out-of-this-world musical entertain-ment and rib-splitting comedy into a coordinated whole that can be com-pared for sheer cinematic know-how with *Gone With the Wind*. This is a pic-ture that's worth seeing over and over again. *A Star Is Born* is the perfect blend of drama and musical—of cinematic art and popular entertainment."

Variety's critic, "Abel," said that the new version was "an even greater pic-ture in its filmmusical transmutation . . . [it] sets a number of artistic stan-dards . . . Integrated into the arresting romance-with-music—the songs are not intrusive, being plausibly spotted as 'benefit' numbers or rehearsal rou-tines—is perhaps the best inside stuff on the Hollywood film production scene that has ever been publicly projected. Whatever the production delays, which allegedly piled up a near $5,000,000 production cost, the end results quite obviously were worth it. . . . The veteran George Cukor directed with a sure hand from a tiptop script by Moss Hart."

However, exhibitors were displeased because the length of the film meant that they could schedule only one showing each night. Eventually, without consulting George Cukor, Warner agreed to allow substantial cutting. The film was sliced to two hours and thirty-four minutes, but the exhibitors wanted the running time to be reduced still further. At last, a two hour and twenty minute version was released. This version—the one that most audiences saw, unfortunately—is a job of inept butchery, omitting so many of the important scenes that the film was quite ruined.

In the early 1980s, film historian Ronald Haver attempted to issue a restored version, including all of the scenes that had been deleted. Many of those scenes had been destroyed, however, so some of the scenes were represented by black-and-white still photographs—some of them provided by George Cukor from his private collection. Fortunately, the sound track was still intact, so viewers can now hear the entire film, although not all of it can be seen.

Chapter 10 TURMOIL: MOSS HART'S DIARY
1953-1954

THE PERIOD 1953–54 WAS ONE OF FRAGILE HEALTH FOR BOTH MOSS AND Kitty Hart. Moss's diseases were no more serious than the flu; nevertheless, he was, he said, "as ill, I think, as I have ever been in my life." Then, on the return to New York, Kitty fell dangerously ill with meningitis. Although her illness lingered and was "agonizing," Hart noted in his diary, "somehow [it] seemed to draw us closer together and I would think that I have known as much happiness in these last three months as I shall ever know or am likely to have."

In December 1953, Hart confessed to his friend, the playwright S. N. Behrman, that he was deeply upset about his inability to write a new play since the failure of *The Climate of Eden*. Behrman suggested that he keep a daily diary for a year, on the theory that writing of any kind would stimulate his creative work. "Writing breeds writing," he said. Behrman himself had kept a journal for ten years that, by 1953, came to over three hundred typed pages. Consequently, Hart maintained a diary between December 2, 1953, and December 5, 1954, and, although he was not scrupulous about writing an entry every day, he recorded his observations as often as possible. Many of the entries simply tell of his insomnia, the succession of lunches and dinners with friends, the almost nightly parties he attended, and the minutiae of life, but many are highly revealing. For example, the diary illustrates more vividly than any other document that Hart's vaunted geniality was paid for by internal turmoil. Entry after entry details his "hostility toward Joe" Hyman, despite their friendship of a quarter of a century, a hostility he felt deeply but took pains not to show. Hart had remained loyal to Hyman for more than twenty years, but the producer's invariable tactlessness was a source of continual irritation.

Perhaps Hyman's remark during the pre-Broadway tryout of *Once in a Lifetime* ("What happened to all that work you were supposed to be doing? This is the same play I saw in Atlantic City") still rankled. In any case, the diary reveals that Hart could barely tolerate Hyman's attitude and behavior in 1953–54.

Hyman and Bernard Hart were producing *Anniversary Waltz* by Jerome Chodorov and Joseph Fields, with Hart directing. Early in December 1953, at an all-day casting session—at which Hart wished to cast Kitty Carlisle but encountered resistance from Hyman—Hart "was [in] a mood of enormous antagonism and rage which fastened itself onto Joe. However, being aware of it I behaved extremely well and let no aspect of it show."

Immediately afterward, Hart noticed that his anger led to "an enormous compulsion to buy something, which apparently goes side by side with both rage and elation. Though I was quite aware of this and its danger, I was unable *not* to go into one or two stores."

On December 5, Hart attempted to break a dinner date with George S. Kaufman for the following week. Kaufman was "extremely testy . . . and very annoyed." Hart immediately attempted to appease Kaufman, which, as he recognized, was an aspect of their relationship that repeated itself again and again. Hart said, "there is still within me a very neurotic orientation toward George." Whenever Kaufman was irascible, Hart sought to placate the older man, leading to "a sense of depression and I suppose inner rage." Hart persevered in this case, however, breaking the date "not so much because I don't want to go, but I think of necessity I must break this pattern of childishness in myself toward George."

Hart's feeling of "rage," whether directed at Hyman, Kaufman, or someone else, is a constant theme of the diary. But he maintained his outward affability at all times. He refers again and again to his "foul moods," "surly moods," and "bad humor"—and to his determination not to let his moods show. One evening in May, when he walked along Broadway, finding it "intolerably ugly," he wrote, "I think it is part of my depressed mood in some masochistic way, wanting to depress myself still further, in which I certainly succeeded."

Carlisle read for the producers, the author, and the director of *Anniversary Waltz* on December 9. Hart thought she read "charmingly, with enormous warmth and when necessary a good deal of bite." Everyone expressed enthusiasm about her audition, "all with the exception of Joe, that is." Characteristically, Hart "made no move to try and talk Joe into it."

While casting *Anniversary Waltz*, Hart was also putting the final touches on *The Nature of the Beast*, a television play he had written for *Omnibus*. The play was to be followed by an on-screen interview with the program's host, Alistair Cooke.

The Nature of the Beast is either a one-act play or the first act of a longer play Hart intended to complete at a later date. The protagonist, hospitalized after having been hit by a bus and believed to be suffering from total amnesia, confides to his nurse that his memory is intact. He has taken advantage of the accident to begin a new life, unencumbered by his past. The nurse, skeptical at first, finally accepts the patient's story, but, as the play ends, says she will need to think over whether or not to give away his secret. *The Nature of the Beast* is not only derivative (of Luigi Pirandello's *Enrico IV*) but extremely heavy on talk and light on action. The discussion between nurse and patient, in which her occasional comments and questions are interspersed with his telling of his story, seems to go on endlessly. At best, the piece is only a thumbnail sketch for a play, but Hart never returned to it.

Mel Ferrer played the patient, and Hart, extremely concerned about Ferrer's ability to act the role believably, worried that the presentation would be disastrous. After the play was presented on December 13, Joe Hyman called Hart as soon as he arrived home to "tell Kitty and myself he thought the show [including Hart's interview] very bad. It seemed to me he took a particular pleasure in doing this. It's astonishing to me what a virtue he makes of this perverse honesty of his. It seems to me in many ways insensitive and un-friendly . . . But I was too pleased and relieved to have the show over to mind anything very much."

Hart and Irving Berlin discussed writing a new musical. On December 17, Hart had "a long telephone conversation with Berlin and a quarrel about the billing of this yet unwritten show. I am not sure I am completely right and I understand his feelings, but it somehow seems unfair and distasteful to me." Hart was able to tell Berlin how he felt and was pleased that he had spoken so directly, writing: "I don't believe this would have been possible for me to do even so short a time as a year ago and this pleases me." The project evapo-rated in January, as Hart decided he did not wish to work with the songwriter.

Although he was able to speak candidly to Irving Berlin, he could not ex-press the "enormous sense of rage and hostility" he felt toward Joe Hyman that same afternoon. At another *Anniversary Waltz* audition, Hyman's candi-dates read for the role of Alice Walters. Hart felt that "none of them held a candle to Kitty. I was pleased in more ways than one to find this to be so, be-cause while I cannot deny that I want very much for her to do it, I was very pleased to find that she is by all odds the best of anyone we have heard and . . . we are very lucky to have her as a candidate." Hart wished to tell Hyman how strongly he believed that Hyman was wasting his and everyone else's time by his refusal to cast Kitty Carlisle. But, he recorded, "I, of course, let none of this spill over or come out into the open." Hart attributed his resentment of Hyman partly to "reality" and partly to "pure childhood rage . . . that I have not resolved."

On December 21, however, everyone, including Hyman, agreed to cast Kitty Carlisle in the role. And a month later Hart had "a long talk with Joe on the phone and I had it out with him. . . . He was very, very good indeed about it; in fact, he astonished me by saying 'I apologize.' This is the first time in 30 years I have ever heard such words escape Joe's lips."

But Hyman's apology did not put an end to the tension between them. Months later, Hyman made a remark that Hart considered "unthinking and unkind and unfair." Hart detailed his encounter: "I sat absolutely silent for a full minute," he said, "not trusting myself to speak, I was so angry. . . . and then I got up and walked away without a word. . . . I then went outside for a breath of air and made up my mind that on no account would I say anything to Joe. . . . I managed to speak to him quite civilly a couple of times through the evening, but driving down to the country afterwards with Rhea and Jerry [Chodorov], for some reason all my rage at Joe came out full-blown." Although Hart recorded that he was "now convinced that Joe is not a good producer," that "he alienates almost everyone he works with," he concluded: "I am stuck with him. I see no way out. . . . I see no way of breaking the tie, either as producer or business manager."

Rehearsals for *Anniversary Waltz* began on February 8, 1954. Hart noticed that, for several days before, Kitty "had what I can only describe as a rehearsal glaze." In order to take her mind off the production, he took her to a round of parties, which "failed to work at all. Kitty slept like a top and I didn't close my eyes."

The first reading of the play went well, but when, at the second rehearsal, Hart began blocking, he "was appalled to find myself in a great state of nerves, approximating real stage fright." Years of analysis had cured this problem, he thought, but he "was very depressed to find the well-known symptoms still there after all these years." He was unable to sleep that night, and staged the first act the next afternoon "through a cloud of weariness." Still, the exhaustion did not prevent him and Kitty from going to George S. Kaufman's apartment after the evening rehearsal. Kaufman's second wife, Leueen McGrath, had recently returned to New York and Hart wanted to welcome her home.

Again that night he could not sleep. Instead, he "spent most of the night in the kitchen re-staging the show with pieces of paper on the kitchen table. I knew I had done a bad two days work out of sheer nerves and fear, and I was determined . . . to pull myself out of it. I threw out everything I had done and," at the next rehearsal, gave the new blocking to the actors, who welcomed the changes. Hart was pleased with his own work, and was elated that "Kitty continues to surprise and delight me by her skill as an actress."

Staging the play was a difficult assignment, "much harder than I had ever anticipated," Hart said. "It [the production] must seem effortless and gay and real and, of course, that is the hardest thing to do."

Hart's one regret about directing Kitty in *Anniversary Waltz* was "that we almost do not see each other [except at rehearsals, where they interacted as director and actress rather than as husband and wife] and though we do see each other at night, we are both so horribly weary we can barely speak. . . . Perhaps when the children are in the country and Kitty and I have two days alone in the city, it will be better."

The play opened in New Haven and, according to Hart, "went extremely smoothly and Kitty covered herself with glory. She was unnervous, extremely deft, with a sure comedic sense, and surprised everyone, including me." Everything proceeded smoothly on the pre-Broadway tour, with Chodorov and Fields doing "extremely good work," in Hart's opinion. Enthusiastic receptions in New Haven, Boston, and Philadelphia persuaded Hart "that we had a solid hit." However, he said, the opening at the Broadhurst Theatre in New York on April 7 was disappointing, because

> the notices in New York, namely, Atkinson [who described the play as a "mechanical comedy" and a sign of the authors' "decline in literary skill"] and the weekly magazines, were devastating and it seems with luck we should only have what can be described as a very moderate hit. It is, of course, a rather bitter disappointment, particularly to Joe Hyman and myself; for I know he was counting on this play economically and in a very large sense, so was I. I must admit I fail to understand the severity and the anger of Atkinson and the others. I have never had any illusions about this play as a piece of fine playwriting, but in its own category it seemed to me, and still seems to me, to serve its purpose extremely well. As a matter of fact, I'm having lunch with Atkinson next Thursday and intend to take it up with him. . . . On examination of this play and my own relationship to it, I cannot help but feel that of its kind it is first-rate and not third-rate, as they all suggest. Even though unpleasant notices are always hard to take, they are somehow less hard when one feels that they are just; and in this particular case I feel they are unjust. . . . I not only enjoyed rehearsals but did what I consider an excellent job on staging and helping the play. However, there are several faults both as a director and author that I have that became obvious to me and which I would like to overcome. For one thing, I tire, it seems to me, a little too quickly for safety plus the fact that had it not been for Jerry and Joe, I doubt whether I would have given the play the exacting polishing job that it had. . . . Jerry in particular, more than anyone I know,

has the capacity for going back and back and back, and improving and tightening, and he also has the saving grace of being able to think quickly on his feet. My great lack is an inability to keep going when I'm weary . . . I was astonished at how tired I was . . .

Joe and Jerry were extremely pleasant to work with and Kitty was an absolute joy. I am not at all sure just what the range of her talent as an actress is yet, but she has a wonderful gift of being able to capture quite quickly from a director exactly what he wants and to keep it that way. . . . I think that to Kitty it has been a completely enjoyable experience and again whatever the outcome, whether failure or success, it has added to our closeness and increased my admiration for her.

Carlisle recalled the rehearsal process somewhat differently. According to her, Hart was reluctant to give her direction, and, with opening day looming, "I cornered him one morning while he was shaving: 'I really need some direction on lines and timing, so if you'll read through the part aloud, I'll simply take your readings and be quite happy.' That is exactly what I did."

Hart's fondest memories of the production were "dining alone on crackers and cheese with Kitty one night after everyone had gone home; having a fashion show in the room one morning and buying some clothes for Kitty—and, perhaps most of all, our return to New York, when we woke up the children at two o'clock in the morning and had a kind of Alice in Wonderland Tea Party until 3:30. They were absolutely wonderful . . . it was one of those rare moments that make parenthood a strange and wonderful bliss."

When Hart and Atkinson had lunch at the *Times* building, Hart "insisted on talking about his notice of *Anniversary Waltz* and though I knew I was on very unsound ground, I was in some way compelled to go through with it. He of course took nothing back, though I did not feel he made any sense whatever. Toward the end I lost my temper in spite of all I could do. For the first time in many years I think we parted a little coldly."

Anniversary Waltz managed to please theatregoers in spite of the lukewarm reviews. One evening when Hart went backstage to visit with the cast, he was "flabbergasted to find that the show, business-wise, has taken a sudden and wonderful upturn . . . How glorious it would be if it were to prove them all wrong and it were to turn into a success instead of a failure." The play moved to the Booth Theatre on December 6, running altogether for more than a year.

In time, however, Hart was able to see and agree with Atkinson's point of view. The failure of *Anniversary Waltz* as an artistic work, he wrote in a diary entry in May, "is because this particular type of play has gone," and that *Anniversary Waltz*, in particular, contained a "lack of surprise or excitement for an audience."

Periodically, Hart returned to watch the production, meeting afterward with the actors to pass on his observations. Kitty Carlisle felt that he did not attend performances as often as he should have. When he did visit, however, his comments were welcomed. After one performance, he held a rehearsal, "and though I was rather harsh, the cast very good about it," he noted.

For a time after the opening of *Anniversary Waltz*, Hart worked with Chodorov and Fields on an idea for a new musical. He never generated much enthusiasm for the project, however. In his diary, he noted, "I have no idea whether this is an aftermath of *Anniversary Waltz* or whether this is the regulation sabotage which goes on with me whenever I start a new project." A few days later, he decided not to pursue the idea. "It seems to me to lack completely any kind of freshness or audacity," he said, "and I have made up my mind more than half, I should think, to tell the boys so before the week is out." He followed through, although he "hate[d] to think that I am tossing in the towel too easily in this instance." However, he "was relieved to see that Joe Fields in part agreed with me that what we were doing was not good."

No longer working with collaborators, he had to return to the solitary business of attempting to write a play. Another constant theme of the diary is Hart's inability to write under those circumstances. "Very dissatisfied with my working days . . . and don't quite know how to organize things better," he wrote on January 7, 1954. "Thoroughly depressed again at my lack of ability to work," he reiterated on January 30. "I am . . . extremely dissatisfied and quite depressed with the way the work schedule is going." On February 1, he attempted to work but instead spent "another long day working through depression and frustration." On May 7, he spent "all day at home trying very unsuccessfully to work; . . . I'm at my wits' end in knowing what to do about this." Later that month he observed that he had "been dreaming nightmarish dreams constantly for the past week. It is of course because I am preparing to face work again. . . . It is going to be a battle . . . it is astonishing what a deep and persistent conscious pain even the prospect of work has for me." On one occasion he suffered through "two days of utter [creative] paralysis." He attempted to "break the spell by writing some letters but I found that even this was impossible. I was in a state of black depression."

Failure to achieve satisfactory results at work produced depression, which produced a further inability to write, which deepened the depression, in what seemed a never-ending cycle. "I tried on Wednesday to work," he wrote on June 9, "read what I had written Wednesday afternoon and tore it up. With this, of course, comes insomnia, and with this dark insomnia horrible nightmares, so that I am worn out and spent in the morning when I try to begin work. It is . . . the old squirrel cage and I fear and dread it."

Hart spoke to his wife about the deep frustrations he felt about being unable to work. She made what he considered a "very perceptive" remark. "She said that she thought that somehow, subconsciously, I had construed work on the book [his autobiographical memoir] . . . as merely a subterfuge or a dodge against writing a play and that I somehow felt, however good or bad [the book] might be, that it was worthless." Her comment made him resolve to "break through this barrier and be able to write . . . or any attempt at a play would be twice as difficult."

Unable to make any progress on a play, Hart spent much of the year (December 1953 to December 1954) during which he kept his diary on the book that eventually became the memoir of his early years, *Act One*. "I let Kitty hear what I had of it and she seemed very taken and intrigued. However, as I read it over it does not seem terribly good to me." Throughout the year Hart read the first ten or twelve pages of the book to friends, most of whom gave him enthusiastic responses. An apparent exception was Jerome Chodorov. "He made the usual polite murmurings of liking it, but I'm sure he did not and it depressed me out of all proportion. I cannot understand this constant reassurance I need in terms of work . . ."

Hart's depressions alternated with moods of euphoria, as on February 16, when "it was suddenly spring and after dinner Kitty and I sat on the terrace smoking a cigarette. I felt strangely and curiously happy and in a sudden burst of happiness and peace within myself, I told Kitty that I thought I would never again reach the low point I had reached in California last winter." The euphoria ended quickly. "Almost immediately after I told her this, I was overcome by a sudden and quick depression. . . . However, the mood passed and I have been fine since."

Shortly afterward, he was able to write productively throughout the afternoon and evening of a single day, words and ideas coming to him comparatively easily. "For the first time in ten days I seemed able to breathe again," he wrote. Perhaps in order to remove any pressure on himself, he noted, "I must keep constantly in mind that it doesn't matter whether the book is good or bad or is ever published. I am doing this as an exercise in discipline or deeper than that, as a therapeutic measure." Working very deliberately—each page took him about four and a half hours, he calculated—he completed the first section of his book on June 12. "It is incredible how deeply the creative mechanism is tied to the whole psyche and all its neurotic manifestations," he wrote. "Three days ago, there was a kind of disintegration of personality and now I feel put together and whole again."

On June 22, he read the material he had written to Joe Fields, Jerome Chodorov, and their wives. This time, Hart was pleased to discover, "They liked it enormously and in fact seemed very impressed with it." Still later, Ruth and Augustus Goetz told Hart how much they liked the work he had done. "They insisted that I drop everything and finish it," which pleased him greatly, but five more years would pass before *Act One* was completed.

Another repeated and unexpected theme in Hart's journal is the boredom he frequently felt in the party world he and Kitty inhabited. One party he called "large, unpleasant . . . and horrendously dull." He and Kitty left early and, while walking home, Kitty asked why the hosts always give "such damn dull parties." Hart answered that he thought "the reason was quite obvious. They are both unwilling and uncomfortable hosts and I think a party is made the moment one walks in the door by the host or the hostess. We, for instance (that is, Kitty and myself), enjoy entertaining whether in the country or in the city. We are easy and relaxed, enjoy our own parties, and I think people immediately sense that; whereas [the host and hostess at the party they attended] are, I think, pushed into giving a dinner party every so often, hate the idea of it, are nervous, unrelaxed, and can't wait till the evening is over." In another entry, Hart describes a dull party which he "was not loath to leave. I have no idea whether it is middle age or not," he wrote, "but I grow to like large parties less and less."

The parties Hart complained of were attended by some of America's most famous and accomplished people, including Greta Garbo, Audrey Hepburn, William O. Douglas, Leonard Bernstein, Oscar Hammerstein II, Jerome Robbins, Henry Fonda, Truman Capote, George Cukor, Robert E. Sherwood, Gene Kelly, and Margaret Truman, among countless others. But, increasingly, he found them becoming tedious affairs. On May 3, he wrote, "I was struck throughout the entire party as I looked at the various people at how unfulfilled they all seemed and how sterile. Here are the people mentioned in the newspapers and magazines of the world and how silly and shallow they seemed . . ." In April, Hart vowed "to be very strict with myself in terms of social activity . . . It is extremely wearing."

On one occasion the Harts gave a dinner party for nine people, among whom were Marlene Dietrich and Dr. Lawrence Kubie.[1] "Larry took a strong

---

1 Christopher Hart recalls that Kubie visited so often he "was practically a member of the family." Although he had no such feelings as a child, he now believes that Kubie's "socializing with his patients and his patients' friends" was "very bad . . . ridiculous."

dislike to her early in the evening," Hart noted. For reasons unknown to Hart, "Larry attacked Marlene first. Marlene held forth on Kubie and all psychoanalysts at great length afterward," and after a time, they "were at it hammer and tongs." Hart observed that the argument represented "very strange behavior for Larry."

Hart, a non-religious Jew who delighted in the pageantry of Christmas, took his children with him to pick out a Christmas tree on December 24. At home, they decorated the tree, with Cathy placing an angel on the top.[2] The next morning, the angel was missing. At last Chris admitted having gotten up early and taken it off the tree himself. Hart observed that Chris's jealousy was "immensely revealing to me. I seem to learn more and more from the children of what my behavior all repressed toward Bernie must have been like."

Throughout the diary, Hart's deep love for his children and his wife is evident. The year 1953 had been "by all odds my best with the children," he wrote. He took Chris to a movie on January 13, 1954. "It was memorable. He was companionable, completely endearing, and it was one of those afternoons when one fantasies [sic] the day a son is born, but which rarely happen. God knows how long this wonderful phase Chris is going through is going to last, but I'm enjoying every single moment of it." On February 3, Hart took his five-year-old son to Sardi's "and," he observed, Christopher "was a great success. It is a little foolish what inordinate pride one takes in one's children . . ." On May 7, he spent "a good deal of time with the children and they grow more and more enjoyable. I'm an absolute fool with Christopher, who can twist me around his finger and tug at my heartstrings by just a melting look." Equally rewarding was the new relationship he was developing with his daughter. "I'm beginning to feel that Cathy genuinely likes me at last and I enjoy her more and more. . . . I find somehow a deep and primitive pleasure in the children."

Of course, children tend to change almost daily. In February 1954, Hart discovered, "Christopher has suddenly become six and is absolutely terrible."

Hart records the many plays he saw during the year, his reactions to them, and his occasional discussions with the playwrights and directors afterward. On January 8, he saw *Tea and Sympathy* ("a very minor effort, saved and made a hit by Kazan's directing"). With the Max Gordons, the Harts saw *Mademoiselle Colombe* on January 14, about which Hart could find nothing at all to praise. He saw *The Teahouse of the August Moon*, *The Caine Mutiny Court Martial*, *The Golden Apple*, and seemingly everything playing on Broadway that season.

---

2 Catherine Hart still remembers the annual occasions on which she and her brother decorated the family Christmas tree, with "Daddy directing the rest of us on the *exact* placement of all the ornaments."

He also went out of town to see pre-Broadway performances when asked. He enjoyed Jeanmaire's performance in *The Girl in Pink Tights*, which he saw in New Haven on January 24, 1954, observing, "It is astonishing how one dazzling personality in a musical show can cover any number of sore spots. This is not quite true of a dramatic show but it is true of musicals." A long session with the creators of the production followed, during which Hart had "a bright notion of fixing it that everyone seemed to like." But he was "seized with a fit of depression" on the train returning to New York the next day. "It seemed to me that I had spent the entire autumn and winter running out of town to see friends' shows, making bright suggestions and yet not being able to write a line of my own." Again on January 30, he discussed a play, *The Immoralist*, with the authors, Ruth and Augustus Goetz. Five days later he revisited the play to see their new ending. He found it "all wrong," he said, and conferred with the Goetzes "until two o'clock in the morning."

In June 1954, he toyed with returning to an idea he had had three or four years before, about a play set in a large, fashionable hotel. "Since I have no other idea, [I ought] at least to begin to think about it," he said. Perhaps he was referring to this idea when he wrote, in July, that he "made a big decision in terms of a play today and feel a good deal better for it. I threw out the main theme and the leading character of the woman and have decided to use the setting and the minor characters and to tell the story in quite different terms." But, like so many of the plays Hart began during this period, he quickly soured on the idea and dropped the project altogether.

Hart's determination to work on a new play was interrupted by the Army-McCarthy hearings, which so fascinated him that he even arranged to be awakened early so that he could watch the morning sessions. He was, he wrote in the diary, "lost to work, friendship, children and life in general for as long as these hearings continue. I haven't been as interested, absorbed and fascinated in years." On June 16 he wrote, "I like to think that [the hearings] have done some good in terms of showing the people exactly how the government operates at high level; though God knows I sometimes despair of both the government and the people." After watching the last day of the hearings later in the month, Hart observed: "It is so hard for me to believe that this country, which behaves sometimes with a kind of genius in times of deep disunity and stress, and which I deeply believe in, will not in some way rise up to stop this climate of fear and hysteria and conformity; but sometimes I despair. . . . I wonder how many mistakes we can afford, even so lucky and rich a country as this."

Periodically, the Harts appeared together on television in 1953 and 1954. One appearance on the Tex and Jinx program, a leisurely talk show, lasted for four hours. Hart "somehow or other . . . always [found] a television appearance more or less humiliating," he said, but was full of admiration for his wife. "Kitty in some wonderful fashion has the ability to be nervous just before the cameras are turned on her, and then to seem very calm and serene the moment the show begins."

Tex McCrary wanted Moss and Kitty to appear regularly on his program, but Hart was reluctant. As he had advised his friends in the past, "I am certain that most of the trouble one gets into is by saying 'Yes' when one means 'No' and hoping it will all turn out for the best. It almost never does." Still, he continued to meet periodically with McCrary before finally breaking off negotiations.

In 1954, the Harts decided to sell Fairview Farm. Kitty thought "that it was ridiculous for a man who was writing plays in New York to have to keep up that kind of real estate," and Moss agreed. Hart wanted to spend one more summer there, however, so he and his valet, Charles, went to the country at the end of April to prepare to open the house for the summer. Hart had not been there for four years, which perhaps accounts for the fact that when he drove his children to New Hope in May, he lost his way.

Hart had forgotten how peaceful and invigorating his country home was, he confided to his diary. "The farm . . . is somehow more lovely than ever and I felt a sudden and new affinity for it . . . I suddenly did not want to sell it at all."

But eventually the Harts received a good offer for the property and he agreed to sell. "It was rather a torturous decision," he wrote in his journal, "but now I feel only relief and anxiety to be rid of it for good and all. It played an important role in my life for 17 years, but now that part of my life is over and done with."

When the Harts closed up the farm in November, Moss "felt no emotion whatever," he wrote. "Certainly no pain or tug at the heartstrings after all these years." But, two days later, when he and his son were taking one last walk around the grounds before leaving, Chris suddenly began crying, "Don't sell the place, Daddy. Why must we sell it?" Hart was moved by Chris's anguish—"It quite undid me," he noted—but he refused to change his mind. "I did not look back, as we rode down the road, for a last look," he wrote.

On June 22, 1954, a front-page story in the newspapers told of the deleterious effect of cigarette smoking on men over the age of fifty. Alarmed,

Carlisle called her forty-nine-year-old husband, insisting that he stop smoking immediately. Hart, who was already burdened with a greater than normal fear of death, agreed to stop at once. Although he had been a four-pack-a-day smoker, he never returned to cigarettes, although he did continue to smoke a pipe. "Curiously enough," he wrote, "my one regret is somehow giving up the gold cigarette case I am so proud of and I must try and find a use for it so that I can carry it with me."

Around 1:30 in the morning on July 17, Kitty arrived home after the performance of *Anniversary Waltz*. She and her husband talked for two hours before going to sleep. "At 4 o'clock," Hart wrote in his journal,

> I awoke with the beginning of a strange pain in my head and chest. The pain was devastating. At first there were just stabs of pain with moments of freedom from it and then the pain became all engulfing. It never occurred to me that it was my heart, though I should have had some hint by the fact that the pain was going down my left arm. I did not awake Kitty, but got out of bed and stayed in the dressing room breathing as well as I could between bouts of pain until 7 o'clock in the morning. In a most idiotic way I felt that we could not call a country doctor [until] 7 o'clock, and I felt there was no point in waking Kitty until we could send for the doctor. I was compelled to wake her at 7, however, because by that time I was thoroughly frightened, though the peak of the pain had passed.

The doctor in New Hope "could make no sensible diagnosis," so Kitty called Hart's physician in New York, who, after hearing Hart's symptoms, "insisted [he] be brought in to New York . . . immediately." He was taken to Harkness Pavilion, where doctors diagnosed a heart attack. There, Hart noted, "I remained flat on my back for the next seven weeks." Never before had he faced such a threatening illness. "When I was informed what it was, I behaved extremely well—too well, in fact," he wrote. "I got the delayed shock full blast about three days later and then I fell into a state of extreme anxiety from which I emerged only intermittently about ten weeks later." One Sunday evening, convinced he was dying, he was given medication and wrapped in blankets "to stop me from shaking apart. It was an experience I shall never forget."

Despite the gravity of his situation, Hart found that "in some strange way and even in the midst of the anxiety at its worst, there were moments that were enjoyable." During the first three weeks he spent in the hospital his wife was the only visitor he was permitted to see. He found that sharing time alone with her ("as we have never been in our life") almost compensated for his fear of imminent death. "It is hard to explain how poignant and joyful some of these days were and how full of laughter we sometimes made them," he wrote.

He insisted that she continue to perform in *Anniversary Waltz* "on the basis of sheer discipline" and because "in a time of illness one member of the family must have some healthy activity to hang onto; otherwise, the entire world becomes a hospital world." When she was not at the theatre, however, she was at Hart's side in the hospital. Her "stamina and courage in a time of crisis," as he put it, created an even stronger bond between them than had existed before.

When, at last, visitors were permitted, Hart spent "a wonderfully ludicrous evening when Marlene Dietrich came to visit me, one arm full of flowers and the other arm lugging a huge record machine on which she solemnly played me for one hour the recording of her opening night in London [in her one-woman show]. She never asked me how I was or what I was in the hospital for, but launched immediately into her London triumph and played the record so loudly that I thought I should be asked to leave the hospital at once."

Sympathetic letters and telegrams arrived by the hundreds. Cole Porter wrote, "I was so distressed to hear about the suffering you have been through for much too long and it was reassuring to hear from Kitty that you are better now and will be home soon." He added, "I am the only man in town who hasn't seen *A Star Is Born* [which had opened in Los Angeles, but not yet in New York] but I congratulate you heartily because everybody says it is terrific and that your script is a thing of beauty and a joy forever."

After leaving the hospital, Hart still felt a "lingering sense of invalidism and anxiety." He began seeing Dr. Kubie again, and forced himself to attend social events. He would rather "go out into the world and risk doing too much rather than too little," he wrote.

He felt that his visits with Kubie were helpful in bringing about his recovery. On November 3 he wrote, "My sessions with Larry are as illuminating as any I've ever had, and I think more rewarding than I had any right to expect." Three days later Kubie suggested "that we stop our sessions for a while and let the dust settle." Hart agreed. "I am forever grateful to him," he noted, "because he always makes time when my need of him is great."

After his heart attack, Kitty relieved her husband of the necessity of doing anything physically demanding. She played baseball with the children in Central Park, took them bowling and ice skating.³ She made certain that Hart never carried a suitcase or attempted to open a window that was stuck.

Instead of athletic activity, all of the Harts played board games and card games together. Catherine Hart recalls regular games of Parcheesi and Canasta.

Kitty attempted to alter Hart's rich diet, with some success. However, he was expert at downing frankfurters and desserts when she wasn't looking.

When he felt well enough to work again, Hart turned to a film about the great nineteenth-century actor Edwin Booth, in the summer of 1954. He had already agreed to write the picture *Prince of Players* for Darryl Zanuck and Twentieth Century-Fox, as the first in a five-picture deal, for which he would receive the unprecedented total sum of $1.5 million, a figure negotiated by his agent, Irving Lazar. Although the necessity to begin the screenplay "comes at a very bad time," he noted in his diary—because he was again attempting to write a new play and working on *Act One*—he "was surprised to find that I was not at all unhappy about going into town for a week of work on the script. One more proof, that any kind of interruption, even the interruption of work on another project, is better or a kind of relief from working on my own."

He met with the director-producer Philip Dunne several times in New York. Dunne had already condensed Eleanor Ruggles's biography of Booth, and Hart thought he had "done a first-rate job." They arranged to meet daily for the next several weeks, working afternoons and evenings.

Working with a collaborator had the usual effect on Hart. If Moss was lazy, his partner could be counted upon to focus his energies upon the play of the moment, and Hart would do the same if his partner became distracted. The writer who was so thoroughly blocked when working alone was freed of that concern when working with a collaborator.

After a week of intensive work, Hart returned to the country, having completed the script on July 10. "It is always astonishing how rapidly one winds

---

3 Hart's only real athletic passion—although, admittedly, the athleticism called for was less than taxing—was croquet, which he often played at Fairview Farm, at Kaufman's Barley Sheaf Farm, and at the homes of other friends. On one occasion in 1953, Hart and George S. Kaufman, representing one team, challenged Richard and Dorothy Rodgers, representing the other, to a match. One must understand that croquet was more than a game to the participants, it was life itself. Dorothy Rodgers said, "Dick takes croquet more seriously than anything outside his work. At a party he's the soul of effortless charm, but on the croquet field he can be as stern and as unyielding as granite." Hart and Kaufman did everything they could think of to distract the Rodgerses, one tactic consisting of whistling brutally mangled versions of several of the composer's melodies, but the Rodgerses won the match. It was a rare loss for Hart, though, for his skill as a croquet player was highly regarded.

up a job," he noted. "It rarely seems in the middle of work that it will ever be finished and then suddenly it is."

On July 16, Dunne told Hart about the actors he hoped to cast in *Prince of Players*. "It chilled my blood," Hart wrote. "This is a gamble, this picture, and if they cast it as disastrously as they seem to be doing, it will be a thumping failure." Hart thought the idea of casting the intense young Welsh actor Richard Burton as Booth was a good one, but he was skeptical of Dunne's other choices, particularly Maggie McNamara and John Derek as Booth's wife and brother.

When *Prince of Players* was released it was praised for its seemingly authentic view of the theatre in the nineteenth century. Excerpts from *Richard III*, *Romeo and Juliet*, *King Lear*, and *Hamlet* particularly impressed the critics (the review in *Variety* said "these scenes come to life with fire and drama to make great entertainment"), as did the performance of Richard Burton (*Variety*'s critic said that his "portrayal stands out due to its fire and strength"). Less successful was Maggie McNamara. Bosley Crowther called her performance "bland" and the romantic scenes between her and Burton "a milk-and-water cliché in the actor's extravagant career, [lacking in] heat and conviction." Hart's concern that some of the casting decisions were unwise proved to be true. McNamara's performance was sincere, even sweet, but her lack of classical acting training was painfully apparent. All in all, *Prince of Players* was a thoroughly pedestrian picture.

Attempting to work again on his own in mid-July 1954, Hart, "sick beyond belief with setting down my work difficulties," found that his old nemesis, writer's block, was still with him. "I wander through the days in a haze of depression and inertia, unable to think or write a word."

He spent all of the next day at work: "—or, rather, all day trying to work, but though I've written a little more on the book I'm getting rapidly nowhere with the play."

On October 23, the night before Hart's fiftieth birthday, he and Kitty gave a party for the entire *Anniversary Waltz* company. The party did not begin until midnight and, at about three in the morning Hart "felt myself wilting fast and overcome with fatigue." Although he enjoyed socializing, the occasion depressed him. He ended his journal entry for the day: "I am 50 years old. There are no words I can add to that somber sentence."

Hart's contract with Twentieth Century-Fox weighed heavily on him. Although the remuneration would have freed him from financial worry for the rest of his life, he was becoming progressively more queasy about fulfilling the contract. Throughout his career in the theatre, he had received the bulk of his pay only *after* having completed work on the play he wrote or directed. Thus the notion of accepting more than a million dollars for work not yet begun upset him. At one point he said to Irving Lazar, "They're nuts to pay that kind of money. I hate to take so much. Can I take less?"

Hart felt oppressed by the notion of having to write four more screenplays. "I can't have that kind of obligation over me," he told Lazar. "I want out." When Lazar protested, Hart said, "I've done screenplays. Sometimes they come off and sometimes not. This is great for the guys in Hollywood who can hack it, but I'm not one of them. I really don't want this deal."

Lazar offered no resistance. "Okay, let's forget about it," he said, and carried the message to Darryl Zanuck. According to Kitty Carlisle, Lazar waived his customary commission in the process.

Hart's decision not to complete the terms of the contract was no doubt prompted in part by his characteristic insecurity. But another factor, his sense of honor, was also clearly at work. He must be one of the few artists in Hollywood history who turned down such an immense sum on the basis of principle.

In November 1954, Hart went to his doctor for a checkup and an electrocardiogram. He received "a very good report indeed and I felt quite set up by it."

George S. Kaufman sought Hart's advice on several occasions in 1954. On one occasion, Kaufman sent Hart two acts of a new play with a letter asking for his reactions. Hart felt the play was "no bloody good at all" and tried to tell Kaufman as tactfully as possible in a long letter. Later, in November, Kaufman asked Hart to see a rehearsal of the musical he had written with his wife, Leueen McGrath, *Silk Stockings*. Hart was "absolutely appalled by what I saw. It seemed to me to be in the most dire muddle, but what was still worse, neither George nor Leueen seemed to know it." Hart barely knew what to say to his old partner, for "there is no doubt that I am still tied very deeply to George." But if Kaufman and McGrath were unaware of the musical's flaws, the same could not be said of Cole Porter, who had composed the score for *Silk Stockings*. As Hart was leaving the theatre, Porter said to him, "This is one of the times when I swear I will never write another show."

In mid-November, Harry Cohn, the head of Columbia Studios, offered Hart a contract to write three pictures. The offer allowed Hart to concoct a "grand strategy" for his career, which consisted of writing the three films, then allowing himself "the indulgence of three years working in the theatre and finishing the book [*Act One*]." Hart had an idea for a film about the pianist and bandleader Eddy Duchin. He went to California to work with Cohn and the prospective director, George Sidney. Before he could complete the screenplay, however, he came to regret his decision, and again turned his attention to the theatre and to his memoir.[4]

Hart's last journal entry was on December 5, 1954. He had, by then, maintained the diary for a full year. He felt that the journal had "served its purpose well. . . . I thought perhaps it would serve to break the log jam of my inability to work and in certain ways, it has. I have managed 15 manuscript pages of a book . . ." He might have added that he had also written two films—but, since he regarded writing for the movies only as a well-paying sideline, he did not include them among his accomplishments. The last entry concludes, "With all its travail, I should set [December 2, 1953 to December 5, 1954] down as a good year, for it is a year most of whose days have been filled with love and I consider myself a lucky man indeed."

---

4 *The Eddy Duchin Story* was produced by Columbia, but the screenplay was not written by Hart.

Chapter 11 *My Fair Lady*
1955–1958

A THEATRICAL PHENOMENON ORIGINALLY TITLED *My Lady Liza* SWEPT the world, beginning with its initial production in New York in 1956. Although Moss Hart had no part in the writing of that groundbreaking musical, he directed it to perfection, and nearly all the subsequent professional productions were either directed by him or closely followed the model he established. The result, *My Fair Lady*, was widely recognized as a brilliant work of art, regarded by some as the greatest musical of all time.

Gabriel Pascal, who had made a film of George Bernard Shaw's 1914 comedy, *Pygmalion*, in 1938, also had the foresight to secure the rights for a musical production. He did not receive permission until after Bernard Shaw died, for Shaw, who was incensed about *The Chocolate Soldier*, the musical derived from his *Arms and the Man*, was adamantly opposed to allowing any of his other plays to be used as the basis for a musical. In 1952, two years after Shaw's death, Pascal suggested that Alan Jay Lerner and Frederick Loewe should attempt a musical adaptation.

Setting *Pygmalion* to music had already been considered by Richard Rodgers and Oscar Hammerstein II, but they gave it up because their temperaments were fundamentally opposed to Shaw's anti-romantic sentiments. Pascal had approached Noël Coward, Cole Porter, E. Y. Harburg, and the team of Arthur Schwartz and Howard Dietz to try their hand at an adaptation, but none had made the attempt.

Lerner had never attempted an adaptation before. All five of his previous musicals, of which only *Brigadoon* had been entirely successful, had derived entirely from his imagination. Now convinced that the often unenthusiastic reaction to his works could be attributed to their shaky librettos, he consciously sought out works that had already proven themselves and were suitable for musical adaptation.

Pygmalion, long recognized as a brilliant play, one of Shaw's finest, offered potential musical adaptors a rich combination of theatrical elements. The characters Shaw created—Henry Higgins, the vain phoneticist who is supremely intelligent in some areas but blind to the needs of human beings (especially women); Eliza Doolittle, the young Cockney flower-girl whose ambitions to improve herself prompt her to call upon Professor Higgins; Alfred P. Doolittle, Eliza's father, whose earthiness and unconventional philosophies of life not only endear him to Higgins but encourage Doolittle to make a highly successful lecture tour of America—were unforgettable. The plot, an adaptation of the Cinderella story, was universally appealing. And the idea, that social mobility was possible even in class-conscious Britain if only one could transform one's appearance and manner of speech, was particularly appropriate for the idealistic, democratic society of the United States.

As Lerner and Loewe labored over the project, they found they were no more successful than Rodgers and Hammerstein had been in attempting to transform *Pygmalion* into a musical. The problem, Lerner said, was that

> *Pygmalion* was basically drawing-room comedy. We felt that it needed enlarging, that it wasn't peopled by enough characters . . . We had all sorts of ideas [to make] our version more populous . . . like making Higgins into an Oxford professor, so there'd be some reason to have more people on the stage. We didn't do that because we didn't want to do violence to the basic structure of Shaw's play. So eventually we abandoned the whole project.

Lerner and Loewe went their own ways during the next two years, working with different collaborators. However, the idea of adapting *Pygmalion* continued to haunt them, and they reunited to return to the job in August 1954. Perhaps the hiatus provided them with fresh insights, for upon their resumption of work they made the startling discovery that enlargement of the plot was unnecessary. All they had to do, Lerner believed, was add scenes that, in Shaw's play, took place offstage. For example, as Lerner said, "at the end of the first scene . . . Eliza Doolittle went home before appearing at Professor Higgins' house the next morning. In *My Fair Lady* we followed her home and showed what happened to her there." Similarly, the elocution lessons given by Higgins to Eliza were only referred to in Shaw's play, but the lessons were turned into one of the most memorable on-stage scenes in the musical. In Shaw's play, Eliza's father is seen only when he visits Higgins, never in his own milieu; in Lerner's adaptation, two scenes are devoted to showing Doolittle in his area of London.

In *My Fair Lady*, Alfred Doolittle became less of a philosopher, an alteration in his character that perturbed some admirers of Shaw's play. It was, however, one of the only ways in which *Pygmalion* was diminished—and, arguably, since something of Shaw's had to be sacrificed in order to make room for the musical numbers, Doolittle's rambling disquisitions were appropriate candidates.

Lerner was also inspired to change the locale of the scene in which Eliza displays her newly acquired diction from Mrs. Higgins's house to the races at Ascot, allowing for the song "The Ascot Gavotte," which proved to be the musical's most elegant and funniest scene. He also created the scene at the Embassy Ball, showing Eliza's Cinderella-like triumph.

Another problem, no less difficult to overcome, was the distant emotional relationship between *Pygmalion*'s leading characters. Higgins feels little more for Eliza than any teacher would for any pupil. After he has brought about her acceptance into society and Eliza has been transformed from a callow girl to a mature woman, Higgins loses interest in her.[1] (The eventual fates of the characters in *Pygmalion* are not shown at all; Shaw explains in a lengthy Afterword that Eliza marries her vacuous young suitor, Freddy Eynsford-Hill, opens a flower shop, and becomes a model of middle-class domesticity.)

However, in *My Fair Lady* (as in the film Pascal had made of *Pygmalion*), Higgins comes to depend upon Eliza emotionally. He does not tell her he loves her but the suggestion is strong that eventually he and Eliza will be married. David Ewen, author of *The Complete Book of the American Musical Theatre*, was one of many who found the change both warranted and desirable: "If a new note of humanity, or sentimentality, was introduced into the play to offset Shaw's irony and malice, this was all to the good, as far as the musical theatre was concerned; so is the welcome presence of genuine romantic feeling, absent in the Shaw comedy, which brings to the [musical play] a radiant glow."

Lerner contended that he and Loewe "did not try to give the play a 'happy ending.' We wanted to complete the character of Higgins, trying to show, from hints in lines Shaw gives Higgins in the last act, a man going through that process of being aware, emotionally, that a vital woman is gone, and then actually and consciously searching for her. And, in the end, having a bleak recognition scene in which Higgins would, in a sense, recognize the loneliness in his life after Eliza has gone."

The decisions to add action Shaw only referred to, and to humanize Higgins's character, solved the problems that had stymied others (including Lerner and Loewe themselves) before they hit upon these solutions in 1954. Perhaps the most remarkable feat Lerner performed in *My Fair Lady* was his creation of Shavian-sounding lyrics. When Shaw's dialogue left off and the songs began, the characters seemed to be speaking and singing with the same,

---

[1] Although the play's name derives from the legend of Pygmalion, the sculptor who falls in love with Galatea, the statue he creates, Shaw virtually ignored the potentially romantic elements in *Pygmalion*.

equally witty voice. Lerner found the lyrics and Loewe the music to express the characters as well as lyrics and music could possibly express them. Stanley Green, a musical comedy historian, offered many examples in *The World of Musical Comedy*:

> In the songs for Professor Higgins there is the biting disdain for his inferiors in "Why Can't the English?"; his witty defense of his own way of life in "I'm an Ordinary Man";[2] his petulant admiration for masculine traits in "A Hymn to Him"; and, in the simply stated "I've Grown Accustomed to Her Face," his admission that he has finally fallen in love with Eliza. Eliza's character is also revealed through song. First, as a poor flower-seller, she dreams only of a life of physical comforts in "Wouldn't It Be Loverly?" Later, after having gone through the rigors of the professor's speech classes, she expresses her secret defiance in "Just You Wait," and her thrill at having succeeded in speaking correctly in "I Could Have Danced All Night." The girl's impatience with all men bursts through in "Show Me," and, at the end, in a bolt of sarcastic fury, she tells Higgins her real opinion of him in "Without You."

Gabriel Pascal had died in 1952, but his estate still held the rights. Since MGM (which hoped to use Shaw's play as the basis for a movie musical) also wished to secure the rights, the final decision about their disposition was up to the Chase Bank, executor of Pascal's will. When Lerner inquired of the vice president in charge of the Trust Department how the decision would be made, he was told simply that the bank, in Lerner's words, "would best serve the interests of the Pascal estate." But how it would arrive at that decision was not divulged.

Fritz Loewe suggested that he and Lerner complete their adaptation as quickly as possible. "My boy," he told Lerner, "there's only one thing to do. We will write the show without the rights, and when the time comes for them to decide who is to get them, we will be so far ahead of everyone else they will be forced to give them to us." Lerner, who would be responsible for the book and lyrics, began writing several of the songs, with Loewe composing the music.

Eventually, the Chase Bank, recognizing that, without knowledge of the theatre, it was not in a reasonable position to award the rights to any party, vested the authority in Harold Freedman, an important literary agent. Freedman decided in 1955 that Lerner and Loewe should be given the rights.

---

2 Moss Hart made a modest contribution to the lyrics of "I'm an Ordinary Man." He mentioned to Alan Jay Lerner that he was often frustrated when Kitty Carlisle looked for her gloves during the performance of a play they were watching. Lerner used the idea for a lyric: "You want to talk of Keats or Milton; / she only wants to talk of love, / You go to see a play or ballet, / and spend it searching for her glove."

Lerner turned his attention to casting even while the writing was in process. The casting was theoretical, since no money had yet been raised to finance the production. Rather, Lerner and Loewe hoped that by securing commitments from leading performers, the job of finding a backer or backers would be simplified. The accomplished British actor Rex Harrison, Lerner felt, was the perfect choice to play Henry Higgins, the world's foremost expert on phonetics, who makes a bet with his friend Colonel Pickering that he can pass off the lowest Cockney guttersnipe as a great lady by transforming her speech. However, the job of convincing Harrison to play Higgins was made difficult because Harrison initially detested the songs Lerner and Loewe had written. Besides, he had never performed in a musical and had no confidence in his singing voice. But Fritz Loewe asked him to sing a song, and, after hearing the first verse, said, "Fine. That's all you need." Harrison, still wishing to think it over, also perused a short list of potential directors Lerner and Loewe had drawn up. Moss Hart's name headed the list. Eventually, as the songs grew on Harrison, he agreed to play Higgins if the backing for the musical could be secured, and seconded the motion that Hart would be the best choice as director.

However, Hart, as Lerner knew, was then working with Harold Rome on the first draft of a musical called *In the Pink*, a satire on big business. The Harts were then living in a house they had rented in Beach Haven, New Jersey. Although Hart and Rome had been working together regularly, the biggest event of the summer to that point had been Kitty Carlisle's receipt of a telephone call from Mark Goodson and Bill Todman, the impresarios of television game shows. They asked her to become one of the weekly panelists on *To Tell the Truth*, and, although she was initially reluctant, Hart encouraged her to accept the offer, particularly because the show only required her to be in New York one day a week. Carlisle decided to accept—and remained on the program as a panelist for the next twenty-three years.

Lerner and Loewe called Hart in Beach Haven, hoping to persuade him—"the great Moss Hart," as Loewe called him—to take over as director. Hart immediately said that he was unavailable to direct because he was occupied with a musical of his own, and, after a cordial conversation, hung up the telephone.

Hart particularly did not wish to hear any of the songs from *My Lady Liza*. "I did not intend to be wooed away by the siren sounds of a composer at the piano and a lyricist standing beside him singing their songs at me," he wrote in a March 1959, article. "It is a fatal enticement. A composer and a lyricist generally perform their own work with uncommon skill. Too often I have walked resolutely into a meeting with my mind firmly made up, and walked irresolutely out of it, my resolve shaken and my good sense frittered away by an adroit rhyme scheme or a musical phrase of subtlety and charm."

But Lerner and Loewe would not accept Hart's refusal. After their third phone call, he agreed to discuss their proposition, although still determined to turn it down. "Having been informed over the telephone of the nature of the musical they were engaged in," he said, "I had come to the private conclusion that Lerner and Loewe were embarked on a quite hopeless task. The idea of musicalizing Shaw's *Pygmalion* seemed to me an untenable proposition. . . . [H]ow music and lyrics were to be fitted into it without violating Shaw's marvelous insouciance, as well as his talent, I could not for the life of me see."

Still, despite Hart's continuing collaboration with Harold Rome, he listened to seven of Lerner and Loewe's songs, including "Why Can't the English," "Wouldn't It Be Loverly," and the "Ascot Gavotte." As "the last note of the music died away on the piano under Fritz Loewe's fingers," Hart said, "I was uneasily aware that my goose was being cooked. In a few deft lyrical and musical strokes Lerner and Loewe had somehow managed to arrive in the most singular fashion at the correct Shavian attitude—the very attitude I thought it impossible to capture in music and lyrics." Hart, who had loved reading and seeing Shaw's plays when he was a teenager in Brooklyn, now gave serious thought to the possibility of directing the musical adaptation of *Pygmalion*.

According to Frederick Loewe, "After [hearing] the first number there was a peculiar look on [Hart's] face. He knocked with his pipe, and after the fourth number all of a sudden he said, 'You sons of bitches, I'm hooked!'"

Hart could not withhold his enthusiasm. "Without further ado, I said I would be delighted to stage the show, and the rest of the afternoon was promptly given over to a discussion of a first act finale and the opening of the second act." Immediately after the meeting, Hart asked Harold Rome to agree to postpone their work on *In the Pink*, even if, as Kitty Carlisle said, "it meant that it might never come to pass."[3]

Hiring Hart to direct *My Fair Lady* was, in the opinion of Alan Jay Lerner, the most important element in its success, for Lerner found Hart to be a master of all things theatrical as well as a splendid human being. He wrote in his autobiography, "Moss Hart, as I was to find out, had no understudies. He is and forever will be irreplaceable to more people in more ways than any man I have ever known. . . . When he turned his hand to directing, he did so with

---

3 Indeed, Hart's withdrawal sealed the fate of *In the Pink*, which was never produced.

the sure hand of a master of his art and an eye that clearly perceived the goal at the far end of the road."

For his part, Hart said he felt that mankind faced two great challenges: one was marriage; the other was "the writing and production of a musical show. . . . Both demand grace under pressure. Both are long, drawn-out affairs, and both harbor the seeds of their own destruction, if the fine, free careless rapture which has seen their beginnings is not to deteriorate into fretful acrimony and finally vanish altogether in the divorce court, or after the tryout in New Haven."

Hart's contract called for him to receive $7,500.00 for the direction of the play, plus three percent of the gross receipts. The contract also stated that he would receive six percent of the proceeds of the motion picture rights.

Normally, the director of a play or musical is hired prior to casting, permitting him or her to participate in the selection of the leading roles. In this case, however, Hart joined the production team knowing that Rex Harrison would play Higgins.

On the first day Lerner and Loewe met with Hart to work on the production, the lyricist and composer arrived in Beach Haven with two completed songs, "On the Street Where You Live" and "Come to the Ball"; a few days later they came back with another, "You Did It." Hart gave his approval to all the material and Lerner and Loewe returned to the piano and the study.

The production team had no thought who might play Eliza, the slum dweller whose speech Higgins makes over, although they hoped it would be a performer as well-known as Rex Harrison.

Mary Martin's husband called Lerner to ask if Martin could hear Lerner and Loewe's songs with the possibility that she might be interested in playing Eliza Doolittle.[4] Mary Martin was a "star" by every standard, better known in America than Rex Harrison. One night, after Martin's performance in *Peter Pan*, she listened to five songs, among them "The Ascot Gavotte" and "Just You Wait." Martin left without saying a word. A week later, her husband told Lerner that her response was, "*How* could it have happened? How *could* it have happened? Those dear boys have *lost their talent*."

With Martin obviously out of the picture, the production team asked Judy Holliday, whose success in *Born Yesterday* on stage and in the film had elevated her to the star status Hart, Lerner, and Loewe sought, to listen to the score. When Holliday elected not to accept the role, the director, librettist, and composer were unable to think whom they should contact next. Soon after-

---

4 According to some accounts, Lerner and Loewe initiated the contact with Mary Martin, hoping to interest her in the role.

ward, they happened to see a production of a British musical called *The Boy Friend*, then playing on Broadway. Making her American debut in that musical was Julie Andrews, then eighteen years old. In Shaw's *Pygmalion*, the author specified that Eliza Doolittle was also eighteen. Traditionally the role had been played by older women,[5] partly because it is so complex, calling for Eliza's transformation from a grubby Cockney flower girl to a mature woman of regal bearing. Previous producers had believed that Eliza required a mature, experienced actress, but Lerner thought "how refreshing it might be if, for the first time since the play was written, a girl of precisely that age [specified by Shaw] played the role." Andrews auditioned for Hart, Lerner, Loewe, and Herman Levin, who had agreed to produce the musical. Shortly before her audition, she had been contacted by Richard Rodgers, who asked her to try out for his new musical, *Pipe Dream*. Now, Andrews told him that she was under consideration for *My Lady Liza*; Rodgers, realizing that the role of Eliza might be a once-in-a-lifetime opportunity, advised her to appear in *My Lady Liza* if an offer were made.

The production team was impressed by Andrews' audition, but not convinced that she possessed the acting ability the role required. They traveled to London, where they auditioned about fifty young British performers, but none of them had quite the charm or the beautiful singing voice of Julie Andrews. Still uncertain, they auditioned Andrews a second time, after which, convinced at last, they offered her the role of Eliza.

As Eliza's father, the dustman Alfred Doolittle, Stanley Holloway, who had performed for more than fifty years in the British theatre, music halls, and films, was the inevitable choice. The scenes Lerner wrote for Doolittle included two musical numbers reminiscent of the music hall era.

At last the producer found a backer for the musical. William Paley, the president of CBS, agreed to finance Lerner and Loewe's musical for $400,000 in exchange for the rights to a television production and the original cast album for Columbia Records.

Oliver Smith, Cecil Beaton, and Abe Feder were hired to design the sets, costumes, and lights.[6] Beaton, an Englishman renowned as a photographer

---

5 Mrs. Patrick Campbell, for whom the role was written, was forty-nine when she played Eliza in *Pygmalion*. Other famous Elizas included Lynn Fontanne, who was thirty-nine, and Gertrude Lawrence, who was forty-four. Wendy Hiller, who acted the role in the 1938 film, had been the youngest Eliza before Andrews. Hiller was twenty-six when the film was released.

6 It should be no surprise to learn that Oliver Smith's changes of settings were brought about by revolving stages. What would a production directed by Moss Hart be without revolving stages?

as well as a costume designer, conferred with Hart, then, afterward, showed him dozens of preliminary designs.

Hart, impressed by their beauty and cleverness, immediately called Lerner, Loewe, and Levin and said

> "I wish you'd take a look at them. I like them very much . . . it's a most expensive [set of costumes] and I'd like you to take a look." So they went down to look at the costumes and we met the next day and I could see they were dubious and I said, "You don't like them. What's the matter?" And they said, "There are two sets [of costumes] we don't like. We don't like the designs for the Ascot scene, because they're just black and white [except for Eliza's contrasting outfit of pink] and they'd look like cartoons on the stage, and we don't like the costumes for the Embassy Ball because they're all different, and they're all pastel shades." The curious thing is that, as director, had I been feeling insecure that day or uncertain, I would have said, "Well, all right, we'll change them." But that was one of my more authoritarian days and I said, "No, I like them, and you have me for my strengths as well as for my weaknesses, and that's the way they're going to stay." Well, I certainly don't think any one element makes a show, but certainly the Ascot costumes were of enormous help . . .

Abe Feder was also present to see Beaton's sketches. He had reservations of another sort. He asked Beaton to bring some of the sketches to his studio, where he bathed them with the light he intended to use. The color of Feder's lights made Beaton's colors disappear, causing Beaton to redesign his color palette. The Ascot costumes remained as Beaton had designed them, however. That scene became the first in a Broadway musical performed almost entirely in blacks, whites, and grays.

Finding the right choreographer was more difficult than hiring the designers. Gower Champion was everyone's first choice, but he asked for more money than Herman Levin could afford. Michael Kidd made a negative impression on Hart when he commented negatively on Lerner and Loewe's material. At last they turned to Hanya Holm, who, having impressed everyone with her ideas, was offered the job.

Lerner estimated that over five thousand performers tried out for the sixteen roles in *My Fair Lady* that were not cast with well-known performers who were offered the roles on the basis of their previous work.[7]

More than a thousand dancers auditioned for an ensemble of twenty-two. In both cases, final casting decisions were made by Hart, Lerner, Loewe,

---

7 In addition to Harrison, Andrews, and Holloway, these included British veteran actors Cathleen Nesbitt as Higgins's mother and Robert Coote as Colonel Pickering. Pickering, like Higgins an expert in phonetics, wagers that Higgins will be unable to pass Eliza off as a duchess after teaching her "proper English."

Levin, Beaton (who needed to know if the actors would look and feel comfortable in his costumes), Holm (who was interested in how singers and actors, as well as dancers, moved), and the musical director, Franz Allers (who was consulted about both the singers and the dancers, since the dancers, too, would have to sing).

Hart worked with Lerner and Loewe to shape the script, perhaps contributing to the dialogue, as Kitty Carlisle has suggested. He expressed his approval or disapproval of each scene and song. When Lerner and Loewe were skeptical about "The Rain in Spain," the song they had written to celebrate Eliza and Higgins's achievement, it was Hart who assured them that the number was appropriate and effective. Otherwise, "The Rain in Spain" would have been eliminated from the musical.

Hart discussed the nature of collaboration on a musical production in his 1959 article:

> Every effort in the theatre is in large degree a collaborative one, but the putting together of a musical production is the essence of collaboration. Without almost complete empathy between the partners in the enterprise, disaster is likely to strike early on. Lerner and Loewe seemed pleasant enough fellows, but I am an old campaigner. My hat has been tossed into the ring too many times for me not to be acutely aware that one can know nothing about human beings until one has lived with them, and Lerner, Loewe and myself were going to be very much married to each other from this moment on. Like any other marriage, it would have to be lived out day by day, and I was fairly certain I was in for one or two genuine surprises.

Perhaps the greatest surprise was how hardworking his partners turned out to be. "They work like stevedores," he said. "They keep unholy hours. It is commonplace for them to part at four o'clock in the morning after a ten or twelve-hour working session, and meet again at nine the next morning." This suited Hart perfectly, for, as he said, "It is my way, once embarked on a show, to live it and breathe it to the exclusion of almost everything else. I go to bed with it at night and wake up with it in the morning. I am by no means convinced that this is the only way to work, or even the best way." Only one year removed from a heart attack, this may not have been the wisest medical course, but, as Hart said, "I know I am incapable of working any other way."

By November 1955, Lerner had not yet completed the book, and three songs remained to be written. Hart, concerned that the process was taking longer than it should and might delay the already scheduled rehearsals, called Lerner to say: "If you have any plans for this weekend, cancel them. We're going away together . . . to Atlantic City, and we're not leaving until you have finished the book and we have had time to discuss every scene together."

For four days, the two of them occupied the penthouse of an Atlantic City hotel. Lerner, who worked best early in the morning, began his work day at seven-thirty. When Hart arose at eleven, he read the material Lerner had written, then made suggestions for changes. The rest of the day was spent on implementing them. Lerner recalled "long, long walks on the boardwalk during which time we discussed every phase of the production from the first moment to the last. I remember them as four of the most delightful days I have ever spent."

After four days the book was complete. Lerner and Loewe wrote the remaining songs in New York, completing the last of Higgins's songs, "I've Grown Accustomed to Her Face," a few days before Christmas—just in time, for at that point, Rex Harrison arrived from London to begin working on his scenes and songs.

Rehearsals for the musical now titled *My Fair Lady* began on January 3, 1956. Hart arranged to have sketches of the scenery and costumes ready for the cast, so that they could immediately become familiar with the environment their characters would inhabit and the clothes they would wear. The cast read the play, Lerner and Loewe performed the songs, and Hart read the stage directions. As a result of the read-through, one problem became apparent: Higgins needed a song in the second act that would flesh out his character. Lerner and Loewe solved the problem by writing "A Hymn to Him" ("Why Can't a Woman Be More Like a Man?").

Continuing an arrangement that had worked for him in the past, Hart chose to begin rehearsals at two o'clock, break for dinner at five-thirty, then reassemble at seven and rehearse until eleven. Other directors began at ten A.M. and rehearsed until seven in the evening. Hart felt, however, that, under that schedule, the cast was exhausted by five o'clock and little productive work was done during the last two hours.

Hart did not anticipate a tradition that regularly eliminated half an hour of rehearsal time. At four o'clock each day, the leading players, all of them British, stopped to have tea, a ceremony that lasted for thirty minutes. The director quickly decided that he would be unable to put an end to a habit that had persisted for centuries, and made no attempt to tamper with it.

Unlike many directors, Hart disliked frequent read-throughs, with the director dissecting each line of the play while the actors took notes. Instead, he preferred to begin blocking after a single read-through. Thus, by the second week of rehearsal, *My Fair Lady* had been blocked and the actors had memorized their lines sufficiently so that they no longer needed to carry their scripts.

Julie Andrews's insecurity was painfully apparent when rehearsals began and her lack of acting training became more evident with each passing day. Andrews, who possessed a singing voice of stunning clarity and beauty, had no difficulty with the songs, but playing Eliza was another matter. For one thing, despite her British origins, she needed a phoneticist to teach her a Cockney dialect.[8]

But that was a minor detail compared to the challenge of convincingly portraying the transformation of Eliza from flower girl to a woman of such poise that other characters took her for an aristocrat. She was, in her own words, "simply terrified. Working with Rex Harrison and Stanley Holloway, and meeting a director I'd never worked with before. Not to mention the giant role of Eliza Doolittle and the image of Shaw hanging over my head." As rehearsals progressed, Andrews seemed to be regressing. She was, she said, "convinced I was going to be sent home any day. It was obvious to everyone that I was out of my depth, and the awful thing was that I knew it."

Hart felt that Andrews "was charming but it seemed to me she didn't have a clue about playing Eliza. About the fifth day [of rehearsals] I got really terrified that she was not going to make it." He asked Kitty Carlisle, who had been observing rehearsals, what she thought. "She needs a bit of help," his wife answered.

Hart then canceled rehearsals for a weekend and suggested to Andrews that the two of them spend the time together, during which they would discuss and rehearse each of Eliza's scenes. Hart called the weekend "the days of The Terror. It was the sort of thing," he said, "you couldn't do in front of a company without destroying a human being."

Andrews described the process:

> I knew that this was the big test. It was one of the hardest weekends of my entire life. I remember driving down Broadway to the New Amsterdam Theatre that Saturday morning, and I felt as if I was going to the dentist to have a tooth pulled. You know the feeling. You've got to go and get it done. It hurts and it won't get better unless you get it done. But it's agony to contemplate.
>
> Deep down I felt I had the ability to play Eliza, but would anybody see that? Would there be someone to pull it out of me? Would there be someone to help me get rid of my inferiority complex? Well, there was Moss. He said, "We don't have time to be easy about this. We've got forty-eight hours and I'm going to be tough." He'd have to be ruthless and brutal, and I'd have to understand why.

---

8 Ironically, her teacher was an American, Alfred Dixon, a former actor.

We began to rehearse. There was just himself and the stage manager, Biff Liff, and the assistant stage manager in this empty theatre. We went over the play, scene by scene and line by line, over and over. It was an amazing time. I think I kind of grew up. Moss bullied, cajoled, pleaded, scolded, encouraged. "You're playing it like a girl guide," he said at one point. "You're too light, much too light," he screamed from the audience. He would yell, "I can't hear you. I want this louder. I want that angrier." And occasionally he would stomp up onto the stage to interrupt and show me exactly how he wanted it done.

I remember tiny little things, like his Cockney accent was atrocious, worse than mine. . . . He padded up and down in those great earth shoes that he'd had specially made, I believe, for comfort. He leaned forward slightly or else, when approving, he would lean back, his arms wide, very expansive about the whole thing: bushy black brows, the ring kind of glinting on his finger, the pipe between the teeth. I remember when he snatched Eliza's purse from my hand and he hit out at an imaginary Higgins, to show me how he wanted it done. And then I have a picture of him holding Eliza's tea cup, very prim and proper with the pinky finger extended. At times he actually became Eliza Doolittle in my eyes and I stood back and watched. But at all times, he was supportive. Nothing was done in an unkind manner. I knew it was going to benefit me. And when I did get something right he would praise me, and it helped my courage—helped me keep trying.

Moss was my Svengali. I knew I had Eliza in me, but I was so inexperienced and so painfully aware of it, and shy, that I just didn't know how to let her out. Moss's trust and our hard work eventually freed her.

He was the strongest force I had come up against to that point; I'd never done anything like it before. I'd been raised in the music halls with no experience other than to hone my instincts—to get on with the business of connecting with an audience. I just wanted to sit down and weep in despair. I got so angry with myself. I had the most enormous respect for him after those forty-eight hours. Eventually, I came to love him dearly.

The weekend of intense work transformed Julie Andrews. At the next full rehearsal, she calmed the fears of those who believed she would never be capable of playing Eliza. "Those two days made the difference," said Hart. "We were both absolutely done in, exhausted, but she made it. She has that terrible English strength that makes you wonder why they lost India."

Later, Andrews said that Eliza was "the greatest role that a woman can play in musical comedy," for "it has everything. You have to scream like a Cockney and then later sing beautifully. There are all the dramatic scenes, the growth of the child into a woman—it's enormous." So enormous that Andrews said she "was never really sure, on any given night, that I had enough strength to do the whole thing flat out. It required such tremendous stamina and I can't remember a single performance when I didn't wonder, 'Am I going to get through it?' or 'I'll have to save myself a little in this song and/or scene so that I have enough voice left for the bigger one later.' There were some nights when it all came together and that was a joy."

Julie Andrews eventually became the bedrock of the *My Fair Lady* company. In contrast to Rex Harrison, who was given to outbursts of temper, and Stanley Holloway, who at one point became so irritated by Harrison's behavior that he complained to the newspapers about it, Andrews always projected "this curious kind of glacial calm," Hart said, "as though she came down from Everest each day to play the show, instead of from a hotel room."

Harrison, a fervent admirer of Bernard Shaw, was at the opposite end of the spectrum from "glacial calm." He frequently interrupted rehearsals to consult his Penguin edition of *Pygmalion* and hotly discuss a point of interpretation with the director. Harrison was by far the best-known performer in the company, and thus had the most to lose. In addition, he was performing in his first musical. Consequently, he was both nervous about his performance and occasionally responsible for outbursts of temperament. For example, one of Lerner and Loewe's songs, "Without You," was written for Eliza to sing to Higgins while Higgins stood onstage. Harrison repeatedly maintained that he had no intention of remaining onstage during Eliza's song. Lerner and Loewe had no idea how to deal with their star, and asked Hart with some desperation, "What are we going to do?"

"I will tell you precisely what we are going to do," Hart answered. "Nothing. At least until everything else in the play is rehearsed. You can't fight every day or you dissipate your strength and it becomes a way of life. In every play there's one battle you have to win, and when we're in the best position we will do battle." Consequently, the song was omitted from rehearsals for more than a week.

Alan Jay Lerner said, "In rehearsal, Moss's authority was total, not because he demanded it but because it was so apparent to everyone he knew what he was doing. If an actor suggested a better move, Moss was the first one to recognize it and be grateful. He was the only director I ever knew who could walk up on the stage and say to the actors: 'I haven't a clue what to do with this scene. Does anyone have an idea?'—and not lose his authority."

Hart and Lerner were able to establish a level of trust and informality seldom established between director and writer. In the middle of a scene Lerner might question some aspect of Hart's staging. Moss would immediately signal the actors and say, "The author is unhappy. Let's try it this way."

Or, on other occasions, Hart might whisper to Lerner, "Are you aware, dear boy, that that is one of the most stinkingest lines ever written in the history of the theatre?" Without resentment or hesitation, Lerner would retreat to his typewriter.

When the company was on the train for New Haven, where the final rehearsals and first performances of *My Fair Lady* would be given, Hart took a seat beside Rex Harrison, who had not deviated an inch from his refusal to stand onstage during "Without You." "Rex," Hart said, "Julie is going to sing 'Without You' in that scene whether you are on the stage or not. It is my personal opinion you will look like a horse's ass if you leave the stage when she begins it and return when she has finished. However, if you will give me the opportunity, I will show you how it can be staged." They arranged to meet onstage in New Haven at the first rehearsal.

Lerner and Loewe had written a verse for Higgins. Just before the end of Eliza's song, in which she explodes with anger at Higgins's insensitivity and egotism, he interrupts, singing/shouting, "I did it. I did it. I said I'd make a woman and indeed I did." Previously, Harrison had refused even to listen to the new material, but, at the rehearsal called especially to stage the scene, he listened to and accepted the material enthusiastically, deciding, in Lerner's words, that "it made all the difference in the world. [Eliza's song would not receive] applause, which would have lengthened the time he would have been standing up there . . . Moss staged the scene and the song and that was that."

Another crisis had been anticipated by Kitty Carlisle, who, knowing that Harrison was insecure about his singing, told Harrison prior to the first New Haven rehearsal, "Rex, at the first orchestra rehearsal you'll be quite disoriented. It's a terrible hazard even for experienced performers. So far you've only sung with the piano, and you can always hear the melody. With full orchestra you'll hear everything *but* the melody. You won't even find your first note, much less anything else. Don't panic. It will eventually sort itself out." But Harrison *did* panic when, for the first time, an orchestra replaced the piano which had accompanied the songs during the New York rehearsals. Unable to pick out the melody from the orchestra of thirty-two musicians, Harrison insisted that the orchestrations made it impossible for him to sing. Although Hart gave him hours to work with the orchestra, hoping that Harrison would become progressively more confident, the star's terror only increased. On the afternoon of the first performance, scheduled for that evening, Harrison announced he would not go on; furthermore, he would not appear in the production until he felt perfectly secure singing with an orchestra.

The scheduled performance was canceled. Hourly bulletins on the radio advised those who had bought tickets that "technical difficulties" had made it impossible to open the production on time. Nevertheless, hundreds of people failed to get the word; hundreds more had come to New Haven specifically to see *My Fair Lady*; not having heard the radio bulletins, they all appeared at the theatre, anticipating a performance. Hart, Lerner, and Loewe held a hasty conference with the house manager, whose anger was so great that he threatened to tell the audience that the performance would not be given because of Rex Harrison's insecurity and temperament. An hour before curtain time, Harrison finally agreed to go on. Bernie Hart, serving as assistant stage manager, then got on the telephone to inform members of the company that there would be a performance that night after all. He also, in Kitty Carlisle's words,

> went to all the nearby movie-houses, asked them to interrupt the film and turn on the lights; then he yelled: "Everybody from the *My Fair Lady* company back to the theatre; we're opening tonight!" He went on to the health clubs and made the same announcement. People were jumping off massage tables, flinging their sheets onto the floor, and heading for the theatre. By the time the curtain went up, not one member of the company was missing.

Despite the difficulties that inevitably occur during the first tryout performance of any production, "the total effect was stunning," said Lerner. Hart's belief in "The Rain in Spain" proved justified when the audience broke into loud, sustained applause after the number. Of all the songs, it was the most spectacularly successful. Eliza's triumph, celebrated vivaciously in a tango-like manner, was irresistible, as was Hart's inventive staging and Holm's choreography. In many ways, "The Rain in Spain" became the emotional climax of the production. And, "when the curtain came down" at the end of the performance, Lerner said, "the audience stood up and cheered."

Two songs and a ballet were cut during the New Haven engagement. The ballet, Julie Andrews said, "was the most exhausting thing for me. It added such an enormous weight to an already long first act. Moss cut all of it and instead put in the tiny little scene where Eliza comes down the staircase to the study—and that was all that needed fixing."

One of the songs cut from the ballet sequence, "Say a Prayer," was later used in the Lerner and Loewe film *Gigi*; the other was "Come to the Ball." Hart said, "It is usual for numbers to be dropped during the tryout, but seldom in my experience" had the composer, lyricist, and choreographer acquiesced so quickly and so pleasantly.

The following week, in Philadelphia, *My Fair Lady* received excellent reviews. Harrison's brilliant portrayal of Higgins—initially arrogant and aloof, ultimately confused and sympathetic—received particular praise. Reports of the show's success reached New York, leading to a flood of mail orders. From the moment the box office opened, a line of people waited to purchase tickets at the window, the length of the line increasing with each passing day.

Among those who eagerly awaited the arrival of *My Fair Lady* was George S. Kaufman, now sixty-six years old. Kaufman, in deteriorating health, was confined largely to his home in 1956, although he had frequent visitors, often including the Harts. Kaufman sent Moss a letter expressing far more sentiment than the writer normally permitted himself:

> I find myself feeling very emotional about *My Fair Lady*, and that, I need hardly add, is due to your participation. Of course I'm looking forward to your opening with great excitement . . .
>
> You've apparently done a wonderful job, and I'm sure you will get gigantic credit.
>
> Anyhow, this is just a letter from a full heart, so far as you are concerned.

The first New York performance, given a month after the Philadelphia opening, was a theatre-party preview. Despite the customary reactions of theatre-party audiences—which, Hart anticipated, would demoralize the company—this one enjoyed the musical thoroughly.

Julie Andrews recalled that the speech Hart gave to the cast on the opening night, March 15, 1956, "convinced the cast and crew before the curtain went up that we were just marvelous and that if the audience didn't like it, well, what did they know anyway? He ended the speech, 'God bless us every one— and screw Tiny Tim.'"

The first-night audience, which had heard so much about *My Fair Lady*'s out-of-town success, behaved quietly and reverentially, applauding after every song but withholding its laughter. The response caused Hart to give way to his customary opening-night nerves. Lerner said, "At the end of the first scene, Moss rushed over to us and it was the first and only time I ever saw him frantic. 'I knew it,' he said. 'It's just a New Haven hit. That's all. Just a New Haven hit.' Fritz [Loewe] looked at him with an amused but sympathetic smile on his face. 'My darling Mossie,' he said, 'If you don't know this is the biggest hit that has ever come to New York you had better come with me and get a drink.' And he led Moss from the theatre to the nearest bar."

By the time Hart and Loewe returned, the audience had warmed up thoroughly, laughing loudly and applauding explosively. "When the final curtain fell," Lerner said, "the members of the audience rose from their seats and surged forward down the aisles, crying 'Bravo,' and applauding with their hands over their heads. There was curtain call after curtain call."

Pandemonium is not unusual backstage after an opening night, but the uproar at the premiere of *My Fair Lady* bordered on hysteria. Exhausted, Hart and his wife, along with Alan Jay Lerner and a handful of others, passed up the opening night party at Sardi's, and got together in a small room at "21."

The reviews could not have been more enthusiastic. Brooks Atkinson, nearing the end of his tenure as drama critic for the *Times*, began his notice, "Bulletins from the road have not been misleading. *My Fair Lady*, which opened at the Mark Hellinger last evening, is a wonderful show." Atkinson had nothing but praise for the authors, the design team, the performers, and for "Moss Hart, who has staged it with taste and skill." Julie Andrews, about whose performance so many had been concerned in the early days of rehearsal, was said by Atkinson to have done "a magnificent job. The transformation from street-corner drab to lady is both touching and beautiful."

Later, in his Sunday article, Atkinson elaborated on Hart's contribution. "Although Moss Hart has been one of the brightest particles on Broadway for years, he has staged *My Fair Lady* without Broadway's usual devices. This is his most impeccable job. In production and performance, the accent is on elegance of style." Later he added that *My Fair Lady* "was brilliantly staged by Moss Hart at the peak of his ability."

William Hawkins described the musical as having "everything. *My Fair Lady* takes a grip on your heart, then makes you exult with laughter."

John Martin, the dance critic for the *Times*, wrote of the choreography, "Hanya Holm should get some sort of specially designed gold medal for what she has done with *My Fair Lady* and Moss Hart deserves at least a silver one for grasping the necessity of having her do it." Martin called the dances in the production "just about as ideal a fusion of the literary-dramatic element of the theatre with the choreo-musical element as has been seen in our time."

Martin also raised an issue that was on the minds of many theatregoers. *Pygmalion* had often been thought to be a play whose characters and ideas were too cerebral for the musical stage. But, as Martin said, *My Fair Lady*'s combination of Bernard Shaw's dialogue with the "revelry and joyousness" of the Covent Garden scenes, "staged with gusto," had proven the skeptics wrong. Martin assigned much of the credit to Holm's dances, but was equally impressed by "Moss Hart's impeccable direction," which seamlessly interwove Shaw's dialogue with Lerner and Loewe's songs.

Congratulations poured in from everywhere. Novelist John O'Hara wrote to Hart, "There is not the slightest doubt in my mind that you did one of the best jobs of direction I've ever seen. Understanding, unobtrusive, and imaginative." Screenwriter and director Nunnally Johnson said, "You are of course going to say there were other people connected with the show who helped you, and all that sort of nonsense, but I'm a fellow not easily hoodwinked, and I can tell you that they all looked better for what you did for that show. A gorgeous affair, and if I ever saw a more beautifully staged production I can't remember it." Producer Herman Shumlin called Hart "a wonder. . . . I was more than ever impressed by the imagination & the skill of the production—the free flow of the show, the remarkable solutions to the problems were not only out of your know-how, but of your fresh, creative imagination." Other congratulatory messages came from John Hersey, Cole Porter ("the best direction of a musical that I have ever known in my life"), Alfred Lunt and Lynn Fontanne, Walter Slezak ("the closest thing to perfection I have ever seen in the theatre"), Joshua Logan, Theresa Helburn, and others. One of the most enthusiastic letters came from Hume Cronyn, who said, "I didn't just enjoy it. I got the kind of kick out of it that you only get very occasionally through years of theatre going. The whole thing, Moss, was so incredibly beautiful, so gay, tender and easy—all the things which are most difficult to bring into the theatre."

The importance of these letters and telegrams to Hart—and the immense pride he took in the job he had done—are evident from the fact that he carefully saved all the letters of congratulations he received.

Typical of the admiration expressed for the achievement of the authors and the production team was the feature article written by the noted humorist and cartoonist James Thurber five months after *My Fair Lady* opened, claiming that the musical "has restored comedy to a position of dignity in the theatre." He defined *dignity* as "the high place attained only when the heart and mind are lifted, equally and at once, by the creative union of perception and grace. . . . This phenomenon," he went on to say, "doesn't happen often in comedy, or in anything else, but when it does it's a time for putting out flags." All too often, comedy in the theatre, Thurber maintained, had "ceased to be a challenge to the mental processes. It has become a therapy of relaxation, a kind of tranquilizing drug." But *My Fair Lady* was both an exception and "an argument in favor of something more inspiring in the comic theatre than what we have been getting."

My Fair Lady was not only a hit, it was immediately recognized as a classic of the musical theatre.

Every production that ran for fifteen weeks on Broadway was obliged to offer a benefit performance for the Actors' Fund. By convention, two tickets were available to all actors appearing in plays and musicals. But the demand for the Actors' Fund performance of *My Fair Lady* was so great that the managers of the fund had to restrict each actor to a single ticket, causing a near-mutiny among the ranks in Actors' Equity. For a time the fund contemplated canceling the benefit, so great was the uproar. Finally, however, the performance was given. A knowledgeable and eager audience responded to the production with ovation after ovation, resulting in what Rex Harrison called "the most exciting night I have ever spent on a stage."

Moss Hart was recognized with a Tony Award as "Best Director of a Musical" for his contribution to *My Fair Lady*. His prize was one of many for the production; more than a third of the Tony Awards that year were given to *My Fair Lady*, including Best Musical, Best Author (Lerner), Best Composer (Loewe), Best Producer (Levin), Best Actor in a Musical (Harrison), Best Costume Designer (Beaton), and Best Scenic Designer (Oliver Smith). To the surprise of many, Julie Andrews lost the Best Actress in a Musical award to Judy Holliday in *Bells Are Ringing*. The New York Critics' Circle deemed it the "Best Musical" of the season and Hart the "Best Director."

Julie Andrews recently characterized Hart's direction: "He was thorough, strong, incisive, but underneath it all there was this wonderful, gentle humanity. He was a very giving man, and especially to me. I owe him the most enormous amount."

Not only was every ticket sold for the first several years of the run, but the number of standees—restricted by law to forty—was always at the maximum. For three years those who hoped to purchase standing room tickets for $3.45 began lining up outside the doors of the Mark Hellinger shortly after midnight, bringing with them blankets and sleeping bags, thermos bottles, bridge tables, food and first-aid kits, patiently waiting until the box office opened at 10 A.M.

Richard Maney, the production's press agent, said, "Three or four times in a generation a show erupts whose success is so explosive, whose merit is so widely hymned, that its press agent becomes the hunted rather than the hunter." So it was with *My Fair Lady*. Maney was besieged with requests for interviews with Rex Harrison and Julie Andrews, for photographic spreads to grace newspapers and magazines, for copies of the costume sketches, for tickets for out-of-town critics. Even William Paley, the head of CBS, which financed *My Fair Lady*, was unable to see the production until he pleaded with Maney to give him tickets.

It is arguable that no production in Broadway history had the influence of *My Fair Lady* on areas outside the theatre. (Cecil Beaton's costumes, for instance, created a rage in women's fashions for several years.)

When throat infections to a number of cast members caused the cancellation of a performance in August, one might have thought a national crisis was at hand. On August 18, Rex Harrison was unable to perform and his stand-by, Tom Helmore, attempted to fill in. However, Helmore, whose throat was similarly affected, could barely speak. He made no attempt to sing "Why Can't The English" in the first scene and spoke only one chorus of "I'm an Ordinary Man." His speaking voice gradually diminished to inaudibility and the curtain was brought down. When a spokesman for the theatre announced that the remainder of the performance would have to be canceled, the audience responded with a groan of dismay. Many of them had waited for months to get tickets to the production, and, because the show was sold out until December, they were informed that their only options were to get refunds at the box office or to apply for tickets at a much later date. Only a handful of spectators elected to take the refunds.

Casting for a road company with Brian Aherne as Higgins began in October. The *My Fair Lady* management intended to cast Anne Rogers as Eliza and two other British actors; Charles Victor as Doolittle and Hugh Dempster as Colonel Pickering. However, Actors' Equity withheld approval on the grounds that the casting would deprive American actors of jobs.

Another aspect of the same controversy arose in January 1957, when Rex Harrison was scheduled to take a four-week vacation from the production. After nearly a thousand actors auditioned, an Irish performer, Edward Mulhare, was selected to replace him. Actors' Equity refused permission, arguing that Mulhare was an alien and that the producers had not proven that a foreign actor was required to play Higgins. *My Fair Lady* Producer Herman Levin explained that he, Lerner, Loewe, and Hart had been seeking a replacement for Harrison for several months and that Mulhare "was by all odds the most satisfactory of all the available candidates we saw and heard." Equity threatened to close the production; Levin threatened to file a damage action against Equity in retaliation. Former New York Governor Thomas E. Dewey was hired by Levin to represent him. Meanwhile, Mulhare began rehearsing in mid-January, with Levin insisting that Mulhare would begin playing Higgins on February 4.

New York City's Department of Labor offered to mediate the dispute (which Hart had taken to calling "The Dreyfus Case"). The city held that if, as

Equity proposed, *My Fair Lady* closed, it would bring "incalculable disappointment and inconvenience to the public."

Mulhare's rehearsals with the company were suspended until the dispute was resolved. Mayor Robert Wagner proposed that the question be submitted to an arbitrator. After a four-hour conference at the offices of the Commissioner of Labor, attended by Hart, Levin, Lerner, and Loewe on behalf of *My Fair Lady* and, on the other side, several officers of Actors' Equity, the mayor's proposal was agreed to. The arbitrator, Theodore Kheel, ruled in favor of *My Fair Lady*, paving the way for Mulhare's appearance. Levin then insisted that Rogers, Victor, and Dempster should be approved for the touring company. Ralph Bellamy, president of Equity, issued the following statement: "Our concern with continuing to regulate alien employment is neither provincial nor capricious. It results from the need to avoid abuses by producers whose interest is primarily with selling American talent and standards short by the indiscriminate use of imported performers." However, on January 25, the U.S. Immigration and Naturalization Service granted permission for the three British performers to join the road company.

The controversy over Mulhare was so intriguing to the public that many New York newspapers reviewed his first performance. Lewis Funke of the *Times* began his review, "Edward Mulhare can take a nice long breath this morning and relax. So can everyone else concerned with *My Fair Lady* [for Mulhare] did remarkably well, particularly so when you consider the spot he was on. . . . His interpretation of the single-tracked Higgins is sound, dynamic, and nicely paced." At the end of the performance, Mulhare (who had rehearsed for only nineteen days rather than the originally scheduled twenty-six) was applauded not only by the audience but by the entire cast.[9]

The road company included an actress named Margaret Bannerman. Kitty Carlisle recalled a time years before when she appeared in an operetta named *Three Waltzes*, replacing Bannerman, who had been dismissed. To Carlisle's surprise, Bannerman sent her a basket of flowers on opening night with an accompanying card, a gesture that was so generous Kitty never forgot it. "I told Moss this story long after," she said, "and he never forgot it either. When he was casting the national company of *My Fair Lady* and saw that Bannerman was up for the part of Mrs. Higgins, he told the casting director to hire her on the spot—no audition necessary."

---

9 Coincidentally, Mulhare later performed in the television version of *The Ghost and Mrs. Muir*, (1968–70) in a role played in the 1947 film of the same name by Rex Harrison.

Performances on the road began in Rochester, New York, on March 19, 1957. The company then moved on to Detroit, the West Coast, and Chicago. Everywhere *My Fair Lady* ran it received rapturous notices similar to those it had received in New York; everywhere audiences were captivated.

Keeping a long-running play fresh is difficult for everyone. Actors' performances, in particular, become dulled by repetition. A performer who has spoken the same words for three hundred consecutive performances finds his mind wandering; rather than remaining focused on his character's reply to another character's question, he thinks, without intending to, of what he'll have to eat after the final curtain. Hart saw a performance of *My Fair Lady* in New York every three weeks to ensure that the production remained fresh. Stone ("Bud") Widney, the production manager, told me of Hart's ability to maintain his objectivity and focus on the entire picture rather than immerse himself in the details:

> Being at his elbow during the performances was very instructive to me. In a musical when you give notes there are usually about fifty notes per performance because somebody is stepping on somebody's laugh line, a light isn't going on, a scenery item comes in late—an incredible amount of things. And I stood at the back of all the performances with Moss and I would note things down like crazy. I was wondering why Moss wasn't saying anything. Why am I writing everything down when he's the director? But he would give me only about two notes—notes that had to do with the architecture of the performance—and those two notes were so meaningful. They affected the shape of the whole piece. He was able to maintain objectivity instead of getting lost in the morass of the details. I so admired that; it taught me a huge lesson as a director. You have got to have two heads on you: you've got to spend some time on the details but you've also got to be able to pull back and just view it like an audience does. That's what Moss did so brilliantly. He was very attuned to what an audience was responding to.

Periodically, Hart would call a rehearsal to sharpen the entire production. He also supervised the road company production, rehearsed understudies and cast replacements, and made arrangements for the London presentation. As Abe Laufe, author of *Broadway's Greatest Musicals*, said, "Moss Hart . . . not only whipped the show into its perfect form for the Broadway opening but also maintained the original perfection of timing and pace with each change in cast."

The extent to which Hart succeeded in maintaining the brilliance and vitality of the performance was also attested to in 1960 by Bennett Cerf, Hart's friend and publisher. Cerf wrote, "It was Lerner and Loewe who wrote the fabulous *My Fair Lady*, but it was Director Moss Hart who whipped the production into shape. By opening night in New York, it was perfect. Four years later, though the leads have changed a half dozen times, it is still perfect. That is because Moss Hart, in play directing, as in every other work he attempts, will accept nothing less."

Even when the leading players left *My Fair Lady*, the production continued to draw standing-room-only crowds. Rex Harrison gave his last New York performance late in November 1957, after having played Higgins more than 700 times. To commemorate Harrison's farewell performance, Kay Kendall, his wife, appeared briefly as the Queen of Carpathia during the ballroom scene. Her escort was Moss Hart, outfitted in formal clothing. Kendall took the small, non-speaking role of a maid in the same performance. After the curtain came down, Harrison, who called the entire experience "very emotional and very touching," gave an onstage party for the cast and stagehands.

In February 1958, Julie Andrews left the New York company. Sally Ann Howes, a British stage and film actress and singer, took over the role of Eliza. Howes had been the management's choice to play Eliza in the national company, but she had turned down that opportunity. Later, when Julie Andrews's departure from the cast became imminent, Lerner and Loewe flew to London, where Howes was then appearing in *A Hatful of Rain*, and successfully persuaded her to take over the role of Eliza.

Many of New York's theatre critics revisited *My Fair Lady* yet again when the musical entered its third year of production. Brooks Atkinson felt that the leading roles were not being played as adroitly as by the original performers, but that the production was "still . . . delightful and moving. . . . Two years have not dissipated the entrancing splendor of an incomparable script and score."

Hart went to London in late February 1958, to cast the British production. Many of the leading performers who had appeared in New York revived their roles. These included Rex Harrison, Julie Andrews, Stanley Holloway, and Robert Coote. The rest of the cast was chosen in London.

Hart, who in the past had observed that the British tabloids concocted one sensational story after another, often by misquoting the words of interviewees, simply invited British reporters to make up whatever they liked and attribute their invented comments to him.

For several reasons the anticipation of British audiences for the premiere of *My Fair Lady* was extraordinary. For one thing, there was the phenomenal reputation the musical had already developed based on its New York run. Second, the leading players were all British; and, finally, the author of the play from which the musical had been adapted was generally regarded as English (although he had been born in and spent his early years in Ireland). Ticket orders were taken seven months before the production opened, an event unprecedented in British theatre history. Ten weeks before *My Fair Lady* was due to open more than a quarter-million tickets had been sold. By February, the box office had no tickets until August, except for some in the farthest reaches of the massive Drury Lane Theatre (which could accommodate 2,247 spectators), known as "the gods."

The British production opened on April 30. The ovation at the end of the performance lasted for more than four minutes. A few critics questioned Lerner and Loewe's temerity in tampering with a classic play, but the reviews were nearly as favorable as those the production had received in New York. Although one columnist called *My Fair Lady* the "most over-publicized, over-sold and over-rated show ever to come to London," his voice was drowned out by the chorus of approval. Harry Weaver, writing in the *Daily Herald*, said, "It can't be true. I don't believe it. No show can possibly live up to the advance raves of *My Fair Lady* . . . but, by George, they did it, yes they did it . . . It fulfilled every extravagant promise." W. A. Darlington in the London *Daily Telegraph* said the show was "good enough to stand up even to the absurdly exaggerated advance publicity and has started off brilliantly." The *Times* called *My Fair Lady* "a beguilingly graceful musical comedy with vastly more wit and more pointed mockery of the period's social distinctions than we expect to encounter" in a musical comedy.

At a party on the opening night, Kay Kendall, after reading the reviews, enlivened the proceedings by turning three somersaults. Kendall, who died from cancer the following year at the age of thirty-three, was a brilliant performer in her own right. Hart remembered "so many evenings when she returned from other theatres and held us all in helpless laughter or sometimes brought us close to tears when she herself had been moved by a fine performance or stirred by a good play. But whether it was laughter or tears—or sometimes rage and temper—she always filled the room with a throbbing and pulsating sense of life. She could make heating soup for Rex over a can of Sterno during the intermission an event of wild suspense."

Everyone who wished to see *My Fair Lady* in London could not possibly have been accommodated. Englishmen by the thousands were turned away, in part because Americans, who were unable to purchase tickets to the production in New York, made reservations for the Drury Lane Theatre in England. Among these was a group of eighty employees of Consolidated Edison in New York, who flew to London and saw the British production on September 29.

Those who saw early performances of both the New York and the London productions felt that Julie Andrews's performance had improved with time. Drew Middleton wrote from London that her "Eliza Doolittle is a more mature, commanding and subtle performance here. In New York Rex Harrison's near miraculous playing as Henry Higgins seemed to throw the musical slightly out of balance. In London Miss Andrews has redressed the balance."

Queen Elizabeth and Prince Philip attended a performance on May 5. During a long intermission, Hart, Kitty, Lerner, and British producer Binkie Beaumont were taken to the anteroom of the Royal box. Hart and his wife spent most of the intermission exchanging polite conversation with the queen. After the performance, the royal couple went backstage to meet and congratulate the cast.

Julie Andrews left the British production on August 8, 1959. By that time, she had played Eliza for more than a thousand performances. A stream of tears rolled down her face as the cast joined in an ovation for her. Andrews ran to her dressing room, but later hosted a party in the theatre. The next night Eliza was played by Anne Rogers, who, coincidentally, had played the role of Polly in the British production of *The Boy Friend* before Andrews assumed the role when the production moved from England to America.

The London production of *My Fair Lady* and the national company touring America were supplemented by others in such locations as Holland, Belgium, Germany, Mexico, Sweden, Denmark, Israel, Australia, Spain, Tokyo, Switzerland, Italy, and South Africa. Each, of course, produced enormous amounts of money—altogether, including the original cast album and the film rights, the production earned more than one hundred million dollars—and Moss Hart, who received a percentage of the income from each production, became, for the first time since the early 1940s, a wealthy man. He remained so for the rest of his life. Of all Hart's commercial successes in the theatre, none brought him a fraction of the income that *My Fair Lady* provided.

The remuneration was highly satisfactory, of course, but Hart was particularly proud of the exuberance of the production that could be seen, he said, "each night in New York, in London, in Australia, in Stockholm, and Lord knows where else," for he insisted that every production be as fresh and inventive as the original.

In 1959, the United States and the Soviet Union negotiated their first cultural exchange, signaling a willingness to reduce political tensions. The Bolshoi

Ballet came to New York's Metropolitan Opera House and an American company of *My Fair Lady* arranged to play throughout Russia.[10]

The production was delayed for some time because Lerner and Loewe refused to give permission unless the Soviets would agree to end their practice of pirating American plays, books, and other creative works, a practice that occurred regularly. (Some American writers had been paid royalties in the past, but only when the Soviets opted to do so.) Lerner and Loewe urged the Authors League of America to support their position. Hart, then president of the League, gave his full endorsement to Lerner and Loewe's argument. He hoped, he said, to help work out an agreement "to pay royalties to all our authors when their works are presented in Russia." He issued a statement: "Our suggestion has been that Russian authors whose works are produced in the United States be paid royalties at the rates usually paid Americans, and that our authors whose works are produced or published in the U.S.S.R. be paid at the rates paid their writers."

When that issue had been resolved, the English-speaking production of *My Fair Lady* in the Soviet Union played in Moscow, Leningrad, and several other cities. Many of the performers were recruited from the American touring company, which shut down temporarily to accommodate the performances in Russia.

On July 1, 1961, the New York company of *My Fair Lady* gave a milestone performance, its 2,213th, making it the longest-running production in Broadway history. When it finally closed in September 1962, it had run for 2,715 performances. Not only did the musical set records for longevity, it earned more money than any production in American history to that time. As it did in New York, *My Fair Lady* broke all records in England for a long-running performance, playing at the Drury Lane for more than six years.[11]

Seldom in the theatre does every detail join together so perfectly that one can hardly imagine how the entire work can be improved. This may happen in a revival, when the play itself has already been tested and approved, but the chances of a new play achieving a state of near-perfection *and* being given a sublime production is so unusual that the conjunction is virtually a once-in-a-lifetime event. That is why *My Fair Lady* was so remarkable. Here was a

---

10 Nikolai Danilov, negotiating on behalf of the Soviets, initially requested a production of *West Side Story*. But the State Department rejected the idea on the basis that its plot, dealing with fights between American and Puerto Rican gang members in New York, was inappropriate for exportation.

11 Both records have long since been broken.

great play turned into a great musical; the performance of every role was magnificent, the choreography extraordinary; and all was tied together by the masterful direction of Moss Hart, in the finest directorial job of his career, his taste and sensitivity ensuring that the production succeeded as an entertaining musical without neglecting Shaw's intellectual content.

In the broader context of Hart's professional career, *My Fair Lady* takes its place among his greatest achievements. If his greatest contribution to American comedy was the three great comedies he wrote with George S. Kaufman; and if his contribution to the development of the American musical was embodied in his creation of *Lady in the Dark*; and if *Act One* is regarded as the finest of all theatrical memoirs; and if the screenplay of *A Star Is Born* is acknowledged as one of the best ever written for an American film, Hart's extraordinary direction of *My Fair Lady* was no less momentous.

Furthermore, *My Fair Lady* restored Hart to his pre-eminent position as one of the leading figures in the American theatre. Such failed plays as *Christopher Blake*, *Light Up the Sky*, and *The Climate of Eden* had damaged his reputation as a playwright whose works invariably appealed to wide audiences and satisfied with wit and elegance. Although Hart's direction of *Miss Liberty* and *Anniversary Waltz* had been praised as astute, neither the musical nor the play will be long-remembered among theatregoers or critics. But *My Fair Lady* will always be fondly recalled as one of the finest musicals, and the production Hart directed will forever be regarded as a model of the directorial art.

No wonder he took such immense pride in his contribution to *My Fair Lady*. With that musical, Moss Hart had once again achieved a success so monumental that few Broadway artists have ever approached it.

Chapter 12 "THE UNHAPPINESS OF A SUCCESSFUL MAN"
1959–1960

MY *FAIR LADY* WAS ONLY THE FIRST OF THREE ENORMOUSLY SUCCESSFUL events for Moss Hart in the five-year period beginning in 1956. One of the most satisfying moments in his life occurred in September 1959, during the third year of *My Fair Lady*'s Broadway run, when Random House published *Act One*, the memoir on which he had been working off and on for years.[1]

At times during that long process, Hart was elated by the way his work on the autobiography was proceeding. "It's going well," he would tell his wife. "It will make our fortune." Since he had earned little money for ten years, the hoped-for financial bonanza was important. On other occasions, however, he would become downcast and say, "The book won't pay the grocery bills. It's an indulgence on my part."

A handwritten copy of an early draft of *Act One*, written in 1953, still exists. It demonstrates that the writer never wavered in the story he had to tell, but the style in which he told it underwent great changes with each succeeding rewrite. The early draft begins somewhat clumsily: "What better way to begin than with my first glimpse of Broadway? One must start somewhere and if this opening sentence falls too [words crossed out] in the time honored tradition of theatrical memoirs, let the unwary reader beware at the very outset."

By contrast, the published version of the book begins far more intriguingly, far less self-consciously: "That afternoon, I went to work at the music store as usual. It was just around the corner from where we lived, and I worked there every afternoon from three o'clock to seven . . ."

The idea of ending the memoir in a novel fashion was obviously a last-minute decision. The final typewritten draft, containing cuts, inserts, and revisions, still concluded with "The End"; perhaps envisioning a sequel, however, Hart replaced "The End" with "Intermission."

Throughout the writing process, he continued to read sections of the book to friends, soliciting their opinions. One evening he read a portion of the

---

[1] As many as eighteen years, according to an item in the April 13, 1941, issue of *The New York Times*, which said Hart "is writing a book on the theatre—autobiographical, anecdotal—which Random House is to publish in the Fall."

book to Bennett Cerf, who had published many of Hart's plays at Random House, and Cerf's wife, Phyllis. Hart was pleased by their reaction to his work, but told Phyllis Cerf that he regarded the book primarily as a writing exercise and suggested that he might never complete it. She then asked to see all that Hart had written, at that point about two-thirds of the whole. In January 1957, she wrote to him, saying, "You must go on with it, you must finish it, and you will." The book was "wonderful," she insisted, "a very special autobiography. . . . I'm so proud of you." She closed by pleading with him to "Go back to your typewriter."

Hart proudly told Edward R. Murrow during an appearance on *Person to Person* in 1959 that his autobiography would appear before the year was out. He credited Kitty Carlisle with having made "an enormous contribution" to the book. "You see, she's a good listener," he told Murrow. "At the end of each day I'd read her what I had written and she listened as though she were listening to [a] radio serial. She couldn't wait for the next episode."

When Hart received an advance copy of *Act One* in July 1959, he immediately sent it to George S. Kaufman, whom he described in the text as the "hero" of his book. Still a profound admirer and close friend of Kaufman's, he waited anxiously to hear what his former collaborator, whose eccentricities he had portrayed candidly in the book, would have to say. Kaufman responded in a telegram, "GEORGE TYLERS OFFICE [where Hart heard that a production of *The Emperor Jones* was being cast] WAS ON THE THIRD FLOOR NOT THE FOURTH BUT THAT IS MY ONLY COMPLAINT THE BOOK IS QUITE WONDERFUL AND . . . I AM PROUD TO BE PART OF IT ALL THANKS AND LOVE."

Reviews of *Act One* were almost unanimously favorable. *The New York Times* ran three separate reviews. "You won't find a more readable theatrical biography in many a season," wrote Charles Poore on September 15. Brooks Atkinson, adding his verdict five days later, called *Act One* "the best book written about the panic and glare of Broadway . . . No one else has told this familiar Broadway odyssey [from obscurity to success] so brilliantly." In the same issue, S. N. Behrman reviewed the book on the cover of the Book Review section. (On the same day, *Act One* was also reviewed on the front page of the book section of the New York *Herald Tribune*, a coup for any writer. Christopher Hart recalled it as his father's "crowning glory.") Behrman, whose encouragement had comforted Hart during the latter's period of writer's block in the mid-1950s, wrote, "This is the best book on 'show business' as practiced in this country in our time that I have ever read; it is entertaining and fascinating through all of its considerable length. . . . His prose is lithe, clean and easy. He is engagingly candid; . . . He is also hilariously funny." According to Kitty Carlisle, Behrman's review elated Hart beyond any notice he had ever received for a play.

John Davenport, in "Book Bag," said: "Books about the theatre are always fascinating, but they are not as a rule very well written. Moss Hart's autobiography is a brilliant exception." The critic for *The New Statesman* observed, "This superb autobiography, bristling with wit, parades before us a fascinating range of characters and experiences and deserves the widest public." Charles Rolo in *The Atlantic Monthly*, calling *Act One* "altogether more substantial than the conventional theatrical memoir," praised Hart for writing "with candor, vitality, and a lack of vanity rare in books about the theatre." Finally, Hollis Alpert, writing in *The Saturday Review*, said that the book was "the most engrossing autobiography I have yet to read by an important figure of the theatre."

Hart, who always had a thin skin where criticism was concerned, wrote a scathing letter to Lillian Hellman when he heard that she had denigrated his book. Earlier, he had asked for her response to his complete manuscript no less than four times. Presumably, she praised it on each occasion, but after publication her opinion became more critical, prompting Hart's angry letter. Hellman responded by saying that she did indeed have reservations about the book, but also thought it charming. Recognizing Hart's erratic mood swings, Hellman wrote, "On another day you will know again that I have always respected you and your work, had great affection for you, and warmth, and pleasure in your success. . . . If I hurt you, God knows I am sorry. But I can't feel guilty. And you have hurt me, too, with [your letter]. . . . I hope that we will not lose each other, but that is up to you."

Bennett Cerf, Hart's publisher, said, "In my thirty-eight years in the publishing business, I have never seen an author derive such unalloyed delight from a best-seller as Moss Hart did from *Act One*. To hear the relish with which he read his fan mail to me over the phone each morning was to understand what fun can be had in this life by a man who knows how to live it. It made no difference to Moss whether the letter came from an Adlai Stevenson or an unsung housewife in Wichita Falls." Indeed, Hart saved hundreds of letters he received from readers. A great number of them were from his friends, among them celebrated writers, directors, and actors;[2] however,

---

2 A sampling includes Alan Jay Lerner, Frederick Loewe, Herman Levin, Henry Luce, Laura Z. Hobson, Binkie Beaumont, Jean Kerr, Norman Krasna, Quentin Reynolds, Oscar Hammerstein II, Edna Ferber, Nunnally Johnson, Thelma Ritter, Emlyn Williams, Howard Lindsay, Alfred Lunt and Lynn Fontanne, Truman Capote, Mel Brooks, Harold Arlen, George Cukor, Somerset Maugham, Spencer

many more were written by readers whom Hart had never met but who wished to thank him for the reading pleasure he had provided. Many of them called his work "inspiring;" some of them wrote at length about their own struggles to achieve success in the arts or in other occupations.

He responded to many of the letter writers. To Madeline Sherwood, the widow of Robert E. Sherwood, he wrote, "It is, as you know, my first venture into prose—and my avidity for praise and my excitement when I receive it from someone like you, must be forgiven. Your words pleased me greatly— more than I can tell you—please be my 'commercial' and tell all your book-buying friends."

Individual buyers of *Act One* sometimes received an unexpected bonus. For example, one day when Hart was out walking he passed an elderly man carrying a copy of the book. "I'm Moss Hart," the author said, unable to contain his pride. "I'm the man who wrote that book," and eagerly offered to inscribe the old man's copy. One can imagine the man's surprise and pleasure.

Act One first appeared on *The New York Times* best-seller list on September 27. By February 21, 1960, it became the best-selling non-fiction book in the country and remained in that position for the next three weeks. It continued to be ranked among the best-sellers until June 26, making a total of forty-one weeks on the list.

Late in 1959, despite the tremendous pride Hart felt in his accomplishment, the enormous success of *Act One* triggered yet another bout of depression. When he was vacationing in Jamaica, he saw many people carrying or reading his book, and, when people discovered he was the author, received a steady stream of lavish praise. Still, Hart sank into despair. Kitty Carlisle said, "Life with Moss was like living on a high mountain range, jumping from peak to peak. The depths were always below; they were Moss's depressions, and I never knew what would trigger them. This time it was the success of *Act One*." She continued:

> I asked Moss how it could be possible that he was so miserable when his dreams [for the book's success] had come true. He said he felt that each success had been sleight of hand, dust in the eyes of the audience and the critics, and he'd gotten away with it again. You strive for success, hoping it will change your life and change you. Then you achieve it; but you wake up the next morning to discover that nothing is changed. You're the same old fellow you were before.

Tracy, Lauren Bacall, Leonard Bernstein, Hume Cronyn, Claudette Colbert, Sidney Lumet, Ilka Chase, Bernard Baruch, William Inge, Richard Burton, Noël Coward (although he scolded Hart for having used too many split infinitives), Joshua Logan, and Russel Crouse.

Kitty, blessed with a sunnier disposition, tried to reason with her husband, assuring him that he had no reason to feel inadequate, "telling him to count his blessings, to look at his successes, what he had made of his life, how much his friends loved and admired him, how much *I* loved and admired him. . . . But [my words] never reached him. It was as if we were in different countries, speaking different languages. I was in a bright, sunlit land, and he was in some dark, stormy region with leafless trees and scorched earth." Kitty could only advise him to once again consult Dr. Kubie, which, when they returned to New York, he promptly did.

Whether or not Hart intended to write *Act Two* is a matter of conjecture. Certainly a volume that ends with the word *Intermission* suggests that another volume will follow. Brooks Atkinson told his readers to "look for *Act Two* eventually." Cecil Smith asked Hart whether he intended to write a sequel. Hart turned the question around. "Let me ask you," he said. "Should I write it?" Smith answered, "Of course . . . *Act Two* would necessarily be the story of continuing and growing success . . . And success—continuing success—is a difficult thing to understand." Hart pondered, then said, "Perhaps for that reason I should write *Act Two*. It seems to me there's a need for a book on the anatomy of success." Unexpectedly, for he rarely shared his bleak outlook with anyone except his wife and closest friends, he added, "Particularly one that probes the mystery of human unhappiness—the unhappiness of a successful man."

In January 1960, Hart said publicly that he was beginning to work on a sequel. Hart's son, Christopher, recalls with certainty that his father was not only giving serious thought to *Act Two* but was compiling preliminary notes for the work. However, Moss was deeply conflicted about it. He asked his friend Jerome Chodorov, "Who wants to read about a guy's success and about his terrible anxieties and his depressions?" Chodorov told me, "And he was right not to do *Act Two* or *Act Three*. He said a success story is one thing, but a successful writer who is going to the analyst for all his troubles is something else."

Joshua Logan, with money furnished by Warner Bros., purchased the film rights to *Act One*, announcing that he would direct the movie for his company, Mansfield Productions. Logan had been one of Hart's many friends who had read sections of the book long before it was published. It never occurred to Logan that the material would lend itself to cinematic treatment, he claimed, until a friend suggested it would make a good movie.

Hart said from the beginning that he would have nothing to do with the movie version; nor, he said, would he have any complaints about the way the book was adapted for film. "I believe a man who sells his work to a studio should take the money and shut up," he said, repeating the attitude he had taken toward his work ever since *Once in a Lifetime*, thirty years before.[3]

∽

When Alan Jay Lerner and Frederick Loewe began work on another musical, there was no doubt that they would ask Hart to serve as director. They had witnessed his ability to mold a group of actors, singers, and dancers into a cohesive unit, to find the appropriate tone for every scene, indeed, every moment of *My Fair Lady*. They had watched him unify the work of the playwright, the composer, the scenic, lighting, and costume designers so that each contribution complemented and enriched the work of the others. Lerner acknowledged Hart's directorial expertise when he said that Moss possessed "the sure hand of a master of his art . . . He was in every sense of the word a man of the theatre . . ."

As early as March 1956, Lerner, Loewe, and Hart had agreed that they would like to work together again one day—and as soon as possible. They discussed the possibilities of adapting several properties into musicals, among them the play *Father of the Bride*, the novel *Huckleberry Finn*, and the French film *Children of Paradise*, but ultimately decided to continue looking. They considered writing a political satire, but that, too, was shelved. They thought of trying their hand at an adaptation of Colette's *Gigi* (which Lerner and Loewe did soon after, creating the Academy Award-winning 1958 MGM musical of the same name) but rejected that idea as well.[4]

Then, in August 1958, while he was still working on *Act One*, Hart read a *New York Times* review of T. H. White's *The Once and Future King*, a novel about the Arthurian legends. On the following day he called Lerner. Although Hart had not yet read White's book, something in the review suggested to him that the novel's combination of fantastic and legendary elements might serve as the basis of an exciting musical. Lerner, who had also been encouraged to consider converting the novel to a musical by his production manager, Stone (Bud) Widney, read the review, then ordered the book. Enchanted by White's tale, he agreed with Hart's and Widney's assessments.

---

3 As it turned out, Logan's friend, who believed that *Act One* would serve as the basis for a compelling film, was wrong. Unable to arrive at a suitable screen treatment, Logan bowed out. Warner Bros. then commissioned a film to be written and directed by Hart's former colleague Dore Schary, with George Hamilton playing Hart and Jason Robards as George S. Kaufman. In the film, released in 1963, somehow all of the gusto of the book was eliminated. Critic Bosley Crowther said, "All that Mr. Schary gives us in this movie . . . is a picture of a patent-leather dullard trying to peddle and then rewrite a play with the help of a cranky old codger who is almost as dull as he . . . [the film] lacks wit, it lacks zip."

4 The stage musical *Gigi*, adapted from the film, did eventually play at the Uris Theatre on Broadway, opening on November 13, 1973. It was unsuccessful, however, playing for only 103 performances.

Lerner surprised Hart by asking him to collaborate on the writing of the book. (One of America's most brilliant lyricists, Lerner understandably reserved the writing of the lyrics for himself.) Hart was delighted. He had not written anything for the stage since *The Climate of Eden* in 1952 and looked forward to resuming his career as a playwright.

But Fritz Loewe had many misgivings about the project. "You must be crazy," he told Lerner and Hart, believing that no one would be interested in a character whose wife is unfaithful to him—except perhaps to laugh contemptuously at him. Lerner disagreed, maintaining that this was not just any character, this was King Arthur, who had retained a grip on the public's imagination for a thousand years. Loewe finally agreed to read White's novel—a vow that he did not keep, so certain was he that *The Once and Future King* was unpromising material for a musical. Still, he ultimately deferred to his collaborators and composed the music for the project that he feared would never reach the stage.

Hart proposed that the three of them should produce the play, in addition to writing it and guiding the rehearsals. Ultimately, this decision, intended to promote creative autonomy, would have negative consequences, as Hart, Lerner, and Loewe had nowhere else to turn when they needed help.

Hart, intending to begin work with Lerner on the musical's book in the spring, simmered with ideas about how to turn a long, complex novel into a three-hour musical, a process that would entail a great deal of cutting as well as shifts of emphasis while highlighting certain characters in White's novel at the expense of others. Moss's enthusiasm for the project increased steadily—until a letter arrived from Lerner, stating that he had decided to write the book as well as the lyrics by himself. Hart was devastated. As one who had collaborated with such masterful playwrights as George S. Kaufman, lyricists Ira Gershwin and Lorenz Hart, and composers Cole Porter, Irving Berlin, Richard Rodgers, and Kurt Weill, Hart knew the intricacies and the rewards of collaboration better than anyone then working in the American theatre, but he realized that it would be pointless to try to change Lerner's mind. Lerner had always written without a collaborator, and to enter into a new arrangement must have seemed to him more awkward than he had originally imagined.

Kitty Carlisle tried to console her husband. "Just direct it," she said, and, knowing how influential directors can be in shaping the script, added, "and help as much as you can."

Lerner arranged to meet with T. H. White in England. When the novelist signed a legal agreement giving Lerner and Loewe the right to adapt his work into a musical, he tried to impress upon them that they needn't consult him about specific changes, being content to let the adaptors alter his work in any way they found appropriate. After receiving a letter from Lerner in which the librettist said that adapting *The Once and Future King* "was less a matter of dramatizing incidents than capturing the spirit," White wrote to Hart on April 4, 1960, "Your friends Lerner and Loewe are misunderstanding me a great deal if they think I have the least wish to interfere . . ." And in October, again in a letter to Hart, White wrote, "Everybody keeps telling me, oh, I do hope you will be pleased with the way they have adapted your book, oh, I do hope you won't think they have altered it too much, etc., etc. Well, I honestly don't care a fart if it has been altered almost out of recognition. I . . . know perfectly well that what has got to succeed is the *musical*, which has different laws to a book."

Converting White's novel to a workable musical proved to be extraordinarily difficult, however. Lerner spent several months on a first draft (originally titled *Jenny Kissed Me*), sending it to Hart in the spring of 1959. Unquestionably, the task of adapting White's novel—which was divided into four sections, each telling different parts of the Arthurian legend, each with a different tone—was incredibly difficult. Even after deciding that the first section of the book could be excluded altogether, there was still so much material, the bulk of it novelistic rather than theatrical, that manipulating it into the form of a play might have stymied anyone. And, indeed, Hart thought that Lerner's first draft was unworkable. The first act, which was essentially romantic and comic, seemed promising. However, some of the songs, he thought, were inappropriately lighthearted for a play whose characters would ultimately experience bitterness and disillusionment. The second act was even more problematic. The somber tone of the proceedings—as Arthur's wife Guenevere has an affair with Lancelot, and the Round Table gradually disintegrates—was true to the spirit of White's book (and to the many versions of the Arthurian legend) but, in Hart's opinion, Lerner's version was static and untheatrical. When Hart discussed the problem with his wife, she suggested that the character of Mordred be given greater prominence, to act as a villainous counterpoint to the other characters. Hart liked her observation and passed it along to Lerner, who expanded Mordred's role in his second draft.

By the time summer had arrived, however, Lerner was still struggling with the material, trying to wrestle it into dramatic shape. The novel contained so many characters in such a variety of situations that Lerner was unable to make satisfactory progress. He asked Hart to visit him in his chateau in Antibes so that they could discuss the work fully. Hart did so, and, as his wife had predicted he would, contributed a great many ideas to the writing of the musical even though he never received official credit.[5]

Eventually, in July 1959, Lerner, Loewe, and Hart believed that the adaptation, now called *Camelot*, was ready to be cast and rehearsed. Everyone agreed that Julie Andrews was a perfect choice to play Guenevere. Andrews, eager to work again with material written by Lerner and Loewe, and equally enthusiastic about being directed by Moss Hart, who had mentored her so successfully in *My Fair Lady*, accepted soon after being offered the role. Hart, remembering Richard Burton's performance in his 1955 film, *Prince of Players*, recommended that Burton be strongly considered to play King Arthur. Lerner and Loewe agreed, for, although Burton's singing voice was not a refined instrument, neither was Rex Harrison's, and that had not been a barrier to Harrison's brilliant success in *My Fair Lady*. Moreover, Lerner had heard Burton sing some Welsh songs at a party, which quelled any fears he might otherwise have had. Hart called Burton in California and arranged a meeting, during which Burton said he was enthusiastic about the project.

Other members of the cast quickly fell into place. Roddy McDowall didn't wait to be contacted. He called Hart to say that Mordred, Arthur's evil son, was a role he was born to play—and it didn't bother him a bit that Mordred did not appear until the second act or that the role was considerably smaller than those he normally played. Robert Coote, a veteran of *My Fair Lady*, was, in Alan Jay Lerner's words, "obviously ideal for Pellinore, the King who had lost his kingdom and could not find it again." Coote's specialty was playing stuffy upper-class British twits, and no one was stuffier than Pellinore. Lerner continued,

> We reached him in London, where he was still playing Pickering. Coote maintained a rigid regime which included fresh air in the afternoon followed by a lie-down, as he referred to it, before the performance, so we called him in the late afternoon. Moss and I were both on the phone. "Cooter," one of us said, "did you ever hear of a book called *The Once and Future King*?" "Got it by my bedside," said Coote. "My favorite book. Want me to play Pellinore?" "Yes," we said. "Love it," came the reply. "Absolutely love it. All that rusty armor. Couldn't be better." And that was that.

The casting of the principals was nearly complete, except for Lancelot. Since Guenevere falls in love with Lancelot, the actor had to possess a charm

---

5 This is by no means an unusual method, and there is no suggestion here that Lerner behaved unethically in taking full credit for the writing of the book of *Camelot*. Directors have far more influence on original scripts than the public generally realizes. Often their contributions are made primarily in rehearsal when they help to reshape the script. In the case of the adaptation of *The Once and Future King*, Hart was involved at an earlier stage, but early involvement by the director is not at all unprecedented.

that would be immediately apparent both to Guenevere and to the audience; an arrogant manner that defines his character when he is first seen, but is somehow not off-putting; and an outstanding singing voice. Laurence Harvey, the British film actor, called the producers to express his strong interest. They were intrigued, but said he would have to sing for them. Kitty Carlisle helped Harvey prepare an audition piece. Although he proved to have a pleasant voice, it was untrained, and the producers agreed that a trained singer would be necessary in the role.[6]

Hundreds of auditions for Lancelot were conducted during the winter of 1959–60, both in England and in America, but no one who had quite the right combination of qualities could be found. The producers met to discuss performers they might invite to prepare an audition. One of those invited, an accomplished actor, explained that his singing voice wasn't up to the role, but suggested they contact Robert Goulet, a performer who already had established himself as a singer on television in Toronto.

Goulet was on vacation, playing golf in Bermuda. Not to be deterred, the producers tracked him down and requested that he come to New York to audition for Lancelot. Goulet was intrigued but had to decline because a dress rehearsal of a stage show in Toronto was scheduled on the precise date the *Camelot* producers wanted him to audition. However, he contacted the producer of his stage show who, to his surprise, gave him permission to audition with the understanding that he would then return immediately to Toronto. Goulet, dressed casually for his holiday, caught the first flight to New York, intending to change clothes before the audition. However, when his luggage was lost at the airport, he arrived at the theatre wearing T-shirt, jeans, and tennis shoes. The stage door opened and the producers crossed the stage on their way to the auditorium. Hart said genially to Goulet, "I can see you've come prepared for action."

The producers, still making their way to their seats, stopped cold as Goulet began to sing in his polished baritone. In the moment that followed, as Lerner, Loewe, and Hart conferred, the pianist whispered to Goulet, "I think you've got it. I think you've got it." The producers then asked Goulet if he could speak French. When he answered, "*Oui, certainment*," Hart, Lerner, and Loewe offered him the role.

Casting of the minor roles progressed as work on the script continued. Although the intention was to pare down the length and the size of the early

---

6 Subsequently, Harvey took singing lessons in London and was cast in the British production of *Camelot*, but as King Arthur rather than Lancelot.

drafts, *Camelot* stubbornly refused to be cut. Indeed, it grew longer with each rewrite, a problem that very nearly drove its creators to distraction.

A more serious occurrence arose after Hart persuaded Adrian, once the premiere costume designer for films, but in 1959 living in retirement, to sketch some designs for the characters in the musical. The designs were perfect, everyone felt, and Adrian was hired as costume designer.

Eight months later, however, before rehearsals began, Adrian suffered a fatal heart attack and was replaced by Tony Duquette.

Although some members of the *Camelot* team had not known Adrian in the past, his death was a shocking blow to all of them. A theatrical company bonds together so quickly that it becomes, for the time of the production, a caring family. Few activities engender the same shared fervor as a theatrical project. On the other hand, once a production is over and those connected with it go their own ways, the bonding frequently disintegrates. Friendships from the production may remain, but the feeling is never again quite as deep or as intense.

In the midst of the planning for *Camelot*, Actors' Equity called a strike against Broadway producers (the League of New York Theatres) in June 1960—or, as the actors contended, the producers provoked a lockout. Actors, concerned about their precarious economic circumstances, rebelled against the situation that typified their lives: periods of work, often brief, during which their compensation was not significant enough—often less than $150 per week—to tide them over long stretches of unemployment. Producers argued, on the other hand, that their own expenses were so high that they were unable to increase performers' salaries. The dispute resulted in a stalemate, shutting down all Broadway theatres.

Both sides agreed that the core of the problem was Broadway's hit-or-miss mentality. A well-reviewed production that caught the public's imagination was likely to run for a year or more; anything less was likely to close in less than a month. But audiences cannot be forced to buy tickets for plays they do not wish to see.

Producers maintained that they were earning smaller profits than before because of rising expenses and were thus in no position to increase salaries. An option was to raise ticket prices, thereby making it possible for actors to be compensated more fairly during their periods of employment, but producers generally believed that the public would not pay higher prices.[7] Each side threatened to sue the other.

---

7 This concern now seems ironic, at best, for the top price for a Broadway musical in 1960 was $9.45. More than forty years later, an orchestra seat can cost in excess of $100.

Hart, then president of the Authors League, was asked to serve as an informal mediator. He worked out an agreement for a four-year contract with the counsels for the League of New York Theatres and Actors' Equity, specifying salary increases for actors on Broadway, in rehearsal, and on the road. In addition, for the first time, Equity performers would be enrolled in a pension plan. The proposal was immediately agreed to by both sides, and, after a week of dark theatres, Broadway's shows reopened.

Hart intended to return to *Camelot*, but an unexpected delay occurred when, toward the end of July, Lerner suddenly found himself unable to concentrate. Moreover, he could not sleep and had no appetite; his entire life seemed to be deteriorating. Hart and Loewe could do nothing until Lerner completed a lyric for an important song, "If Ever I Would Leave You." But Lerner, groggy from lack of sleep, was unable either to complete the lyric or to revise the second act. Thus, work that *had* to be completed before the production could go into rehearsal, came to a standstill. And the first rehearsal, scheduled for early September, was only a few weeks away.

Lerner called Hart, hoping to consult the director's psychoanalyst. Dr. Kubie was then practicing in Baltimore, but he gave Lerner the name of a psychiatrist in Great Neck, New York, to whose office Lerner immediately drove. The doctor diagnosed depression, a disease with which Hart was all too familiar, but was a new—and devastating—experience for Lerner. With no time to undergo lengthy psychiatric treatment, Lerner asked for medication, which the doctor agreed to prescribe with the understanding that Lerner would see him twice a week. As the medication took hold, Lerner's symptoms subsided and he completed the script on the last day of August— but only by laboring all day and well into the evening, then, after a brief sleep, beginning the process once again.

On September 3, rehearsals began on schedule. Robert Goulet recalled that Hart arranged a "very civilized" schedule, rehearsing from 11 A.M. until 5 P.M., then, after a leisurely dinner, resuming at 8:30 until 11:00.

The first read-through made the producers aware how much work needed to be done, for the play was still far too long: considerably more than three hours. Still, Lerner said, "no one fully realized the extent of the problems"— except Moss Hart, who, with the approval of his co-producers, began making cuts during nearly every rehearsal. A less-respected director might have aroused animosity with his frequent recommendations for cutting material that highly accomplished artists had labored over for months, but Hart was universally respected, even revered, by the *Camelot* company. When he cut an entire ballet that Hanya Holm had choreographed—a ballet of stunning beauty but one that failed to advance the plot or develop the characters—the decision was accepted without resentment, for it was apparent that it had improved the production.

Hart also believed that Lerner and Loewe should excise a twelve-minute musical sequence, but, not wanting to overrule his collaborators without their wholehearted approval, suggested that the sequence be seen by an audience before a final judgment was reached. As it turned out, it took only one performance in Toronto to convince the composer and lyricist that Hart was right. The sequence was dropped.

Every director possesses a unique style when relating to actors. Some are dictatorial, insisting that performers adopt their approach to the exclusion of all others. Such directors refuse to allow their actors to interpret their roles in ways that clash with the director's view. Some go so far as to give line readings, eliminating nearly all of the actor's creativity. At the other extreme, some directors have only the vaguest idea about how the actors should approach their roles, hoping that the performers will make meaningful discoveries on their own. And still others, although they have firmly decided upon an interpretation, prefer to make suggestions, gently guiding the actors to the best possible performances, thus allowing the actors more latitude than the dictatorial director but less than the *laissez-faire* director.

None of these approaches can be termed "correct," for directors of every sort have presented successful productions. However, most actors prefer to be nurtured rather than commanded, and most are frustrated by a director who seems to have abdicated directorial responsibility. Hart's style was to be meticulously prepared for each rehearsal but not to impose his will upon performers. Rather, he sought to work collaboratively with each one, while slowly, painstakingly, bringing out the best each performer had to offer.

"He was a very helpful director," Robert Goulet said, "always very kind. Instead of telling me what to do, he'd say, 'Bobby, try this.' He had a great sense of humor, and, of course, he was very bright." Goulet recalls Hart taking him out to Sardi's one night, helping to establish a sense of camaraderie between director and performer. "Bobby," Hart said, "stick with me and you'll be wearing platinum."

Goulet, charmed by Hart's manner throughout the rehearsal process, savored his relationship with the director. "I adored the man," he said.

Goulet's comment could be applied to virtually all the members of the company. Hart's calm demeanor and his firm control of rehearsals encouraged the actors to believe that each of them would succeed and that the production, too, would win plaudits.

Everyone hoped that Hart's cutting would reduce the musical to a more acceptable running time. Somehow, though, the reverse occurred. At the first performance prior to the Broadway opening, given at Toronto's O'Keefe Center on October 2, 1960, the final curtain of *Camelot* did not descend until 12:40 A.M. Everyone was dismayed. In addition, the theatre itself presented difficulties. *Camelot* was the first production given there, and, even as rehearsals were progressing, workmen were hammering and sawing away. In addition, the theatre's problems—poor acoustics, a mammoth auditorium containing more than 3,000 seats, mechanical equipment that refused to function—became *Camelot*'s problems, making the show seem all the more laborious.[8] Indeed, the producers felt that *Camelot* was in such ragged shape that, despite having cut fifteen minutes from the running time, they contemplated delaying the New York opening from November 19 to December 3.

The producers had agreed to open in Toronto in the hope that the usual Broadway crowd that attended openings in New Haven or Philadelphia would not venture north of the Canadian border. When a show is in rough shape—and *Camelot* was in *extremely* rough shape—the last thing one needs is well-wishers (or those who pretend to be well-wishers but are secretly delighted that the play is in trouble) who will commiserate with the authors and director, then eagerly spread the news in New York that the production is in disarray. But the O'Keefe Center's publicity department, trying to promote their new theatre and not realizing the mischief their scheme would cause, paid for two planes to bring curious theatergoers, most of them theatrical insiders, to Toronto from New York.

When the insiders returned to Manhattan, they let it be known, gleefully or regretfully, that *Camelot* was destined for failure. Fortunately for the company, their comments had little impact on the theatregoing public, for *Camelot* seemed to be one show that was gossip-proof. Surely, the public felt, Alan Jay Lerner, Frederick Loewe, Moss Hart, and Julie Andrews, fresh from their triumph with *My Fair Lady*, would present another smash hit. Consequently, advance sales for the musical broke all records. A single advertise-

---

8 No new theatre is problem-free. Eventually, with luck, the problems are ironed out and the theatre functions smoothly. But that transformation requires time—sometimes months, sometimes years. In the case of *Camelot*, there was not enough time. Although the acoustics were adjusted after the opening performances, little could be done about the other problems. The production was, therefore, performed in a space that was ill-equipped to show it at its best.

ment in *The New York Times* brought in a flood of mail orders. Long before *Camelot*'s New York opening at the Majestic Theatre in December, 1960, the box office was selling tickets through June, 1961.

That the public should be enthusiastic about a forthcoming production would ordinarily be pleasing to its creators. In the case of *Camelot*, however, the enthusiasm, bordering on hysteria, only added to their concern. Unrealistic expectations of unalloyed success could result in surly critics and disappointed audiences. Lerner and Loewe felt the pressure even more keenly when *Time* magazine featured them in a cover story. When the story, which predicted failure for *Camelot*, appeared, the librettist and composer, as well as many of the performers in the company, felt that they had been victims of a hatchet job.

One unqualifiedly positive aspect of the enormous advance sale for *Camelot* was that the producers were as free of budgetary concerns as it is possible for producers to be. If writing a new scene entailed new costumes or sets, the budget could always be expanded to cover the expenses, as long as CBS, the production's funding source, agreed.

Lerner, Loewe, and Hart worked furiously to cut unnecessary material and to reshape what remained. After each performance, they would retreat to a hotel room and rewrite portions of the play. In the morning the new material was given to the cast, who, after a brief time for memorization, rehearsed it in the afternoon and played it at night. Then the cycle began all over again. For Hart, in particular, the schedule was grueling. As the director, he had to watch every performance and rehearse the cast; and as an unofficial collaborator on the script—not to mention his involvement as co-producer—he had to be present at all rewriting sessions. The pressure of work left little time for thought and no time whatever for rest. This prompted him to say publicly that *Camelot* was the most difficult show with which he had ever been associated, an admission that carried particular weight, coming as it did from a man who had worked as playwright or director (and sometimes as both) on some of the largest, most complex productions ever mounted on Broadway. Directing *My Fair Lady* had been "a picnic" compared with *Camelot*, he said later. Moreover, he vowed that he would never have anything to do with a musical again. Julie Andrews "sensed that [Hart] did not have the huge energy he had on *Fair Lady*. He was clearly tired, perhaps due to the weight of the enormous task of trying to do justice to the T. H. White novel."

As stressful as the process was for Hart, however, Lerner was the first of the producers to collapse. A series of dizzy spells prompted him to call a doctor, who insisted that Lerner, who was hemorrhaging internally, be taken to Toronto's Wellesley Hospital. Ultimately, his doctors determined that the bleeding was caused by an ulcer, and Lerner was confined to the hospital for two weeks. Hart sent a message to Lerner's room, saying that he should not worry about the production but should concentrate on recuperation.

Until that time, a postponement of the Broadway opening was only a theoretical possibility. Lerner's illness made a delay inevitable. Hart announced to the press on October 11 that *Camelot* would require an additional two weeks on the road. "The likelihood is that [Lerner] will be in the hospital for ten days," Hart said. "Obviously, nothing can be done until he gets out . . ." He meant precisely what he said, refusing to make any further cuts until he could discuss them with Lerner. To do otherwise, he felt, would be disloyal and unfair.

Hart, despite experiencing a severe toothache that alarmed Kitty Carlisle (because his heart attack in 1954 had been preceded by a toothache), continued to rehearse and refine the production but now under the added pressure of having to do so without the contributions of the librettist. The strain proved to be too much. At the very moment that Lerner was being released from the hospital, on the late afternoon of October 14, Hart was being admitted. He had suffered a heart attack in his hotel room after having worked much of the day at the O'Keefe Center.

Hart's family had just arrived in Toronto from New York. As Catherine Hart, who was ten years old at the time, vividly recalls, she, her mother, and her brother had just gotten into a taxi.

> We were just going to meet him at the hotel and the radio was on and there was music playing. Then there was suddenly no music and it was a news report and here we were in the cab going to meet him at the hotel. It was a bulletin about "Moss Hart, heart attack." We couldn't quite hear. There was static and for the rest of the taxicab ride to the hotel it was just horrible because my mother, of course, feared the worst. I had no idea what was going on, really. We got to the hotel and we took the elevator and there was a long hallway leading from the elevator. A bunch of people were outside his room. And I saw my mother running from the elevator to his room and realized that something horrible had happened.

Kitty spoke to the doctor, who assured her that the attack was a mild one and that Hart would be out of the hospital in two weeks. But this was Hart's second heart attack within six years, and, mild though it might be, it was cause for great concern. Hart had been a cigarette and cigar smoker from the time he was a young man until his wife persuaded him to stop in 1953. Afterward, he continued to puff on a pipe and, on stressful occasions, went back to cigarettes. His diet had always been rich. And he was fifty-five years old.

Kitty entered the hospital room, which, she said,

> was very small and dark, and the bed was so low it was almost as if Moss were on a stretcher on the floor. He looked awful. He'd had the aching tooth pulled, and there was blood at the corner of his mouth. I knelt down on the floor to be nearer, and murmured words that were really just cooing noises. Moss took my hand and held it with surprising strength. "Go immediately to Alan's room and tell him to take over the direction of the play until I'm well enough to come back, and not to look for anyone else." I hesitated to leave him, but he said, "It's important. Go now."

After delivering the message, Kitty returned to the room, only to find it empty. She was overwhelmed with the thought that her husband had died. But someone led her to another room, where she found Hart asleep in a proper bed.

The doctors did not consider Hart's attack to be critical and described his condition to the press as "satisfactory," but, as Lerner said, "he was a very sick man and there was no doubt he would be a very sick man for a very long time." He was placed in an oxygen tent and told that the doctors' original prediction that he would need to be hospitalized for only two weeks might have to be revised upward. The chance of his rejoining *Camelot* before its New York opening was virtually nonexistent.

The theatrical world was saddened by Hart's illness. George S. Kaufman wrote to express his distress at his former collaborator's plight. Brooks Atkinson wrote to Hart on November 2, "Dear Moss: I was in Boston when I read about your heart attack. It was front-paged on the Boston newspapers, which gives you some notion of the national importance of anything that happens to you. You have been flourishing so breezily for so many years that I had forgotten your medical history in this respect. I am sure you are recovering, and that sooner or later you will be as healthy as you have been for several years." Helen Hayes wrote, "I think about you all the time. Who doesn't?"

Hart's friends outside the theatrical community also rallied to his support. Whitney Griswold, the president of Yale, wrote, "hoping that it is not serious and that you will soon be back in the fray. How you have managed to survive all these openings this long has always been a mystery to your ever-admiring fellow hypochondriac but you have; and you will, therefore, survive this one."9

---

9 Hart and Griswold had become friends earlier in 1960 when Hart spent a week at Yale as Visiting Fellow of Arts and Letters. He attended seminars and met with students of playwriting, directing, acting, and design.

And Adlai Stevenson wrote, on October 28, "I just want you to know that you have been very much in my thoughts these past two weeks . . . If Kitty has any trouble keeping you under control, tell her that I am available!"

The cast of *Camelot* remained unaware of the severity of Hart's condition, according to Goulet, who said they only knew that Hart was ill. Julie Andrews said, "It did cause a great deal of worry," but she, too, knew only that Hart "was really unwell" rather than having suffered a heart attack. Therefore, when Lerner told the performers that he would temporarily be taking over the direction, they were not unduly alarmed.

Lerner's task was made easier by the support of the highly respected Richard Burton. "Both on stage and off he was the King in every sense of the word," Lerner said. Julie Andrews also recalls the effort having been "spearheaded by Richard." So the cast followed him in accepting Lerner's modifications without resistance.

The company was, in Julie Andrews's words, "unique. We had such a sense of family. *The Once and Future King* was such an amazing body of work that we all felt a tremendous obligation to somehow make it work."

Lerner claimed that the directorial assignment would be temporary. Loewe strongly believed that a new director should be hired, leaving the authors free for rewriting sessions. Equally important, he felt that a new director could give them a fresh perspective on the production. Ultimately, Lerner and Loewe agreed to look for a new director after *Camelot* completed its run in Toronto. Their choice was José Ferrer, but Ferrer was not available. For a while it was rumored that Joshua Logan, who had directed *South Pacific* eleven years before, would take over. In the end, however, the search for a new director was unsuccessful.

Lerner, who had planned to shepherd the production to Boston and then to New York, periodically was forced to take some time off in order to rewrite the book and lyrics. When he did, Philip Burton stepped in, less in a directorial capacity than to provide someone to keep the rehearsals progressing smoothly. For the most part, however, Lerner remained in charge until the Broadway opening.

Philip Burton was Richard Burton's mentor. The actor, whose real name was Richard Jenkins, had taken Philip Burton's last name to honor the man who gave him vocal coaching, inspired his love for the theatre, and helped him win a scholarship to Oxford University. In the words of Bud Widney, Philip Burton was asked to take over during Lerner's absences because Lerner "was very anxious to have somebody who would give Richard Burton security. Richard was drinking very heavily and, although he was marvelous, he was an unknown factor in terms of emotional stability—and Alan needed him desperately because he [Lerner] was in a very vulnerable situation."

Camelot continued to take a terrible toll on those associated with the production. Added to the list of those who suffered illness or death during their connection with *Camelot* was Hugh Walker, the director of the O'Keefe Center, who, like Lerner, developed a bleeding ulcer and was hospitalized late in October. Frederick Loewe also suffered from illness throughout the rehearsal process. Julie Andrews recalls that Loewe "seemed more ill than Lerner."

In mid-November, Hart returned home to New York, where he was confined for two more months, permitted only to speak on the telephone for five minutes every other day. When *Camelot* opened at the Majestic Theatre in New York on December 3, he was unable to attend. Still terrified by the memory of his 1954 heart attack, he made no attempt to visit the theatre, and suffer the stress that opening nights always caused him.[10]

Lerner had done a solid job (he did not receive directorial credit, just as Hart received no authorial credit). Thus the *Camelot* that opened in New York was both better and somewhat shorter than the *Camelot* Hart had last seen in Toronto—but not enough to make a difference. The tone of the second act still clashed jarringly with the tone established in the first act. Before the New York opening, Oliver Smith, the scenic designer, had strongly urged Lerner to cut the second act entirely and expand the first, but Lerner elected not to act on the suggestion. Instead, he gave some thought to beginning the play with its final scene, thus alerting the audience to the tragic dimensions the play would eventually assume, then flashing back to the beginning. But, concerned about making such a major change so late in the process, Lerner decided against it, having already rewritten "more than half of the first act . . . and most of the second."

Most of the New York reviews regarded the production as a failure. All of the critics had serious reservations about its quality, and nearly all of them compared it unfavorably to *My Fair Lady*.

---

10 When I interviewed Julie Andrews, she said she had a memory of Hart's having seen the opening night in New York and speaking with her afterward, saying, "We'll be back after a few months to rework" the production. But *The New York Times'* version of the event—that Hart did not see *Camelot* until February—is supported by Bud Widney. Kitty Carlisle Hart confirms she attended the opening without her husband, who was under doctors' orders to remain at home. Perhaps, as Andrews allows, it may have been Lerner rather than Hart who spoke to her after opening night.

Howard Taubman, the new critic for *The New York Times*, called *Camelot* only "a partly enchanted city. At the outset the new musical . . . glows with magic [but] unfortunately *Camelot* is weighed down by the burden of its book. The style of the storytelling is inconsistent. It shifts uneasily between light hearted fancy and uninflected reality."

In his Sunday piece written on December 11, Taubman added, "It is no longer a secret that *Camelot* is not another *My Fair Lady*. . . . What everyone . . . hoped for was a musical that would have a freshness and fragrance of its own. *Camelot* merely hints at what might have been."

Each critic seemed to have his own prescription for *Camelot*. One thought the material should have been treated farcically. Another wished the unhappy ending had been omitted. Many felt that the comedy provided by Pellinore and Morgan Le Fay was labored.

Julie Andrews felt that the critics were "puzzled" by the production. As she described *Camelot* and the critical reaction it received, she told me, "The first scene is a little play within itself; it is enchanting. The press seemed to hope that it would continue from there, but the piece becomes very dark as it goes on. I think the press felt cheated of that opening deliciousness—the look of it, the joy of it. But Alan wanted to lead the audience to a darker place; the original novel had a heartbreaking ending. The press implied that they didn't wish to be taken there." However, neither she nor Robert Goulet felt a negative response from the audience. Indeed, Goulet recalls audience reaction as "enthusiastic." Andrews attributes much of the enthusiasm to Richard Burton's performance. Burton "was such an awesome talent," she said, "and the audiences adored him. In a way it was Richard's show. People came to see the great actor. He was brilliant. He could do no wrong even on a night when he was somewhat the worse for wear."

Lerner recalled things differently, however. According to him, theatregoers, as well as reviewers, appeared to resent the fact that the new musical was not up to the standard of *My Fair Lady*. Many audience members attended the production with a sense of resignation, he said, having already decided that *Camelot* would be a letdown. Lerner believed this attitude was clearly felt by the performers who became apprehensive about facing each new audience—with the result that, in Lerner's estimation, whatever buoyancy the production had had before its New York opening slowly drained away. However, neither Julie Andrews nor Robert Goulet felt nearly as unhappy as Lerner did.

Andrews does not recall audience reaction as particularly negative. She knew that the production needed work, but Lerner assured her that he intended to make changes in the script and that Hart would take over the direction once again. Based on those assurances, she was confident that the necessary alterations would eventually be made. In the meantime, her spirits remained high, as did Goulet's.

Not until two months after its opening did Hart see the production. After his first viewing of *Camelot*, he defended the musical. Yes, "there are imperfections," he said in the course of an interview, "but at least it aspires and it has quality." However, he knew very well that *Camelot* still needed rewriting and that the production was badly in need of polishing. Fortunately, he had ideas about how to accomplish both goals—and not a moment too soon, because by February 1961, the ticket sales for *Camelot* had all but dried up. Lerner took stock of the dismal reality, as he perceived it: "There was hardly any window sale at all and people were walking out of the theatre not by the dozens, but some nights by as much as two to three hundred. . . . [T]he word of mouth was not good . . ."

But no one else can recall such dissatisfaction on the part of the audience. Bud Widney, the production manager, suggests that Lerner's view was far bleaker than anyone else's. Widney agrees that "we were boring our audience; we were still too long and some people's patience ran out and they left," but is certain that Lerner's estimate that two to three hundred people walked out on some performances is greatly exaggerated. Widney said when I spoke to him, "That was Alan's way of dramatizing the trouble we were in." In general, Widney recalls, "We were sold out for the first six months and they were responsive houses, although not as responsive as they could have been and as they ultimately became. But I don't remember any disgruntled cast and I don't remember anybody calling up their agent and saying, 'Get me out of this turkey.' I think that the person who was disgruntled was Alan because he knew the piece could and should have been a lot better."

As production manager, Widney stayed in constant touch with Lerner and Hart, saying, "Fellas, we've got work to do. . . . This thing is too long. Let's get to work on it." As a result of Widney's prodding, Lerner, Loewe, and Hart met as soon as Hart's doctors allowed. "Alan, Moss and Fritz all sat together and analyzed what needed to be done and did it," Widney said.

The course of *Camelot* was changed by two events. The first was Hart's reinstatement as director. Viewing the production once again after such a long interval, he was able to see clearly what needed to be altered. When he announced to the cast that the production would be re-rehearsed during the day while the performances continued at night, the actors welcomed the alterations. Hart discussed his suggestions for improving the production with

Lerner and Loewe, after which Lerner did some rewriting of the book and, with the agreement of all the collaborators, two songs—one performed by Julie Andrews, the other by the chorus—were cut. Hart assembled the cast and, working primarily on the second act, made additional cuts and revisions, which, all in all, were substantial. It was, Julie Andrews said, "the first time I know of a piece being reworked once it had actually opened on Broadway." Without sacrificing the musical's best qualities, Hart found a way at last to end the production at eleven-fifteen rather than just before midnight.

Still, Hart's work might have gone for naught if it were not for the second event: CBS, the backer of the production, arranged to present four of the musical numbers and some of the dialogue on its highly rated television series, *The Ed Sullivan Show*. One Sunday in March 1961, Sullivan not only devoted his program entirely to Lerner and Loewe, he gave them permission to structure the show as they liked. Rather than perform songs from previous productions by the composer and librettist, as was standard on such occasions, the producers decided to present Richard Burton, Julie Andrews, and Robert Goulet in a seventeen-minute segment comprised entirely of songs from *Camelot*. Conventional wisdom said that to present so much material from the production would only further harm its prospects because the television audience would conclude that they had seen the best of *Camelot* and would not purchase tickets. But conventional wisdom was wrong. The very next morning, long lines formed at the box office. These spectators proved to be vastly different from those who had previously demonstrated dissatisfaction. The new audiences that came to see the production had neither read the reviews nor heard the negative reports. They knew only what had been shown on the Ed Sullivan show, and they liked what they saw in the theatre: a much-improved *Camelot*.

"The change in audience reaction . . . gathered momentum as the play progressed," Lerner said, "and as the wave of approval came sweeping over the orchestra pit it not only raised [the cast's] spirits, but the level of the performance." Indeed, Julie Andrews said that the actors were elated by the audience's more enthusiastic reception.

Hart's cuts, Lerner's rewriting, and the newly rehearsed material gave the musical the sharpness and clarity that had eluded it for so long. "The reaction and the applause were overwhelming," Lerner said. "The people came up the aisles raving. *Camelot* was finally a hit." Lerner, beaming, saw Hart onstage after the show that night and acknowledged the directorial magic he had wrought. "You son of a bitch!" he said. "How dare you give me an inferiority complex?"

Julie Andrews agreed that the production "certainly did get better," but she believes "it was never quite the show that we thought it could be. We knew we didn't have it completely. Everybody, Alan, Richard, Moss, myself, the entire company felt that it could be extremely special, but we never did quite pull it off." Still, audiences "were in awe of Richard and his great speech at the end of the first act [and] the sadness at the end of the second act."

Even a full year after the opening, the company discussed and attempted to improve the production. "There were many evenings," Julie Andrews recalled, "when we would go and have a drink after the show and someone would say, 'Do you think if I did this here that it would help there?'—that kind of thing. I have never known a company so in love with the message of the piece. We all felt the same, and with Richard as our leader, we were fanatical. It had to have been partly inspired by the magic of T. H. White's original piece."

The satisfaction of the audiences can be seen in the length of the run: ultimately, *Camelot* gave 837 performances on Broadway, playing successfully in London[11] and on tour throughout the United States. It is one of the few cases on record of an American theatrical production that faltered at the beginning of its Broadway run but became a runaway success. *Camelot* was helped immeasurably by the enormous sales of its original cast album. And, of course, the very name of the play became the symbol of John F. Kennedy's presidency, a development that did not harm the play's popularity at all. Even today, the melody of the title song evokes a wistful longing in a certain segment of the population for a political leader whose promise was cut short so tragically.

One day during the run of *Camelot*, Hart encouraged Julie Andrews to think about playing Liza in a revival of *Lady in the Dark*. "To my shame," she now says, "I didn't bite. Having been so dazzled by *My Fair Lady* and *Camelot*, it was not something that appealed at the time. It felt a little dated. But of course I now wish that I had jumped at the chance." (Andrews did eventually play Gertrude Lawrence, however, in the 1968 film musical *Star!* in which she sang "The Saga of Jenny.")

For Hart, his achievement with *Camelot* was bittersweet. Was the ultimate triumph worth the years of frustration while he and Lerner tried to put together a workable book, the months of grueling rehearsals, the deaths and illnesses of his friends, and his own heart attack? If he had been aware in advance

---

11 *Camelot* claimed still another victim in 1963, when the London production opened. Fritz Loewe asked Kitty Carlisle Hart to attend the opening night. As she descended from the plane, she was given the news that her brother-in-law, Bernie Hart, who had been an assistant stage manager on *Camelot*, had died of a heart attack.

that *Camelot* would represent a Faustian bargain—his health in exchange for one more theatrical triumph—would he have initiated the project? In the throes of the production he never gave a hint that he wanted to withdraw, but his vow never to do another musical certainly indicates some regret that he had become involved.

Kitty Carlisle Hart, asked whether, given all the stresses associated with *Camelot*, her husband had at any time given any thought to withdrawing from the production, answered, "No. That was not the sort of thing he would do when the going got tough. You don't moan and groan and say, oh dear, I shouldn't have gotten into this one. You put your shoulder to the wheel and you do the best you can. And after the heart attack, when he was allowed to go back to the theatre, he went back and he fixed it as well as it could be fixed."

Chapter 13 FINALE
1960–1961

DESPITE THE PRIDE HART TOOK IN THE EVENTUAL SUCCESS OF *CAMELOT*, he could not escape another bout of depression. And this time the source of the depression was hardly mysterious: his recent heart attack had given him good reason to be concerned about how much longer he had to live, and he must have wondered if he could continue to be productive as an artist in the theatre.

After the second heart attack, he lost much of the vitality that had characterized him in the past. The man who had been a veritable mountain of energy for more than thirty years aged rapidly. His wife observed, "he couldn't walk in the wind, he grew tired easily, and worst of all he was frightened"— frightened of death, frightened of becoming an invalid, frightened that he could no longer summon the creative force that had sustained him for so many years.

Chris Hart and his sister, Cathy, then thirteen and ten, respectively, were not aware of their father's depressions. "Depression," Chris said recently, "didn't manifest itself in terms of feeling sad or blue or being mopey." When his father was depressed, Chris observed, "it was done in a solitary way. He certainly didn't impose it on the family."[1]

It must have taken a superhuman effort for Moss not to burden his children with his feelings, for he was often so downcast that each day was an ordeal. "One morning in Beach Haven," Kitty Carlisle said, "I woke up early and found the bed empty. I looked out of the window and saw a lonely figure walking way down the beach. I pulled on some clothes and ran and ran and finally caught up with him. He turned, put his hands on my shoulders, and leaned heavily on me, his beautiful eyes veiled with misery. 'I couldn't make it without you,' he said."

Despite his private anxieties, on occasion Hart could create at least the appearance of the jovial, debonair personality of the past. In March 1961, he and his wife appeared jointly on the Academy Awards television program,

---

1 Chris believes that his father suffered from what is now called bi-polar disorder (formerly manic-depression). "My understanding of it was he was more manic depressive than clinically depressed," he said. "I noticed the sort of wild upswings when he was being effusive and buying stuff and redecorating the different houses."

handing out the Oscars for best screenplay based on material from another medium to Richard Brooks (for *Elmer Gantry*) and for best story and screenplay written directly for the screen to Billy Wilder and I. A. L. Diamond (for *The Apartment*). He looked the very picture of robust health and confidence. Edna Ferber wrote to the Harts, "It was refreshing and reassuring to see you two civilized, self-possessed, well-dressed and cerebral human beings as contrast to the dullness and bad taste that dominated the Oscar Awards program. You were like beings from another planet." But prodigies of energy were needed to summon up the strength for such moments.

Hart suffered another blow when George S. Kaufman died on June 2, 1961, at the age of seventy-one. Kaufman's death was devastating to all the people he had known and worked with, but particularly to his long-time partner. Two days later, at Kaufman's funeral in New York, Hart delivered the eulogy, which said, in part,

> The people who worked with him in the theatre and all of us, his friends, owe him a . . . debt, a very special one. He was a unique and arresting man, and there are few enough unique people in anyone's time. Nature does not toss them up too often. And part of our loss is that we will not know again the uniqueness and the special taste and flavor that was George. But part of our solace is that we were lucky to have known him—that he lived in our time.

One of the things that sustained Hart during this difficult time was his love for his family. For example, he wrote a letter to his daughter, Cathy: "Dearest Muffin Girl, I can hardly wait to see the kind of grown-up you are going to become. But even when you are an old, old lady you will always be my Muffin Girl. I will always be jealous of *all* your boy friends and I will HATE your husband until I get used to the idea. I love you like a Sputnik up to the moon."

He also hoped to find fulfillment in writing another play. He was beginning work on a new comedy at the time of Kaufman's death. However, his increasing states of depression had robbed him of confidence in his ability. He wrote to the playwright Howard Lindsay, "I've just started a new play—and I cannot believe I ever wrote a decent line of dialogue in my life. Absolute and terrifying stage-fright! Does it never stop?"

His insecurity is poignantly evident in a conversation he had with Alan Jay Lerner, in which he described the plot of his new play, but, he said, he was not certain he was capable of finishing it satisfactorily. Instead, Hart offered the plot to Lerner, suggesting that he complete the project. Lerner protested that Hart could write the play far better than he, Lerner, could. "Everything about this little incident touched me deeply," Lerner said, "because it was so typical of everything that was Moss. I knew his offer was sincere. At the same time I knew that one of the reasons he was reluctant to write it was because of the hell of his own insecurity. In spite of all his years of success and the universal recognition of his talents . . . I know of no man so tortured by self-doubt and so nobly gifted at concealing it."

Lerner thanked Hart for his offer, but declined, encouraging his friend to continue working on the play.

The Harts sold their duplex apartment in New York and moved to Palm Springs in November 1961, intending to live permanently in California. According to Christopher Hart, Moss's "doctors thought the New York winters would be too hard on his health" and suggested that he "move to a warmer climate."[2]

Hart's thirty-one-year career in the cauldron of the New York theatre had taken its toll. More than anything else, he needed peace and quiet, at least for most of the year. Then, if all went well, he and his family planned to travel to various locations during the summer months, when the heat in Palm Springs became unbearable. No longer in need of money, thanks to the continuing income from *My Fair Lady*, he could concentrate on his new play without pressure of a deadline.

Christopher was sent ahead of the rest of the family in order to start the new school year in September at a boarding school, the Cate School, in Santa Barbara. The rest of the family arrived in Palm Springs at the beginning of December.

In mid-December 1961, Moss experienced a pain in his jaw. Both his heart attacks in 1954 and 1960 had been preceded by toothaches, so his wife was instantly alert to the possibility that this new pain might be a warning of another heart attack.

Hart's physician gave him an electrocardiogram and reported that no new heart damage had occurred, but Kitty remained concerned. Of course, the children had no such fear. Christopher, home from boarding school for Christmas vacation, said, "I knew that he had been sick before, and it was serious, but he always got better, and everything got back to normal each time." But the pain in Hart's jaw did not go away.

Early in the morning of December 20, Kitty backed the car out of the garage to take her husband to the dentist when he collapsed on the grass next to the driveway. Kitty and the Harts' servants managed to carry Moss inside,

---

2 "How my father imagined he could live without New York, the city of his birth, or more specifically Broadway, I'll never really understand," Chris said.

where they attempted artificial respiration, but it was too late. "I was awakened by my mother screaming," Christopher said. "I knew immediately what had happened. A woman makes a sound like that only once in her life, hopefully." Almost two months after observing his fifty-seventh birthday, Moss was dead, probably before he hit the ground. In any case, he spoke no final words before he died.

Christopher, in a bedroom off the living room, sat up in bed, whispering out loud, "Please don't let him die, please don't let him die." He heard his mother and the butler, Charles, bring Moss's body inside and call the doctor, but did not come out of his room, "perhaps because I was petrified, or perhaps because I thought I could forestall the reality of the situation by not going out there and witnessing it."

Shortly afterward, however, Christopher entered the living room and saw his father dead on the sofa. "My mother was touching him and holding him as she explained he was gone. I tried to comfort her, but to no avail." He suggested that Kitty tell Cathy what had happened.

Cathy, whose bedroom, like Christopher's, was off the living room, was asleep when her father collapsed. She recalled being "awakened by some noise or commotion, and I peeked out in the hall and saw all these strange people, I guess the doctor and maybe a nurse, and there were other people in the living room. I didn't know what it was about but I didn't want to go out there and meet all these strange people. And then some time later, maybe half an hour, my mother came in and took me in her lap and said, 'Daddy's gone.'"

Kitty suggested that she and the children should return to the living room and say farewell to Moss. They all kissed him goodbye for the last time.

Cathy repressed her memory of the next several months; consequently, she has few recollections of the aftermath of her father's death. She does remember two details, however. One was her feeling of isolation at school. "I remember that other kids treated me differently," she said. "You know, at that age, any difference, any distinction, any uniqueness is dealt with by distancing. So I felt very different and estranged from the other kids for a while. And I remember that we recited the Lord's Prayer every day in class: 'Our Father, who art in heaven.' And every time I said that I thought of my father and it made me sad all over again." She also remembers taking the horse, Chester, that her parents had bought her, "out to the desert after school, usually by myself, and just riding."

Of all Hart's friends, several were particularly supportive. One was Irving Lazar, who, among other acts of kindness, made arrangements for Moss's funeral. Another was Joan Axelrod, the wife of playwright George Axelrod, who "looked after Kitty and Cathy and me," Christopher recalled. "Joan took my sister and me out of the house to do things like bowling and horseback riding. Joan allowed the three of us to mourn in our separate ways," but prevented any of them from yielding to total despair. "She understood we were living through a tragedy, but at the same time we had to continue to live. She articulated the irony we felt about the 'holiday spirit' and the 'joyous season of a palm tree yuletide in the desert,' and made us laugh, and for a moment forget."

Kitty Carlisle also mentioned Bennett and Phyllis Cerf as two people who comforted her and helped her through the trying moments in the months after Moss's death. "They were wonderful," she said.

It was not just Hart's family and close friends who felt his loss so keenly. "DEAR MRS HART," a telegram to Kitty began, "NOTHING CAN SAY WHAT IS IN OUR HEARTS TODAY AT SUCH SAD NEWS. AS A GROUP THAT PERFORMS HIS WORK EVERY DAY WE WILL SORELY MISS HIM AND AS INDIVIDUALS WE EACH FEEL A DEEP PERSONAL LOSS." The message was sent by the entire company of *My Fair Lady*, which was still playing on Broadway.

"Much of those three or four days before the funeral was a blur," Chris says now. "I do remember Mom spending every afternoon at the funeral home with the body. She wanted me to come with her one afternoon, so I went. She asked me to wait in the hall while she went into a small viewing room, and I heard her talking to someone. She opened the door [to the hallway], saying, 'Mossie, look who I brought you this afternoon.' The room was just big enough for the open coffin and one chair. She spent an hour chit-chatting and filling him in on the news of the day as though he'd just come home from work." Chris was "extremely uncomfortable" with this conversation, but he recalls being thankful that his mother "was still connected" to his father, "and happy to be with him, still sharing her life with him." When Kitty asked Chris if he wished to be alone with the body, however, Chris "drew the line." That would simply be too morbid for Chris, who "never cried" during the days leading up to the funeral.

Cathy Hart recalls "that the thing that was most helpful to [Kitty], and kind of got her back on track, was commuting to New York once a week to do *To Tell the Truth*. And she was forever grateful to Goodson and Todman for giving her the opportunity to do that, because when my parents moved to Palm Springs she had left the show. But [when she returned to it] she had to pull herself together once a week, so she traveled and became a functioning professional."

Hart's funeral was held in the Temple Isaiah in Palm Springs on December 22. The three hundred mourners included Frederick Loewe, Harpo Marx, Frank Sinatra, William Goetz, and Billy Wilder. Neither Kitty nor Cathy Hart recalled anyone speaking at the funeral, but Kitty freely admits that "I was totally disoriented for about six months." Hart's body was then taken to Montecito Memorial Park in San Bernardino for cremation. Later, his ashes were interred at Ferncliff Cemetery in Westchester County, north of New York City.

Alan Jay Lerner was asked to write a commemorative essay about Hart for *The New York Times*. He wrote it, he remembered, "with trembling hands and . . . through blurred eyes:"

> Occasionally in one's life there comes a tragedy so vast, so deep, so intense that it reaches out and into so many areas of habit, feeling and living that all words to express it seem false and foolish and even tears are but a meager token. For those of us who were friends of Moss, his death is that kind of tragedy. We will not be the same again.

Later, in his autobiographical memoir, *The Street Where I Live*, Lerner wrote that Hart "forever will be irreplaceable to more people in more ways than any man I have ever known. When he died in 1961, it was more than simply the death of one man. It seemed as if the gods had broken in and robbed us of some of our most precious humanity. For me hardly a day goes by that I do not find myself beginning a sentence with, 'As Moss used to say . . .' He was always the great Moss Hart—and the adjective, for once, is accurate."

If no one spoke at Hart's funeral, many of his friends took the opportunity to pay tribute to him at a memorial service, held in the Music Box Theatre in New York. Eleven hundred people attended, filling every seat and every inch of standing room, to hear Moss eulogized.

Bennett Cerf recalled Moss's ability to bring out the best in others. Somehow those who felt less than eloquent under normal circumstances found that with Moss they became dazzling conversationalists. Cerf commented that people "began living up to Moss's conceptions immediately and saw themselves for the rest of their days as Moss recreated them." He also recalled, "No sooner did [Hart] appear at a party than everybody in the room became a little brighter, a little more assured, just because Moss was there."

On the same occasion, Brooks Atkinson spoke of Hart's exuberance, Edna Ferber about his integrity, ambition, and discipline, and Alan Jay Lerner about his "dignity and grandeur." Dore Schary summed up his view of his old friend in this way:

In a dispute he was logical but firm.
In a conversation he was original and candid.
In a crisis he was resourceful and determined.
He could comfort you in sadness and soothe you in pain.
An act of thoughtfulness toward him would receive extravagant thanks.
But the sharp and acid wit could be turned on, if needed, to quiet the fakir or
 the boor.

დ

When Hart died, the play he had been writing, a comedy about a middle-aged woman and her divorced neighbor, was approximately half-completed. Kitty Carlisle offered Hart's old friend Jerome Chodorov the opportunity to complete it. Knowing that extensive changes would be required in the material and that more than half the play remained to be written, she asked that Hart's name not be listed on the program or included in the advertising. Consequently, Jerome Chodorov is listed as the sole author of *A Community of Two*. The play was produced in 1973, with Claudette Colbert and George Gaynes in the leading roles. The first performances occurred in Wilmington, Delaware, as the first stop on a tour that, it was hoped, would end on Broadway. But the play closed before it reached New York. Reviews from newspapers in Wilmington and Boston found the play tepid, "superficial, old-fashioned . . . [but] amusing and [with] flashes of wit."

For several years after Hart's death, *My Fair Lady* continued to run in New York. Altogether, the musical played on Broadway for six and a half years, closing on September 29, 1962—although it was still turning a considerable profit. Subsequently, Lerner and Loewe generously gave Hart's widow a small percentage of the royalties of *My Fair Lady*, whose companies continued to perform around the world. And when *My Fair Lady* was sold to the movies, the proceeds from the film served as an annuity for Hart's family for many years.

დ

For Kitty, "the bitterness of my loss was constant, and at times unbearable. The worst was the morning I woke up and Moss's black umbrella of despair opened over my head." She even contemplated suicide. But work proved to be the medicine she needed. She remained on *To Tell the Truth*, acted in summer stock, played Prince Orlovsky in *Die Fledermaus* at the Metropolitan Opera, and, at the age of sixty-four, accepted the position of Vice Chairman (later Chairman) of the New York State Council on the Arts. Among the many awards she received was the first-ever Lifetime Achievement Award from Marymount Manhattan College, "in recognition of her distinguished record of excellence in her profession and dedication to the support of humanitarian concerns in the community and society at large."

Christopher Hart gained his first theatrical experience shortly after his father died. When he was fourteen, he served as a "gofer" (his job called for him to go for coffee and go for cigarettes) for *Banderol*, a Broadway play written by Dore Schary. Christopher was then attending the Trinity School in New York City and preparing to transfer to the Millbrook School for boys in Millbrook, New York. Subsequently, he majored in general studies at Harvard, graduating in 1970. He became a producer, director, and writer (for the stage and for television) in California, where he directed several of his father's plays. In 2005, he relocated to the East Coast to continue his theatrical career. He and his wife, Beth, are parents of a daughter, Emma.

Like her brother, Catherine Hart went on to study at Harvard. Later, she earned a graduate degree at the University of Pennsylvania Medical School. She is now in private practice in New York, specializing in internal medicine and infectious diseases. She and her husband, Mark Stoeckle, also a physician, have two children.

Moss Hart's death at a relatively early age was a dreadful misfortune in every sense. But that he should have failed to see his children grow up to become so accomplished in their professional careers and fulfilled in their personal lives is especially poignant.

❧

Hart's primary interest was the theatre and the essence of his personality was theatrical. It has been said of him that he arranged his life like a play. He readily agreed, speaking in *Act One* of his tendency to see events in life as scenes in a play, resolving themselves into three clearly defined acts. He arranged social events at his home with all the precision of a stage director. His passion for designing his homes has obvious parallels with a theatrical designer. He carefully selected clothing for himself and his wife, assuming the function of the costume designer. His behavior was often flamboyant, larger-than-life, theatrical. In his plays, too, he often focused on the theatre. The characters he created were frequently either theatrical personalities or individuals who behaved in a highly theatricalized fashion. "His plays," critic Richard Mason noted, "offer ample evidence that the work was an exceedingly personal extension of the man."

All too often, theatrical historians have dismissed American playwrights who have primarily written comedies and farces as insignificant, trivial, mere commercial hacks. Perhaps that opinion prevails because of the popularity of comedies, including musical comedies, over more somber fare. The attitude of the historians—that whatever is popular cannot be significant—does not extend to fiction, however, where Mark Twain, Kurt Vonnegut Jr., Joseph Heller, and other American comic writers are highly regarded; few critics have dismissed their work or accused their readers of being undiscriminating. It is, therefore, somewhat baffling that American theatregoers have been castigated for their acceptance of comedies, while American readers have been praised for their discernment at discovering outstanding comic writers.

Of course, one could easily enumerate American comic plays that are neither fresh nor inventive nor skillfully written, but have, nonetheless, enjoyed long Broadway runs. But to assume that an entire genre is inferior because of the successes of some inferior plays is an unreasonable judgment. On the contrary, the best American comic plays have enriched our drama as the best comic novels have enriched our fiction.

Is it possible that the tendency for American intellectuals to denigrate comic playwrights derives from our collective experience with serious, sometimes tragic events? Has our national experience with rebellion, war, the betrayal of the native American population, slavery, economic depression, the struggle for civil rights, the care of the needy made comedy seem merely frivolous? Edna Ferber thought so. "We, as a nation, are timorous of the sparkling, the fresh, and the gaily trenchant," she said, adding, "it is the Puritan sourpuss . . . which clings to the belief that if it's gloomy it's good."

Perhaps it is for that reason that Moss Hart's contributions to the American theatre have received less critical praise than they deserve. His gift was undeniably for comedy, and too many critics of the late twentieth, and early twenty-first, century seem to be unaware of the virtues of that form.

Before he achieved success in the theatre, Hart himself, as he said in *Act One*, always thought of himself as a writer whose sensibility would produce tragic drama. But his greatest successes proved to be in the comic vein. Unable to suppress his desire to write in the tradition of "serious drama," he eventually attempted to write more solemn material. Surely the attempt was praiseworthy, for an artist's reach should always exceed his grasp. But it is clear that his forays into non-comic drama were only fitfully successful.

When one focuses on Moss Hart's body of work, the very range of his talent and the extreme variety of those works render it difficult to offer a reasoned critical judgment of his literary-theatrical career. He wrote some plays and films (*Once in a Lifetime, You Can't Take It With You, The Man Who Came to*

Dinner, A Star Is Born, Gentleman's Agreement) that may justly be described as examples of brilliant theatrical writing. *Act One* is by any standard an outstanding memoir, and remains in print more than forty years after it was first issued. *The Climate of Eden*, a vastly underrated play, is a solid contribution to American dramatic art. Several of his works can be categorized as ambitious, but less than fully realized (*Winged Victory, Christopher Blake*). Others, such as *Light Up the Sky, Hans Christian Andersen*, and *George Washington Slept Here*, can only be described as workmanlike, while some of the collaborations with Kaufman (*Merrily We Roll Along, The Fabulous Invalid*, and *The American Way*) are—at least as seen from the perspective of a later generation—interesting but unsatisfactory theatrical experiments.

Hart's contribution to the writing of books for musicals and sketches for revues should not be overlooked. Only *As Thousands Cheer* and *Lady in the Dark* could be described as groundbreaking, but, as musical historian David Ewen said, Hart brought to every musical he wrote "his incisive wit, his trenchant intelligence, his sparkling dialogue, and his impertinence of spirit that made him one of Broadway's foremost writers."

It is impossible to know how much credit to assign Moss Hart for the help he gave to other playwrights who requested his assistance, particularly since he received no credit on those occasions. At times, however, it seems that his help was not only substantial but crucial. In 1954, Billy Rose, who was less than friendly with Hart, sent him a grateful telegram regarding *The Immoralist*, a decidedly non-comic play the showman was producing: "RUTH AND AUGUSTUS GOETZ [the play's authors] READ ME THE FINAL SCENE A FEW MINUTES AGO AND TOLD ME HOW MUCH YOU HAD HELPED THEM. . . . I WOULD BE AN INGRATE IF I DID NOT THANK YOU FOR YOUR CONTRIBUTION . . ."

Hart's best comedies, particularly those written in collaboration with Kaufman, are intriguing both for the traditions they borrowed from earlier American comedy and for the advances they represented. An example of the former is the character of George Lewis from *Once in a Lifetime*; the unsophisticated bumpkin who, against all odds, achieves more success than the ultra-smart characters who surround him.

As an example of an advance in American comedy represented by the Kaufman and Hart comedies, the collaborators created a series of important roles for shrewd, wisecracking women in their plays at a time when few female characters in American comedy rose above subservience to men. Examples from the plays of Kaufman and Hart include May in *Once in a Lifetime* and Annabelle in *George Washington Slept Here*. In addition, although they were less witty, Penny in *You Can't Take It With You* and Maggie Cutler in *The Man Who Came to Dinner* (not to mention Liza in Hart's *Lady in the Dark*) offered actresses large, often pivotal roles. Thus, Kaufman and Hart helped to create a series of roles for women who were, for the most part, brighter and more complex than most female characters who inhabited American comedies.

Although critics may quibble about the value of the plays Hart wrote, there is little division of opinion within the theatrical community itself. One significant sign of the esteem in which he was held was his election in 1972, more than a decade after his death, to the Theatre Hall of Fame. Another, vividly demonstrating Hart's importance to American culture, was the issuance of a postage stamp bearing his image on October 25, 2004.

Given the enormous success of *Once in a Lifetime*, *You Can't Take It With You*, and *The Man Who Came to Dinner*, Kaufman and Hart's influence on the playwrights of their time and on those of future generations was vast. Their best comedies have never gone out of fashion. They are performed continually in America: at regional theatres, in revivals on and off-Broadway, in colleges and universities, at community theatres, and in high schools. The continuing popularity of these comedies assures that playwrights of the future will continue to be influenced by Kaufman and Hart's examples.

Woody Allen told Kitty Carlisle that his life was changed when, as a boy, he read Random House's collection *Six Plays by Kaufman and Hart*. Certainly one can see the influence of Kaufman and Hart in any number of Allen's comic films. (And in Allen's *Radio Days*, he uses Moss Hart's name as a symbol of sophistication and urbanity—and casts Kitty Carlisle in the same film, as another representative of the same qualities.) Larry Gelbart is another gifted comic writer of the present day who indicated that he was "aware at a very young age of these two extraordinary guys," Kaufman and Hart, who were "among those in the torrent of influences early in my life. Their plays were as funny as hell to me." Neil Simon, in his autobiography, *The Play Goes On*, said of Kaufman and Hart, "They were giants; I was not."

When a dramatist chooses to work almost exclusively in collaboration with other writers, it is difficult to generalize about his work. However, one statement can be made about Moss Hart's career as a writer: unlike playwrights who achieve success after success by writing plays so similar that they can hardly be distinguished from one another, Hart seldom fell into a pattern. He (and, if he was working with collaborators, his partners) strove continually to explore fresh territory. Such attempts were occasionally unsuccessful, but the goal—not to permit his art to become stagnant by repeating well-worn formulae—is surely praiseworthy.

Moss Hart's most singular contribution as a playwright was his willingness to reinvent himself with nearly every play he wrote. In this way, he resembles Eugene O'Neill, who attempted to transform himself continually, writing in the forms of realism, expressionism, mask drama, adaptations of Greek drama, the vocalization of inner thoughts. Hart was certainly not as adventurous as O'Neill, but he did explore diverse subjects in a variety of forms.

Hart's record as a director was one of considerable distinction. His productions of plays and musicals as varied as *Winged Victory* and *My Fair Lady* demonstrated an uncommon versatility. Few people outside the theatre are aware of the magnitude of the director's contribution, for, unlike the work of the actor or the designer of sets, lights, and costumes (which can be seen), the director's work is invisible to the audience. Without a knowledgeable, skillful director, however, even the best play will fail to connect with audiences. Moss Hart was a master of that least-understood aspect of theatrical art.

⌘

In late 2004, the hundredth anniversary of Moss Hart's birth, a celebration of Moss and Kitty Carlisle Hart was held at Avery Fisher Hall in Lincoln Center. In the program, hosted by Julie Andrews and Beverly Sills, appearances were made by Rosemary Harris, Robert Goulet, Thomas Hampson, Celeste Holm, Audra McDonald, and many others.

Beverly Sills referred to Kitty Carlisle's "continued presence as a New York living landmark," and Julie Andrews spoke of her twenty-five-year participation on the New York State Council on the Arts: serving as vice-chairman from 1971 to 1976 and as chairman from 1976 to 1996, during which her budget increased from $27 million to $60 million.

Andrews also paid tribute to Moss Hart as the director of *My Fair Lady* and *Camelot*, crediting him with giving her the most profound acting lesson of her career. She also noted, "Very few Americans in the arts have been deemed worthy of appearing on a stamp. That the United States Postal Service has recently selected Moss for this singular honor is a measure of his lasting contribution to our culture."

Chris Hart said that when he was a child, Moss "was my protector, my teacher, and my friend." As an adult, Chris directed many of his father's plays, and said, "Tearing each scene apart as a director is wont to do, I got to watch my father create unique and indelible characters, marvel at the exquisite mechanisms of plot and storytelling, and be moved by the real human emotions generated by his characters, who still have the power to make us laugh and make us cry, even today."

As the occasion at Lincoln Center made clear, Moss Hart had by no means been forgotten. As a writer, a director, and as the friend of many, he remained a beloved figure. One hundred years after his birth and not more than five miles from where he had been born, more than two thousand people had gathered to pay tribute to his (and his wife's) life and career.

෨෮

As readers of *Act One*, Moss Hart's autobiography, will recall, the book ends not with the words *The End*, but with the single word *Intermission*, signaling one or more installments to follow. Now, at the conclusion of *Moss Hart: A Prince of the Theatre*, it seems only appropriate to conclude this book with another word:

CURTAIN

BIBLIOGRAPHY

Among my most important sources were the letters Moss Hart wrote and received from hundreds of people. These are collected at the State Historical Society of Wisconsin and the Billy Rose Theatre Collection of the New York Library of Performing Arts. I have also drawn from many published and unpublished sources, which are listed in the bibliography. *Not* included in the Bibliography are reviews of the plays Moss Hart wrote and directed; the reviews can be found in newspapers published a day or two after the opening of the plays, and in magazines a week or two afterward. Dates for most reviews are given in the Notes.

The following abbreviations are used in the bibliography:

MH = Moss Hart

GSK = George S. Kaufman

KCH = Kitty Carlisle Hart

SHSW = State Historical Society of Wisconsin

NYT = New York Times

BRTC = Billy Rose Theatre Collection, Performing Arts Research Center, New York Public Library for the Performing Arts

I. BOOKS AND MAGAZINE ARTICLES

Arntz, James, and Thomas S. Wilson. *Julie Andrews*. Chicago: Contemporary Books, 1995.

"As Thousands Cheer," *The Stage*. [undated clipping from the State Historical Society of Wisconsin—hereafter abbreviated as SHSW—but evidently from 1933].

Atkinson, Brooks. *Broadway*. New York: The Macmillan Company, 1970.

———, "Introduction," *Six Plays by Kaufman and Hart*. New York: The Modern Library, 1942.

Bach, Steven. *Dazzler: The Life and Times of Moss Hart*. New York, Alfred A. Knopf, 2001.

Ballet, Arthur, "*You Can't Take It With You*," *International Dictionary of Theatre—1: Plays*. Chicago and London: St. James Press, 1992.

Beavan, John, "London Queues Up for Eliza," *New York Times Magazine*, March 9, 1958.

Beebe, Lucius, "Going to It" [clipping from SHSW; no date; unidentified magazine]

Beeson, Paul B. and Walsh McDermott, *Cecil-Loeb Textbook of Medicine*, Twelfth Edition. Philadelphia and London: W. B. Saunders Company, 1967.

Behrman, S. N., "Curtain Going Up! Curtain Going Up!", *New York Times Magazine*, September 20, 1959.

——, "They Left 'em Laughing," *New York Times Magazine*, November 21, 1965.

Bergreen, Laurence, *As Thousands Cheer: The Life of Irving Berlin*. New York: Viking, 1990.

Bigsby, C. W. E. *A Critical Introduction to Twentieth-Century American Drama*, Volume I. Cambridge: Cambridge University Press, 1982.

Blum, Daniel. *Theatre World*. Various seasons, no publisher or dates given.

Boardman, Gerald. "Moss Hart," *The Oxford Companion to the Theatre*. New York and Oxford: Oxford University Press, 1984.

Brenner, Marie. "The Art of Mrs. Hart," *The New Yorker*, July 5, 1993.

——, *Great Dames*. New York: Crown Publishers, 2000.

Brooks, Tim, and Earle Marsh. *The Complete Directory to Prime Time Network TV Shows, 1946-present*. New York: Ballantine Books, 1979.

Brubaker, Howard, "I'd Rather Be Right," *Stage* [clipping from SHSW; no date given].

Carlisle, Kitty. "About the Author," *Theatre Arts*. October 1949.

Celebration of Moss Hart, A. Los Angeles: Friends of the [University of Southern California] Libraries, 1970.

Cerf, Bennett, "With Gaiety and Gusto," *Saturday Review*, January 20, 1962. (Eulogy for MH)

Clarke, Gerald. *Get Happy*. New York: Random House, 2000.

Contemporary Authors, Volume 109. Detroit: Gale Research Company, 1983.

Cook, Bruce. *Dalton Trumbo*. New York: Charles Scribner's Sons, 1977.

Coward, Noël. *Future Indefinite*. London: William Heinemann Ltd., 1954.

Dunning, John. *Tune In Yesterday*. Englewood Cliffs, NJ: Prentice-Hall, 1976.

Eells, George. *The Life That Late He Led: A Biography of Cole Porter*. New York: G. P. Putnam's Sons, 1967.

Eliscu, Edward, *With or Without a Song*. Lanham, MD, and London: The Scarecrow Press, 2001.

Eustis, Morton, "*The Man Who Came to Dinner* With George Kaufman Directing," *Theatre Arts Monthly*, November 1939.

Ewen, David. *Complete Book of the American Musical Theater*. New York: Henry Holt and Company, 1958.

Farber, Stephen and Marc Green, *Hollywood on the Couch*. New York: William Morrow and Company, Inc., 1993.

Fearnow, Mark, *The American Stage and the Great Depression*. Cambridge: Cambridge University Press, 1997.

——, *Clare Boothe Luce*. Westport, CT: Greenwood Press, 1995.

Fenichel, Otto. *The Psychoanalytic Theory of Neurosis*. New York: W. W. Norton & Company, 1945.

Ferber, Edna, "A Rolling Moss Gathers Considerable Heart," *Stage*, December 1936.

Ferguson, Donita, "Mad Marvels." [clipping from SHSW; no date given; magazine unidentified]

Gardner, Mona, "Byron from Brooklyn," *Saturday Evening Post*, undated clipping at SHSW.

Gianakos, Larry James. *Television Drama Series Programming, 1947–1959*. Metuchen, NJ: The Scarecrow Press, Inc., 1980.

Gilbert, Julie Goldsmith. *Ferber: A Biography*. Garden City, NY: Doubleday & Company, Inc., 1978.

Gilder, Rosamond, "The Fabulous Hart," *Theatre Arts*, February 1944.

Goldstein, Malcolm. *George S. Kaufman: His Life, His Theater*. New York and Oxford: Oxford University Press, 1979.

Gordon, Joanne. *Art Isn't Easy: The Theater of Stephen Sondheim*. Updated Edition. New York: Da Capo Press, 1992.

Gould, Jean. *Modern American Playwrights*. New York: Dodd, Mead & Co., 1965.

"Great Waltz, The." [clipping from SHSW, unidentified magazine], 1935.

Green, Stanley. *Ring Bells! Sing Songs! Broadway Musicals of the 1930s*. New Rochelle, NY: Arlington House, 1971.

——, *The World of Musical Comedy*. New York: Grosset & Dunlap, 1962.

Harriman, Margaret Case. *Take Them Up Tenderly: A Collection of Profiles*. Freeport, NY: Books For Libraries Press, originally published 1944, reprinted 1972.

Hart, Kitty Carlisle. *Kitty*. New York: St. Martin's Press, 1988.

Hart, Moss. *Act One*. New York: Random House, 1959.

——, "Before Thousands Cheered," *The Stage* [no date], in MH collection at SHSW.

——, "Foreword" to *The Cole Porter Songbook*. New York, Simon and Schuster, 1959. (A typed copy is at SHSW)

——, "A Graduate Academy," *Theatre Arts*, April 1950.

——, "Men At Work" [on collaboration with GSK], *Six Plays by Kaufman and Hart*. New York: The Modern Library, 1942.

——, "Men At Work" [on collaborations with Irving Berlin and Cole Porter], *Stage*, November 1936.

——, "Moss Hart." *Esquire*, January 1962.

Haver, Ronald. *A Star Is Born: The Making of the 1954 Movie and Its 1983 Restoration*. New York: Alfred A. Knopf, 1988.

Hawkins-Daly, Mark, ed. *International Dictionary of Theatre—2: Playwrights*. Detroit: St. James Press, 1994.

Higham, Charles, and Ray Moseley. *Cary Grant: The Lonely Heart*. New York: Harcourt, Brace, Jovanovich, 1989.

Jablonski, Edward. *Irving Berlin: American Troubador*. New York: Henry Holt and Company, 1999.

"Jubilee Over Here," *Stage* [clipping from SHSW; no date given].

Katz, Ephraim, *The Film Encyclopedia*. New York: Harper Perennial, 1994.

Kaufman, Beatrice, and Joseph Hennessey, eds. *The Letters of Alexander Woollcott*. New York: The Viking Press, 1944.

Kaufman, George S. "Forked Lightning," *Six Plays by Kaufman and Hart*. New York: The Modern Library, 1942.

Krutch, Joseph Wood. *The American Drama Since 1918*. New York: George Braziller, Inc., 1957.

[Kubie, Lawrence; the "author" is listed as "Dr. Brooks"] "Preface" to *Lady in the Dark*. New York: Random House, 1941.

Laufe, Abe. *Broadway's Greatest Musicals*, revised edition. New York: Funk & Wagnalls, 1977.

Lazar, Irving (written in collaboration with Annette Tapert). *Swifty: My Life and Good Times*. New York: Simon & Schuster, 1995.

Lerner, Alan Jay. *The Street Where I Live*. New York and London: W. W. Norton & Company, 1978.

——, "Of 'Sleepers' and 'Wakers,'" *New York Times Magazine*, December 3, 1961.

"*Look* Calls on Moss Hart," *Look Magazine*, March, 1940.

"Mad Marvels," unidentified magazine, clipping, SHSW.

Maney, Richard. "Fabulous Six Months of a Fabulous *Lady*," *New York Times Magazine*, September 9, 1956.

"Many Props," *The New Yorker* [clipping from SHSW; no date given].

Maslon, Laurence. "George S. Kaufman," *American National Biography*. New York and Oxford: Oxford University Press, 1999.

——, "Moss Hart," *American National Biography*. New York and Oxford: Oxford University Press, 1999.

Mason, Richard, "The Comic Theatre of Moss Hart: Persistence of a Formula," *Theatre Annual*, Volume 23, 1967.

Matuz, Roger, ed. *Contemporary Literary Criticism*, Vol. 66. Detroit and London: Gale Research Inc., 1991.

McBrien, William, *Cole Porter*. New York: Alfred A. Knopf, 1998.

McClung, Bruce, Joanna Lee and Kim Kowalke, eds. *Lady in the Dark: A Sourcebook*, second edition. New York: Kurt Weill Foundation for Music, 1977.

McClung, Bruce, "Life after George [Gershwin]: The Genesis of *Lady in the Dark*'s Circus Dream," *Lady in the Dark: A Sourcebook* [see above].

——, "Psicosi per musica: Re-examining *Lady in the Dark*," *Lady in the Dark: A Sourcebook* [see above]

——, "The Saga of *Lady in the Dark*" in the program of the Royal National Theatre's production of *Lady in the Dark*, 1997.

Memorial Tribute to Moss Hart, A. [a booklet issued of the remarks at the Music Box Theatre, January 9, 1962] No publisher or date given.

Meredith, Scott. *George S. Kaufman and His Friends*. Garden City, NY: Doubleday and Company, Inc., 1974.

Merrick, Gordon. *The Lord Won't Mind*. No city specified: Bernard Geis Associates, 1970.

Millstein, Gilbert, "Flowering of a 'Fair Lady,'" *New York Times Magazine*, April 1, 1956.

——, "The Playwright's Ordeal by Fire, Etc.," *New York Times Magazine*, December 12, 1954.

Mordden, Ethan. *The American Theatre*. Oxford: The Oxford University Press, 1981.

Morella, Joseph, and George Mazzei. *Genius and Lust: The Creativity and Sexuality of Cole Porter and Noel Coward*. New York: Carroll & Graf Publishers, Inc., 1995.

"Moss Hart," *Contemporary Literary Criticism*, Volume 66.

"Musical Comedy Express" [about *As Thousands Cheer*]. [Undated clipping from SHSW; perhaps from *The Stage* or *Theatre Guild Magazine*]

Rodgers, Richard. *Musical Stages*. New York: Random House, 1975.

Rogers, Ginger. *My Story*. New York: Harper Collins, 1991.

Ross, Walter W., "Moss Hart" in *Dictionary of Literary Biography*, Volume VII (Twentieth-Century American Dramatists). Detroit: Gale Research Co., 1981.

Schary, Dore. *Heyday*. Boston: Little, Brown and Company, 1979.

Schlesinger, Herbert J., ed. *Symbol and Neurosis: Selected Papers of Lawrence S. Kubie*. New York: International Universities Press, 1978.

Schwartz, Charles. *Cole Porter: A Biography*. New York: The Dial Press, 1977.

Secrest, Meryle. *Stephen Sondheim: A Life*. New York: Alfred A. Knopf, 1998.

"Seventy-five Miles From Broadway," *American Heritage*, May-June, 1999.

Sievers, W. David. *Freud on Broadway, A History of Psychoanalysis and the American Drama*. New York: Cooper Square Publishers, 1970.

Simon, Neil. *The Play Goes On*. New York: Simon & Schuster.

Smith, Cecil. *Musical Comedy In America*. Clinton, MA: The Colonial Press, 1950.

Spindle, Les. *Julie Andrews: A Bio-Bibliography*. New York: Greenwood Press, 1989.

Stang, Joanne, "My (New) Fair Lady," *New York Times Magazine*, January 5, 1958.

Tallmey, Allene, "The Biography of *Merrily We Roll Along*," clipping, SHSW.

Teichmann, Howard. *George S. Kaufman: An Intimate Portrait*. New York: Atheneum, 1972.

Terrace, Vincent. *The Complete Encyclopedia of Television Programs, 1947–79*, Second Edition. South Brunswick and New York: A. S. Barnes and Company, 1979.

"Torch Song for Depression" [about *Face The Music*], *Theatre Guild Magazine*, March 1932.

Turner, Elaine, "Once in a Lifetime," *International Dictionary of Theatre—1: Plays*. Chicago and London: St. James Press, 1992.

"Two Parfit Broadway Knyghts," *Time*, November 14, 1960.

Valentine, Elizabeth R., "Moss Hart: A Drama in 3 Acts," *New York Times Magazine*, October 31, 1943.

Walker, John, ed. *Halliwell's Film Guide*, 8th Edition. New York: Harper Collins, 1991.

Windeler, Robert. *Julie Andrews: A Biography*. New York: St. Martin's Press, 1983.

Zolotow, Maurice, "To Couch or Not to Couch," *Theatre Arts*, February 1954.

II: NEWSPAPERS

Hundreds of clippings from newspapers throughout the United States can be found in BRTC. Many of them do not indicate either the name of the newspaper or the date of publication. All articles below are from *The New York Times* unless otherwise noted. Reviews of all of Moss Hart's plays (beginning with *Once in a Lifetime*) and screenplays are included in the *Times*, as are hundreds of articles. Only the most significant articles are noted below.

"And Now Rests the Weary Hart," October 8, 1933.

"And Who, Pray Tell, Is Moss Hart?" September 28, 1930.

"Aperitif to a Dinner," September 17, 1939.

Arthur, Art, "Reverting to Type" [profile of MH in a clipping from an unidentified newspaper, no date, but written around 1934].

Atkinson, Brooks, "Country Manners," October 27, 1940.

———, "White Owl of Lake Bomoseen," October 22, 1939.

"Backstage American," March 5, 1939.

Barclay, Dorothy, "Playwright Has Script of Own on Parenthood," October 6, 1959.

[*Brooklyn*?] *Eagle*, April 27, 1941 [clipping in BRTC].

Calta, Louis, "Playwrights Seek Sounder Theatre," January 10, 1950.

———, "Broadway Pays Tribute to Hart," January 10, 1962.

Cerf, Bennett, "A Few Words About Moss Hart," March 27, 1960.

Doll, Bill, "On Filming 'Winged Victory,'" December 17, 1944.

"Fabulous Invalid, The," October 30, 1938.

Funke, Lewis, "News of the Rialto: Hart Back," January 22, 1961.

Gelb, Arthur, "Fair Lady' Nods Toward Moscow," May 7, 1959.

Hall, Mordaunt, "Carl Laemmle Jr. and His Pictures, Including 'Once in a Lifetime,'" November 6, 1932.

Hart, Moss, "Amateur Dramatics in the Centres," unidentified newspaper [clipping from SHSW; no date given]

———, "Before Thousands Cheered," *The Stage* [undated clipping from SHSW].

———, "First-Night Thoughts of a Playwright," clipping in BRTC from an unidentified newspaper, 1948.

———, "How A. W. Came to Dinner, and Other Stories," October 29, 1939.

———, "Inside ANTA," July 4, 1948.

———, "Let the Shuberts Be Warned," December 17, 1944.

———, "A Playwright's View," November 2, 1952.

———, "The Saga of Gertie," March 2, 1941.

———, "What Does He Know About Children?" *Boston Post* [clipping from BRTC; no date, but written in 1946].

———, "Why I Will Vote for Franklin D. Roosevelt," *The Independent*, September 21, 1944.

———, "A Winged Victory," November 14, 1943.

"Hollywood Proves It Can Take the Drama's Joke," February 1, 1931.

Horner, Harry, "Of Those Four Revolving Stages," April 6, 1941.

Hughes, Elinor, *Boston Herald*, no date [clipping in BRTC], but written in 1946.

Lerner, Alan Jay, "Shavian Musical Notes," March 11, 1956.

———, "Hart: Footprints Too Deep to Fill," December 24, 1961.

Maney, Richard, "Press Agent's Plight," May 27, 1956.

Millstein, Gilbert, "The Playwright's Ordeal by Fire, Etc.," December 12, 1954.

"Moss Hart and His Success," *Newark News*, November 1, 1934 [?] clipping in SHSW.

"Moss Hart Felled by Heart Attack," October 15, 1960.

"Moss Hart Is Dead: Playwright Was 57," December 21, 1961.

New York Herald Tribune, January 12, 1941 [clipping in BRTC].

New York World Telegram, March [?], 1939 [clipping in BRTC].

———, May 14, 1941 [clipping in BRTC].

"On a Hart and Its Beat" [about *Merrily We Roll Along*], clipping, no date, unidentified newspaper, SHSW.

"Preface to 'Jubilee,' A." October 20, 1935.

"Prelude to a 'Jubilee.'" September 15, 1935.

Reynolds, Ruth, "Notables, Spoofed on Stage, Show They Can Take It," [*New York*?] *Sunday News*, January 21, 1934 [clipping in SHSW].

Rice, Robert, "Rice and Old Shoes," *PM*, February 3, 1941.

Stanley, Fred, "The Hollywood Slant," August 6, 1944.

Talmey, Allene, "The Biography of *Merrily We Roll Along*," *Stage* [undated clipping from SHSW].

Toohey, John Peter, "Regarding Those Who Would Rather Be Right." November 7, 1937.

"$25,000 Burglary At the Moss Harts," December 27, 1946.

Variety, June 24, 1942 [clipping in BRTC about *The Lunchtime Follies*].

"Why 'You Can't Take It With You,'" December 20, 1936.

"Winged Victory in Production," *Theatre Arts*, February, 1944.

Zolotow, Sam, "'Fair Lady' Role Barred to Alien," January 11, 1957.

III. UNPUBLISHED MATERIALS

Address given by MH to the American Academy of Dramatic Arts at their graduation exercises, April 5, 1960, SHSW.

Brochures and programs for the Crescent Country Club, the Brooklyn Jewish Center, the "Y" Stagers, the Flagler Hotel, etc., SHSW.

Commemorative Premiere Booklet of *Hans Christian Andersen*.

Contract between Columbia Pictures Corporation and MH, dated December 9, 1954, SHSW.

Federal Bureau of Investigations File for Moss Hart (obtained through the provisions of the Freedom of Information Act and the Privacy Act).

Grammar school report card for MH, 1910–19, SHSW.

Hart, Barnett, "The Man Who Came to Dinner," sheet music, Irving Berlin, Inc., in SHSW.

Hart, Moss, address to the American Academy of Dramatic Arts at their graduation exercises, April 5, 1960, SHSW.

———, address to the first National Assembly of Authors and Dramatists, SHSW.

———, article [evidently unpublished] about directing *My Fair Lady*, dated March 3, 1959, in typescript, SHSW.

———, *As Thousands Cheer*, handwritten script, SHSW.

———, *The Beloved Bandit* (see *Lad O'Laughter* below)

———, "A Devil's Dictionary of the Theatre," SHSW.

———, Diary, December 2, 1953 to December 5, 1954, SHSW.

———, Eulogy for George S. Kaufman, SHSW.

———, Eulogy for Kay Kendall, SHSW.

———, *Face the Music*, typed manuscript, SHSW.

———, *Gentleman's Agreement* (screenplay), SHSW.

———, *The Great Waltz*, typed manuscript, SHSW.

———, handwritten drafts of *Act One*, SHSW.

———, handwritten notes for *Christopher Blake*, SHSW.

———, *Hans Christian Andersen* (screenplay), SHSW.

———, *Jubilee*, handwritten manuscript, SHSW.

———, *Lad O'Laughter* [also known as *The Beloved Bandit*], typed manuscript, SHSW.

———, *Merrily We Roll Along*, typed manuscript, SHSW.

———, *Music by Duchin* (partial screenplay), SHSW.

———, "My Trip Around the World," unpublished manuscript, SHSW.

———, *The Nature of the Beast* (television play), SHSW.

———, *Once in a Lifetime* [original version-before MH's collaboration with George S. Kaufman], SHSW.

———, "One World-One Trip-One Play" [about *Winged Victory*], SHSW.

——, "Please Don't Eat the Critic," SHSW.

——, preliminary notes for *Prince of Players* screenplay, SHSW.

——, *Prince of Players* (screenplay), SHSW.

——, *A Star Is Born* (screenplay), SHSW.

——, "These Pretty People," an "Original Screen Story," SHSW.

——, various revue sketches, SHSW.

——, *Winged Victory* (screenplay), SHSW.

—— and Harold Rome, *In the Pink*, typewritten manuscript, SHSW.

Moss Hart Collection (newspaper clippings, correspondence, programs, photographs, etc.), Billy Rose Theatre Collection, New York Public Library for the Performing Arts.

Moss Hart Papers (correspondence, scrapbooks, audiotapes, telegrams, contracts, newspaper clippings, school records, programs, handwritten manuscripts, typescripts, diary, awards, contracts, etc.), State Historical Society of Wisconsin.

Moss Hart Collection (films and videotapes), Wisconsin Center for Film and Theatre Research.

My Fair Lady Souvenir Program, Theatre Royal, Drury Lane.

"Person to Person" videotape from 1959 in Wisconsin Center for Film and Theatre Research (interview with MH and KCH by Edward R. Murrow).

Script of the celebration at Lincoln Center in 2004 honoring Moss Hart and Kitty Carlisle Hart.

"35 Years of Broadway Musicals," audiotape of radio program broadcast on WQXR in New York on June 17, 1960; at SHSW (Participants are MH and Brooks Atkinson).

Untitled article about directing *My Fair Lady*, SHSW.

Videotape of MH and KCH presenting Academy Awards in 1961 in the Wisconsin Center for Film and Theatre Research.

IV. PUBLISHED PLAYS BY MOSS HART

American Way, The (with George S. Kaufman) in *Six Plays by Kaufman and Hart*. New York: The Modern Library, 1942.

Christopher Blake. New York: Random House, 1946.

Climate of Eden, The. New York: Random House, 1953.

Community of Two, A [by Jerome Chodorov; based on MH's unfinished play]. New York: Samuel French, Inc., 1974.

Fabulous Invalid, The (with George S. Kaufman). New York: Random House, 1938.

George Washington Slept Here (with George S. Kaufman) in *Six Plays by Kaufman and Hart*. New York: The Modern Library, 1942.

I'd Rather Be Right: A Musical Revue (with George S. Kaufman, Lyrics by Lorenz Hart, Music by Richard Rodgers). Whitefish, MT: Kessinger Publishing, 2005.

Lady in the Dark (with Lyrics by Ira Gershwin and Music by Kurt Weill). New York: Random House, 1941.

Light Up the Sky. New York: Dramatists Play Service, Inc., 1949.

Man Who Came to Dinner, The (with George S. Kaufman) in *Six Plays by Kaufman and Hart*. New York: The Modern Library, 1942.

Merrily We Roll Along (with George S. Kaufman) in *Six Plays by Kaufman and Hart*. New York: The Modern Library, 1942.

Once in a Lifetime (with George S. Kaufman) in *Six Plays by Kaufman and Hart*. New York: The Modern Library, 1942.

Winged Victory. New York: Random House, 1943.

You Can't Take It With You (with George S. Kaufman) in *Six Plays by Kaufman and Hart*. New York: The Modern Library, 1942.

V. INTERVIEWS

(all conducted between 1999 and 2005)
Albert, Eddie
Andrews, Julie
Bertsche, John, M.D.
Chodorov, Jerome
Gelbart, Larry
Goldstein, Malcolm
Goulet, Robert
Hart, Catherine
Hart, Christopher
Hart, Kitty Carlisle
Hornblow, Leonora
McCriskin, James, M.D.
Murch, Anna Crouse
Peck, Gregory
Schneider, Anne Kaufman
Widney, Stone (Bud)
Williams, Macon

The sources for each chapter are given below. Abbreviations used in notes:

MH = Moss Hart

KCH = Kitty Carlisle Hart

GSK = George S. Kaufman

K&H = Kaufman and Hart

AO = *Act One* by Moss Hart

GSKLT = *George S. Kaufman: His Life, His Theater* by Malcolm Goldstein

SWL = *The Street Where I Live* by Alan Jay Lerner

NYT = *New York Times* (in which all of MH's plays, from *Once in a Lifetime* on, are reviewed)

SHSW = State Historical Society of Wisconsin

BRTC = Billy Rose Theatre Collection, Performing Arts Research Center, New York Public Library for the Performing Arts

Information concerning how long individual plays ran on Broadway is taken from Daniel Blum, *Theatre World* (various editions); Abe Laufe, *Broadway's Greatest Musicals*; Stanley Green, *The World of Musical Comedy*; Stanley Green, *Ring Bells! Sing Songs! Broadway Musicals of the 1930s*; David Ewen, *Complete Book of the American Musical Theatre*; and Walter H. Ross, "Moss Hart," *Dictionary of Literary Biography*.

Chapter One

Most of the material in this chapter, and many of the quotations (all except those specifically indicated), come from *AO*. Additional details about MH's early years came from Margaret Case Harriman's "Hi-yo, Platinum" in *Take Them Up Tenderly* (pp. 81–88); Scott Meredith's *George S. Kaufman and His Friends* (hereafter abbreviated as *George S. Kaufman*), p. 469 ff.; *GSKLT* (pp. 73–75); "Broadway Pays Tribute to Hart" (quoting Dore Schary, "a green velour hat . . .") and "And Who, Pray Tell, Is Moss Hart?" in *NYT* (which briefly mentions *Jonica*); "A Drama in 3 Acts," *NYT*; an interview by MH on *Person to Person*, 1959 (in which MH refers to the theatre as "the refuge for many unhappy children"); KCH's *Kitty*; Edna Ferber's "A Rolling Moss Gathers Considerable Heart" (in which she details the duties of a summer camp social director); Rosamond Gilder's "The Fabulous Hart"; "Dore Schary's Tribute to Moss Hart" in *A Memorial Tribute to Moss Hart*, "*Look* Calls on Moss Hart" in *Look* Magazine; Mona Gardner's "Byron From Brooklyn" (which discusses, among other things, Bernard Hart's childhood diseases), as does MH, "What Does He Know About Children?" *Boston Post*, undated clipping, BRTC; various undated newspaper clippings in SHSW; "Moss Hart and His Success," *Newark News* (about his directing of amateur groups). MH's claim that he "is a graduate of the Morris High School in New York and took several extension courses at Columbia University" is from an undated clipping at SHSW; he repeated the claim to Jean Gould in *Modern American Playwrights*. The certificate MH won as Junior Four Minute Speaker is at SHSW, as is his grade school report card. The program for the National Cloak and Suit Company's Entertainment and Dance in 1922 is at SHSW. Clippings in the scrapbook at SHSW also offer details about the plays MH staged for the Labor Temple Players, the "Y" Stagers, the American Co-Optimists, the Park Players of the Young Folks League of Congregation Shari Zedek, The New Jersey Federation of the YMHA and YWHA, etc. Summer camp programs from Camp Greater Utopia, the Flagler Hotel, and the Crescent Country Club (where MH taught) are included in the scrapbook. Dore Schary in *Heyday* discusses MH's activities as a little-theatre director and as a social director (pp. 16–29); Schary also identifies the regulars who met with MH for coffee in the 1920s; he states that the group met at Childs, the Tavern, and the Cadillac Cafeteria. Charles Higham in *Cary Grant: The Lonely Heart* says the group met at Rudley's (as MH does in *AO*). MH, in "What Does He Know About Children?" discusses his brother's childhood illnesses and MH's consequent absences from school; he also discusses the performers he saw in vaudeville. MH, in "Amateur Dramatics in the Centres," writes about his experiences directing amateur groups, his wish to write "the Jewish prize play," and "do for the Jewish soul what Eugene O'Neill has done for the American."

MH's typewritten script of *Lad O' Laughter* is at SHSW. Various clippings at SHSW in MH's scrapbook offer reviews of and publicity materials (and sheet music) for *The Beloved Bandit* or *The Hold-Up Man*—from Rochester, Youngstown, Dubuque, etc. Other clippings about *The Beloved Bandit* from *The Fort Wayne, Indiana, Journal Gazette*, *The Youngstown Vindicator*, August 16, 1925, and other newspapers are at BRTC.

Edward Eliscu's version of events is from his autobiography, *With or Without a Song*.

The reviews of *The Emperor Jones* at the Mayfair Theatre are taken from newspaper clippings in SHSW. GSK's statement, "I simply feel . . ." is quoted from Howard Teichmann's *George S. Kaufman: An Intimate Portrait*.

Richard J. Madden's letter of encouragement and his suggestion that Hart write comedies are in the scrapbook, as is the clipping in which Jed Harris is reported to have optioned *Panic* for a Broadway production. The plot of *No Retreat* and its production by The Hampton Players are documented in a magazine clipping at SHSW. Brooks Atkinson mentions it in "Introduction" to *Six Plays by Kaufman and Hart*, p. xi; newspaper clippings about the play are at *SHSW*. A program and photographs of the production of *No Retreat* are at BRTC.

GSK told Howard Teichmann that *Act One* should be classified as fiction: Teichmann, *George S. Kaufman: An Intimate Portrait*, p. 288.

In a letter from Lester Sweyd to MH, dated July 18, 1959, Sweyd claims to have shown *Panic* to Richard Madden, and to have taken the play to Frieda Fishbein who, according to Sweyd, "got you to write material for Fannie Brice for a revue which Billy Rose was doing." Sweyd claims that the meetings of the coffee klatsch occurred at the Paramount Cafeteria. *Panic* is also discussed by Harriman, *Take Them Up Tenderly*, p. 95. Billy Rose's interest in MH's sketches appears in newspaper clippings in SHSW.

Information about *Jonica* comes from clippings—promotional material, programs, and many reviews—in MH's scrapbook at SHSW. Some of the newspapers (e.g., *The Washington Post, The Atlantic City Press*) are identified, many are not. More reviews are at BRTC. MH's contribution to *Jonica* is noted in Jean Gould's *Modern American Playwrights*. Brooks Atkinson quotes from the *NYT*'s anonymous critic's review of *Jonica* in *NYT*, September 20, 1959. MH took credit for *Jonica* in the *My Fair Lady* Souvenir Book distributed in London.

Chapter Two

I have relied heavily on MH's account of the New York productions of *Once in a Lifetime* in *AO*. Again, all quotations in this chapter are from *AO*, unless otherwise noted. Other sources include Margaret Case Harriman's "Hi-yo Platinum," who also describes MH's redecorating at the Edison Hotel, as does Mona Gardner in "Byron From Brooklyn" (both refer to it as the Ansonia); MH's "Men at Work;" Scott Meredith's *George S. Kaufman and His Friends* (pp. 175–86); *GSKLT*; the play is analyzed in *International Dictionary of Theatre— 1: Plays*; the length of the run is mentioned in *NYT*, October 30, 1962. The contract between MH and Sam Harris, dated January 17, 1930, is at SHSW. Reviews are in MH's scrapbook at SHSW.

MH's original script (before it was submitted to GSK) is at SHSW. It demonstrates that GSK was right: 80% of the play *was* written by Moss Hart. GSK's statement is quoted in Laurence Maslon, "Moss Hart," p. 242, Scott Meredith, *George S. Kaufman* (p. 10 and p. 477), and many other sources. GSK insisted that MH receive sixty percent of the royalties: *GSKLT*, p. 185, and an undated clipping from *The New Yorker* in SHSW.

Reviews of the production in Atlantic City, Brighton Beach, and Philadelphia are in MH's scrapbook at SHSW. A clipping in BRTC discusses the Brighton Beach production.

The Philadelphia production is further discussed in *NYT*, September 7, 1930. MH in "Men at Work," p. xxv, mentions that Beatrice Kaufman disliked the new third act. The California production of *Once in a Lifetime* is detailed in Meredith, *George S. Kaufman*, p. 475 and pp. 480–83; *GSKLT*; *NYT*, February 1, 1931. Jean Dixon's disparagement of MH's performance is in *GSKLT*, p. 223. The film version is discussed in *NYT*, June 12, October 9, and November 6, 1932. Clippings in MH's scrapbook discuss the deluxe treatment and the offers to write screenplays he received in Hollywood. His comments about Hollywood ("I would rather . . ." and "to take picture writing . . .") appear in other clippings at SHSW.

Intermission

The quotation beginning, "It just damned well . . ." is from a letter from MH to Brooks Atkinson, c. 1948, in BRTC.

Chapter Three

The play MH began but did not finish, *Twentieth Century Limited*, is mentioned in a clipping from a Los Angeles newspaper in MH's scrapbook, SHSW.

Rumors of MH's bisexuality: Charles Higham in *Cary Grant: The Lonely Heart* speaks of the "sexual ambiguity" of MH and Archie Leach (Cary Grant), pp. 37–8; Charles Schwarz writes in *Cole Porter* that Porter and Monty Woolley proselytized Hart "on behalf of the gay cause;" according to Malcolm Goldstein (in our interview), Gordon Merrick, who acted in the original production of *The Man Who Came to Dinner* in 1939, claimed to have had an affair with

MH. And letters MH received from a male friend seems to hint at a sexual (or, at the very least, a passionate) relationship. One begins "Dearest Boy;" another begins "Dear Heart" and concludes, "will end with the love and tenderness I have for you, my dear boy . . . no one will ever know what I've been through these past days, watching and waiting for news of my prince." (SHSW) Also, two telegrams MH received on the opening night of *Once in a Lifetime*, both sent by men, began "WELL DARLING" and "MOSS DEAR."

MH's attitude toward the movies: interviews with KCH; Anne Kaufman Schneider; Christopher Hart. The quotation beginning "Well, here I am . . ." is from "Moss Hart and His Success," *Newark News*.

The story of MH's being assigned the wrong treatment by MGM is from *The New York Herald-Tribune*, February 5, 1933. Hart's attempts to "pitch" *The Merchant of Venice* and *Hamlet* in Hollywood: *New York World Telegram*, March [?], 1939 (clipping, BRTC).

Information about MH's early films come from Jay Robert Nash and Stanley Ralph Ross, *The Motion Picture Guide*; Ephraim Katz, *The Film Encyclopedia*; John Walker, ed., *Halliwell's Film Guide*.

Reviews of specific films include the following: *Flesh: NYT*, December 10, 1932; clipping, SHSW; *Variety*, December 19, 1932; *Frankie and Johnnie*, *NYT*, May 25, 1936; *The Masquerader: Variety*, September 5, 1933.

Information about and reviews of *Face the Music*: MH, "Men At Work," *Stage Magazine*, November, 1936; Edward Jablonski, *Irving Berlin: American Troubador*, pp. 149–53; *Philadelphia Inquirer* ("The audience, which filed in . . ."), February 4, 1932; Malcolm Goldstein, *GSKLT*; *NYT*, February 18 (which mentions that Jimmy Walker was in the audience on opening night and praised the musical's "impudent sense of humor"), February 28 and November 2, 1932; and October 15, 1933; *New York World Telegram*, February 18, 1932; Stanley Green, *The World of Musical Comedy*, pp. 94–5; Stanley Green, *Ring Bells! Sing Songs! Broadway Musicals of the 1930s*; Cecil Smith, *Musical Comedy in America*, p. 286; David Ewen, *Complete Book of the American Musical Theatre*; "Torch Song for Depression," *Theatre Guild Magazine*, March, 1932; original typed script in SHSW; clippings of reviews from Philadelphia and New York, SHSW.

MH's appearance and personality: interviews with Anne Kaufman Schneider, KCH, Christopher Hart, Catherine Hart, Julie Andrews, Gregory Peck, Leonora Hornblow, Jerome Chodorov; *NYT*, December 21, 1961 (obituary); Brooks Atkinson, "An Enthusiasm for Life," *NYT*, October 27, 1940, December 21, 1961, and January 10, 1962. Margaret Case Harriman, "Hiyo Platinum," *Take Them Up Tenderly*, p. 81; Brooks Atkinson's "Introduction" to *Six Plays by Kaufman and Hart*; GSK's "Forked Lightning" in the same volume; Alan Jay Lerner, *The Street Where I Live*; Scott Meredith, *George S. Kaufman* (which includes the anecdote about Kaufman and Hart whistling in order to distract Mr. and Mrs. Richard Rodgers during a game of croquet, p. 175); Malcolm Goldstein, *GSKLT*; Bennett Cerf, "With Gaiety and Gusto: A Tribute to Moss Hart," *The Saturday Review*; KCH, "About the Author," *Theatre Arts*; Elizabeth R. Valentine, "Moss Hart: A Drama in 3 Acts;" Alan Jay Lerner, "Hart: Footprints Too Deep to Fill;" S. N. Behrman, "They Left 'em Laughing;" *Time*, December 29, 1961; *Newsweek*, January 1, 1962; Richard Rodgers, *Musical Stages*; Brooks Atkinson, *Broadway*; KCH, *Kitty*; letter from Phil Silvers to MH, 1960, in SHSW; Rosamond Gilder, "The Fabulous Hart"; *A Memorial Tribute to Moss Hart*; Mona Gardner, "Byron From Brooklyn;" Bennett Cerf, "A Few Words About Moss Hart," *NYT*, March 27, 1960; Edna Ferber, "A Rolling Moss Gathers Considerable Heart" (in which she uses five adjectives to describe MH), pp. 41–3; Jean Gould, *Modern American Playwrights*; Julie Goldsmith Gilbert, *Ferber: A Biography*; Dore Schary, *Heyday*; George Cukor, Garson Kanin, Louis Jourdan, Gregory Peck, Frederick Loewe, Danny Kaye, quoted in *A Celebration of Moss Hart*; Irving Lazar (with Annette Tapert), *Swifty: My Life and Good Times* (hereafter abbreviated as *Swifty*); MH, in "Moss Hart," *Esquire*, p. 31, called his extravagance "senseless."

MH's relationships with women: Elizabeth R. Valentine, "Moss Hart: A Drama in 3 Acts"; Edna Ferber, "A Rolling Moss Gathers No Heart"; Walter W. Ross, "Moss Hart." The wisecrack about Edith Atwater ("Here comes Moss Hart . . .") has often been told; one source is Harriman, *Take Them Up Tenderly*, p. 92; another is Leonard Lyons, *New York Post*, December 9, 1942. Jerome Chodorov said in an interview that Levant was the source of the wisecrack. Leonard Lyons also attributed the remark to Levant in the *New York Post*, December 9, 1940. Scott Meredith, in *George S. Kaufman*, asserts that Greta Garbo flirted with MH, p. 479; K&H's relationship with the young actress is mentioned in *GSKLT*, p. 327; Scott Meredith's book is also the source of the story about MH's invention of a schoolteacher and his remark ("My God . . .") to Beatrice Kaufman (p. 529), as is Mona Gardner's "Byron From Brooklyn"; Anne Kaufman Schneider said in an interview that GSK (her father) was unaware of any bisexuality on the part of (or rumors of bisexuality

about) MH. MH's relationship with Beatrice Kaufman is best described in
GSKLT, pp. 179, 185, 229, 373.

Information about and reviews of *As Thousands Cheer*: MH's handwritten
script is at SHSW; *NYT*, January 29, September 2, September 3 (in which
MH is described as the director, albeit uncredited, of the Broadway produc-
tion), October 2, October 7, October 8, and October 15, 1933; *New York
Herald-Tribune*, December 25, 1932 and August 1, 1933; Stanley Green, *The
World of Musical Comedy* (pp. 95–7); Cecil Smith, *Musical Comedy in America*
(pp. 286–88); Laurence Bergreen, *As Thousands Cheer: The Life of Irving Berlin*;
David Ewen, *Complete Book of the American Musical Theatre*; Brooks Atkinson,
Broadway; clippings from various newspapers in MH's scrapbook, SHSW;
clippings from various newspapers, BRTC; MH, "Before Thousands
Cheered" (which describes the near-closing of the production and Clifton
Webb's demands; the article also includes the quotations beginning, "I began
to think . . ." and "I had a show again! . . ."); "As Thousands Cheer," SHSW;
MH, "Men at Work," *Stage* (from which the quotation, "Either we had
grown . . .") is taken; Ethan Mordden, *The American Theatre*; Edward Jablonski, *Irving Berlin: American Troubador* (which discusses the racist attitudes expressed by the revue's stars to Irving Berlin), p. 159; Burns Mantle, in a clipping at SHSW, called *As Thousands Cheer* "a civic institution."

MH's response to opening nights is described in *AO*; in Brooks Atkinson's "Introduction" to *Six Plays by Kaufman and Hart*; *NYT*, September 28, 1930 and October 8, 1933; Gilbert Millstein, "The Playwright's Ordeal by Fire, Etc."; KCH,
Kitty; Mona Gardner, "Byron from Brooklyn;" MH, "Before Thousands
Cheered" (from which the quotation "I have tried telling myself . . ." is taken).

MH's legendary extravagance: The following quotations can be found in the
following sources. "I have none of the money . . ." in *Newsweek*, January 1,
1962. "I feel as if every bit . . ." is from KCH's *Kitty*, pp. 133–34; "He didn't
buy things . . ." in Bennett Cerf, "With Gaiety and Gusto"; "I never had any
curtains . . ." in Margaret Case Harriman, "Hi-yo, Platinum!"; "I have never
known anyone . . ." in Edna Ferber, *A Memorial Tribute to Moss Hart*; MH
called his buying habits "senseless" in "Moss Hart," *Esquire*, p. 31. Also, see
Harriman, *Take Them Up Tenderly*, pp. 80–1; Atkinson, "Introduction," p. xiii;
GSK, "Forked Lightning," pp. xxxi–xxxii; Mona Gardner, "Byron from
Brooklyn," p. 11; MH, "My Trip Around the World" in SHSW, pp. 1–2; *NYT*,
October 27, 1940 and December 21, 1961 (obituary); Brooks Atkinson,
Broadway; Alan Jay Lerner, *The Street Where I Live*; Malcolm Goldstein,

GSKLT; KCH, *Kitty*; Mona Gardner, "Byron From Brooklyn;" Edna Ferber, "A Rolling Moss Gathers Considerable Heart;" Irving Lazar (and Annette Tapert), *Swifty*, and various newspaper clippings at SHSW.

More Cheers: NYT, October 7, 1934; Art Arthur, "Reverting to Type;" *New York American*, October 7, 1934; Jablonski, *Irving Berlin: American Troubador*, p. 164. The decision not to produce *More Cheers*: Bergreen, *As Thousands Cheer*.

Information about and reviews of *The Great Waltz*: Margaret Case Harriman, "Hi-yo, Platinum"; *NYT*, September 24 and September 30, 1934 (which discusses the size of the Center Theatre); Stanley Green, *Ring Bells! Sing Songs! Broadway Musicals of the 1930s*; Cecil Smith, *Musical Comedy in America*; clippings from various newspapers at SHSW; *New York Evening Post*, May 8, 1934; MH's typed copy of the libretto at SHSW (from which Mr. Ebeseder's monologue is taken); "The Great Waltz," clipping [possibly from *Theatre Guild Magazine*] at SHSW; the quotation ("is to divorce operetta . . .") is taken from an unidentified clipping at SHSW; MH's claim that the Strausses were his favorite collaborators is from MH, "Men at Work," *Stage Magazine*. Bernard Hart being mistaken for MH: clipping at SHSW.

Chapter Four

Telegram to Sam Harris ("TENTATIVE TITLE . . .") is from a clipping in SHSW. MH's decision not to continue with *Wind Up an Era: NYT*, December 10, 1933; *GSKLT*, p. 229; Scott Meredith, *George S. Kaufman*, p. 487. GSK's statement, "I very quickly knew . . ." is from S. N. Behrman, "They Left 'em Laughing," p. 7. K&H's library research for *Merrily We Roll Along*: Allene Talmey, "The Biography of *Merrily We Roll Along*." Writing *Merrily* in chronological order, then reversing it: Tallmey; Art Arthur, "Reverting to Type." MH's claim "There are other women . . ." is in Art Arthur's "Reverting to Type." Dorothy Parker's wisecrack, "I've been too fucking busy . . ." is from Scott Meredith, *George S. Kaufman*, p. 489. The account of MH spending his days at rehearsals of *Merrily We Roll Along* and his evenings at rehearsals of *The Great Waltz* is from Allene Talmey, "The Biography of *Merrily We Roll Along*." Sam Harris's decision to forego an out-of-town tour for *Merrily*: GSKLT, pp. 230–31.

Reviews of *Merrily We Roll Along*: John Anderson, from an unidentified clipping at SHSW; Brooks Atkinson, *NYT*, October 1, 1934 (Atkinson offered a very different opinion—a wholly negative one—in his book, *Broadway*, p. 235); Percy Hammond, from an unidentified clipping at SHSW.

MH's interview with George Ross, beginning "We find ourselves . . ." is from an unidentified clipping at SHSW. *Merrily We Roll Along* results in loss of investments: Harriman, *Take Them Up Tenderly*, p. 89; *GSKLT*, p. 33; "Hart, Moss," *American National Biography*, Oxford University Press, New York and Oxford, 1999. Herman Mankiewicz's comment, "It's about this playwright . . ." can be found in Harriman, *Take Them Up Tenderly*, p. 89; Scott Meredith, *George S. Kaufman*, p. 490; and *GSKLT*, p. 235. MH's screenplay for *Broadway Melody of 1936* and its resemblance to his screenplay, *Miss Pamelo Thorndyke*: *Los Angeles Times*, April 4, 1934.

MH's meeting with Cole and Linda Porter and the quotation "of fashion and glitter . . ." MH, "Foreword" to *The Cole Porter Song Book*. Porter's invention of his past: Charles Schulz, *Cole Porter*. Porter's comments, "Let's do a show together . . ." and "Why not do both?"—as well as the subsequent account—are from MH, "Men at Work," *Stage Magazine*, p. 61. The account of writing on the *Franconia* and the quotation "he was scrupulous . . ." are from MH, "Foreword" to *The Cole Porter Song Book*. The following are from MH's "My Trip Around the World" (which is at SHSW): "Whatever has been written . . ." (p. 22), "are worth going to the other end . . ." (p. 28), "a traveler's paradise" (p. 40), and "I am more impressed . . ." (p. 4). The passenger's question "Mr. Hart, do you get . . ." is from "Jubilee Over Here," *Stage*. Lily Hart's comment about Cole Porter's mother is from George Eells, *The Life That Late He Led*. MH and Porter reading the script and singing the songs for Harris and Gordon: *New York World Telegram*, June 5, 1935. MH's assertion "was surprised, but quickly agreed" is from MH's "Foreword" to *The Cole Porter Song Book*. The characters in *Jubilee* based on real-life models: *NYT*, September 23, 1935. Casting of Mary Boland: "Jubilee Over Here." The audition of Kitty Carlisle and her comments are from KCH's *Kitty*, pp. 74–5. The cost of production: *NYT*, October 27, 1935. Cole Porter sitting in the front row during rehearsals and MH's comment "a glorious party . . ." are from MH, "Men at Work," *Stage*, p. 62; also see KCH, *Kitty*, pp. 165–66. The firing of Monty Woolley as dialogue director: George Eells, *The Life That Late He Led*, p. 126. Eells also tells of the threatening letters and backstage fires (pp. 126–29). Steven Bach, in *Dazzler*, claims that Kate was the arsonist, on p. 140.

Reviews of *Jubilee*: Percy Hammond, clipping at SHSW; Robert Garland, clipping at SHSW; John Mason Brown, in the *New York Post*—from an undated clipping at SHSW. MH renting Frances Marion's home in 1935: *NYT*, December 20, 1936. The account of *Frankie and Johnnie* is from *The New York*

Herald-Tribune, December 31, 1933; the review is in *NYT*, May 25, 1936. *Variety*'s review is from a clipping at BRTC. The article calling MH "Broadway's current wonder boy . . ." is from Art Arthur, "Reverting to Type." Article claiming that MH was "making more money . . ." is from "Moss Hart and His Success." ($3,000 per week in 1935 equaling $2,500,000 per year in 2000 dollars: Bureau of Labor Statistics Data, Consumer Price Index, December 6, 2000.) K&H's work on *Washington Jitters*: Bruce Cook, *Dalton Trumbo*, pp. 95–6. MH's work on *The Maurizius Case*: *NYT*, August 18, 1935 and March 8, 1936; and "Jubilee Over Here." GSK's question "What about your other idea?" is from *NYT*, December 20, 1936. W. David Sievers's description of *You Can't Take It With You* (hereafter abbreviated as *YCTIWY*) is from *Freud on Broadway*, p. 290. GSK's letter to Beatrice Kaufman ("the way to live . . .") is quoted in *GSKLT*, p. 291. "Many of the plays . . ." is from Ethan Mordden, *The American Theatre*, p. 159. The telegram to Sam Harris ("DEAR SAM WE START WORK . . .") is from *NYT*, December 20, 1936. S. N. Behrman's evaluation of *YCTIWY* is from "They Left 'em Laughing," *NYT Magazine*. Searching for titles: *NYT*, December 20, 1936; and *GSKLT*, pp. 271–72. Harris's booking of theatres and signing actors: *NYT*, December 20, 1936. More than 700 props: "Many Props." GSK's and MH's apprehension about audience reaction: Donita Ferguson, "Mad Marvels." Out-of-town performances of the play ("back muscles . . ."): report from Philadelphia in *NYT*, December 6, 1936. Brooks Atkinson's review is in *NYT*, December 15, 1936; John Anderson's review is in *The New York Journal*, December 15, 1936. The account of Sam Harris's collecting the NY critics' reviews and mailing them to locations outside New York: *NYT*, May 2, 1937. Winning the Pulitzer Prize for *YCTIWY*: *NYT*, May 4, 1937; a telegram from the Pulitzer Prize judges to MH is at SHSW. Edna Ferber's diary entry is quoted in Julie Goldsmith Gilbert's *Ferber: A Biography*, p. 315. The *New York News'* editorial about *YCTIWY* is quoted in Scott Meredith, *George S. Kaufman*, p. 539; the *NYT* editorial appeared on May 5, 1937. The *Times* of London review is quoted in *NYT*, December 23, 1937. Virginia Gordon accusing K&H of plagiarism: *NYT*, November 14, 1937. The run of *YCTIWY* not being affected by the film version: Scott Meredith, *George S. Kaufman*, p. 537. Information about the televised versions of *YCTIWY*: MH's scrapbook at SHSW; Tim Brooks and Earle Marsh, *The Complete Directory to Prime Time Network TV Shows, 1946–present*. The anecdote of MH's visit to his school in the Bronx appears in GSK's "Forked Lightning," pp. xxix-xxxi. Marc Connelly's comment, "Moss is in such . . ." is from Scott Meredith, *George S. Kaufman*, p. 557. Beatrice Kaufman's recommendation of Dr. Gregory Zilboorg: Meredith, pp. 555–56. Information about Drs. Zilboorg and Kubie was taken primarily from Farber and Green, *Hollywood on the Couch*, pp. 56–64. Steven Bach in *Dazzler* is highly critical of Kubie (pp. 213–215). Chris Hart, in an interview with me, confirmed Kubie's preoccupation with homosexuality as a curable disease. The quotation "It was said by his contemporaries . . ." is from Marie Brenner, "The Art of Mrs. Hart," *The New Yorker*, p. 46. MH's contemplation of suicide and the letters to Dore Schary are from Bruce McClung, et. al., *Lady in the Dark: A Sourcebook*, p. 70. The quotation, "To the casual eye . . ." is from Elizabeth R. Valentine, "Moss Hart: A Drama in 3 Acts," *NYT Magazine*, October 3, 1943, p. 4. GSK's skepticism about psychoanalysis: *GSKLT*, p. 270. MH's statement, "The great mystery of unhappiness . . ." is quoted in Meredith, *George S. Kaufman*, p. 556. Meredith also quotes MH ("I practically had to be carried . . .") on p. 191.

Chapter Five

Dore Schary's description "Moss never saw himself as . . ." is from Schary's *Heyday*, p. 29. An avid reader: interviews with Christopher Hart and KCH. Review of *The Show Is On* by Brooks Atkinson is in *NYT*, December 26, 1936. MH's involvement with *The Women* and Clare Boothe Luce's decision to write her own dialogue: Mark Fearnow, *Clare Boothe Luce*, pp. 81–82, 94, 96, 176; Scott Meredith, *George S. Kaufman*, pp. 566–67; *GSKLT*, p. 279. MH's investment in *Stage Door*: clipping from unidentified newspaper in BRTC. The material concerning Fairview Farm comes from an interview with KCH; KCH, *Kitty*, pp. 104–05; Harrison, *Take Them Up Tenderly*, p. 92; *NYT*, October 27, 1940; Mona Gardner, "Byron from Brooklyn"; *Variety*, November 22, 1944. MH leased his 57th Street apartment: *NYT*, May 15, 1939. MH's statement "Buying houses all over the place . . ." is from MH, "Moss Hart," *Esquire*, January 1962. The quotation "He was determined . . ." is from an interview with Leonora Hornblow. MH's aborted screenplay for Garbo: *NYT*, November 15, 1936; clipping, January 19, 1937, in BRTC. Returning the advance payment to MGM: interview with Jerome Chodorov; *NYT*, February 18, 1937; *New York World Telegram*, July 26, 1937. Consideration of the revue about the writing of a revue: *NYT*, November 7, 1937; *GSKLT*, p. 289; Scott Meredith, *George S. Kaufman*, p. 542. Writing a screenplay for Norma Shearer: *GSKLT*, p. 301. Writing a musical for Marlene Dietrich: *NYT*, November 7, 1937; *GSKLT*, pp. 289–90.

Sam Harris recommends Charles Winninger for *I'd Rather Be Right*: *GSKLT*, p. 290. GSK's suggesting George M. Cohan: *NYT*, November 7, 1937.

Lily Hart's funeral: *NYT*, September 7, 1937, and *New York Herald Tribune*, November 7, 1937; Steven Bach, *Dazzler*, p. 166. MH's phone call to Edna Ferber: Gilbert, *Ferber*, p. 319. Anecdote about MH's mother and the mysterious crosses: Donita Ferguson, "Mad Marvels;" Mona Gardner, "Byron from Brooklyn;" clipping (June 28, 1935) in BRTC; Harriman, *Take Them Up Tenderly*, p. 79 and pp. 82–3.

Material on *I'd Rather Be Right* can be found in Cecil Smith's *Musical Comedy in America*. Cohan's reaction to Rodgers and Hart's songs: Richard Rodgers, *Musical Stages*, p. 184. From the same source: "Don't take any wooden nickels" (p. 185), Cohan referring to Rodgers and Hart as "Gilbert and Sullivan" (p. 185), Cohan's substitution of his lyrics for Lorenz Hart's in Boston (p. 186), and "*I'd Rather Be Right* may well have been . . ." (p. 187). "All four of the authors . . ." is from *NYT*, November 7, 1937. The quotation from the editorial "Love to laugh at plays . . ." is from *NYT*, October 14, 1937. Promotion and advance sale: *GSKLT*, p. 298; Stanley Green, *The World of Musical Comedy*, p. 153. Brooks Atkinson's review of *I'd Rather Be Right* is in *NYT*, November 3, 1937. Commercial success of the production: Scott Meredith, *George S. Kaufman*, p. 546. GSK telling newspaper interviewer that MH was his favorite collaborator: *GSKLT*, p. 299.

MH's investment in *Sing Out the News*: Meredith, *George S. Kaufman*, p. 570. Harold Rome said K&H wrote sketches for the revue: Meredith, p. 570. Rome's disappointment with K&H"s approach: *GSKLT*, p. 305. Backers lost their investment: *GSKLT*, p. 307. *Sing Out the News*'s problems in Philadelphia: *GSKLT*, p. 307.

About *The Fabulous Invalid*: MH's purchase of old *Theatre* magazines is from *NYT*, October 30, 1938. MH's claim that he and GSK were the first to use the phrase "the fabulous invalid": MH, "A Devil's Dictionary of the Theatre." K&H's hope that Lunt and Fontanne would appear in the play: *NYT*, October 30, 1938. K&H's decision to use scenes only from twentieth-century plays: *NYT*, October 30, 1938. GSK reads play to Sam Harris: *NYT*, May 21, 1938.

Alexander Woollcott approaches MH with an intriguing proposal: MH, "How A.W. Came to Dinner, and Other Stories," *NYT*, October 29, 1939. Woollcott's previous acting experience: Beatrice Kaufman and Joseph Hennessey, eds., *The Letters of Alexander Woollcott*, pp. xv–xviii. Woollcott's disagreeable behavior at Fairview Farm: MH, "How A. W. Came to Dinner," *NYT*, October 29, 1939. Woollcott's note "I wish to say . . ." is quoted in *GSKLT*, p. 318. Quotation from MH "By 4 o'clock in the morning . . ." is from MH, "How A. W. Came to Dinner," *NYT*, October 29, 1939. MH's question "Wouldn't it have been awful . . ." is quoted in Meredith, *George S. Kaufman*, p. 551.

The Fabulous Invalid had New York previews rather than a road tour: *GSKLT*, p. 308. Brooks Atkinson's review: *NYT*, October 10, 1938. MH calling *The Fabulous Invalid* "unmourned and over-sentimental:" MH, "A Devil's Dictionary of The Theatre." Suit brought by Federal Nut against K&H: *Variety*, April 5, 1939; Meredith, *George S. Kaufman*, p. 126.

Beatrice Kaufman's request that K&H write an anti-fascist play: *GSKLT*, p. 310. Decision by K&H, Harris, and Gordon to donate a share of the profits of *The American Way* to political charities: *NYT*, January 29, 1939. From *NYT*: number of actors in the play (January 23, 1939 and March 5, 1939); salaries of the extras: February 9, 1939. K&H choosing not to make Martin Gunther Jewish: *GSKLT*, p. 313. Details about the production at the Center Theatre: Meredith, *George S. Kaufman*, pp. 549–50; *GSKLT*, p. 314. Postponing the opening of *The American Way*: *NYT*, October 13, 1938. John Anderson's review: *The New York Journal American*, January 22 (?), 1939 [clipping, SHSW]; Richard Watts's review: *The New York Herald-Tribune*, January 22 (?), 1939 [clipping, SHSW]. Cost of production, box-office gross, length of run, lowering of admission prices: *NYT*, August 28, 1939. Production losing $60,000: Harriman, *Take Them Up Tenderly*, p. 89. U. S. Flag Association award to K&H: *NYT*, February 21, 1939. RKO's purchase of rights to *The American Way*: *NYT*, March 31, 1940, and August 24, 1941. Columbia's purchase of the rights: *NYT*, February 1, 1942.

K&H beginning a musical with Cole Porter for W. C. Fields: *GSKLT*, p. 317. Quotation from MH "I received the royal command"—and Woollcott's angry explosion—are from MH, "How A. W. Came to Dinner," *NYT*, October 29, 1939. MH's investment and participation in *From Vienna*: *GSKLT*, pp. 316–17.

Chapter Six

About *The Man Who Came to Dinner*: MH's statement "We decided to use only . . ." quoted in *GSKLT*, p. 320. K&H reading the play to Woollcott: Meredith, *George S. Kaufman*, p. 551; *GSKLT*, p. 321. Woollcott's letter to Sybil Colefax is in Beatrice Kaufman and Joseph Hennessey, eds., *The Letters of Alexander Woollcott*, p. 230–32 (letter is dated February 19, 1940). From the same source: Woollcott's quote, "It struck me that it . . ." p. 322 (letter, dated March 3, 1941, is to Edmund Wilson); Woollcott's suggestion of Robert Morley, p. 322 (letter, dated March 3, 1941, is to Edmund Wilson). Adolphe Menjou turns down role: *GSKLT*, p. 321. Lorraine Sheldon based on Gertrude Lawrence: *GSKLT*, p. 324. Relationship of MH and Edith Atwater: *GSKLT*, p. 322. Rehearsals of *The Man Who Came to Dinner* (hereafter abbreviated as *MWCTD*) and all quotations attributed to K&H: *NYT*, September 17, 1939; Morton Eustis, "*The Man Who Came to Dinner* with George Kaufman Directing," *Theatre Arts Monthly*, November, 1939, pp. 789–98. Postponement of NY opening: *NYT*, September 17 and October 17, 1939. Monty Woolley's drinking affecting his performances: *GSKLT*, p. 325. Richard Watts's review is in *The New York Herald-Tribune*, October 17, 1940. Brooks Atkinson's review in *NYT*, October 17, 1940. Monty Woolley appearing on "Information Please" and delaying the play until 9:00: *NYT*, July 15, 1940. GSK saying he preferred *MWCTD* to *YCTIWY*: *NYT*, September 26, 1939; MH saying *MWCTD* was K&H's best work: Rosamond Gilder, "The Fabulous Hart," p. 91. Woollcott deciding to play Whiteside in Chicago, then on the West-Coast tour: Meredith, *George S. Kaufman*, p. 552; *GSKLT*, p. 329. K&H supervising rehearsals in Los Angeles: *GSKLT*, p. 329. From Los Angeles review ("a vastly entertaining performance . . .") is from *NYT*, February 18, 1940 (report is dated February 16). GSK playing Whiteside: Scott Meredith, *George S. Kaufman*, p. 187. Woollcott's refusal to cut back his activities: Letter from Woollcott to Cornelia Otis Skinner, February 19, 1940, in Beatrice Kaufman and Joseph Hennessey, eds., *The Letters of Alexander Woollcott*, p. 235. Observation of Cecil Smith's ("only partly an actor") is from *The Chicago Tribune*, April 10, 1940. Woollcott's heart attack and the decision to close the play while he recuperated: *NYT*, April 24, 1940. Woollcott's letter to Lynn Fontanne ("thinking to surprise everybody") is from Beatrice Kaufman and Joseph Hennessey, eds., *The Letters of Alexander Woollcott* (letter is dated November 20, 1940). Woollcott's curtain speech ("Due to the magnificent reception . . .") is from *The New York Herald-Tribune*, February 9, 1941. Woollcott's letter to Alan Campbell is from Kaufman and Hennessey, eds., pp. 350–51 (letter is dated August 11, 1942); also see *NYT*, May 6, 1941. July, 1941 production at the Bucks County Playhouse: *New York Post*, July 30, 1941; *New York Herald-Tribune*, July 29, 1941; KCH, *Kitty*, pp. 122–23; *GSKLT*, pp. 352–53. Harpo's performance: Harriman, clipping in BRTC; *Take Them Up Tenderly*, p. 86; *GSKLT*, p. 353. July, 1941 production at the

Cape Playhouse in Dennis, Mass.: *New York Post*, July 14, 1941 and *NYT*, July 19, 1941. Review in *Cape Cod Standard-Times*: clipping in BRTC. Film of *MWCTD*, including the saga of the casting: *NYT*, March 31, 1940; March 28, 1941; April 6, 1941; April 9, 1941; July 1, 1941; September 21, 1941; and January 2, 1942. Woollcott refusing to give permission for film: Meredith, *George S. Kaufman*, p. 553. Woollcott's statement ("I thought and still think . . .") is from the same page. Woollcott's practical joke, "I'm sure you're wondering who this young man . . ." is quoted in KCH, *Kitty*, p. 104. Bosley Crowther's review of *MWCTD* (film) is in *NYT*, January 2, 1942.

Edith Atwater's marriage to Hugh Marlowe: *New York World Telegram*, November 15, 1941; *NYT*, November 21, 1941; Atwater's obituary: *NYT*, March 17, 1986. Jerome Chodorov recalled MH's shock in an interview. MH's diary, which contains the words, "feelings of deep hostility . . ." is at SHSW.

MH on committee of American Theatre Wing: *GSKLT*, p. 330. Set of *George Washington Slept Here* (hereafter abbreviated as *GWSH*) resembling MH's house at Fairview Farm: *NYT*, October 19, 1940. In 1941, Kubie told MH to break with GSK: Scott Meredith, *George S. Kaufman*, p. 556. GSK's unhappiness when MH announced he would write independently: Interview with Anne Kaufman Schneider. MH's suggestion that GSK direct *My Sister Eileen*: *GSKLT*, p. 339; Meredith, *George S. Kaufman*, p. 577. Ernest Truex' accident: *NYT*, October 6, 1940. Berton Churchill's death: *NYT* and *New York Herald-Tribune*, both October 10, 1940. Reviews of *GWSH*: Sidney Whipple in *The New York World Telegram*; Richard Watts in *The New York Herald-Tribune*; John Mason Brown in *The New York Post*: all October 19, 1940. *GWSH* making a slight profit despite requiring twenty-three stagehands: *Variety*, March 12, 1941. *GWSH* as the most popular play in summer stock in 1941: clipping, BRTC; *GSKLT*, p. 339. Warner's purchase of the movie rights: *NYT*, February 18, 1941. After their break, K&H continued as friends: *GSKLT*, p. 333.

Collaboration with GSK: Jean Gould, *Modern American Playwrights*, pp. 165–66. The quotation "Mr. Kaufman applies the discipline . . ." is from Brooks Atkinson, "Introduction" to *Six Plays by Kaufman and Hart*. pp. xiv–xv; and Rosamond Gilder, "The Fabulous Hart."

Intermission

MH's insomnia: KCH, *Kitty*, p. 182; MH's diary in SHSW; Mona Gardner, "Byron from Brooklyn." "Again, no sleep" is from MH's diary. MH's anxiety and depression and dependence upon psychoanalysis: interviews with Dr. Catherine Hart and Dr. Macon Williams. Kurt Weill told Lotte Lenya about MH's sessions with Dr. Kubie: quoted in Bruce McClung, et. al., *Lady in the Dark: A Sourcebook*, p. 4. The quotation "I doubt if anyone . . ." is from an interview with Jerome Chodorov. "All of his life . . ." is from Bennett Cerf's "With Gaiety and Gusto," p. 31. Brooks Atkinson's comment on MH's "genuine and possibly dangerous" melancholia is from Brooks Atkinson's tribute in *A Memorial Tribute to Moss Hart*, p. 10. Alan Jay Lerner's statement "When one is plagued . . ." is from *SWL*, p. 249. The quotation "He never, ever burdened you . . ." is from an interview with Leonora Hornblow. The quotation "He was a wonderful listener" is from an interview with Anne Kaufman Schneider. "I have a snapshot . . ." is from an interview with Jerome Chodorov. Also: See Notes for Chapter Four.

Chapter Seven

A great deal of information about *Lady in the Dark* can be found in Bruce McClung, et. al., *Lady in the Dark: A Sourcebook* (hereafter abbreviated as "McClung, et al") and some material is in Cecil Smith's *Musical Comedy in America*, pp. 339–40. MH's suggestion to GSK that they write "a show based upon . . . the psychoanalytic technique" is from *NYT*, November 7, 1937. MH and Kurt Weill expressing interest in working together: *Boston Evening Transcript*, December 28, 1940; [*Brooklyn?*] *Eagle*, April 27, 1941; MH, "Preface" to the Chappell Piano/Vocal Score, reprinted in McClung, et. al., p. 6. Weill wanting to write a full score: *NYT*, February 26, 1940. Purchase and sale of Lyceum Theatre, 1940–45: Meredith, *George S. Kaufman*, pp. 570–71. MH asking Ira Gershwin to write lyrics: Stanley Green, *The World of Musical Comedy*, p. 231; *Boston Evening Transcript*, December 28, 1940; McClung, et al., pp. ii and 64. Weill's quote, "three one-act operas . . ." is from McClung, et al., p. 7. *Lady in the Dark* written in New York and at Fairview Farm: McClung, et al., p. 8. Cost and financing of production: McClung, et al., p. iii. Marshall Field's investment: *New York News*, January 9, 1941. MH's wish to write a play for Katharine Cornell: MH, "The Saga of Gertie," *NYT*, March 2, 1941; McClung, et. al., p. 12. Edith Atwater's audition for MH: Leonard Lyons, *New York Post*, September 12, 1940. K&H seeing Gertrude Lawrence at a British War Relief Benefit: MH, "The Saga of Gertie." From the same source: MH's quote "As I watched her sing and dance . . ." MH's discussion with Sam Harris and his staff: *New York Herald-Tribune*, January 12, 1941. MH's long pursuit of Gertrude Lawrence: MH, "The Saga of Gertie," *NYT*,

March 2, 1941. Quotation "I went to [Hart's] office . . ." is from an interview with Gregory Peck. Quotation from MH "I hate night clubs, but . . ." is from a radio program in which MH appeared with Brooks Atkinson: "35 Years of Broadway Musicals;" the audiotape is at SHSW. Gertrude Lawrence's discussions and rehearsals with MH at Fairview Farm: clipping, BRTC. Three-week rehearsal period for *Lady in the Dark*: MH, "The Saga of Gertie." From the same source: MH's statement "I privately decided . . ." The quotation from MH ("a very bad rehearser") is on the audiotape of "35 Years of Broadway Musicals" at SHSW. Gertrude Lawrence ("the chorus was busy in another . . .") is quoted in Helen Ormsbee, *New York Herald-Tribune*, February 9, 1941. MH's concern that "Tschaikowsky" might stop the show and irritate Gertrude Lawrence: audiotape of "35 Years of Broadway Musicals" at SHSW, which is also the source for MH's "Please, for goodness' sake . . ." as are Gertrude Lawrence's response ("This is not a song for me") and MH's reply ("You must do it . . .") and "In rehearsal, when a star . . ." (Also see McClung, et. al., pp. 10, 22, 66-7.) Danny Kaye's rapid-fire singing of "Tschaikowsky" and Ripley's claim: Stanley Green, *The World of Musical Comedy*, p. 233; *A Celebration of Moss Hart*; and *The New York Journal American*, April 21, 1941. MH's comment to Julie Andrews that he found Gertrude Lawrence "maddening" is from an interview with Julie Andrews. Harry Horner's set for *Lady in the Dark*: *NYT*, April 6, 1941. Sam Harris's decision not to have an extensive tryout tour: *GSKLT*, p. 341. MH's characterization to the response to "Tschaikowsky" ("thunderous") is from the audiotape of "35 Years of Broadway Musicals" at SHSW. Maurice Abravanel cuing the trumpets: McClung, et. al., pp. 67-8. MH's statement that Gertrude Lawrence "then sang 'Jenny' . . ." is from the audiotape of "35 Years of Broadway Musicals" at SHSW. Elliott Norton's review of *Lady in the Dark* is in *The Boston Post*, December 31, 1940. K&H working together to cut the length of the musical: *GSKLT*, p. 342. Gertrude Lawrence's influenza causing Sam Harris to postpone the New York opening: clipping, BRTC. Gertrude Lawrence's observation "The nurses and doctors are trying . . ." is quoted in Helen Ormsbee, *The New York Herald-Tribune*, February 9, 1941. Reviews: Brooks Atkinson in *NYT*; John Mason Brown in *The New York Post*; Richard Watts in *The New York Herald-Tribune*: all January 24, 1941. Gertrude Lawrence's eleven-week vacation: *Toledo Blade*, July 14, 1941; *NYT*, September 3, 1941, and November 23, 1941. The vacation adding $23,000 to the production cost: *NYT*, November 23, 1941. National tour followed by a return to Broadway: *NYT*, March 9, 1942, October 18, 1942, and October 26,

1942. MH's earnings from *Lady in the Dark* allowing him to build "the Gertrude Lawrence Memorial Wing:" KCH, *Kitty*, p. 128. The quotation from "Dr. Brooks" [Lawrence Kubie], "for the first time on any stage . . ." is from the "Preface" to the published version of *Lady in the Dark*, p. viii. Purchase by Paramount for $283,000: *NYT*, February 18, 1941. Addition of scenes to the film: *NYT*, January 23, 1944. Casting of Liza (Irene Dunne, Greta Garbo) in the film: *New York Journal American*, February 5, 1941. Jesse Zunser's review is in *Cue*, February 26, 1944. Quotation "*Lady in the Dark* was not one of my happiest . . ." is from Ginger Rogers, *Ginger*, pp. 252–55.

MH's interview with Robert Rice and the quotation "One reason for writing . . ." are from Robert Rice, "Rice and Old Shoes," *PM*, February 3, 1941. Joseph Fields and Jerome Chodorov asking MH to direct *Junior Miss*: clipping, BRTC. MH's opting to take a share of the weekly box-office receipts rather than a salary: Meredith, *George S. Kaufman*, p. 368, and Brooks Atkinson, *Broadway*, pp. 236–37. MH's directorial style and the statement "The actors loved him" are from an interview with Jerome Chodorov. (Also, see Irving Lazar, *Swifty*, p. 77.) Alan Jay Lerner's statement "He was a superb constructionist . . ." is from *SWL*, p. 72. The quotation from Alan Jay Lerner ("Only those writers who . . .") is from Lerner's tribute in *A Memorial Tribute to Moss Hart*, p. 22. The assertion by MH ("In some ways I think . . .") is from his diary at SHSW. The comment "Once rehearsals of a new play . . ." is from Bennett Cerf, "A Few Words About Moss Hart," *NYT*, March 27, 1960. MH writing material for American Theatre Wing sketches: *NYT*, March 28, 1943. MH applying to the army and being rejected: *New York World Telegram*, May 14, 1941; *NYT*, December 21, 1961; clipping, BRTC; Harriman, *Take Them Up Tenderly*, p. 93. MH's being granted a deferment: Steven Bach, *Dazzler*, p. 232. An account of "The Lunchtime Follies" is in *NYT*, June 23 and June 24, 1942; *GSKLT*, p. 362. The quotation praising MH "selfless interest in the plight . . ." is in *The National Jewish Monthly*, BRTC.

About *Winged Victory*: the genesis of the play is discussed in Elizabeth R. Valentine, "Moss Hart: A Drama in 3 Acts," *NYT Magazine*, October 31, 1943; MH, "A Winged Victory," *NYT*, November 14, 1943; MH, "One World—One Trip—One Play," SHSW; and Irving Lazar, *Swifty*, pp. 70–4. Lazar asking MH, "would you like to do a show . . .": MH, "A Winged Victory," *NYT*, November 14, 1943. General Arnold's question "Do you think you can do this show? . . ." and MH's reply are quoted in Irving Lazar, *Swifty*, p. 71. MH's description of his meeting with Gen. Arnold is from MH, "A

Winged Victory," *NYT*, November 14, 1943 and from MH, "One World—One Trip—One Play," SHSW. All of MH's description of the places he went and the things he did in preparation for writing *Winged Victory* are from MH, "A Winged Victory," *NYT*, November 14, 1943, and from Elizabeth R. Valentine, "Moss Hart: A Drama in 3 Acts," *NYT Magazine*, October 31, 1943. MH's description ("very simple, very . . .") is from Valentine, p. 2. Seven thousand applicants are considered: "*Winged Victory* in Production," p. 94. (Elizabeth R. Valentine, in "Moss Hart: A Drama in 3 Acts," puts the figure at three thousand.) 500 soldiers arrive in New York: *NYT*, August 29, 1943. MH picking up meal checks for soldier-actors: newspaper clipping, BRTC. Production cost raised by civilian committee headed by Gilbert Miller: *NYT*, October 28, 1943, and November 21, 1943. MH's refusal of pay and donation to the Army Emergency Relief Fund: *NYT*, October 28, 1943; *A Celebration of Moss Hart*; and "Person to Person," appearance in 1954 (videotape in Wisconsin Center for Film and Theatre Research). Two-and-a-half week rehearsal period: *NYT*, August 29, 1943. Elinor Hughes's review is in a Boston newspaper, November 3 (?), 1943 (clipping in SHSW). Eighteen curtain calls at the Broadway opening: *A Celebration of Moss Hart*. Lewis Nichols's reviews are in *NYT*, November 22, and November 28, 1943. Burton Rascoe's review is in *The New York World Telegram*, November 22, 1943. Design process for *Winged Victory*: "Winged Victory in Production," *Theatre Arts*, February, 1944, pp. 93–6. MH winning Donaldson Award as Best Director: clipping, SHSW. The letter from MH to Gen. Arnold ("I kept waiting . . .") is from a letter dated January 28, 1944, in SHSW. Payment of backers' investments: *NYT*, January 10, 1943. 20th Century-Fox obtains rights to the play: *NYT*, December 16, 1943. Bosley Crowther's review is in *NYT*, December 21, 1944. MH's letter to Gen. Arnold ("My feeling is that . . .") is dated January 28, 1944, in SHSW. Arrangements for the cast in the film: *NYT*, March 12, 1944. Where scenes were shot: *NYT*, August 6, 1944. Wives of the soldiers playing small roles: *NYT*, December 17, 1944; and a letter from MH to M/Sgt. Jerry Whyte, July 19, 1944, SHSW. Bosley Crowther's review is in *NYT*, December 21, 1944. Letter from Gen. Arnold to MH beginning "Not quite three years ago . . ." is dated February 9, 1946, in SHSW.

MH supports FDR for re-election: MH, "Why I Will Vote for Franklin D. Roosevelt," *The Independent*, September 21, 1944; Meredith, *George S. Kaufman*, p. 443. MH appears on "Hollywood Fights Back": *NYT*, October 31, 1947. MH and others file anti-trust suit against MPAA: *NYT*, May 31, 1948. MH speaks out against McCarthyism: *NYT*, December 21, 1961; Walter H.

Ross, *Dictionary of Literary Biography*. MH supports Adlai Stevenson for presidency: letter from Stevenson to MH dated October 31, 1955, in SHSW. MH and others produce closed circuit telecast for Stevenson: *NYT*, October 6, 1956. Stevenson's letter to MH ("your support and encouragement") is dated October 31, 1955, in SHSW.

Chapter Eight

Reviews of *Seven Lively Arts*: *NYT* and *New York Herald-Tribune*, both December 8, 1944. MH directed *Dear Ruth* for Bernie Hart and Joseph Hyman: "Let The Shuberts Be Warned," *NYT*, December 17, 1944. Reviews of *Dear Ruth*: Lewis Nichols in *NYT*, December 14, 1945; Howard Barnes in *The New York Herald-Tribune* and Burton Rascoe in *The New York World Telegram*, both clippings in BRTC. The tour of *MWCTD* in the South Pacific: quotation from MH, "Don't ask me why . . ." is from an unidentified army newspaper, clipping, SHSW. GSK's farewell party for MH and the dialogue from "Moss Hart at the Analyst's" are in *GSKLT*, pp. 293–94. A review of the production of *MWCTD* is in *The Midpacifican*, April 14, 1945; other reviews are at SHSW. MH's relationship with Dora Sayers: interview with Anne Kaufman Schneider. MH's casting of Charles Matthies: KCH, *Kitty*, p. 130. Production schedule: several clippings, BRTC. Review of *MWCTD* in an army newspaper, "pretty good in the part . . ." is from an undated clipping, SHSW. Col. De Haven's letter (*MWCTD* "is ideally suited . . .") to MH is dated April 21, 1945; in SHSW. About *The Secret Room*: Lewis Nichols's review is in *NYT*, November 8, 1945. MH permits melodramatic acting: Burton Rascoe's review in *The New York World Telegram*, November 8, 1945. Reviews by Louis Kronenberger and Ward Morehouse are in *PM* and in *The New York Sun*, November 8, 1945.

Much of the information about MH's pursuit of and marriage to Kitty Carlisle is from many interviews with KCH and from KCH's *Kitty* (hereafter referred to only as *Kitty*). Beatrice Kaufman's death: *GSKLT*, p. 389; Scott Meredith, *George S. Kaufman*, p. 592. Anne Kaufman Schneider's comments about Beatrice Kaufman's relationship with MH: from an interview with Anne Kaufman Schneider. MH invites Norman Krasna to Fairview Farm: *Kitty*, p. 103. Krasna is quoted saying "If I can get her away . . ." is in *Kitty*, p. 103, which is also the source for MH telling Krasna that marriage to KCH would be a mistake (p. 105). Sinclair Lewis and George Gershwin in love with KCH: letters from Lewis and Gershwin to KCH in SHSW. The following several items are all from *Kitty*: MH invites KCH to lunch at "21" (p. 112); "He was quite different . . ." (p. 112); "I find I wanted to make . . ." (p. 114); "told me that one of . . ." (pp. 117–18). KCH's question to MH, "Are you homosexual?" is from Marie Brenner, "The Art of Mrs. Hart," *The New Yorker*, p. 49. GSK's quote, "This afternoon I am having . . ." is taken from *GSKLT*, pp. 394–95. The next several items are all from *Kitty*: MH's comment, "I didn't like the placement . . ." (p. 127); MH and KCH in *MWCTD* at Bucks County Playhouse (pp. 122–23); "I said everything . . ." (p. 127). The quotation "From the day . . ." is from an interview with Anne Kaufman Schneider. KCH's statement "We lived in each other's pockets . . ." is from Marie Brenner, "The Art of Mrs. Hart," which also quotes from MH's letter, "Is there a way of saying . . ." KCH's statement "I never bought a dress . . ." is from Meredith, *George S. Kaufman*, p. 529. She said "quickly realized that 'order' . . ." is from *Kitty*, p. 138; that is also the source for "I felt I was in a . . ." (p. 152). KCH's miscarriage, then the birth of her children: *Kitty*, pp. 137, 139, 142, 145–46; letter from MH to Brooks Atkinson, undated, in BRTC. In the same letter is MH's reference, "cute as a button . . ." MH's avowal that he and KCH "try to be sure . . ." is in *NYT*, October 6, 1959. "We were standing in line . . ." is from an interview with Christopher Hart. The quotation "making him laugh" is from an interview with Catherine Hart. KCH's "Moss handled his depressions . . ." is from *Kitty*, p. 165. "She told me one time . . ." is from an interview with Anne Kaufman Schneider.

About *Christopher Blake*: MH's alternate ending is at SHSW. Production cost of $180,000: clipping, dated February 18, 1947, in BRTC. Invited audience responding favorably to *Christopher Blake*: *Kitty*, p. 135; the same source speaks of the disastrous Broadway tryout (p. 135). Undated review of the play by Elinor Hughes is in *The Boston Herald*, clipping in BRTC. Robert Garland's review, in *The New York Journal American*, and Richard Watts's review, in *The New York Post*, are both dated December 2, 1946. MH's angry letter to John Chapman (and a similar letter to George Jean Nathan) are at SHSW. MH's admission that *Christopher Blake* was "smothered in production:" *NYT*, November 2, 1952. Sale of *Christopher Blake* to the movies: Letter from Warner Bros. to Joseph Hyman, December 9, 1946, in SHSW; and Irving Lazar, *Swifty*, p. 118. Problems on the set of the film: *NYT*, August 19, 1947. Bosley Crowther's review is in *NYT*, December 11, 1948.

MH's election as president of the Dramatists Guild: *NYT*, November 12, 1947; November 9, 1949; December 21, 1961. KCH's description of MH running the Dramatists Guild with an iron hand: interview with KCH.

About *Gentleman's Agreement*: significant information was derived from an interview with Gregory Peck. Darryl Zanuck announcing that MH will write the screenplay: *NYT*, March 16, 1947. MH's eagerness to write the film and his acceptance of minimum salary: interview with KCH; *Kitty*, p. 140. Louis B. Mayer was quoted as saying, "Why stir up . . ." by Gregory Peck, in an interview. Cecilia Ager's review of the film is in *PM*, November 12, 1947. Bosley Crowther's review is in *NYT*, November 12, 1947. *Gentleman's Agreement* wins NY Film Critics Award: *NYT*, December 30, 1947. Wins Academy Award: *SWL*, p. 73. 20th Century-Fox gives MH a station wagon: interview with KCH; *Kitty*, p. 141.

Reviews of *Inside USA*: *NYT*, May 3, 1948; *Baltimore Evening Sun*, April 5, 1949.

Concerning *Light Up the Sky*: MH's description of the play as "a simple story . . ." is from MH, "First-Night Thoughts of a Playwright," unidentified newspaper clipping, BRTC. Owen as a self-portrait of MH: *New York Sunday News*, October 10, 1948. Irene based on Gertrude Lawrence: *NYT*, November 14, 1948—which is also the source for the producer and his wife being based on Billy Rose and Eleanor Holm. Rose threatening to sue Hart: two newspaper clippings in BRTC. KCH's quote ("conferences took place . . .") is from *Kitty*, p. 136. Changes in *Light Up the Sky* (cuts, new third act, etc.): two newspaper clippings, BRTC. Reviews of *Light Up yhe Sky*, all dated November 19, 1948: Brooks Atkinson in *NYT*; John Chapman in *The New York Daily News*; William Hawkins in *The New York World Telegram*. CBS telecast: *NYT*, June 9, 1949. Review in *Variety* ("one of the top treats . . ."), June 15, 1949. Continued popular success of *Light Up the Sky*: interview with Christopher Hart. MH's statement that he "had hoped, in . . ." is from *NYT*, November 2, 1952.

MH's friendship with Brooks Atkinson is described in Atkinson's tribute in *A Memorial Tribute to Moss Hart*, pp. 9–10. MH's attitude toward critics: "They are notoriously unable . . ." is from MH's address to the American Academy of Dramatic Arts, April 5, 1950. Other sources are *NYT*, June 10, 1950 and October 23, 1950 (which includes "almost nothing about directing"); MH, "A Devil's Dictionary of the Theatre," SHSW. About *Miss Liberty*: Advance sale of $430,000: *NYT*, July 15, 1949. Rehearsal problems: *NYT*, June 15, 1949; Edward Jablonski, *Irving Berlin: American Troubador*, p. 261. Jablonski's book also tells of MH cutting and adding dialogue (p. 261 and p. 264). Also: interview with Eddie Albert. Allyn Ann McLerie's comments are from Bergreen, *The Life That Late He Led*, p. 488. The reviews from Philadelphia are summarized in *NYT*, June 15, 1949. Postponement of New York opening of *Miss Liberty: NYT*, June 10 and June 15, 1949. Brooks Atkinson's review: *NYT*, July 16, 1949. Ward Morehouse's review: *New York Sun*, July 16 (?), 1949 (clipping, BRTC). *Miss Liberty* barely breaking even: *Kitty*, p. 137.

Chapter Nine

Answer—Yes or No: Vincent Terrace, *The Complete Encyclopedia of Television Programs, 1947–79*. Jack Gould's review of *Answer—Yes or No* is in *NYT*, May 14, 1950.

About *Hans Christian Andersen*: Samuel Goldwyn had rejected twenty screenplays before hiring MH: American Movie Classics telecast. Goldwyn's wish to ignore Andersen's biography: *NYT*, March 15, 1952. Frank Loesser's collaboration with MH: *NYT*, November 16, 1952; interviews with KCH and with Christopher Hart. MH's quote "The spirit of the film . . ." is in the Commemorative Premiere Booklet for *Hans Christian Andersen* at SHSW. Goldwyn's insistence on a rewrite after the California preview: *Kitty*, p. 161. MH's response, "how terrible," is from his diary, SHSW. Reviews of *Hans Christian Andersen: NYT*, November 26, 1952; *Variety*, November 26, 1952. MH nominated as "author of the best American musical:" clipping, February 16, 1953, BRTC; *Contemporary Authors*, Volume 10.

About *The Climate of Eden*: quotation from MH "nothing that excited or pleased me . . ." is from MH, "A Playwright's View," *NYT*, November 2, 1952. MH wrote to Mittelhölzer for permission to adapt *Shadows Move Among Them*: letter from Edgar Mittelhölzer to MH, December 4, 1951. "The very difficulties . . ." is from MH, "A Playwright's View"—which is also the source for "I think *The Climate of Eden* is by far . . ." MH's casting of *The Climate of Eden* in England: *Theatre Arts*, November, 1952; *Kitty*, pp. 159–60. Brooks Atkinson's review: *NYT*, November 7, 1952. MH believing that he had miscast the role of Gregory: interview with KCH. KCH's comment "Almost no one in Washington . . ." is from *Kitty*, p. 160. Brooks Atkinson's letter to MH ("There is so much that is good . . ."), dated November 10, 1952, is at SHSW. Ward Morehouse's undated letter to MH ("There's a great deal of beauty . . .") is at SHSW. Reviews: Richard Watts in *The New York Post*, John Chapman in the *Daily News*, both November 7, 1952. Chapman's subsequent discussion of the play is in *The New York Daily News*, November 16, 1952. MH's undated letter to Brooks Atkinson ("I have no regrets") is in

BRTC. Productions on WNTA-TV: *Variety*, March 2, 1960. Quotation from editors "that it is a worthwhile play . . ." is from *Theatre Arts*, May, 1954. Laurence Olivier's letter to MH, dated February 4, 1954 ("I have just finished . . .") is at SHSW. MH's note that he was "very pleased indeed . . ." is in MH's diary, SHSW. N. Gwatkin's list of recommended changes in *The Climate of Eden*, dated March 17, 1954, is at SHSW. Olivier's request for "rewriting the second act . . ." is from a letter to MH dated March 26, 1954, SHSW. Olivier's withdrawal and his letter to MH beginning "Dorothy Tutin . . ." dated June 22, 1954, is at SHSW. Anthony Quayle's letter to MH "a really fascinating piece of work . . ." dated January 15, 1957, is at SHSW. MH submitting *The Climate of Eden* to Tony Richardson: letter from Richardson to MH, dated May 12, 1958, at SHSW. MH's statement "a failure that hurt . . ." is from MH's diary, SHSW. MH's quote, "tantalizing and frustrating," is from MH's prefatory note to the published version of *The Climate of Eden*.

About MH's father: Barnett Hart's song, "The Man Who Came to Dinner," is at SHSW. KCH describes the Commodore's songs in *Kitty*, pp. 118–19. Also, see Mona Gardner, "Byron from Brooklyn." KCH loved the Commodore: interview with KCH. MH's observation "a touching moment . . ." is from MH's diary, SHSW—as is his comment "looks very hale . . ." Barnett Hart died on October 5, 1960: *NYT*, October 6, 1960.

MH being offered the direction of *Two's Company*: two newspaper clippings, dated November 18 and November 19, 1952, at BRTC.

About Edna Ferber: MH's aborted collaboration on *Saratoga Trunk: Kitty*, pp. 150–52. Ferber's question "Who is this Arlen fellow?" is from Julie Goldsmith Gilbert's *Ferber: A Biography*, p. 123. MH referring to the play as *Saratoga Junk*: interview with KCH. MH's comment "I simply cannot work with her . . .:" *Kitty*, p. 151. Ferber said MH called her "old granite face": letter from Ferber to KCH, October 3, 1954, SHSW. MH said he simply said "as stubborn as a piece of granite": interview with KCH. Letter from Rodgers and Hammerstein to MH and Edna Ferber, dated November 3, 1953, is at SHSW. Ferber's letter to KCH ("friendship, understanding, appreciation . . ."), dated October 13, 1954, is at SHSW. Julie Goldsmith Gilbert's statement ("the only maternal instincts . . .") is from *Ferber*, p. 100. MH running into Ferber in 1954 ("Hello, Edna") is from MH's diary, SHSW. MH and Cathy Hart meeting Ferber backstage at *Peter Pan*: interview with KCH; *Kitty*, p. 151. MH saying he and Ferber "looked right through each other . . ." is from MH's diary, SHSW. MH and Ferber ending their feud in London: interview with KCH.

About *A Star Is Born*: much information for this section was derived from Ronald M. Haver's *A Star Is Born: The Making of the 1954 Movie and Its 1983 Restoration*. Also see Gerald Clarke, *Get Happy*. Inscriptions by Sid Luft and Judy Garland are in MH's bound filmscript at SHSW. MH's opinion of Judy Garland ("completely enchanting . . .") is from MH's diary, SHSW. Party at Irving Lazar's house attended by the Harts and by Judy Garland: interview with KCH; Irving Lazar, *Swifty*, pp. 151–52. Garland's undated letter to MH, "How can I possibly tell you . . ." is at SHSW. George Cukor's letters to MH about *A Star Is Born*, dated September 24, 1953, September 30, 1953, March 30, 1954, and August 18, 1954, are all at SHSW. MH's undated responses to Cukor's letters are at SHSW. From MH's diary at SHSW: "It may be that I had heard," "sent them a scorching wire" and "a number of letters and telegrams . . ." Jack Warner supervises the editing of the film: Letter from Jack Warner to MH, May 28, 1954, SHSW. MH's letter to Jack Warner, "apprehensive that what may appear . . ." is from a letter dated May 25, 1954, at SHSW. Warner's response "Between you and me, Moss . . ." is from a letter to MH dated May 28, 1954, at SHSW. Warner's telegram ("JUST IMPOSSIBLE TO FIND WORDS . . ."), dated August 4, 1954, is at SHSW. Quotation from Cukor, "extraordinary occasions," is in a letter to MH dated August 18, 1954, at SHSW. Cukor resumes control of editing: letter from Cukor to MH dated March 30, 1954. MH's comment on *A Star Is Born*, "The picture itself . . ." is from MH's diary, SHSW. Bosley Crowther's review is in *NYT*, October 12, 1954. Review in *The Hollywood Reporter* is dated September 29, 1954. Exhibitors demanding cuts in *A Star Is Born* and Ronald Haver's restoration: Ronald M. Haver, *A Star Is Born: The Making of the 1954 Movie*, pp. 202–04, 212–14, 222, 229, 264.

Chapter Ten

Most of the information from this chapter was taken from Moss Hart's 1953–1954 diary, at SHSW. Unless otherwise noted, all quotations are from the diary. S. N. Behrman's "Writing breeds writing": clipping at SHSW. *The Nature of the Beast* is at SHSW. (The program was telecast on December 13, 1953.) Review of *Anniversary Waltz*: Brooks Atkinson, *NYT*, April 8, 1954. Christopher Hart's observation (Kubie "was practically a . . .") is from an interview. Quote from MH "I am certain that most of the trouble we get into is

by saying . . ." is from MH, an (apparently) unpublished article about directing *My Fair Lady*, SHSW. Alan Jay Lerner, in *SWL*, paraphrases MH's remark
as well. Quote from KCH "that it was ridiculous . . ." is from an interview
with KCH. Sale of Fairview Farm: *NYT*, October 7, 1954. KCH calling up
MH to demand that he stop smoking: *Kitty*, pp. 172–73. K&H's croquet
game with Richard and Dorothy Rodgers: Scott Meredith, *George S. Kaufman*, p. 175. KCH relieving MH of all demanding physical activity: *Kitty*, pp.
173–74. Irving Lazar negotiates a five-picture deal for MH with 20th Century-Fox: Irving Lazar, *Swifty*, p. 181. *Variety's* review of *Prince of Players*: January 4, 1955. Quote from MH ("I can't have that kind of . . .") is from Irving
Lazar, *Swifty*, p. 182—as is Lazar's reply ("Okay, let's forget . . ."); also, see
Kitty, pp. 164–65. Harry Cohn's offer for MH to write three screenplays: interview with KCH. The contract between Columbia Pictures and MH for a
three-picture deal, dated December 9, 1954, is at SHSW. Quote from MH,
"the indulgence of three years . . .," is from MH's diary, SHSW.

Chapter Eleven

Much of the information about *My Fair Lady* was derived from several inter-
views with Julie Andrews and from Alan Jay Lerner's autobiography, *The Street
Where I Live (SWL)*. Lerner and Loewe began casting *My Fair Lady* (hereafter
abbreviated as *MFL*) before MH became director: *SWL*, pp. 55–65; interview
with Stone Widney. Quote from Loewe, "Fine. That's all you need" is from
SWL, p. 59. Lerner and Loewe draw up list of potential directors: *SWL*, p. 71.
MH's collaboration with Harold Rome on *In The Pink*: *Kitty*, pp. 175, 177;
SWL, p. 66. The script of *In the Pink* is at SHSW. Offer to KCH to appear on *To
Tell the Truth*: *Kitty*, pp. 183–86. Quote from Loewe, "the great Moss Hart," is
from *SWL*, p. 73. MH's statement, "Having been informed over . . ." is from
MH's article about directing *MFL*, SHSW. "As the last note of music . . ." is
from the same source. "Harold was very gracious . . ." is from an interview
with KCH. Lerner's quote "Mrs. Hart, as I was to find out . . ." is from *SWL*,
p. 71. MH's statement "the writing of a musical show . . ." is from MH's article about directing *MFL*, SHSW. Mary Martin turned down the role of Eliza:
SWL, pp. 50–51; Stanley Green, *The World of Musical Comedy*, p. 278. Judy Holliday turned down the role: interview with Stone Widney; Abe Laufe, *Broadway's Greatest Musicals*, p. 198. Quote from Lerner ("how refreshing it might
be . . .") is from *SWL*, p. 52. Julie Andrews's several auditions for *MFL*: Les
Spindle, *Julie Andrews*, p. 5; Stanley Green, *The World of Musical Comedy*, p. 278.
CBS's financing of *MFL*: Richard Maney, "Fabulous Six Months of a Fabu-

lous Lady," *NYT Magazine*, September 9, 1956, p. 27. Quote from MH, "I wish you'd take a look . . ." is from the radio program MH appeared on with Brooks Atkinson, "35 Years of Broadway Musicals," audiotape in SHSW. MH may have contributed to some of the dialogue in *MFL*: interview with KCH. Lerner's use of KCH's searching for her gloves in "I'm an Ordinary Man:" *Kitty*, p. 186. MH telling Lerner and Loewe to retain "The Rain in Spain": *SWL*, pp. 100 and 107. "Every effort in the theatre . . ."; "They work like stevedores . . ." and "It is my way . . ." are from MH's article on directing *MFL*, SHSW. Quote from MH "If you have any plans . . ." is from *SWL*, p. 88. Also from *SWL*: Lerner writing book and songs in Atlantic City and New York (pp. 88–9); sketches of scenery and costumes at the first rehearsal (p. 90); MFL's rehearsal schedule (p. 92); daily tea breaks during rehearsals (p. 93); MH's custom of blocking after a single read-through (p. 98). Quotation from Julie Andrews "simply terrified working with . . ." is from *A Celebration of Moss Hart*, p. 32. MH's observation that Julie Andrews "was charming but it seemed . . ." is from Gilbert Millstein, "Flowering of a Fair Lady," *NYT Magazine*, April 1, 1956, p. 47. Quote from KCH, "She needs a lot of help," is from *Kitty*, p. 178. Quote from MH "the days of the Terror . . ." is from Millstein, "Flowering of a Fair Lady," p. 47. The lengthy quotation from Julie Andrews beginning "I knew that this was the big test" was taken originally from *A Celebration of Moss Hart*, pp. 32–4; the quotation was then modified by Julie Andrews during our interview in 1999. Quote from MH, "Those two days made the difference," is from Millstein, "Flowering of a Fair Lady," p. 47. Quotation from MH that Julie Andrews projected "this curious kind of glacial calm": Gilbert Millstein, "Flowering of a Fair Lady," p. 24. Rex Harrison's temperamental outbursts at rehearsals: *SWL*, pp. 99ff. The quotation from MH ("I will tell you precisely . . .") is from the same source (p. 100), as are the following: "In rehearsal, Moss' authority . . ." (p. 96); "The author is unhappy" (p. 96); "Rex, Julie is going to sing . . ." (p. 101); and "It made all the difference" (p. 101). KCH's statement "Rex, at the first orchestra rehearsal . . ." is from *Kitty*, p. 179. Harrison announcing he would not perform on opening night in New Haven: *SWL*, p. 104. The house manager threatening to tell the audience of Harrison's fit of temperament: *SWL*, p. 104. Quote from KCH "went to all the nearby . . ." is from *Kitty*, p. 180. Both "the total effect was stunning . . ." and "when the curtain came down the audience . . ." are from *SWL*, p. 105. Julie Andrews said "It was the most exhausting thing . . ." in an interview. MH's comment "It is usual for numbers . . ." is from MH's article on directing *MFL*, SHSW. People lining up at box office in New York as a result of the out-of-town reviews: *SWL*, p. 110. GSK's letter to MH "I find my-self feeling very emotional . . ." is undated, SHSW. ". . . convinced the cast . . ." is from an interview with Julie Andrews. From *SWL*: "At the end of the first scene . . ." (p. 116); "When the final curtain fell . . ." (p. 117); MH, KCH, Lerner and others going to "21" (p. 117). Brooks Atkinson's review of *MFL*:*NYT*, March 16, 1956. Sunday article by Atkinson ("although Moss Hart . . .") is from *NYT*, March 25, 1956. Quotation from Atkinson that *MFL* "was brilliantly staged . . ." is from Brooks Atkinson, *Broadway*, p. 445. Let-ters and telegrams to MH from John O'Hara, Nunnally Johnson, Herman Shumlin, Hume Cronyn, and many others: at SHSW. Tony awards for *MFL*: Abe Laufe, *Broadway's Greatest Musicals*, p. 199. Quotation from Julie Andrews "He was thorough, strong . . ." is from an interview with Julie Andrews. MH's casting of Margaret Bannerman in the road company: *Kitty*, p. 92. "Being at his elbow . . ." is from an interview with Stone Widney. "Moss Hart . . . not only . . ." is from Abe Laufe, *Broadway's Greatest Musicals*, p. 204. "It was Lerner and Loewe who . . ." is from Bennett Cerf, *NYT*, March 27, 1960. MH and Kay Kendall appearing in *MFL* in November 1957: *NYT*, November 30, 1957. Rex Harrison is quoted saying "very emotional and very touching" in *NYT*, November 30, 1957. One quarter of a million tickets sold in London be-fore *MFL* opened there: *NYT*, May 4, 1958; John Bevan, "London Queues Up for Eliza," *NYT Magazine*, March 9, 1958, p. 22. Harry Weaver's review in *The London Daily Herald* is quoted in *NYT*, May 11, 1958. Eighty employees of Consolidated Edison fly to London to see *MFL*: *NYT*, September 30, 1958. Review by Drew Middleton of the London production: *NYT*, May 4, 1958. Queen Elizabeth and Prince Philip attend performance of London produc-tion: *Kitty*, pp. 192–93; *SWL*, p. 129; *NYT*, May 7, 1958. Production, record album and film rights exceeded $100,000,000 and made MH rich: Robert Windeler, *Julie Andrews*, p. 50; "Person to Person" videotape. Quotation from MH, "each night in New York, in London . . ." is from MH, article about di-recting *MFL*, SHSW. Taking *MFL* to the Soviet Union: *NYT*, May 6, May 7, May 14, and November 24, 1959.

Chapter Twelve

About *Act One*: MH's statements "It will make our future" and "The book won't pay . . ." are both from *Kitty*, p. 182. The handwritten draft of *Act One* is at SHSW. "You must go on with it . . ." is in a letter from Phyllis Cerf to MH, January 22, 1957, SHSW. GSK's undated telegram, "GEORGE TYLERS OFFICE . . ." is in SHSW. Reviews: Charles Poore's review of *Act*

One is in *NYT*, September 15, 1959; both Brooks Atkinson's and S. N. Behrman's reviews appeared on September 20, 1959. The quotation "crowning glory" is from an interview with Christopher Hart. KCH's observation that Behrman's review elated MH is in *Kitty*, p. 193. "In my thirty-eight years . . ." is from Bennett Cerf, "With Gaiety and Gusto," *Saturday Review*, January 20, 1962, p. 36. Hundreds of letters from readers of *Act One* are at SHSW. MH stopping the elderly man and saying "I'm Moss Hart:" Bennett Cerf, "With Gaiety and Gusto." *AO* on *NYT* bestseller list for 41 weeks: *NYT*, December 21, 1961. "Life with Moss was like . . .": *Kitty*, p. 193. Quotation from Brooks Atkinson, "look for *Act Two* eventually . . ." is from *NYT*, September 20, 1959. MH musing, "Perhaps . . . I should write *Act Two* . . ." is from an article by Cecil Smith in an unidentified newspaper clipping, SHSW. Question from MH, "Who wants to read . . ." is from an interview with Jerome Chodorov. KCH believes MH never intended to write a second volume: interview with KCH. Joshua Logan purchases film rights to *AO*: *NYT*, September 28, 1959. Bosley Crowther's review of the film of *Act One*: *NYT*, December 27, 1963. Quotation from MH, "I believe a man who sells his work . . ." is from a clipping in SHSW.

About *Camelot*: Much of the information derives from interviews with Julie Andrews and Robert Goulet, and Alan Jay Lerner's *The Street Where I Live* (*SWL*). MH was "a master of his art . . .": *SWL*, p. 72. Lerner, Loewe, and Hart discuss various possibilities for musical adaptation: *NYT*, November 27, 1960. MH calls Lerner about *The Once and Future King*: *SWL*, pp. 189–90. Stone Widney calls Lerner about the same book: interview with Stone Widney; *SWL*, p. 189. Lerner asks MH to collaborate on the book of *Camelot*: *Kitty*, p. 195. Frederick Loewe's response, "You must be crazy . . ." is from *SWL*, p. 190. MH receives letter from Lerner saying that Lerner wishes to write the book for *Camelot* himself: *Kitty*, p. 196. "Just direct it . . ." is from *Kitty*, p. 196. MH, Lerner and Loewe decide to produce *Camelot* themselves: *SWL*, p. 190. Difficulty of adapting *The Once and Future King* to the stage: *SWL*, pp. 191ff. From *Kitty*: MH thought Lerner's first draft was unworkable (pp. 196–97); KCH suggests Mordred be given more prominence (p. 197); MH joins Lerner in Antibes (p. 197). From *SWL*: Lerner had heard Richard Burton singing Welsh songs (p. 195); Laurence Harvey's wish to play Lancelot (p. 197); Robert Goulet's audition for *Camelot*: interview with Goulet. Goulet also quoted MH "I see you've come prepared . . ." and "I think you've got it" in our interview. Text of *Camelot* growing longer with each rewrite: *SWL*, pp. 206ff. Death of Adrian: *SWL*, p. 202. MH helping to resolve the Equity strike (or producers' lockout): *NYT*, June 5 and June 10, 1960. Lerner's depression: *SWL*, p. 205. Rehearsal schedule for *Camelot*: interview with Robert Goulet. From *SWL*: quote from Lerner, "no one fully realized the extent . . .": (p. 206); MH's cutting Hanya Holm's ballet (p. 211); MH suggesting that Lerner and Loewe cut a twelve-minute musical sequence (pp. 211–12). Observations about MH's directorial style came from interviews with Julie Andrews, Jerome Chodorov, Robert Goulet, and from *SWL*, p. 76. "He was a very helpful . . .": interview with Robert Goulet. Final curtain comes down at 12:40 a.m. at first performance in Toronto: *SWL*, p. 214. Advance sale breaks all records: *NYT*, September 27, October 28 and November 27, 1960; *SWL*, p. 202. Attempts to cut *Camelot* and the pressure on MH: interview with KCH; *SWL*, pp. 214ff. Quotation from MH, "a picnic," is from *NYT*, October 15, 1960. The quotation "sensed that [MH] did not have . . ." is from an interview with Julie Andrews. Lerner collapses and is taken to Wellesley Hospital: *NYT*, October 6, 1960; *SWL*, p. 216. Broadway opening is postponed and MH says, "The likelihood is that . . .": *NYT*, October 10 and October 11, 1960; Alan Jay Lerner, "Of Sleepers and 'Wakers,'" *NYT Magazine*, December 3, 1961, p. 34. MH suffers toothache: *Kitty*, p. 200. MH suffers heart attack in Toronto: *NYT*, October 15, 1960; *Kitty*, pp. 200–01; *SWL*, pp. 216–17. Quotation "We were just going . . ." is from an interview with Catherine Hart. The description from KCH "was very small . . ." is from *Kitty*, p. 201. Lerner's statement "he was a very sick man . . ." is from *SWL*, p. 217. Robert Goulet knew only that MH was ill: interview with Robert Goulet. The quotation "it did cause . . ." is from an interview with Julie Andrews. Lerner's statement about Richard Burton "Both on stage and off . . ." is from *SWL*, p. 211. The quotation from Julie Andrews "unique. We had . . ." is from an interview with Julie Andrews. Information about the accepted treatment for heart attack in 1960 came from Beeson, Paul B. and Walsh McDermott, *Cecil-Loeb Textbook of Medicine*, Twelfth Edition, Philadelphia and London: W. B. Saunders Company, 1967, and from interviews with Dr. James Bertsche and Dr. James McCriskin. Search for a new director: *SWL*, p. 95; *NYT*, October 18, 1960. Hugh Walker's hospitalization: *NYT*, October 18, 1960. Loewe"s illness and Julie Andrews's statement "seemed more ill . . ." are from an interview with Julie Andrews. MH released from hospital and confined to his home: *NYT*, November 27, 1960; interview with KCH. Reviews of *Camelot* by Howard Taubman: *NYT*, December 5, 1960 and December 11, 1960. Critics offering different prescriptions: Abe Laufe, *Broadway's Greatest Musicals*, p. 275. "The first scene . . ." is from an interview with Julie Andrews. Robert Goulet's recollection of audience response: interview with Goulet. Quotation "was an awesome talent . . ." is from an interview with Julie Andrews. Lerner's account of audience reaction and its influence on the production: *SWL*, p. 244. Quote from MH "there are imperfections": *NYT*, January 22, 1961. Quotations "we were boring our audiences . . ." and "Fellas, we've got work . . ." are from an interview with Stone Widney. MH's cutting and redirection of *Camelot*: *SWL*, p. 244; *NYT*, January 22, 1961. Quotation "the first time I know of . . ." is from an interview with Julie Andrews. Appearance on *The Ed Sullivan Show*: interview with Julie Andrews; *SWL*, pp. 244–45. Quotation "The reaction and applause . . ." is from *SWL*, p. 245. The following quotations: "certainly did get better . . ."; "There were many evenings . . ."; and "To my shame . . ." are all from interviews with Julie Andrews. KCH receiving the news that Bernard Hart had died: KCH, *Kitty*, pp. 213–14. MH suffering from depression after the success of *Camelot* is from *Kitty*, p. 203. Quotation "No. That was not the . . ." is from an interview with KCH.

Chapter Thirteen

Quotation from KCH "he couldn't walk . . ." is from *Kitty*, p. 203. "One morning in Beach Haven . . ." is from *Kitty*, p. 194, and MH suffering from depression after the success of *Camelot* is from the same source, p. 203. MH and KCH appearing on Academy Award program: videotape of the ceremony in the Wisconsin Center for Film and Theatre Research. Edna Ferber's letter, "It was refreshing . . ." is quoted in Julie Goldsmith Gilbert, *Ferber: A Biography*, p. 100. Important sources used in this chapter were interviews with Catherine Hart, Christopher Hart, and Kitty Carlisle Hart about their recollections of the circumstances surrounding Moss Hart's death, and a script of the celebration at Lincoln Center in 2004 honoring Moss Hart and Kitty Carlisle Hart. A copy of MH's eulogy for GSK is in SHSW. Quotation from Alan Jay Lerner "Everything about this little incident . . ." is from *SWL*, p. 249. The Harts' move to California in 1961: interview with KCH; *NYT*, December 21, 1961. MH's toothache in December 1961: *Kitty*, p. 205; *NYT*, December 21, 1961. [Dr. John Bertsche, in an interview, confirmed that a toothache could be a precursor of a heart attack, as did Dr. Catherine Hart] MH's death: *Kitty*, pp. 205–06; *NYT*, December 21, 1961 (obituary). Alan Jay Lerner's essay "with trembling hands . . ." appeared in *SWL*, p. 249. MH's funeral: *NYT*, December 23, 1961. Quotation "His plays offer ample . . ." is from Richard Mason, "The Comic Theatre of Moss Hart: Persistence of a Formula," *The Theatre Annual*. Quotation from Bennett Cerf "began living up to . . ." is from Cerf, "With Gaiety and Gusto," p. 31. KCH offers MH's un-finished play to Jerome Chodorov: interview with KCH. Reviews of *Two's Company* appeared in the *Boston Phoenix*, February 26, 1974, and in a clipping (April 1974) about the production when it appeared in Wilmington, BRTC. Quotation from KCH "the bitterness of my loss . . ." is from *Kitty*, p. 209. Christopher Hart's one-paragraph biography: interview with Christopher Hart; *NYT*, September 8, 1962. Catherine Hart's one-paragraph biography: interview with Catherine Hart. Quotation "his incisive wit . . ." is from David Ewen, *Complete Book of the American Musical Theatre*, p. 983. Telegram from Billy Rose ("RUTH AND AUGUSTUS GOETZ . . .") is dated February 5, 1954, SHSW. Woody Allen's admiration for MH: *Kitty*, p. 236. Larry Gel-bart's quotation is from an interview. Neil Simon's statement is quoted from Simon's *The Play Goes On*. Quotations from the event at Lincoln Center are from the written script of the event.

INDEX